Delivering
Human Services

Delivering
Human Services

A LEARNING APPROACH TO PRACTICE

FOURTH EDITION

Alexis A. Halley
Meridian International Institute

Judy Kopp
Late, University of Washington

Michael J. Austin
University of California–Berkeley

With assistance from
Amy R. Olk

LONGMAN

An imprint of Addison Wesley Longman, Inc.

New York • Reading, Massachusetts • Menlo Park, California • Harlow, England
Don Mills, Ontario • Sydney • Mexico City • Madrid • Amsterdam

Editor-in-Chief: Priscilla McGeehon
Executive Editor: Alan McClare
Acquisitions Editor: Janice E. Wiggins
Project Management and Text Design: Ruttle, Shaw & Wetherill, Inc.
Senior Marketing Manager: Wendy Albert
Supplements Editor: Tom Kulesa
Editorial Assistant: Katya McElfresh
Cover Designer: Kay Petronio
Electronic Production Manager: Christine Pearson
Manufacturing Manager: Willie Lane
Electronic Page Makeup: Ruttle, Shaw & Wetherill, Inc.
Printer and Binder: Maple-Vail Book Manufacturing Group
Cover Printer: Coral Graphic Services, Inc.

For permission to use copyrighted material, grateful acknowledgment is made to the copyright holders on pp. 649–650, which are hereby made part of this copyright page.

Library of Congress Cataloging-in-Publication Data
Halley, Alexis A.
    Delivering human services : a learning approach to practice /
Alexis A. Halley, Judy Kopp, Michael J. Austin. — 4th ed.
      p.   cm.
    Includes bibliographical references (p.   ) and index.
    ISBN 0-8013-1797-5
    1. Social work education—United States—Programmed instruction.
I. Kopp, Judy. II. Austin, Michael J. III. Title.
HV11.H323   1998
361'.06'077—dc21

                                      97-33624
                                        CIP

ISBN 0-8013-1797-5

45678910—MA—0099

OCLC # 37341528

Contents

Preface

Floods of change are surging through the human service work world and are likely to continue through the dawning of the twenty-first century. America's population and its families are experiencing major reforms and increasingly complex human problems of living in health, welfare, mental health, education, poverty, race relations, violence, child and adult homelessness, AIDS, drug abuse, aging, immigration, and work itself, to name a few. Our governments and the private and nonprofit sectors struggle with competing, increasingly fragmented, and contradictory views of the role of the state and other sectors in assuring a social safety net for citizens and non-citizens. There are national calls for voluntarism amidst assertions that America is experiencing an extreme crisis in caring and in public cynicism and distrust of government.[1] Models and methods of helping abound—in social welfare, psychology, counseling, human and organizational development, alternative medicine, and education. In many human service fields, the emphasis is shifting to helping clients to acquire skills (e.g., of self-help, self-management, and self-change) and achieve economic independence.[2] Human service organizations face increasingly tough choices as the American welfare state is restructured (e.g., determining which clients are most in need and most at risk in order to target scarce resources to priority populations). And numerous "work life experiments" are under way, ranging from total quality management to business process reengineering, performance budgeting, organizational democracy, virtual teams (workers linked by computer/internet), and high performing work teams, all of which place greater decision-making responsibility for service quality and effectiveness with those who deliver the services.

These are demanding times to be delivering human services. Pressure, uncertainty, ethical dilemmas, political conflict, scarce resources, and the desire to address both individual needs and environmental conditions characterize this work. Now and in the foreseeable future, the quality and results of services produced by social service, health care, and related human service organizations translates into the quality of life for the nation.[3] Who can make these differences? This book is targeted to those who are—the people who actually deliver human services.

THEME

The fourth edition of *Delivering Human Services* revolves around a central theme: *empowering human service workers and consumers through reflective learning*. This is a

---

[1]Suzanne Gordon, "A National Care Agenda," *Atlantic Monthly* (Jan. 1991): 64–68; John McKnight, *The Careless Society* (New York: Basic Books, 1995.)

[2]See the Personal Responsibility and Work Opportunity Reconciliation Act of 1996, summarized in: BASSC, *Social Welfare at a Crossroads: A National, Statewide, and Local Look at Poverty and Public Assistance* (Berkeley, CA: Bay Area Social Services Consortium, University of California–Berkeley, 1997).

[3]David M. Austin, *The Political Economy of Human Service Programs* (Greenwich, Conn.: JAI Press, 1988), p. xiii.

framework of practice oriented toward a positive, responsible view of the human condition and a capacity for change in both individuals and the environment.

Learning enables empowerment: the belief that all individuals have the capacity for growth and change and can shape their own destiny to benefit self and society. Workers who deliver human services need knowledge and skill in ongoing learning to meet rapidly changing situations. Those who are continually learning can diagnose unique situations as they are occurring and use the insights as opportunities to improve their performance. The single competence that workers must possess in any facet of delivering human services is the ability to learn and the ability to engage consumers in a collaborative learning process that leads to positive results. Learning about learning, learning about self, learning about consumers, learning how consumers achieve well-being, learning about the social environment, and learning from experiences working with consumers and colleagues—these themes are reflected throughout the book.

The goal of empowerment recognizes that it is a two-way process. For example, there are social impediments to healthy, self-initiated growth, particularly among the poor and oppressed. Environmental conditions create service needs and can adversely affect consumers' ability to take charge of their own lives. Yet many consumers can reshape their situation. To do so, both consumers and human service professions must engage in continual learning.

The framework of practice in this book refers to the "client" as a *consumer* or *customer*. *Consumer* reflects an approach to serving people that emphasizes we are all human and that we differ only according to our needs. We view it as less stigmatized than *client, patient, inmate, student* or *resident*. Human service consumers, like human service workers, face often profoundly difficult circumstances. The single critical competence that consumers must possess is the ability to learn—to acquire skills to take charge of their lives, to receive services or move beyond services, and to learn from their experience. Human service workers can facilitate these results.

The overall objectives of the fourth edition are that the student should (1) acquire a beginning understanding of the basic skills required of entry-level personnel performing as human service generalists and (2) be capable of successfully applying the basic vocabulary and practice principles to real-life practice situations.

CONTENTS

The fourth edition of *Delivering Human Services* is divided into four units that reflect a generic framework for learning and delivering human services:

- **Unit One** introduces a set of knowledge areas intended to be "gateways" that open the learner to the practice of delivering human services. It includes discussions of learning, language, and systems thinking skills as the basic orientations to service delivery. The human service institution is introduced by examining the conditions creating human needs and the people responding to those needs. The historical view of human services is presented in Chapter 2, Lesson 2 through three major waves of social changes—the agricultural wave, the industrial wave, and the information/electronic wave. The combination of learning, language, and systems thinking with the content of human needs and the characteristics of the people responding to them provides a solid conceptual foundation for the service delivery skills that follow in the next units.

- **Unit Two** describes the process of getting services to people in need through the roles of brokering, consumer advocating, and mobilizing. These three roles are rarely described together and in depth in entry-level human services texts.
- **Unit Three** focuses on ways of helping consumers to function more effectively. It describes the stages and approaches of the helping process; the foundation skills for conducting the process (e.g., interviewing and relationship building); and selected advanced intervention models that augment the helping process. Special attention is given to learning, empowerment, and the development of an effective, collaborative helping relationship.
- **Unit Four** examines working across boundaries (e.g., of hierarchy, program, and information) for competent practice. It emphasizes skills needed to work, create, and survive in rapidly changing service delivery systems. Integrating—through self-assessment, attention to service quality, and professional accountability—is introduced. These boundary-spanning skills are rarely found in entry-level human service texts. Yet working across boundaries is critical to effective practice as we look to the twenty-first century of delivering human services.

Features new to the fourth edition include:

- Substantially revised and new material on policy practice (Chapter 2, Lesson 3), considerations in the relationship between self-awareness and effective delivery of human services (Chapter 3), rights issues in the human services (Chapter 5, Lesson 2), and managing the transitions to new service delivery systems (Chapter 11).
- Reorganization and updating of material describing the helping process and elimination of dated clinical methods (Unit Three).
- Updating of case material to achieve a greater emphasis on diversity (e.g., in human service setting, culture, ethnicity).
- Substantial updating and reorganization of "chapter summary and further study" sections to augment and extend the material developed in each chapter.
- Suggested answers to exercises now appear at the end of the book rather than after each lesson.
- Curriculum assumptions underpinning the book and background about how the curriculum has been evaluated for impact and effectiveness.
- A revised, updated test bank available in Macintosh or Windows format from your Longman sales representative.

ASSUMPTIONS

Traditional approaches to staff development and training in the human services have emphasized the uniqueness of each human service setting in terms of knowledge, skills, and values, rather than the common knowledge, skills, and values on which all human service practice is based. With the current trend toward comprehensive and unified delivery of human services and the corresponding need for workers who can function in a variety of human service settings, *setting-specific* training is no longer sufficient. A training model is needed to meet worker demands for career mobility and to provide consumers with flexible and knowledgeable resource guides.

This text identifies a generic framework of knowledge and skills required for beginning competence in delivering human services. Our definition of beginning competence is only part of the full spectrum of knowledge, skills, and values required for effective entry-level performance. For example, the text does not include the in-depth knowledge needed about the social, political, or economic environment or the behavioral science concepts found in abnormal psychology, adolescent psychology, family sociology, sociology of deviance, cultural anthropology, child development, and gerontology. The organizational and societal constraints prevalent throughout the human services require beginning workers to have a thorough understanding of the social science concepts of health and welfare economics; of federal, state, and local government and nonprofit and for-profit organizations; of the sociology of complex organizations; and of the sociology of group and community behavior. We hope that the suggestions for further study and references found at the end of each chapter will provide some assistance for continuing study in these and other areas. In addition to the social and behavioral sciences, the entry-level worker also needs to acquire a thorough understanding of the values and attitudes necessary for effective service delivery.

In regard to the how-to aspect of the text, our statements of practice principles are in no way intended to serve as absolute rules to be followed in delivering human services. We do believe that it is possible to learn from experience and to translate the practice wisdom derived from this experience into principles that can guide new workers entering human service agencies. Users should reflect periodically on the significant gap between the seemingly simple issues and principles described in the text and the actual complexity involved in working with consumers who have a variety of human problems and individual differences in age, gender identity, personality, and life experiences. The ideas in this text also need to be implemented and tested by each learner under appropriate supervision through on-the-job training or practicum experiences.

Finally, a few words on the method of programmed instruction. This text is directed to the entry-level worker as an adult learner whose training needs will be met most efficiently through programs based on the adult learning process. We assume that entry-level training will be most effective when

1. The learner is given the opportunity to learn by doing and by practicing.
2. Learning is problem centered.
3. The method provides the learner with frequent feedback about her or his progress.

The text is based on the concept of adjunct autoinstruction, which means it is a self-contained text and includes questions and exercises to help learners assess their mastery of the content. While one of the strengths of this approach is separating and analyzing the component parts of human service skills, a corresponding limitation is the temptation to assume that an understanding of the components leads directly to a mastery of the skills. In the final analysis, skills are developed only through a combination of knowing and doing. It is important to recognize that this text emphasizes the knowing, while discussions, role playing, and on-the-job experiences emphasize the doing.

DISTINCTIVENESS

When compared with current texts in the human service field, this book differs in the following ways: (1) It is unique in developing the theme of a learning approach to practice as an orientation toward a future of rapid individual and social change. (2) It is one of the few texts that thoroughly engages the learner in a self-instructional process. (3) It is more comprehensive and balanced in its approach to the functions performed by a human service worker. (4) It does not overemphasize the counseling function but places it in the context of other worker functions. (5) It is more practical in its emphasis on skill development. (6) It provides an opportunity to integrate and connect different subject areas so that a big picture emerges. (7) The text provides job-related knowledge and practical techniques to be acquired by a learner. In addition, many examples are used to illustrate the material.

Several features of the book make it accessible to the reader. Each unit, chapter, and lesson opens with an introduction and overview section, including a statement of the relevant learning goal. Each lesson identifies the specific learning activities that will be undertaken to achieve the learning goal. Each chapter concludes with a summary and suggestions for further reading. Within most of the lessons, the material is presented in an interactive format that engages the learner in self-application and testing of the ideas. Because the format of the presentation is "programmed," we encourage readers to review the section on "How to Read This Book," which follows this preface. A *Test Bank* of multiple-choice and essay items to accompany each chapter is available to adopters.

The answers used in each lesson are designed as preferred responses. This means that both the learner and the instructor should find numerous areas of disagreement with the text based on their prior and current experience. This disagreement should lead to fruitful discussions.

EFFECTIVENESS

Field evaluations have been conducted to assess the effectiveness of the text from two perspectives. First, for all four editions of the text, human service educators, practitioners, and experts in instructional design were asked to review both the content and the design in order to assess the appropriateness of the text in various human service settings. Second, as part of the development of the first edition, measures of the actual effects of the program were obtained from preprogram and immediate postprogram tests of two groups of target population learners. The results of these field evaluations were as follows.

Faculty members in programs related to human services and instructional design at Florida State University, Hunter College, the University of Georgia, Morgan State College, Santa Fe Community College, and St. Petersburg Community College reviewed the content. Practitioners in Florida health and human services agencies also provided extensive feedback.

College and university educators thought the program innovative and most useful for undergraduate students beginning their study of the human services and students involved in field placement and internship activities. The text design evoked interest in introducing complex concepts and skills at the entry level, the depth versus breadth of coverage, and the method of programmed instruction. All the reviewers indicated that the text would be a valuable resource in their programs.

Community college faculty were extremely positive about the method of programmed instruction and content. They indicated that the text would have a wide range of immediate applications in their programs. They were impressed with the broad definition of human services and felt that the community college student needed such a broad perspective as a foundation for effective practice and further specialized studies. This group was intrigued with the presentation of interpersonal skills in a programmed format.

Practitioners, particularly those responsible for orientation and in-service training for entry-level workers, considered the program to be a valuable resource. This group viewed the text as one component of a larger staff development program.

Most of the students and workers participating in these evaluations were initially unfamiliar with the method of programmed instruction and responded to it in a number of interesting ways. At first they were intrigued with the novel effect of self-instructional material. One commented, for example, "This book talks to me—it's fun to read." They experienced a feeling of confidence derived from mastering a wide range of information, and they began to show marked interest in pursuing additional areas of study and adapting the content to their personal work experiences. As a result of their success with and exposure to such a wide range of information, they began to realize the tremendous responsibilities and personal value conflicts inherent in human service work, and thus found the generalist framework of the text a useful schema to further their understanding of delivering effective human services.

We considered the results of these evaluations important indications of the effectiveness of the program.

AUDIENCE

The text can be a resource in community college and university social work/human service education programs, staff development programs in human service organizations, and volunteer organizations.

1. Community colleges. Community colleges across the country offer programs in human services, social work, family and consumer studies, family services, childcare management, guidance and counseling, interdisciplinary studies, mental health and rehabilitation counseling, occupational therapy, law enforcement and corrections, and health care including nursing. An introduction to the baseline knowledge and skills required for effective delivery of human services is important in these programs, and can expand students' knowledge of the total human service industry and prepare them for more advanced study.

2. College and university programs. Undergraduate university programs in social work and social welfare can also use this text. Many of these programs include field placements in human service agencies where student practicum experiences could be supplemented by this text, which has a strong agency orientation. Each chapter lends itself to potentially rich learning discussions between a student and the agency supervisor.

3. Staff development programs in human service organizations. The text can be used in many areas of agency in-service training, not only in the umbrella human service agencies—which include public welfare, vocational rehabilitation, mental health, health, mental retardation, youth corrections, drug abuse, and aging—but also within any of these specific programs. Organizations interested in orienting new entry-level workers and developing the skill of workers already employed in entry-level jobs will find this comprehensive introduction to the human service industry useful for a wide range of workers.

4. Volunteer organizations. Volunteer groups working in various human service settings will find the text helpful in clarifying their understanding of the skills needed for human service work and in expanding their own volunteer activities.

In any setting, the programmed format lends itself to computer-assisted instruction because the entire text could be programmed on the computer for learners to use on terminals in the institution or agency.

APPLICATIONS

A variety of procedures can be used to structure and present the content of this text. For example, it can be used as part of an intensive one-week workshop for agency personnel or as part of a semester or quarter course focused on working with individuals and families in need of human services. The four units can be used separately in several courses or in a different sequence.

Several recommendations ought to be considered in any application. Through self-instruction the learner is encouraged to test his or her understanding of the content in frames that either reinforce learning or require the learner to apply the content to a real-life situation. We view the instructor as playing a crucial role in this translation process. The answers indicated as the correct responses represent preferred answers but are not necessarily the only answers. There are few situations in which there is only one correct action. Instructors and learners should be encouraged to argue and present alternative interpretations based on new knowledge, prior experiences, or special situations. If our preferred responses serve as focal points for discussion and debate, we shall have accomplished one of our major objectives—to stimulate further thinking about the concepts, skills, and practice principles needed for effective performance of entry-level human service work.

Group discussions regarding the actual concepts and practice principles, as well as discussions of related topics that are not included in the chapters, are essential to the program. For example, discussions regarding values, attitudes, racism, and sexism can lead to insights regarding ways of seeking change within an organization. Similarly, group discussion should explore and contrast a systems perspective to understanding consumers and human service agencies, humanistic or behavioral perspectives, which are interwoven in this book.

We strongly encourage instructors to use the experience of a variety of workers involved in human service organizations by including them in discussion sessions and role-playing activities. For example, discussion of the role of consumer advocating can be greatly enhanced by involving civil rights or consumer rights attorneys. Psychologists and social workers experienced and trained in the use of various counseling techniques can add considerably to classroom discussions and serve as role models to be observed through one-way mirrors or other devices as they apply the techniques discussed in helping consumers function more effectively.

The separate *Test Bank* has objective-referenced items specially constructed for this program. The tests focus on knowledge acquisition and can easily be augmented with the instructor's own testing instruments, applying the material to "real life" practice situations.

ACKNOWLEDGMENTS

Longman Publishers, Alexis Halley, and Michael Austin deeply regret the untimely death of Judy Kopp just after the final manuscript for the fourth edition was completed. Professor Kopp had a very deep commitment to and affection for the subject and approach of this book and the clinical material she creatively authored.

This fourth edition has benefited from very helpful reviews and recommendations for improvements. We thank the following: Armand Lauffer, The University of Michigan; Guy Stephen Wylie, Kansas State University; Gerald Rubin, Central Virginia Community College; Dolores Finger Wright, Delaware State University; Patricia J. Sawyer, Middlesex Community Tech College; Jane S. Gore, State University of New York–Plattsburgh; and Richard Blake, Seton Hall University.

We are also grateful to numerous colleagues, students, and agency workers who have used and commented on earlier editions since the original in 1977. We especially thank our teachers—the pioneering hundreds of Florida Department of Health and Rehabilitative Services workers who participated in defining a human service task bank that deepened our understanding of human service work and sharpened our appreciation for the commonalities and differences in settings in which it is performed.

For the fourth edition, special thanks go to Amy Rebecca Olk, a recent Phi Beta Kappa graduate of Stetson University, who is in the process of building a career in international and domestic humanitarian work. Amy is the author of the new lesson on policy challenges in delivering human services. She also updated the lesson on rights issues in the human services and rewrote and reconceptualized the *Test Bank* to accompany the book. Amy provided invaluable overall research assistance in updating all the chapter references and suggestions for further study.

We want to single out Janice Wiggins, Longman's Social Work Acquisitions Editor, for her unusual commitment to quality, her invaluable support to the senior author, and her very special professional role in nurturing the project to completion. Thank you, Janice. Peg Markow, Senior Project Manager at Ruttle, Shaw and Wetherill, Inc., devised incredible motivational and coordination schemes to bring the book to publication on time. We are also grateful to Susan McIntyre, whose insightful copyediting has produced a much crisper presentation.

Delivering Human Services was conceived as a partial response to incredibly difficult, enduring, and interesting questions. Who are human service workers? How can we describe what human service workers do when delivering services? What knowledge and skills do workers need to derive satisfaction from their work and to increase the quality of service delivery in any setting? How can we impart the ever-changing body of human service knowledge and practice in ways that appreciate learners (instructors, students, and consumers) as adults and engage them actively in the learning process? This text is but a partial answer to these questions. While each human service profession has a valuable, essential, and specialized body of knowledge, we offer *De-*

livering Human Services: A Learning Approach to Practice, Fourth Edition, in the spirit of a scholarship of integration that seeks human service connections across the disciplines and the professions. We hope this approach will stimulate intense curiosity and a desire for lifelong learning in delivering effective, accountable, and quality human services.

Alexis A. Halley
(Late) Judy Kopp
Michael J. Austin

How to Read This Book

FRAME

1

THE MAIN PARTS OF THIS BOOK

You are about to be introduced to a book that may be quite different from the traditional books with which you are familiar. This is a programmed textbook or instructional program. If you follow the instructions here, you should find using this book to be a rewarding learning experience.

The text contains much of the same kind of information you would expect to find in other textbooks. The difference is the manner in which this information is organized and presented. Figure 1 illustrates this organization.

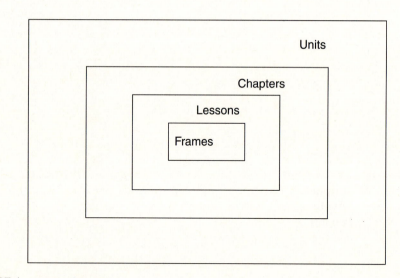

FIGURE 1   How information is organized in this book.

The book has four large *units*. Each unit is divided into *three chapters*. Information in each chapter is conveyed in *lessons,* and lessons are organized into *frames* labeled with numbers (1, 2, 3, 4, etc.) Looking at a frame in this text is like looking at a screen on your computer.

You have now completed Frame 1, so continue reading with Frame 2.

UNITS AND CHAPTERS

Each unit opens with a brief introduction and overview—a preview of the unit and a statement of the overall goal we are trying to accomplish in that unit.

Once you have read the unit preview, you turn to a chapter. Each chapter also opens with an introduction and a statement of the overall goal we are trying to accomplish.

LESSONS AND FRAMES

The details of the book—and the place where it looks most different from other textbooks—are inside the chapters, in what we call "lessons" and "frames."

Each lesson in this book is made up of two parts:

- Each lesson begins with a goal that specifies what you should be able to do at the conclusion of the lesson, and what *learning activities* you will pursue to achieve the goal.
- Following the lesson goal and learning activities, content is presented in blocks of information called *frames,* which are numbered (e.g., Frame 1) and separated by solid lines that run across the page.

In general, you "read" each lesson by reading each of the frames—that is, you proceed from Frame 1 to Frame 2 to Frame 3 and so on to the last frame in the lesson. We will not prompt you to move from frame to frame unless the material in the frame is a question or exercise. Since this frame is not a question, you should now move directly to Frame 3.

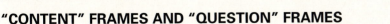

"CONTENT" FRAMES AND "QUESTION" FRAMES

Some of the frames in a lesson simply present content (e.g., definitions of concepts, assumptions, skills, or practice dilemmas and guidelines). Other frames contain questions or exercises to test your understanding of the content or to suggest ways of applying it to your work. When it makes sense to do so, you will be given immediate feedback on each question when you turn to the answer that is provided at the end of the book.

Suppose Frame 3 is the following question. **If you apply yourself to this material, you will**

_____ A. Be unable to answer most questions.

Turn to Answer 1 on page xxi

_____ B. Be able to answer most questions.

Turn to Answer 2 on page xxi

(We suggest you look at both of the above answers for instructional purposes.)

F R A M E

If for some reason you do not want to take the time to look up the answers, you could continue directly with the next frame—in this case, Frame 4. If you do this, however, you risk missing possible supplementary content and suggestions. You also miss the opportunity to actively involve yourself in the material.

Many question or exercise frames throughout this program will ask for some form of response. In some cases, such responses will require that you choose one of several given alternatives. In other cases, you will be asked to construct short descriptions or to engage in some specific application (e.g., conduct a discussion and report back the results).

Be sure to follow directions, and when asked to write a response, do so in the spaces provided or on a separate page. Since this program is designed to help you learn through the presentation of a wide variety of material, do not spend time attempting to write perfect answers. Answer each question as best you can and move on. Remember: After you have selected a response, turn to the indicated answer number at the end of the book. This answer will tell you whether your response choice was correct. A correct response will send you to the next frame. An incorrect response will give you the information you need to answer the question correctly. The important thing is to follow the directions and *write down* your answers.

F R A M E
5

You should be able to finish each programmed lesson during one study session. If you find that you must take breaks during a lesson, try to make them short. For most effective learning, it is recommended that you do not wait more than one day between study sessions for any single programmed lesson.

When you are ready to begin the program, turn to Unit One. We hope you enjoy this experience of learning!

Answers to "How To Read This Book"

ANSWER 1

If you selected A, then you either have not read the material carefully or have little confidence in your own abilities, since you have said that you will be unable to answer most questions if you apply yourself to the material presented. Whatever the case, this is an incorrect answer.

If, during the program, you should choose the wrong answer to a question, you will often be given further information to clarify any misunderstanding or be asked to review the material you may have missed.

You should return to Frame 3 to answer the question correctly.

ANSWER 2

We hope you selected B—be able to answer most questions. If you apply yourself to this material in the manner we are suggesting, this will be the result. Great work!

You can see that answering a question correctly will typically move you ahead to the next frame; answering a question incorrectly will often send you back to a prior frame.

Return to Frame 4.

UNIT**ONE**

GATEWAYS TO THE PRACTICE OF DELIVERING HUMAN SERVICES

Preview of Unit

People who deliver human services act in a complex world of work. They deal with a wide range of problematic situations and are often challenged to respond with sensitivity and creativity. As practitioners seek both to find people who need human services and to establish helping relationships during service delivery, they rely on a knowledge base to orient their actions. This knowledge base provides a framework that enables practitioners to structure their thoughts in action.

The core theme of Unit One is knowledge to guide your *learning about* service delivery and knowledge to use *while doing* service delivery. The framework presented in this unit provides three broad perspectives from which you can view human service work situations: skills, conditions, and people. It is organized to respond to three key questions:

1. What basic *skills* do human service practitioners need that will enable them to meet today's service delivery requirements and those of the next decade?
2. What are the *conditions* giving rise to the need for human services?
3. Who are the *people* who deliver human services?

Chapter 1 introduces three basic skills that are critical for your meeting current and future service delivery needs: the ability to learn, the capacity to be sensitive to the language you use in delivering human services, and the ability to use systems thinking. All three of these skills are concerned with how you approach your work; how you think about yourself and the people you work with; how you interpret your experiences; and how you rely on your insights to make decisions, take actions, and live with the consequences of those actions. Practitioners who are able to approach service delivery using the skills of learning, language, and systems thinking will be able to create an ongoing inquiry process. They will be better able to be *aware of self* in a demanding setting, observing the results of their actions with others, and continually experimenting to make themselves more effective.

Chapter 2 is concerned with your developing and using a framework for understanding why there are human services. Three conditions are proposed as useful concepts: personal needs, changes in society, and service delivery issues. At an individual level, we all share in addressing basic requirements that enable us to lead successful lives. Everyone has difficulty at times in coping with the problems and frustrations of daily living. When these difficulties are such that they exceed our capacity to address them, we may require special assistance. Why would such problems arise? Chapter 2 suggests that a broad cause is the changes in our society. As society changes, the problems and opportunities of living change. How do human service workers connect changes in society with the problems people face? Chapter 2 introduces the idea of service delivery issues that identify the key human conditions being addressed by human service systems. Since service delivery issues are both wide-ranging and often changing, we lead you through a step-by-step process that helps you to "scan" the critical issues in a human service area of interest to you.

The third part of the knowledge base for delivering human services is the people who respond to human needs. Three elements are important: workers, work organizations and work groups, and the work itself. A distinguishing characteristic of human service work is that it requires highly effective use of self. Human service workers must be interpersonally competent to deliver human services, since so much of their success hinges on the ability to relate to other people. In turn, this requires the ability to recognize your own feelings, values, and intuitions; to connect the personal self with the values commonly held by human service professions; and to use these insights to establish a work identity. Human service workers typically practice in some organizational context. Chapter 3 discusses the characteristics of human service work organizations and emphasizes the importance of skillful membership in a (usually smaller) work group. Finally, Chapter 3 discusses the content of human service work—what people delivering human services actually do.

The overall objective of Unit One is to enhance your ability to learn how to learn while delivering human services in three ways: first, by helping you know yourself better; second, by offering you a conceptual framework for organizing your experience while delivering services; and third, by helping you develop skills that will enhance your capacity to produce the results you, and others, really want—now and in the future.

Chapter 1

Basic Orientations to Delivering Human Services

We could begin this text by immediately presenting a lot of very specific content about the human services. For example, we could begin by defining the human services. Or we might start by discussing the history of the human service professions. But another approach is to start with the following question: What basic skills do human service practitioners need that will enable them to meet today's service delivery requirements *and* those of the next decade?

Employers—today and tomorrow—are looking for a skilled workforce that is capable and flexible.[1] Employers of workers delivering human services face a special challenge. As our society becomes more complex, new human problems are created, and existing human problems can become more difficult to address. Thus, employers are looking for workers who are resourceful, flexible, and competent. People experiencing the numerous problems of living that can confront any of us at any time are also looking—for institutions, services, and fellow human beings who can offer a wide range of help.

The basic purpose of this chapter is to develop three sets of skills that will be the foundation for meeting today's service delivery requirements and those of the next decade. These three skills—the *ability to learn,* the *capacity to be sensitive to language,* and the *ability to use systems thinking*—are strategies that will enable you to acquire the additional skills developed in other chapters of the text. They are also the same skills you will be using as you deliver human services. Effective human service workers are continually learning. They are sensitive to the implications of their own and others' language. And they are able to see the world and its people as systems. With skills in learning, language, and systems, a human service worker can transform the process of service delivery into an experience that produces knowledge—about self and about the people in need.

Lesson 1 may surprise you. It's about learning as a basic orientation to delivering

---

[1]Anthony Carnevale, Leila J. Gainer, and Ann S. Meltzer, *Workplace Basics: The Essential Skills Employers Want* (San Francisco: Jossey-Bass, 1990), pp. 1–4. Also see Anthony P. Carnevale, *The American Mosaic: An In-Depth Report on the Future of Diversity at Work* (NY: McGraw-Hill, 1995).

human services. Learning, both an attitude and a skill, is essential to being able to deliver human services. Learning is a developmental activity. It helps you to grow, enabling you to make sense out of your experiences. It is a process by which you discover the problems being experienced by another human being, a process by which you develop competence in recognizing and understanding human problems. Learning is also an attitude. People who know how to learn, and who make learning an ongoing habit, approach situations by asking questions. Learners are not committed to fixed points of view; instead, they are constantly inquiring into their situations. Because we think the ability to learn—about yourself, the people you are helping, and your organization—is so essential to delivering human services, it is the first skill we introduce. Working through this lesson should provide you with two kinds of learning skills: First, you will learn about learning itself; second, you will explore the connections between how you learn, how we approach learning through this text, and how you actually deliver human services.

> Real learning gets to the heart of what it means to be human. Through learning, we re-create ourselves. Through learning we become able to do something we never were able to do. Through learning we reperceive the world and our relationship to it.[2]

Lesson 2 introduces the second basic orientation to the human services: sensitivity to language. Language is a reflection of who we are. It plays an important role in shaping the behavior, attitudes, images, and values of personal, organizational, and professional life. Workers in the human services use a particular vocabulary to describe their experience and the experience of the people they are helping. Lesson 2 demonstrates the significance of language by exploring the term *human services*. What words are used to explain the human services? What can we learn about ourselves and this area of work by examining these words? Lesson 2 also explores the terms we use to label the people receiving human services. Are people who receive human services clients? patients? victims? consumers? inmates? residents? recipients? working class? The labels we assign to people are powerful. They orient our actions and our thinking in particular situations. We raise a number of issues surrounding the labels we use for people receiving human services and provide a rationale for the label we use in this text: the human service consumer.

Lesson 3 develops the third basic orientation we believe to be essential to meeting the service delivery requirements of today and the next decade: systems thinking. The tools and ideas in this lesson are for seeing the big picture and "destroying the illusion that the world is created of separate, unrelated forces."[3] Systems thinking is the ability to see and approach human service problems by organizing them into coherent stories that suggest the causes of the problems and how they might be remedied. Lesson 3 explores what constitutes systems thinking and how systems thinking is used in the practice of delivering human services. We show how systems thinking can be used to understand a complex enterprise—the human service social institutional system. We also suggest how systems thinking can be used to distinguish different levels of

---

[2]Peter M. Senge, *The Fifth Discipline: The Art and Practice of the Learning Organization* (New York: Doubleday, 1990), p. 14.

[3]Senge, *Fifth Discipline,* p. 3.

consumer populations or levels of helping. Successful problem solving and problem intervention hinge on the consideration of interrelated elements without becoming overwhelmed by them. Systems thinking, in combination with learning and language skills, provides a framework for learning about the human service world and taking effective and responsive action in it.

The overall objective of Chapter 1 is to provide you with a foundation of three key skills for delivering human services. These three skills—learning, language, and systems—will help you to be effective in seeing the human service world, taking action in the human service world, and continually enhancing your own and others' capacities in that world.

LESSON 1

Learning and the Delivery of Human Services

The human services can be understood in many ways, but a fundamental orientation is that of learning. Learning is a developmental activity. It helps you to grow, to make sense out of everyday events. Learning is an attitude and a skill. As an attitude, learning reflects an ongoing stance of curiosity, wonder, inquisitiveness, sensitivity, and desire to be competent. As a skill, learning is the ability to act effectively on the basis of understanding what to do in different situations. Learning is a process that people pursue throughout their lives. But self-aware learning is a skill that must be developed.

The ability to learn is a critical skill in delivering human services for at least three reasons. First, the very essence of delivering human services is to learn about people—to understand who they are, what problems they are facing, and what services might be useful to them. Second, to be able to deliver human services, you must have awareness about how you act and what makes you effective and what you can do to be more effective. Third, our world, and the smaller sphere of human services, is in a state of rapid change. Thus, the effective human service practitioner of today and tomorrow will be distinguished more by the ability to adapt to and master the changing demands of people, service delivery, and life (especially in the job or career) than by the possession of a fixed body of knowledge and skills. Another way of saying this is that the effective human service practitioner is characterized by *the ability to learn*.

Lesson 1 pursues these ideas about learning and delivering human services. Our exploration will take us down three roads. One journey will develop some basic understanding about learning as a concept and a process. This is based on our conviction that being highly skilled at learning requires knowing something about it. A second journey will ask you to reflect on how you learn in an effort to increase your self-awareness. And the third will be a voyage linking learning and human services by introducing the framework for this book, including guidelines for using it.

This lesson asks you to pursue the possible connections among "learning," "delivering human services," and "yourself." Our hope is that it will be an experience of reflection and discovery that will extend beyond a single lesson.

Goals

To appreciate the capacity to learn as a key attitude and skill for effective delivery of human services. To translate this appreciation into an approach for using the program of learning in this book.

Learning Activities

To accomplish these goals, we will:

1. Develop an understanding of the characteristics of learning.
2. Examine basic attitudes toward learning and reflect on our own.
3. Consider a model of the learning process.
4. Discuss and experiment with skills of effective learning.
5. Introduce the framework and learning principles of this book to illustrate the connections between learning and delivering human services.

F R A M E

1

AN ORIENTATION TO LEARNING[1]

Learning is hard to define because it can be understood in many ways. Two ways that are descriptive include understanding learning as an outcome and as a process.

- Learning as an *outcome,* or *result,* refers to what you are able to *do* after some learning experience. For example, after an internship in a human service agency, a person might be perceived as having acquired skills in interviewing, a knowledge of the kinds of work performed in a human service agency, and an ability to discuss career plans with an agency personnel representative.
- Learning can also be described as a *process,* or the things that *happen* while learning is taking place. Questioning, rehearsing, reflecting, repeating, making connections, memorizing, testing, performing, and making mistakes illustrate some of the actions that might be observed during the process of learning. For example, during a discussion with a co-worker concerning how best to address some problem a consumer is facing, you both are likely to ask questions about the person's situation in an effort to learn what the issues are and how they got that way. The things that happen during this conversation that increase your understanding of how to help might be described as a process of learning.

What is common to learning as an outcome and learning as a process is an element of *newness to you*—something that you did not know existed or did not grasp or something that was being done incorrectly is brought to light.

Learning means an approach, both to knowledge and to life, that emphasizes human initiative. It encompasses the acquisition and practice of new methodologies, new skills, new attitudes, and new values necessary to live in a world of change. Learning is the process of preparing to deal with new situations.[2]

---

[1]Unless otherwise noted, the ideas in this frame draw on a synopsis of Robert M. Smith, *Learning How to Learn: Applied Theory for Adults,* © 1982, pp. 87–93. Adapted by permission of Prentice-Hall, Englewood Cliffs, N.J.
[2]James W. Botkin, Mahdi Elmandjra, and Mircea Malitza, *No Limits to Learning: Bridging the Human Gap* (Elmsford, N.Y.: Pergamon, 1979), p. 8.

Some generally accepted observations about learning that sum up its key aspects include the following six points:[3]

1. Learning goes on throughout life. Learning can be intentional—"I plan to learn how to skate"; or unintentional—"I never realized that there was a faster route to the office until I accidentally took a wrong turn."
2. Learning is a personal and natural process. It takes place within you. No one can learn for you.
3. Learning involves change. Something is added or taken away. The change may be as small as attaching a name to a face or as large as making an in-depth reorientation in values and self-perception.
4. Learning is bound up with human development. Learning affects and is affected by the biological and physical changes in personality, values, roles, and tasks that usually occur over the normal human life span. Examples of learning at different life stages might range from learning how to tie shoes, learning how to walk, and learning how to read and write, to learning how to date, learning how to leave home, learning how to have children, and learning how to cope with death.
5. Learning pertains to experience and experiencing. Learning is doing. To learn is to experience and to interact with the environment, however that is defined.
6. Learning has an intuitive side. Knowledge can come from the environment within. Some of our most important and creative insights can come through what is called tacit knowing—for example, by letting ideas and problems simmer inside, by dreaming, or by meditating.

FRAME 2

"Thinking About Learning" Exercise[4]

Describe a *really good learning experience* you have had—one you found to be peak or really enjoyable.

Describe a *particularly unpleasant learning experience* you have had—one you found to be somehow displeasing or ineffective.

Using these experiences, discuss or reflect on how you think you learn most or least effectively.

Then continue with Frame 3.

FRAME 3

Learning Attitudes Exercise

People differ in how they go about the activities associated with learning. Some of us like to learn by doing, others by thinking. Some like to start with examples and then build up to a larger picture; others like to start with the big picture and then work

---

[3]Smith, *Learning How to Learn,* pp. 35–36.
[4]Adapted from Smith, *Learning How to Learn,* p. 173.

through the details. Some like a lot of examples and exercises; others prefer just the bare outline of the main points.

There is no one right way to learn. But as a result of our past life experience and the demands of our present environment, we develop attitudes toward learning that predispose us to act in certain ways. As a result, each of us develops a learning style that likely has some strong and weak points. Answer the questions below to reflect on your attitude toward learning

What is the most significant learning you have experienced in the recent past? What do you know now that you did not know, say six months ago? Describe one significant learning experience—about yourself, your job, your society, your recreation, or your daily living (e.g., how to operate new entertainment or computer equipment)—you've had in the past six months:

Answer the following five questions about this significant learning experience and compare the answers with those for Frame 2. Use a separate sheet of paper.

1. How did you set learning goals? Did you first write down what you wanted to learn, or did you decide what was to be done as you went along?
2. What resources did you use to help you learn? Did you interact with people or did you rely chiefly on nonhuman resources (books, cassettes, or videotapes), or did you do both?
3. What approaches did you use? Did you start at the back of the book and work forward? Did you look for something with which you were familiar and start there? Did you start with the first page and systematically work your way through the material? Did you start by talking about yourself or asking about the other person? Did you become frustrated and overwhelmed at the difficulty of it all?
4. Did you chart your progress? Did you use forms or take tests, or did you rely more on how you felt about your efforts as you were carrying them out?
5. How would you describe the experience of the learning process? When things did not go as you expected, what was your reaction? What were the chief difficulties you encountered? What was most enjoyable?

NOTE: We will be discussing clients, or consumers, the people who need or are entitled to human services in the next lesson. But as you conduct this exercise for yourself, you might also begin to think about how it might apply in your relationship with consumers. That is, how do you learn about your consumers? How do your consumers learn?

Look back at your responses to the two learning exercises (Frame 2 and this frame). How would you characterize your attitude toward learning? Consider, for example, how you acted in the learning experience you described in Frame 2. Did you place the responsibility "out there" or "within you"? What about your description of a significant learning experience? Was it one for which you took responsibility and created choices for yourself? Was it peak or really enjoyable?

F R A M E
4

A WHEEL OF LEARNING[5] FOR HUMAN SERVICE PRACTITIONERS

The philosophy of this book is that delivering effective human services is a process full of opportunities for proactive learning—about yourself, your consumers, your co-workers, your workplace, and the society and world of which you are a part. We have just discussed one element you bring to this process—either a proactive or a reactive learning attitude. How you use the experiences you have, whether they occur in the classroom or during the actual delivery of human services, is also critical. You can consciously choose to use your experiences as sources for learning if you become an *observer of your own thinking and acting*. The basic idea comes from David Kolb and is illustrated in the figure below as a "wheel" of learning by Peter Senge and his colleagues.

How do you understand the *cyclical process* in this figure? The idea of the picture is to show a process at work when you are learning from your experience.

Reflecting. When reflecting, you become an observer of your own thinking and acting. For example, you notice that the agency eligibility form or record you had to fill out was really complex; you got frustrated because the form seemed to ask you for the same thing in different ways; you complain that it leaves out some important items.

Connecting. You look for connections between changes you might make and actions you have taken in the past. To continue with the example just started: You now have more thoughts and feelings about what you are doing, but at this point you notice some patterns. You notice that almost every time you fill out one of these forms, you are frustrated with how difficult they are. You notice that you've had four very difficult meetings with your supervisor, where you have been angry and not very receptive to her feedback about your performance—yet you now notice that you have not discussed your frustrations about the agency's forms with your supervisor. So you begin to think about some options to do things differently. You consider writing a memo to your supervisor, pointing out some ideas you have about making this form easier to fill out and more complete. Or you play with the idea that you'll ask one of your co-workers to act as if she were your supervisor so you might practice sharing some of your ideas to improve the agency's form and feel more comfortable about making such suggestions. That leads you to think you'll examine some library resources to see if they address your question.

Deciding. You settle on what you are going to do from among the options generated in the connecting stage. You decide what you will do and why.

Doing. You spend half an hour doing the role-playing, going to the library, developing a memo identifying some of your concerns about the agency

---

[5]Richard Ross, Bryan Smith, and Charlotte Roberts, "The Wheel of Learning: Mastering the Rhythms of a Learning Organization," in Peter Senge, Charlotte Roberts, Richard Ross, Bryan Smith, and Art Kleiner, *The Fifth Discipline Fieldbook* (New York: Doubleday, 1994), p. 59.

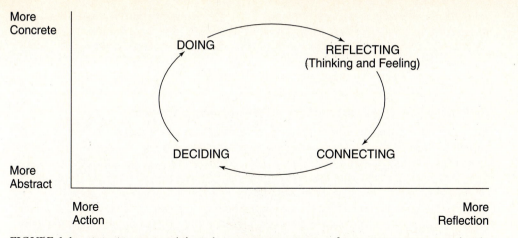

FIGURE 1.1   How We Learn While Delivering Human Services [*Source:* Peter Senge et al., *The Fifth Discipline Fieldbook* (New York: Doubleday, 1994), p. 60 and David A. Kolb, Irwin M. Rubin, and James M. McIntyre, *Organizational Psychology: Readings on Human Behavior in Organizations,* 14th ed. (Englewood Cliffs, N.J.: Prentice Hall, 1994), p. 128].

form, and identifying ideas you and others with whom you have spoken have to improve the form. You discover your supervisor liked the memo you wrote proposing some changes to the form and suggested you meet with an analyst in the policy group to discuss your ideas. Trying to do a role-play pretending your co-worker was your supervisor was a disaster, so maybe you'll address your concerns more directly. You just realized you respond to your brother in ways that are similar to how you interact with your supervisor. When you finish these actions, you move to another reflecting stage.

Repeating the Process. As you keep repeating the process of "reflecting-connecting-deciding-doing" for different experiences you have, eventually you reach a point where you are doing your work with an inquiring and experimental mindset. Your actions are increasingly supported and followed by the reflective and connecting and deciding stages. Knowing this increases your self-awareness and ability to learn from your own experience.

Practiced regularly, the wheel of learning can beome a way of life, in the same way that the scientific method is a way of life for people in laboratories. Work done in rhythm with the learning wheel is reassuringly cyclical. No matter how frantic things get, you know your action will be mindful, because time for reflection is built in. Yet when it is time to act you can move instantly.[6]

This book is an attempt to engage you in a reflective conversation about what you are or will be doing as a human service practitioner. We hope that the book will also be a catalyst for you to continue developing and using these learning and self-reflective skills while you are delivering human services, and that you will approach

---

[6]Ross et. al., "The Wheel of Learning," p. 61.

your responsibilities as an ongoing process of learning, so that you are continually inquiring into what you are doing, how you are doing it, how well it worked, and what actions you might take in the future to maintain, change, or improve patterns you observe.

FRAME 5

Reflections from One of the Authors, on "Learning from Experience"

I was attending a four-day seminar on human behavior. On the first day, the instructor presented a model of experiential learning and suggested that the key to effective practice was to be able to transform experience into knowledge and to link knowledge back into experience. I thought all of this sounded really interesting but didn't think much more about it.

Then, on the second day of the seminar, we had a six-hour role-playing experience where we all took on different jobs in an organization we created. I got the part of a human service supervisor. For a while, the game didn't really mean much, but then I became really engaged in my part. As I did, I noticed myself acting out a range of behaviors, some of which were effective in my group and others less so.

At the end of the six-hour role-playing experience, we gave one another feedback about our behavior during the game. The way we structured it was to tell one another one thing we each did well and one area we thought would be an opportunity for growth. My group really liked my high energy level and commitment, but one person thought I wrote too much and another thought I talked too much! At the time, I was good natured and receptive to the feedback. After all, it was just a game.

For two days after the game and the feedback, I kept feeling like I was going to cry, but I didn't know why. Then I began to think about my experiences during the game, and I started to realize that some of my behaviors there were similar to things I had done in other aspects of my life. I talked with friends and colleagues and read some books that discussed some of what I felt. At this point, I remembered the model of learning that the instructor talked about, and I realized I was using it. He had mentioned how you sometimes feel when you really learn something—when you really make a connection between your experience, how you feel about the experience, and what you know intellectually. Basically, he suggested that you feel it in your gut. I had that feeling, and I used it to try out some different ways of behaving. I have to say it was not easy, but it made that model come alive in my work and other aspects of my life.

Not all learning experiences will be difficult or "felt in your gut." However, those involving major changes often will be. The point is that there are many ways to learn from experience, and the process for doing so usually involves having an experience, thinking about what the experience means, connecting the experience to others you have had or are having, and using the results to experiment with new or more effective ways of behaving.

FRAME 6

"LEARNING" AND THE FRAMEWORK FOR DELIVERING HUMAN SERVICES USED IN THIS BOOK

Human services, broadly applied, include public welfare, mental health, corrections, mental retardation or developmental disabilities, vocational rehabilitation, services to the elderly, pupil personnel, public health, employment services, services to delinquent youth, hospital and health care, Social Security, and related areas. Two kinds of knowledge and skills are needed to deliver services in these areas: setting-specific and generic. *Setting-specific content* is specialized and tailored to the requirements unique to a particular set of services. For example, working with the elderly requires knowledge of the aging process and the special needs and problems likely to arise during these periods of development. This is in contrast to working with delinquent youth, which would suggest the need for different knowledge, such as more attention to the needs of adolescents, family issues, drug issues, and career or educational planning issues. *Generic content,* on the other hand, argues that there is a body of knowledge and skills that is important to all of these areas of human services—in addition to the setting-specific information.

Delivering Human Services is a program of learning designed around a framework of generic content for effective practice at the entry level. The framework of the book has three parts:

1. A set of learning guidelines or principles
2. A knowledge base
3. A set of skills for service delivery

The following is a brief introduction and overview of these elements. They are also displayed in more detail in the figure in Frame 9 for those who like to learn visually. All of this material will be developed in more detail in the rest of this text.

I. Learning Principles Underlying the Use of This Book

Four learning principles are important to keep in mind as you complete this curriculum:

1. Learning processes are important to understand and deliver effective human services. How people go about learning to deliver human services will affect how they actually deliver them.
2. It is practically impossible to define human services in one sentence or even in one page because there are many aspects involved. So each lesson in this book is really an attempt to define one piece of the total mosaic of delivering human services. For example, this lesson suggests that the human services can be understood and practiced as learning processes. Other lessons will consider the human services as systems, as helping processes, or as advocating or mobilizing processes, to name a few. No one lesson stands alone. Each one is a way to look at your practice of delivering human services.
3. Effective delivery of human services will in part be based on the acquisition of a set of experiences that include certain knowledge, values, and skills.
4. Effective learning through this text will best be accomplished by using the activities in the program as "experiences" and applying the model of learning from experience to classroom, agency, and personal settings.

II. Knowledge Foundation

Unit One of the text is concerned with laying a foundation of knowledge for your practice. Each of its three chapters provides information about the different contexts of your work, including yourself and how you see things (e.g., through learning, language, and systems). Unit One also describes the big picture of service delivery. On the one side of the picture are the conditions creating the need for services, including the personal needs of consumers and the conditions in our society that can act to turn needs into collective problems. On the other side are the people responding to human needs, including human service workers, the work they do, and the organizations through which their services are delivered. Each lesson in this unit is constructed as one door, gate, or window you can "open" to understand and deliver human services. Thus each lesson is only a partial view of the human service world.

Knowledge in the human services is not absolute because there is no "one way" of doing things or "one right answer." The more important point about knowledge for delivering human services is how you use it to approach your work—what questions you ask, how effectively you are able to know what you don't know and search for alternatives, how well you know yourself and how effectively you use yourself, and how well you are able to link what you know and what you are doing through a variety of sources. The "conversations" in this program of learning are intended to challenge you to imagine alternatives, to experiment with different ideas and practices, and to test what you are learning with your notions of who you are.

An important component of the knowledge foundation for delivering human services is knowledge about values or preferred beliefs about human nature and preferred ways of translating these beliefs into helping consumers. Lessons in Unit One call attention to the importance of awareness of personal, professional, and societal values as well as the values of the consumer receiving services.

III. Skills for Delivering Human Services: Three Goals and Nine Roles

A skill is measured by how you perform. It is how you connect your knowledge and values with your actions in delivering human services.[7] The skills needed to deliver human services are the focus of this book.

Three goals for delivering entry-level human services are getting services to consumers in need; helping consumers to function more effectively; and working across boundaries for competent practice. Certain skills are needed to accomplish these three general goals. These skills can be organized into major clusters of activities called roles. Units Two, Three, and Four develop skills for delivering human services according to the major roles involved for each goal.

- Unit Two defines the roles performed in getting services to consumers in need and includes linking the consumer with appropriate community resources, advocating on behalf of the consumer when services are unjustly denied, and developing new consumer services where none exist. The roles of brokering, consumer advocating, and mobilizing are emphasized in the three chapters in this unit.
- Unit Three defines the roles performed in helping consumers to function more effectively. Emphasis is placed on helping consumers to modify or change their behavior, either through short-term helping and counseling or

---

[7]Louise C. Johnson, *Social Work Practice: A Generalist Approach,* 2nd ed. (Boston: Allyn & Bacon, 1986), p. 62.

long-term treatment in a controlled environment, such as a mental hospital. While all human service work involves relationship building, special attention is given to interviewing and mapping the consumer's system of resources and supports. The three key roles are relating to consumers, collaborating with consumers, and intervention models.

- Unit Four defines the administrative, organizational, and professional practice roles performed to work across boundaries (of organizations, programs, cultures, problems, etc.) for competent practice. Three key roles are performed to span the numerous divisions that exist in the human services in order to deliver the full array of services that a particular consumer might require. These roles are managing information, managing the transition to new service delivery systems, and integrating or developing skills in combining and synthesizing the big picture of practice when delivering human services.

FRAME
7

Indicate with a check mark whether each of the following would be classified as generic human service content or setting-specific content.

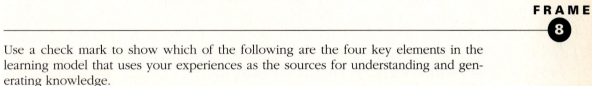

	Generic Content	*Setting-Specific Content*
1. Being able to identify the diagnostic labels used to classify consumers receiving mental health services.	_____	_____
2. Being aware of the values underlying human service work in a variety of settings.	_____	_____
3. Understanding the formulas used to determine whether a consumer is eligible for a particular form of financial aid.	_____	_____
4. Being skilled in the role of collaborating with (helping) consumers to empower them to acquire needed services and behaviors.	_____	_____
5. Being familiar with the causes, processes, and treatments for drug addiction in particular populations.	_____	_____

Turn to Answer 1 on page 591

FRAME
8

Use a check mark to show which of the following are the four key elements in the learning model that uses your experiences as the sources for understanding and generating knowledge.

_____ **1.** Finding patterns in your experience.

_____ **2.** Writing down learning goals.

_____ **3.** Thinking about your experience.

_____ **4.** Using a variety of resources to meet your learning needs.

_____ **5.** Having concrete experience.

_____ **6.** Experimenting with new behaviors based on your experiences.

_____ **7.** Charting your progress toward learning goals.

_____ **8.** Taking extensive notes to doc000ument what you have learned.

Turn to Answer 2 on page 591.

FRAME

9

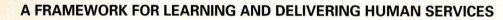

A FRAMEWORK FOR LEARNING AND DELIVERING HUMAN SERVICES

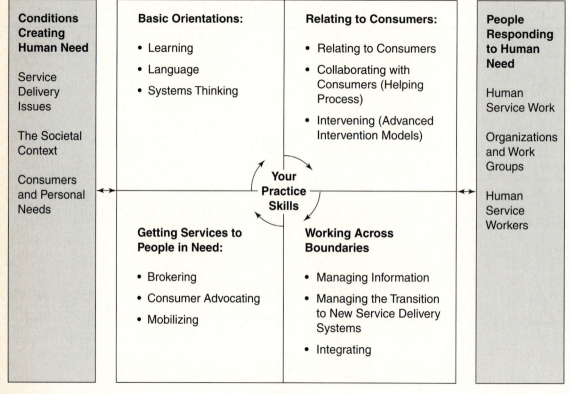

FIGURE 1.2

FRAME

10

LEARNING PRINCIPLES AND DELIVERING HUMAN SERVICES

Seven learning principles can facilitate a reflective learning attitude and an ability to learn from experience. These are important not only to complete the program of learning in this text successfully but also to put into practice the model of learning just described. Quite likely, your basic goal will be to sharpen your skills rather than to start from scratch. These learning principles are introduced here and then developed further, to varying degrees, throughout this text.

1. Listening reflectively. To listen reflectively is to wonder about the meanings and connections among actions and concepts, self and other, this book versus that book. To listen reflectively is to be able to embrace error and uncertainty, including an openness and freedom to say, "I don't know the answer." To listen reflectively is to hear what is going on within and about you and what is being said by people speaking. Listening reflectively is the art of "developing deeper silences in yourself, so you can slow your mind's hearing to your ear's natural speed, and hear beneath the words to their meaning."[8] To listen reflectively is to be open to deep learning about self and world.

2. Reading actively. In much the same way that good listeners interact with speakers and seek to understand what is said, active readers enter into a transaction with the printed word. They constantly put questions to themselves: What is being communicated here? What would be an example? Does that relate to the course objectives? Reading actively also implies watching for opportunities to apply the new ideas.

3. Observing sensitively. We often hear, "I learn a lot by just keeping my eyes open." However, it is often difficult to really "see." Skills of observing include paying attention to aspects of the setting you are in (e.g., furniture, equipment, ventilation, clothing, eye movements, facial expressions, physical conditions, hand gestures, and pictures) and using these as additional sources of understanding.

4. Cultivating an openness to change. How can we cultivate and revive the curiosity and the experimental attitude toward living and learning that seem to come naturally in childhood? We might accomplish it through a series of taking risks, however small. For example, deciding to read an unfamiliar book, trying an exercise frame in *Delivering Human Services,* viewing a film we are not immediately drawn to, engaging in a conversation with someone whose beliefs we do not share, or visiting strange surroundings. The more we reach out to new experiences, the greater our effectiveness in dealing with a variety of situations, and the easier it may be to reach out again.

5. Cultivating variety. Effective learners will have the capability and flexibility to learn from and in a variety of situations. Examples include learning from self, instructors, mentors, television, agencies, classroom discussions, friends, consumer interactions, conferences and workshops, radios, computers, nature, books, and the arts. Effective learners will also be distinguished by how they view mistakes. The "trained" learner will use mistakes as sources of insight and suggestions for improvement. Closely linked to these characteristics is *imagination,* or the ability to use all kinds of experiences as sources for inventing new ideas and figuring out how different concepts might combine into changed or improved ways of doing things.

6. Increasing self-awareness. Experiences that increase your awareness of yourself can result in greater learning effectiveness. For example, completing self-assessment exercises in this text, keeping a diary or writing autobiographical essays, and asking for feedback from friends and co-workers are ways of discovering how you are perceived and understood.

7. Cultivating a healthy skepticism or ability to think critically. Some of the above habits, such as listening reflectively, reading actively, observing sensitively, and cultivating variety and imagination, might leave you with the impression that you do

---

[8]Peter Senge et al., *The Fifth Discipline Fieldbook: Strategies and Tools for Building a Learning Organization.* New York: Doubleday Currency, 1994, p. 377.

not evaluate the information you receive. Not so! Once you understand what is being proposed, effective learning will be enhanced if you challenge it, check it out, and add to it or otherwise adopt or reject it as your own. Part of what it means to be a developing or learning person is this ability to question and reflect on what is being proposed and then to act in ways that are linked to what you discover through that process.

The point of all of these principles is to be able to use them at appropriate stages of the learning process and throughout the process of delivering and studying human services. If there are two common themes, they are the following: (1) ask, then judge, and (2) connect ideas with actions—or achieve understanding prior to evaluation, and continually develop your ability to link what you learn or know to what you do.

F R A M E

11

Match each characteristic of learning in column A with the appropriate learning principle in column B.

<table>
<tr><td align="center">*Column A*
Characteristics of Learning</td><td align="center">*Column B*
Learning Principle</td></tr>
</table>

_____ **1.** Questioning the rationale for a particular answer choice and suggesting an alternative.

_____ **2.** Being able to learn from a variety of situations—such as self, instructors, supervisors, consumers, and television.

_____ **3.** "I learn a lot by keeping my eyes open."

_____ **4.** Being more interested in "I don't know" than "I have the answer."

_____ **5.** Taking someone to lunch whose beliefs you do not share.

_____ **6.** Keeping a journal of the feelings you have as you complete the program of learning in this text.

a. Observing sensitively
b. Listening reflectively
c. Thinking critically
d. Increasing self-awareness
e. Cultivating variety
f. Openness to change

Turn to Answer 3 on page 592

F R A M E

12

An Exercise in Active Reading Applied to Delivering Human Services[9]

This exercise is offered as an illustration of how to use active reading skills to become familiar with the program of learning in this text. The approach is also useful in becoming familiar with other written materials (e.g., agency procedure manuals and other textbooks).

_____

[9]From Smith, *Learning How to Learn,* p. 171.

1. Read what the publisher has to say about the book and its authors on the inside and outside covers.
2. Turn to the frontmatter (preface and instructions) and read the authors' orientation to the book.
3. Turn to the table of contents and see how the authors have organized the information into parts (units, chapters, lessons, or other sections).
4. Leaf through the book, rapidly scanning or reading the occasional paragraph or heading that interests you. Try to get the feel of the book.
5. Put the book down and write three questions concerning matters you have become curious about as a result of this preliminary examination.
6. Review your first question and find in it a key word or phrase that you think might be in the index. Go to the index and look for the key word; if you draw a blank, try to come up with a synonym. If the synonym isn't there, see if the table of contents leads you to where the question can be answered.
7. Turn to the part of the book that deals with your question and look for the answer. If the author refers to material in other parts of the book, follow the leads until you have enough information relevant to your question.
8. Use the same procedure with your second and third questions.

F R A M E

13

An Exercise in Self-Awareness: How Do You Learn Best?[10]

This exercise provides an opportunity to assess how you learn best and to use that insight to identify the learning you would like to achieve using this book. As you increase *your* understanding of your learning style, you are in a better position to create your own learning opportunities. You are also better able to inform others (e.g., colleagues, supervisors, and instructors) about the ways in which you learn best. The exercise has two parts, with instructions provided separately for each.

Part I: How Do I Learn Best?

This part of the exercise proposes that you think about how you learn best with respect to five broad conditions: motivation, energy, rewards, involvement, and individuality. To make this material "come alive" for you, we suggest you personalize each condition using the following steps:

STEP 1. Consider the following six conditions under which you might learn best. After reading all the statements, rank them in order according to how you learn best, beginning with "*1*" to indicate what is most important to you.

_____ a. I learn best if I am highly *motivated* to learn.

---

[10]Adapted from Alfred Kadushin, *Supervision in Social Work,* 3rd ed. (New York: Columbia University Press, 1992), pp. 183–200.

_____ b. I learn best when I can devote most of my *energies* in the learning situation to learning.

_____ c. I learn best when my learning is attended by positive satisfactions—when it is successful and *rewarding*.

_____ d. I learn best if I am actively *involved* in the learning process.

_____ e. I learn best if consideration is given to my *uniqueness* as a learner.

STEP 2. Discuss how each of the six conditions is important to your learning. Examples of how each condition might be important are offered below.

Examples of the Learning Conditions

How This Condition Is Important to Your Learning

Motivation

I learn best if:

1. I am highly motivated to learn.
2. I understand the usefulness of the content to be taught.
3. Learning is made meaningful in terms of my motives and needs.
4. Areas of low motivation are tied to areas of high motivation.
5. I am highly interested in the material.
6. Someone else motivates me.

Energy

I learn best when:

1. My role as a learner is clearly differentiated from the role of the instructor.
2. The performance expectations are clear and progress is measured against them.
3. I can comfortably open myself to saying, "I don't know."
4. The anxiety I may feel from the risk of changing (my attitude, values, behaviors) is positively acknowledged—with appropriate performance expectations.
5. There is acceptance that learning is a growth process and takes time.

Rewards

I learn best when:

1. Learning is attended by positive satisfactions—when it is successful and rewarding.
2. Conditions of learning are set to ensure high probabilities of success.

Examples of
the Learning Conditions

How This Condition Is
Important to Your Learning

3. Success in professional accomplishment is praised.
4. Praise is given through positive feedback.
5. Feedback on performance is provided at frequent intervals.
6. Learning is divided into small, manageable components.
7. Material is presented in graded sequences from simple to complex.
8. I am prepared for failure.

Involvement

I learn best if:

1. I am actively involved in the learning process.
2. I am encouraged to participate in planning the agenda for learning.
3. I am encouraged to question, discuss, object, or express doubt.
4. I have an opportunity to use and apply the knowledge that I am learning.
5. I take responsibility for interacting with the material (successively building toward greater complexity) and for integration (relating different contents to one another).

Uniqueness

I learn best if:

1. Consideration is given to my uniqueness as a learner.
2. My learning is tailored to me, based on a diagnosis of my competencies.
3. I am actively engaged in an assessment of what I already know and what I want to learn.
4. The educational diagnosis is used for periodic updating.

Part II: Using How You Learn Best to Develop a Learning Plan

STEP 1. Identify a specific activity that you want to learn or want to learn to do better. This activity should be related to what you want to do or are doing as a human service worker.

STEP 2. Select what you consider to be your top three learning conditions—the things that are most important to ensure you will learn best.

STEP 3. Apply your top three learning conditions to this activity in the form of a learning plan or learning contract with yourself and one significant other person.

Activity/Activities You Want to Learn (e.g., from this book):

Three Conditions Most Important to How You Learn Best	*Application of Each Condition to What You Want to Learn: What Do You Need to Do to Make It Happen?*
1.	
2.	
3.	

LESSON 2

Language and the Delivery of Human Services

Experience becomes possible because of language.[1]

The structure of language determines not only thought, but reality itself.[2]

A feature that distinguishes the human services from other areas of work activity is the language practitioners use to communicate. Helping you to understand the basic human service vocabulary and to apply it to real-life agency situations are major objectives of this book. But knowing what the words are and being able to use them in specific situations are only part of the story. Particularly in the human services, where working *with people and through people* is the essence of the work, workers must be sensitive to the implications of the language they use—both for themselves and for others. For example, cultivating such an appreciation requires an awareness of how human service language interacts with issues of human diversity (e.g., cultural, ethnic, gender, health, race, education, and employment). Lesson 2 illustrates these ideas by pursuing two primary aspects of the human service language—the term *human services* itself and the terms for the people receiving human services. The aim throughout is to use the discussion to consider possible principles of practice.

Goals

To demonstrate the significance of the language human service workers use to talk about their work, with particular emphasis on understanding the term *human services* and the terms labeling the people receiving human services. To translate these considerations into an ability to discuss the practice implications of the language you choose.

Learning Activities

To accomplish these goals, we will:

1. Examine a basic definition of language and the overall role it plays in an area of work.

---

[1]Noam Chomsky, in Ruth Nanda Anshen, *Biography of an Idea* (Mt. Kisco, NY: Moyer Bell Limited, 1986), p. 196.
[2]Anshen, *Biography of an Idea*, p. 206.

2. Explore three key dimensions that characterize the term *human services*.
3. Develop sensitivity to the numerous labels that are used for the people receiving human services and consider their implications.
4. Develop an ability to listen to our language by considering six possible principles of practice that emerge from our survey of the use of language in the human services.

FRAME

THE ROLE OF LANGUAGE IN AN AREA OF WORK

Language is the unique combination of symbols, signs, and words with which a particular group of people communicate meaning and regulate their activities. Language has many aspects and plays an important role in shaping the behavior, attitudes, images, and values of personal, organizational, and professional life.

You will recall that each lesson in this book offers a different view of the human services. In this lesson, we consider human services as an area of work in which a particular language is used. As an area of work, human services can be compared with other areas, such as law, theater management, business management, physical science, and forest or park service. Every area of work has its own characteristic language that makes it possible to understand everyday events. In fact, to function effectively in any specialized group situation—be it work, a community college or university, a spiritual or church group, or an athletic club—it is essential that we understand the language used.

Language has at least two important aspects: content and form. The content of a language includes words, symbols, and signs. The forms of language are how or through what means the words, signals, and signs are communicated. Many forms of language appear in a culture such as ours, and these language forms differ widely in how they convey ideas, emotions, and experiences.

Examples of Forms of Language[3]

Art (e.g., music and painting)	Body language	Poetry	General verbal expression	Concepts peculiar to a particular field (e.g., disease)	Computer languages	Mathematics

Language plays an important role in creating and maintaining an area of work for at least two reasons:[4]

1. It enables people in a given area to communicate with one another. Those engaged in an area of work tend to communicate more among themselves than

---

[3]Adapted from Richard L. Daft and John C. Wiginton, "Language and Organization," *Academy of Management Review,* 4, 2 (1979): 179–191.

[4]Roger Evered, "The Language of Organizations: The Case of the Navy," in Louis R. Pondy, Peter J. Frost, Gareth Morgan, and Thomas C. Dandridge, *Organizational Symbolism* (Greenwich, Conn.: JAI Press, 1983), pp. 125–143.

TABLE 1.1   **Preview of the Vocabulary of the Human Service Language**

Words	Symbols	Signs	Means of Communication
Human services	Seal of the state on agency	Acronyms (e.g., DRG,	Face to face
Consumers	letterhead	HHS, AFDC, AIDS)[a]	Bulletin boards/walls
Clients	Office furniture (desks,	Hand gestures	Telephone
Patients	beds, wheelchairs)	Facial expressions	Memos
Citizens	Forms or paperwork that	Phones ringing	Mail
Social work	must be completed	Sirens	Messengers
Helping	Office equipment	Locks/alarms/security	Computers
Black	Office space (private	systems	Televisions/VCRs
Male	offices, large room with		Intercoms
Chinese	many desks)		Paging systems
Diversity	Office location		Fax systems
Poor	Size of building		Brochures
Mentally ill	Job titles		
Disabled	Educational degrees		
Counselor	Clothing (uniforms,		
Blind	business attire)		
White	Retirement dinners		
Female	Annual picnics		
Russian			
Generalist			

[a]DRG stands for diagnostic related group, or patient illness category. DRG is a concept used in a federal government policy called the Prospective Payment System for Hospitals under Medicare; HHS stands for the federal Department of Health and Human Services; AFDC stands for Aid to Families with Dependent Children, a program that provides financial support to families with dependent children and was changed in 1996 to a new program called Temporary Aid to Needy Families (TANF); and AIDS refers to acquired immune deficiency syndrome.

with those in other activity fields. To understand one another, they need shared understandings for events, objects, words, and people. Language is part of what enables this sense of a common view to exist.

2. It differentiates the activity in one area of work from that in other areas. Every group creates its own "in" words that mark both belonging to that group as well as the world view of the group. Thus, moving from one area of work to another—for example, moving from the human services to forestry—will necessitate learning a new language.

Table 1.1 illustrates elements of language for the human services. We will pursue these ideas further in this lesson and throughout the book; thus the table is offered as a preview of what is to come. The point for now is not to define each term you see; rather, it is to be aware that a unique and changing vocabulary exists in the human services. As you review the examples in the table, you might want to add your own based on what you already know about the human services.

If you consider experiences you have had entering new organizations—a school, a job, a neighborhood, a state, or a country you have never visited—you may recall that one important aspect of becoming both familiar and effective in that setting was learning the language. As Table 1.1 suggests, this is more than simply knowing the words. The language also includes meanings attached to objects in the environment, ranging from furniture to specific events. For example, having a computer terminal in your office might symbolize direct access to critical data files and the fact that you have a security clearance to information not available to others. But it is your personal experience with unfamiliar situations that most strikingly illustrates the role that language plays in shaping what you do and how you do it.

> It is probably safe to assume that most people of working age have had the experience (at least once) of joining a new organization, especially a different kind of organization from those they have previously encountered. The initial experience is often described as confusing, scary, surprising, unintelligible, giving rise to a need to comprehend the new and unfamiliar surroundings in order to act. New situations characterized by unfamiliar terminology, data, signals, and symbols are difficult to make sense of because the critical vocabulary and rules for relating are not known. In short, organizational events and actions have no meaning until we learn the *language* of the particular organization that provides the context for meaning.[5]

FRAME

UNDERSTANDING THE TERM *HUMAN SERVICES*

Saying that an area of work such as the human services has a unique vocabulary to distinguish it from other areas is certainly true. But the term *human services* can be confusing because it allows for multiple meanings and interpretations.[6] We would like to take advantage of this variety by exploring some of the language that helps us to understand the term *human services*.

Human services is a very broad term that includes at least three dimensions:

1. **Services,**
2. **Providers,** and
3. **Recipients.**

Watch the use of language as we consider each of these dimensions. Circle terms that strike you as being unique to the human services as an area of work or terms to which you have any kind of strong reaction.

Services: Nature of the Services Delivered

Webster's defines *service* as "the work performed by one that gives good, use, or benefit to others." However, if we took this as the definition of human services, we would include virtually any act that produces a good effect on at least one person.

When we focus on the nature of professional services, "human" services are intentional, organized, ongoing efforts designed to provide good to others through the work

---

[5]Evered, "Language of Organizations," p. 125.
[6]Richard S. Sauber, *The Human Services Delivery System* (New York: Columbia University Press, 1983), p. 16.

of specially designated people.[7] Human services are provided to improve the quality of living for the most needy members of our society (e.g., individuals or groups who, for whatever reason, have failed to be included in the mainstream of the society or culture or who experience the pain and anguish of life in these complex times).[8]

The possible services offered can be extensive, ranging from providing information to helping prevent problems to providing specialized services (such as training, crisis intervention, outreach, and financial assistance) to helping people with serious problems related to major disabilities or law violations. All of them, however, are variations on a basic theme of sustaining (e.g., health care), supporting (e.g., financing), or enhancing (e.g., education) life.[9]

Because the nature of services is so broad, people look for different languages to describe them. Two approaches are typical: People either simply list examples of the services without trying to categorize them or they try to find a few categories that will summarize the different kinds of services provided. These two approaches are illustrated here.

"Listing" Examples of Human Services

Advice and counseling for individuals with personal psychological problems.
Care and protection of dependent persons.
Care and treatment of individuals with disabilities.
Care and treatment of individuals who are sick, including the mentally ill.
Control of dangerous or deviant behavior.
Development of social interaction skills involved in group participation and in collective decision making.[10]
Development of work skills.
Education and socialization of children and youth.
Mutual assistance in emergencies and catastrophies.
Organization of problem-solving groups.
Recreation and social activities.
Transfer of economic resources—or the direct provision of food, shelter, and medical care to individuals and households without such resources.

"Categorizing" Examples of Human Services

Example 1: Access, protective, survival, and personal growth services.
Human services include those services providing *access* to other services, such as programs to provide referral information, outreach, transportation, and escort

---

[7]Francis X. Russo and George Willis, *Human Services in America* (Englewood Cliffs, N.J.: Prentice-Hall, 1986), p. 3.

[8]Joseph Mehr, *Human Services: Concepts and Intervention Strategies,* 5th ed. (Boston: Allyn & Bacon, 1992), p. 1.

[9]Roy S. Azarnoff and Jerome S. Seliger, *Delivering Human Services* (Englewood Cliffs, N.J.: Prentice-Hall, 1982), pp. 1–3. Also see Harold Wilensky and Charles Lebeaux, *Industrial Society and Social Welfare* (New York: The Free Press, 1958) and Ralph Dolgoff, Donald Feldstein, and Louise Skolnik, *Understanding Social Welfare,* 3rd ed. (New York: Longman, 1993).

[10]David M. Austin, *The Political Economy of Human Service Programs* (Greenwich, Conn.: JAI Press, 1988), p. 1.

services. A second category, *protective* services, includes those services that offer guardianship for abused children or youthful offenders and prevention of drug abuse. A third category includes basic services necessary for *survival,* including health care and housing. Finally, there are services aimed at *personal growth,* or enhancement of the quality of life, such as recreation, education, and arts programs.[11]

Example 2: Eligibility-based and developmental services.[12]

Some human services are available only after people meet a set of rigorous eligibility criteria. A detailed investigative process analyzes a person's specific situation to establish need and eligibility for services. The assessment may be quite extensive and require the submission of rent and medical bills; bank books and Internal Revenue Service forms; and explanations for the causes of crises such as alcoholism, drug abuse, and divorce. Often the person is then stigmatized by the negative public sentiment directed toward the service. Examples include certain forms of financial support, such as Aid to Families with Dependent Children.

Developmental human services meet the normal living needs of average people facing ordinary circumstances without subjecting people to rigorous investigations in which they have to "prove" their worth and eligibility. Examples of developmental human services include public education, day care, and providing financial benefits to the elderly solely on the basis of age.

Example 3: Direct and indirect services.

Human services can be *direct* or *indirect.* Direct human services are concerned with the immediate welfare of individuals or groups. They are intended to deal with specific problems or to meet well-defined needs of recipients. A service is direct as long as it is intended to benefit the recipient individual or group immediately. Examples of direct services are family counseling and health care.

Indirect human services are more concerned with improving the general social welfare, and the well-being of individual recipients is incidental. For example, incarcerating convicted criminals may or may not benefit them, but it is usually justified in terms of reducing the incidence of crime and improving public safety. Many services are both direct and indirect (e.g., education benefits the individual and society). Whether a specific service is direct or indirect depends on the immediacy of the delivery of goods and services, the intentions of the providers, and the justifications offered for the service.[13]

It is important to note that both approaches—"listing" services and "using broad categories"—to describing the kinds of services provided are valid. Each provides a different language to understand what is delivered. Indeed, full comprehension of the nature of services requires the ability to discuss both.

---

[11]Azarnoff and Seliger, *Delivering Human Services,* p. 2.
[12]See David Macarov, *Social Welfare: Structure and Practice* (Thousand Oaks, Calif.: Sage, 1995) and Howard Karger and David Stoesz, *American Social Welfare Policy* (New York: Longman, 1990) for more in-depth distinctions of the conceptions of social welfare in American society.
[13]Russo and Willis, *Human Services in America,* p. 10.

Providers: Who Delivers Human Services?

Clearly the range of the services offered is broad; so, too, is the range of organizations and people who provide them.

Organizations. Human services may be offered by governmental agencies at the federal, state, or local level (e.g., a welfare department), by private nonprofit agencies (e.g., a family service agency), by private for-profit agencies (e.g., most nursing homes), by individuals in private practice, or by voluntary organizations (e.g., a senior citizen's organization).

Service personnel. Service providers include members of established human service professions, such as medical professionals, psychologists, social workers, and rehabilitation counselors. Service providers may also be members of more recently established paraprofessional groups—or, as they are sometimes called, "new professionals." These groups include workers trained as human service generalists (in contrast to specialists in a particular service area), mental health technicians, allied health professionals, child care workers, drug and alcohol abuse counselors. Volunteers are also an important category of human service providers. The formal training of people working in the broad field of human services ranges from on-the-job training for high school graduates to AA/AS, BA/BS, MA/MS degrees to training at the doctoral level.

Together, these agencies, service institutions, and workers form a vast network for the delivery of human services.

FRAME

Stop and personalize your understanding of the material thus far by reflecting on the following. Use the prior frames and your own experience as resources.

1. Identify two different ways of describing the kinds of services that are human services.

2. Name three organizations in your neighborhood, town, city, or state that deliver what you consider to be human services.

3. Give two examples of people whom you would consider to be providers of human services, including their job titles.

4. List three dimensions that capture the important aspects of the term *human services*.

a. _____

b. _____

c. _____

5. In your own words, describe your understanding of the term *human services* at this point.

6. What are some questions you have about the human services at this point?

FRAME

4

RECIPIENTS: WHO RECEIVES HUMAN SERVICES?

The third dimension important to understanding the term *human services* is who receives them. Human services are delivered to individuals and families and other groups from a wide variety of economic backgrounds and in a wide range of difficult circumstances. Indeed, we may think ahead to a time, or already be in a time, when the market for human services will expand to include the total society.[14] For these reasons, we may derive significant insights by reflecting on how we characterize people when they—or we—are obtaining a human service. One way to begin is by exploring the labels we apply when people receive or request a human service.

The people who receive human services are known by a wide variety of titles. The specific term used depends in part on the kind of service being provided.[15] For example:

- Medical services often use the term *patient*.
- School or educational services use the term *student* or *learner*.
- Recreation services might use the term *citizen*.
- Financial aid services might use the term *client*.
- Clinical social workers typically use the term *client*.
- Correctional services might use the term *inmate, criminal, offender,* or *law violator*.
- Counseling services for people with developmental disabilities living in a group home or elderly persons living in a nursing home might use the term *resident*.
- Crisis intervention services might use the term *victim* (e.g., rape victim).

These are powerful, possibly helpful, and potentially confusing labels to apply to people. Special language such as these terms is characteristic of any area of work activity. It is one thing to apply different labels to automobiles, fax machines, VCRs, clothing, or food. But it is quite another to apply labels to people. Consider some of the defini-

---

[14]Austin, *The Political Economy of Human Service Programs,* p. xiv.

[15]See Louise C. Johnson, *Social Work Practice: A Generalist Approach,* 2nd ed. (Boston: Allyn & Bacon, 1986), p. 145.

Patient: "An individual awaiting or under medical care and treatment; the recipient of any of various personal services; *one who is acted upon.*"

Victim: "One who is injured, destroyed, or sacrificed; *one who is acted on and usually adversely affected* by a force or agent; one who is subjected to oppression, hardship, or mistreatment; one who is tricked or duped."

Student: "One who *attends* a school; an attentive and systematic *observer.*"

Consumer: "One who uses economic goods; *one who buys* economic goods."

Customer: "One who *purchases* a commodity or service."

Citizen: "An inhabitant of a city or town, especially *one entitled to the rights and privileges* of a freeman; a native or naturalized person *who owes allegiance* to a government and is entitled to protection from it."

Constituent: "*One who authorizes another to act* for him; one of a group who elects another to represent him in public office."

Resident: "*One who dwells* at a place—lives there."

Client: "*One who engages* the professional advice or services of another (e.g., a lawyer); a person serviced by or using the services of a social agency; *one who is under the protection of another—dependent.*"

Recipient: "*One who receives, comes into possession of, or acquires (as a gift); one who suffers the hurt or injury of.*"

tions offered in the dictionary. As you reflect on these, think of the different ways you react when someone applies each label to you.

One major issue that arises in surveying these definitions is the question of how we perceive the people who receive human services. Do we perceive them as

- dependent?
- sick?
- generally self-reliant and able to make decisions?
- capable of taking initiative to make improvements?
- capable only of simply surviving?
- buyers of services who are informed about what they are purchasing, concerned about prices, and desirous of the highest quality for the least cost?
- entitled by law to the services?
- partners in a transaction with us as the workers or partners?
- objects or raw materials on which we act?
- persons under our protection—as a lawyer protects his client—on whose behalf we advocate?
- passive?

Are these different perceptions linked to the language we use to label people? If you call someone a victim, do you simultaneously treat her as self-reliant? If you label someone as a patient, do you also view him as a valued consumer who should get the best quality service and who has an interest in the costs of that service?

Traditional labels of *victim, patient,* and *client* have come to be regarded by many as stigmatizing, accentuating differences, and relegating those receiving human services to passive and dependent roles. *Consumer, customer,* and *citizen* have been proposed as alternative terms that should apply to anyone receiving human services. New definitions of *client* have also been suggested. All of these contemporary terms—*consumer, customer, citizen,* and *client*—are advocated to communicate a new perception of people receiving human services. The newer labels are intended to communicate in very clear language that people who use human services ought to be perceived and empowered as active partners, coparticipants, or buyers in the service planning and delivery process.

There is no one right answer to the question "What is the correct label?" Moreover, any label selected is likely to raise additional questions. For example, buyers are not always viewed as business partners. And who is responsible for "empowering" buyers to know which purchases will offer them the greatest quality for a reasonable or least cost? *The more important issue may be what we gain and what we lose by selecting one term over another.* To help you develop this understanding, we will illustrate some of the common implications associated with two terms: *client* and *consumer.* We do this, first, to demonstrate the power of language; second, to note some of the confusion about even these terms; third, to provide a rationale for the language we use in this book; and, fourth, to empower you to make your own choice about how you will label the people you work with.

FRAME
5

LABELS FOR RECIPIENTS OF HUMAN SERVICES: CLIENTS OR CONSUMERS?

Service Recipients as Clients?

First consider the term *client,* perhaps the most commonly used reference for a recipient of human services. It is also used frequently by lawyers, advertisers, consultants, and beauticians, to name a few. What messages do you send to yourself and to others when you think of and talk about service recipients as *clients?* We discovered at least two different usages or messages conveyed by the term *client:* (1) Clients are human beings who are passive, dependent, and need help; and (2) clients are human beings who are active participants in the helping endeavor.

John is my client: John is material to work on.[16] With this usage of *client,* a worker would view people receiving human services as neutral "other parties" in the endeavor to deliver human services. Clients are the people who ask for help or are served by an agency employing a human service worker. Clients are recipients and consumers of human services even when services may be forced on them (e.g., prisoners or children in a public school). *Client* represents raw material to be worked on, people who must cooperate and comply with service requirements. This usage of *client* reflects a benign form of professional paternalism. The worker is the professional who ultimately knows what is "best" for the client.

Sarah is my client: Sarah decided to . . . Another worker might use the term *client* to reflect a relationship that calls for active participation in the helping endeavor.[17] With this usage, the worker would refer to recipients as clients, but mean

---

[16]See Johnson, *Social Work Practice,* p. 144; Yeheskel Hasenfeld, *Human Service Organizations* (Englewood Cliffs, N.J.: Prentice-Hall, 1983), p. 177; and Beryl Radin and Terry Cooper, "From Public Action to Public Administration: Where Does It Lead?" *Public Administration Review* (Mar./Apr. 1989): 167.
[17]Johnson, *Social Work Practice,* p. 144.

that her clients had a right and responsibility to participate with leverage in the service delivery process. That participation might include furnishing appropriate information to aid in the decision-making process, setting and selecting goals, mutually agreeing to specific tasks, or sitting on an agency advisory board. Those who use the term *client* in this way also tend to take the notion of active participation one step further. They suggest that using the term *client* implies a process of empowering others by giving them the skills and knowledge needed to handle their worlds effectively.[18]

Service Recipients as Consumers?

Consumers are generally considered to be persons who purchase, buy, and use goods and services. To appreciate usage of the term in the human services, it is helpful to look at its recent origins.

General usage of consumer—*We are all consumers in this society.* The mass prosperity that followed World War II created a society of people who consumed increasing amounts of complex and specialized goods and services. Initially, consumer well-being was defined as getting the largest quantity of goods from a given income. Over time this shifted, so that now the consumer is viewed as a problem solver who recognizes buying problems in terms of a choice among competing alternatives and actively acquires and uses information in an attempt to solve the buying problem in a satisfactory manner.[19] There is a tremendous emphasis in our service society on buying, and this is often related to an urge to find something newer or better. Consumer education and intensive advertising now play prominent roles to help us all reach higher consumption levels and to help or persuade us to make choices in favor of product or service A over product or service B.

> Consumerism is an essential part of the service society. The negative aspect is easy to perceive: the commercialism, the waste reflected in gadgets and trivia, the hucksterism. *On the positive side, there is the involvement of the consumer in scrutinizing, evaluating, and questioning all areas of life,* from the environment to education to automobiles, and to some extent, even to politics, as in the concern about the representatives of the political process. Moreover, particular groups in the society, in their consumer roles, have raised important questions with regard to basic rights, personal liberation, the quality of living and so on (e.g., women, youth, minorities).[20] [Italics added.]

Consumers of human services? In the 1970s, the general language of consumerism was picked up in the human services. Human services, it was argued, should be an integral part of the consumer movement because a consumer is or should be *actively involved* in the delivery of a human service.

> Passivity on the part of consumers is a special problem in the human services. Unlike the goods sector where the production process by itself can adequately fill a consumer's demand, the consumer is a *producer* in the human services. . . .

---

[18]Barbara Solomon, *Black Empowerment: Social Work in Oppressed Communities* (New York: Columbia University Press, 1976), pp. 26–29.
[19]Raymond L. Horton, *Buyer Behavior: A Decision-Making Approach* (Columbus: Charles E. Merrill, 1984).
[20]Alan Gartner, "Consumers in the Service Society," *Social Policy* (Nov./Dec. 1977): 3.

in health and mental health care, it is the patient who is the key factor in producing his or her own return to or maintenance of good health. Human service work is *consumer-intensive* and the key to increasing productivity and consumer satisfaction lies in effectively engaging and mobilizing the consumer.[21] [Italics added.]

Thus, consumerism in the human services was proposed to convey that workers needed to do more than deliver human services. They needed to engage consumers in learning *how to consume* human services. This had at least three implications:

1. Human service consumers must be actively engaged as effective producers of the services.
2. Consumers of human services require adequate information so they can make informed choices.
3. Human service consumers' complaints must be addressed directly rather than being whitewashed or buried.

While these viewpoints may have been clear in the 1970s, contemporary use of the term *consumer* will likely evoke mixed reactions. For example, in the economic sense, consumers are not voters or citizens or even community members. Consumers are individual persons who use goods and services for their own purposes.

What about the perspective of a human service recipient who has been labeled a consumer? Consider the following comment by Judi Chamberlin, a person labeled as a patient in the mental health system, a long-term activist in the self-help and advocacy movement in mental health, and a member of the National Association of Psychiatric Survivors:

> In the field of mental health, it has become fashionable to refer to recipients of mental health services as consumers, a term that I and many other ex-patients find objectionable because *it implies that we have choices and power.* In fact, we are seldom consulted about whether we want services at all or what form services should take, or asked whether we are satisfied with the services we have received. Whereas corporations spend millions of dollars to try to find out what their customers or potential customers want, mental health systems often work with a captive population that cannot take its business elsewhere. The term consumer in itself is not empowering; in fact, it is often used to obscure the true power relationship in which the service recipient has no leverage at all.[22] [Italics added.]

Chamberlin raises some important issues. She clearly suggests that the term *consumer* implies a particular perception of service recipients as active participants in the service delivery process who are treated as *valued customers—whose choices and reactions are important to those defining and providing the services.* And she argues strongly

---

[21]Gartner, "Consumers in the Service Society," p. 7.
[22]Judi Chamberlin, "Planning a Community-Based Mental Health System," *American Psychologist* (Nov. 1990), p. 1242.

that from her experience, this is not the case. Moreover, she points out that the mere fact of labeling a recipient as a consumer does not mean that he will actually be involved as a consumer in business might be.

In sum, the terms *client* and *consumer* suggest very different perceptions of recipients of human services. In some settings and by some workers, *client* is used to refer to a relationship that is highly participative between worker and recipient, with the recipient playing a major role in the entire service delivery process. This has some similarities to the intent behind the use of the term *consumer*. In the same settings, other workers might use the term *client* to refer to recipients as "them," as "objects of our work," and "as people who have no choices and certainly aren't capable of framing them." The term *client* has a long history within helping professions such as law, psychiatry, social work, and counseling. As such, it has acquired the mixed baggage of empowerment and dependency. In our view, today, the term *client* does not evoke a clear image of participation, choice, or empowerment. By contrast, the term *consumer* has its origins in business. As Judi Chamberlin so clearly illustrates, the term *consumer* leaves little doubt as to what is intended. The prevailing sense of the term is that of an informed buyer who is involved in a transaction to purchase a service or a good. The term also suggests there is a provider who is very interested in reaching and satisfying consumers effectively for both parties. Yet just labeling a service recipient a consumer does not guarantee that the person is actually being treated as an informed buyer.

FRAME
6

What Do You Think?

What are some of the potential risks in using the term *consumer?* One colleague with whom we had such a discussion replied that, to her, *consumer* implied shared decision making between the provider and the buyer—but it also suggested a "let the buyer beware" caution. That is, if the person receiving human services is a consumer or buyer, she will need to assume responsibility for getting the "right" service—and if she buys a service that is wrong or of poor quality, then she assumes the major responsibility for not getting the right information. *What do you think?*

FRAME
7

THOUGHTS ON RESOLVING THE LABELING DILEMMA

Labels are important; they are more than mere semantics. If you look for some themes in the foregoing discussion of the implications of *client* and *consumer,* you should notice at least two. One theme is the notion of *difference*. Are the people who receive human services apart from or somehow less than the people who deliver those services? *Client, patient, inmate, resident,* and *student,* for us, are all labels that emphasize difference rather than commonality.

The second theme is the notion of *relationship*. In the human services, the label for a person who receives services also characterizes the nature of the relationship that will be created between the provider and the recipient. It may help to draw a contrast between two different kinds of relationships that seem to be at the extremes of our exploration of client and consumer. At one end is a dependent relationship in which the provider is generally considered the expert and the receiver is expected to do as he is told. At the other extreme is a partnership relationship in which the parties are mutually engaged in figuring out what to do. The table below contrasts these extremes using six elements that, when considered together, define the nature of a relationship.

Six Elements That Determine the Nature of a Relationship[23]

Dependent Relationship	Elements	Partnership Relationship
Directed; need not be shared	Goals and priorities	Jointly developed; must be shared
Spelled out	Expectations	Understood
Spelled out	Roles	Understood
Formal; less frequent	Communication	Informal; frequent
Unequal	Control	Shared
Formal: spelled out	Processes	Informal; understood

Our choice. We are all consumers and all citizens, if not of a country then certainly of the planet. In this book, we have chosen to use the term *consumer* to reflect an approach to serving people that is hopefully less stigmatized than *client, patient, inmate, resident,* or *student.* Instead, *consumer,* for us, emphasizes that we are all human and differ only according to our special needs. *Consumer* also suggests a relationship between a worker and a consumer that is somewhere between a pure "client" relationship and a pure "partnership." That is, we use the word *consumer* to convey a relationship that is empowering, helping, and moving constantly in a direction toward full partnership.

FRAME

8

LISTENING TO OUR LANGUAGE: POSSIBLE PRINCIPLES OF PRACTICE

What ideas might you take from this lesson with respect to language and delivering human services? Consider the following six ideas:

1. Language and perception. If anything emerges from this discussion, it is the importance of being able to make connections between the language you use and the world you see. Be aware of these linkages. Language builds images in your mind that become the filters for how you view the world. If you use a vocabulary that includes ideas of action, empowerment, involvement, and partnership, you are likely to perceive a far different human service world than if you speak in terms of illness, deviance, blame, or other party (a human being as object).

---

[23]U.S. Environmental Protection Agency (EPA), *The Nation's Hazardous Waste Management Program at a Crossroads* (Washington, D.C.: Office of Solid Waste and Emergency Response, July 1990), p. 13.

2. Appreciate how human diversity interacts with language. People can be talking together, using the same language, and still be at cross-purposes. One reason has to do with human diversity. We are diverse because of age, race, gender, education and training, physical or mental ability, religious affiliation, ethnicity, and socioeconomic status, among other things.

A teacher using the term *client* may not mean the same thing as a lawyer or social worker using the same term. A white male counselor in Florida working with a Haitian family or an Iraqi family that has just moved to the United States may discover they hold very different understandings of what it means to be actively involved as a human service consumer. A Ph.D. psychologist defining the term *human services* may construct an understanding that differs from the one proposed in this book.

Diversity can also work the other way. A white female counselor and a black male psychiatrist, who have discussed how they separately understand the term *human service consumer,* may reach a common definition that will greatly simplify their discussions about particular consumers.

The point is to be able to use the human service vocabulary to find commonalities across the wide range of differences that characterize our society. At the same time, we must ensure that our language does not prevent us from appreciating what is unique about being a particular human with a particular problem or need.

3. Listen to the language of others. Develop an ability to attend to the language of others so that you can raise questions to yourself and others about how it fits within your human service vocabulary. For example, a consumer in a dependent relationship with a human service worker might be heard to say, "I'm in your hands." A consumer in an interdependent relationship with a provider might be heard to say, "I have a question about that—what other options exist?"

4. Seek feedback from others about the language you use. Videotape or record your discussions and review them or appoint an observer who can later discuss with you what you said and how you said it.

5. Know what you are giving up and getting with important terms. Not every word or symbol in your vocabulary needs a deep examination. But for those terms you find significant—*clients, consumers,* and *human services* are three—explore what they imply and how they are used. What does one term give you and others that the other terms do not? What does one term prevent you from doing that another might not? Ask yourself how you might feel if someone applied that term to you.

6. Awareness of self. Our language is a very real indicator of how we understand the world. It also offers us some clues as to how we see ourselves. Embracing the language of the human services involves a fundamental look at who you are and what you believe—about services, the people who deliver them, the people who receive them, and the relationships that you want to form. Those who are self-aware will listen to what they say and how it affects others; listen to what others say and explore what they mean; and be willing to add new terms or change the use of current ones when circumstances suggest such changes to be appropriate or meaningful.

Systems Thinking and Delivering Human Services

Lesson 3 is about a particular way of thinking about the world, especially the human service world. It is about *systems thinking* and about the use of a particular set of ideas—systems ideas—to try to understand complexity and solve human service problems. The concept of system has been a mainstay in the human services for over two decades, and it is rare to find a leading practice theory or human behavior text that does not use it centrally.[1] Systems thinking can be a wellspring for creative insights; it can also be rather esoteric unless the language can be linked to everyday events.

An approach is a way of seeing a problem. Examples are the scientific approach, the psychoanalytic approach, the religious approach, the historical approach, and the humanistic approach. The systems approach is central to effective delivery of human services because it considers the whole—the totality of persons, groups, organizations, and societies in their environments. It recognizes that nothing exists by itself and offers tools for taking a broad view of problems. The penalties for *not* taking such a perspective are legion. Reflect, for example, on the following human service situations in which practitioners did not use systems thinking:[2]

- A physician prescribed a diet for a diabetic patient without regard for her limited income or for her husband's reluctance and intellectual inability to comprehend his wife's condition or needs.
- A teacher expected maximum learning from a gifted child who was performing poorly, whose peer group did not accept him, and whose familial values did not support acquiring academic knowledge.
- A nurse could not comprehend or accept an individual's reaction to pain and illness, which had been defined by a culture different from her own.
- A child protective services worker removed a disturbed individual from his family for treatment and then returned him to the pressures of an unhealthy, unchanged environment.
- A psychiatrist treated an adolescent for substance abuse without regard for the crushing reality of her family's poverty, debt, and paternal alcoholism.

What constitutes systems thinking? How is systems thinking relevant to the practice of delivering human services? These are the central questions we will pursue in this lesson.

---

[1]John F. Longres, *Human Behavior in the Social Environment* (Itasca, Ill.: F. E. Peacock, 1990), p. 19.
[2]Naomi Brill, *Working with People: The Helping Process,* 4th ed. (New York: Longman, 1990), p. 104.

Goals

To understand the systems approach as a way of thinking that applies throughout the practice of delivering human services. To apply this understanding to describing the human service system from multiple perspectives.

Learning Activities

To accomplish these goals, we will:

1. Use examples to understand "system" as a way of thinking.
2. Consider three key attitudes that facilitate systems thinking in the human services.
3. Introduce the connection between systems thinking and drawing.
4. Apply the concepts of the systems approach to mapping the human service social institutional system from five different perspectives.
5. Apply the concepts of the systems approach to mapping the human service consumer from five different perspectives.
6. Explore the advantages and limitations of systems thinking.

FRAME

1

SYSTEM AS A WAY OF THINKING

System is a common, contemporary term. "This is a lousy system," "you can't beat the system," "the solar system," "the welfare system," "the health care system," "the computer system," and "the space system" are but a few examples of phrases that are part of our everyday language. *System* has so many meanings that it can evoke utter frustration when you seek to understand it. But maybe there's another way to look at it. Consider some examples of what different people have proposed to see as systems:

Examples of Systems[3]

"A sheep can be considered a system: It takes in fodder and produces wool and lamb chops."	"A volcano is part of a system by which the Earth ventilates excessive internal heat."
"System stands for what we do not yet know how to manage—for example, the solar system and the nervous system."	"System stands for what man creates for his own use—for example, a language, a school system, and a weapons system."
"The great blue whale is a system."	"A tiny atom composed of only a few sub-atomic parts is a system."
"The process of solving a problem is a system—you take the ingredients in a problem, alter them, replace them, supplement them, or realign them, and thus produce a solution."	"A machine can be thought of as an inanimate system, and a plant can be thought of as an organic system."

[3]Ideas from Joel Kurtzman, *Futurecasting: Charting a Way to Your Future* (Palm Springs: ETC Publications, 1984), pp. 22–23; Gerald Nadler and Shozo Hibino, *Breakthrough Thinking,* 2nd ed., (Rocklin, Calif.: Prima Publishing and Communications, 1994), pp. 197–229; Harlan Cleveland, "Systems, Purposes, and the Watergate," *Public Administration Review* (May/June 1974): 265–268; and Longres, *Human Behavior,* pp. 18–20.

Some people look at these examples and argue that they are so different it is virtually impossible to be clear about what a system is. Why is this the case? Some clues may be forthcoming if we look more closely at what the term *system* means. Consider how some of these same people have defined *system* by itself (i.e., without examples):

Examples of Definitions of *System*

Webster's *dictionary*	"A system is a regularly interacting or interdependent group of items forming a unified whole."
Anatol Rapoport	"A system is a bundle of relations."
Ralph Waldo Emerson	"Man is a bundle of relations, a knot of roots, whose flower and fruitage is the world."
Harlan Cleveland	"A system is a bundle of relations which is first aimed at a sub-jective human purpose and second so large and complicated that the connections among its parts cannot be known by any one person even if that person is said to be in charge."
Fritjof Capra	"Systems are integrated wholes whose properties cannot be re-duced to those of smaller units."
John F. Longres	"A system is a dynamic order of parts and processes standing in mutual interaction."
Gerald Nadler and Shozo Hibino	"A system is a group of related entities that does something—it receives inputs, affects them in some way, and produces out-puts to achieve some purpose."

When reading these definitions, what words are repeated? We see at least five themes:

- A bundle of relations
- Interrelated, interdependent, interaction
- Parts
- Wholes
- In and out (inside and outside, input and output)

Notice how these themes are in a language that makes it relatively easy to apply them to just about anything. Therein lies the beauty of systems thinking: Its concepts are so general as to enable seeing many things in terms of their parts, relations, and wholes. Thus, the point of these examples is that a "system" is a way of seeing or a way of thinking that looks for connections, purposes, and wholes—*irrespective* of *what* is being looked at (e.g., atoms, animals, poverty, homelessness, disease, people, machines, organizations, or processes such as thinking). It is a way of seeing that asks, "What is this related to? What is going on in other settings that may be influenc-ing what I see?"

Can you imagine knowing very much about a total human being by studying just one bone? Or understanding the African American, Navajo, or Russian cultures by talk-ing with just one person from each? Clearly these tactics would produce some insights, but certainly few that would enable you to comprehend the whole person or cultural system. In the systems approach, the issue is not so much what you concretely define as a system—that is, whether this or that is a system—rather, it is how you "see or approach" problems: Do you search for relationships and connections? Do you try to think in holistic terms and map the big picture (e.g., whole person in some settings such as a family and a neighborhood)? We can summarize these observations by suggesting that *systems thinking looks for elements, relationships, and purpose:*

Elements. All systems have elements. If we look at an automobile as a system, then the tires, batteries, steering wheel, and brakes are examples of its elements. If we look at a human being as a system, then the circulatory system, digestive system, respiratory system, and legs are examples of its elements. If we look at a community mental health center, examples of its elements are the consumers' problems (e.g., adolescent difficulties attending school, relating to parents or peers, sexual abuse, inadequate housing, alcoholic family problems, and unemployment); counselors' activities with consumers (individual and family counseling, referrals to employment, and referrals to support and self-help groups); and services provided (number of job referrals and number of persons employed).

Relationships. The "whole" of a system is formed by patterns of relationships. The same elements are connected in different ways for different systems. Patterns can be described verbally, visually, or symbolically. For example, "adult children of alcoholics" is a verbal label for a pattern of behavior, family history, and feelings associated with some individuals raised by one or more alcoholic parents. Most of the figures in this lesson are examples of visual patterns being used to show different ways of systems thinking and to aid in displaying the elements and relationships of a system.

Purpose. Systems have goals, and their behavior is an attempt to achieve those goals. The unemployed head of a single-parent family of four likely has goals of basic physical survival (keeping food on the table) and perhaps education (how to train for a new kind of skill). An individual abusing drugs may have goals of getting more drugs to avoid withdrawal, or getting more drugs to avoid dealing with some incredibly painful emotions, or both.

FRAME

2

THREE ATTITUDES THAT FACILITATE SYSTEMS THINKING

Effective systems thinking in the human services is linked to attitudes of openness, humility, and confidence to act.[4]

Openness. Systems can be *closed* or *open* with respect to an *environment*. Closed systems do not depend for their existence on the outside world; to understand them,

[4]Discussion from Richard Daft, *Organization Theory and Design,* 3d ed. (St. Paul, Minn.: West Publishing, 1989), pp. 14–15; and Kenneth Boulding, "General Systems Theory: The Skeleton of Science," *Management Science* 2 (1965): 197–207.

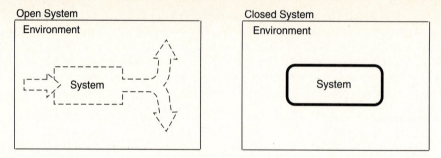

FIGURE 1.3   Open System vs. Closed System Thinking [*Source:* Wayne A. Chess and Julia M. Norlin, *Human Behavior and the Social Environment: A Social Systems Model* (Boston: Allyn & Bacon, 1988), p. 43.]

we focus exclusively on their internal workings. Open systems, by contrast, must interact with the outside world in order to survive. (See Figure 1.3.)

If you are a closed systems thinker, you see situations so that external influences do not affect system behavior. So, for example, if you were working with an adolescent abusing substances and thinking in closed systems terms, you would be uninterested in how the family situation might be influencing the substance abuse; you would consider the problem to be solely with the adolescent. If you were an open systems thinker working with the same adolescent, you would be interested in learning about the person's family and school situations, dating and other peer group relationships, and possible employment influences at key points throughout your interactions.

The condition of an open system at any one time is a function of how it is interacting with its environment. You shiver when it's cold to burn more calories and create more heat. You sweat when it's hot to lose body heat. Your system is always in the process of adjusting itself to your physical environment. The behavior of an open system thus has two important aspects: *internal* and *external* in relation to the environment. The internal task is to maintain a balanced relationship among the elements of the system. The external task is to relate to the environment. *The notion of environment is the essence of an attitude of openness.* It says that for any system there is always some context. For an open system, that context will be critical to its survival and behavior.

Humility. A second attitude of systems thinkers and actors is an appreciation of the complexity of human systems and the fact that there will always be some aspect not fully understood. This appreciation is gained, in part, by recognizing different levels of systems. Richard Daft illustrates this in Figure 1.4, which shows that systems can be arranged in order from simple to complex.

The simplest level of system is the *framework system,* such as an atom, a bridge, or a building. Frameworks sometimes include movement among elements in a predictable manner, such as a clock or solar system. *Control systems* are the second level of complexity. These systems are self-regulating and include thermostats or assembly lines. The purpose of these systems is maintaining a certain state, such as a temperature. The third level of complexity is the *biological system,* which is a living, self-maintaining system. Plant and animal systems are far more complex than either control systems or frameworks. They also exchange resources with the environment and can adapt on their own to changes in the environment. The fourth level, the *human,* or

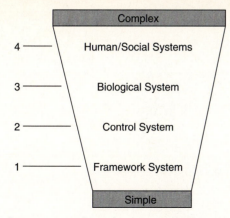

FIGURE 1.4   Scale of System Complexity [*Source:* Daft, *Organization Theory,* p. 15]

social, system, is the most complex of all. The sources of this complexity are characteristics found only in human groups: values, music, art, self-awareness, language, and use of tools such as computers. The individual, as a system, is the basic human system. In the human services, human beings or social systems are the obvious major interest. But human service workers must be sensitive to the complex nature of the social systems with which they are interacting if they are to be truly effective. If human service workers oversimplify consumer issues, they can make mistakes. All of this leads to the sobering realization that it will always be impossible to fully understand or represent any human situation.

   Confidence. Systems thinking is characterized by openness to the existence of an environment and a humility that recognizes the complexity of a human system. One undesirable result of these two attitudes could be an inability to act. For example, trying to understand a human service consumer as a system might lead you to become overwhelmed by the complexity or frustrated that perhaps something important is left out. This leads to the third attitude of systems thinking—confidence to act—to deliver human services while recognizing that you can never know all there is to know. Because systems thinking emphasizes doing your best to map key relationships and to figure out the important parts of the big picture, an attitude of confidence with humility emerges *when the steps of systems thinking have been followed.*

F R A M E

3

SYSTEMS THINKING AND DRAWING

One of the results of using the systems approach with human systems is typically an urge to draw—to visualize your understanding of elements, relationships, and purpose. These pictures are models that simplify reality. Some elements are always missing. Otherwise, the models wouldn't be models—they would be reality. Circle diagrams, charts, tables, boxes with arrows, and circles within circles are all ways of

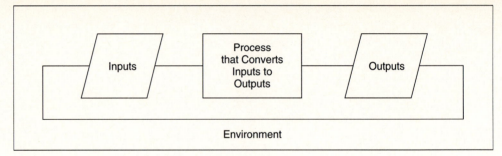

FIGURE 1.5   The Input-Output Model of a System

helping the human mind to better visualize a "whole" or a system with respect to some particular question or situation.

Although human beings and their situations are complex, a very simple model can give great insight with respect to what's going on and some options concerning solutions. The simplest model of a system is the "input-output model" (see Figure 1.5.). An input-output model is a system that takes inputs and, using some process or processes, changes them into outputs. We begin to understand the system by identifying and connecting these inputs and outputs.

Now consider applying the input-output model to the human services. *Inputs* are generally a consumer's problems—for example, inadequate housing, family problems, or unemployment. Outputs involve the empowerment of consumers, either through coping strategies or an enhanced capacity to function. *Outputs* are the results that consumers experience as a consequence of the services provided. The principal desired output, or result, is that consumers are empowered to address their problems—for example, consumers are now better able to finish school, find a job, stay in school, live more independently, enjoy life, adopt a child, stop abusing their child, or locate affordable housing. The *processes* that convert consumer problems into the experience of empowerment include the things providers actually do during their interactions with human service consumers. For example, they talk, find out what the problems are, develop helping relationships, broker, advocate, and mobilize. In many respects, *human service workers, as they interact with consumers, are the process that converts consumer problems into an ability to cope with or resolve those problems*. Figure 1.6. illustrates this application using the service delivery framework we develop in this book.

When you use systems thinking with human service consumers or in other aspects of your work, you'll find yourself drawing diagrams and pictures to aid your understanding of a situation. This book will provide many examples, so it is not necessary to start from scratch. Models that you draw help you to visualize the elements, relationships, and purposes of a system. They can aid your thinking by permitting you to examine many aspects of a problem simultaneously.

F R A M E

Pause for a moment to test your understanding of the material presented thus far.

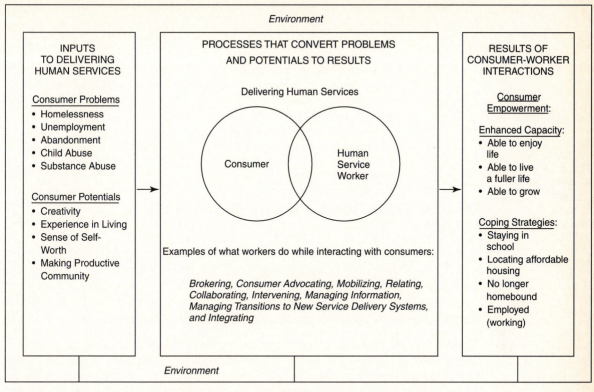

FIGURE 1.6   The Input-Output Model of Systems Applied to Delivering Human Services

1. Indicate with a check mark whether each of the following is true or false. The systems approach or systems thinking stresses:

	True	*False*
a. wholeness.	_____	_____
b. relationships.	_____	_____
c. arguments about what is and is not a system.	_____	_____
d. environments.	_____	_____
e. using drawings and tables to display the system.	_____	_____
f. searching for the one complete model.	_____	_____
g. understanding the purpose or goal of a system.	_____	_____
h. that all systems are equally complex.	_____	_____

2. Describe in one sentence your understanding of the material you have read thus far in this lesson.

3. Describe in one word your impression of the material you have read thus far.

4. Why should a human service worker consider the four levels of system complexity—the framework system, the control system, the biological system, and the human or social systems?

Turn to Answer 4 on page 593.

Turn to Answer 4 on page 593.

FRAME
5

SYSTEMS THINKING AND THE HUMAN SERVICE SYSTEM

In this frame, we begin to apply the general concepts of systems thinking to a discussion of the different ways of viewing the human service system—its purposes, elements, and relationships.

Human Services as a Single Social Institutional System

In today's society, human services can be viewed as a social institution, one that is charged with the responsibility for addressing human problems and helping human beings to realize their greatest potential when other social institutions (such as the family, religion, the political system, and the economic system) fail to do so. Viewed as a social institution, the functions of the human service system are (1) *prevention,* which means preventing human problems from becoming overwhelming by helping persons maintain their highest level of functioning; (2) *rehabilitation,* which means helping to restore individuals to their highest possible level of functioning; (3) *maintenance,* which means providing ongoing care or support to impaired individuals when their full restoration of functioning cannot be accomplished; and (4) *systems advocacy,* which means helping other institutions become more responsive to human needs and problems.

Despite the complex nature of human services in the United States, it is important to view human service agencies and programs as part of an organized system. Systems thinking helps us to understand the complex human service institutional system in the United States by suggesting that we take different snapshots of it, each giving us a partial view. The human services as a single social institutional system can be understood (1) by program area, (2) by a concept called areas of functioning, (3) as networks of agencies, (4) as service delivery approaches, and (5) through the eyes of consumer populations.

1. Mapping the contemporary human service system as subsystems of programs. A program is a category of services, such as programs for the elderly and educational programs. Programs are long-term affairs with wide applications.[5] In its

---

[5]Roy S. Azarnoff and Jerome S. Seliger, *Delivering Human Services* (Englewood Cliffs, N.J.: Prentice-Hall, 1982), p. 8.

broadest and most comprehensive form, we can define the contemporary human service system in the United States as consisting of five major program components or subsystems: health, mental health, education, social welfare, and criminal justice.[6]

A distinguishing feature of the behavior of the human service system when we look at it by major programs is the presence of many goals that can overlap or conflict with the goals of other social institutions. Education provides a good example of overlapping goals. One goal of education is to teach children to become good citizens, a form of political socialization. Thus, part of the educational system overlaps with the political system. Many goals of schools are also oriented to social welfare and include helping people maximize their potential by empowering them to deal with problems. Criminal justice, by contrast, provides a dramatic example of conflicting goals. One goal of the criminal justice subsystem is to punish offenders and protect the general public; this is a political and social control function. Another goal of the criminal justice subsystem is to provide resources to offenders and engage them in rehabilitative programs; this is a human service goal. The general implication is that we must always be sensitive to the multiple goals that govern the different components of the human services when we view them as a system of programs.

2. Mapping the contemporary human service system as areas of functioning. A second approach to understanding the human service system is through a concept called areas of functioning.[7] This refers to the environments in which people live or function: physical, emotional, education and employment, financial, transportation, family, housing, safety and security, spiritual and aesthetic, and leisure and recreation. Building on the notion of human service programs just discussed, an areas-of-functioning snapshot of the human service system might look like Table 1.2.

TABLE 1.2   Human Service System and Areas of Functioning

Areas of Need	*Examples of Human Service Programs*
PHYSICAL	Public health programs: immunization, communicable disease control, maternal and child health, family planning, and sanitation
	Medical treatment: publicly supported "free clinics" and privately supported medical "missions"
	Medical benefits program (subsidies): employer contribution to health insurance (private or public); union contribution to health insurance (private); public (tax-supported) subsidies of Medicare and Medicaid, veterans benefits, and vocational rehabilitation
	Early detection–prevention programs: medical screening (industrial, armed forces, public schools, etc.); public education (American Cancer Society, Easter Seals, etc.)
	Rehabilitation maintenance and grant programs: veterans benefits, vocational rehabilitation, nursing homes, programs for retarded citizens, and alcohol- and drug-abuse counseling

(continued)

---

[6]See Richard S. Sauber, *The Human Service Delivery System* (New York: Columbia University Press, 1983), p. 17.

[7]Adapted from "domains of living" categories presented by Robert J. Teare and Harold L. McPheeters in *Manpower Utilization in Social Welfare* (Atlanta: Southern Regional Education Board, 1970), p. 14.

Areas of Need	*Examples of Human Service Programs*
EMOTIONAL	Inpatient hospital programs: publicly supported hospitals and clinics and private psychiatric hospitals
	Community-based programs (therapeutic): community mental health centers, group homes, halfway houses, and private practitioners
	Individual and family counseling programs: state, county, and private agencies and private practitioners
	Supportive services: public school programs (school social work, guidance and counseling, psychological testing, etc.), shelter-care programs, foster-care programs, correctional counseling (institutional, community based, probationary), and nursing home social services
EDUCATIONAL AND EMPLOYMENT	Public schools: general, academic programs, vocational/technical training, and professional preparation
	Programs related to self-development: child development programs (Head Start, exceptional child programs, etc.) and programs for development of self-awareness and social skills (parenting programs, self-actualization programs, etc.)
	Job training and placement: state employment agencies, federally supported job programs (WIN, CETA, CEP, Job Corps, etc.)
	Occupational subsidies: training allowances, work-related grants, and farm subsidies
	Support services: day care, counseling, medical services, and recreational services
FINANCIAL	Money grant programs: AFDC, SSI, Social Security, General Assistance, unemployment benefits, strike benefits, farm subsidies, tax incentives, private charity, government-subsidized loans, and veterans benefits
	Market substitutes: food stamps, rent subsidies, fringe benefit programs, private charities (food, clothing, shelters), medical insurance (public and private), Medicare, and Medicaid
	Instructional programs: budgeting, home economics, and financial planning
TRANSPORTATION	Public transportation programs
	Transportation support services (for children, elderly, disabled, etc.)
FAMILY	Preventive programs: family life education, parent effectiveness training, and communication programs
	Treatment programs: family counseling, marital counseling, and family therapy
HOUSING	Programs to aid in securing housing: public housing, rent subsidy programs, loan programs for purchase and/or housing improvements, and emergency shelter programs
	Maintenance programs for the disabled and elderly: nursing homes, independent living homes, group homes, foster care, and institutions
SAFETY AND SECURITY	Consumer and Legal Aid programs: Better Business Bureaus, Legal Aid Societies, American Civil Liberties Union, Public Defender programs, and programs to aid crime victims
	Public education and action programs: crime prevention programs, fire prevention programs, and block club programs
	Emergency relief programs: Civil Defense and the American Red Cross

Areas of Need	Examples of Human Service Programs
SPIRITUAL AND AESTHETIC	Spiritually related study and discussion groups: meditation and activity groups
	Programs related to the arts: museums, art galleries, and performing arts
	Programs related to various ethnic groups
LEISURE AND RECREATION	Public programs: city, county, state, and federal parks; recreation programs; museums; and community centers
	Private programs: church or civic group or private agency programs for athletics, special interest, group projects, social activities, and cultural activities

3. Mapping the contemporary human service system as networks of agencies. The human service system represents a mixture of public agencies, private agencies, and voluntary organizations. Together, these agencies and service institutions form a vast network for delivering human services. To illustrate one part of this perspective, we will concentrate on the organization of public agencies at the federal, state, and local levels.

As you can see in Figure 1.7 on page 50, we have described, in simplified form, each of the three levels of public human services at the federal, state, and local levels. The federal Department of Health and Human Services (HHS) is primarily concerned with policy making and the funding of programs on a national basis. The consumer group serviced by HHS is drawn from the entire population of the United States.

The state is the next major level in the hierarchy of public services. Many states have independent agencies, such as health departments and welfare departments, and each provides a specific range of services. Other states have organized these agencies into one agency in order to provide more efficient and effective services. These agencies are called umbrella agencies. The Florida Department of Health and Rehabilitative Services is one such agency, and it administers a broad range of state and federally financed human services—including health, welfare, mental health, developmental disabilities, family and children's services, vocational rehabilitation, and substance abuse. The community served by this organization is the entire state of Florida.

The level with which most workers have the greatest familiarity is the local community level. This is where policy and program are translated into specific services for individuals. There is usually a wide range of services available to consumers with special needs. Some examples of community services and consumers are:

Local Human Services	Community Consumers Served
Mental health centers and hospitals	Emotionally disturbed persons
Public health departments	Physically ill persons
Public welfare departments	Financially dependent persons
Retardation centers and hospitals	Developmentally disabled persons
Youth services institutions and programs	Delinquent minors
Vocational rehabilitation programs	Physically and emotionally disabled persons
Prisons, halfway houses, and community correctional centers	Convicted offenders

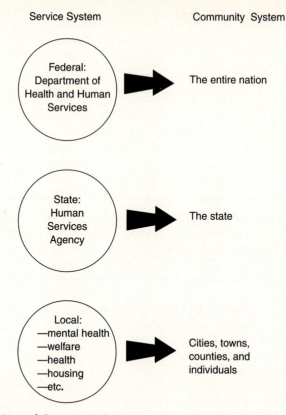

FIGURE 1.7   Service and Community Systems

This is not a complete listing of the public community human service agencies but is intended to be generally representative. You should eventually be familiar with the full array of human service agencies operating at your local level, a subject we will address more fully in Chapter 4. Examples of local human service agencies include:

Other Local Public Agencies
These are generally supported by local public funds, sometimes matched with state and federal funds. Public housing authorities fall into this category, as do some urban renewal programs.

Private Social Service Agencies
These usually exist for a specific purpose. For example, a children's home society primarily handles child care and adoptions.

Church-Affiliated Social Services
Every major denomination offers some services to people. Catholic Charities, Jewish Family Service, and the Salvation Army are typical.

4. Mapping the contemporary human service system according to approaches to service delivery. A fourth angle we can take to understand the human service system is to look at the models used to organize the delivery of human services.

There are generally two ways of organizing to provide human services—the comprehensive service center and the traditional separate agency. The comprehensive service center (CSC) brings together a wide array of human services in one location where the consumer can go for assistance. Staff from agencies that have been separate and disconnected from one another work together to provide such services as public welfare, vocational rehabilitation, youth services, public health, and mental health.

The more traditional pattern of service includes independent, separate agencies at the local level maintaining separate offices and procedures for delivering services where the health department is in one place, welfare in another, and vocational rehabilitation somewhere else. Usually little effort is made to locate these offices in a central area that is convenient for consumers. Each agency functions as a system virtually independent of the others, and, as a result, coordination between them is often poor. Consumers often find themselves spending considerable time and money going from one to another and repeating the application and interview procedure in efforts to find the services they need.

The table that follows compares these two approaches to service delivery in terms of systems thinking. Please review it carefully.

TABLE 1.3   Two Approaches to Service Delivery

Elements of Systems Thinking	Comprehensive Service Center (CSC)	Separate Local Agencies
PURPOSE	*Integration.* To enable the consumer to obtain all the needed services in one location (or through an integrated service system).	*Specialization.* To require the consumer to obtain needed services from separate service systems, usually in different locations.
ELEMENTS	The various agencies, and the services they offer, are housed in the center. These would include most of the public social services (such as public welfare, youth services, health, and vocational rehabilitation) and perhaps some of the locally financed social services (such as public housing and legal aid).	The programs and services offered by a particular agency would be directed toward a certain set of social needs and consumers.
RELATIONSHIPS	Generally there is a person in charge of coordinating the different service agencies represented; however, it is up to the various agencies to accept a consumer for service and to plan and deliver the needed services. Some mutual concerns of all the agencies are information exchange, service planning, record keeping and handling, traffic flow, hours of operation, and referral procedures. Each influences the others by having particular needs and objectives.	Within the office or offices of the local agency are many workers attached to different programs and with specific responsibilities. There are several administrative levels as well. There is considerable interaction as each attempts to do a particular part of a much larger total operation.

5. Mapping the contemporary human service system through the eyes of consumer populations. A fifth way to view the human service system is through the eyes of consumer populations. Population groups may be defined according to age, sex, race, marital status, or the acute or chronic nature of their problems or experiences. From this perspective, human services are organized in terms of children, the elderly, women, minorities, families, the disabled, and alcohol or drug abusers.

Consumer populations may also be defined according to the level at which providers are working with them. There may be several such levels of providing human services to any particular consumer population group, ranging from individuals obtaining personal counseling and therapy to organizations working in conjunction with other organizations or to legislators developing laws intended to impact large populations.

The first four views of the human service system focused on social institutions, programs, areas of functioning, and approaches to service delivery. The consumer population view is the first to emphasize the people who get the services. This raises at least one important point: The people who get or need human services have numerous interactions with each of the other four aspects of the human service system we have described. This communication is integral to the basic process of receiving services; however, it may in some instances be characterized by conflict.

> **Example:** A human service agency controls the expenditures of local, state, and federal funds allocated for services. Consumer organizations may seek to influence the operations of the organization. This may generate conflict, since the sharing of decision making in agency programs may threaten those in control of the agency. Whether that conflict is constructive or destructive depends on agency responses to the consumer actions and whether the two systems—agency and consumer—are able to reach an acceptable accommodation.

Consumers have won some significant victories with respect to influencing agency operations and services in recent years, but the service systems continue to exercise strong control over what help is available and the conditions under which it may be obtained. Recent efforts to organize citizen advisory committees as an integral part of human service agencies indicate the beginning recognition of the importance of consumer involvement in the operation of human service systems.

FRAME 6

We have just described five approaches to viewing the system of human services. Try to apply your understanding to a brief example of a problem situation. Read the example and then fill in the blanks in the statements that follow.

> Mr. and Mrs. Jones seek the services of a local agency because their 10-year-old son is acting out in school and showing very aggressive, sometimes violent, behavior toward his classmates. The school social worker has been working with the child but feels that he needs more intensive counseling services and refers the family to a local agency. After seeing the family, the agency counselor learns that the father refuses to accept the fact that his son's behavior is not normal. This is causing problems between the husband and wife, and the counselor suggests counseling for the parents while the child is in treatment. The parents consent, and they and the child become clients of the agency.

1. The Jones family has been served by at least two of the five program subsystems described in Frame 5 of this lesson. Recall that these five program subsystems were health, mental health, education, social welfare, and criminal justice. The first human service worker to help the Jones family was from the education subsystem. The agency to which the family was referred is probably part of the _____ subsystem.

2. The agency to which the Jones family was referred was intervening in two primary areas of functioning. They are _____ functioning and _____ functioning.

3. Two approaches to service delivery are the comprehensive service center and separate independent agencies. Which approach to service delivery is illustrated in the Jones's case?

4. Two ways of viewing consumer populations are by broad categories, such as age or nature of the problem, and by level of helping. If you were to describe consumer populations in the Jones's case by age, which of the following would apply?

_____ Infants

_____ Children

_____ Adolescents

_____ Parents

_____ Elderly

5. If you were to describe the levels of consumer populations or levels of helping in the Jones's case, which of the following would apply? That is, at which level(s) were services provided in this case?

_____ Individual

_____ Family

_____ Organization

_____ Community

_____ Society

Turn to Answer 5 on page 593

F R A M E

7

SUMMING UP: HUMAN SERVICES AS A SINGLE SOCIAL INSTITUTIONAL SYSTEM

We've covered a lot of material. Now we can put it together using some of the tools of systems thinking.

The human service system, as a social institutional system, is complex, so it is helpful to examine it in several ways. Figure 1.8 on page 54 provides a visual display of five "snapshots" we took of the system. We looked at it as subsystems of five programs; as areas of functioning; as networks of agencies; as service delivery approaches; and as consumer populations. We said each of these captured some aspects of the human services that helped us to grasp what they're all about, but not one of them had everything we needed.

Now look at Figure 1.9 on page 54. This picture summarizes the human services as a social institutional system. It shows the four primary purposes or functions of the

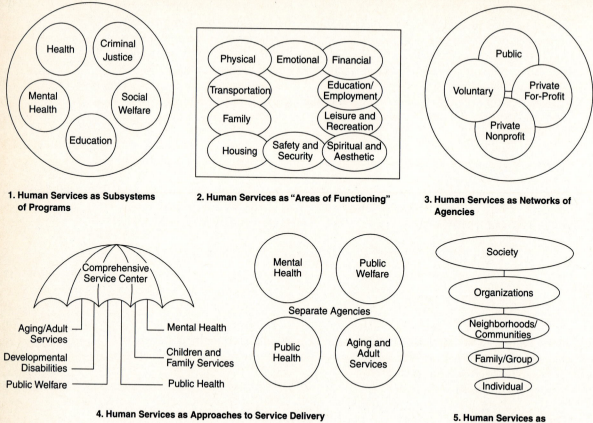

1. Human Services as Subsystems of Programs

2. Human Services as "Areas of Functioning"

3. Human Services as Networks of Agencies

4. Human Services as Approaches to Service Delivery

5. Human Services as Consumer Populations

FIGURE 1.8   Applying the Systems Approach to Understanding the Human Service System

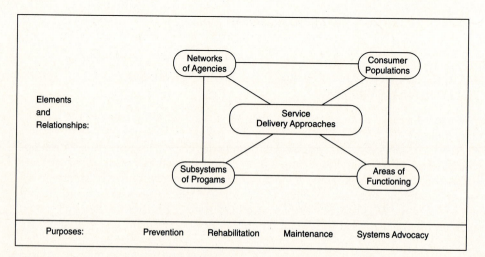

FIGURE 1.9   Summary View of Human Services as an Institutional System

human service system: prevention, rehabilitation, maintenance, and systems advocacy. It also shows the five different ways we looked at it.

The purpose of this discussion and these drawings is to illustrate how the tools of systems thinking can help us to cut through the complexity and begin to understand some of what is important. If nothing else, we hope you walk away from this at least somewhat convinced of three things. First, the human service social institutional system is indeed highly complex. Second, this material introduces some of the important aspects of the system rather than covering it in depth. And third, even though the human service system is complex, it is possible to act effectively in it—provided you approach it with the key attitudes of systems thinking: *openness, humility in the face of complexity,* and *confidence.*

FRAME

8

SYSTEMS THINKING AND THE HUMAN SERVICE CONSUMER

How can you use systems thinking in your work with human service consumers? Two ideas are important: levels of consumer populations and being able to "see" a consumer's many environments.

A consumer may be an individual, a group or family, a community or neighborhood, an organization, or a society. We can apply systems thinking to each of these levels to develop different ways of understanding problems. Figure 1.10 on page 56 illustrates these ideas. At the individual level, a consumer is a system and represents biological, spiritual, physical, social, intellectual, and psychological subsystems. The individual consumer is also part of other, larger systems. A family is a well-known system that includes parents, children, and grandparents as components. Organizations that include consumers are also systems, for example, inmate associations, associations for retarded or developmentally disabled persons, and senior citizen associations. Other groups of consumers that may be considered as systems include church organizations, civic and fraternal groups, social and recreational groups, and kinship and friendship groups. Society as a system is made up of a vast number of different subsystems or groups.

Seeing a consumer's many environments. If Patricia is a diabetic, she can be seen entirely as a biological system that has a disease. From this point of view, Patricia is understood as having to take insulin, follow a certain diet to complement the insulin, check her blood sugar, and take special care of her eyes and feet. But what if attention to these matters still leaves problems? Patricia can also be seen as the youngest member of a family, none of whom really understands her condition or her reaction to it. Then again, Patricia can be seen as a person whose interior includes not only her diabetes but also her psychological makeup, her spiritual and aesthetic preferences, her intelligence, and her amazing sense of humor. If Patricia is in a hospital, you can understand how she is reacting by focusing exclusively on her, *or* you can focus on her interactions with her visitors, nurses, physicians, nurses aides, and orderlies. Once you start thinking in systems, each of these views becomes a snapshot that helps you to understand one aspect of Patricia in different situations. Faced with any kind of problem, you begin to ask, "Well, what if I looked at it this way—or that? And how might I weave all of this together in working with Patricia?"

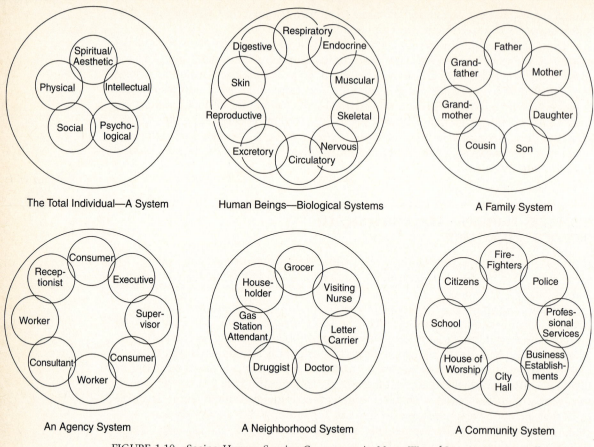

FIGURE 1.10   Seeing Human Service Consumers in Many Ways [*Source:* Naomi Brill, *Working with People: The Helping Process,* 4th ed. (New York: Longman, 1990), p. 110.]

FRAME

9

SYSTEMS THINKING: ADVANTAGES AND LIMITATIONS

From all that we have said, you might conclude that systems thinking is *the* answer. Taking a learning attitude toward this material, we hope you are skeptical about assertions that the systems approach—or any approach—is *the* correct one to understanding our society. Let's explore some of the possible advantages and disadvantages of systems thinking as a way of guarding against such a conclusion.

Possible Advantages of Systems Thinking

Systems thinking:

1. Protects against the complacency arising from the assumption that the solution or answer to a situation is simple.

2. Provides a mental discipline for critical thinking in any circumstance—committee meetings, political discussions, analysis of a theatrical performance, and counseling a family.
3. Shows that human behavior must be understood in the context of a number of interacting factors.
4. Can make focusing on and including the important elements and dimensions of a situation more likely.
5. Helps the human service worker to see the world through the eyes of another.
6. Better ensures that the human service worker will search for more than one way to look at a situation.
7. Helps in realizing that the person or group seeking help is not always the major target—that the problem may be in a different system.

Possible Limitations of Systems Thinking

Systems thinking:

1. Is only as effective as those who use it.
2. Can lead to overconfidence that this map is *the* solution.
3. Can result in making things worse if applied to only part of a situation.
4. Can scare people by portraying the complexity of a situation they would prefer to see simply.
5. Is a tool that still needs to be developed and improved.

What additional benefits and limitations can you suggest for using the systems approach?

As a way of balancing the advantages and limitations of the systems approach, we offer a quote from C. West Churchman, a well-known systems thinker:

> Well, then, what is the systems approach? On the one hand, we must recognize it to be the most critical problem we face today, the understanding of the systems in which we live. On the other hand, however, we must admit that the problem—the appropriate approach to systems—is not solved. . . . It's not as though we can expect that next year or a decade from now someone will find the correct systems approach and all deception will disappear. . . . Instead, what is in the nature of systems is a continuing re-viewing of the world, of the whole system, and its components. The essence of the systems approach is *confusion as well as enlightenment*.[8] [Italics added.]

Churchman acknowledges the importance of a critical view of the systems approach; however, in noting that, he still concludes that the systems approach is not a bad idea. As you see the many applications of systems thinking throughout the lessons of this book, we hope you'll be better able to reach your own conclusions.

---

[8]C. West Churchman, *The Systems Approach* (New York: Dell, 1979), p. 231.

Summary and Further Study

Chapter Summary

Chapter 1 explored answers to this question: What basic skills do human service practitioners need that will enable them to meet today's service delivery requirements and those of the next decade? Three essential skills were developed as the basic orientations to delivering human services: learning, language, and systems thinking.

Lesson 1. The major theme of Lesson 1 was that how you learn about human services may parallel how you actually deliver human services, and therefore the effective human service practitioner will be characterized by an ongoing ability to learn. Learning is an attitude, a process, and an outcome—an approach to living and working that enables a person to deal effectively with new situations.

As an attitude, learning is characterized by curiosity, openness, reflection, and flexibility. We distinguished proactive learners from reactive learners and expressed a preference for a proactive orientation. Reactive learners are passive and expect others to take care of their learning needs. Proactive learners take initiative for meeting their own learning needs—they ask questions and seize the experiences of work and life as opportunities for learning. We argued that effective human service practitioners will be proactive learners. As such, they will know how to use their experiences as sources of learning by becoming skillful in talking and thinking about what they do.

As a process, learning is concerned with the things that happen while learning is taking place—for example, questioning, rehearsing, giving feedback, and making changes based on feedback. The basic elements of the learning model that will be used in this text as well as during a learning approach to the delivery of human services include: concrete experience, thinking about the experience, finding patterns in experiences, and using the patterns discovered to try new behaviors.

As an outcome, learning refers to what you are able to do after some learning experience. We introduced the contents of this book as a framework for having experiences of learning about and actually delivering human services. We stressed that each lesson in the book ought to be regarded as one window for viewing and practicing what is involved in delivering human services. This learning program is distinguished as a generic or generalist approach rather than a setting-specific approach to practice. In addition, it is based on a set of learning guidelines, a knowledge foundation, and generic skills or roles that define the actions taken to deliver human services. Life is full of learning experiences. The situations experienced with consumers during the process of delivering human services are fundamentally learning experiences for both workers and consumers.

Seven learning principles were suggested as being important to the successful use of this book and to the practice of delivering human services: listening reflectively, reading actively, observing sensitively, cultivating an openness to change, cultivating variety, increasing self-awareness, and cultivating a healthy skepticism or ability to think critically.

Lesson 2. The human services can be understood, in part, by the words, symbols, and signs used and by the meanings given to them. The central theme of this lesson was that the vocabulary of the human services is distinct and personal. What we say provides many clues about who we are and how we are going to behave. We discussed the general role that language plays in any area of work, including enabling people in one area to distinguish themselves from people in other areas of work.

With this as background, we explored three key dimensions of the term *human services:* the nature of the services, who provides the services, and who receives the services. Services can be enumerated in lists or in a few categories, such as direct and indirect or residual and developmental. Both approaches are useful. Public, private nonprofit, private for-profit, and voluntary organizations provide human services through service personnel from a number of different professions (e.g., medicine, psychology, and social work). A variety of people and organizations provide human services and will be discussed further in Chapter 3.

Several issues were raised with respect to the language used to label the people who receive human services. Labels and specialized vocabulary are an essential characteristic of areas of work. The central question was what these labels might imply about basic perceptions of people in need. Two major themes emerged as we examined the terms *client* and *consumer:* whether a label emphasized that human service consumers were different from those providing the service, and what the label suggested about the nature of the relationship that ought to exist between the worker and the consumer.

After discussing different views of client and consumer, we explained why we chose to use the term *human service consumer* in this book. However, we stressed the importance of reaching your own decision in the matter. The lesson concluded with a suggestion of six possible principles of practice with respect to language skills.

Lesson 3. Lesson 3 explored a third orientation to delivering human services: systems thinking. We asked two questions at the outset: (1) What constitutes system thinking? and (2) How is systems thinking relevant to delivering human services?

We discovered that people who are able to think in systems approach problems by looking for elements, relationships, and purpose. Openness, humility in the face of complexity, and confidence to act were proposed as three attitudes critical to effective systems thinking. Open systems thinkers are those interested in the relationships inside and outside the system, whether that system is an individual, a group, or something else. The attitude of humility is generally aroused when we truly appreciate the complexity of human systems and understand how little we really know. But systems thinking is also characterized by confidence when appropriate steps have been followed. In addition to attitudes that facilitate systems thinking, one critical skill was illustrated throughout the lesson: the urge to draw or otherwise visually represent the various understandings of systems. We introduced this idea by discussing the input-output model of a system, then applying it to delivering human services as it is organized in this book.

To begin the practice of using systems thinking, we took on a big task. We used this introduction to the basic ideas of systems thinking to better understand the human service social institutional system and the different perspectives we can use to "see" human service consumers. Five snapshots provided different angles on the human service institutional system: program areas, areas of functioning, networks of agencies, approaches to service delivery, and consumer populations. Another way of saying this is that the human service institutional system has at least these five elements. The idea of levels of consumer populations or levels of helping was introduced. Consumers can be individuals, groups, communities or neighborhoods, organizations, or societies. This insight provides different frames of reference for delivering human services; that is, we might focus on an individual as a member of a family, exclusively on the individual as a total system, or on the individual in a family and the family in a neighborhood.

The principal focus of this text is delivering human services to individual consumers. However, since individuals function in groups, communities, organizations, and societies, characteristics of these levels are also introduced. The lesson concluded with the observation that there are advantages and limitations to systems thinking, and that human service workers should retain their ability to judge the approach critically.

Suggestions for Further Study

A great deal of material was introduced in this chapter. The skills identified in each lesson are the subject of an emerging body of literature that will yield beneficial insights.

Learning
The skill of learning is receiving increasing attention today. Additional study is needed concerning the process of learning in the human services and the learning process in general. Topics such as stages of learning, learning as part of the helping process, and styles of learning are important to address.

Adler, M. J. *Guide Book to Learning for the Lifelong Pursuit of Learning*. New York: Macmillan, 1986.

Argyris, Chris. *Reasoning, Learning, and Action: Individual and Organizational*. San Francisco: Jossey-Bass, 1982.

Brookfield, Stephen. *Understanding and Facilitating Adult Learning*. San Francisco: Jossey-Bass, 1986. (reprint 1988).

Brookfield, Stephen. *Becoming a Critically Reflective Teacher*. San Francisco: Jossey-Bass, 1995.

Carnevale, Anthony and Susan Stone. *The American Mosaic: An In-Depth Report on the Future of Diversity at Work*. New York: McGraw-Hill, 1995.

Covey, Stephen, A. Roger Merill, and Rebecca R. Merrill. *First Things First: To Live, to Love, to Learn, to Leave a Legacy*. New York: Simon & Schuster, 1994.

DeRoos, Yosikazu S. "The Development of Practice Wisdom through Human Problem-Solving Processes." *Social Service Review* (June 1990): 276–287.

Dollar, Bruce. "Students as Co-Producers of Their Own Learning." *Social Policy* (Nov.–Dec. 1977): 69–72.

Friedlander, F. "Patterns of Individual and Organizational Learning." In *The Executive Mind: New*

Insights on Managerial Thought and Action, edited by S. Srivastva & Associates. San Francisco: Jossey-Bass, 1984.

Kegan, R. *The Evolving Self.* Cambridge, Mass.: Harvard University Press, 1982.

Keirsey, D., and M. Bates. *Please Understand Me: Character and Temperament Types,* 4th ed. Del Mar, Calif.: Prometheus Nemesis Books, 1984.

Landon, Pamela S. "Generalist and Advanced Generalist Practice." In *Encyclopedia of Social Work,* 19th ed. Washington, D.C.: National Association of Social Work, 1995: 1101–1108.

Loevinger, J. *Ego Development.* San Francisco: Jossey-Bass, 1976.

Miley, Karla, Michael O'Melia, and Brenda DuBois. *Generalist Social Work Practice: An Empowering Approach.* Boston: Allyn & Bacon, 1995.

Nadler, Gerald, and Shozo Hibino, with John Farrell. *Creative Solution Finding: The Triumph of Full-Spectrum Creativity Over Conventional Thinking.* Rocklin, Calif.: Prima, 1995.

Osterman, Karen F. and Robert B. Kottkamp. *Reflective Practice for Educators: Improving Schooling Through Professional Development.* Newbury Park, Calif.: Corwin Press, 1993.

Schon, Donald A. *The Reflective Practitioner: How Professionals Think in Action.* New York: Basic Books, 1983.

Torbert, William A. *Learning from Experience: Toward Consciousness.* New York: Columbia University Press, 1972.

Wolfe, Donald M., and David A. Kolb. "Career Development, Personal Growth, and Experiential Learning." In *Organizational Psychology: Readings on Human Behavior in Organizations,* 4th ed., by David A. Kolb, Irwin Rubin, and James McIntyre. Englewood Cliffs, N.J.: Prentice-Hall, 1984.

Language

The vocabulary of the human services will be developed throughout this text, but it will certainly not be complete. You may wish to pursue in more depth the notion of language in general and how it influences and reflects who we are, how we see, and what we do. Moreover, although we indicated that each lesson in this text was one view or definition of the human services, other resources should be studied to gain different perspectives. It would also be beneficial to study the role of language in different cultures—for example, how the same idea can be symbolized and interpreted in very different ways and even similar ways.

Barker, Robert L. *The Social Work Dictionary,* 3rd ed. Silver Spring, Md.: National Association of Social Workers, 1995.

Berger, Peter L., and Thomas Luckmann. *The Social Construction of Reality.* New York: Doubleday, 1966.

Devore, W., and E. Schlesinger. *Ethnic-Sensitive Social Work Practice,* 4th ed. Boston: Allyn & Bacon, 1996.

Dixon, Lisa, Nancy Kraus, and Anthony Lehman. "Consumers as Service Providers: The Promise and Challenge." *Community Mental Health Journal,* 30 (December, 1994): 615–625.

Gartner, Alan, Colin Greer, and Frank Riessman. *Consumer Education and the Human Services.* New York: Pergamon, 1979.

Goffman, Erving. *Asylum: The Social Situation of Mental Patients and Other Inmates.* Garden City, N.Y.: Doubleday Anchor, 1961.

Jung, Carl G. *Man and His Symbols.* New York: Dell, 1964.

Martin, Patricia Yancey, and Gerald G. O'Connor. *The Social Environment: Open Systems Applications.* New York: Longman, 1989.

Minsky, Marvin. *The Society of Mind.* New York: Simon & Schuster, 1988.

Moore, Stephen T., and Michael J. Kelly. "Quality Now: Moving Human Services Organizations Toward a Consumer Orientation to Service Quality." *Social Work,* 41 (January, 1996): 33–40.

Pei, M. *The Language of the Specialists.* New York: Funk & Wagnalls, 1966.

Pei, M. *The Story of Language.* New York: New American Library, 1965.

Popple, Philip L., and Leslie H. Leighninger. *Social Work, Social Welfare, and American Society,* 3rd ed. Boston: Allyn & Bacon, 1996.

Shore, M. F. "Patient or Client?" *Hospital Community Psychiatry* 39 (Dec. 1988): 1247.

Whorf, B. L. *Language, Thought, and Reality.* Cambridge, Mass.: MIT Press, 1964.

Wolfensberger, Wolf. *The Origin and Nature of Our Institutional Models.* Syracuse, N.Y.: Human Policy Press, 1975.

Systems Thinking

As indicated, most human service texts include systems thinking skills as part of their approach to delivering human services. You can develop a deeper understanding of the basic skills of systems thinking by consulting other works, some of which are listed below. As Brill notes, human service workers should reflect on three systems questions: (1) What are the boundaries of the system with which they are dealing? (2) What are the patterns and channels of communication within the individual system under consideration (e.g., individual, family, and neighborhood) and related external systems (e.g., network of agencies and network of family relations)? (3) What explicit and implicit rules govern the relationships among the parts, both internally and externally, particularly with respect to input (openness to new ideas and materials, processing (working with these materials), and output (results of this work and feedback)?[1] The concept of feedback is an important one that will be discussed in later sections of this text. It should also be pursued as a separate line of inquiry using some of the resources provided.

The concept of human services as a major social institution is becoming increasingly important and useful as attempts are made to consolidate and improve the delivery of human services. A growing literature on human service organizations addresses the problems of defining and studying this special kind of system (also see Chapter 3).

It is also important to use systems concepts to analyze the process by which you help consumers. Meyer addressed this perspective as follows:

> In a systems framework, where concepts of input and output and reciprocity take on meaning, we can cease our unending search for cause and effect. We find in the notion of equifinality (i.e., the same final results may be achieved with different starting conditions, with varying inputs, and in different ways) that there is more than one way to achieve an outcome in a case, because each action taken will rebound upon another one which will set in motion yet other movements for change. The case might be defined as a person, a family, a hospital ward, a housing complex, a particular neighborhood, a school population, a group with particular problems and needs, or a community with common concerns. The case might then be defined geographically, functionally, or according to problem or interest groupings. The systems framework does not make individual assessments in a case unnecessary. On the contrary, it provides a conceptual structure that insures a true transactional understanding of the person-in-situa-

---

[1]Naomi Brill, *Working with People: The Helping Process,* 5th ed. (New York: Longman, 1990).

tion. Its most salutary feature is that it provides for multifaceted interventions, determined by the needs of the case and made possible by the opportunity to utilize the available manpower from all levels of education, experience, and expertise.[2]

These additional perspectives should serve as the basis of further reading and discussion, perhaps consulting the sources below.

Anderson, R., and J. Carter. *Human Behavior in the Social Environment: A Social Systems Approach,* 4th ed. New York: A. de Gruyter, 1990.

Berrien, K. *General and Social Systems.* New Brunswick, N.J.: Rutgers University Press, 1968.

Bertalanffy, Ludwig. *General Systems Theory: Foundations, Development, Applications.* New York: George Braziller, 1968. (revised edition: New York: Braziller, 1988).

Buckley, W. *Sociology and Modern Systems Theory.* Englewood Cliffs, N.J.: Prentice-Hall, 1967.

Capra, F. *The Turning Point: Science, Society, and the Rising Culture.* New York: Bantam Books, 1982.

Emery, F. E. *Systems Thinking,* vol. 1 and vol. 2. New York: Penguin Books, 1981.

Friedman, Robert M. "Restructuring of Systems to Emphasize Prevention and Family Support," *Journal of Clinical Child Psychology* 23 (Suppl., 1994): 40–47.

Hampden-Turner, C. *Maps of the Mind.* New York: Collier Books, 1982.

Hearn, Gordon. *The General Systems Approach: Contributions Toward a Holistic Conception of Social Work.* New York: Council on Social Work Education, 1969.

Janchill, Sister Mary Paul. "Systems Concepts in Casework Theory and Practice." *Social Casework* 50 (Feb. 1969): 74–82.

Longres, John F. *Human Behavior in the Social Environment,* 2nd ed. Itasca, Ill.: Peacock, 1995.

Martin, Patricia Yancey, and Gerald G. O'Connor. *The Social Environment: Open Systems Applications.* New York: Longman, 1989.

Oshry, Barry. *Seeing Systems.* San Francisco: Berrett-Koehler, 1995.

Salamon, Lester. "The Nonprofit Sector and the Evolution of the American Welfare State." In Robert D. Herman and Associates, *The Jossey-Bass Handbook on Nonprofit Leadership and Management.* San Francisco: Jossey-Bass, 1994, pp. 83–99.

Sauber, S. Richard. *The Human Services Delivery System.* New York: Columbia University Press, 1983.

---

[2]Carol H. Meyer, "Direct Services in New and Old Contexts," in Alfred Kahn (ed.), *Shaping the New Social Work* (New York: Columbia University Press, 1973), pp. 49–51.

Chapter2

Conditions Creating the Need for Human Services

Throughout the ages, there have been social and human problems. Society has responded, to varying degrees and in different ways, to those problems. Along with human problems are human capacities for growth and development. These two conditions—the recognition of human problems, specifically the problems we all face in the process of living, and the conviction that change and human betterment are possible—are the major conditions creating the need for human services.

In Chapter 1, the principal question was this: How should you approach the practice of delivering human services? The answer was to be able to travel through the human service world with at least three basic skills: an attitude of learning, a sensitivity to language, and an ability to use systems thinking.

Chapter 2 asks another question: Why human services? This is not a simple inquiry, and there are many perspectives to draw on in developing a response. We will develop five themes:

1. Needs. The human services are fundamentally a response to basic human needs. The human services thus have two aspects: conditions creating needs and some system responding to those needs.

2. Society. Human needs are linked to conditions in our society. A society that is principally concerned with mass-producing items in large organizations and increasing wealth will have human problems different from one that is principally concerned with creating shelter and individually producing food supplies.

3. Change. Our society is continually changing. As it changes, so do our needs, our problems, and our human services.

4. Making connections. Human service workers are very much a part of this complex and changing society. To be effective, they need to be able to make connections that link people's needs with social changes and service delivery.

5. Simplifying complexity. Human services cover a wide range of needs and professional responses. No one can have in-depth knowledge of the entire spectrum. Instead, it is necessary to develop skills for appreciating the fullness and complexity of the human condition and for simplifying it in a way that makes effective responses possible.

This chapter explores the personal and societal conditions that create human needs and turn them into problems that demand a response. We start at a *personal level*. Lesson 1 develops a framework for understanding the range of needs and problems of consumers and ourselves. This lays the foundation for assessing a situation in terms of the need, the level of functioning in the need, and the nature of obstacles to effective functioning.

Lesson 2 broadens the concept of need by shifting attention to the *societal level*. Here, the aim is to cultivate an appreciation for change—as a condition of our existence, as a feature of the development of the human services, and as a basic human need with implications for the human service practitioner. We illustrate this by exploring the longstanding connection between changes in our society and the human needs that become the focus of an increasingly complex system of human service organizations and individual providers.

Lesson 3 develops entry-level skill in policy practice. It suggests that, for the human service practitioner, the result of the interaction between needs of consumers and broad forces of change is *service delivery issues* related to social policy. It provides an opportunity to survey examples of current challenges in practice and introduces skills for conducting your own initial scan of a service delivery area of interest. Scanning skills are introduced as a way of staying connected to the rapid changes in society as well as gaining general and reasonably quick familiarity with policy issues affecting your practice.

The overall objective of the chapter is to develop skills of sensitivity in linking individual needs and social changes and to use these experiences to recognize and explore the consequent "issues in practice." The world of human service work is immensely diverse, complex, changing, disturbing, and rewarding. We hope this chapter reflects that challenge and inspires you to raise questions to guide your practice for some time to come. That is, we hope you use the perspectives of Chapter 1—an attitude of learning, a sensitivity to language, and an ability to use systems thinking—to develop a personal understanding of your answers to the question of this chapter: Why human services?

Human Service Consumers: Unmet Needs or Untapped Capacities?

People become human service consumers because they are experiencing problems in meeting their needs. In fact, the two concepts of "needs" and "needs that turn into problems of living" define the core of the human service field and distinguish it from other kinds of services. But there are questions behind these general statements: What kinds of needs do people have? What problems fall within the scope of the human services? Is there a way of thinking about needs and problems that will focus understanding of the consumer's situation and be useful in planning what to do?

These questions, of concern to every human service worker, are answered during a systematic process of assessing the consumer's situation to gain a clear understanding of the consumer's problem and plan a response to the specific areas that require intervention. This is not a simple process, so a framework helps. This lesson proposes three ways of thinking about capacity for daily living: (1) specific kinds of needs, (2) the consumer's level of functioning with respect to each need, and (3) obstacles preventing effective functioning in each need.[1] Additional skills are necessary to conduct a complete assessment process (e.g., interviewing). Lesson 1 focuses on the concepts of needs and problems, which are central to the field and therefore extend beyond assessment.

Goals

Given a description of a consumer, to be able to identify his or her needs and the degree to which each is a problem area. For each problem area, to be able to identify specific obstacles preventing effective functioning.

Learning Activities

To accomplish these goals, we will:

1. Identify 10 areas of human needs.
2. Consider the kinds of problems that can develop in meeting human needs.

---

[1]See Robert J. Teare and Harold L. McPheeters, *Manpower Utilization in Social Welfare* (Atlanta: Southern Regional Education Board, 1970), pp. 11–17. Also see Robert J. Teare and Bradford W. Sheahy, *Practice-Sensitive Social Work Education* (Alexandria, Va.: Council in Social Work Education, 1995).

3. Discuss five categories that can be used to describe how well a consumer is functioning with respect to each problem area.

4. Identify four general categories of obstacles that can prevent a consumer from effective functioning.

5. Practice applying a framework of needs analysis using case illustrations.

6. Explore the experience of needing human services, including characteristics that may influence the behavior of consumers.

7. Consider some limitations of seeing people in terms of needs and suggest a few alternatives.

F R A M E

1

AREAS OF HUMAN NEEDS

Consider the following case example:

As a human service worker in a neighborhood service center, you have been visiting residents at their homes to discuss their need for services. Today you met Mr. Davis, who is 73 years old, retired, and living alone in a small efficiency apartment. Mr. Davis enjoys good health for his age and has Medicare coverage.

The neighborhood is slowly deteriorating. To get to stores, doctors, or recreation, Mr. Davis must walk through areas that are considered unsafe, especially after 5:00 P.M. The local bus system does not have a stop close to him, and he cannot afford a taxi.

In the course of your conversation with him, he states that he would like very much to find a place to live that would be closer to a recreation center for people in his age group and also closer to shopping. He feels he cannot pay more rent than the $500 a month he is paying now.

How should you think about the problems presented in such a case? First, there is the concept of *areas of needs*. An independent, fully functioning human being is generally able to be self-sustaining in a limited number of areas. There are many definitions of what these areas are, but one that is useful for the practice of the human services proposes ten areas that sustain human beings:

Ten Areas of Human Needs

1. Physical functioning	6. Family functioning
2. Emotional functioning	7. Housing
3. Education and employment	8. Safety and security
4. Financial functioning	9. Spiritual and aesthetic functioning
5. Transportation	10. Leisure and recreation

Next, there is the concept of *problems* or *unmet needs*. Usually human service consumers are having difficulty in one or more of these ten areas of need. Examples of the kinds of problems that might occur in each area are listed below:

Human Needs and Possible Problems

AREAS OF NEED	EXAMPLES OF PROBLEMS
1. Physical functioning	Chronic (long-term) or acute (brief and severe) illness or disease; physical deterioration or disability; lack of needed medical care
2. Emotional functioning	Mental illness or emotional disorder; problems related to getting along with peers or other important people in the person's environment
3. Education and employment	Significant lack of education; difficulty in securing and retaining employment; poor or dangerous working conditions
4. Financial functioning	Inability to earn an income or to maintain an income; inability to manage available funds adequately
5. Transportation	Lack of reliable and inexpensive transportation; inability to use normal modes of transportation; need for special transportation
6. Family functioning	Problems in family relationships, such as husband–wife, parent–child, brother–sister, or extended family involvements
7. Housing	Problems with shelter: inadequate facilities, poor condition, too many people living there, rent too high, etc.
8. Safety and security	Problems with the physical environment such that the consumer does not feel safe where he or she lives or works; inadequate fire and police protection; lack of access to other necessary services, such as legal advice and health care
9. Spiritual and aesthetic functioning	Problems making an acceptable adjustment to life and the world around; problems with lack of contentment and accomplishment in life; feeling there is nothing to live for
10. Leisure and recreation	Inadequate opportunities to relax and enjoy recreational activities, either individually or in a group

Given this framework of areas of need and potential problems, what are your initial impressions of the areas where Mr. Davis has problems? Place a check mark beside each area where you think Mr. Davis might be experiencing a problem, then continue to Frame 2. You'll have the opportunity to check your answers shortly.

FRAME 2

LEVELS OF FUNCTIONING

You may have experienced some difficulty in identifying which areas of need might be problems for Mr. Davis. For example, you may have wondered about the degree to which something was a problem. This suggests that additional information might be helpful.

The second aspect of an analysis of need that will hopefully yield a more precise answer to the question of whether Mr. Davis's problems require a human service response involves the concept of *levels of functioning for each area of need.* The levels of functioning range from well-being, at the highest level, to disability at the lowest. The entire range is difficult to describe except in broad stages, such as these:

$$1 \rightarrow 2 \rightarrow 3 \rightarrow 4 \rightarrow 5$$

well-being   stress   problem   crisis   disability

Stages 2 and 3 are the points at which intervention would be most effective, but workers are seldom able to become involved this early. Disability, however, is a state workers probably see often. A definition of each stage should help you locate any given consumer on the continuum.

1. Well-being. This is a high level of functional health. The consumer is getting along well in all vital areas of functioning. Intervention of any kind at this stage is unlikely.

2. Stress. No problems of functioning have developed at this point, but the risk has increased considerably. Ideal intervention at this point, if assistance were requested, would be in the form of some sort of support to prevent problems from occurring.

3. Problem. At this stage problems have begun, but they remain within the consumer's ability to deal with them. Any intervention at this point is focused on preventing the consumer from reaching a point of crisis.

4. Crisis. The crisis stage indicates that the problems are beyond the consumer's ability to deal with them. This is the point at which most service agencies become involved. Continued crisis-level functioning may lead to disability. Intensive services of whatever type needed should be employed at this stage.

5. Disability. At this stage considerable damage has occurred. Problems will be chronic or permanent. The usual services are remedial, that is, aimed at attempting to help the consumer adapt to the situation or learn compensating methods of functioning.

Whereas most human services relate to helping consumers solve problems related to their level of functioning, increased attention is now being given to preventing problems (e.g., more playgrounds and youth activities to prevent delinquency or more home health services to prevent social and physical deterioration and to keep the elderly out of costly institutions).

FRAME

Adding the concept of levels of functioning to the ten areas of need creates the framework on page 70. For each area of need, place a check mark in one of the five levels of functioning columns to indicate your view of Mr. Davis's level of functioning. Make any notes you wish on why you made each selection in the last column. After completing this exercise, continue with Frame 4.

Analysis of Mr. Davis's Level of Functioning in Each Need

	Well-being	Stress	Problems	Crisis	Disability	
			Levels of Functioning			
Areas of Need	(1)	(2)	(3)	(4)	(5)	*Notes on Mr. Davis*
Physical functioning						
Emotional functioning						
Education and employment						
Financial functioning						
Transportation						
Family functioning						
Housing						
Safety and security						
Spiritual and aesthetic functioning						
Leisure and recreation						

FRAME 4

OBSTACLES TO FUNCTIONING

The third concept to consider in understanding the needs and problems of human service consumers involves the identification of *obstacles that prevent them from functioning effectively.* Obstacles may come from one or more basic sources and are important to identify so that appropriate services can be planned with a consumer. There are four general categories of obstacles to functioning:

1. Personal deficiencies. Deficiencies may relate to physical handicaps, whether congenital or from accidents, as well as psychological handicaps, either from early childhood or more recent experiences. Obstacles to functioning in this area include learning disabilities; physical limitations, such as blindness, deafness, and physical defects; and emotional problems relating to deficiencies in the opportunities for personal growth.

2. Environmental deficiencies. A range of consequences can result from certain deficiencies in the environment that are usually beyond the control of individual consumers. Poor housing with inoperative sanitary facilities; torn or missing screens that do not keep out flies and mosquitoes; rats; poor garbage collection; and many other environmental defects can have consequences that negatively influence an individual's entire life. Similarly, an institution such as a prison or a mental hospital may create dependency and thereby become an environment that does not contribute to consumer rehabilitation. Other environmental defects include racist and/or sexist attitudes of significant people in the consumer's environment.

3. Rigid laws and policies. Policies, regulations, and laws sometimes play a part in keeping an individual from obtaining a certain job or type of employment. Restrictive policies and practices based on race, creed, or color often bar access to jobs, education, and housing. Restrictive policies and procedures may even prevent an individual from obtaining needed agency services.

4. Catastrophes. Unexpected devastating events are potential obstacles for everyone. These events include sudden death, illness, and disability. Automobile accidents and home accidents also may be the source. Natural disasters such as storms, earthquakes, and fire are well known. Most of these catastrophes are subject to little control and may require extensive remedial treatment and maintenance, especially at the individual level.

FRAME
5

For the following statements, write in each blank the letter of the obstacle that best completes the sentence. Statement 1 is an example.

Obstacles

P = personal deficiency
E = environmental deficiency
R = rigid laws and policies
C = catastrophe

1. Blindness is an example of ___**P**___.
2. A company policy not to hire Chinese taxi drivers is an instance of _____.
3. Being struck by lightning and left paralyzed is _____.
4. A child who cannot pay attention in class because he is hungry is probably suffering from _____.
5. Being kept awake all night by insects and rats in your home is a case of _____.
6. Having a realtor refuse to sell you a house in an all-White suburb because you are Black is a result of _____.
7. Having the head of the household die unexpectedly is _____.

Turn to Answer 6 on page 595

FRAME
6

PULLING IT ALL TOGETHER

The preceding material has outlined a framework for organizing consumer information about ten areas of need, five levels of functioning in each area of need, and four categories of obstacles to well-being in each area of need. Return to Frame 1 and reread the case about Mr. Davis. Then review the chart below and see if you agree with it. Discuss those aspects where you differ. Then continue with Frame 7.

Analysis of Mr. Davis's Needs

	Levels of Functioning					
Areas of Need	**Well-being** (1)	**Stress** (2)	**Problems** (3)	**Crisis** (4)	**Disability** (5)	**Obstacles to Functioning** (Personal, Environmental, Rigid Laws, Catastrophes)
Physical functioning	X					
Emotional functioning		X				There appears to be an environmental deficiency related to the deteriorating neighborhood, distance from shopping, etc., that is causing him stress.
Education and employment	X					
Financial functioning			X			Due to a personal deficiency, age, he is not employed and probably could not get a job. His low Social Security benefits may make him eligible for public assistance.
Transportation			X			One of the obstacles in this area is simply a lack of inexpensive transportation. He is physically capable of walking, but this may be unsafe. This is an environmental deficiency.
Family functioning	X					
Housing		X				The obstacle here is the nature of the neighborhood, which is slowly becoming run down. A more convenient location would be much better. This is an environmental deficiency.
Safety and security			X			He definitely feels, with apparent good reason, that he is not safe walking along the streets. This reality serves to restrict his activities. This is an environmental deficiency.

Levels of Functioning

Areas of Need	Well-being (1)	Stress (2)	Problems (3)	Crisis (4)	Disability (5)	Obstacles to Functioning (Personal, Environmental, Rigid Laws, Catastrophes)
Spiritual and aesthetic functioning	X					
Leisure and recreation		X				One of his primary concerns is to be situated more conveniently, near friends and recreation. The obstacles here are environmental—the type of neighborhood he lives in and the area he must walk through to get to stores and recreation.

F R A M E

7

Practice Exercise

It is important to remember that through your work experience in a human service agency, you should be able to increase your skills in making judgments about the range and types of consumer problems. Practical experience is needed in order to use this approach effectively to assess a consumer's needs.

Are you ready to try one on your own? Here's the situation:

Mrs. Collins is 34 years old and supports herself and three children (ages 16, 14, and 12) on an AFDC grant of $540 a month. She seems to be doing a commendable job as a money manager. The two older children have part-time jobs through the work study program.

You are a public health nurse and have just been told by your supervisor that X-rays of Mrs. Collins's abdomen confirm the presence of a large tumor that needs to be removed immediately. There is some chance that it is cancerous, but the doctor thinks this unlikely. The supervisor has talked to Mrs. Collins about making preparations to have the operation. Mrs. Collins was very upset but agreed to come in for further medical examination. Since that time, she has failed to show up for two appointments, explaining that she is "very busy." The supervisor wants you to arrange a home visit with Mrs. Collins and help resolve the problem. After some trouble and delays, you finally see her at home. She is obviously scared and gives three reasons why she can't consider having an operation now:

- There is no one to take care of her children while she is in the hospital.
- She doesn't have anyone to help her at home after she leaves the hospital.
- If she dies, her children will be orphans.

Complete the following chart. Leave blank those areas of functioning for which the example does not give information.

Analysis of Mrs. Collins's Needs

	Levels of Functioning					
	Well-being	*Stress*	*Problems*	*Crisis*	*Disability*	
Areas of Need	*(1)*	*(2)*	*(3)*	*(4)*	*(5)*	*Obstacles to Functioning (Personal, Environmental, Rigid Laws, Catastrophes)*
Physical functioning						
Emotional functioning						
Education and employment						
Financial						
Transportation*	X					
Family* functioning	X					
Housing*	X					
Safety and security*	X					
Spiritual and aesthetic* functioning	X					
Leisure and recreation*	X					

*Since this is a crisis situation, the focus is on the major problem. No information was received that any of these areas were causing problems.

Turn to Answer 7 on page 595

Turn to Answer 7 on page 595

FRAME

8

ISSUES IN APPLYING THE NEEDS ANALYSIS FRAMEWORK

It is one thing to have a framework and to try it out on a few case examples, but it is another to apply it to a real human being. This raises three issues to which human service workers should be sensitive: (1) what it's like to experience problems of living, especially as they escalate; (2) applying the framework with a recognition of the total person and his or her situation; and (3) keeping perspective.

The Experience of Problems of Living

It's not easy to have problems; it can be difficult and humiliating to share personal information with a stranger and to know you are being judged by that person. It can also be ultimately rewarding when someone perhaps understands the situation and helps you set goals to address the problems. These skills will be further developed in subsequent sections of the book. For now, the point is awareness and reflection. Naomi Brill's comments on vulnerability, dependency, resistance, and ethnic diversity offer a perspective:

> To be poor in an affluent society; to be old and slow in a world that values youth and speed; to be a child when family structures are weakened and changing and when proliferating no-fault divorces are mainly concerned with the rights of adults; to be a member of a minority group that is considered inferior; to be so handicapped as to be unable to use available resources—to be any one of these is to be isolated, stereotyped, and dehumanized. It is also to know that within the society there are institutionalized supports that tend to maintain prejudice and discrimination and close the doors of opportunity. It is to know the frustration of powerlessness, the bitterness of the knowledge that prejudice and powerlessness tend to be self-perpetuating, the loneliness of being the outsider, the deadening defeat of unfulfilled potential. It is to be afraid.[2]

Recognizing the Total and Unique Person

Human service workers may define needs differently depending on their backgrounds. It is important to recognize the many different characteristics that reflect the diversity of being human. Being aware of and appreciating the fact that a person is male or female; Black, White, or some other race; young or old; from an urban or rural area; or from the United States or another country, will enhance your ability to understand problems from multiple points of view and thereby (hopefully) to deliver effective, sensitive, and responsive services. Consider the diversity of practice reflected by the following library entries found under "social work clients":

Aliens	Asian Americans	African Americans
Cancer patients	Children	Chinese Americans
Divorced people	Drug addicts	Gays
Hispanic Americans	Homeless people	Native Americans
Men	Mexican Americans	Minorities
Prostitutes	Puerto Ricans	Refugees
Southeast Asians	Aged people	Deaf people
Disabled people	Mentally handicapped people	West Indians
Women	Youths	Arab Americans

These "labels" do not determine whether a person becomes a consumer of human services. Rather, they suggest both the need to be sensitive and to develop an awareness and appreciation for other cultures *and* how people from different cultures

---

[2]Naomi Brill, *Working with People: The Helping Process,* 5th ed. (New York: Longman, 1995), pp. 209–210.

may *experience* our human service system and our society.[3] For example, if you are working with a consumer who is a member of a racial minority, you should be aware of the frustration caused by discrimination and the resulting lack of trust and confidence that may occur. On the other hand, you should be careful about assuming that all racial minorities have some, or the same, experience of discrimination. Elderly consumers may not display the same vigor that you may see in the young, and they may be physically incapable of participating in certain kinds of services. Yet just because a person is elderly, it does not follow that he is less able or willing to use, or less interested in, services that may seem more appropriate for "the young." A person from a small rural community may have a difficult time adjusting to the pace of the big city, and her values may come into conflict with life in a new neighborhood. Sex discrimination in employment may be a factor in working with female or male consumers. The point is to be aware of diversity and its consequences *and* of your reactions to people who are different from those you are familiar with.

Keeping Perspective

Placing these issues back into the context of the three-part framework for needs analysis reinforces the point that the total assessment process is not a simple one. For example, an emotionally upset consumer may be bothered by the fact that the welfare check has not arrived or upset over the loss of a family member. These are two very different problems. In addition, problems may be momentary crises or longstanding problems that affect the consumer's level of functioning. Level of functioning is a result of the impact of problems on consumers. Are they so immobilized or paralyzed by their problems that they cannot continue their jobs or rear their children, or are they only momentarily blocked from carrying out their normal duties? In assessing the obstacles to functioning, you might find that a call to the welfare department will resolve the problem of the missing check, whereas several supportive counseling sessions may be necessary to overcome the shock of a lost family member. In the first case you might be dealing with the consumer's environment and/or personal resources and deficiencies.

The needs analysis framework helps you to discriminate conditions in what can seem at times to be a swirl of complexity. We hope that with this framework and an awareness of these characteristics, their consequences, and how they affect people, you will have a better understanding of the consumers you serve.

If your goal is to be sensitive in applying the needs analysis framework, you may be interested in the consequences of seeing individuals primarily in terms of their "needs." John McKnight challenges human service workers to think about some possible implications of focusing on needs:

> Each of us can be conceived as a half-glass of water. We are partly empty. We have deficiencies. We are also partly full. We have capacities. Human service professionals focus on deficiencies and call them "needs," and have expert skills in giving each perceived deficiency a label. This process of focusing on deficien-

---

[3]See, for example, James W. Green, *Cultural Awareness in the Human Services* (Englewood Cliffs, N.J.: Prentice-Hall, 1982); Elsie Y. Cross, "Issues of Diversity," in Dorothy Vails-Weber and W. Joseph Potts, *Sunrise Seminars,* vol. II (Alexandria, Va.: National Training Laboratories, 1985). Also consult the suggestions for further study at the end of this chapter.

cies may force us to focus on the empty half when the appropriate focus may be the full half.[4]

As an alternative, McKnight proposes that human service workers engage in capacity-oriented development, and act as catalysts and resources for releasing the skills or potential contributions of the persons who are said to be in need.

What is your reaction to these issues? Do you think consumers should be perceived and helped in terms of *needs and problems*—or needs *and* problems *and* capacities—or just *capacities?* This would be a worthwhile topic to pursue in discussions as well as in further independent study.

---

[4]John McKnight, "Do No Harm: Policy Options That Meet Human Needs," *Social Policy* (Summer 1989): 7. Also see Dennis Saleebey, ed. *The Strengths Perspective in Social Work Practice* (New York: Longman, 1992).

The Societal Context: Riding the Waves of Change

What we consider to be needs and human services are shaped by the society in which we live. Although some human needs might be considered as unchanging, the prevailing pattern over time is that society changes. Many aspects of the human services reflect these shifts and require practitioners and others to develop new response mechanisms. To understand the connection among social changes, human needs, and human services practitioners need to be aware of the broader context of which they are a part. Because this context changes so often, the key issue that commands attention is the ability to manage change—for ourselves, our clients or consumers, and our agencies or organizations.

Goals

To develop an appreciation for the connection between the changes in society and the human needs that become the concern of human service practitioners. To translate this appreciation into an awareness of the need and ability to manage change.

Learning Activities

To accomplish these goals, we will:

1. Explore the meaning and significance of change, especially social change.
2. Develop a basic understanding of human needs in relation to social changes.
3. Look at examples of the connections among social changes, human needs, and human services in the United States.
4. Highlight some contemporary examples of how social changes have dramatically affected human needs and, therefore, human services.
5. Explore differing views of change.
6. Consider "managing change" as an emerging, essential human need of central importance to the practice of human services.

GROWTH AND CHANGE: WHAT'S IT ALL ABOUT?

Change is avalanching upon our heads and most people are grotesquely un-prepared to cope with it.[1]

Growth and change are the essence of living. *Webster's* defines *grow* as "to spring up and develop to maturity." Change can be a form of growth, but it can include an element of the unexpected. *Webster's* defines *change* as "to make different; to undergo loss of or modification of; to move to another; to undergo transformation, transition, substitution."

Change has always been a part of the human condition and a necessary part of any society's growth and development. Individuals change over the course of a lifetime—physically, emotionally, and intellectually. Organizations are constantly changing who works for them, what is important, and what is rewarded. And conditions in society, in the world in which we live, are constantly changing. What is different today is not the fact that there is change; rather, more changes seem to take place at a much faster pace.

Not too far in the past, most people lived their whole lives in one place. The friends of their childhood were the friends of their old age. The skills they learned early in life served them for decades, if not for a lifetime. The rate of change was relatively slow, and change came at a predictable, steady rate. To really see it required looking at a variable in terms of centuries.

For the past 50 to 75 years, we have begun to experience "exponential change," a change curve that comes at increasing speed and must be measured in shorter and shorter units of time. For example, the information technology industry illustrates exponential change: a relatively new technology in which knowledge expands rapidly and may become obsolete within months, even weeks. This is the environment in which we live, a time of rapid change. So much has transpired in such a short period that we are still in shock. For example, a fashion, a taste, or a style of doing business hardly has time to become entrenched before it is replaced by another. Something new is always happening: Mars landings, test-tube babies, video games, financial crises, computers, changes in eastern Europe, increasing divorce rates, population changes, single parenthood, changing family structures, career shifts, and earlier and later retirement. Today's changes can be seen much more rapidly, sometimes in days and months in contrast to years. Yet most of us were raised and educated as if the old world still existed. Our basic expectations about work and family may well be rooted in a lifestyle that no longer exists. No wonder most of us struggle with change; no wonder it causes us stress.

Change can be understood from at least two perspectives: as something that is happening to us or outside of us (e.g., in society) and to which we are responding; or as something that we are doing to others. Social changes are generally perceived as happening to us or outside of us. They are necessary ingredients of any society's growth and development and form the environment in which we live. However, by

---

[1] Alvin Toffler, *Future Shock* (New York: Bantam, 1970), p. 12.

their very nature, social changes can also disrupt the functioning of individuals, families, and institutions such that new conditions, both positive and negative, are created.

FRAME

HUMAN NEEDS AND SOCIAL CHANGES

A human life is lived in a complex process of meeting needs.[2] Human needs are those resources people require if they are to survive as individuals and to function appropriately in society.[3] They are created and met in a complex of interactions between the individual and society. Lesson 1 of this chapter presented a framework of human needs in ten areas:

Physical functioning   Family functioning
Emotional functioning   Housing
Education and employment   Safety and security
Financial functioning   Spiritual and aesthetic functioning
Transportation   Leisure and recreation

Conditions in society can create situations in which people are unable to meet their needs in one or more of these areas so that they experience problems in living. Four obstacles have been recurring themes in the development of the human services. First, *conditions of adversity can create needs for basic physical survival.* Catastrophes, such as floods, pestilence, war, and economic collapse, leave otherwise self-maintaining individuals, families, and communities temporarily without the basic necessities for life. Second, *conditions of uneven distribution of economic resources that result from economic activity that force some households to live at a level grossly below the standard for society can create poverty.* Third, *conditions of conflicts between majority society and minority groups can create denial of access to resources for some citizens or racism and discrimination.* Fourth, persons with disabilities, infirm elderly individuals, and children without families that can provide care are examples of *conditions of dependency* that have both societal and individual causes.[4]

Such problems or unmet needs can be individually caused (e.g., through illness or disability) or societally caused (e.g., through changes in the environment over which individuals have no control).[5] Whether needs are created from individual or societal actions, the human services have arisen as a major response. How those human

---

[2]Dean Pierce, *Social Work and Society: An Introduction* (New York: Longman, 1989), p. 118.
[3]Louise C. Johnson and Charles L. Schwartz, *Social Welfare: A Response to Human Need* (Boston: Allyn & Bacon, 1988), p. 3.
[4]This paragraph is based on David M. Austin, *The Political Economy of Human Service Programs* (Greenwich, Conn.: JAI Press, 1988), pp. 85–86; and Johnson and Schwartz, *Social Welfare,* pp. 47–59.
[5]Naomi Brill, *Working with People: The Helping Process,* 5th ed. (White Plains, NY: Longman, 1995), p. 3.

services are defined with respect to human needs is closely related to the changing conditions in our society.

FRAME
3

EXAMPLES OF SOCIAL CHANGES: THE THREE WAVES[6]

Alvin Toffler has pointed out that Western society has experienced three major waves of technological advances, each of which changed all aspects of living and working. The first wave developed when man discovered agricultural technology and switched to settlement from a subsistence and nomadic hunting and gathering society. This social change began thousands of years ago. The second wave began with the transition to industrial organization and technology about a century ago for most of the world, though much of the world has remained in the agricultural first wave. The third wave—the information/electronic wave—began its major impact in North America and the world in about 1970, with the invention of the microchip. Each of these waves required the demise of a previous social structure and its values, replacing it with new structures and values. Each shift was significantly wrenching and demanding.

One way to illustrate the dramatic transformation in our society through each of these three major waves of social change is to look at how the means, methods, and materials with which we work have changed during each. The chart in Table 2.1 illustrates some of these changes.

[6]H. Alan Raymond, "Management in the Third Wave," in *Careers Tomorrow: The Outlook for Work in a Changing World* (Washington, D.C.: World Future Society, 1988).

TABLE 2.1 **Changes Through the Ages**

Characteristic	*Agricultural Age*	*Industrial Age*	*Information Age*
Defining technology	Craftsman	Clock	Instruction-based systems
Key resource	Raw materials (seeds, water, soils, land)	Capital (money)	Ideas (minds)
Transforming resource	Natural energy (sun)	Processed energy (coal, electricity)	Synergy (minds working together)
Rhythm	Nature	Machine	Self
Product	Food	Mass-produced items	Information
Place of work	Farm, cottage	Central plant, office, bureaucracy	Cyberspace; home office plus traditional office
Communication	Conversation (transfer ideas locally)	Face-to-face conference (transfer ideas by transporting people)	Teleconference (transfer ideas by transmitting images)

Sources: Samuel E. Bleecker, "Rethinking How We Work: The Office of the Future," in *Careers Tomorrow: The Outlook for Work in a Changing World* (Washington, D.C.: World Future Society, 1988), p. 38; and Martin Morf, *The Work/Life Dichotomy* (New York: Quorum Books, 1989), p. 22.

FRAME 4

THE THREE WAVES OF CHANGE AND THE DEVELOPMENT OF THE HUMAN SERVICES IN THE UNITED STATES

To better appreciate the connections among social conditions, human needs, and human services, as well as the increasing overall pace of social change, we will examine the emergence of the human services during each of the three major waves of change identified in Frame 3—the agricultural wave, the industrial wave, and the information/electronic wave. We will highlight three features for each wave of change: the major social changes, society's view toward the human problems arising as a consequence of those changes, and society's responses. A few questions to check your general understanding are also included. We suggest you spend some time reviewing the emergence of the human services throughout these three major waves of change. There are two important things you should try to achieve during your review. First, try to get a feel for the connections among social conditions, human problems, and society's responses. Second, notice the kinds of changes taking place from one wave to the next. Do you get a sense of a faster pace and intensity, a difference in human needs and society's responses?

THE AGRICULTURAL AGE AND THE HUMAN SERVICES (ABOUT 1600–1800)

Review of General Characteristics of the Agricultural Age

Technology	Key Resource	Transforming Resource	Rhythm	Product	Place of Work	Communication
Craftsman	Raw materials (seeds, water, soils, land)	Natural energy (sun)	Nature	Food	Farm, cottage	Conversation (transfer ideas locally)

Highlights of the Relationships Among Social Change, Human Needs, and Human Services in the United States During the Agricultural Age[7]

Social Changes	Society's View of Human Problems	Society's Response to Human Problems
1600–1700		
Poverty and hardship of pioneer society; battles with	Human problems—poverty, ill health, mental deficiency,	Responsibility for human problems rested with the

[7]The idea for this conceptualization is from Brill, *Working with People,* pp. 4–5. While some of the content in the table is from Brill, other sources include Michael J. Austin, Judy Kopp, and Philip L. Smith, *Delivering Human Services,* 2nd. ed. (New York: Longman, 1986), pp. 6–12; and David M. Austin, *The Political Economy of Human Service Programs* (Greenwich, Conn.: JAI Press, 1988).

Social Changes	Society's View of Human Problems	Society's Response to Human Problems
1600–1700 (continued)		
Native Americans; isolation of colonies leading to sense of community and responsibility for selves.	physical disability, and dependency—are acts of God or nature. Helping others is a duty to God and to the community.	individual experiencing them and with the family, kinship group, and colony to which the individual belonged. The church or organized religion placed a high value on charitable acts. Help on a personal basis by individuals in their homes.
1700–1800		
French and Indian Wars; problems with England culminating in American Revolution; establishment of a loose federal government; opening of the West, resulting in personal mobility; results of wars: broken families, displaced people, poverty, epidemics.	A growing feeling that in a land of affluence, people should be able to care for themselves, that poverty and unworthiness are equated, that poverty need not exist; emphasis on the Puritan ethic.	Separation of church and state, resulting in many sects that cared for their own. Development of both public aid and organized private philanthropy. Emphasis on states' rights, with programs largely local but with some state support.

F R A M E

5

Stop here and check your understanding of the emergence of human services in the United States. During the agricultural age, America was a pioneer society with much of its population making its living from the land. During this period, human services were

_____ a. provided by the government, which sought to address virtually all of the human problems experienced by the population.

_____ b. the sole responsibility of the individual who experienced them.

_____ c. a combination of individual and family responsibility supplemented by some public aid and private charitable organizations.

Turn to Answer 8 on page 596

FRAME

THE INDUSTRIAL AGE AND THE HUMAN SERVICES
(ABOUT 1800–1980)

Review of General Characteristics of the Industrial Age

Technology	Key Resource	Transforming Resource	Rhythm	Product	Place of Work	Communication
Clock	Capital (money)	Processed energy (coal, electricity)	Machine	Mass-produced items	Central plant, office, bureaucracy	Face-to-face conference (transfer ideas by transporting people)

The Relationships Among Social Change, Human Needs, and Human Services in the United States During the Industrial Age

Social Changes	Society's View of Human Problems	Society's Response to Human Problems
1800–1900		
Expansion across the continent; rapid urbanization; increasing wealth; Industrial Revolution; Civil War; lack of sanitation in new cities; epidemics; poverty of workers who lost their jobs; families at risk; displaced people; growth of unions.	Causes of human need are understandable and preventable; poverty and need are an individual matter, and people are responsible for their own plight; public services to which people have a "right" are pauperizing and destructive.	Stage is set for future development of expanded human services. State funds used extensively to provide economic relief to families in their own homes. Federal government becomes involved at modest level with creation of Freedmen's Bureau—when local facilities did not suffice; also created Bureau of Indian Affairs. Population density in major cities leads state governments to expand their roles in the provision of public health services, treatment of mentally ill, and responsibility for the care of dependent children. Development of "scientific" charity requiring highly trained professionals.

Social Changes	Society's View of Human Problems	Society's Response to Human Problems
1900–1940		
World War I; stock market crash and economic depression; dust storms; many people of money and prominence find their lives devastated by economic conditions beyond their control.	Americans begin to realize that many human problems are created by environmental conditions rather than personal deficiency.	Extensive involvement of federal government in human service programs. Franklin Roosevelt's New Deal creates the framework of our contemporary human service system and establishes what many call "the American welfare state." Social Security Act and Amendments are passed as part of New Deal—variants of these programs still exist today. Federal government a major funding source for programs that dealt directly with some aspects of poverty.
1940–1980		
World War II; the Korean conflict; the Cold War; Vietnam; the Middle East wars; beginning movement from an industrial to a technological or information society; increasing affluence; civil rights movement.	Human need can and should be eradicated for the welfare of all; eradication can be achieved by laws and extensive social programs. Human beings are constantly at risk from factors in the environment. Society is responsible for dealing with human problems.	The provision of human services becomes a permanent part of American society. Youth service "character-building" programs (YMCA, YWCA, Boy Scouts, Girl Scouts, Campfire Girls) are created. Community-based mental health and mental retardation programs for the elderly and indigent (Medicare and Medicaid). Food Stamp program. Community self-help organizations, stimulated by available federal money, grow and prosper.

(continued)

Social Changes	Society's View of Human Problems	Society's Response to Human Problems
1940–1980		
		Community mental health centers develop all across the country with funding from federal, state, and local governments as well as private sources of revenue.
		Local affiliated agencies of the Family Service Association of America expand rapidly with the support of United Way funds.
		Private, for-profit human service agencies grow rapidly (e.g., counseling centers, nursing homes, psychiatric hospitals).
		Significant increase in the number of individual private practitioners, such as psychiatrists, psychologists, social workers, marriage and family counselors, and other mental health professionals.

FRAME

7

Now check your understanding of the emergence of the human services during the industrial age.

1. During the industrial age, conditions in America changed radically. Many people moved to cities and began to work in organizations outside of their homes. There were numerous wars and financial upheavals. These social changes

_____ a. retarded the growth of a comprehensive human service system.

_____ b. helped the growth of a comprehensive human service system.

_____ c. didn't have any influence one way or the other.

2. Changes during the industrial age created new concerns about

_____ a. problems of unemployment, poverty, working conditions, and civil rights.

_____ b. national defense and foreign policy.

_____ c. the separation of church and state.

Turn to Answer 9 on page 596

THE INFORMATION/ELECTRONIC AGE AND THE HUMAN SERVICES (ABOUT 1970 OR 1980 TO THE PRESENT)

Review of General Characteristics of the Information Age

Technology	*Key Resource*	*Transforming Resource*	*Rhythm*	*Product*	*Place of Work*	*Communication*
Instruction-based systems	Ideas (minds)	Synergy (minds working together)	Self	Information	Cyberspace, home office and traditional workplace	Teleconference (transfer ideas by transmitting images)

Highlights of the Relationships Among Social Change, Human Needs, and Human Services in the United States During the Information Age

Social Changes	*Society's View of Human Problems*	*Society's Response to Human Problems*
Increasing affluence and increasing poverty; drastic changes in how people communicate; unemployment and underemployment; hunger; increasing drug use; national deficits; drastic changes in foreign affairs; an increasingly interdependent world; shift to a service economy or an economy based on the creation and distribution of information; overpopulation; environmental problems, rising health costs; enormous budget and trade deficits; rising crime rates.	Human problems cost society enormous sums of money to address. As a society, we have a responsibility to continue to address the problems, but in different ways. A return to the Puritan ethic and local, state, and private responsibility. Tremendous tension and conflict over the increasingly pressing and complex needs of a variety of special populations (e.g., children, elderly, homeless, disadvantaged), and who has responsibility for their welfare and quality of life.	Efforts to drastically reduce federal expenditures in and fundamentally reform the design and delivery of human services (e.g., welfare reform, health care reform). Efforts to return as much control and responsibility as possible to the states. Calls on private charitable or voluntary organizations to increase their contributions to many human services. Increased action on the part of advocacy groups and non-profit organizations for special populations. Larger segments of American society experiencing economic hardship and limited resources are inadequate to respond. Growth of for-profit human service firms in health, mental

(continued)

Social Changes	Society's View of Human Problems	Society's Response to Human Problems
		health, day care, and residential institution services of all types.
		Some state governments becoming actively involved in new program and policy initiatives—in adult and juvenile corrections, mental health and mental retardation services, services for older adults living in their own homes, job training for mothers receiving AFDC payments and child welfare.

FRAME 9

You are living in the information age and experiencing the conditions just described. We will continue to explore many facets of the human services as we know them today. But for now, which of the following best characterizes the relationship between social changes and human services during the information age? The social changes during the information age have

_____ a. solved many longstanding human problems as a consequence of increased contributions from private charities.

_____ b. resulted in a significant expansion of federal human service programs, including the creation of major new national programs.

_____ c. brought a new ideological approach to human services focused on efforts to reform delivery systems, reduce federal expenditures, eliminate or cut back programs, and increase competition for scarce resources.

Turn to Answer 10 on page 596

FRAME 10

When Naomi Brill surveyed the range of social and human service changes in the United States, she came away with two important observations.[8] First, we have not arrived at any consensus on dealing with our social problems. Second, it is possible to find individuals and groups within the present total society who are operating on the basis of attitudes and approaches in each of the major waves of change.

What are your impressions at this point? To expand your perspective a bit more, review the box below:

---

[8]Brill, *Working with People,* p. 4.

Nine Forces Reshaping America[9]

1. **The maturation of America.** The maturing of the baby-boom generation and the graying of America with the growth of the 65-and-over population mean the United States is leaving an era obsessed with youth and moving into one that will be more realistic, more responsible, and more tolerant of diversity.
2. **The mosaic society.** Rising levels of education, increased ethnic diversity, a growing population of elderly individuals, more single-person households, and other diversity-related trends are moving American society away from "mass society" toward a "mosaic society."
3. **Redefinition of individual and societal roles.** There will be a blurring of the boundaries that have traditionally defined the roles of the public sector and the private sector, as well as individual versus institutional responsibilities. Wellness activities will become increasingly important, and the self-help movement will grow.
4. **The information-based economy.** Information technologies are changing the way people communicate, work, and play. The most profound effect is that it is creating a new context in which it is necessary to try the unprecedented because the usual no longer works.
5. **Globalization.** The movement of products, capital, technology, information, and ideas around the world is continuing to increase. There is increasing foreign ownership of the U.S. industrial base and a growing presence of U.S. firms in other countries. U.S. citizens are experiencing more cultures through travel. An increasing globalization of tastes and ideas is occurring.
6. **Personal and environmental health.** Quality-of-life issues, particularly the health of the individual and the state of the environment, are beginning to emerge as areas of public concern.
7. **American business is being restructured.** Entire industries are being globalized and restructured. Small firms are being created in increasing numbers. The rapid pace of technological change is continuing.
8. **Family and home are being redefined.** Many functions once handled predominantly by families—such as meal preparation and child care—are offered by commercial services outside the home. Information technologies are bringing shopping and banking and other services into the home. The family has become a diverse institution and will grow in importance as a stabilizing force. Yet the stresses on family life may make the family less able to fulfill its support-giving role without help from outside the family structure.
9. **Rebirth of social activism.** The public agenda pendulum is swinging decisively in the direction of social concerns (environmental degradation, pervasive homelessness, lack of affordable housing, racial tensions, and extensive child poverty). Accompanying this shift is likely to be less tolerance for business actions that the public perceives as harmful to society.

---

[9] *What Lies Ahead: Countdown to the 21st Century,* United Way Strategic Institute, 701 N. Fairfax Street, Alexandria, Va., 1989, a portion of which was reprinted as "Nine Forces Reshaping America." Reprinted by *The World Future Society,* 4916 Saint Elmo Ave., Bethesda, Md., 1989.

FRAME

BEING AWARE OF DIFFERENT VIEWS OF CHANGE

Naomi Brill's observations raise questions: Does everyone in our society think change is a good thing? Are there different viewpoints or social attitudes that shape our beliefs and behaviors in the United States—especially those concerned with the human services? Would everyone view the emergence of the human services through the agricultural, industrial, and information/electronic ages as positive? As the heading suggests, people, including human service workers, debate these questions. This frame illustrates one set of differences about change to alert you to some of the complexities in our society that shape our practice.

Philip Popple and Leslie Leighninger suggest three general social attitudes that can be used to illustrate the fact that there are strong differences of opinion on how to approach the human services in our society and on change in general.[10] They use the

Comparison of Three Social Attitudes[11]

Attitudes toward:	Conservative	Liberal	Radical
Change	Change is generally not desirable; it is better to keep things as they are.	Change is generally good; it brings progress. Moderate change is best.	Change is good, especially if it means fundamental change in the system.
Human Nature	People are essentially selfish; they need to be controlled.	People are basically good; they need structures to reinforce good impulses.	People are basically good; they can be corrupted by institutions.
Individual Behavior	Individuals have free will; they are responsible for their own lives and problems.	Individuals are not entirely autonomous or self-governing; environment plays a part in the problems they face.	Individual behavior is strongly influenced by social and economic structures.
Family	The traditional family is the basic unit of society; it should not face government interference.	The family is changing; it needs social and governmental supports.	The traditional family is oppressive; the changing family needs government supports.
Society	Society is inherently fair; it functions well on its own, and it is a system of interrelated parts.	Society needs regulation to ensure fair competition between various interests.	Society contains inequalities, conflict between those with power and those without, and thus it needs change.

[10]This discussion is taken from Philip Popple and Leslie Leighninger, *Social Work, Social Welfare, and American Society* (Boston: Allyn & Bacon, 1990), pp. 3–23.
[11]Popple and Leighninger, *Social Work,* p. 19.

terms conservative, liberal, and radical to describe and to differentiate three quite different sets of social attitudes, political perspectives, or ideologies for improving the human condition. Obviously these are highly charged terms in our times, and they are difficult to portray simplistically. These three social attitudes are, however, worth examining as concepts, if for no other reason than to push all of us to examine what we believe about the world in which we live and how that might affect our views toward and action in the human services.

As the table on page 90 suggests, the conservative view emphasizes tradition, and believes that change generally results in more negative than positive consequences. The liberal view holds that pervasive inequities in our society can be rectified with reform rather than radical restructuring of existing institutions. The radical view is skeptical about moderate change (such as reform) to fix inequities in society, and stresses the need for fundamental changes in the social system.

There is no "correct" perspective on the premises that should govern how we improve the human condition, or how we deliver human services. Liberal, conservative, and radical viewpoints are all part of a larger picture. They are also *rarely* seen "purely" in the real world. E. J. Dionne, for example, shows how complicated and messy these distinctions can be:[12]

> Conservatives claim to be the true communitarians because of their support for the values of family, work, and neighborhood. Unlike liberals, conservatives are willing to assert that "community norms" should prevail on such matters as sex, pornography, and the education of children. Yet the typical conservative is unwilling to defend the interests of traditional community whenever its needs come into conflict with those of the free market. If shutting down a plant throws thousands in a particular community out of work, conservatives usually defend this assault on "family, work, and neighborhood" in the name of efficiency. Many of the things conservatives bemoan about modern society—a preference for short-term gratification over long-term commitment, the love of things instead of values, a flight from responsibility toward selfishness—result at least in part from the workings of the very economic system that conservatives feel bound to defend. For conservatives, it is much easier to ignore this dilemma and blame "permissiveness" on "big government" or "the liberals."
>
> The liberals often make that easy. Liberals tout themselves as the real defenders of community. They speak constantly about having us share each other's burdens. Yet when the talk moves from economic issues to culture or personal morality, liberals fall strangely mute. Liberals are uncomfortable with the idea that virtuous community depends on virtuous individuals. Liberals defend the welfare state, but are uneasy when asked what moral values the welfare state should promote—as if billions of federal dollars can be spent in a "value-free" way. Liberals rightly defend the interests of children who are born into poverty through no choice of their own. Yet when conservatives suggest that society has a vital interest in how the parents of these poor children behave, many liberals accuse the conservatives of "blaming the victim." When conservatives suggest that changing teenage attitudes toward premarital sex might reduce teen pregnancy, many liberals end the conversation by accusing the conservatives of being "prudes" or "out of touch."

---

[12]E. J. Dionne, *Why Americans Hate Politics*. (New York: Simon & Schuster, 1991), pp. 13–14.

Not all conservatives and liberals fall into the neat categories I have just de-scribed, and the questions each side raises about the other's proposals are often legitimate.

Dionne goes on to develop the idea that these perspectives can end up framing issues as false choices. He says, "wracked by contradiction and responsive mainly to the needs of their various constituencies, liberalism and conservatism prevent the nation from settling the questions that most trouble it."[13]

FRAME

Reflecting on Practice

The important point for you as a human service practitioner is to realize that you work in a political environment. You need to begin to think about what you believe about change and how you think society should respond to the human problems that emerge on their own and as a consequence of change.

Take some time to discuss your views of the changes in our society and how we have responded to human needs. Try to find people who hold different views from yours and see if you can present a brief statement of their thoughts and ideas and how they compare with yours. Present an ongoing debate on some highly charged human service or social controversy from each of the three perspectives on change.

You might also take some time to discuss the labels of liberal, conservative, and radical. Are they helpful? Are they complete? For what purpose? What other ways would you suggest to describe the different views on change in our society?

FRAME
14

THE CENTRAL ISSUE FOR PRACTICE: "MANAGING CHANGE" AS A CRITICAL HUMAN NEED

No matter how you view change, the inescapable conclusion is that it happens.[14] Man-aging change should thus be viewed as a need similar to the need for food, shelter, and clothing; for community and companionship; for security and safety.

Dean Pierce suggests that what all human service problems have in common is the fact that they reflect some kind of change that has to be addressed. He says:

A variety of changes—in individuals and institutions—account for the emergence of many problems and needs: children without parents, the frail elderly, alco-holics, abused children, the hungry, homeless people, the mentally ill, impover-ished communities. There are changes in social structures, changes that amount to a loss, changes that come from the processes of human growth. Moreover, certain changes are necessary to restore the social functioning in each case pre-

---

[13]Dionne, *Why Americans Hate Politics,* p. 11.
[14]Pierce, *Social Work and Society;* Brill, *Working with People;* and Dorri Jacobs, *Change: How to Live with, Manage, Create, and Enjoy It* (New York: Programs on Change, 784 Columbus Avenue, 1981).

sented. . . . Whether problems stem from processes of psychological and social development, from unexpected changes in people's lives, or from the structures of social institutions where people interact and obtain resources to meet their needs, all people have to manage change in their lives.[15]

What does all of this suggest for understanding and delivering human services? If managing change is both a critical human need and a characteristic of the problems that you will be addressing in the human services, it will affect your definition of the purpose of the human services, as well as the knowledge and skills you bring to your practice.

Purpose

A major purpose of the human services can initially be understood as helping people to change their pattern of functioning—helping them to better manage change and to bring about change. The human services help people to complete growth processes; replace existing psychological or cognitive approaches to living that have been destroyed by changes; rehabilitate parts of people's lives in relation to human or social changes; or take care of people who have been completely or partly damaged by change.

Knowledge and Skills

To strengthen the ability to manage change, it will be important to understand concepts about how growth and change affect our society and the growth and functioning of individuals and institutions, and to develop skills in:

- confronting change
- planning for change
- avoiding change
- managing necessary growth and change
- redirecting change

Practice

Human service practitioners who view the ability to manage change as an essential human need (and who view change as an opportunity for people to learn and improve their lives) will be aware of the conditions in society and how these link with human problems and societal and personal responses. They will also explore their feelings and attitudes about change and compare them with other points of view.

A strong component of helping people to manage change is supporting them while they confront how they feel about what the change has done or will do to their life. This confirmation is at the core of people's need to manage change because in confronting their feelings about change, people take their first step in meeting this need.[16]

---

[15]Pierce, *Social Work and Society,* p. 121.
[16]Pierce, *Social Work and Society,* p. 134.

The Emotions of Change?

Think of some major change you have recently experienced personally. Next think of some change outside of you that surprised you. Individually or in a small discussion group, consider answers to the following questions.

- How did you respond to these events?
- What were some of the emotions you experienced?
- How did they affect you?
- How did they affect others?

If you are in a discussion group, share your emotions and reactions, not the event that triggered them.

The emotions people experience during major changes can range from feeling energized and motivated to actualize their potential to feeling confused, depressed, overwhelmed, and even physically ill. A major factor in identifying and understanding such emotions is your skills in learning to effectively manage change, especially seeing and feeling the potential connection between conditions in the world and conditions in the immediacy of your daily life.

Scanning Key Issues: The Policy Challenges in Delivering Human Services[1]

This lesson begins to link what you do in delivering human services to social policy. To do that, Lesson 3 highlights the ways in which personal needs and the changes in society get translated into problems and issues, and it shows how these problems and issues are addressed through seeing your work, in part, as policy practice.

Social policy is highly complex and there are many written materials available to describe it. The aim of this lesson is to introduce you to the idea of "service delivery issues" as a way to connect what you do in delivering human services to social policy. A service delivery issue is something that entry-level human service workers can experience quite directly. It is the particular connection that emerges from:

- a troubling condition in our society;
- a pattern or regularity in problems confronted by the consumers you work with; and
- a possible response (or lack of response) from some level of the human service community.

A service delivery issue can thus be thought of as the policy intersection of a problem or issue and the attempt of the human service professions to resolve it. Lesson 3 concentrates on developing skills that will enable you to "see" service delivery issues that emerge from frustrations you experience while you are delivering human services. While not all frustrations are "policy" related, Lesson 3 points the way to recognizing those that might be.

Social policy is not only complex but it is always changing. The aim of this lesson is *not* to make you a policy expert in all or any particular area of the human services. You should approach this lesson with a focus on *developing your learning skills* (your

---

[1]Amy Rebecca Olk, a freelance writer and volunteer with local and international humanitarian organizations, took the lead in reconceptualizing and rewriting this lesson for the fourth edition.

issue scanning skills) from the perspective of policy, so that you will be able to "see" service delivery issues in your practice, and to take a variety of steps to discover more about them. "Issue scanning" to learn about areas of policy in your direct practice is really the focus of the lesson.

The ability to see your work as contributing to the creation of social policy is an essential skill you need to manage societal change. It helps you to forge a link between your practice and the broader context in which you live and work, including changes needed or under way in the human services.

Goals

To gain an overall picture of the range and focus of human services by examining the links among problems, issues, policies, and delivery of human services. To develop an awareness of the complexity of resulting service delivery issues, and to illustrate how to learn more about issue areas of interest to you.

Learning Activities

To accomplish these goals, we will:

1. Explore the linkage among problems, issues, and social policy and develop an awareness of the complexity of these concepts.
2. Reflect on the relationship between policy and the practice of delivering human services.
3. Scan examples of service delivery issues in eight major policy areas relevant to delivering human services.
4. Introduce the skill of "issue scanning" as a way to see service delivery issues and learn more about them.
5. Illustrate creative, in-depth approaches to scanning three specific service delivery issues.
6. Develop a perspective for appreciating service delivery issues as opportunities for change.

FRAME
1

PROBLEMS AND ISSUES

Webster's defines a *problem* as "a question raised for inquiry, consideration, or solution; an intricate unsettled question, or a source of perplexity, distress, or vexation."

While the words "issue" and "problem" are sometimes used interchangeably, issues are different in that they develop *in response* to a question or problem. An issue arises when the answer to a question is either unknown or very complex, or when people disagree about how a problem should be solved. Issues are basically conflicts of interests or values.[2] As such, an issue can almost never be definitely and completely resolved to the full satisfaction of all parties. Rather than "solving issues," the focus is on identifying issues and then managing them by exploring a range of options and taking a variety of actions.

To better understand how human problems get translated into issues, consider this specific example: Nearly everyone would agree that poverty is a broad social problem of great concern. It is clear that poverty in and of itself generates and exacerbates many other human problems. However,

> [c]onflict over poverty begins with conflict over the definition of poverty and differing estimates of its extent in the United States. Proponents of large-scale government programs for the poor, on the one hand, frequently make broad definitions of poverty and high estimates of the number of poor people. They view the problem as a persistent one, even in an affluent society. They contend that millions suffer from hunger, exposure, and remediable illness, and that some people starve to death. Their definition of the problem of poverty practically mandates immediate and massive governmental programs to assist the poor.
>
> On the other hand, opponents of large-scale governmental antipoverty programs frequently minimize the number of poor in America. They see poverty diminishing over time, without major public programs. They view the poor in the United States as considerably better off than the middle class was fifty years ago—and even wealthy by the standards of most other societies in the world. They deny that Americans need to suffer from hunger, homelessness, or remediable illness, if they make use of the services and facilities available to them. Their definition of the problem of poverty minimizes the need for massive public programs to fight poverty.[3]

Thus, the first difficulty in addressing the problem of poverty lies in agreeing on a definition, and because this process is complicated by differences in how the problem is viewed, the definition of poverty becomes an issue in itself. However, a consensus is needed in order to visualize goals and to develop a strategy for attaining them.

FRAME

2

WHAT IS SOCIAL POLICY?

Policy in its broadest sense is a set of carefully chosen guidelines that steer present and future decisions. Policy is a kind of overall plan that sets forth general goals and acceptable procedures.

---

[2]Joseph F. Coates, *Issues Management: How You Can Plan, Organize, and Manage for the Future* (Mt. Airy, Md.: Lomond Publications, 1986), p. 19.
[3]Thomas R. Dye, *Power and Society: An Introduction to the Social Sciences,* 5th ed. (Pacific Grove, Calif.: Brooks/Cole, 1990), p. 254.

Policy and law are not synonymous, although the two overlap. Laws are formal and specific rules, while policies are more informal and general plans. Policy can proceed with the law, absent the law, or even be contrary to the law. For example, the Reagan administration's policy of denying certification to eligible Social Security disability applicants and of decertifying recipients continued after federal courts ruled that it was illegal.[4]

Public policy in the United States is divided into three major areas: social, economic, and national security. Of these three, social policy accounts for over half the total cost of public policies.[5] Social policy is a complicated network of programs and services that are difficult to capture in a few words. Some define social policy as "action to influence the course of societal change and to allot societal resources among various groups."[6] Others define it as "a collective strategy to address social problems."[7]

Until the 1990s, social policy education in the helping professions was primarily concerned with the history of social welfare and the kinds of services it provided, and human service workers focused more on specific practice skills than on the policy aspects of their work. These trends have resulted in certain inconsistencies within human service professions:

> In American social welfare, a wide gulf separates social welfare policy from social welfare practice. It is commonplace for students entering the human service professions to focus on intervention with clients around discrete problems or direct practice. Rarely do they express an interest in social policy. Over the years, welfare institutions have come to reflect these preferences. The result is not without considerable cost to professionals who find themselves having to work by— and frequently around—social policies that have little consonance with the needs of the practitioner or the client.[8]

These trends, however, must also be viewed in the context of the culture in which they occur. For example, Specht and Courtney (1994) argue, for the case of social work, that this human service profession needs to develop what amounts to a new practice model—the social problems are that critical:

> Many Americans fail to understand that a number of the problems we experience as individuals can be dealt with most effectively when they are perceived to be social problems that require social solutions. . . . Generations of Americans . . . identify the individual as the source of many problems that are basically social in origin. . . . Social welfare policy and social welfare practice are closely related. Family and community policy is eventually seen in the ways professionals and public institutions go about helping people and, especially, in the extent to

---

[4]George T. Martin, Jr., *Social Policy in the Welfare State* (Englewood Cliffs, N.J.: Prentice-Hall, 1990), p. 9.
[5]Richard Rose and Guy Peters, *Can Government Go Bankrupt?* (New York: Basic Books, 1978), p. 68. Cited in Martin, *Social Policy in the Welfare State,* p. 10.
[6]Martin, *Social Policy in the Welfare State,* p. 1.
[7]Bruce S. Jansson, *Social Policy: From Theory to Policy Practice* (Pacific Grove, Calif.: Brooks/Cole, 1994), p. 5.
[8]Howard J. Karger and David Stoesz, *American Social Welfare Policy: A Structural Approach* (New York: Longman, 1990), p. ix.

which [those efforts] support the resources of families and communities to help themselves. Social work . . . needs a new practice model. . . .[9]

Policy is the link between broad forces of change in the environment that create problems of human living and responses from society at large regarding how those problems will be addressed.

Reflecting on Practice

In Lesson 1, we used a needs analysis framework designed to point you and the consumer in directions that will overcome the obstacles to functioning. We practiced assessing the needs of hypothetical consumers such as Mr. Davis, who was experiencing some problems due to a lack of financial resources. What happens once these needs are identified? Describe a profile for two or three other consumers who may have similar, but not identical needs to Mr. Davis. What steps will you, can you, and should you, as a human service provider, take in order to help Mr. Davis and the consumers in similar situations? What questions might arise as you do this? What frustrations might you, personally, experience?

Practitioners have many ways of helping consumers to meet their needs. One important variable influencing that help (e.g., what services are provided, how they are provided, to whom, when, and by whom) is what is, what might, and what actually becomes policy.

FRAME
3

LINKING PROBLEMS, ISSUES, AND SOCIAL POLICY: THE LIFE CYCLE OF PUBLIC POLICY ISSUES

One way we can link problems, issues, and social policies is to think of policy as *developing* from problems and issues. In policy practice, this development is called "the life cycle of public policy issues."

Figure 2.1 illustrates the life cycle of a public policy issue and suggests where you can find issues. It shows issues moving through four stages: *development, visibility, action,* and *clarification.* In its early stages, an issue takes the form of felt needs and dissatisfactions by those who will be the relevant actors. The issue then moves through an increasingly visible stage of discussion among workers, leaders, and the public. Existing or new intellectual leadership may come forward and dramatic events may occur. Actions to resolve how the issue will be handled for broad segments of the population will occur if the issue moves into the legislative or regulatory cycle, and from there to clarification, sometimes by the courts. With the passage of time, our ability to reshape the issue steadily decreases as the issue becomes more well defined.

---

[9]Harry Specht and Mark Courtney, *Unfaithful Angels: How Social Work Has Abandoned Its Mission.* (New York: The Free Press, 1994), pp. 130–131.

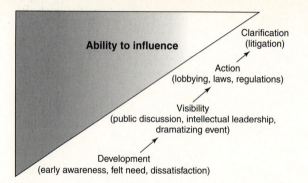

FIGURE 2.1.   Life Cycle of a Service Delivery Issue [*Source:* Adapted from Jane Work in Joseph F. Coates, *Issues Management: How You Can Plan, Organize, and Manage for the Future,* (Mt. Airy, Md.: Lomond Publications, 1986) p. 22; and Alice Chambers Wygant and O. W. Markley, *Information and the Future: A Handbook of Sources and Strategies* (Westport, Conn.: Greenwood Press, 1988), p. 121.]

Once again, issues are basically conflicts of interests or values. Rather than "solving" issues once and for all, policy is generally an ongoing effort to manage issues and problems.

FRAME

4

LINKING "POLICY" TO THE PRACTICE OF DELIVERING HUMAN SERVICES

Human service practitioners make, advance, retard, and shape policy all the time during their interactions with consumers and with each other.[10] For example, in the human services, policy responses occur:

1. when human service practitioners work directly with consumers; or
2. when human service practitioners work more closely with policy makers (e.g., legislators, heads of agencies, judges) to design, implement, modify, or analyze policies that determine what services are available and to whom.

"Social policy connects individuals with society."[11] At any level of human service practice, existing social policy will affect what human service practitioners "see" as "problems" as well as how those problems are addressed. Policy practice in delivering human services is thus the effort to influence the development, enactment, implementation, or assessment of social policies.[12]

Some human service practitioners and educators have resisted defining and developing policy practice as part of delivering human services. The ensuing debate is il-

---

[10]Martin, *Social Policy in the Welfare State,* p. 16.

[11]Demetrius S. Iatridis, "Policy Practice," *In Encyclopedia of Social Work,* 19th ed., (Washington, D.C.: National Association of Social Work, 1995), p. 1856.

[12]Bruce S. Jansson, *Social Policy: From Theory to Policy Practice* (Pacific Grove, Calif.: Brooks/Cole, 1994), p. 8; and Demetrius S. Iatridis, "Policy Practice," p. 1864.

lustrated in the table below, which shows, in the left column, three reasons why policy *is not* part of delivering human services and, in the right column, accompanying reasons why policy *is* part of delivering human services at all levels.[13]

Policy IS NOT Part of Delivering Human Services Because of:	*Policy IS Part of Delivering Human Services Because:*
The expert myth: which suggests that policy making belongs to policy specialists with advanced analytic skills (e.g., economists, program evaluators, policy analysts).	Human service workers see social problems first hand and actually implement policies. Therefore, they should help shape policies by sensitizing policy makers to shortcomings in existing policies.
The myth of powerlessness: which suggests that professionals and ordinary citizens cannot contribute to policy making because they lack the power resources of interest groups and politicians.	Direct social workers can sometimes develop and use power resources to positive policy use within their practice settings.
The legislative myth: which suggests that all policy is public policy, and that all public policy is made by legislative bodies (such as city councils, state legislatures, or Congress).	Social policy is developed by public and nonpublic agencies within parameters set by legislatures. But legislatures and judiciaries and other government bodies leave many details undefined that those who implement policies can and do define. Human service practitioners, as they deliver human services, are engaged in just such an act, whether or not they are aware of it.

The work of delivering human services is linked to all aspects of social policy. This lesson develops the idea that all human service workers should have an awareness of social policy and the forces that shape it:

> Direct social workers confront social policies at every turn of the road, whether agency, legislative, or administrative. Few of these policies are trivial. They determine who gets what services, whether personal rights such as confidentiality are protected, and the kind of staff who will provide the service. Human service workers need to be acquainted with existing policies because they have to help consumers navigate the network or programs and services. They also need skills to change existing policies or to propose new policies. They cannot help their clients or protect the prerogatives of their professions without these skills.[14]

In later chapters of this book, notably the chapters on advocating and mobilizing, specific skills are introduced to change existing policies and propose new policies. This lesson focuses on developing the skill of seeing the policy elements of service

---

[13] Myths are from Jansson, *Social Policy,* p. 21.

[14]Jansson, *Social Policy,* p. 27–28.

delivery situations, principally in the form of service delivery issues—how you "see" them and how you "learn about" them.

EXAMPLES OF SERVICE DELIVERY ISSUES IN POLICY AREAS RELEVANT TO DELIVERING HUMAN SERVICES

There are many ways to conceptualize the world of human services in terms of problems, issues, and social policies. One approach might be to think of the populations served (e.g., elderly, children, poor, homeless, disabled). A second approach might be to identify the service systems (e.g., health, mental health, education, correctional, and child and family).

We have chosen a *policy area framework* to illustrate the categories into which service delivery issues might fall. Policy areas generally correspond to different populations and also act as a backbone for service systems and institutions. We can thus loosely refer to these policy areas as fields of practice, social welfare policy areas, and populations served. Policy areas are reasonably illustrative categories, correspond to common social problems addressed by human service practitioners, and contain service delivery issues that have no clear-cut answers.

The cluster drawing in Figure 2.2 is designed to help you visualize the interrelations among eight major social policy areas and examples of the service delivery issues they address. Frames 6–13 contain brief summaries and reflections for each segment of the cluster drawing as further background for the connection between policy area and service delivery issues. As you scan each of these summaries, you may wish to make notes on where your curiosity is sparked, what emotions you feel, or what questions you have. The aim of the summaries is to interest you in linking social policy and the practice of delivering human services. The summaries do not provide an in-depth look at the history or structure of any one policy area. Presenting a comprehensive analysis of such complex topics in the space of about a page each would be an impossible task. Instead, we provide introductory overviews that we hope will enable you to appreciate the complexity of each topic and to connect it to your delivery of human services.

Following the policy area summaries, we provide information about further developing your "issue scanning skills" and then offer examples of how you can use these skills to "capture" your own service delivery issue.

Reflecting on Practice

The information in Figure 2.2 is far from an exhaustive list of issues. Before you read the frames summarizing these topics, consider what could be added to this scheme based on what you already know. Experiment with adding issues by drawing new lines between policy areas. For example, if a line were drawn across the center of the diagram from AGING to HEALTH, what issues might these two areas share?

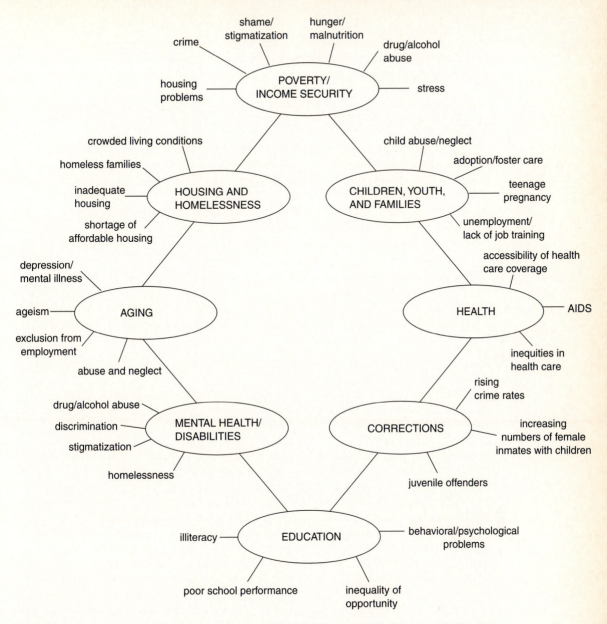

FIGURE 2.2.   Cluster Drawing of Major Human Service Policy Areas and Accompanying Service Delivery Issues.

FRAME
6

POVERTY AND INCOME SECURITY: POLICY AND SERVICE DELIVERY

Earlier in this lesson, we discussed the difficulties in agreeing on a definition of poverty. Despite conflicting views about what poverty is, an official definition is needed in order to formulate policies to prevent and alleviate it.

The U.S. government has defined poverty in terms of a poverty threshold, calculated on the basis of the number of dollars needed to purchase resources necessary to basic survival. These poverty thresholds take into account total family income, family size, and an adjustment each year for inflation in consumer prices. According to recent poverty thresholds, families with less than the following amounts of annual cash income in 1992 were considered poor:[15]

One person (not in a family)	$7,143
Family of two people	$9,137
Family of three people	$11,186
Family of four people	$14,335
Family of five people	$16,952

Based on these figures, 36.9 million people were defined as living in "official" poverty in 1992, 14.6 million of them children.

While not all human service consumers are poor, human service problems are significantly more frequent among people who live in poverty. The network of programs and policies designed to reduce poverty is highly complex, as are the arguments for and against such programs. *Income security* is the basic floor of income that all individuals, regardless of their stage in the life cycle, need to live in any type of economic system. *Income security policy* provides this floor of income to individuals who are otherwise unable to meet their basic needs. The Social Security Act of 1935 laid the groundwork for the contemporary U.S. income security policy, bringing two pillars into the system: social insurance and public assistance, otherwise known as "welfare."[16] Social insurance benefits are paid by worker and employer contributions that are redistributed by the government to replace wages lost due to unemployment, old age, disability, and death of the breadwinner. Public assistance, on the other hand, is based purely on need. Public assistance programs are not created for everyone, but for specific categories of citizens whose benefits are determined by a *means test*, which amounts to demonstrating proof of poverty directly. Below are some examples of social insurance programs and public assistance programs:

---

[15]Children's Defense Fund, *Wasting America's Future: The Children's Defense Fund Report on the Costs of Child Poverty* (Boston, Mass.: Beacon Press, 1994), p. 3

[16]Martha N. Ozawa, "Income Security Overview," in *Encyclopedia of Social Work,* 19th ed., (Washington, D.C.: National Association of Social Workers, 1995), p. 1453. Also see: BASSC, *Social Welfare at a Crossroads: A National, Statewide, and Local Look at Poverty and Public Assistance* (Berkeley, CA: Bay Area Social Services Consortium, University of California–Berkeley, 1997).

Social Insurance Programs

- Hospital Insurance (HI)
- Old-Age, Survivors, and Disability Insurance (OASDI)
- Public employee retirement
- Railroad retirement, unemployment, and temporary disability insurance
- State temporary disability insurance
- Supplemental Medical Insurance
- Unemployment Insurance
- Worker's Compensation

Public Assistance Programs

- Temporary Assistance to Needy Families (TANF), formerly AFDC*
- Food Stamps
- General Assistance (A residual program for those who do not qualify for other income security programs)
- Housing Assistance
- Medicaid
- Supplemental Security Income (SSI) (Serves the aged, the blind, and the disabled)

Many human service systems address the problem of poverty directly. Thus, a general familiarity with service delivery issues in poverty as well as the major components of income security policy is a necessity for every human service practitioner. Suggested references are provided at the end of this chapter.

Reflecting on Poverty and Income Security

What are some of the common images of welfare and welfare recipients? Try making a list, then challenge yourself to investigate one or more of the items on your list. Are these images supported by research?

FRAME

7

HOUSING AND HOMELESSNESS: POLICY AND SERVICE DELIVERY

Housing becomes a human service problem when there is not enough of it; when it becomes too expensive for people to afford; or when its design, location, or quality cause problems for those who live in it.[17] According to some analysts, America's housing problem seems to be worsening in light of a series of emerging trends in the housing market:[18]

1. *Home ownership has declined.* In 1975, the average family needed an income of $15,775 to buy an average new home; by 1985, that family needed an income of $37,657.

---

*The Personal Responsibility and Work Opportunity Reconciliation Act of 1996 replaced AFDC with TANF.
[17]Philip R. Popple and Leslie H. Leighninger, *Social Work, Social Welfare, and American Society* (Boston: Allyn & Bacon, 1990), p. 512.
[18]Robert M. Moroney, *Social Policy and Social Work: Critical Essays on the Welfare State* (New York: Aldine de Gruyter, 1991), pp. 78–81.

2. *The affordability and availability of rental housing has decreased* to the point where 30 million tenants live in substandard housing. Since the mid-1970s the housing market has lost over one million low-income units each year due to abandonment, arson, demolition, condominium conversion, and gentrification.

3. *The quality of existing housing is declining.*

4. *The number of homeless families has dramatically increased.*

Homelessness is only one facet of the housing problem in the United States, just as the shortage of adequate, affordable housing is only one dimension of the highly complex problem of homelessness. While there have been individuals living without permanent dwellings since America's early days, it was not until the 1980s that homelessness emerged as a distinct problem in the United States. The newly invented label of "homeless" came to designate an increasingly demographically diverse population of poor people who began to appear on the streets in record numbers (estimates vary from 250,000 to 3 million). Sharp cutbacks in federal spending on low-income housing, strategies of urban "revitalization," increases in poverty and unemployment, deinstitutionalization, and the elimination of many poor people from government programs due to changes in eligibility rules have all contributed to the growing problem of homelessness. Other problems affecting the homeless population of the 1990s are drug and alcohol addictions, mental illness, lack of education, and low self-esteem. This wide range of problems makes addressing the needs of the homeless as a group extremely difficult.

Shelters for the homeless, operated by voluntary social service agencies, have sprung up all over the country. Supporters of these organizations argue that shelters do a good job caring for the homeless, providing medical and other services and offering protection against inclement weather, violence, and crime. Opponents of the shelter movement claim that shelters are an inefficient and haphazard response to a housing problem that should be addressed at the national level through adequate government intervention.[19]

Reflecting on Housing and Homelessness

Do you think that housing policy should be social policy? That is, should the goal of housing policy be to make the distribution of housing efficient and equitable and to ensure decent living conditions for all citizens? To what degree do you think the government should be responsible for the housing needs of American citizens?

Do you think that shelters are a good response to the problem of homelessness? Why or why not? What might be some other ways to address the needs of the homeless?

---

[19]Howard J. Karger and James Midgley, ed., *Controversial Issues in Social Policy* (Boston: Allyn & Bacon, 1994), p. 131.

CHILDREN, YOUTH, AND FAMILIES: POLICY AND SERVICE DELIVERY

Programs and policies that address the needs of children, youth, and families are as diverse as the types of needs experienced. Traditionally, the child welfare delivery system has provided programs and policies for child and family concerns. For all individuals, the family is probably the most significant social system within which they function. But how well a family is able to meet the needs of its members depends on the capabilities of those members as well as on other systems within the family's environment (e.g., workplace, neighborhood, community, and society). When referring to the needs of children and families, a family is usually considered to include a parent figure or figures and at least one child. But no two families are alike. Moreover, an even broader definition of a family might be "any group of individuals who are bonded together through marriage, kinship, adoption, or mutual agreement."[20]

An organization that focuses on issues concerning children is the *Children's Defense Fund (CDF)*. Its goal is to educate the nation about the needs of children and encourage preventive investment in children before they get sick, drop out of school, suffer family breakdown, or get into trouble. Although its main office is in Washington, D.C., the CDF reaches out to towns and cities across the country to monitor the effects of changes in national and state policies and to help people and organizations concerned with what happens to children.

A 1994 Children's Defense Fund publication entitled *Wasting America's Future* sets forth the findings of the Costs of Child Poverty Research Project, begun in 1991 to bring attention to the growing crisis of poverty among America's children. These findings not only vividly illustrate the costs of child poverty in terms of human suffering, but also translate these sometimes intangible costs into dollar figures: the CDF estimates that future losses to the economy stemming from the effects of just one year of poverty for 14.6 million children reach as high as $177 billion.[21] The following example illustrates how the consequences of child poverty translate into costs for society:[22]

> Sam and Sarah, an Indiana couple, could not afford prenatal care. Their son Josh was born two months prematurely and was subject to chronic ear infections. When their daughter, Amy, was conceived, Sarah and Sam's relationship deteriorated, and Sam left the state. Sarah applied for food stamps and Aid to Families with Dependent Children (AFDC), which provided assistance far below the poverty line. She had to make difficult choices among food, housing, clothing, and incidental expenses for her children.
>
> At the grocery in the winter of 1980, 3-year-old Josh pulled a jar out of a display and a pyramid of grape jam toppled over him, breaking half the items on

---

[20]Paragraph summary from Joseph Heffernan, Guy Shuttlesworth, and Rosalie Ambrosino, *Social Work and Social Welfare: An Introduction* (St. Paul, MN.: West Publishing, 1988), pp. 138–140, 167.

[21]Children's Defense Fund, *Wasting America's Future*, p. xix.

[22]Case study adapted from Indiana Youth Institute Occasional Paper No. 1, 1991, as cited in Children's Defense Fund, *Wasting America's Future*, p. 100.

display. The storekeeper insisted that Sarah pay for the damage, which amounted to $27. This figure represented a sizable portion of her monthly income. Sarah paid for the damage at the expense of Amy's diaper budget. After Sarah rationed Amy's disposable diapers, Amy developed a diaper rash, which became infected. Amy was unable to sleep and developed a fever. Concerned, Sarah took both children to the public health clinic. The nurse who examined Amy was legally compelled to report the child's condition to the family's welfare case worker. Josh was rambunctious in the doctor's office. Tired, overwhelmed, and angry with Josh, Sarah lost control. She slapped Josh in the face and blamed him for her current situation.

An inexperienced, newly hired caseworker was assigned to investigate the referral from the nurse. The rural county welfare department did not have sufficient staff to keep up with the high volume of referrals. Unable to monitor Sarah's situation, the caseworker recommended temporary foster care. The court removed both children to a foster home 30 miles away. The new caseworker could provide transportation for monthly visits only.

- Separated from their mother, the children stayed in foster care for years. Total foster care expenses for both children grew to an estimated $104,000.
- Josh never adjusted well to his foster placements. He became delinquent and required an additional estimated $58,400 in Boy's School and residential care.
- Josh's latest caseworker reported that he met the profile of many children who pass through the child welfare system. "Prognosis for the future is poor. If his behavior doesn't improve, Josh will likely spend as much time incarcerated in the adult correctional system as he will on the streets"—at an estimated cost of $25,000 per year of incarceration.

Reflecting on Children, Youth, and Families

The above scenario illustrates many different policy areas and issues that present challenges to the family involved as well as to the human service community. Make a list of the problems Sarah and her children experienced, as well as some that they are likely to experience in the future. How can these problems be translated into service delivery issues? How are these issues dealt with through policy? Following the example in Figure 2.2, make a cluster drawing that could provide another human service worker with a guide to the problems, issues, and policies involved in this situation.

FRAME
9

HEALTH: POLICY AND SERVICE DELIVERY

U.S. health care is a highly complex and contradictory system that has developed to address our physical needs. U.S. medical services have five major components: (1) physicians in solo practice; (2) group outpatient settings, including groups of physicians sharing facilities; (3) hospitals—private, nonprofit, and public; (4) public health services delivered on state, local, regional, national, and international levels and including health counseling, family planning, prenatal and postnatal care, school health services, and maintenance of health statistics, to name a few; and (5) numerous corollary health services, such as home health, physical rehabilitation, group homes, and nursing homes.[23] Most public health services are provided by government agencies. Most personal health care services are provided by the private sector or by nonprofit organizations.

In recent decades, two major structural changes have occurred in the nation's health care system. First, service delivery has moved away from physician's offices and hospitals and into outpatient clinics, nursing homes, and other health care arrangements. Second, financing of health care has shifted dramatically since 1965, when the federal government began to pay for the health care of certain low-income groups (via the Medicaid program) and for those over 65 (via Medicare).

The U.S. health care system is a paradox. The quality of care most Americans receive for acute illness is unsurpassed anywhere in the world—but millions of Americans cannot afford, and are therefore denied, care that many other industrialized countries treat as a routine right guaranteed to all residents. And although Americans are hospitalized less than residents of many other industrialized countries and their hospital stays are shorter than those of people anywhere else in the world, the American hospital system is the world's most costly.[24]

Private and public health services are now in a "reform scramble" because of rising costs and inequities in access to health care. The debate about health care reform raises fundamental questions. Is health care a public good, which government should make available to all as a right? Is health care a limited resource that must be rationed? Perhaps conditions are ripe for a fundamental restructuring of health care. However formal debates play out, market forces are already at work to reshape the way Americans receive medical care and pay for it. All levels of government are also likely to continue to experiment with reforms in the years ahead.

Reflecting on Health Care

AIDS (acquired immune deficiency syndrome) has become a serious health threat. Worldwide, nearly 160 countries have reported a total of 2.6 million AIDS cases and an estimated 13 million more people infected with HIV, at a rate of about 5,000 new cases a day. As of September 1993, an estimated 339,000 people in the United States had contracted the AIDS virus.[25] Because of these growing numbers, human service practitioners in all areas of service delivery are likely to come into contact with consumers who have AIDS or are HIV positive. Do you feel comfortable in your knowledge about the AIDS virus? If called on to address AIDS-related concerns, what are

---

[23]Howard J. Karger and David Stoesz, *American Social Welfare Policy: A Structural Approach* (New York: Longman, 1990), p. 192.

[24]Henry J. Aaron, "A Prescription for Health Care," in *Setting National Priorities: Policy for the Nineties* (Washington, D.C.: Brookings Institution, 1990), p. 249.

[25]Michael P. Soroka and George J. Bryjak, *Social Problems: A World at Risk* (Boston: Allyn & Bacon, 1995), p. 374.

some initial steps you might take to learn more about delivering human services in this area?

AGING: POLICY AND SERVICE DELIVERY

Working with the elderly is a fairly recent addition to the human services because they were traditionally considered as part of the family. But with many elderly persons living alone and with a growing elderly population, the needs of older people have been recognized as an area of concern that must be given separate attention. This service area is sometimes referred to as gerontology and usually includes people 60 years and older. The Gerontological Society was formed in 1945 as a forum for professionals working with the elderly. The National Council on Aging was established in 1960.[26]

The estimated life expectancy at the beginning of the 19th century was 35 years, and by 1900, the average had reached 47 years. Today, the average American can expect to live until the age of 75.

In 1990, people over 65 constituted 12 percent of the population, or 32 million people. Demographers estimate that by the year 2030, almost 65 million people in the United States (or approximately 20 percent of the population) will be 65 or older.[27] These demographic trends will likely necessitate a reconceptualization of the programs, benefits, and services available to the elderly, making aging policy an important domestic concern for the 21st century. While poverty in the elderly population has been reduced significantly over the last three decades, it remains a problem, particularly among the minority elderly. The growing need for long-term care is also a major area of concern. Given the high cost and low quality of many nursing homes, more and more middle-aged people are likely to be caring for their elderly parents in their homes. This can create a great deal of stress for family caregivers, which sometimes leads to elder abuse. Other examples of service delivery issues in aging include:

- How can we define elderly and old age. Is it an incurable disease, an inevitable decline, or a stage of growth and development? When does it begin?
- Coordination and adequacy of community services among many types of public and private organizations (hospitals, hospices, county departments of social service, churches, visiting nurse associations, and home health care agencies).
- Advocacy to address ageism, discrimination against those 65 and over.
- Abuse and neglect, ranging from self-neglect when older persons are socially isolated to family neglect when the older adult lives with a son or daughter (e.g., improper clothing and diet, denying transportation, and ignoring daily needs) to physical, psychological, or emotional abuse (e.g., giving no spending money, reminding them they are a burden, and placing older adults in restraints).

---

[26]Paragraph from Louise C. Johnson and Charles L. Schwartz, *Social Welfare: A Response to Human Need* (Boston: Allyn & Bacon, 1988), p. 255.

[27]Soroka and Bryjak, *Social Problems,* p. 85 (based on figures from Ahmed & Smith, 1992; *America in the 21st Century,* 1989).

- Quality of life—living longer but enjoying it less (e.g., mandatory retirement, more older women than men, fewer children available to care for aging parents, and declining physical capacity).

Reflecting on Aging

There is much concern about the impact that the growing elderly population will have on the nation's economy and material resources. Imagine that it is ten years from now. How do you think that the demographic changes and economic concerns will affect society's attitudes toward the aged? Do you think current attitudes *should* change in ten years? How?

F R A M E

11

MENTAL HEALTH AND DISABILITIES: POLICY AND SERVICE DELIVERY

One of the factors that contributes to inability to meet basic needs is the state of a person's mental health. The recognition of mental illness has existed throughout history. Today, however, the definitions of mental health and mental illness are especially difficult due to a wide range of individual and cultural differences. It is therefore useful to consider mental health services as those provided by mental health agencies, including community mental health centers, psychiatric hospitals or psychiatric units in general hospitals, and child guidance clinics. Generally those agencies use a multidisciplinary approach to provide services, with psychology, psychiatry, nursing, counseling, and social work as some of the key disciplines involved.[28] Examples of service delivery issues in mental health include:

- Lack of community resources for persons who have been released from institutions.
- Substance abuse crisis (e.g., increased availability of low-cost, highly addictive drugs on the street; cocaine babies; misuse of alcohol and drugs; addictions).
- Homeless people with mental illness.
- Who defines mental illness and how.

Disability is defined in various ways by individuals, organizations, and government agencies. Despite these various definitions, there seems to be some consensus that a person with a disability can have either a permanent physical or mental impairment or a chronic health or mental health condition. Perhaps the best-known estimate of the size of the U.S. disabled population is 43 million, the figure cited in the Americans with Disabilities Act of 1990. The passage of the Americans with Disabilities Act of 1990 represents a civil rights landmark for the disabled. This Act acknowledged that the disabled have been subject to serious and pervasive discrimination, and provides protection against discrimination comparable to that afforded by Title VII of the Civil Rights Act of 1964 for race, sex, national origin, and religion.[29]

---

[28]Johnson and Schwartz, *Social Welfare,* pp. 208–210.
[29]Adrienne Asch and Nancy R. Mudrick, "Disability," in *Encyclopedia of Social Work,* 19th ed. (Washington, D.C.: National Association of Social Workers, 1995), pp. 752–758.

Services for disabled adults are shifting away from institutions and toward community-based programs, such as group homes, employment training, and paid employment. There is a growing tendency to focus on the strengths and capacities of the disabled rather than on their weaknesses, a change typified by the use of the term "mental health" rather than "mental illness." This field is extremely broad due to the high numbers of individuals with disabilities and the wide range of problems that the disabled experience either due to their own physical limitations or as a result of discrimination. Examples of service delivery issues are unemployment due to injury, social stigmatization and exclusion from participation in employment and recreational activities, and individual and family stress or depression due to a sudden, disabling injury or onset of an acute illness.

Developmental disabilities refers to lower-than-average functioning that affects people's adaptive behavior. Examples of service delivery issues are:

- How to integrate developmentally disabled students into regular classrooms and schools.
- How to reduce utilization of institutional care (e.g., by increasing community-based employment opportunities).
- Approaches to facilitate independent living.

Reflecting on Mental Health and Disabilities

Read a biography written by someone with a disability or a biography about an individual with a disability. You might consult C. Abernathy, *Detours: Biographies of Physically Disabled Achievers* (Salem, Or.: TEAMS, 1988); M. Daly, *Marie's Voice* (Dublin: Wolfheus, 1992); S. Han, *A Share of Loving* (London: J. Cape, 1987); T. Helms, *Against All Odds* (New York: Warner, 1978); R. Kovic, *Born on the Fourth of July* (New York: Pocket Books, 1989); or O. Sacks, *An Anthropologist on Mars: Seven Paradoxical Tales* (New York: Knopf, 1995). What barriers to employment and other major life activities did the individual face? How did he or she feel about and cope with these daily barriers? Did the book's content suggest policy or attitudinal changes that would help the disabled succeed in society?[30]

FRAME

12

CORRECTIONS: POLICY AND SERVICE DELIVERY

Every modern society has an institutionalized, formal mechanism of social control that it utilizes to apprehend, try, and punish those individuals found guilty of violating criminal laws. In the United States, these functions are fulfilled by the Criminal Justice System (CJS), which is composed of the police, the courts, and the prisons. Crime in the United States is a major social problem, and criminal justice in the United States is

---

[30]Exercise and suggested readings from Sandra Kopels, "The Americans with Disabilities Act: A Tool to Combat Poverty," in *Journal of Social Work Education* 31, 3 (Fall 1995), p. 343.

TABLE 2.2   **Incarceration Rates Worldwide: 1990–1991**

Country	Rate of Incarceration (per 100,000 population)	Country	Rate of Incarceration (per 100,000 population)
United States	455	Denmark	71
South Africa	311	Albania	55
Venezuela	177	Ireland	44
Canada	111	Japan	42
China	111	India	34
Australia	79		

Source: Michael P. Soroka and George J. Bryjak, *Social Problems: A World at Risk* (Boston: Allyn & Bacon, 1995), p. 283.

very expensive, costing over $60 billion in 1993. Approximately 48 percent of CJS expenditures go for police protection, 22 percent for the courts' legal services and public defenders, and most of the remaining 30 percent for corrections.[31]

Corrections as a policy and service delivery area provides for the administration of treatment and rehabilitation of criminal offenders through a program of penal custody (imprisonment), parole, and probation. Rehabilitation can occur through a number of systems. Human service workers in probation and parole systems deal with people who are under the supervision of the court after committing a crime. Imprisonment has at least three goals: rehabilitation, punishment, and deterrence. Of these, only rehabilitation is a service provided for the offender; punishment and deterrence are services for society. Prisons are oriented more toward containing criminals than rehabilitating them. Some rehabilitative services do exist, however: Human service workers provide work-training programs, education, counseling, and recreational services, among others. The impact of a human services perspective in correctional institutions is only beginning to be felt.[32]

The United States has the greatest per capital prison population in the world. In 1966, approximately 200,000 people were behind bars in the United States. By 1982, that figure approached 400,000, and in 1993, there were 925,000 prisoners in state and federal correctional facilities.[33]

Reflecting on Corrections

Today, a year in prison for one inmate costs U.S. taxpayers more than a year's tuition at an Ivy League university. How do you think that the increasing rate of incarceration

[31]Michael P. Soroka and George J. Bryjak, *Social Problems: A World at Risk* (Boston: Allyn & Bacon, 1995), pp. 282–283.
[32]Paragraph from Joseph Mehr, *Human Services: Concepts and Intervention Strategies,* 4th ed. (Boston: Allyn & Bacon, 1988), p. 120.
[33]Soroka and Bryjak, *Social Problems: A World at Risk,* p. 286.

will affect funding in other service systems? Do you think that more funds should be allotted for rehabilitation of offenders? Why or why not?

FRAME
13

EDUCATION: POLICY AND SERVICE DELIVERY

Of all the provisions of the American welfare state that we have discussed thus far—income security, health care, housing, and the variety of services reserved for special populations—the right to a free, public primary and secondary education is the only commodity that the government assures to all citizens. The government has a strong interest in providing this universal right, as education is the primary means by which children learn about the culture and norms of their society and are prepared for an adult life as a member of the workforce. Because education is such an important societal function, the accompanying social policy is quite political and this is reflected in our learning institutions:

> Because education is an essential task and because the school is its common ground, the school is an important and oft-used locale of social policy. For example, in the United States the social policy of free public schooling serves as a means by which a large and diverse population can be integrated into a coherent society. In the same vein the school serves as a means of fostering racial desegregation, which is another integrative social policy. The public school is viewed as a route by which children of the working class can become upwardly mobile. Even if the school cannot eliminate social inequality, it is a moral imperative to devote the school to the goal of equal opportunity. Thus, while "getting an education" is the acknowledged purpose of schooling, the school is also an agency of social policy.[34]

As society changes, the goals and purposes of education are redefined to accommodate new conditions and shifting concerns. Americans have always placed great faith in the power of education to right all of society's social, economic, and political problems, an attitude that is reflected in the many cycles of reform through which the educational system has passed since the creation of the first free schools in the early 19th century. In recent decades, high rates of unemployment, economic difficulties, and crime have contributed to widespread public dissatisfaction about public education, despite the fact that these problems can be regarded as external to education per se.

Today public education in the United States is undergoing a reform movement that has been termed "restructuring." Among the many proposed alternatives to the traditional system, there is one innovation in particular that, if implemented on a large scale, would have major implications for human service workers in all service systems. The "full-service school" model is essentially a school center in which health, mental health, social and/or family services may be colocated, depending on the needs of the particular school and community.[35] It recognizes the neighborhood school as a crucial

---

[34]Martin, *Social Policy in the Welfare State,* pp. 107–109.
[35]Joy G. Dryfoos, *Full-Service Schools: A Revolution in Health and Social Services for Children, Youth, and Families* (San Francisco: Jossey-Bass, 1994), p. xvi.

link between public services and at-risk families and youth. Nurses have been part of the K–12 scene for many years. If the idea of full-service schools catches on, the delivery of noneducational human, social, and other services from school sites will bring in other human service providers.

Researchers estimate that about one-third of the school-age population, or approximately 15 million children in 1992, are at risk of failing in school. Academic failure increases the likelihood that these children will drop out of school. One study estimated that males who drop out can expect to earn $260,000 less and pay $78,000 less in taxes during their lifetimes than males who graduate from high school, while comparable estimates for female dropouts were $200,000 and $60,000 respectively. Studies have also shown that school dropouts are more likely to be poor, have costly medical problems as a result of their economic status, and require job training. Currently, many school dropouts populate U.S. prisons.[36]

Reflecting on Education

Michael Kirst, an advocate for full-service schools, maintains that "What's needed is a complete overhaul of children's services, bringing together public and private organizations to meet the comprehensive needs of children, adolescents and parents. Schools should constitute one of the centers of a coordinated network of total children's services."[37] What do you think of this statement? Can you think of any barriers or problems that might arise with the school-linked service delivery approach (e.g., What happens after the school year ends? What if the school lacks space for additional programs? What about those who do not attend school?)?

FRAME
14

DOING YOUR OWN SERVICE DELIVERY ISSUE SCAN

We began this lesson by talking about problems, issues, and policies and their connection to human service delivery. Next we provided you with a "big-picture" perspective of some of the challenges addressed in the human services using a policy framework, along with a short description of each area designed to give you a taste of the services, issues, and policies involved. In this section of the lesson, our goal is to help you combine what you've learned with the most important resource there is: your own interest and curiosity.

Here are some questions you might be pondering:

- How might I further investigate a particular service delivery issue of interest to me or my organization?
- Given all of this information and the fact that it is constantly changing, how can I ever hope to stay current?

[36]U.S. General Accounting Office, *School-Linked Human Services* (Washington, D.C.: GAO, 1994). Report No. GAO/HRD 94-21.

[37]Michael Kirst, "Improving Children's Services: Overcoming Barriers, Creating New Opportunities." *Phi Delta Kappa* (Apr. 1991), pp. 615–618, as cited in Dryfoos, *Full-Service Schools,* p. 6.

- What is the best way to get background information on a particular service delivery issue?

Issue scanning is a method of discovering and monitoring what's going on in a particular policy area of delivering human services. Many organizations use issue scanning as one part of a broader program of issues management.[38] Issues management is a tool for gaining an earlier understanding of what issues will affect the future of the organization and what plan will be used to deal with them. The same idea applies to human service practitioners who are interested in expanding their knowledge of a problem, issue, or policy. Whether your focus is on the past, the present, or the future of an area of service delivery, and regardless of how much or how little you know about it, issue scanning is a skill that will serve you well.

An issue scan is like taking a snapshot. It's a dynamic, interactive approach to capturing some of the conflicts and trends in a particular area, such as the warring opinions in the debate over health care reform in the United States. Once these conflicts and trends—and your interest—are captured, you can begin to explore the issue in greater depth.

Organizing Your Search

More information about practically any issue you can imagine is available now than at any time in our history. Sometimes people seeking information will jump immediately into an unfocused search without thinking about what they hope to gain from it. Your search will be more fruitful and less time consuming if you begin with some kind of plan in the form of a few basic questions:

- What question are you trying to answer, or what issue do you want to explore further? What are some alternative ways of expressing this question or issue? It is important that your question be manageable. For example, a broad question involving a complex ethical argument such as "Is welfare good or bad?" could be narrowed down to "What exactly *is* welfare?" or "What are the predominantly held views of welfare in the United States in the 1990s?" As you become engaged in your search, you will begin to develop and refine your own arguments, thus naturally forming responses to the broader questions as you answer the more specific ones.
- Why are you trying to answer the question?
- How are you going to use the information you find?
- What sources will you consult to begin your issue scan?

Being Aware of Resources That Will Identify Service Delivery Issues

The list of resources that can be of use to you in your search is endless. Service delivery issues are often of great interest to the general public, making newspapers, journals, magazines, professional and lay publications, fiction and nonfiction books, newsletters, television, radio programs, documentary films, and on-line computer databases excellent places to find discussions of current issues as well as early warn-

---

[38]For example, see Joseph F. Coates, Vary T. Coates, Jennifer Jarratt, and Lisa Heinz (1986). *Issues Management* (Mt. Airy, Md.: Loman Publications, 1986).

ings of issues that might appear in the future. When you are interested in the history of an issue, an ideal way to find out more about it is to do a keyword search using the library database.

The library is of course an obvious place to go to get more information, but you need not confine yourself to this setting. Communicating with other people— be they consumers, other human service practitioners, professors, students, friends, volunteers, or employees of organizations—can be an excellent source of information about current and emerging issues, and can help you to establish valuable contacts in your field of interest. If you have an ongoing interest in a particular topic, it makes sense for you to find others with similar concerns. Some groups publish brief summaries or newsletters identifying and briefly describing the issues they discover.

Improving the Scanning Process

Some suggestions that might improve the scanning process and the results include:

- Keep the amount of information manageable. An increase in the quantity of information cannot always be equated with an increase in its quality: burying yourself in photocopies can be both frustrating and expensive. It is often more efficient to process the information in small chunks.
- Scan a full range of potential sources that might address your interests. Keep up with developments on the issue by continuing to watch, observe, and check your sources.
- Discuss issues with other human service practitioners, particularly as they relate to specific consumer problems.

The next three frames illustrate some of the approaches to issue scanning mentioned above. Each frame makes use of different elements of the issue scanning process in order to emphasize that your search need not be rigidly structured in order to be effective. It is important to have some direction, but you can feel free to adapt your issue scan to best suit your needs and interests.

F R A M E

15

EXAMPLE 1: SCANNING THE ISSUE OF "TRANSRACIAL ADOPTION" USING THE LIBRARY

Adoption is a service delivery area subject to many rules, regulations, and policies that can vary from one state or agency to another. One particularly sensitive issue in this area is that of transracial adoption, which refers to the adoption of a child by parents of a different race.

As of 1990, according to the U.S. Department of Health and Human Services, 442,000 children were in foster care nationwide. Federal officials said Latino and African American children spend an average of twice as long as white children in foster care before being adopted.[39] Due to its controversial nature and the passage of recent legislation that has led to an intensification of the debate, the subject of transracial adoption has lately attracted a great deal of public attention. The central question

---

[39]Rhonda Smith, "Marchers Revitalized to Act on Social Ills," *NASW News* 41, 2 (Feb. 1996), p. 3.

in transracial adoption is this: Should children and prospective adoptive families be strictly "matched" on the basis of racial background? This question does not yield a single, clear-cut answer given that responses to it will reflect the status, interests, and moral views of the respondents. Consider the following excerpt from the Multiethnic Placement Act of 1994. This act states that no agency or entity receiving federal assistance may:

> categorically deny to any person the opportunity to become an adoptive or foster parent, solely on the basis of race, color, or national origin of the adoptive or foster parent, or the child, involved; or delay or deny the placement of a child for adoption into foster care, or otherwise discriminate in making a placement decision, solely on the basis of race, color, or national origin of the adoptive or foster parent, or the child involved." (S.553[a]1[A&B]).

Now consider the following situation:

> Tamika is a 10-year-old African American child who has lived in three different foster homes since age 2. Her younger brother was adopted four years ago by an African American family, but the agency managing Tamika's case, which places strong emphasis on racial matching of parents and children, has not been able to find an African American adoptive family for her. A white family has indicated an interest in adopting Tamika, but the agency continues to resist placing her with them in the hopes of finding a "more suitable" family.

Both the passage of the Multiethnic Placement Act and the efforts of Tamika's adoption agency reflect an attempt to act in the "best interests" of the children involved.

Transracial adoption is clearly a complex issue. How can we use issue scanning to find out more about it? As stated earlier, the best way to begin a search is by posing a manageable question. Here is one possible formulation: "There seem to be a number of conflicting opinions about transracial adoption. What are they, and who holds these opinions?" Our objective is thus to explore the multiple perspectives involved in this debate.

Because the media has devoted a lot of attention to the issue, doing a keyword search on "transracial adoption" at the library is a good place to start. Here are some examples of headlines and titles of articles that our keyword search turned up:

- "Transracial Adoption: The Truth Comes in Shades of Gray." *New York Times* (July 27 1994).
- "In Adoptions, Race Does Matter, But Should It?" *National Journal* 27, 26 (July 1 1995).
- "'What I Need Is a Mom': The Welfare State Denies Homes to Thousands of Foster Children." *Policy Review* 73 (Summer 1995).
- "Adoption Should Be Color-Blind." *ParentsMagazine* 70, 7 (July 1995).
- "Black Children, White Parents: The Difficult Issue of Transracial Adoption." *The Chronicle of Higher Education* 40, 4 (Sept. 15 1993).

Here are some of the different opinions on transracial adoption that emerge:

1. If not adopted by parents of the same race, children will be denied exposure to their own cultural heritage and be less prepared to cope with racism. Transracial adoption should only be allowed as a last resort. The National Association of

Black Social Workers has denounced transracial adoption, maintaining that it represents a form of racial and cultural genocide.

2. Giving preference to adoptive parents of the same race is a practice that makes sense. Children who grow up in a same-race family will be more emotionally healthy and comfortable with their racial identity.

3. Numerous investigators (Feigelman & Silverman, 1983; Grow & Shapiro, 1972; Simon & Alstein, 1987; Vroegh, 1992) have found that children adopted transracially are as well adjusted as other adopted children.[40]

4. The classifications used by social service agencies charged with placing children with parents of the same race are racist and fail to account for the many children of multiracial ancestry. Such classifications deny multiracial persons an identity.[41]

5. Race should not be a factor in adoption. What is important is finding loving, caring families for children in foster homes.

Continuing to Scan "Transracial Adoption"

What could you do to find out more about transracial adoption at this point? One possibility would be to call a local adoption agency and ask about their policies in this area. You could also call the National Association of Black Social Workers in order to request information about their efforts to recruit more African American adoptive families. By finding a few recent articles on the issue of transracial adoption, we have succeeded in identifying some of the major arguments both for and against it. Keep in mind that no one source can provide all of the answers—it is important to become aware of as many facets of an issue as possible to develop a balanced perspective.

FRAME
16

EXAMPLE 2: SCANNING SERVICE DELIVERY IN "CORRECTIONS" BY INTERVIEWING A VOLUNTEER

We began our scan of the issue of transracial adoption at the library. But an issue scan need not begin there: linking with people already involved in the field of human services is an extremely valuable way to learn more about a service delivery issue, or to discover an entirely new one. If you are interested in speaking with someone, come up with a few questions and make sure you tell the person you are interviewing what you plan to do with the information they give you. As details of interaction with consumers are often protected by client confidentiality, it is important that the terms of your interview be clearly established.

K. T. is a self-employed writer and healing-arts educator with a master's degree in education who has worked in many different human service organizations and institutions. Among the institutions she has worked in are a Florida county jail and a federal

---

[40]Richard P. Barth, "Adoption," in *Encyclopedia of Social Work,* 19th ed., (Washington, D.C.: National Association of Social Workers), p. 55.

[41]Julie C. Lythcott-Haims, "Where Do Mixed Babies Belong? Racial Classification in America and Its Implications for Transracial Adoption," *Harvard Civil Rights-Civil Liberties Law Review* 29, 2 (Summer 1994): pp. 531–558.

prison, where she teaches journaling and poetry once a week. In our summary of corrections, we noted that of the three main components of the correctional system—punishment, deterrance, and rehabilitation—the latter is given the least emphasis. Because there are few funds allocated for rehabilitative services, K. T. does most of her work in the prison on a volunteer basis. Below are some excerpts from an interview with her.

AUTHOR: *How did you become involved in working with prisoners?*

K.T.: I had been interested in working in the prison system for a number of years. When I moved to Oakland, I met a very interesting man who was the G.E.D. [graduation equivalency diploma] teacher at the county jail. I told him I was interested in teaching journaling and poetry in the prison system, and he suggested that I come in once a week. I worked there for over a year, and we put together two literary magazines from material I collected from my students—the inmates. At some point my friend left the county jail, and I left too. A year went by, then I called up the local prison and got an appointment with the director. I said "I want to teach a writing class in your G.E.D. program." I showed him the publications from my work at the county jail. He was so happy to welcome me into his prison. And both the supervisor and the G.E.D. teacher are very supportive.

AUTHOR: *What kind of an impact do you think your teaching has on the people you work with?*

K.T.: People in prison are really searching for meaning. They have time—it's kind of like people who are dying, who are terminally ill. If you can activate these beings, you can just get such rich material from them. I feel there are certain kinds of things that, when you give them to people like tools, the benefits are immediate and lasting. I did an evaluation at the end of the last class to ask the men what they had gained from their experience. This is an excerpt from one of the evaluations. It's by a Hispanic man who had had little experience with writing:

"This writing class has brought a bunch of men from many different races or religions together. Inside these walls, we must all be on the alert at all times from one another. But in this small writing class, we're all together as one as we express our feelings and emotions in this journal. It's funny how a small class like this could bring a bunch of men together to make them better human beings."

Even people who come to one writing class or one movement class contact a part of themselves that has been hidden or unknown or longing for expression.

AUTHOR: *How do you think that rehabilitation in the correctional system is viewed today?*

K.T.: I'm really talking from my personal experience, but I've sensed that there are two things going on. On the one hand, more people like me are getting into the prison system. There's this movement that wants to give people the keys to their own liberation. But then you have the conservative voices saying, "Why should prisoners have anything but punishment?" Because of the public's fear, their passion to keep themselves safe by getting these people off the streets, they want to keep them locked up. They don't want them to have education or weight rooms and things like that. But in terms of preventing children from ever going to prison, you have to give them an alternative. Everybody has that yearning to be all that they can be—no one wants to be a bad person who goes to prison. At what point do you transform this potential into something positive?

AUTHOR: *What would you tell someone interested in this field or in any field of the human services?*

K.T.: When you go into an institution and have something to give, you step into a forcefield of possibility. Much good can happen within these walls and come out of it—it will create a ripple effect. It's not highly paid, but it can be incredibly gratifying. People in the human services should look at what they really love to do. You shouldn't be giving or teaching or working in something you don't really love, because then people won't connect with you. We need to remember that we're *all* potentially down and out—and that human service workers are at a point in the cycle where we can give. What I believe is the greatest gift that one can give is a sense of loving respect—when you give it you receive it.

Continuing to Scan "Corrections"

Do you agree with K.T. when she says, "People in the human services should look at what they really love to do. You shouldn't be teaching or working in something you don't really love, because then people won't connect with you"? Why do you think people go into the human service professions? What are some of the reasons for your own interest in the human services?

F R A M E

17

EXAMPLE 3: SCANNING THE ISSUE OF HOMELESSNESS BY INTERACTING WITH CONSUMERS

We are all influenced by popular beliefs, by the opinions of people we know, and by things we've heard and read. Sometimes the only way to get a sense of what *you* believe is to create opportunities for yourself that will test your own ideas and expectations. A textbook such as this one can provide you with concepts, definitions, and reflections that you can take with you into practice, but it cannot simulate real, human interaction. This is why contact with consumers and other human service practitioners is often your best resource for broadening your knowledge of an issue as you develop a sense of yourself as a human service provider. It is also a good way to experiment with translating theory into practice and practice into theory. As K.T. noted, human service providers are constantly giving and receiving. In opening yourself up to opportunities to learn from consumers, you may find that the roles of "consumer" and "provider" are no longer so clear-cut.

If you do not already work within an organization, or even if you do and are curious about some other setting, volunteering can be one way to learn more about an issue of interest to you. Most organizations will be glad to use your services, but if you are volunteering strictly to conduct research on a particular issue, it would probably be best to make that clear to the volunteer coordinator at the outset. Below is the narrative of one college student's experience as a volunteer at a homeless shelter.

I volunteered on a Saturday night. I had not taken a conscious inventory of my preconceived notions about homeless shelters prior to arriving, yet the moment I walked up to the door, expectations I didn't know I had began to manifest themselves in the form of surprise. Perhaps I had expected the men, waiting singly or in clusters to be let in the back gate, to stare as men often do when a woman approaches, or to make me feel threatened in some way. Instead, they went on with their conversations, their hands jammed deep in their pockets as they stamped their feet on the ground to warm up. A man seated on the sidewalk noticed that I wasn't sure where to go in. He looked up at me with a friendly smile, and said, "You just knock on the window right there and they'll come and let you in." "Thanks," I said, to which he replied, "Thanks for volunteering. We sure appreciate it." This was my first surprise.

My first impressions of the inside of the shelter produced the same, unexpected feelings. I was struck by the inviting warmth of the kitchen lights, the homey smell of turkey pot pie, and the general quiet; the clean sheets and blankets on the neat rows of bunk beds, the sign-up sheet for wake-up calls, and the coffee and hot chocolate all set out and ready to be poured. I was surprised by the visible nervousness of the mostly college-age volunteers—as well as those there to put in community service hours for infractions of the law—and the general irritability of the regular shelter staff. What had I expected? Roaches and dim lighting? Staff who were overflowing with energy and enthusiasm?

I was hastily instructed to sit behind the desk on the men's side (the fifteen or so women were confined to a separate wing) where my job was to sign out towels. Each man was assigned a bed number that also corresponded to the plastic drinking cups and the towels. There was a fifteen minute limit on the shower, and only eight men allowed in the bathroom at one time. If soap was needed there was an enormous box full of it; tiny, pearly-pink and white bars imprinted with "Radisson," "Marriott," and "Holiday Inn" logos. Each man had the right to two cough drops, his own hotel shampoo and conditioner, the use of communal bottles of hydrogen peroxide and moisturizing cream, and a single, blue-green stick of deodorant. Each was also entitled to one toothbrush per month and one razor a week, items which were to be logged in a separate notebook.

During the course of the evening, there were few opportunities to engage in conversation with the "guests," as the volunteers learned to refer to them. I felt very awkward as I fumbled through the pages of the notebook looking for a guest's name as he stood there with a bemused expression, reminding me that it was one month for a toothbrush, so why was I looking on the list from two months ago? Some of the men sighed with impatience as I searched for combs, soap, or shaving cream (on the top shelf to your right, they pointed out wearily). I quickly realized that my only function was to act as a conveyor belt for towels, toothbrushes, and toiletries, since the vast majority of the shelter's 90 or so guests knew how the place functioned far better than

I did. Most of them were tolerant of my disarray, although one man's irritation provoked a scene which, in retrospect, provided me with a valuable learning experience.

"I need a blanket," he announced loudly, as I was busy trying to locate a razor for another guest. "I'll be right with you," I replied, searching through the drawers of the filing cabinet.

"Hey," he snapped, "I *said* I needed a blanket. Don't just brush me aside." I looked up at him. He was leaning over the desk, his dark eyes flashing.

"Why don't you go ask the director if you can have another blanket?" I said, trying to keep my cool. "I'm trying to help someone else right now."

"NO," he shot back at me. *"You're* going to go ask him for a blanket." He had his finger pointed at me, his eyes narrowed.

I reacted reflexively. "I am *not* your servant," I erupted. "And you can't talk to me like that. Everyone here can make an effort to be pleasant."

Whoa. Suddenly everyone was looking at me—the guests, the staff, the other volunteers. My "antagonist" was glaring at me, his muscular chest in its white undershirt expanding and contracting with each breath. "Why are you letting him get to you?" another volunteer whispered to me, looking surprised. She turned to the guest. "Let me get you another blanket, sir. Will this one be all right?" He yanked the blanket from her and headed for his cot with a parting glare in my direction.

The director of the shelter came to see what was going on. "Hey, you can't let them get to you like that," he told me. "Yeah, why are you upset?" another volunteer chimed in. Suddenly, I felt very confused. How was I *supposed* to react? Why wasn't I supposed to "let them get to me," and why was everyone so surprised that one of "them" had? What exactly was my role? I had gone there because I wanted to learn and because I felt I had something to offer. I was concerned about these people. But there was still a part of me that wanted to yell at that guest, "Hey—I'm volunteering my time for you. You should be grateful." My reaction had been spontaneous; I had not chosen my words with care. Interestingly, the ones I had chosen told me something about the way I perceived both myself and the guest. "I am not your servant." Or was I? In providing my services, was I to cater to the needs of the consumer with no regard for the way the consumer treated me? I tried to imagine how I would have reacted if I had been, say, an employee of Motel 6, and this man a paying client. I do not think I would have concealed my irritation, but I know I would not have chosen the same words.

The rest of the evening went by without incident, but I continued to ponder the nature of my interaction with this guest. While this part of the experience at the shelter was confusing and somewhat troubling for me, it was this very uncertainty that guided me in subsequent readings about the issues of homelessness.

If all we expect from the homeless is gratitude, and if what and how we give is contingent on how "deserving" they show themselves to be, how is this empowering to the consumer? On the other hand, if we expect nothing in return—writing off rude behavior as unimportant or invalid so that it doesn't "get to us"—we place the consumer in a category separate from other human beings who "matter"—the general population that we expect to comply with the rules of social etiquette. In the effort to be unshakably tolerant and forgiving, are we shutting out the voices of those who are asking for more than to simply be tolerated?

Continuing to Scan "Homelessness"

How do you think you would have reacted in a situation similar to the one this volunteer describes? How do you think she should have reacted?

What does the word "guest" mean to you? Think about the labels of "guest" and "consumer." Are a guest and a consumer the same thing? Why or why not? How does language define relationships between people?

FRAME 18

VIEWING SERVICE DELIVERY ISSUES AS OPPORTUNITIES FOR IMPROVEMENTS

Remaining open to the complexity of the policy aspects of human services can be draining. "Why can't there be an easy solution?" you may sometimes be tempted to ask. "How will I be able to make a difference?" Mapping examples of the issues that are challenges to current notions of service delivery can leave you feeling angry, frustrated, depressed, and overwhelmed by the scope and range of the social problems facing our society. However, it is important to remember that in confronting these problems, you are dealing not only with challenges, but with opportunities for changes that will better link resources to human needs. Here are some examples of problems and issues that provided opportunities for change:

Problems or Issues	*Changes*
Racial discrimination	Civil rights movement—1954
School segregation	*Brown* v. *Board of Education*
Poverty in the aged population	Social Security benefits—Social Security Act of 1935
Polio	Polio vaccine developed in 1955 by Jonas E. Salk
Child labor	Child labor laws

Today these changes are generally considered positive, although as noted earlier, the very nature of an issue defies perfect, permanent resolution. There is much disagreement about the ways policies and programs are implemented, as well as concern about new problems and issues that arise due to changing societal conditions, shifts in public opinion, or dissatisfaction with the outcomes of change. There is evidence of this range of conflict in the ongoing debate over social welfare programs and policies. Some view government policy as creating poverty by destroying work incentive and breaking up the family, whereas others contend that the government is responsible for the well-being of its citizens and has an obligation to take care of them. While these conflicts can be frustrating, they too can be viewed as opportunities, for it is only when society acknowledges the existence of a problem that action can be taken to solve it.

Summary and Further Study

Chapter Summary

Chapter 2 examined the question of what conditions create the need for a system of human services. We proposed two primary sources: (1) consumers who become such due to obstacles that prevent effective functioning in accepted areas of need and (2) conditions in society that shape both the state of human needs and the system of human services that develops in response.

Lesson 1. At the personal level, we emphasized sensitivity to individual differences and careful application of a needs analysis framework. We also considered some limitations of seeing people primarily or exclusively in terms of needs and suggested replacing that with the concept of capacities, skills, and potential or strengths. Lesson 1 developed a framework for analyzing the needs of human service consumers according to ten needs, five levels of functioning in each need, and four obstacles preventing effective functioning. We showed how the needs analysis framework can sometimes quickly point you and the consumer in directions that will help the consumer to overcome the obstacles to functioning.

It is important to cultivate a sensitivity in applying the needs analysis framework. You should (1) appreciate what it is like to experience problems of living that may exceed your capacity to handle them; (2) apply the framework with a recognition of the total person and his or her life situation; and (3) keep perspective. Possible consequences of viewing people exclusively in terms of needs and deficiencies were identified. To further familiarize yourself with the material in this lesson, we suggest you apply the framework to yourself and discuss, or at least reflect on, the results.

Lesson 2. The thesis of this lesson is that rapid change is pervasive in society at large, the human services, and our personal lives. We discussed change in four ways:

1. Broadly, in terms of the three waves of social change through which our society has been transformed—the agricultural, industrial, and information/electronic waves.
2. Interactively, by showing how the social changes in each major wave were linked to society's attitude and response to human problems. Here we sought to gain a general understanding of the development of the human services in terms of the links among social changes, human needs, and human services to meet the needs that become problems.
3. Attitudinally, by showing that there are different beliefs about change in society and in the human services.

4. Personally and professionally, by suggesting that our cumulative experience implies a need to manage the changes in our lives and in the lives of our consumers or clients. It also indicates a need for the human service practitioner to be aware of the changes taking place in society.

Lesson 3. One extension of skills in managing change is being aware of some of the service delivery issues in our particular specialization and cultivating a curiosity to know more about them. Issues were defined as conflicts or areas in which the solutions are not clear. We portrayed the human service practitioner to be involved in "policy practice"—in addressing and shaping a range of often vexing social problems when delivering human services. Five points were made about how such a policy practice orientation ought to be viewed and can be developed.

1. Issues develop over time in response to a question or problem, generally through four stages: (1) felt needs or early awareness, (2) societal and political developments that make the issue visible, (3) legislative or other policy actions, and (4) clarification by courts and other rule-making or interpreting bodies. This is important because some human service issues have been around for a long time, whereas others are more emergent (e.g., homelessness). It also suggests that practitioners should be sensitive to both possibilities.
2. Policy is the link between broad forces of change in the environment that create problems of living and responses from society at large regarding how those problems will be addressed. Policy develops from problems and issues.
3. When delivering human services, human service practitioners shape policy all the time. One immediate way to see this is to discover service delivery issues. Service delivery issues are intimately connected to practice. They are the policy intersection that you can experience among a troubling condition in our society, a pattern or regularity confronting consumers you work with, and a possible response (or lack of response) from some level of the human service community.
4. We examined different personal orientations people bring to defining issues. Service delivery issues can evoke strong feelings of depression or anger. They can be viewed creatively as opportunities for improving painful conditions; and they can be viewed with balance in the sense that some issues express society's hopes while others reflect its fears.
5. People will disagree or at least have different interpretations about issues. Depending on your purposes, it will be important to acknowledge and explore these perspectives.

To emphasize the fact that issues develop and change, some initial guidelines and exercises were proposed for conducting your own "scan" of a consumer problem, area, or issue. We provided a broad scan of eight human service policy areas, and then specific illustrations that showed different scanning techniques applied to three different service delivery issues (in different stages of formulation). We focused on documents likely to be found in a library or your agency but also opened the possibility to other media as resources. Being able to conduct a limited issue scan was offered as a preliminary means of linking service delivery issues "out there" to "problems you are trying to solve in practice." These skills and linkages will be developed further in other sections of this text (e.g., brokering, advocating, and mobilizing). The point in this lesson was to lay a foundation and to develop learning skills specialized in "seeing" and linking issues in practice (i.e., service delivery issues) to social policy.

A Closing Reflection

After reading about the incredibly wide range of complex issues that we've addressed in this chapter, it may seem to you that the human service community bears the weight of the world's problems on its shoulders. Does the responsibility for dealing with these problems fall entirely to those who have chosen to go into the human service professions? Can the human service community do it all alone?

Jonathan Kozol is a writer and teacher who is concerned with the care and education of children. His most recent book, *Amazing Grace: The Lives of Children and the Conscience of a Nation,* is a nonfiction account of his day-to-day interactions with poor inner-city children and their families. In this book, Kozol makes a reflection on a card he picks up in the New York subway, which announces what the president of the transit system has described as the new "gospel" that New York will henceforth "preach" in regard to subway beggars:

> "When you're on a train," the card instructs the passengers, "don't give money for *any* purpose. . . . The best way to help panhandling is not to give . . . don't give." The message on the card is cleverly constructed. It does not prohibit charity but recommends an arm's length version. If we feel upset, it says, "Look in the Yellow Pages under . . . Human Services."[42]

What does the professionalization of "giving" and "caring" mean for our society and for the human services? Should these responsibilities be left up to those who are trained in the helping professions?

Suggestions for Further Study

The lessons in this chapter are introductory sketches of an enormous body of knowledge and experience describing aspects of the historical and contemporary human service delivery environment. Further study will be necessary and rewarding in each area, but this will probably be more manageable if you can focus it around a few particular interests. Comments to guide your learning follow. These are supplemented by the suggestions for further reading.

Human Needs and Human Potential

A number of theories and approaches underlie the needs analysis framework of Lesson 1. Some will be addressed in Unit Three of this text. Examples are structural functional and symbolic interaction theories, ego psychology, and cognitive development. A good summary is found in John F. Longres's *Human Behavior in the Social Environment* (Itasca, Ill.: F. E. Peacock, 1990). One important aspect is awareness of the issues that arise at different stages of human development and how these interact with cultural, ethnic, gender, and other differences. There is also a continually expanding literature on consumer problems and characteristics in specific areas (see section below

---

[42]Jonathan Kozol, *Amazing Grace: The Lives of Children and the Conscience of a Nation* (New York: Crown Publishers, 1995), p. 222.

on service delivery issues). Suggestions for further reading about human needs and human potential in general are:

Chapin, Rosemary Kennedy. "Social Policy Development: The Strengths Perspective." *Social Work* 40, 4 (July, 1995): 506–514.

DeJong, Peter, and Scott D. Miller. "How to Interview for Client Strengths." *Social Work* 40 (November, 1995): 729–736.

Devore, Wynetta, and Elfriede Schlesinger. *Ethnic-Sensitive Social Work Practice.* 4th ed. Boston, MA: Allyn & Bacon, 1996.

Green, James W. *Cultural Awareness in the Human Services,* 2nd ed. Boston: Allyn & Bacon, 1995.

Latting, Jean E., and Claudia Zundel. "World View Differences Between Clients and Counselors." *Social Casework* 67 (Nov. 1986): 533–541.

Macarov, David. "Human Needs." *Social Welfare: Structure and Practice.* Thousand Oaks, Calif.: Sage, 1995: 17–28.

McKnight, John. "Are Social Service Agencies the Enemy of Community?" Excerpt from *Social Policy* (Winter, 1987). *Utne Reader* 62 (July–August, 1992): 88–91.

Schlesinger, Elfriede G., and Wynetta Devore. "Ethnic-Sensitive Social Work Practice: The State of the Art." *Journal of Sociology and Social Welfare* XXII 1 (March, 1995): 29–58.

Soriano, Fernando I. *Conducting Needs Assessments: A Multidisciplinary Approach.* Newbury Park, Calif.: Sage Publications, 1995.

Towle, Charlotte. *Common Human Needs.* Silver Spring, Md.: National Association of Social Workers, 1987 (first published in 1948).

Linkages Among Societal Context, Evolution of Human Services, and Managing Change

There is a rich literature documenting the history of the development of the human services that you should consult for a deeper appreciation. One example is David M. Austin in *The Political Economy of Human Service Programs* (Greenwich, Conn.: JAI Press, 1988); he devotes two excellent chapters to the subject. The literatures in organizational development, humanistic and clinical psychology, death and dying, and business and public management contain numerous useful perspectives on and skills for managing change at individual, group, organizational, and societal levels. Another aspect we did not discuss was the tension in the human services between orientations toward social control versus social change. The Longres book and most other general reference works in social work and the human services deal with these questions. Suggestions for further reading are:

Managing Change, Understanding Waves of Change, and Awareness of Future Social Trends

Bell, Wendell. *Foundations of Futures Studies: Human Science for a New Era.* New York: Transaction, June 1996.

Bridges, William. *Transitions: Making Sense of Life's Changes.* Reading, Mass.: Addison-Wesley, 1980.

Cetron, Marvin J., and Owen Davies. *American Renaissance: Our Life at the Turn of the 21st Century.* New York: St. Martins Press, 1989. Also see Marvin Cetron, "An American Renaissance: 74 Trends That Will Affect America's Future—And Yours." Bethesda, Md.: World Future Society, 1994.

Coates, Joseph F., and Jennifer Jarratt, editors. *The Future: Trends into the Twenty-First Century.* Newbury Park, Calif.: Sage Publications, 1992.

Cook, Lauren B., Jack Osterholt, and Edward C. Riley. *Anticipating Tomorrow's Issues: A Handbook for Policymakers*. Washington, D.C.: Council of State Policy and Planning Agencies, 1988.

Drucker, Peter. "The Age of Social Transformation." *The Atlantic Monthly* (November, 1994): 53–80.

Haynes, Karen S., and Karen A. Holmes. "The Future of Social Work." In *Invitation to Social Work*. New York: Longman, 1994: 405–420.

Henderson, Hazel. "The Three Zones of Transition: A Guide to Riding the Tiger of Change." *Futures Research Quarterly* 2, 1 (Spring, 1986): 19–38.

Kennedy, Paul. *Preparing for the Twenty-First Century*. New York: Vintage Books, 1993.

Marien, Michael. "Infoglut and Competing Problems: Key Barriers Suggesting a New Strategy for Sustainability." *Futures* 26, 2 (March, 1994): S1(7).

Mary, Nancy L. "The Future and Social Work: A Global Perspective." *Journal of Multicultural Social Work* 3, 4 (1994): 89–101.

McGrath, J. E., ed. "Social Issues and Social Change: Some Views from the Past." *Journal of Social Issues* 139, 4 (Winter 1983): 1–239.

National Association of Social Workers. *A User's Guide to Social Work Abstracts*, 2d ed. Silver Spring, Md.: NASW, 1989.

Royse, David, Surjit Dhooper, and Elizabeth Rompf. "Pragmatic Concerns: How Do I Prepare for Social Work Practice in the Next Century?" In *Field Instruction: A Guide for Social Work Students*. New York: Longman, 1996.

Schilling, Robert F., Steven Paul Schinke, and Richard A. Weatherly. "Service Trends in a Conservative Era: Social Workers Rediscover the Past." *Social Work* (Jan.–Feb. 1988): 5–9.

Tannenbaum, Robert, and Robert W. Hanna. "Holding On, Letting Go, and Moving On: Understanding a Neglected Perspective on Change." In *Human Systems Development*, by Robert Tannenbaum, Newton Margulies, Fred Massarik, and associates. San Francisco, Calif.: Jossey-Bass, 1987, pp. 95–121.

Toffler, Alvin. *Creating a New Civilization: The Politics of the Third Wave*. Atlanta: Turner Publishing, Inc., 1994.

Evolution of the Human Services

Axinn, June, and Herman Levin. *Social Welfare: A History of the American Response to Need*, 3rd ed. New York: Longman, 1992.

DiNitto, Diana M., and Thomas R. Dye. *Social Welfare: Politics and Public Policy*, 4th ed. Boston: Allyn & Bacon, 1995.

Dolgoff, Ralph, Donald Feldstein, and Louise Skolnik. *Understanding Social Welfare*, 3rd ed. New York: Longman, 1993.

Epstein, William M. *The Dilemma of American Social Welfare*. New Brunswick, N.J.: Transaction Publishers, 1993.

Johnson, Louise C. *Social Work Practice: A Generalist Approach*, 2d ed. Boston: Allyn & Bacon, 1986.

Leiby, James. *A History of Social Welfare and Social Work in the U.S.* New York: Columbia University Press, 1987.

Logan, Sadye M. L., Edith M. Freeman, and Ruth G. McRoy. *Social Work with Black Families: A Culturally Specific Perspective*. New York: Longman, 1990.

Mehr, Joseph. *Human Services: Concepts and Intervention Strategies*, 4th ed. Boston: Allyn & Bacon, 1988.

Pincus, Allen, and Anne Minahan. *Social Work Practice: Model and Method*. Itasca, Illinois: F. E. Peacock, 1973.

Popple, Philip R. "Social Work Profession: History." In *Encyclopedia of Social Work*, 19th ed. Washington, D.C.: NASW, 1995: 2282–2292.

Posner, Wendy B. "Common Human Needs: A Story from the Prehistory of Government by Special Interest." *Social Service Review* 69 (June, 1995): 188–225.

Reed, P. Nelson. "Social Welfare History." In *Encyclopedia of Social Work,* 19th ed. Washington, D.C.: NASW Press, 1995: 2206–2225.

Russo, Francis X., and George Willis. *Human Services in America.* Englewood Cliffs, N.J.: Prentice-Hall, 1986.

Schmolling, Paul, Merrill Youkeles, and William Burger. *Human Services in Contemporary America,* 2d ed. Pacific Grove, Calif.: Brooks/Cole, 1989.

Skocpol, Theda. *Social Policy in the United States: Future Possibilities in Historical Perspective.* New Jersey: Princeton University Press, 1995.

Vasey, Wayne. *Government and Social Welfare.* New York: Henry Holt, 1958.

Wilensky, Harold L., and Charles N. Lebeaux. *Industrial Society and Social Welfare.* New York: Free Press, 1965.

Service Delivery Issues and Policy Practice

The examples of resources included with the service delivery issues were intended to underscore the fact that there is a great deal more required to appreciate not only each area but also its issues. Practically any introductory text in social welfare and introductory and advanced works on human service policy in general will include in-depth discussions of the history and current context of each major field. A good resource for staying current, not only in human service issue areas but also about the world in general, is The World Future Society (phone: 301–656–8274), especially its Future Survey Newsletter (a monthly abstract of books, articles, and reports concerning forecasts, trends, and ideas about the future).

For each policy area below, we have tried to include one reference pertaining to the history of the policy area, one relating policy to service delivery, and one dealing with general policy/service delivery issues.

Scanning Service Delivery Issues (Policy Practice: General)

Aaron, Henry J., Thomas E. Mann, and Timothy Taylor. *Values and Public Policy.* Washington, D.C.: The Brookings Institution, 1994.

Dye, Thomas. *Understanding Public Policy.* Englewood Cliffs, NJ: Prentice-Hall, 1995.

Ginsberg, Leon. *Social Work Almanac,* 2nd ed. Washington, D.C.: National Association of Social Work, 1995.

Ginsberg, Leon. *Understanding Social Problems, Policies, and Programs,* 2nd ed. Columbia: University of South Carolina Press, 1996.

Harris, Howard S., and David C. Maloney, eds. *Human Services: Contemporary Issues and Trends.* Boston: Allyn & Bacon, 1996.

Jansson, Bruce S. *Social Policy: From Theory to Policy Practice.* Pacific Grove, Calif.: Brooks/Cole Publishing Co., 1994.

Karger, Howard Jacob, and James Midgley. *Controversial Issues in Social Policy.* Boston: Allyn & Bacon, 1994.

Martin, George T., Jr. *Social Policy in the Welfare State.* Englewood Cliffs, N.J.: Prentice Hall, 1990.

McKnight, John. "Do No Harm: Policy Options That Meet Human Needs." *Social Policy* 20, 1 (Summer 1989): 5–15.

Mendelsohn, Henry Neil. *A Guide to Information Sources for Social Work and Human Services.* New York: Oryx Press, 1987.

Moroney, Robert M. *Social Policy and Social Work.* New York: Aldine de Gruyter, 1991.

Popple, Philip and Leslie Leighninger. *Social Work, Social Welfare, and American Society,* 3rd ed. Boston, Massachusetts: Allyn & Bacon, 1996.

Skocpol, Theda. *Social Policy in the United States: Future Possibilities in Historical Perspective.* Princeton, N.J.: Princeton University Press, 1995.

Specht, Harry and Mark E. Courtney. *Unfaithful Angels: How Social Work Has Abandoned Its Mission.* New York: Free Press, 1994.

Mental Health/Disabilities

American Coalition of Citizens With Disabilities, 1346 Connecticut Ave., NW, Suite 817, Washington, DC 20036, (303) 785–4265.

Americans With Disabilities Act, 42 U.S.C. 12101 et. seq., 1990.

Brown, P. *The Transfer of Care: Deinstitutionalization and Its Aftermath.* Boston, Massachusetts: Routledge & Kegan Paul, 1985.

Clearinghouse for Mental Health Information, 5600 Fishers Lane, Rockville, MD 20857, (301) 443–4515. Clearinghouse for information about all aspects of medical disorders, treatment programs, and preventative mental health care.

Grob, Gerald N. *The Mad Among Us: A History of the Care of America's Mentally Ill.* New York: The Free Press, 1994.

Kesey, Ken. *One Flew Over the Cuckoo's Nest.* New York: Viking, 1996.

National Alliance for the Mentally Ill, 2101 Wilson Boulevard, Suite 302, Arlington, VA 22201, (703) 524–7600 or 1–800–950–NAMI. Fax: 703–524–9094.

Romel W. Mackelprang and Richard O. Salsgiver, "People with Disabilities and Social Work: Historical and Contemporary Issues," *Social Work* 41, 1(January 1996), pp. 7–13.

Wilk, Ruta J. "Are the Rights of People with Mental Illness Still Important?" *Social Work* 39, 2 (1994): 167–175.

Aging

Cox, E. O., & Parsons, R. J. *Empowerment-Oriented Social Work Practice with the Elderly.* Pacific Grove, Calif.: Brooks/Cole, 1994.

Gelfand, Donald E. *Aging and Ethnicity: Knowledge and Services.* New York: Springer, 1994.

National Council on the Aging, Inc., 600 Maryland Avenue, SW, West Wing, Washington, DC 20024, (202) 479-1200, Fax 202-479-0735. Works to improve the lives of older persons; provides information, training, technical assistance, advocacy and research on virtually every aspect of aging.

Olson, Laura Katz, editor. *The Graying of the World: Who Will Care for the Frail Elderly?* Binghamton, N.Y.: Haworth Press, 1994.

Siegel, Jacob S. *A Generation of Change: A Profile of America's Older Population.* New York: Russell-Sage Foundation, 1993.

Torres-Gil, F. M. *The New Aging: Politics and Change in America.* Westport, Conn.: Auburn House, 1992.

Warnes, Anthony M. "Being Old, Old People, and the Burdens of Burden." *Aging and Society* 13, 3 (Sept. 1993): 297–338.

Housing and Homelessness

Blau, Joel. *The Visible Poor: Homelessness in the United States.* New York: Oxford University Press, 1992.

Fagan, Ronald W. "Homelessness in America: Causes, Consequences, and Solutions." *Journal of Interdisciplinary Studies* 7, 1–2 (1995): 101–118.

National Coalition for the Homeless, 1621 Connecticut Ave., N.W., Washington, DC 20009, phone: (202) 265-2371.

Schwartz, David C., Richard Ferlauto, and Daniel M. Hoffman. *A New Housing Policy for America: Recapturing the American Dream*. Philadelphia: Temple University Press, 1988.

Timmer, Doug A., Stanley Eitzen, and Kathryn D. Talley. *Paths to Homelessness: Extreme Poverty and the Urban Housing Crisis*. Boulder: Westview Press, 1994.

Poverty/Income Security

Bane, Mary Jo, and David T. Ellwood, *Welfare Realities: From Rhetoric to Reform*. Cambridge, Mass.: Harvard University Press, 1994.

Katz, Michael B. *In the Shadow of the Poorhouse: A Social History of Welfare in America*. New York: Basic Books, 1986.

Mead, Lawrence M. "Poverty: How Little We Know." *Social Service Review* 68, 3 (Sept. 1994): 322–350.

Piven, Frances Fox, and Cloward, Richard A. *Regulating the Poor: The Functions of Public Welfare*. New York: Vintage, 1993.

Social Security Administration, 6401 Security Boulevard, Baltimore, MD 21235.

Steinbeck, John, *The Grapes of Wrath*. New York: Knopf: Distributed by Random House, 1993.

Children, Youth, and Families

Berrick, Jill Duerr, and Lawrence-Karski, Ruth. "Emerging Issues in Child Welfare." *Public Welfare* 53, 4 (Fall 1995): 4–11.

Berrick, Jill Duerr. *Faces of Poverty: Portraits of Women and Children on Welfare*. New York: Oxford University Press, 1995.

Child Welfare League of America, 440 First Street, N.W., Suite 310, Washington, DC 20001-2085, (202) 638-2952, Fax (202) 638-4004.

Children's Defense Fund, 25 E. Street, Washington, DC 20001, (202) 628-8787, Fax (202) 783-7324.

Dickens, Charles. *Oliver Twist*. New York: Knopf: Distributed by Random House, 1992.

Pecora, P., Whittaker, J., & Maluccio, A. *The Child Welfare Challenge: Policy, Practice, and Research*. New York: Aldine de Gruyter, 1992.

Simon, Rita J., and Altstein, Howard. *Adoption, Race, and Identity: From Infancy Through Adolescence*. New York: Praeger, 1992.

Health

Fox, Daniel M. *Power and Illness: The Failure and Future of American Health Policy*. Berkeley, Calif.: University of California Press, 1993.

Ginzberg, Eli. *Critical Issues in U.S. Health Reform*. Boulder, Colorado: Westview Press, 1994.

Lipson, Debra. *State Health Policy: A Sourcebook*. Portland, Maine: National Academy for State Health Policy, 1991.

National Health Information Center, P.O. Box 1133, Washington, DC 20013–1133, (301) 565-4167, 1-800-336-4797, Fax (301) 468-7394.

Shelby, R. Dennis, editor. *People with HIV and Those Who Help Them*. Binghamton, N.Y.: Harrington Park, 1995.

Starr, Paul. *The Social Transformation of Medicine*. New York: Basic Books, 1982.

Webber, Henry S. "The Failure of Health-Care Reform: An Essay Review." *Social Service Review* 69, 2 (June 1995), pp. 309–322.

Corrections

Department of Human Services—Youth Services Administration, Office of Juvenile Justice and

Delinquency Prevention, Indiana Building, 633 Indiana Ave., N.W., Washington, DC 20531, (202) 307-5911, Fax (202) 514-6382.

Douglas C. McDonald, editor. *Private Prisons and the Public Interest*. New Brunswick, N.J.: Rutgers University Press, 1990.

National Criminal Justice Reference Service (NCJRS), 1600 Research Blvd., P.O. Box 6000, Rockville, MD 20850, 301-251-5500 or 1-800-851-3420, Fax 301-251-5212.

Pisciotta, Alexander W. *Benevolent Repression: Social Control and the American Reformatory-Prison Movement*. New York: New York University Press, 1994.

Severson, Margaret M. "Adapting Social Work Values to the Corrections Environment." *Social Work* 39, 4 (July 1994): 451–456.

Stephen D. Gottfredson and Sean McConville, editors. *America's Correctional Crisis: Prison Populations and Public Policy*. New York: Greenwood Press, 1987.

Straus, Martha B. *Violence in the Lives of Adolescents*. Evanston, Illinois: W.W. Norton, 1994.

Education

Dryfoos, Joy G. *Full-Service Schools: A Revolution in Health and Social Services for Children, Youth, and Families*. San Francisco: Jossey-Bass, 1994.

Kozol, Jonathan. *Savage Inequalities*. New York: HarperPerennial, 1991.

National Education Association, 1201 16th Street, N.W., Washington, DC 20036, (202) 833-4000, Fax (202) 822-7974.

National Head Start Association, 201 N. Union Street, Suite 320, Alexandria, VA 22314 (703) 739-0875, Fax (703) 739-0878.

Tyack, David, and Larry Cuban. *Tinkering Toward Utopia: A Century of Public School Reform*. Cambridge: Harvard University Press, 1995.

Vinovskis, Maris A. "Early Childhood Education: Then and Now." *Daedalus* 122, 1 (Winter 1993): 151–176.

Racism in Human Services

Agency for Health Care Policy and Research (1996). *Race/Ethnicity and Treatment of Children and Adolescents in Hospitals by Diagnosis*. Rockville, MD: U.S. Department of Health and Human Services, Public Health Service.

James, Carl R., ed. *Perspectives on Racism and the Human Services Sector: A Case for Change*. Buffalo, NY: University of Toronto Press, 1996.

Chapter 3

People Responding to Human Needs

In Chapter 1 we asked this question: What basic skills do human service practitioners need that will enable them to meet today's service delivery requirements *and* those of the next decade? Three critical skills were proposed as the basic orientations for delivering human services: an attitude and skill in learning, a sensitivity to language, and an ability to engage in systems thinking. In Chapter 2 we examined the conditions creating human needs that have been the catalyst for the rise of the human services. Chapter 2 asked this question: *Why* human services? Individual needs and the constantly changing conditions in our society were discussed, along with how these needs become service delivery issues in the human services. In Chapter 3 we continue the process of understanding human services by asking these questions: Who is involved in delivering these services? Who are the people who respond to human needs, and in what context do they deliver their responses?

For most of us, work occupies one-third or more of our lives. Millions of women and men experience a variety of work situations, pleasures, and problems every day. Because so much time and effort are spent at work, it is important to understand its characteristics. You have chosen human service work as the central activity around which you are organizing your work life. To deliver effective human services, you should be committed to helping others and should find personal satisfaction in your work. The starting point for these things is examining who you are, where you work, why you work, and the kind of work you perform.

This chapter provides you with the opportunity to learn about the important factors that affect your ability to function in the world of human service work. Much of human service work requires using the self as an instrument of change. Thus Lesson 1 addresses the process of establishing a work identity, the importance of developing an awareness of your own value system, and linking your values to those commonly held by human service professions. Your work identity unfolds and is continuously shaped by a specific work environment. Lesson 2 examines the characteristics of human service work settings, specifically human service organizations. Because so much time in organizations is spent in the context of work groups, Lesson 2 also discusses the characteristics of effective work groups, including teams. Finally, Lesson 3 discusses the nature of the work itself—the purposes, goals, roles, and processes involved in delivering human services. The overall objective of this chapter is to provide you with a beginning understanding of the major characteristics of the world of human service work.

The Worker Perspective: Human Services as Self-Awareness

Knowing about yourself is an extremely important part of delivering human services. Although we recognize that the process of learning about your true feelings, biases, and values is a lifelong activity, the delivery of human services requires all of us to spend time sorting out our feelings and reactions to the problems presented by consumers as well as to the problems presented by our agencies. Working with people who suffer from such problems as poverty, mental illness, and abuse requires those of us who really care about the needs of others to develop an increasingly deeper understanding of ourselves. In addition, we must all find ways to recharge our batteries, which can often be drained by the physical and emotional needs of our consumers. Working with human problems on a daily basis also requires a clear understanding of the values we hold. These values are tested constantly by our awareness of the sometimes oppressive conditions our consumers experience. Knowledge of your needs, feelings, attitudes, and values contributes to what we call your work identity, which is the primary focus of this lesson.

Goal

To begin the process of establishing a work identity by exploring possible connections between your personal self and your ability to work effectively with people.

Learning Activities

To accomplish this goal, we will:

1. Describe the context for developing a work identity by introducing the helping professions providing human services and exploring a definition of the generalist human service worker.
2. Review some of the concrete steps you can take to begin the process of understanding yourself.
3. Explore how you deal with your fundamental needs.
4. Examine the connection between your value system and the commonly held values of human services.

5. Relate the development of a work identity to stages of career development.
6. Introduce self-leadership skills as a way of exercising your responsibility to shape a work identity.

FRAME

PROVIDERS OF HUMAN SERVICES

In the early history of human services, in both Europe and the United States, the primary providers of human services were volunteers, well-meaning persons (frequently the clergy) concerned with the plight of those experiencing human problems, and members of charitable voluntary organizations concerned with poverty, poor health, and mental illness. With the exception of medicine, the human service professions had not yet developed. Not until the late 19th and early 20th centuries did the social and behavioral sciences—especially psychology, sociology, and anthropology—begin to develop a coherent body of knowledge to help us better understand the dynamics of human behavior. For example, one of the first helping professions, social work, was formally organized in 1921 with the founding of the American Association of Social Workers, although the roots of social work can be traced to the charity organization and settlement house movements of the late 1800s. By the 1920s social work was recognized as a helping profession complete with a professional course of study designed to prepare people for professional practice.

By the 1960s a number of human service professions had developed in the United States. Drawing from the body of knowledge produced by the social and behavioral science disciplines, as well as biological and medical sciences, the staffs of human service agencies grew to include representatives from such disciplines as psychiatry, clinical psychology, counseling psychology, social work, rehabilitation counseling, psychiatric nursing, marriage and family counseling, child development, communicology (speech and hearing), gerontology, and correctional counseling. Academic programs in colleges and universities grew rapidly in the post–World War II era to prepare people for entry into these human service professions.

With the proliferation of new human service programs in the 1960s came a recognized need for the development of new helping professions. On the one hand, existing professional schools could not produce enough graduates to keep up with the demand for trained human service professionals. On the other hand, human service workers with generalist skills were needed because many of the human service professions had become highly specialized. The rapid expansion of human services, the de-emphasis on institutional care, and the growing programs as the community level led to the need for more human service workers trained from a generalist (as opposed to specialist) perspective. Also, in certain program areas, such as mental health and mental retardation, there was a recognized need for technical training of a relatively short duration for the increasing number of technician positions previously filled by untrained personnel. As a result, there was a rapid growth of training programs primarily at the community or junior college level to prepare people for new human service positions. This nationwide movement came to be known as the "paraprofessional," or "new professional," movement.

Today a number of new professions have taken their place alongside the older, established human service professions. This new professional group includes persons trained as human service generalists, mental health technicians, mental retardation technicians, allied health professionals, child care workers, drug and alcohol abuse counselors, and others.

HELPING PROFESSIONS AND LEVELS OF PRACTICE[1]

There are many professionals who work within the human "helping" services. Most of these helping professions include workers at different levels of work activity based on educational background and the complexities of consumer problems encountered. To meet a wide range of consumer needs, the professions typically define levels of practice. In turn, levels of practice are linked to education and degrees, ranging from the Ph.D. (doctoral degree) to M.S. (masters degree), B.S. (bachelors degree), A.A. or A.S. (associate of arts or sciences degrees), to high school education. These distinctions are illustrated below using four very different helping professions: medicine, law, theology, and social work.

A Comparison of Four Helping Professions[2]

Levels of Practice	Medicine	Law	Theology	Social Work
Professional (Ph.D., M.D., J.D., M.Div., M.S.W., M.S., or B.S. degrees, depending on profession)	Internist Neurologist Surgeon Obstetrician Orthopedist Psychiatrist	Corporate lawyer Criminal lawyer International lawyer Maritime lawyer Tax lawyer	Minister Priest Rabbi	Correctional social worker Community planner Psychiatric social worker School social worker
Paraprofessional (B.A. or A.A. or A.S. degrees, special training)	Laboratory technician Paramedic Operating room assistant X-ray technician	Court stenographer Legal secretary Paralegal aide	Lay deacon Lay Sunday school director	Case aide Child care worker Psychiatric technician Correctional officer (guard)
Volunteer (no special training except orientation sessions)	Candy striper Friendly visitor Home visitor	Intake aide Research aide	Advisory board member Sunday school teacher Youth activity leader	Hotlines Meals-on-Wheels Volunteers in probation

[1]Robert P. Scheurell, *Introduction to Human Service Networks: History, Organization, and Professions* (Lanham, Md.: University Press of America, 1987), chap. 2; and Joseph Heffernan, Guy Shuttlesworth, and Rosalie Ambrosio, *Social Work and Social Welfare: An Introduction* (St. Paul, Minn.: West Publishing, 1988), p. 15.
[2]Scheurell, *Introduction to Human Service Networks*, p. 53.

Thus "helping professions" have three major characteristics. First, their primary function is the delivery of a social service that usually involves the development of a relationship with the client served. Second, such service delivery uses knowledge of human behavior and skills in forming relationships with people in need. And third, most helping professions have educational qualifications that usually define different levels of work activity with clients or consumers.

HUMAN SERVICE WORKERS?

Given the variety of helping professions, what is a "human service worker"? Joseph Mehr offers an intriguing idea that is quite congruent with the curriculum we develop in this text:[3]

> A human service worker is an individual who, through training and experience or formal education in a human services curriculum, develops a role identity as an entry-level professional possessing the knowledge, skills, and attitudes that characterize the generic field of human services. The field of human services and entry-level human service professionals are characterized by a multidisciplinary or interdisciplinary viewpoint, a concern for the whole person, and a recognition that the field of human services can lay claim to a philosophical uniqueness that continues to evolve dynamically. . . . (T)here is something different about people who are human service workers. They contribute something new and different to the helping services, something beyond what the traditional professions offer. The human service professional is a new type of worker: a generalist change agent.

Strong ideas. But they are seconded by Harold McPheeters, who said:[4]

> I feel there needs to be a differentiation in the roles of human services and social work. I feel that human services has much more of an orientation to helping the client in any possible way. . . . Human service workers are not constrained by any single philosophical orientation or technology. They are much more oriented to helping a client solve a problem whatever it takes, using a range of biological, social, and psychological approaches. . . . To me, this generic orientation of getting the job done is philosophically the difference between human service workers and other professions.

Is it possible to be, simultaneously, a social worker and a human service worker, or to be a lawyer and a human service worker? Mehr and McPheeters might say no, but perhaps it is possible that the generalist orientation of human service workers they describe is an approach and attitude that professionals such as social workers and lawyers can incorporate. This is a good topic to discuss throughout this lesson and this text.

---

[3]Joseph Mehr, *Human Services: Concepts and Intervention Strategies,* 5th ed. (Boston: Allyn & Bacon, 1992), p. 12.
[4]T. McClam and M. R. Woodside, "A Conversation with Dr. Harold McPheeters," *Human Service Education* 9 (1989).

DEVELOPING SELF-UNDERSTANDING

Human service work requires the establishment of relationships with other people—consumers, fellow workers, and people in the community. In dealing with people, the human service worker faces the challenging task of defining effective ways of working with others. However, it takes more than technical knowledge and skills to accomplish this. It takes an understanding of oneself. How does a worker establish an identity that successfully combines his or her technical knowledge with self-knowledge? What should a human service worker be like?

In order to develop effective working relationships, it is essential for workers to possess an awareness of themselves and of their relationships with others. The key to beginning this process of self-understanding is accepting and recognizing the fact that what you are will affect what you can do. Workers who understand themselves are more likely to develop a clear identity as human service workers, which is important in developing meaningful and productive relationships with others.

Before reviewing some concrete steps you can take to begin this process, make sure you understand what you are striving for. Self-understanding means more than simply collecting a lot of information about yourself. The word *understanding* signifies perceiving, comprehending, and knowing. Therefore, understanding yourself involves getting in touch with your feelings, attitudes, values, goals, beliefs, and ways of behaving—and this is usually a lifelong process.

How can you begin? In striving to understand yourself, you can begin by trying to answer some basic questions:[5]

1. How do I think and feel about myself?
2. How do I deal with my own fundamental needs?
3. What is my value system, and how does it define my behavior and my relationships with others?
4. How do I relate to the society in which I live and work?
5. What is my lifestyle?
6. What is my basic philosophy?
7. What do I present—and represent—to those with whom I work?

Eight specific questions you may ask yourself to begin the process of self-understanding are listed below. Take a few minutes to think carefully about each of these questions as they relate to you and then place a check mark in one blank for each question.

	Yes	Sometimes	No
1. Do I have a positive view of myself? Am I okay?	____	____	____
2. Do I recognize my own needs to be respected, loved, involved, left alone, etc.? Do I deal with them successfully?	____	____	____

[5]Naomi Brill, *Working with People: The Helping Process,* 5th ed. (New York: Longman, 1995), p. 19.

	Yes	*Sometimes*	*No*
3. Do I clearly understand how my values affect my relationships with others? For example, do I think all people are basically good? Do I give everyone a chance?	____	____	____
4. Am I involved in my community—talking with neighbors, joining clubs, going to parades, etc.?	____	____	____
5. Do I clearly understand my lifestyle as evidenced, for example, by a fancy car, lots of clothes, few records, a modest home, etc.?	____	____	____
6. Do I like to work with people in need, such as consumers?	____	____	____
7. Do I like to work with other workers?	____	____	____
8. Do I believe that work is important? Does my work have meaning for me?	____	____	____

The rest of this lesson provides you with some suggestions for answering these questions, in addition to discussing some related issues that are important to the human service worker.

FRAME
3

HOW DO YOU DEAL WITH YOUR NEEDS?

Developing insight does not come automatically. It is achieved through systematic self-study and effort to understand what is happening in you in a variety of situations. One major resource for understanding yourself is examining how you deal with your needs.

The development of the total individual rests on the fulfillment of certain basic needs. The way in which you meet these needs defines how you achieve satisfaction in your life and therefore your work. Lesson 1 of Chapter 2 identified ten areas of human need: physical functioning, emotional functioning, education and employment, financial functioning, transportation, family functioning, housing, safety and security, spiritual and aesthetic functioning, and leisure and recreation. To begin the process of systematic self-study, first consider your level of functioning in each need. Second, since a major purpose of your analysis is to lay a foundation for developing your work identity, focus on how you meet these needs through your work relationships. (See the chart on page 141).

These ten needs can be considered in two overall categories: (1) the need for security and (2) the need to accommodate the drive for growth (see Figure 3.1). Security includes the material needs to sustain life (e.g., food, clothing, and shelter) and the less concrete needs for loving and being loved and for meaningful association with others. Growth is a continuous and essential part of the life process. Each of us possesses the drive to grow—to mature to the point that is our maximum capacity. According to Naomi Brill:

> Healthy security provides the firm floor upon which individuals can stand with confidence and assurance as they grow. They can depend on this essential base and can move from it to try new ways; they can return to it when faced with failure, to regroup and start again.

· · ·

Levels of Functioning

Areas of Need	Well-being (1)	Stress (2)	Problems (3)	Crisis (4)	Disability (5)	How I Meet this Need at or Through Work
Physical functioning						
Emotional functioning						
Education and employment						
Financial functioning						
Transportation						
Family functioning						
Housing						
Safety and security						
Spiritual and aesthetic functioning						
Leisure and recreation						

People require stimulation to trigger development in all life areas, but it must be in good balance, determined by their needs at a particular time.[6]

Human service workers must be aware of the existence of these needs within themselves and of how they are meeting these needs. It is particularly important to be clear about how one's needs are being met through working relationships, especially relationships with consumers.

While helping relationships can be a source of personal satisfaction that is normal and useful, human service workers whose personal lives do not fulfill their own needs may find themselves manipulating those with whom they are working, making them overly dependent, using them to satisfy needs for power, prestige, or self-fulfillment. This does not mean that workers get no satisfaction from their successes, no pleasure—and no frustration!—from their working relationships. Rather, it means that the satisfaction derives from the client's freedom to develop and to be successful as a person apart from the worker.[7]

---

[6]Brill, *Working with People*, pp. 22–24.
[7]Brill, *Working with People*, p. 25.

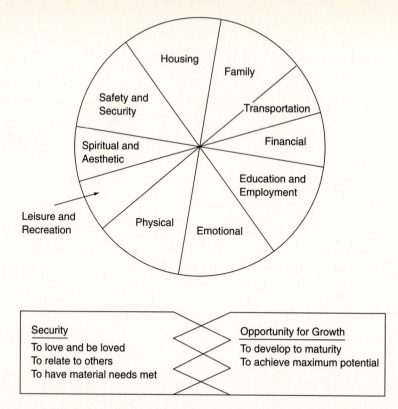

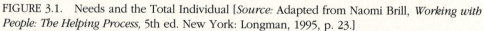

FIGURE 3.1.   Needs and the Total Individual [*Source:* Adapted from Naomi Brill, *Working with People: The Helping Process,* 5th ed. New York: Longman, 1995, p. 23.]

FRAME

4

Clarifying Beliefs

Read each of the following questions and place a check mark by one answer for each question.

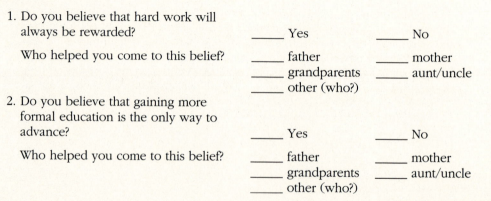

1. Do you believe that hard work will always be rewarded?

_____ Yes   _____ No

Who helped you come to this belief?

_____ father   _____ mother
_____ grandparents   _____ aunt/uncle
_____ other (who?)

2. Do you believe that gaining more formal education is the only way to advance?

_____ Yes   _____ No

Who helped you come to this belief?

_____ father   _____ mother
_____ grandparents   _____ aunt/uncle
_____ other (who?)

The questions you just answered relate to examining what you believe and how you think and behave. Since many factors affect what people believe and think and how they behave, it might be helpful to consider four of these factors.

A person's *family background* will affect what that person believes. If a man has been brought up in a poor, hard-working family, he might feel that getting ahead depends on a good education. On the other hand, if a person has grown up in a family that owns and operates a small but successful restaurant, she might believe that going to college or even finishing high school is a waste of time. Such a person might believe that hard physical work and long hours in one's own business are the keys to success. You can see that these two people would have very different beliefs about education, stemming from influences in their family backgrounds.

A second influence on a person's beliefs stems from the expectations of the groups to which the person belongs. These *group expectations* are manifested in the common groups to which people belong, such as church groups, clubs, and work groups. Church groups are a good example of how groups affect what people believe. People from religious groups sometimes have a difficult time discussing their beliefs with those outside their group because different church groups often have very different ideas about what to believe and how to behave. The groups people join will have an effect on what they believe.

The *life experiences* of a person will also influence personal beliefs. For example, if an older man has been in a nursing home for some time where no one has paid much attention to him, it might be difficult for a worker to establish a relationship with him. The older person's experiences over a period of time have led him to believe that no one really cares about him.

A fourth influence on what a person believes comes from his or her *feelings about human nature*. Some people believe that others are basically bad and that they can therefore be expected to behave in the most unacceptable way possible. Other people believe that human beings are basically good but that they sometimes make mistakes. The way a person treats other people may be related to how he or she feels about human nature, whether he or she thinks people are basically good or basically bad.

FRAME

5

Now that you have clarified some thoughts about influences on the way you think and believe, try this brief exercise, which will carry you one step further in getting at *who you are*.[8] Answer the following ten questions in terms of most of your own experiences and responses to people. Place a check mark for one response for each question.

	Yes	Sometimes	No
1. Do you feel you are an open person?	_____	_____	_____
2. Would you prefer that people not know too much about you?	_____	_____	_____

[8]Exercise from Eveline D. Schulman, *Intervention in Human Services,* 4th ed. (New York: Merrill/Macmillan Publishing Company, 1991), p. 25.

	Yes	Sometimes	No
3. Do you feel free to tell people about yourself?	_____	_____	_____
4. Do you get upset if someone is told something about you that you preferred he or she did not know?	_____	_____	_____
5. Do you like people to ask you questions about yourself?	_____	_____	_____
6. Do you feel exposed when people seem to know too much about you?	_____	_____	_____
7. Have other people told you that you are frank?	_____	_____	_____
8. Do you like people to know you better?	_____	_____	_____
9. Would you feel comfortable writing or talking about your life experiences?	_____	_____	_____
10. Do you feel people are prying if they ask you questions about yourself?	_____	_____	_____

FRAME

Turn to Answer 11 on page 597

VALUING

Human service workers are continually faced with work situations that call for thought, opinion, decision, and action. In almost all these situations, every action a worker takes is consciously or unconsciously based on his or her beliefs, attitudes, and values. One important aspect of understanding yourself is knowing your value system and how it relates to the value system of the human service professions. Values are based on beliefs, preferences, or assumptions about what is desirable or good for people.[9] Values are the customs, standards of conduct, and principles considered desirable by a culture, a group of people, or an individual.[10] Since values grow from a person's experiences, different experiences will result in different values. These values may shift as a person gains more experience and adapts to change.

A value is a thing or condition that you consistently act on to get or to keep. Thus the more consistently and energetically you commit your time or money to something, the more you apparently value it. This means that you can get a pretty clear idea of your values by studying your calendar and your checkbook. . . . To explore your values is to become more thoroughly aware of your priorities, and consequently, to live in closer harmony with your beliefs. . . . Values are not right or wrong or true or false. They are personal preferences.[11]

[9]Allen Pincus and Anne Minhan, *Social Work Practice: Model and Method* (Itasca, Ill.: F. E. Peacock, 1973), p. 38.

[10]Robert L. Barker, ed. *The Social Work Dictionary,* 3rd ed. (Washington, D.C.: National Association of Social Workers, 1995), p. 399.

[11]Richard J. Leider, *Life Skills: Taking Charge of Your Personal and Professional Growth* (San Diego, Calif.: Pfeiffer, 1994), pp. 61, 64, 65.

In order to clarify the meaning of a value and assist you in defining your own values, we suggest three tests for determining whether something is a value. In describing or defining a value, three requirements must be met.[12]

1. **Choosing.** If something is a value, it must be a result of free choice. A value results when you choose from different things, after carefully considering what each means.
2. **Prizing.** When you value something, you are happy with it. You prize it and respect it and are proud of it. You will share your choice with others. If you are ashamed of a choice, or would not make your position known when asked, then you do not really have a value.
3. **Acting.** Finally, when you have a value, you will do something about it—it will affect your life. It will reappear on a number of occasions and will tend to become a pattern in your life.

Values are thus based on a process of choosing, prizing, and acting. Values are those aspects of our lives that are so important and pervasive that they include thoughts, feelings, and behavior.[13] If you doubt whether something is a value, ask yourself whether it is (1) prized; (2) freely and thoughtfully chosen from alternatives; and (3) acted on, repeated, and shared with others. If it is, then it is a value.

F R A M E

7

Making your values explicit can be somewhat difficult. Following are four questions that you might use to begin the process:[14]

1. Identify three people who have had the deepest impact on your life (at least one outside your immediate family). For each person, what specific advice, philosophy, or value has stuck with you?
2. List three books, tapes, movies, poems, sermons, or sayings that have contributed to your own values. For each, what insight has stuck with you?
3. List five peak experiences that have profoundly shaped your life/career direction. For each experience, what value do you think was demonstrated?
4. List as many answers as you can to the question: Why do you work (e.g., security, recognition, advancement, comfort, environment, relationships, opportunity to make a contribution, adventure, variety, money, challenge, authority to make decisions and plan work, artistic appreciation of things, competition with others, teamwork in a group with common goals, variety of assignments, creative design

[12]Sidney B. Simon, Leland W. Howe, and Howard Kirschenbaum. *Values Clarification: A Practical, Action-Directed Workbook* (New York: Warner Books, 1995), p. 9.
[13]Simon et al., *Values Clarification*, p. 10.
[14]Leider, *Life Skills*, p. 62–68.

of new programs, working on the frontiers of new knowledge)?[15] Of all the reasons you gave to why you work, which five are most important, and are they being satisfied in your current job?

Use your answers to these four questions as background to preparing a short address to a group of human service workers from a variety of practice areas who are interested in learning your values, especially what you believe constitutes a successful life and how you would describe your ideal job.

FRAME
8

ETHICS OF THE HUMAN SERVICE PROFESSIONS

We have discussed how beliefs are formed and the process of how values are formed from both an individual and a professional viewpoint.

One of the defining characteristics of a profession is that it has a code of ethics, or code of conduct, that defines the attitudes, beliefs, values, obligations, and actions that constitute right and wrong. Values are thus much broader in scope than ethics. The problems of ethics are not simply value problems, but problems of duty and obligation.

Professional organizations such as the National Association of Social Workers, the Association for Counseling and Development, the American Psychological Association, the American Medical Association, and the American Nurses Association have all developed codes of ethics that are the basis for regulating the conduct of their members. The human services encompass a range of professions, and there is as yet no nationally recognized single professional standards group for human service workers, and thus there is no single code of ethics.[16] However, there have been efforts to identify values that are basic to ethical behavior among those who are engaged in the helping professions. Among the values typically regarded as ethical in character are:[17]

1. Dignity and respect. Treat consumers with dignity and respect. Recognize and accept each consumer as a person different from all others. Do not treat consumers like second-class citizens because they cannot cope as well as you. Avoid using demeaning words such as *junky, nut case, ex-con,* or *hillbilly*. Help every consumer to the best of your ability, irrespective of their circumstances, what they did, how they look, or how they behave.

2. Self-determination. Self-determination involves letting consumers make up their own minds. For example, a person who is eligible for old-age assistance from the state and who could use the money, might, nevertheless, turn it down. This is really the individual's decision to make, regardless of what you might do if you were in her situa-

---

[15]Two excellent resources for insights about work values are: Michael Maccoby, *Why Work? Motivating the New Workforce,* 2nd ed. (Alexandria, Va.: Miles River Press, 1995), and Edgar Schein, *Career Anchors: Discovering Your Real Values* (San Diego, Calif.: Pfeiffer, 1990).

[16]Mehr, *Human Services,* 5th ed., p. 304. Mehr notes that two active human service organizations are the National Organization for Human Service Education (NOHSE) and the Council for Standards in Human Service Education (CSHSE). He says the development of these two formal organizations is of major significance in the establishment of the human services approach as a viable field of study for the helping professions.

[17]Adapted from Mehr, *Human Services,* 5th ed., pp. 304–305.

tion. Remember, however, that it is not possible for all service consumers to have total freedom in making their choices. An inmate, for example, may choose vocational training, what to eat, and recreation, but may not be allowed to choose to go home for a weekend. Thus, self-determination is the consumer's right to determine his own course of action from the opportunities and limitations presented, even if it means failure.

3. Confidentiality. Have you ever been tempted to talk or joke about a consumer with your friend or fellow workers? Most workers have done this at one time or another, but this conflicts with the value of confidentiality. Confidentiality is your guarantee to consumers that their personal situations will not be discussed in public. It also ensures consumers that they will not be the subject of social conversation or gossip. However, this does not mean that information about a consumer's case cannot be shared, such as in case conferences with other workers and a supervisor, where the objective is to help the consumer.

4. Privacy. Respect the consumer's right to privacy. Learn only what you need to know.

5. Competence. Engage only in activities at which you are competent. If consumers require services you are not trained to provide, refer them to appropriate sources or get the training and supervision you require, or both. Do not use your consumers to satisfy the needs that should be satisfied by your friends, spouses, and relatives. Continue to upgrade your skills as a lifelong process. Respect your colleagues and acknowledge what each profession has to contribute.

More recently, these basic or traditional values have been extended to include *cultural sensitivity* (e.g., designing programs and services around the needs and values of consumers), *valuing diversity* (whether of gender, color, sexual orientation, social status, economic status, religion, politics, ethnicity, etc.), and *multiculturalism* (e.g., helpers' awareness of their own cultural values and biases, helpers' understanding of the world views of their clients, and helpers' ability to use culturally appropriate intervention strategies).[18] Later chapters will further develop these and other values with particular reference to the nine roles and skills involved in delivering human services. Chapter 12 is especially relevant.

FRAME 9

The five values that are basic to ethical behavior in the human services are dignity and respect, self-determination, confidentiality, privacy, and competence. In the space provided, write in the value that is operative in each of the following descriptions. (Each value is only used once.)

_____ **1.** A worker assigned to a ward for the criminally insane seeks to understand each individual patient's situation.

---

[18]See, for example D. W. Sue, P. Arrendondo, and R. J. McDavis (1992), "Multicultural Counseling Competencies and Standards: A Call to the Profession," *Journal of Counseling and Development* 70: 477–506; Gerard Egan, *The Skilled Helper: A Problem Management Approach to Helping,* 5th ed. (Pacific Grove, Calif.: Brooks/Cole, 1994), and Robert L. Berger, James T. McBreen, and Marily J. Rifkin, *Human Behavior: A Perspective for the Helping Professions,* 4th ed. (New York: Longman, 1996).

_____ **2.** A worker believes that a consumer should change his approach to his family but gives the consumer the freedom to make his own choices.

_____ **3.** A worker who would like to tell a friend about a funny incident concerning a consumer decides to keep it to herself.

_____ **4.** A worker refers a consumer to a colleague who specializes and is trained in law, even though the consumer requested the service from the worker.

_____ **5.** A worker wants very much to ask a consumer about his religious background, but realizes it is irrelevant to the problem and does not bring it up.

Turn to Answer 12 on page 597

FRAME
10

PERSONAL VALUES AND PROFESSIONAL VALUES

Some might argue that the human services are just too diverse and too complex to say there is anything like a set of commonly held values. Gerard Egan wisely cautions that values cannot be handed to prospective helpers on a platter.[19] He notes that you need to be proactive in your search for the beliefs, values, and norms that will govern your interactions with consumers. Effective human service workers will be clear about the value system they are using to drive their delivery of human services. Yet they will also recognize that the values we say we believe in do not always coincide with our actions, and they will use this awareness as an ongoing resource to clarify what they believe.

Now that you are familiar with some of the values underpinning the ethics of the human service professions, it is important for you to spend some time trying to define your own value system in relation to the human service values. Remember that it is easy to pay lip service to these values, but it is another thing to act on them in your daily work. Also recall the three requirements for a value. For each human service value, ask yourself whether it is (1) prized; (2) freely and thoughtfully chosen from alternatives; and (3) acted on, repeated, and publicly known. In addition, you might consider the following as suggestions for integrating your personal self with your work self:

1. Be aware that you are a living system of values. This system is so much a part of you that you are, more often than not, scarcely aware of its existence.
2. Use all means possible to become conscious of what your biases are. For example, consider how you may use the word *they: They* don't support their families; *they* always wear bright colors and yell too loud; *they* can never be helped to change. A worker who becomes aware of doing this has taken the first step toward understanding her value system and seeing how it conflicts with the human service values.
3. Strive to evaluate yourself and your values objectively and rationally. Look at the origins of these values and the purposes they serve and try to think about whether they will also serve these purposes for others.

---

[19]Egan, *The Skilled Helper,* 5th ed., p. 48.

4. Finally, strive to change those values that, on the basis of your evaluation, need changing so that you may use yourself more effectively in helping others.[20]

At the beginning of this lesson we stated that human service work involves establishing relationships with other people. These relationships are formed for a purpose and are based on your ability to step outside of your own personal feelings and needs and be sensitive to the needs of others.[21] In order to accomplish this, you need to establish the kind of work identity we have been discussing in this lesson. Basically this work identity involves translating and integrating your own values, knowledge, and skills into your daily work behavior. Once you know who you are and how others perceive you and are willing to accept yourself, you will be able to make effective use of yourself in relationships with others.

F R A M E

⑪

STAGES OF CAREER DEVELOPMENT AND WORK IDENTITY

The development of a work identity is closely linked to major stages of your career.[22] We try to understand stages of personality development as background for working with consumers, such as adolescents or the elderly. It is equally important to gain insight into where you are in your career, and how your career progression (and that of others with whom you work) might affect your self-concept.

Edgar Schein, building on the work assessing career and life stages, suggests that people move through the stages of career development outlined below. He says that these stages are an internal timetable for every worker. Though we share in the possibility of moving through all the stages, some of us will spend more or less time in one stage or another, and, as we move from one career to another, we may repeat stages. Knowing where you are at any particular time, and knowing where you would like to move next, is an important part of your work identity.

Major Career Stages

Stage 1. Growth, fantasy, and exploration. In this period, usually associated with childhood and early adolescence, an occupation is a mere thought and a career has little meaning except in general terms. The person at this stage prepares to enter the necessary training or educational process for whatever occupation is tentatively chosen.

Stage 2. Education and training. Depending on the occupation, this can be a very elaborate or very minimal process lasting anywhere from a few months to 20 or more years. In some occupations, early decision making is required to en-

---

[20]Adapted from Brill, *Working with People,* 5th ed., p. 28.
[21]Pincus and Minahan. *Social Work Practice,* pp. 69–70.
[22]Edgar Schein, *Career Anchors: Discovering Your Real Values* (San Diego, Calif.: Pfeiffer, 1990). Also see Edgar Schein, *Career Dynamics: Matching Individual and Organizational Needs* (Reading, Mass.: Addison-Wesley, 1978).

sure that all the prerequisites for later entry are achieved during the period of education.

Stage 3. Entry into the world of work. For most people, entry into the world of work is a time of major adjustment as they learn about the realities of work and their own reactions (e.g., work involves logic and reason as well as working with people and their feelings). Major personal learning begins at this point. An occupational self-concept begins to take shape as the career incumbent begins to test his or her talents, motives, and values in doing real work.

Stage 4. Basic training; socialization. This stage is a major source of personal learning because the organization now begins to make demands to which the individual must respond. The length and intensity of this period differ by occupation, organization, complexity of the work, the organization's assumptions about the importance of teaching elements of the culture to new members, and the degree of responsibility society assigns to the occupation.

Stage 5. Gaining of membership. At some point, an individual recognizes through formal rituals or the kinds of assignments received that he or she has passed beyond the trainee stage and has been accepted as a full contributor. It is at this stage that a meaningful self-image as a member of the occupation or organization begins to emerge. Values, motives, talents, strengths, and weaknesses begin to be clarified through recognizing responses to different challenging situations.

Stage 6. Gaining of tenure; permanent membership. Within the first 5 to 10 years of a career, most organizations and occupations make a tenure decision that tells the individual whether she or he can count on a long-term future in the organization. Tenure is formally or symbolically granted with the proviso that tenure exists only so long as the job exists.

Stage 7. Midcareer crisis; reassessment. Although it is not clear whether this is a crisis or a stage, there is mounting evidence that most individuals go through some kind of serious reassessment of themselves when they are well into their careers. They struggle with questions such as: Have I entered the right career? Have I accomplished all I hoped to accomplish? Were my accomplishments worth the sacrifices? Should I continue what I am doing or make a change? Such reassessment can be traumatic, but many people find it leads to a rediscovery of who they are and greater awareness that they are doing more of what they really want to do with their lives.

Stage 8. Maintaining momentum, regaining it, or leveling off. The insights resulting from reassessment result in personal decisions about how the remainder of a person's career will be pursued. For some this is a determination to climb the ladder in their organization as high as possible. For others, it is a redefinition of the areas of work they wish to pursue. For many, a complex assessment is made about how to balance work, family, and personal concerns. Those whose talents force them to level off realize that their talents, motives, and values do not require them to aspire any further, but instead to develop more deeply and fully where they are.

Stage 9. Disengagement. Inevitably, a person slows down, becomes less involved, begins to think about retirement, and prepares for that stage. Some people aggressively deny the reality of retirement by avoiding the attempts of others to get them involved in such preparation.

Stage 10. Retirement. Finally, whether or not a person has prepared for it, inevitably the organization or occupation no longer makes a meaningful role available and the individual must adjust. What happens to the occupational self-image at this point is very important and depends on how the person has prepared. Some people develop second careers. For others, retirement is traumatic, resulting in loss of physical or psychological health, sometimes to the point of premature death.

Source: Edgar H. Schein. *Career Anchors: Discovering Your Real Values* (San Diego, Calif.: Pfeiffer, 1990), pp. 10–12.

F R A M E
12

Take some time to examine the present stage of your career development, to describe what you did and what you learned in prior stages, and to imagine what you would like to be doing in future stages. You can explore your descriptions and questions with a friend, a colleague, a family member, or a supervisor. You might also interview people you know who are at career stages different from yours to learn more about their experiences and how they apply to your own development (e.g., someone occupying a position or role to which you aspire).

F R A M E
13

SELF-LEADERSHIP AND WORK IDENTITY

The greatest difficulties in getting what you want in life are figuring out what you really want or who you are, and then taking the first step. Doing this is your responsibility and requires self-leadership—the capability to continually monitor how you are growing and changing and to prioritize what you want from work and life.[23]

Using self-leadership to shape your work identity requires skill in self-listening, or the ability to listen to messages from your internal voices.[24] These voices take many forms: feelings, body symptoms, intuitions, and so forth. You may feel joyous inside, or angry, hurt, and threatened. But when you suppress feelings, you in effect lose touch with yourself and may create physical distress. When you learn to unravel these messages, you gain access to tremendous energy reserves and inner sources of wisdom that can make your self-awareness, and therefore your work, much more effective. The differences between human service workers who are self-aware and have high energy and those who are not are often apparent in the things they do: how they approach new tasks, how they work with consumers, how they work in groups, how they relate informally. These outer behaviors are only the reflections of a climate that begins deep inside—your inner world of needs, beliefs, and values.

Learning to listen to your internal signals in relation to external experiences in the world of work, you develop a self-concept that includes some explicit answers to these questions:[25]

1. What are my talents, skills, and areas of competence? What are my strengths and weaknesses?
2. What are my main motives, needs, drives, and goals in life? What do I want? What do I not want, either because I have never wanted it or because I have reached a point of insight and no longer want it?

---

[23]Leider, *Life Skills*, p. 5.
[24]Dennis T. Jaffe and Cynthia D. Scott, *Take This Job and Love It* (New York: Simon & Schuster, 1988), chap. 5; and Brill, *Working with People*, 4th ed., chap. 2.
[25]Schein, *Career Anchors*, p. 17.

3. What are my values, the main criteria by which I judge what I am doing? Am I in an organization or job that is congruent with my values? How good do I feel about what I am doing? How proud or ashamed am I of my work and career?

Your work identity or self-concept cannot be mature until you have had enough occupational experience to know your talents, motives, and values. If you have many varied experiences and get meaningful feedback from each, a clear work identity will likely develop more quickly. With accumulation of work experience and feedback come clarification and insight, providing a basis for more informed career decisions. According to Schein:[26]

> The self-concept begins to function more as a guidance system and as an anchor that constrains career choices. A person begins to have a sense of what is "me" and "not me." This knowledge keeps a person on course or in a safe harbor. As people recount their career choices, they increasingly refer back to things they have strayed from or figuring out what they really want to do or finding themselves.

Five practical steps to realize the ongoing self-leadership required in shaping a work identity are:[27]

1. *Ask yourself some tough questions.* What am I trying to accomplish in the years that are left to me? How am I spending my time right now? Am I living the kind of life I want to live?

2. *Write a master dream list.* List all the things you dream of doing before you die (e.g., in personal, work, relationships, and financial areas). Let yourself go. Quantity is what is wanted. List as many of your dreams as you can recall without heeding the usual time and money limitations.

3. *Talk with a partner.* As you dream and change, there is bound to be stress on your closest relationships. It can therefore be useful to do this exercise with your partner or even to make it a family project. You might each do a list and then exchange lists. Children can create their own lists. Listen carefully to everyone's dreams. The core question is: What dreams do you need to act on to feel you have lived a life of no regrets when you reach the end?

4. *Choose four major goals for this year.* Using your master dream list as a reference, identify one personal, work, relationship, and financial goal for this year.

5. *Develop an action plan for each goal.* Identify the specific steps you need to take to accomplish each goal and the due date for each. Then go public with a few important people and let them in on your goal.

Self-leadership thus means taking charge of your life, your career, and your work identity. Effective human service workers need to know themselves and be aware of the views and needs of others. Who you are and how you respond to your work environment will be shaped by your goals, values, and beliefs. In today's rapidly changing world of work, taking charge means recognizing that the best way to predict your future is to know who you are and to create what you want.[28] This is easier said than done, but it is critical to surviving during the years ahead.

---

[26]Schein, *Career Anchors,* p. 18.
[27]Steps from Leider, *Life Skills,* pp. 141–156.
[28]Leider, *Life Skills,* p. 157.

Human Service Organizations and Work Groups

Most human services are delivered by people working in organizations. Our society is characterized by a great many organizations: banks, government agencies, private companies, social welfare agencies, social clubs, recreation groups. As a human service worker, you are likely to be in one of the many organizations that have been formed to deal with people's social and personal needs. Understanding the characteristics of organizations, especially those that are human service organizations, plays a crucial role in effective service delivery.

In organizations, the face-to-face work group is where workers typically feel the greatest affiliation. Work groups take a variety of forms in the human services. For example, there are permanent work units with a supervisor and a range of workers with different titles. There are temporary work groups, such as treatment teams and task forces formed to address some specific issue and then disbanded once the issue is resolved. Work groups are a principal means for workers to satisfy personal needs, serve consumers, and influence the organization. Understanding the important characteristics of work groups is thus essential to your success in delivering human services.

As a human service worker, you have an important set of relationships with your work group and the larger organization. These relationships are illustrated in Figure 3.2, which may be helpful to keep in mind as you work through this lesson.

Goals

To develop an understanding of the essential characteristics of human service organizations and the work groups within them. To apply this knowledge to considering concepts and skills useful for effective organization and work group membership.

Learning Activities

To accomplish these goals, we will:

1. Consider the definition and importance of organizations in our society.
2. Identify common features of human service organizations as systems.
3. Ask you to analyze your organization as a system.

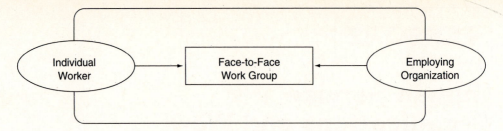

FIGURE 3.2. Relationships in Organizations [*Source:* Gordon L. Lippitt, *Organizational Renewal: A Holistic Approach to Organizational Development* (Englewood Cliffs, N.J.: Prentice-Hall, 1982), p. 197.]

4. Discuss the distinctiveness of human service organizations, including a typology based on service technologies and types of consumers.
5. Describe the characteristics of work groups in human service organizations.
6. Discuss properties of effective membership in teams.
7. Ask you to describe and evaluate your work group in terms of the characteristics we discuss.
8. Identify possible conflict areas that exist for workers within a human service organization.

FRAME

1

WHAT IS AN ORGANIZATION?[1]

Organizations are hard to see. We see aspects of an organization such as a tall building, an employee, or an advertisement—but being familiar with the whole organization can be difficult. We know organizations are there because they touch us every day. We are born in organizations and are educated in organizations so that we can later work in organizations. Organizations supply us, entertain us, govern us, and even harass us. Yet few people really understand these strange collective beasts that so influence our daily lives.

Ours has become, for better and for worse, a society of organizations. Hospitals, churches, schools, community colleges, universities, construction companies, real estate agencies, banks, grocery stores, corporate farms, moving companies, police departments, department stores, and armed services are but a few of the common examples of organizations we take for granted. Organization means collective action in pursuit of a common mission. More simply, organization means people coming together under an identifiable label (e.g., Department of Mental Health, Riverside Nursing Home) to produce some product or service. The more you know about the agency or organization in which you work, the more effectively you may be able to contribute to (1) its responsiveness to consumers and (2) its effectiveness in meeting your needs.

---

[1]Discussion points from Richard L. Daft, *Organization: Theory and Design,* 3rd ed. (St. Paul, Minn.: West Publishing, 1989), pp. 9–10; and Henry Mintzberg, *Mintzberg on Management: Inside Our Strange World of Organizations* (New York: Free Press, 1989), pp. 1–3.

UNDERSTANDING HUMAN SERVICE ORGANIZATIONS AS SYSTEMS

Although organizations have important differences, they also have certain common characteristics. For example, all organizations:

- are complex systems.
- are composed of people.
- exist for a purpose.
- perform deliberate work activities.
- have a formal structure and processes.
- have an informal structure and processes.
- produce output.
- have boundaries that identify which elements are inside the organization and which are outside.

Using the systems thinking skills we developed in Chapter 1, it is possible to connect these common features of organizations. To do this, we need three major elements: input, throughput, and output. For illustration, we will discuss these elements from the perspective of a human service organization.

The first important element of Figure 3.3 is *policy inputs.* Human service organizations have policies derived from human needs; available resources; their history; and other sources, such as requirements of federal, state, and local governments, and related bodies, such as boards of directors. Policies tell you two things about an organization. First, policies tell you what the organization is supposed to do, that is, the goals and objectives of the organization. Second, policies tell you how the organization goes about accomplishing its goals and objectives, that is, what regulations you as a member must observe in delivering services to consumers.

The second important element is *throughputs,* the mechanisms that turn policies into outputs, or results. Three organizational throughputs are important: structure and processes, people, and work activities.[2]

Organizational Throughputs

1. Organizational structure and processes. Organizational structure refers to how tasks, responsibilities, and authority are formally divided among various workers. Most organizations have what is called a "chain of command" that defines who will give orders and make decisions in each area of work activity and who will carry out the orders and decisions. The most common way to represent an organization's formal structure is by drawing an organization chart. They are composed of boxes with lines to connect them, each box representing a unit work (a position or a division). The lines between the boxes designate the lines of authority or communication connecting them, showing who is directly responsible to whom. Figure 3.4 shows the relationships among several units in a mental health clinic: accounting, intake, treatment (counsel-

---

[2]See Armand Lauffer, *Understanding Your Social Agency* (Beverly Hills: Sage, 1977); Harold W. Demone, Jr., and Dwight Harshbarger, *A Handbook of Human Service Organizations* (New York: Behavioral Publications, 1974); Yeheskel Hansenfeld and Richard A. English, eds., *Human Service Organizations* (Ann Arbor: University of Michigan Press, 1974); and Richard F. Boettcher, "The Service Delivery System: What Is It?" *Public Welfare* (Winter 1974): 45–50.

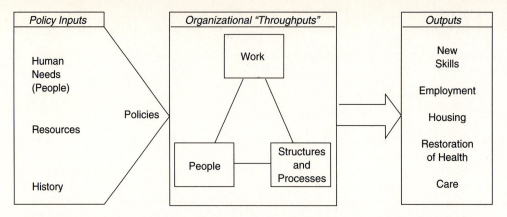

FIGURE 3.3.   Understanding Human Service Organizations as Systems [*Source:* Adapted from David A. Nadler and Michael L. Tushman, *Strategic Organization Design: Concepts, Tools, and Processes* (Glenview, Ill.: Scott, Foresman, 1988), pp. 22–32.]

ing), staff development, and research and development. This chart shows only the formal reporting relationships in the agency. It gives no information about what happens within a work unit, the roles of individuals, or interpersonal relationships.

Organizational processes are mechanisms that support service delivery. For example, construction and maintenance of adequate sites; sound fiscal systems; selecting, evaluating, and training competent staff and volunteers; securing and maintaining equipment and supplies; and designing and operating record-keeping systems. It may be difficult to realize how attention to clean offices, courteous telephone manners, an efficient interoffice mail system, timely payment of bills, preventive maintenance of office motor vehicles, and an attractive consumer waiting room have anything to do with important policy and program issues that affect hundreds and thousands of the agency's consumers.[3] But all of us have a desire for a work environment that runs smoothly and provides the necessary tools supportive of service provision.

2. People. All organizations are systems of people who interact with one another in ways that lead toward or away from accomplishment of the organization's goals. People are at the heart of a human service organization. People bring knowledge and skills to the organization and their interactions with consumers, as well as needs, preferences, and expectations. As workers, they occupy positions established within the organization, from the director to a clerk. These positions shape the people in them, in part by defining with whom the worker interacts. For example, a director may spend a lot of time interacting with agency managers, the governor, advocacy groups, and legislative committees. A counselor, however, is likely to interact more directly with human service consumers. People also shape organizations by virtue of what they bring to and how they respond to a particular setting. Since the core activities of any human service organization center on people working with people, an organization's personnel are important factors in assuring that goals are achieved in delivering services.

---

[3]Lauffer, *Understanding Your Social Agency*, p. 32.

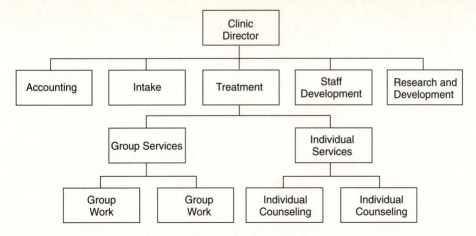

FIGURE 3.4. Example of an Organizational Chart Showing the Formal Structure of an Agency

3. Work activities. A third aspect of the throughput that converts policies into results is the actual work activities. The emphasis is on the specific work tasks that must be carried out to deliver a service. Lesson 3 of this chapter discusses work activities in more depth. Units Two, Three, and Four of this book focus on the knowledge and skills needed to perform specific work activities in delivering human services.

The last important element for understanding a human service organization as a system is *output,* or *results*. This refers to what the organization produces as a consequence of its policy inputs and throughputs. A great deal of emphasis is placed on policy inputs (e.g., human needs) and throughputs (e.g., the interactions that take place between workers and consumers) in delivering human services. But it is important not to lose sight of the results of all of these activities. For example, have consumers acquired the skills needed to parent a recently disabled child? Have they located housing and developed a means to sustain it? In terms of the larger system, desired results might be increasing the number of companies willing to provide child care and hire and train youth, the disabled, and the disadvantaged.

Human service organizations, understood as systems, are thus a means of turning policies into services that meet the needs of consumers and hopefully achieve intended results. The three elements—policy inputs, throughputs, and outputs—or results, combine to form a human service organization. They must function together for the organization to operate effectively.

F R A M E

You have just read a description of policy inputs, throughputs, and results as common features of all human service organizations understood as systems. Consider

now how these characteristics apply to the organization in which you work or to the college in which you study by answering the questions in this frame and Frames 3 and 4.

ANALYZING YOUR ORGANIZATION AS A SYSTEM: ORGANIZATIONAL POLICY

What are some of the goals of your organization? What is your organization trying to accomplish? Can you list four goals of your organization? If you are using an educational institution as the organization, consider going to the registrar's office and getting policies covering the admissions process (similar to the intake process of a human service agency). Or you might call the president's office or the budget office and ask for a copy of the college's three- to five-year plan, annual report, or other document that might contain statements of goals or policies.

Examples of Organization Goals

1.

2.

3.

4.

Your organization may have long-range as well as immediate goals. For example, a mental health agency may have an immediate goal of locating and providing help to seriously emotionally disturbed children who would otherwise be unassisted. It may also have a long-range goal to help as many seriously mentally ill persons (adults and children) as possible to become self-supporting and able to care for themselves in the community. Understanding your organization's goals will help to clarify why you perform certain tasks and how these tasks might affect consumers and the community. If you lose sight of the reasons for performing tasks, they will simply become routine chores with little meaning for you or the consumer.

Now take one of the goals you listed above and describe how that goal is accomplished. What program do you have in your agency to accomplish the goal (e.g., Food Stamp program, nutrition education program, income assistance program, program of outreach services to the homeless mentally ill, congregate feeding, meals on wheels, language classes, and teen peer sex information)? Who does the program serve? What specific services can a consumer receive in that program?

> The organization goal:
>
>
>
> The program to accomplish the goal:
>
>

Remember: Regulations that say who can or cannot be served by a given program and what services can or cannot be provided are all part of agency policy that you must observe in delivering services to consumers.

FRAME
3

ANALYZING YOUR ORGANIZATION AS A SYSTEM: ELEMENTS OF THROUGHPUT

1. Organization structure and processes. What is the chain of command in your organization or college? Ask for a copy of the organizational chart. What are the job titles of the senior management team? Is there a board of directors or one or more advisory boards? How is work divided in the organization—do people work in different offices that focus on different programs? How are decisions made about who does what work in the organization? Do all staff members share in the decision-making process?

> In the space below, describe a specific work or learning assignment you have been given. Tell how the decision was made that you would be responsible for that assignment, the extent to which you shared in making that decision, and how communication went up and down the chain of command relative to that assignment.
>
>
>
>
>

It is important to understand the chain of command in your organization, since through it work is defined and decisions are made as to who does what. Obviously, at higher levels in the chain of command a greater degree of administrative discretion exists in how any given work assignment will be accomplished. The better you understand the chain of command and the more you can participate in the decision-making process, the greater your contribution can be to your organization and to your consumers. Perhaps the lesson from all of this is to ask at least three questions when engaging in a work assignment: How will this contribute to the goals and objectives of the organization? How will this help serve the consumers of the organization? How did I receive this assignment and to whom am I accountable for the results?

2. People. What are the different kinds of workers in your organization (e.g., administrators, physicians, psychologists, social workers, professors, instructors, human service counselors, administrative assistants, clerks, accountants, aides, and activities directors)? What are their responsibilities? Do they serve different types of consumers?

In the space below, list three different kinds of workers in your organization and briefly describe what they do. Be sure to indicate what kind of direct involvement they have with human service consumers or the types of consumers with whom they interact.

WORKERS   **WHAT THEY DO (E.G., INVOLVEMENT WITH CONSUMERS)**

1.

2.

3.

In understanding how your organization functions, it is important to know the different kinds of personnel who work in the organization and how they contribute to its goals and objectives. As you better understand the roles and responsibilities of your coworkers, you come to a better understanding of the organization of which you are a part.

3. Work activities. What are some examples of specific work activities performed by two different workers in this organization? What do they do in a typical work week? What do they spend most of their time doing? Ask to see a job description. Also talk with them to compare what they actually do with what is stated in their job description. In describing these work activities, include the workers' perspectives on the consumers they serve. (Use a separate sheet of paper if you need more room.) Remember that the only reason for your human service organization to exist is to provide services to the consumer. In the rush of everyday work, particularly when you get bogged down in meetings and paperwork, it is easy to lose sight of this simple but critical fact.

ACTIVITIES OF WORKER A   **ACTIVITIES OF WORKER B**

ANALYZING YOUR ORGANIZATION AS A SYSTEM: OUTPUTS OR RESULTS

What are some examples of results your organization has achieved in the past two or three years? How many consumers has it served? How many students graduated? What kinds of things happened as a result of these services? Are there any reports describing consumer outcomes? How many students went on to higher education? Identify five results for consumers that your organization achieved during the past year (e.g., provided meals to 400 elderly poor five days a week in three sites during a 12-month period). You might also identify five results the organization achieved that better enabled it to support its service delivery (e.g., more timely receipt of funds as a consequence of purchasing computers to automate accounting records, higher levels of worker and consumer satisfaction as a result of redecorating the waiting room or office areas, and fewer record-keeping errors as a result of three training seminars).

	Examples of *Consumer Outcomes*	*Examples of* *Outcomes Supporting Service Delivery*
1.		
2.		
3.		
4.		
5.		

THE DISTINCTIVENESS OF HUMAN SERVICE ORGANIZATIONS

You have just completed several exercises designed to help you better understand the organization in which you work or may work in the future. However, you may have noticed that the characteristics of human service organizations as systems could be applied to virtually any organization. What is it, then, that makes human service organizations unique? To answer this question, let us look again at the following characteristics of how systems operate:

The nature of the system process distinguishes human service organizations from organizations such as factories, banks, or retail stores. At least six characteristics distinguish human service organizations from these other organizations:[4]

1. The "raw materials," or inputs, to a human service organization are people who come to the organization with their unique qualities and capabilities. Thus, what is done "with" consumers must be tailored to meet their needs within the capabilities of the funds made available by taxpayers and donors.

2. The goals of human service organizations are sometimes ambiguous because it is difficult to achieve desirable outcomes for all the needs of consumers.

3. The ambiguity that surrounds human services means that human service organizations operate in a turbulent environment composed of many diverse interest groups (community leaders, legislators, taxpayers, and consumer groups).

4. Human service organizations operate with helping techniques (the throughput phase of the process) that do not provide complete knowledge about how to achieve desired outcomes. This is because consumers (inputs) are complex systems and extremely variable, and our knowledge about how they function is incomplete.

5. The core activities of human service organizations consist of relationships between staff and consumers. Thus the critical determinant of the success of the organization is the quality of these relationships. Yet these relationships are difficult to monitor and control because they are affected by so many different factors, including the personal attributes of staff and consumers.

6. Human service organizations do not have a sufficient number of reliable and valid measures of effectiveness (outputs). This is the result of problems in the ambiguous nature of goals, the service technologies, and the influence of human attributes.

Simply stated, the inputs of human service organizations are people with problems. They enter a human service organization that is under pressure from many forces (often contradictory) that seek to shape its goals. Consumers bring attributes to the service situation (behaviors, beliefs, etc.) that are difficult to measure accurately. They are served by a diverse staff that uses helping technologies (methods of service) that are often nonspecific in order to produce service outcomes that are difficult to measure. While this description may sound overwhelming, its intent is to make you aware of the unusual complexities that make human service organizations unique. In contrast, at General Motors, materials such as steel and plastics are processed through a standardized set of operations to produce a car that either does or does not conform to a standard set of measures. Subsequently, specific measures (e.g., sales figures and repair records) will indicate whether the product is acceptable. Human service organizations do not have such standardized, consistent, or predictable methods of operating or measuring results.

---

[4]Yeheskel Hasenfeld, *Human Service Organizations* (Englewood Cliffs, N.J.: Prentice-Hall, 1983), pp. 9–11.

THROUGHPUT AND HUMAN SERVICE ORGANIZATIONS

Throughput is a particularly critical component of the system process, since it involves what workers do for or with consumers. In this section we examine a way to classify the various functions of human service organizations according to the nature of the throughput.

Hasenfeld classifies the nature of the service technologies utilized by human service organizations into three major categories: people processing, people sustaining, and people changing.[5]

1. People-processing technologies. One of the things that we do with consumers in the human services is to certify them as eligible for one form of service or another. This involves conferring on them a classification or status—for example, "permanently and totally disabled," "chronically mentally ill," "abused child," or "developmentally disabled." By means of these classifications, human service personnel link consumers with appropriate services. Dealing with consumers in a people-processing manner does not alter or change consumer behaviors.

2. People-sustaining technologies. These technologies attempt to prevent, maintain, or retard the deterioration of consumers who are suffering problems. They are not aimed at changing the personal attributes of consumers. They would include, for example, income maintenance programs and nursing home care.

3. People-changing technologies. These technologies attempt to alter the personal attributes or behaviors of consumers in order to improve their well-being. They would include, for example, training programs, counseling, and therapy.

Obviously these categories are not always clear-cut and mutually exclusive. For example, a program may involve income maintenance (people sustaining) and job training (people changing) simultaneously. However, if the primary goal of a program is maintenance, it would usually be categorized as a people-sustaining program.

A Typology of Human Service Organizations

Type of Consumer	People Processing	People Sustaining	People Changing
	Type I	*Type III*	*Type V*
Normal functioning	College admissions office Credit rating bureau	Social Security Retirement home	Public school YMCA
Malfunctioning	Juvenile court Diagnostic clinic	Public assistance Nursing home	Hospital Residential treatment center

Consumers can also be categorized in terms of certain attributes. As you may recall from Chapter 2, consumers can be assessed in reference to their "level of functioning." If we consider that there is a point, though it may be debatable as to precisely where it

---

[5]Hasenfeld, *Human Service Organizations,* p. 5.
[6]Hasenfeld, *Human Service Organizations,* p. 6.

falls, that distinguishes relatively normal functioning from malfunctioning, then we have a mechanism for dividing consumers into one of these two categories. Thus it can be said that human service organizations serve both normal functioning consumers and consumers with serious problems through services that are people processing, people sustaining, or people changing. We can use these three categories to classify consumers and services into a typology of human service organizations (see page 163).[6]

In looking at the typology of human service organizations in the table above, you should note that some organizations may reflect more than one "type," depending on the nature of services they offer. For example, a community mental health center may have a diagnostic unit (Type II), operate an apartment facility for the elderly (Type IV), and have a residential treatment program for the acutely mentally ill (Type VI).

FRAME
6

DEVELOPING YOUR OWN TYPOLOGY

Using the organization or sections in which you work or one with which you are familiar, or by otherwise gaining information about one, analyze each program offered by the organization in reference to the category of services provided (e.g., people processing, people sustaining, and people changing) and to the nature of the consumer served (e.g., normal functioning or malfunctioning). Identify the program "type" (Type I to Type VI). Write a brief description of each program, explaining your reason for categorizing each program as you did.

FRAME
7

WORK GROUPS IN HUMAN SERVICE ORGANIZATIONS

In the world of human services, workers spend much time in groups. Indeed, the basic building block of an organization is the face-to-face work group, typically consisting of the supervisor and those individuals immediately responsible to him or her. There are two ways to think about and to experience groups in organizations. One is the *organizational view,* which pictures the organization as systems of many overlapping, or interlocking, groups. The second is the *single group view,* which focuses on what happens inside a particular work group. Our interest in the next few frames is to use these two perspectives to understand some important characteristics of work groups, especially how to contribute to making them effective. Our discussion focuses on task groups composed of workers inside the human service organization. We are specifically concerned with how the workers interact with one another, as opposed to how the workers may interact with consumers. The numerous relationships formed between workers and consumers, individually and in groups, require specialized helping skills that are addressed later in this book (Units Two and Three).

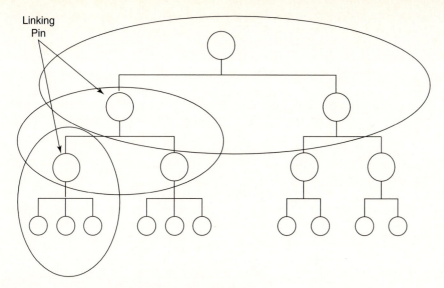

Linking
Pin

FIGURE 3.5.   Overlapping Work Groups in Organizations

Organizational View of Groups

Organizations of all sizes can be viewed as systems of small groups. More specifically, organizations are systems of *overlapping,* or *interlocking, groups* as indicated in Figure 3.5. These groups are connected by linking pins—individuals who occupy membership in two groups—as a subordinate in one group and a supervisor in the other. People are also usually members of an informal group, such as the carpool or coffee-break group. Groups link the parts of the organization. In this scheme, management personnel are often the key links because of their multiple group responsibilities and involvements. But in human service organizations, and increasingly in others, all workers are viewed as "links" because consumers' problems seldom fit neatly into organizational boxes. That is, at least in the ideal case, workers at many levels and across many programs link with one another in the process in delivering human services.[7] Thus a key reality in organizations is that individuals function as members of groups or teams. Sometimes the team consists of members of a work unit who report to a single supervisor (as shown in Figure 3.5). Other times the team consists of workers from different work units who form task groups to address specific organizational issues.

Looking Inside a Single Work Group

A second, and perhaps more familiar, perspective is people's behavior toward one another within particular work groups. Since World War II, behavioral scientists have conducted significant research in an effort to understand the hows and whys of group

---

[7]Gordon L. Lippitt, *Organizational Renewal: A Holistic Approach to Organizational Development* (Englewood Cliffs, N.J.: Prentice-Hall, 1982), pp. 196–197.

phenomena. The result is that we now know a great deal about group forces and processes:

1. Successful group outcomes depend on the members' ability to exchange ideas freely and clearly and to feel involved in the decisions and the processes of the group.
2. A collection of capable individuals does not always produce a capable group. Mature adults often form an immature working team, unless they take explicit steps to prevent this.
3. Using appropriate procedures, groups can become more productive, channel energies into effective work, and eliminate or replace internal conflicts that block progress.
4. A group's ability to function properly is not necessarily dependent on the leader. No group can become fully productive until its members are willing to assume responsibility for the way the group acts.[8]

FRAME 8

Select a human service organization with which you are familiar or one about which you would like more information. Get a copy of an organizational chart for either the whole organization or some division. Indicate the overlapping or interlocking groups in the organization as well as some of the "linking pin" positions, using Figure 3.5 as your guide.

Next, select one work group in the organization. For that work group, identify the supervisor by job title and the job titles of all the workers reporting to the supervisor. Then find out how often they meet as a group and what they discuss, whether they have group objectives, and how they make decisions. Also inquire about what responsibilities individual workers have to make the group function effectively.

FRAME 9

CHARACTERISTICS OF EFFECTIVE TEAMS

Not all groups can be characterized as teams. Teamwork is manifested in the way a group is able to solve its problems. As described by William Dyer:[9]

Teams are collections of people who must rely on group collaboration if each member is to experience the optimum of success and goal achievement. It is obvious that in order to score touchdowns and prevent the opponent from scoring, a football team has to play together. It should be just as obvious that a work unit or a special task group must also work together to ensure success. A football team practices over and over again how it will execute its plays. The team has "skull" practice, when they talk over plans and strategies. They review films of past games, identify mistakes, set up goals for the next week.

---

[8]Lippitt, *Organizational Renewal,* p. 199.
[9]William G. Dyer, *Team Building: Issues and Alternatives,* 2d ed. (Reading, Mass.: Addison-Wesley, 1995), p. 7.

What are some of the characteristics of teamwork? What makes a team effective in accomplishing its goals and also satisfying the personal and interpersonal needs of its members? A good team is likely to be characterized by the following conditions:[10]

1. **Informality.** The atmosphere tends to be relaxed, comfortable, and informal.
2. **Clear purpose.** The group's task is well understood and accepted by the members.
3. **Listening.** The members listen well to one another; there is a lot of task-relevant discussion in which most members participate.
4. **Open communications.** People express both their feelings and their ideas.
5. **Civilized disagreement.** Conflict and disagreement are present but centered on ideas and methods, not personalities and people.
6. **Self-assessment.** The group is self-conscious about its own operation.
7. **Consensus decision making.** Decisions are usually based on substantial agreement through thorough discussion, not majority vote.
8. **Clear roles.** When actions are decided on, clear assignments are made and accepted by the members.
9. **Style diversity.** The members have a broad range of group process and task skills.
10. **Shared leadership.** While there is a formal leader, everyone shares responsibility for task, process, and results.
11. **External relations.** Members pay attention to developing outside relationships and resources.

When these conditions are met, it is likely that the team is successfully accomplishing its mission and satisfying its members' needs.

Participating Effectively as a Team Member

Teamwork depends as much on the behavior and contribution of each member as it does on the skill of the leader. But leadership need not reside in one person. In a highly effective group, many functions are performed by both the leader and the members, depending on the situation or the requirements of the moment. For example, the leader and members establish and maintain an atmosphere and relationships that enable the communication, influence, and decision-making processes of the group to be performed effectively. This means creating positive conditions, such as a supportive atmosphere, and eliminating any negative or blocking factors. Groups sometimes have to deal with members who are insensitive or hostile, who talk too much, or who otherwise behave in ways that adversely affect the group's capacity to function. In a highly effective group, members handle these situations by making the troublesome members aware of the problem, but in a sensitive and considerate manner that assists the whole group.[11] There is considerable evidence that group leadership roles are best performed when they are shared. Group leadership is sometimes described in terms of task leadership and social leadership: Task leadership helps the

---

[10]Douglas McGregor, *The Human Side of Enterprise* (New York: McGraw-Hill, 1960), pp. 232–235; and Wendell L. French and Cecil H. Bell, Jr., *Organization Development,* 5th ed. (Englewood Cliffs, N.J.: Prentice-Hall, 1995), p. 170.

[11]Rensis Likert, "The Nature of Highly Effective Groups," in David A. Kolb, Irwin M. Rubin, and James M. McIntyre, *Organizational Psychology: Readings on Human Behavior in Organizations,* 4th ed. (Englewood Cliffs, N.J.: Prentice-Hall, 1984), p. 161.

group to examine content issues, while social leadership attends to how the group does its work and maintains its relationships.

There are three areas in which a member of a work group can contribute to the team's effectiveness: process, content, and feelings. These are the three levels at which groups work—simultaneously.[12]

1. Process. Groups operate according to certain procedures that may be either consciously determined or derived through happenstance. For example, groups may arrange themselves in open circles or sit around long, narrow conference tables. Groups may have a formal agenda and a sequence for moving through it. Some groups will carefully consider the contributions of even the least active group members; others may attend only to the more vocal or more influential. Some groups evaluate happenings in their sessions; others deal openly with conflict; and others smooth it over or repress it.

2. Content. When a group addresses the "stated agenda," it is engaging in the content of the work. Solving work problems, making decisions, and learning through discussion are all part of the substantive life of a group. Explicit processes are designed to assist groups in moving through their agendas. However, even in the most focused of groups, there are side trips, humorous interjections, and numerous other events that ostensibly take the group away from its content issues. All of these behaviors can be important for a well-balanced, effective group.

3. Feelings. We all have feelings that influence our behavior and how we relate to others. How members feel about one another as well as about the formal leader of the group can enhance or detract from both the content and the process. Some groups focus so much on feelings that they are unable to attend to the content of their work; others are too "product-oriented" and do not admit that feelings exist. Effective groups are able to surface and admit their feelings and deal with them realistically.

FRAME
10

EVALUATING YOUR TEAM

Select a team or work unit with which you are familiar, preferably as a participating member. Use the following questionnaire to explore some of the key characteristics of the group.[13] Circle the number of the one response that best expresses the conditions you experience or observe in the team.

1. To what extent do I feel a real part of the team?

1	2	3	4	5
Completely a part all the time.	A part most of the time.	On the edge, sometimes in, sometimes out.	Generally outside, except for one or two short periods.	On the outside, not really a part of the team.

---

[12]Neely Gardner, *Group Leadership* (Washington, D.C.: National Training and Development Service Press, 1974), pp. 6–7.
[13]William G. Dyer, *Team Building: Issues and Alternatives,* 3rd ed. (Reading, Mass.: Addison-Wesley, 1995), pp. 96–99. Reprinted with permission.

2. How safe is it in this team to be at ease, relaxed, and myself?

1	2	3	4	5
I feel perfectly safe to be myself.	I feel most people would accept me, but there are some I'm not sure about.	Generally, you have to be careful what you say or do in this team.	I am quite fearful about being completely myself in this team.	A person would be a fool to be himself in this team.

3. To what extent do I feel "under wraps," that is, have private thoughts, unspoken reservations, or unexpressed feelings and opinions that I have not felt comfortable bringing out in the open?

1	2	3	4	5
Almost completely under wraps.	Under wraps many times.	Slightly more free and expressive than under wraps.	Quite free and expressive much of the time.	Almost completely free and expressive.

4. How effective is our team at getting out and using the ideas, opinions, and information of all team members in making the decisions?

1	2	3	4	5
We don't really encourage everyone to share his or her ideas, opinions, and information with the team in making decisions.	Only the ideas, opinions, and information of a few members are really known and used in making decisions.	Sometimes we hear the views of most members before making decisions, and sometimes we disregard most members.	A few are sometimes hesitant about sharing their opinions, but we generally have good participation in making decisions.	Everyone feels his or her ideas, opinions, and information are given a fair hearing before decisions are made.

5. To what extent are the goals the team is working toward understood and to what extent do they have meaning for you?

1	2	3	4	5
I feel extremely good about the goals of our team.	I feel fairly good, but some things are not too clear or meaningful.	A few things we are doing are clear and meaningful.	Much of the activity is not clear or meaningful to me.	I really do not understand or feel involved in the goals of the team.

6. How well does the team work at its tasks?

1	2	3	4	5
Coasts, loafs, makes no progress.	Makes a little progress, but most members loaf.	Progress is slow, spurts of effective work.	Above average in progress and pace of work.	Works well, achieves definite progress.

7. Our planning and the way we operate as a team are largely influenced by:

1	2	3	4	5
One or two team members.	A clique.	Shifts from one person or clique to another.	Shared by most of the members, some left out.	Shared by all members.

8. What is the level of responsibility for work in our team?

1	2	3	4	5
Nobody (except perhaps one) really assumes responsibility for getting work done.	Only a few assume responsibility for getting work done.	About half assume responsibility.	A majority of the members assume responsibility for getting work done.	Each person assumes responsibility for getting work done.

9. How are differences or conflicts handled in our team?

1	2	3	4	5
Differences or conflicts are denied, suppressed, or avoided at all cost.	Differences or conflicts are recognized but remain unresolved mostly.	Differences or conflicts are recognized, and some attempts are made to work them through by some members, often outside the team meetings.	Difference and conflicts are recognized, and some attempts are made to deal with them in our team.	Differences and conflicts are recognized, and the team usually works them through satisfactorily

10. How do people relate to the team leader, chairperson, or "boss"?

1	2	3	4	5
The leader dominates the team, and people are often fearful or passive.	The leader tends to control the team, although people generally agree with the leader's direction.	There is some give and take between the leader and the team members.	Team members relate easily to the leader and usually are able to influence the leader's decisions.	Team members respect the leader, but they work together as a unified team with everyone participating and no one dominant.

11. What is one thing you would like to do to improve the functioning of your team?

RESPONSIBILITIES AND CONFLICTS IN ORGANIZATIONS

To be a member of a work group or an organization is to be a citizen in that community.[14] The basis of this relationship is minimally the economic contract between the employer and the employee. This contract defines the responsibilities of both parties to each other. But there is more to it than that. Organizations today are complex communities that can be healthy or unhealthy, successful or unsuccessful, in part as a function of how well their members are able to work individually and together toward desired results.

One of the essential properties of living in an organization is conflict. For example, some of the resources of human service organizations are used to meet consumer needs, while others operate to keep the organization going. Sometimes these two needs can work against each other and result in a conflict, which is soon felt by the workers and even the consumers of the organization.[15] For example, some human service organizations are known to place more emphasis on procedures, methods, and record-keeping activities (which help maintain the organization) as opposed to emphasizing the services and needs of consumers (which are represented as goals of the organization). In these cases, it is important to understand that these organizations are not purposely withholding services from consumers; rather, they structure themselves so that it becomes difficult to change, and conflicts soon develop.

As a worker in a human service organization, you need to recognize that there will be conflicts and tensions in your organization. For example, at times you may discover that rules are emphasized to such an extent that the purposes for which the rules were formulated have been forgotten. Or you may find that your desires for promotion, status, and security do not agree with those of the organization. Whether the organizational conflicts relate to consumers, to you, or to both, it is important that you not become too frustrated. On the other hand, you should also realize that sometimes rules in the organization that do not seem to make good sense to you do serve a purpose. For example, rules related to working hours, punctuality, and so forth, may carry a personal implication to you that the organization does not trust you. However, within a large organization that employs hundreds of workers, enforcement of such rules is often necessary if the organization is to maintain control of itself and function efficiently. Remember that these problems exist to some degree in all organizations. Solving problems requires that you stay in the organization and engage in the ongoing but difficult process of seeking necessary changes.

It is always well to keep in mind that all organizations must spend part of their resources simply to keep the organization going. When an organization loses sight of its goals and objectives, it is in trouble. It is also well to remember that rules and regulations are the laws by which organizations operate. They are necessary if the organization is to maintain control of itself. However, when the organization be-

---

[14]Daniel Katz in Karen M. Hult and Charles Walcott, *Governing Public Organizations: Politics, Structures, and Institutional Design* (Pacific Grove, Calif.: Brooks/Cole, 1990), p. 121.
[15]Bernard Gelfand, *The Window: Toward an Understanding of Human Need* (Toronto: Training and Staff Development Branch, Ministry of Community and Social Services, undated), pp. 82–83.

comes overly rigid, both the consumer and the worker suffer. As a member of a human service organization, it is your responsibility to abide by the rules of the organization, but it is *also* your responsibility to offer the constructive criticism needed to help the organization modify its goals and objectives in order to improve services to consumers and create a healthy work environment.

FRAME 12

Given some of the problems that naturally occur in organizations, answer the following questions from the perspective of a worker attempting to serve both the organization and the consumer. If you do not have any experience in human service organization, consult with others in order to gain insight into the questions below.

1. What kinds of activities do you engage in that do not appear to be directed toward meeting consumer needs? Can you think of ways in which these activities could help meet consumer needs?
2. What kinds of rules and regulations exist in your agency that personally frustrate you or your career goals? What do you think you, as a worker, could do to change these rules and regulations?

FRAME 13

THE CHANGING CONTRACT BETWEEN EMPLOYEES AND ORGANIZATIONS

Today and likely into the future, the relationship between individuals and their employing organizations is undergoing extraordinary change.

> People are losing their jobs more frequently, questioning their careers, redefining their identities, consolidating their debts, expanding their options, and shifting their loyalties. Organizations are laying off, doing more with fewer employees, building self-directed work teams, and buying services from a growing contingent: a part-time workforce. . . . The old foundation is gone. . . . Loyalty to the organization no longer guarantees job security. . . . (We need) a new social contract: that we are self-employed inside and outside of organizations.[16]

Can you describe examples of human service organizations undergoing rapid changes in the way services are delivered? What have been some effects on the relationships among the human service employees, their supervisors, and the consumers?

When rapid organizational change is combined with the reforms proposed or under way in many human service policy areas, and with changes brought about by information technology, the organizational setting is likely to become more rather than less conflicted. It will be important, under these circumstances, to take a self-directed approach to the interface between your future and that of your organization (how they connect, how they differ). The exercises throughout this text (see especially Chapters 11 and 12) are possible steps in this direction.

---

[16]Cliff Hakim, *We Are All Self-Employed* (San Francisco, Calif.: Berrett-Koehler, 1994), pp. ix, xii.

LESSON 3

The Work Perspective: Human Services as Jobs, Roles, and Process

In addition to understanding your work setting and developing a positive work identity, it is necessary to have a clear understanding of the work itself, of the things that workers do in the human services. Although human service work is carried out in a variety of settings with a wide range of people, it is important to recognize that there is a common foundation of knowledge, attitudes, and skills that defines the nature of all human service work. To assist in the development of your understanding of the nature and meaning of human service work, this lesson defines what human service workers do to achieve the purposes and goals of their organizations.

Goal

To develop an understanding of the nature and meaning of human service work.

Learning Activities

To accomplish these goals, we will:

1. Review some of the reasons why work is important in our society.
2. Identify some of the worker needs that jobs fulfill.
3. Examine the components of work.
4. Identify the general purposes of human service work.
5. Recognize some of the major roles and activities involved in delivering human services.
6. Explain delivering human services as an ongoing and systematic problem-solving process.

FRAME
1

THE FUNCTIONS OF WORK

When most people are asked, "Why do you work?" their first response is usually, "To earn a living." Yet, earning money for the purchase of goods and services is only one of the functions of work. To fully appreciate the meaning of work in our society, we need to examine some of the other functions accomplished by working.[1]

1. Work regulates activities. The pattern of work activity during the day, the week, and the month affects not only the activities of workers while employed on the job but also their participation in nonwork activities. In addition, the patterns of activity of the workers' families are affected. For example, the family life of a worker on the night shift in a prison is obviously affected in a different way from the family life of a worker on a regular eight-to-five shift.

2. Work provides the opportunity for relationships with others. The personal relationships between a worker and others who occupy related positions in an organization will frequently continue into nonwork activities. Thus, a person's friends and companions off the job are frequently his or her associates at work.

3. Work provides identity. Work provides one of the main answers to the question "Who am I?" Some possible responses are, "I am a mental health technician," "I am a correctional guard," and "I am a welfare worker." Of course other things go into making up a person's identity, but the work a person does is one of the chief components.

4. Work provides a means of human development. Work contributes to human development by helping people express themselves and giving them the opportunity to learn and demonstrate new skills. Work also helps satisfy people's social and psychological needs and provides much of the content and meaning in life.

Considering these functions of work, we might define *work as the effort or activity of an individual, performed for the purpose of providing goods and services of value to others; it is also considered to be work by the individual so involved.*[2] Work is purposeful and sustained action. In today's society, work takes many forms, ranging from agricultural work to sales, teaching, assembly-line work, child rearing, counseling, and management.

The nature and place of work has a long history. In preindustrial society, most work was done on the farm or in the cottage. In industrial society, work is done in large-scale central plants and office buildings, where major power sources can be tapped and where supervisors can observe employees and exercise control over work actions. New forms of work are also emerging. For example, some corporations distribute their workforce over satellite work centers throughout a geographical area. Some people work at home on computers connected to other computers; their homes have become electronic cottages.[3] Still other people are concerned with the design of work in space stations.[4] All of which is to suggest that work is a central function in human life.

---

[1]Adapted from Walter L. Slocum, *Occupational Careers: A Sociological Perspective,* 2nd ed. (Chicago, Aldine, 1974), pp. 19–21.

[2]Richard H. Hall, *Dimensions of Work* (Beverly Hills: Sage, 1986), p. 13.

[3]Paragraph to this point from Martin Morf, *The Work-Life Dichotomy: Prospects for Reintegrating People and Jobs* (New York: Quorum Books, 1989), p. 23.

[4]See, for example, Claudia Bird Schoonhoven, "Sociotechnical Considerations for the Development of the Space Station: Autonomy and the Human Element in Space," *Journal of Applied Behavioral Science,* 22, 3 (1986): 271–286.

F R A M E
2

THE JOB: SATISFYING OR DISAPPOINTING?[5]

Jobs are positions in particular workplaces such as agencies, hospitals, and institutions. An important factor to consider in any job is whether you, as the worker, will find the job satisfying or disappointing. In other words, does your job really satisfy your needs? Examples of needs that can be satisfied by a person's job include:

1. Economic security satisfies the need for income and adequate standard of living.
2. Recognition and approval satisfy the need to have one's work activities known and approved by others.
3. Mastery and achievement satisfy the need to perform well according to one's own standards and abilities.
4. Dominance satisfies the need to have some power or influence and control over things or people.
5. Socioeconomic status satisfies the need to have money and material goods that measure up to community standards.
6. Self-expression satisfies the need for personal behavior to be consistent with one's self-concept.
7. Affection and interpersonal relationships satisfy the need to feel accepted by other people.
8. A moral values scheme satisfies the need to have one's behavior be consistent with some moral code in order to feel good and worthy.
9. Dependence satisfies the need to be directed by others, to avoid feeling alone and totally responsible for one's own behavior.
10. Creativity and challenge satisfy the need to meet and attempt to solve new problems.
11. Social well-being satisfies the need to help others and to have one's efforts result in benefits to others.
12. Independence satisfies the need to direct one's own behavior rather than be completely controlled by others.

Obviously, any job has both positive and negative aspects. For example, in any one job, a worker may experience friendship, a sense of accomplishment, pleasure, frustration, nervous strain, and boredom. The key to a general feeling of job satisfaction is the extent to which the job adequately meets the individual's needs. A worker who is generally satisfied with a job will be able to manage both the positive and the negative aspects of daily work situations.

F R A M E
3

We have just discussed examples of needs that may be met in various jobs. What is most important to your own job satisfaction? What factors cause you to be dissatisfied with a job? You may find it helpful to discuss your perspectives with your fellow students, workers, and so forth.

---

[5]Adapted from Robert L. Darcy and Philip E. Powell, *Manpower and Economic Education: A Personal and Social Approach to Career Education* (Denver: Love Publishing, 1973), pp. 30–35.

FRAME

4

Underline the correct response in each statement below:

1. When correctional guards exert influence by preventing inmates from breaking a prison regulation, they fulfill their own need for (dependence/dominance).
2. When social workers feel satisfied after helping a client with a family problem, they are fulfilling the need for (social well-being/economic security).
3. When a new employee successfully completes a training program, the needs of (creativity and challenge/affection and happiness) are fulfilled.

Turn to Answer 13 on page 598

FRAME

5

THE COMPONENTS OF WORK

Work is an activity that produces something of value for other people. It may involve physical activity (e.g., typing, driving, and cooking) or mental activity (e.g., reading, thinking, and listening).[6] However, an activity must always have a specified purpose if it is to be considered work. Consequently, a homemaker caring for her children is working because she is being productive for her family and has a specified purpose in raising her children a certain way. Writing a report regarding a particular consumer represents productive work for both the consumer and the organization and has a particular purpose related to services for the consumer. Performing voluntary tasks in a hospital represents productive work for the community and the hospital residents and has the purpose of assisting the hospital staff and residents. Therefore, paid or not, voluntary or required, hard or easy, *work is always an effort with a specific purpose that produces something of value for other people.*

What are the components of work activity? What are you actually doing when you are working? In performing the activities that are part of their jobs, workers act in relation to three primary components of work activity—data, people, and things.[7] No matter where a person works or what she or he actually does, any job at some time will involve the worker with information and ideas (*data*), with other workers and consumers (*people*), and with machines, equipment, or supplies (*things*). Obviously there are an infinite number of combinations of data, people, and things in any given job, but all are necessary components of work activity in any organization.

FRAME

6

We have said that the three components of work activity are data, people, and things. In the blank beside each of the statements below, write in the name of the work component being described.

---

[6]Report of a special task force to the Secretary of Health, Education and Welfare, *Work in America* (Cambridge, Mass.: MIT Press, 1973), p. 3.
[7]Sidney A. Fine and Wretha W. Wiley, *An Introduction to Functional Job Analysis: A Scaling of Selected Tasks from the Social Welfare Field* (Kalamazoo, Mich.: W. E. Upjohn Institute for Employment Research, 1971).

_____ a. This work component involves the worker with other workers and consumers.

_____ b. This work component involves the worker with information and ideas.

____ c. This work component involves the worker with machines and equipment.

Turn to Answer 14 on page 598

F R A M E

7

THE GENERAL PURPOSES OF HUMAN SERVICE WORK

Human service work focuses on the interactions between people and the systems in their environment in an effort to help them solve their problems.[8] Human service work involves a vast range of activities related to data, people, and things, which are performed to produce something of value for others. Since human service work requires constant interactions with people, it is important to recognize that it requires unique mental and emotional involvement. Human service work usually involves problem solving with consumers and fulfilling basic human needs. A great deal of effort is required in planning the strategies to resolve the problems.

You will recall that one of the major characteristics of any work activity is that there is a specified purpose. To understand the nature and meaning of human service work, it is useful to consider its general purpose. All the activities performed by human service workers are designed, according to Pincus and Minahan, to achieve one or more of the following purposes:[9]

1. To provide material resources. Many activities in the human services are performed in order to provide people with the resources and services they need in order to survive. Tasks related to providing financial assistance, food, homemaker services, and foster home placements are all examples of activities performed to provide people with necessary material resources.

2. To connect people with the systems that provide them with resources, services, and opportunities. One of the major purposes of human service work is connecting people with the services they need. To accomplish this purpose, human service workers engage in activities related to finding people who need services, connecting them with the appropriate resources, and making sure that the services are received.

3. To help people use their problem-solving and coping capacities more effectively. Everyone has difficulty at times in coping with the problems and frustrations of daily living, but some people find it so difficult that they develop inappropriate behaviors. Therefore, activities related to talking with, understanding, and supporting people, in addition to helping them develop plans to solve their problems, are performed to achieve this purpose.

4. To serve as a resource for social control. Some human service systems have been granted the authority and have the purpose of serving as agents of social control for people whose behavior violates the laws or who are physically or mentally unable to care for themselves. Activities related to enforcing rules and regulations in

---

[8]Allen Pincus and Anne Minahan, *Social Work Practice: Model and Method* (Itasca, Ill.: F. E. Peacock, 1973), p. 3.

[9]Pincus and Minahan, *Social Work Practice,* pp. 9–33.

providing services and maintaining security and control in settings such as prisons and mental hospitals are performed for the purpose of social control.

These four purposes of human service work are not separate from one another in practice but are related to all human service jobs. In performing your daily activities, you should be able to recognize the purpose(s) guiding each situation you are confronted with.

FRAME

Beside each of the following statements, write the number of the purpose being accomplished (as listed in Frame 7).

_____ a. A prison officer places an inmate in custody.

_____ b. A human service worker provides a woman with Food Stamps.

_____ c. A psychiatric aide discusses a patient's personal problems with him.

_____ d. A case worker visits a welfare recipient to explain about a new child care program.

Turn to Answer 15 on page 598

FRAME

9

SPECIFIC GOALS AND ROLES IN DELIVERING HUMAN SERVICES

Earlier, in Lesson 1 of Chapter I, we introduced the framework of this book as a resource for organizing your present and future learning about delivering human services. You will recall that the basic learning framework had three major parts:

Part I: Learning guidelines or principles for using the book. This corresponds with the major message of the lesson on learning, namely, how to be an effective learner and how to apply learning skills to the practice of delivering human services.

Part II: A knowledge foundation or gateways to the practice of delivering human services. This corresponds with all of Unit One of this book, which seeks to lay a beginning knowledge foundation for entry-level practice.

Part III: Specific skills for delivering human services: Three goals and nine roles. This corresponds with Units Two, Three, and Four of this book, which focus on the "how-to" aspects of delivering human services.

All of these elements—learning guidelines, knowledge foundation, and specific practice skills—are ways of defining the nature of human service work. In this frame, we link the general discussion of the purposes of human service work to the specific goals and skills required for entry-level practice.

In order to accomplish the four general purposes of human service work, the human service practitioner must be able to achieve at least three specific goals: (1) getting services to people in need; (2) helping consumers to function more effectively; and (3) managing work for competent service delivery. Performing each of these goals requires competence in a range of skills. One useful way of organizing the skills needed is to look at the various roles or activities workers perform to accomplish each goal. With this as a focus, nine major roles can be differentiated in human service work. All nine of these roles are described in the remaining chapters of this text; here we give a general overview of each, with examples of how they are performed in human service systems.

Specific Service Delivery Goal 1: Getting Services to People in Need

The first three roles relate to the skills and activities required to get services to people in need. These roles include brokering, consumer advocating, and mobilizing:

1. Brokering. Brokering involves the actual physical connection between the individual(s) with a problem and the services needed to resolve or reduce the problem. It includes assessing the situation to identify the problem, knowing the various community resources available, preparing the individual for a positive contact with the resources available, and making sure the individual gets there and is served. Brokering also involves actively reaching out into the community to locate people with problems. It is more than providing information and making referrals.

2. Consumer advocating. The primary focus of consumer advocating is pleading and fighting for services for an individual whom the service system would otherwise reject. The consumer advocate literally stands in the place of the individual to bring about a change on the part of the rejecting organization in favor of the individual involved.

3. Mobilizing. Mobilizing involves community work directed toward bringing the residents together to effect changes for the better in their community. It also includes activities related to identifying specific unmet community needs and developing new facilities, resources, and programs needed to meet these needs. It is sometimes called community organizing.

FRAME

10

The following is a list of three tasks that might be performed in the roles of brokering, consumer advocating, and mobilizing. Beside each task, write in the role that is being performed.

_____ a. Worker contacts the appropriate resource for a consumer in order to make an appointment for the consumer and advise the resource of the consumer's referral.

_____ b. Worker reports unfair treatment of a consumer to the proper source in order to initiate a review of the action.

_____ c. Worker organizes a group of consumers having a common unmet need in order to help them develop the means to resolve their problems.

Turn to Answer 16 on page 598

FRAME

Specific Service Delivery Goal 2: Helping Consumers to Function More Effectively

The fourth, fifth, and sixth roles of human service work relate to helping consumers use their problem-solving and coping capacities more effectively. The roles workers perform to achieve this goal include relating to consumers, collaborating, and intervening.

4. Relating to consumers. The ability to communicate effectively with consumers is central to all facets of effective service delivery. Interviewing skills, relationship-building skills, and general assessment skills are important throughout the process of building helping relationships with consumers. They are also crucial to getting services to people in need and to the roles involved in managing work for competent practice. That is, achieving both general and specific human service goals depends on the worker's ability to develop relationships with consumers and with other workers.

5. Collaborating. Collaborating activities are concerned with the ability to engage in a systematic process of problem solving or helping. Specific stages of the process include assessment, goal setting, service planning, contracting, implementation, and evaluation. Collaborating involves a helping relationship between the worker and the consumer that seeks to empower the consumer. The expected result is improved understanding and/or skills on the part of the consumer.

6. Intervening. This involves those worker activities directed toward changing or modifying a consumer's behavior using specialized, structure-setting, advanced treatment or intervention techniques. Intervention strategies supplement or extend the generic helping approaches, and may range from controlling or maintaining consumers in institutional settings to using specialized techniques such as reality therapy, behavior therapy, cognitive or cognitive-behavior therapy, and crisis intervention.

FRAME

12

Listed on the right are some of the tasks that might be performed in the roles of relating to consumers, collaborating, and intervening. Match the roles on the left with the tasks on the right.

1. Intervening

_____ a. A worker introduces herself to a consumer and talks about feelings and needs in order to establish an open and trusting relationship for the future.

2. Collaborating

_____ b. A worker evaluates efforts to achieve helping goals in order to determine the future course of the helping process.

3. Relating to consumers _____ c. A worker leads regular group sessions of residents using reality therapy as the treatment modality in order to modify individual behavior.

Turn to Answer 17 on page 599

FRAME

13

Specific Service Delivery Goal 3: Working Across Boundaries for Competent Service Delivery

The last three roles necessary for delivering human services are concerned with the skills needed to manage the fragmented world of work itself. This includes the ability to perform responsibilities in a network of actors starting with self and extending to relationships with consumers, other workers, the specific agency or organization, other human service agencies, and the larger community and society in which services are delivered. The critical roles are managing information, managing the transition to new service delivery systems, and integrating.

7. Managing information. Information is the lifeblood of human service work because it is crucial to answering questions such as: Who am I in relationship to this consumer? Who is this consumer and what are her needs? What are the needs of my co-workers with respect to this consumer? What role does the broader community play in creating and resolving these needs?[10] Human service workers create and manage consumer-related information in part through the skills of recording and reporting. Workers perform these skills in many media, including face-to-face discussions, telephone conversations, written letters and memos, formal reports, and interactions with computers that may contain automated client information systems.

8. Managing the transition(s) to new service delivery systems. Numerous changes are under way in how human service delivery systems are designed, and this trend is likely to continue, especially with the twin forces of an emerging information age and decreasing resource availability. Many skills are required to manage the frequent transitions to these emerging new service delivery systems, but two that are important are supervising "up" (or working across the boundaries of hierarchy) and networking across organizations and programs in and outside your immediate work setting. These activities serve to span frequently changing boundaries within and among the organization, programs, networks of organizations, and consumers.

9. Integrating. Integrating is concerned with the ongoing process of self-development in relationship to the worker's profession and total life context. It is concerned with creating and maintaining the vitality of being a helper through reflection, planned learning experiences, and active solitication of feedback.[11] Integrating asks questions about effectiveness: What is effective human service work? What is an effective helper? What actions need to be taken to create the conditions for effective helping? What do I know? What do I not know? How am I managing the relationship between my life and my work?

---

[10]Concepts drawn, in part, from Richard L. Daft, *Organization Theory and Design,* 3d ed. (St. Paul, Minn.: West Publishing, 1989), p. 309.
[11]Donald F. Krill, *Practice Wisdom* (Beverly Hills: Sage, 1990), p. 11.

FRAME

14

Underline the role being performed for each of the following tasks:

1. A worker inventories the services provided to consumers at the end of each week, using case records and standard reporting forms, in order to provide a record of services for the files and program accountability. (consumer advocating/managing information)
2. A worker requests a meeting with the supervisor in order to review past performance and identify job assignments that will contribute to career goals. (supervising "up"/intervening)
3. A worker seeks feedback from co-workers concerning effectiveness of communication skills and develops a learning plan to refine skills. (brokering/integrating)

Turn to Answer 18 on page 599

FRAME

15

DELIVERING HUMAN SERVICES AS A PROBLEM-MANAGEMENT AND OPPORTUNITY DEVELOPMENT PROCESS[12]

We have described human service work as having general purposes, specific service delivery goals, and roles or skills that facilitate the achievement of goals. We have not suggested how all of this fits together. Underlying the apparent diversity of human service delivery systems is a basic process focused on *identifying and helping consumers to manage problems of living and to develop opportunities*. There are three important ideas in this thought: problem, process, and opportunity.

Problems are a part of life. In fact, we might consider that all human living is effective problem management. Formal human service work becomes relevant when people cannot readily meet their needs with their own resources—in other words, human service work is centrally concerned with recognizing human problems and developing strategies to address those problems. Usually the solutions are jointly developed with the consumer and are aimed at strengthening the consumer's capacity to cope more effectively with life. Thus, one way that the general purposes, service delivery goals, and roles are linked is that they have all been developed as specialized resources to address human problems.

Training to deliver human services is fundamentally an in-depth experience of learning how to use a systematic process of managing human problems and developing opportunities for betterment. It also involves a lifetime of updating and expanding knowledge and skills relevant to this work. The idea of a *process* common to delivering most human services suggests something that takes place over time, in a particular direction, according to a particular pattern. The concept of process indicates a systematic and reliable manner of critical thinking in reaching solutions with

---

[12]This frame is a synthesis of Gerard Egan, *The Skilled Helper,* 5th ed. (Belmont, CA: Brooks/Cole Publishing, 1994), pp. 12–15; Beulah R. Compton and Burt Galaway, *Social Work Processes,* 4th ed. (Belmont, Calif.: Wadsworth, 1989), pp. 370–413. Also see Louise C. Johnson, *Social Work Practice: A Generalist Approach,* 3rd ed. (Boston: Allyn & Bacon, 1989).

a consumer. So, in addition to recognizing that human service work is centrally concerned with addressing problems of living, it is also important to understand that delivering human services is fundamentally the skill of performing specialized processes of problem management and opportunity development. In this text, the nine roles offer the human service worker a range of options to use throughout this process.

Basic Steps of Problem Management and Opportunity Development

Work activities in practically any field can be thought of as problem management endeavors. The distinction is that each profession or occupation focuses on different kinds of problems and therefore needs different knowledge and skills with which to address them. But there are common steps taken to address any problem, even though in practice they may not always occur in exact sequence or one at a time. The steps can be useful to keep in mind as you complete the chapters in this text (you will see variations on these steps in the nine roles involved in delivering human services). The basic steps are:

1. Perceiving a need and then defining the problem that must be addressed.
2. Stating a purpose to be achieved by addressing the problem.
3. Collecting data related to the situation.
4. Using the data to generate alternative responses, opportunities, or solutions to the problem.
5. Assessing the costs of pursuing different solutions and weighing the choices.
6. Selecting one or more solutions.
7. Implementing the solution.
8. Evaluating the results and beginning again, drawing on what is learned.

The third important idea is *opportunity*. Gerard Egan describes opportunity as the goal of developing the unused resources of consumer's lives effectively and fully. In Chapter 2, we made a similar point when we suggested focusing on the untapped capacities, skills, and potential contributions of consumers in addition to, or even instead of, descriptions of their needs, deficiencies, diagnoses, and problems.

Identifying and managing problems are essential characteristics of human service work. Whether brokering, consumer advocating, mobilizing, relationship building, collaborating (helping), intervening (with advanced intervention models), managing information, managing the transition to new service delivery systems, or integrating, the human service worker is engaged in an ongoing process of problem management and opportunity development. According to Beulah Compton and Burt Galaway:[13]

> This means that the worker is not involved in treating an illness, or in bringing about a cure for client troubles, but rather is joining the forward motion of the client system and is, along with helping the client, strengthening the client's capacity to cope more effectively with life.

---

[13]Compton and Galaway, *Social Work Processes,* 4th ed., p. 371.

And according to Gerard Egan:[14]

> The problem management and opportunity development model is not one-sided or dogmatic. It is ready to give up the most time-honored and revered methods if new evidence contradicts them. It constantly grows and develops. . . . Even though it takes different forms in different cultures, its basic structure is recognized around the world.

FRAME 16

As a way of reviewing this lesson, see if you can give an example of a task you (or another worker) might perform in each of the nine major roles. Make sure you include what activity is performed and what might be accomplished by that activity.

Role	Activity	What Is Accomplished?
1. Brokering		
2. Consumer advocating		
3. Mobilizing		
4. Relating to consumers		
5. Collaborating (helping)		
6. Intervening		
7. Managing information		
8. Managing the transition to new service delivery systems		
9. Integrating		

---

[14]Egan, *The Skilled Helper,* 5th ed., p. 13.

Chapter Summary

Chapter 3 was concerned with the people who deliver human services and the world of work that is the context of their responses to human needs. We looked at: (1) human service workers, (2) human service work organizations and work groups, and (3) the content and process of the work itself.

Lesson 1. Because human service workers use themselves to deliver services, it is imperative that they have a well-developed self-awareness. We presented the process of learning about yourself as a lifelong activity but stressed the importance of focused efforts to develop a work identity. This involves familiarity with other workers who may be delivering services to consumers, and an appreciation of the different levels of practice and where you position yourself. It also requires an ongoing awareness of how you are dealing with your fundamental needs and how your personal professional values are linked. Schein's stages of career development were discussed and suggested as a major referent to the development of a work identity. The skill of self-leadership emphasized that effective human service workers take the responsibility for knowing what they want, monitoring how they (and the world around them) are growing and changing, and imagining and realizing personal plans for development and career transitions.

Lesson 2. Most human services are delivered by people working in organizations. Organization was defined as collective action in pursuit of a common mission—or simply people coming together under an identifiable label, such as the Department of Family Services or the Bay County Community Mental Health Center, to produce some product or deliver some service.

We developed a definition of human service organizations as systems with three major elements: input, throughput, and output. The distinctiveness of human service organizations was described using a typology based on service technologies and types of consumers. People (consumers) are the inputs as well as an integral part of the throughput and output; goals can be ambiguous; and outputs can therefore be difficult to measure. The variety of human service organizations was captured through a scheme that used consumers and services to classify six different kinds of human service organizations. These included people-processing, people-sustaining, and people-changing organizations for both normal and malfunctioning consumers.

The general knowledge about human service organizations was then applied to the work group, especially how to be an effective member. Work groups are sometimes able to form teams that are highly effective in solving their problems. Good teams are characterized by how they accomplish their goals and how well they satisfy the personal and interpersonal needs of their members.

We defined the work group as consisting of the supervisor and those individuals immediately responsible to him or her. We proposed two ways of looking at work groups. The first was a "big picture," or total organization view, that enabled us to understand an organization as a system of many groups, some of which overlap or interlock through managerial positions called "linking pins." The second perspective looked inside a single work group to determine the characteristics of effective work groups. We discussed teamwork as the way a group is able to solve its problems and identified eight characteristics of effective teams. We emphasized the importance of all members sharing responsibility for the successful functioning of the group and identified three levels at which contributions might be made: process, content, and feeling. Finally, we presented a comprehensive questionnaire for evaluating a familiar team and extending your understanding of effective team behavior.

Lesson 2 concluded with a brief discussion of organizational citizenship and sensitivity to the pervasiveness of organizational conflict. We suggested that being a member of a work group or an organization is equivalent to being a citizen in that community, thereby implying that both parties have responsibilities to each other. Knowledgeable organizational citizens recognize the existence of numerous conflicts and tensions in their settings of practice and take responsibility for effective participation, including proposing solutions and seeking changes when appropriate. Knowledge and skills relating to different "groups" and the total human service organization will be addressed again in later sections of this text. For example, in Unit Two you will learn about forming and leading community groups. In Unit Three you will be introduced to treatment processes used to counsel groups of consumers. And in Unit Four you will explore the relationship-building aspects of supervising and networking that contribute to a positive working environment.

Lesson 3. The third aspect of human service delivery is the nature of the work itself. Lesson 3 delved into some of the reasons why work is important in our society and suggested 12 needs that jobs can fulfill. Work is purposeful and sustained action that provides goods and services of value to others and is considered to be work by the person doing it. All work involves the individual with information and ideas (data), with people, and with things.

Human service work was characterized as having four general *purposes*: providing material resources; connecting people with the systems that offer the resources they need; helping people use their problem-solving and coping capacities more effectively; and serving as a resource for social control. To achieve these general purposes, entry-level human service workers focus on three specific delivery *goals*: getting services to people in need; helping consumers to function more effectively; and managing work for competent practice. Nine *roles* define the sets of skills or competencies human service workers need to deliver services: brokering, consumer advocating, mobilizing, relating to consumers, collaborating (helping), intervening (advanced intervention models), managing information, managing the transition to new service delivery systems, and integrating. The tasks related to these roles are assigned to various levels of workers in human service organizations, with the result that many workers are performing similar activities. However, even though workers at different levels of education and experience appear to perform similar kinds of activities, it is important to recognize that these activities differ in terms of the closeness of supervision required, the extent of responsibility and decision making, and the complexity of problems addressed.

A fundamental characteristic of human service work, which links purposes, goals, jobs, and roles, is the idea that the work is essentially a process of problem management, critical thinking, and opportunity development. The worker will perform a wide range of roles in delivering human services. But within each role, the worker will be engaged in an identifiable sequence of activities that have as their purpose the development of solutions to human problems. The basic steps are: defining the problem to be addressed; stating a purpose to be achieved; collecting data related to the problem; using the data to generate options to address the problem; assessing the costs of pursuing different solutions; selecting one or more options; implementing a solution; evaluating the results; and beginning again based upon what is learned. These general steps are treated in various ways in each of the nine roles involved in delivering human services that are developed in this text.

Thus, understanding the nature and meaning of human service work includes the ability of each worker to have a clear understanding of his or her job. By knowing the personal needs fulfilled by your job, what activities and skills are required, and what is accomplished by the many tasks you perform, you will have a basis for making your work in the human services important and personally satisfying.

Suggestions for Further Study

Although the suggestions for further study and reading below are organized according to worker, work organization, and work, many of the materials cover all three topics. So if a title looks interesting, we recommend pursuing it even if it seems not directly related.

Human Service Workers

Any material aimed at better understanding yourself as a total person will be an important part of developing a work identity. Further study is highly recommended on the subject of values. The expanding literature on values and the process through which they are acquired should prove to be useful. We suggest reading biographies of human service workers to further develop your work identity in the context of your career. Some readings below will refer to either values or ethics or both. The interrelationships of values and ethics are quite complex and require careful study. As a start, further study might involve comparing the codes of ethics for different helping professions (e.g., social workers, counselors, marriage and family therapists, and lawyers) to illustrate the specific value bases central to their work (some are listed below; also see Chapter 12 of this text).

Abbott, Ann A. *Professional Choices: Values at Work.* Silver Spring, Md.: National Association of Social Workers, 1988.

Austin, Michael J. *Professionals and Paraprofessionals.* New York: Human Sciences Press, 1978.

Bartlett, Harriet. *The Common Base of Social Work Practice.* Silver Spring, Md.: National Association of Social Workers, 1970.

Bateson, Mary Catherine. *Composing a Life*. Boston: The Atlantic Monthly Press, 1989.

Chenhall, Pamela. "Who Are Our Models Now?" In David G. Martin and Allen D. Moore, *First Steps in the Art of Intervention: A Guidebook for Trainers in the Helping Professions*. Pacific Grove, Calif.: Brooks/Cole, 1995: 468–479.

Coles, Robert. *The Call of Service: A Witness to Idealism*. Boston: Houghton Mifflin, 1993.

Collison, Brooke B., and Nancy J. Garfield, eds. *Careers in Counseling and Human Services*, 2nd ed. Washington D.C.: Taylor & Francis, 1996.

Corey, Gerald, Marianne Schneider Corey, and Patrick Callanan. *Issues and Ethics in the Helping Professions*, 4th ed. Pacific Grove, Calif.: Brooks/Cole, 1993.

Corey, Marianne Schneider, and Gerald Corey. *Becoming a Helper*. Pacific Grove, Calif.: Brooks/Cole, 1993.

Dillick, Sidney, ed. *Value Foundations of Social Work: Ethical Basis for a Human Service Profession*. Detroit: School of Social Work, Wayne State University, 1984.

Dubin, Robert. *Central Life Interests: Creative Individualism in a Complex World*. New Brunswick, N.J.: Transaction Publishers, 1992.

Etzioni, Amatai. *The Semiprofessions and their Organization*. London: Collier-Macmillan, 1969.

Gilbert, Neil, and Harry Specht. *Handbook of the Social Services*, 3rd ed. Englewood Cliffs, N.J.: Prentice-Hall, 1993.

Greenwood, Ernest. "Attributes of a Profession," *Social Work* 2 (July 1957): 44–45.

Hirschhorn, Larry. *The Workplace Within: Psychodynamics of Organizational Life*. Cambridge, Mass.: MIT Press, 1988.

Hopps, June G. "Valuing Others: The Bedrock of Ethics," *Social Work* 32 (May-June 1987): 179–180.

Hughes, Everett. *Education for the Professions of Medicine, Law, Theology, and Social Welfare*. New York: McGraw-Hill, 1973).

International Federation of Social Workers. "Ethics of Social Work—Principles and Standards." In *Encyclopedia of Social Work*, 19th ed. Washington, D.C.: National Association of Social Work, 1995: 2661–2664.

Kagle, Jill Doner, and Pam Northrup Giebelhausen. "Dual Relationships and Professional Boundaries," *Social Work* 39, 2 (March, 1994): 213–220.

Lammert, Marilyn. "Experience vs. Knowing: Using Therapist Self-Awareness," *Social Casework* 67 (1986): 369–376.

Levy, Charles S. "Personal vs. Professional Values: The Practitioner's Dilemma," *Clinical Social Work Journal* 4 (1976): 110–120.

Levy, Charles S. *Social Work Ethics on the Line*. New York: Hayworth Press, 1993.

Mehr, Joseph. *Human Services: Concepts and Intervention Strategies*, 5th ed. Boston: Allyn & Bacon, 1992.

Morales, Armando, and Bradford W. Sheafor. *Social Work: A Profession of Many Faces*. Boston: Allyn & Bacon, 1995.

National Association of Social Workers. *Code of Ethics of the National Association of Social Workers*. Washington, D.C.: National Association of Social Workers, as adopted by the 1979 NASW Delegate Assembly and revised by the 1990 and 1993 NASW Delegate Assemblies.

Reamer, Frederic G. *Social Work Values and Ethics*. New York: Columbia University Press, 1995.

Roberts, Cleora S. "Conflicting Values in Social Work and Medicine," *Health and Social Work* 24 (Aug. 1989): 211–218.

Russo, J.R. *Serving and Surviving as a Human Service Worker*. Monterey, Calif.: Brooks/Cole, 1980.

Saladin, Michael E., and David V. Ness. "The Therapist: Some Thoughts on Living Well." In David G. Martin and Allen D. Moore, *First Steps in the Art of Intervention: A Guide for Trainers in the Helping Professions*. Pacific Grove, Calif.: Brooks/Cole, 1995: 450–467.

Schervish, Paul G., Virginia A. Hodgkinson, and Margaret Gates, eds. *Care and Community in*

Modern Society: Passing On the Tradition of Service to Future Generations. San Francisco, Calif.: Jossey-Bass Publishers, 1995.

Schindler, Ruben, and Edward Allan Brawley. *Social Care at the Front Line: Paraprofessionals Worldwide*. New York and London: Tavistock Publications, 1987.

Schulman, Eveline D. *Intervention in Human Services: A Guide to Skills and Knowledge,* 4th ed. New York: Macmillan, 1991. See appendixes for:
- Ethical Standards of the American Association for Counseling and Development
- Principles of Medical Ethics, American Psychiatric Association
- Code for Nurses' American Nurses' Association
- Ethical Principles of Psychologists, American Psychological Association

Tebb, Susan. "An Aid to Empowerment: A Caregiver Well-Being Scale," *Health and Social Work* 20, 2 (May, 1995): 87–92.

Teicher, Morton, ed. *Values in Social Work: A Re-Examination*. Silver Spring, Md.: National Association of Social Workers, 1967.

Watkins, Sallie A. "Confidentiality and Privileged Communications: Legal Dilemma for Family Therapists," *Social Work* 34 (Mar. 1989): 133–136.

Wells, Carolyn Cressy, with M. Kathleen Masch. *Social Work Ethics Day to Day: Guidelines for Professional Practice*. Prospect Heights, Ill.: Waveland Press, 1991.

Human Service Organizations and Work Groups

Further study is needed to fully understand the components and properties of human service organizations and work groups and how these relate to effective work behavior. Additional reading concerning teams and the variety of team roles and processes in human service organizations will also be rewarding.

Adams, John D. *Transforming Work*. Alexandria, Va.: Miles River Press, 1984.

Argyris, Chris. *Personality and Organization: The Conflict Between the System and the Individual*. New York: Garland, 1987.

Austin, Michael J., and Jane Issacs Lowe, eds. *Controversial Issues in Communities and Organizations*. Boston: Allyn & Bacon, 1994.

Brill, Naomi I. *Teamwork: Working Together in the Human Services*. Philadelphia: J.B. Lippincott, 1976.

Demone, Harold W., Jr., and Dwight Harshbarger. *A Handbook of Human Service Organizations*. New York: Behavioral Publications, 1974.

Ezell, Mark, and Rino J. Patti. "State Human Service Agencies: Structure and Organization," *Social Service Review* (Mar. 1990): 22–45.

Garner, Howard G., and Fred P. Orelove. *Teamwork in Human Services: Models and Applications Across the Life Span*. Boston: Butterworth-Heinemann, 1994.

Goodman, Paul S., and Associates. *Designing Effective Work Groups*. San Francisco: Jossey-Bass, 1986.

Hackman, J. Richard, ed. "Part V: Human Service Teams." In *Groups That Work (And Those That Don't): Creating Conditions for Effective Teamwork*. San Francisco: Jossey-Bass, 1990.

Hasenfeld, Yeheskel. *Human Services as Complex Organizations*. Newbury Park, Calif.: Sage Publications, 1992.

Hirschorn, Larry. *Managing in the New Team Environment*. Reading, Mass.: Addison-Wesley, 1991.

Holland, Thomas P. "Organizations: Context for Social Services Delivery." In *Encyclopedia of Social Work,* 19th ed. Washington, D.C.: National Association of Social Workers, 1995: 1787–1794.

Martin, Patricia Yancey, and Myra Marx Ferree, eds. *Feminist Organizations: Harvest of the New Women's Movement*. Philadelphia: Temple University Press, 1995.

Mills, Theodore M. *The Sociology of Small Groups,* 2nd ed. Englewood Cliffs, N.J.: Prentice-Hall, 1984.

Organ, Dennis W. *Organizational Citizenship Behavior: The Good Soldier Syndrome*. Lexington, Mass.: Lexington Books, 1988.

Powell, Thomas J. *Understanding the Self-Help Organization: Frameworks and Findings*. Thousand Oaks, Calif.: Sage Publications, 1994.

Smith, Kenwyn. *Groups in Conflict: Prisons in Disguise*. Dubuque, Ia.: Kendall/Hunt, 1982.

Weiner, Myron E. "Designing and Executing Effective Human Services Organizations," *Public Administration Quarterly* (Spring 1988): 32–59.

Human Service Work

The nature and meaning of human service work is worthy of further investigation. This might include researching additional skills necessary for effective human service work, how work content and process affect job satisfaction, and other definitions of human service work (e.g., other descriptions of purposes, goals, roles, and tasks).

Austin, David M. *The Political Economy of Human Service Programs*. Greenwich, Conn.: JAI Press, 1988.

Bell, Winifred. *Contemporary Social Welfare,* 2nd ed. New York: Macmillan, 1987.

Dolgoff, Ralph, and Donald Feldstein. *Understanding Social Welfare,* 3rd ed. New York: Longman, 1993.

Dubin, Robert. *The World of Work*. Englewood Cliffs, N.J.: Garland Publications, 1987.

Epstein, Charlotte. *An Introduction to Human Services*. Englewood Cliffs, N.J.: Prentice-Hall, 1981.

Gambrill, Eileen. *Critical Thinking in Clinical Practice*. San Francisco, Calif.: Jossey-Bass, 1990.

Heffernan, Joseph, Guy Shuttlesworth, and Rosalie Ambrosino. *Social Work and Social Welfare: An Introduction*. St. Paul, Minn.: West, 1988.

Hepworth, Dean H., and Jo Ann Larsen. *Direct Social Work Practice: Theory and Skills,* 4th ed. Pacific Grove, Calif.: Brooks/Cole, 1990.

Hollis, Florence. *Casework: A Psychosocial Therapy*. New York: Random House, 1964.

Landon, Pamela S. "Generalist and Advanced Generalist Practice." In *Encyclopedia of Social Work,* 19th ed. Washington, D.C.: National Association of Social Workers, 1995: 1101–1107.

Martin, Patricia Yancey, and Gerald G. O'Connor. *The Social Environment: Open Systems Applications*. New York: Longman, 1989.

Mcmahon, Maria O'Neil. *The General Method of Social Work Practice: A Problem-Solving Approach,* 2d ed. Englewood Cliffs, N.J.: Prentice-Hall, 1990.

Mcmahon, Maria O'Neil. *Advanced Generalist Practice: With An International Perspective*. Englewood Cliffs, N.J.: Prentice Hall, 1994.

Nadler, Gerald, and Shozo Hibino. *Breakthrough Thinking,* 2nd ed. Rocklin, Calif.: Prima Publishing and Communications, 1994.

O'Looney, John. *Redesigning the Work of Human Services*. Westport, Conn.: Quorum, 1996.

Pinderhughes, Elaine. "Direct Practice Overview." In *Encyclopedia of Social Work,* 19th ed. Washington, D.C.: National Association of Social Workers, 1995: 740–751.

Saleebey, Dennis, ed. *The Strengths Perspective in Social Work Practice*. New York: Longman, 1992.

Schumacher, E. F. *Good Work*. New York: Harper & Row, 1979.

Simons, R., and S. Aigner. *Practice Principles: A Problem-Solving Approach to Social Work*. New York: Macmillan, 1985.

Wessells, D. T. *Professional Burnout in Medicine and the Helping Professions*. New York: Haworth Press, 1989.

Other Sources

Akabas, Sheila H., and Paul A. Kurzman. *Work, Workers, and Work Organizations: A View from Social Work*. Englewood Cliffs, N.J.: Prentice-Hall, 1982.

UNIT**TWO**

GETTING SERVICES TO PEOPLE IN NEED

Preview of Unit

One of the major goals of human service work is getting services to the people who need them. In order to accomplish this goal, human service workers reach out to people who need services, provide information about available services, connect people who have problems with appropriate community resources, and make sure that the people who need these services receive them. This process is known as *brokering*. In cases where people are denied services to which they are entitled, workers frequently find they must actively protect and defend the rights of consumers. This process is known as *consumer advocating*. Activities aimed toward developing new entitlements and rights are also called social action[1] and planned social change.

In making sure that services are delivered to people in need, workers also discover many problems or needs that are not being met by existing resources in the community. Thus human service workers are also engaged in activities that help the people in the community work together in developing new community services to handle these needs or problems. This process is known as *mobilizing*.

Since one of your primary goals as a human service worker is to get services to people in need, this unit helps you examine three human service work roles—brokering, consumer advocating, and mobilizing. When you refer a consumer to another agency and follow up to see that appropriate services have been provided, you are engaging in the brokering role. If you find that consumers have been denied services or benefits to which they are entitled, such as public assistance or Social Security, the activities of negotiating for consumers are part of the advocating role. When you find, for example, that no day care services are available for a consumer, the activities that you complete to help develop a new day care center are part of the mobilizing role. The goal of this unit is to assist you in developing your knowledge of these roles so that you will be more effective in making sure that services are delivered to the people who need them.

---

[1]Ronda S. Connaway and Martha F. Gentry, *Social Work Practice* (Englewood Cliffs, N.J.: Prentice-Hall, 1988).

Chapter 4

Brokering

As human service systems grow larger and more complex, it becomes increasingly difficult for people who are not familiar with them to find and use the resources that will meet their needs. You may be familiar with people called real estate brokers, so you know that a broker is generally a person who brings a client together with another party and helps him or her find and purchase goods and services. Human service workers act as brokers when they help consumers find and use the resources they need.

When you are working in the human services, you have an obligation to try to help a person who comes to you with a problem. You also have an obligation to find people in your community who need help and are entitled to receive your agency's services but are not aware that they can get assistance with their problems. As a broker, you may think of yourself as the "person in the middle." You will be guiding, advising, and actively helping people to access the services they need. You will also be making sure that people do not get lost in the shuffle or give up their efforts to get help.

If you are working in a community setting, you are probably already familiar with the brokering process. For example, if you work in a welfare agency, you probably spend a lot of your time giving consumers information and referring them to other sources for help. However, if you work in an institutional setting, such as a prison or a mental hospital, brokering may be a new activity for you. Keep in mind that even though consumers who are in institutions are there for help with certain problems, they will also face some problems that are related to institutional living. Brokering is a process that can alert you to the problems of institutional settings and the resources and information needed to resolve these problems.

In this chapter you will learn some of the basic skills you need in brokering. In Lesson 1 you will learn how to get to know the resource systems in your community. In Lesson 2 you will be introduced to some guiding principles underlying two of the main activities in brokering—giving information and making referrals. In Lesson 3 you will examine some techniques used in reaching out to a community to identify unmet needs. The overall objective of this chapter is to provide you with a framework for understanding and practicing the process of brokering.

The brokering tasks that might appear in a human service job description can be divided into two groups: (1) assessing the formal and informal resources available to consumers and (2) linking consumers with existing services.

Assessing Resources

1. Observe or inspect consumers' homes in order to assess security or hazards, determine deficiencies, or evaluate their status.
2. Visit day care, residential care, or foster home periodically in order to evaluate services provided or the suitability of the environment for persons cared for or to solve any problems.
3. Visit and/or investigate potential service resources or providers in order to assess their suitability or to license them for use by the agency.
4. Evaluate goods and services, price lists, and bids in order to decide which supplier or contractor offers the best quality at the best price.

Linking Consumers to Existing Services

1. Inquire about and discuss job vacancies or positions with employers in order to help consumers find jobs.
2. Collect information and follow leads in order to locate a missing individual (e.g., spouse, parent, or offspring).
3. Fill out standard forms or write letters and memos to refer consumers to appropriate services.
4. Use telephone, make home visits, or talk with consumers in order to locate people who might need services or financial help.
5. Provide or arrange for transportation in order to get consumers to service or treatment resources.
6. Tell consumers about services and/or resource locations in order to promote their use by consumers.
7. Give information to consumers, relatives, call-ins, or other people in order to explain and interpret agency programs, policies, or procedures.
8. Follow up or monitor consumers' referrals in order to ensure that services are being provided.

LESSON 1

Identifying Community Resource Systems

You will need considerable knowledge of the resources in your community if your brokering activities are to be successful and helpful. Equally important is your ability to accurately assess consumers' needs, their ability to access resources, and the extent to which they need help with accessing resources. In this lesson you will learn about the resource systems found in most communities.

Goal

Given a description of a community, you will be able to identify and describe components of the available resource systems.

Learning Activities

To accomplish this goal, we will:

1. Review the definition of *resource system*.
2. Identify three kinds of resource systems and study examples of each.
3. Consider the inadequacies of each kind of resource system.
4. Examine three ways of identifying and describing resource systems.

FRAME

1

WHAT IS A RESOURCE SYSTEM?[1]

You will recall from Unit One that an understanding of service and consumer systems is basic to effective human service work. In discussing resource systems, your knowledge of systems will be valuable since the resource *system* is based on the same concepts as service and consumer systems.

During the early days of American society, the family was the primary system that provided people with the necessary resources to cope with their needs and problems. Neighbors were also a resource. However, as society grew and became increasingly

---

[1]The concepts and discussions in Frames 1–5 are adapted from Allen Pincus and Anne Minahan, *Social Work Practice: Model and Method* (Itasca, Ill.: F. E. Peacock, 1973), pp. 3–9.

complex, people became more dependent on other resource systems for assistance. Today a resource system includes services and opportunities along with the material, emotional, and spiritual resources available in the community. In almost all communities, this help is available from three kinds of resource systems: informal, or natural, resource systems; formal, or membership, resource systems; and societal resource systems.

FRAME

2

THREE KINDS OF RESOURCE SYSTEMS

Informal (Natural) Resource Systems

The first major resource system available in all communities is the informal, or natural, resource system. This system consists of family, friends, neighbors, co-workers, and others who serve as informal sources of help in meeting needs and solving problems. The aid given through these informal relationships includes emotional support, affection, advice, and information, as well as concrete services such as babysitting, help in filling out forms, and assistance in locating appropriate resources.

Since today's resource systems have moved far beyond the functions originally fulfilled by the family, they have also become increasingly complex and difficult to negotiate. Relying on the informal resource system may not bring about the required assistance for several reasons:

1. A person may not have an informal resource system. For example, a person may be new to a community and not have any friends.
2. A person may be hesitant to turn to friends, relatives, or neighbors for help.
3. Even if people do turn to an informal resource system, it may be unable to meet their needs. This is frequently the case in extraordinary or crisis situations, where informal systems may lack the resources necessary to help.

Formal (Membership) Resource Systems

The second major resource system is the formal resource system, which includes membership organizations and formal associations that exist to promote the mutual benefits and common interests of their members. These systems may supply resources directly to members or help them negotiate with various societal systems. For example, a social club may provide recreational activities for its members in addition to helping them buy food cooperatively at a reduced rate. When formal resource organizations negotiate with societal systems, both the organization members and other people who need help may benefit. Examples of formal resource systems include labor unions, welfare rights groups, Boy/Girl Scouts, neighborhood associations, social clubs, youth clubs, Better Business Bureaus, the American Medical Association, the National Association of Social Workers, and the National Association for Retarded Persons.

A variety of factors may prevent people from receiving the necessary help from formal resource systems, including the following:

1. In some communities, such groups may not exist. There may not be a welfare rights group to help recipients in receiving adequate services from the welfare department or to inform consumers of their rights.

2. People may be reluctant to join a membership organization or association for a variety of reasons. For example, they may fail to see how it can help them, or they may be unacceptable to the other members.
3. People may be unaware of the existence of a formal resource system.
4. Existing organizations may not have the necessary resources to provide services or negotiate with societal systems for members.

Societal Resource Systems

The third major resource system is the societal resource system, which has been established through social legislation and voluntary citizen action to deliver services. Most people are linked to several of these systems, which include hospitals, adoption agencies, schools, day-care centers, libraries, welfare departments, Social Security programs, family services agencies (Lutheran, Catholic, Jewish, public, etc.), and Easter Seal centers. Some of these systems provide services through public or tax-supported agencies; others provide services through private or voluntary agencies.

Societal resource systems are the most complex of the three resource systems and are probably the most difficult to negotiate. As a result, people often encounter problems in receiving help from these systems. Some of the inadequacies of societal resource systems are:

1. The needed resources may not exist or may not exist in sufficient quantity to provide adequate services for all who need them.
2. The needed resources or service may not be geographically, psychologically, or culturally available to those who need it. For example, a Chicano migrant family may be hesitant to ask for help from an agency employing white middle-class workers who speak only English.
3. The needed resource may exist, but people may not know about it or how to use it.
4. When a person is linked to more than one resource system, the systems may work at cross-purposes and overwhelm the person with conflicting demands and messages.
5. The policies of the various societal resource systems may create new problems for people. For example, some of the requirements of being a consumer of a resource system that reduces welfare payments as soon as a consumer finds employment may create new problems, such as insufficient child-care resources in the family, leading to dependency on a day-care agency.

FRAME
3

Marc S. lives in the city of Big Bend and works for the state division of developmental disabilities. Marc is trying to identify and classify some of the resources that are available in Big Bend and has come up with the following list of ten community resources. How would you classify these resources? Place a check mark in the correct column after each resource.

	Informal Resource System	Formal Resource System	Societal Resource System
1. City of Big Bend Welfare Department	_____	_____	_____
2. Big Bend Red Cross	_____	_____	_____
3. A Girl Scout troop interested in volunteer work with the developmentally disabled	_____	_____	_____
4. Federal Social Security office	_____	_____	_____
5. A private agency that tests the developmentally disabled	_____	_____	_____
6. A Salvation Army center	_____	_____	_____
7. A privately owned day care center	_____	_____	_____
8. Relatives of developmentally disabled clients	_____	_____	_____
9. Special classes for the developmentally disabled offered by the public schools of Big Bend	_____	_____	_____
10. Neighbors of parents of developmentally disabled children	_____	_____	_____

Turn to Answer 19 on page 600

FRAME
4

IDENTIFYING COMMUNITY RESOURCES

How can you find out about the resources in your community? Whether you live or work in a large community or a small community, it is difficult for both consumers and workers to have a full knowledge of all available resources. The following are some of the ways you can begin to identify and describe the resources in your community:

1. Consult city, neighborhood, or agency directories. Many cities have a directory published by an association to which many human service resources belong (e.g., a health and welfare council, or a council of social agencies, such as the United Way). In addition, some neighborhoods have guides to agencies serving neighborhood residents, and organizations such as the chamber of commerce usually publish guides that list the resources available within a community. Your organization may have developed some guides to resources available within the community. Community resource directories usually list the services and resources each agency provides. These directories should be updated yearly. Even if updates are fairly frequent, the listed services may not actually be available, or may not be available to all consumers. You may need to call agencies to get their specific eligibility requirements and to learn whether a certain service is currently available. Sending consumers on dead-end resource leads is discouraging and can be further debilitating.

2. Develop your own file of community resources. Beyond consulting directories that list available resources, you can develop a resource file of your own that is related to the common needs of consumers. In developing your own resource file, you need to know more than the fact that the resource exists. You need to know, for example, the special functions of the resource, what kinds of services are offered, and to whom. The following is a checklist of some of the important information you should collect about each resource:

a. Name, address, phone number of resource
b. Hours when resource can be contacted and when services are provided
c. Types of problems handled or services offered
d. Eligibility, including important facts about special groups served

3. Visit various resources. Talking with workers to find out what they are doing and how your consumers can use any of the services offered is another way to find out about a community and its resources. Getting to know some of the people who live and work in a community; talking with community leaders, clergy, and volunteers who work in various agencies; and talking with relatives of consumers and workers in your own and other agencies are good ways to gain an understanding of each resource and what it has to offer to meet the needs of consumers. Your knowing the worker to whom the referral is being made can help the consumer to actually obtain the service.

FRAME

5

Alice has recently moved to the city of Flatlands and started working as a house-parent in a community halfway house for delinquent boys. She soon discovers that some of the boys are in need of clothes and blankets. She also finds that the boys have a lot of free time, and she would like to help them get part-time jobs in the community. But Alice is new to the community and has only recently started working for this agency. Can you identify two things she might do to get to know her community and the resources it contains?

1.

2.

Turn to Answer 20 on page 600

Giving Information and Making Referrals

People who are not familiar with human service agencies often discover that they have a difficult time finding and using the resources that will meet their needs. Brokering is the process in which you identify people's service needs, see that they have the information they need, and see that their unmet needs are met through the provision of an appropriate community resource. In this lesson you will learn about two of the primary activities in brokering: giving information and making referrals.

Goals

Given a description of an individual with an unmet need, you will be able to (1) identify the necessary information the individual needs to receive assistance; and (2) plan and explain the steps you would follow in referring the individual to an appropriate resource.

Learning Activities

To accomplish these goals, we will:

1. Recognize the process of determining an individual's unmet needs.
2. Identify the skills needed to understand a problem situation faced by a consumer.
3. Examine the process of preparing individuals to receive help with their unmet needs.
4. Consider three questions that need to be answered before initiating a referral.
5. Outline the process of referring an individual to another resource.
6. Review ways of assisting consumers when they are having trouble getting help from another resource.

FRAME

IDENTIFYING AN INDIVIDUAL'S UNMET NEEDS

How do you find out about an individual's problem or unmet need? What do you need to know about this unmet need? You need to consider several points when an individual comes to you for help with a problem or a need that is not being met.

1. Find out as much as possible about the exact need. In finding out what the exact need is, you should consider how the person came to your attention, why he is asking for help now, and how he identifies his need. While you are finding out about the specific need, you should also get enough facts about the person, such as age and marital status, so you will be able to understand the nature of the problem. You will use this information later to determine the individual's eligibility for resources and services.

2. Find out what the person wants to do about the need or problem. Once you and the individual both think you understand the unmet need, you should find out how the consumer feels about this need. You also have to know what, if anything, has already been done to meet this need. You should find out what the person wants *you* to do about the need as well as what *he* wants to do.

3. Begin to determine who can handle this request best. Once you know what the need is, what the person wants to do about it, and what he expects from you, you can begin to determine whether your agency has the resources to meet this need. If you find out that your agency can be of help, you can explain the services of your agency and, if possible, answer questions the individual asks. If your agency does not have the necessary resources, you must begin to think about other resources that are available for help.

F R A M E
2

ASSESSING UNMET NEEDS[1]

Identifying an unmet need may be a simple matter when consumers know what they will need and you can link them with an existing resource. However, there will also be situations where it is difficult to identify the unmet need. For example, a consumer may be able to state only part of the problem or may ask for help with something other than the real problem or even avoid discussing the real problem altogether. No matter how involved or difficult the situation, certain skills can be employed in identifying an unmet need:

1. Give the information the individual requests either at once or gradually, as indicated.
2. Listen, wait, and relax as needed; and, above all, be yourself.
3. Emphasize the present situation and secure only the essential information from the person.
4. Try to recognize early the kind of person you are working with and continue to be sensitive to his or her needs.
5. Take hold of and use information as the person shows the interest and capacity to use help.
6. Do not pursue the deeper emotional or psychological problems that may appear, and avoid long, drawn-out discussions.

Also consider the following in assessing consumer needs for resources or referrals and potential resources in order to maximize your effectiveness in the broker role.

---

[1]Ronda S. Connaway and Martha E. Gentry, *Social Work Practice* (Englewood Cliffs, N.J.: Prentice-Hall, 1988).

1. Is the consumer at risk without additional resources?

2. Consider consumer demographic characteristics, culture, and skills in assessing the extent to which consumer and/or consumer support persons can participate in obtaining resources and in selecting agencies. For example, a Jewish agency might assist a Russian Jewish immigrant, whereas another agency might not provide resources to Jewish immigrants.

In addition to culture, consider the consumer's skills, such as verbal ability, stability, self-esteem, intelligence, commitment to change, and appearance in assessing the consumer's ability to access resources and the extent to which your help is needed in order for the consumer to successfully approach other agencies. Consider as well the extent to which the consumer is in crisis. Consumers (in fact, all of us) have diminished abilities when we have just experienced a crisis such as death, an accident, or a natural disaster. In these situations, we all need extra help until our equilibrium is reestablished.

3. Resource agencies, including your own agency, need to be assessed in terms of the purpose and structure of the agency, the extent of worker discretion in allocating resources, the values of the agency administrators, staff resources to respond to the consumer's needs, physical accessibility in terms of consumer mobility and geographical location, agency-held behavior norms for consumers, service costs, and how well the agency functions, including the extent to which the agency honors appointment times and how the agency manages information and records.

F R A M E

3

Read the following passage and then answer the question below.

> Mr. Lane came into the office to get the addresses of some foster homes for his mother, and he seemed very hesitant and nervous. Kim, the worker, gave him the information he requested and listened carefully to his questions. Accepting him as deeply concerned, she gave him time to offer more and more examples of his mother's extreme behavior. He became more confident—and then suggested that his mother did not need a foster home. Kim agreed. They discussed this further, and Kim explained the services her agency could offer. Then they decided that Mr. Lane should seek the advice of a psychiatrist. Mr. Lane left, relieved that he had taken the first step in admitting something that he had been ashamed of.[2]

In the situation above, Kim was faced with a consumer who was asking for help with something other than the problem he presented. Which skill or skills did Kim use?

_____ 1. Explain the function and purpose of your agency as it relates to the individual's request.

_____ 2. Give the information the individual requests either at once or gradually, as indicated.

---

[2]Adapted from a case description found in Janet Rosenberg, *Breakfast: Two Jars of Paste* (Cleveland: Case Western Reserve University Press, 1972), p. 79.

_____ 3. Listen, wait, and relax as needed.

_____ 4. Emphasize the present situation and secure only the essential information from the person.

_____ 5. Try to recognize early the kind of person you are dealing with and continue to be sensitive to the individual and his or her needs.

_____ 6. Take hold of and use information as the person shows the interest and capacity to use help.

_____ 7. Do not pursue deeper problems that may appear, and avoid long, drawn-out discussions.

_____ 8. Kim used all these skills.

Turn to Answer 21 on page 601

F R A M E

4

REFERRING

Sometimes the solution to an individual's unmet need simply involves giving her information about a resource, such as the address of another agency. Frequently, however, the situation will not be so clear-cut, and you will need to do more than provide an address and a phone number. When an individual's unmet physical, emotional, or social needs require services from another agency, you may need to make a referral. The process of *referring* involves more than simply sending a person to a resource. You need to be actively involved in helping the person to find and use the resource and you must stay in touch with the person to make sure that the appropriate service has been received.

In addition to identifying an individual's unmet need and deciding who can best handle this need, you have to find out whether the individual is ready to accept help. Some people will be able to accept the assistance you are offering and will be able to take the steps necessary to receive help. More often, however, people who have unmet needs will be fearful and confused and will need your assistance in understanding why they need help and what the help will do for them. There are three ways you can prepare an individual to receive help:

1. Talk. Discuss the individual's feelings toward getting help. Should you discover that the person is afraid, feels guilty, or is acting hostile, you should make it possible for him or her to talk about these feelings. For example, you might say, "Let's talk about the pros and cons of this plan" or "Do you have some idea what this is going to be like?" Do not always assume that individuals have these feelings, but when they do, make it possible for them to talk.

2. Share responsibility. Involve individuals in planning how they will find and use the resource they need. You can help individuals to see the need for getting help by working *with them* in contracting the resource (whether it is someone in your agency or another resource). Will you make the phone call to the agency for them? Will you go with them? Do they know how to get there? Do they need to rehearse or practice what they need to do?

3. Explain the resources that are available. Sometimes individuals will be afraid to use another resource because they do not know or understand how this resource can help them. Using your knowledge of your community's resource systems, you should explain the functions of these resources as accurately as you can. However, in doing this, it is usually *not* a good idea to discuss the details of how other agencies operate or how the individual will be treated there because you cannot always be certain this information will be accurate and up to date. By being direct, sincere, and realistic, you will be able to help the individual understand the resource and how it might assist him or her.

Remember that people might be hesitant to accept help from another source for many reasons. For example, the resource may be far away from where they live or may seem large and impersonal. You should recognize when a person is not ready to accept help from another resource and use your brokering skills in preparing consumers to accept and use the help they may need.

Initiating a Referral

Before initiating a referral, there are three questions you need to answer. *When, how,* and *where* will you refer? Let's look at each of these questions so that you will understand how the referral process works.

When to refer. A referral is necessary when the consumer and you have identified an unmet need and discovered that meeting this need requires social, health, educational, or some other community service. Thus, meeting this need may require the services of your own agency and/or other community resources. You can determine if a consumer has certain needs by (1) meeting the consumer who comes and tells about the problem, (2) observing the consumer's circumstances, and/or (3) locating consumers in your community with unmet needs. Referrals are made after you have identified an individual's unmet need and have decided that meeting this need will require directing the person to some community resource.

How to refer. Referring a consumer to a resource is not just a simple matter of telling him where that resource is located. As explained above assessment precedes referral. Steps involved in the referral process include:

1. *Discuss* thoroughly with the consumer the purpose of the referral. Let the consumer know how and why you think this resource will be helpful to enhance her knowledge.

2. Assess the consumer's ability to contact the resource and how much help the consumer needs in doing so. If the consumer is to make the contact, a part of preparing the consumer might be role playing initiating the contact. You want to help the consumer acquire the skills that will ensure success.

3. If you are making the contact, make certain the resource can meet the consumer's needs. Even if the consumer is to make the contact, you may first need to screen the resource to make certain it is appropriate.

4. When the referral is accepted, get an *appointment time* from the resource and give this information to the consumer or help the consumer in making the appointment.

5. Make sure the consumer knows the appointment time, where the resource is located, and the name of the person to see when he arrives. Offer any support that is needed to help the consumer keep the appointment and get the needed service.

Intervention planning and contracting as described in Chapter 8 are part of the brokering process. A plan and contract reflecting the consumers' goals precede making the actual referral. Finally, it is critical to follow up to learn whether the referral was effective. Did the consumer receive the needed service and, if so, was the consumer's need met?

FRAME

5

Read the following passage and then answer the question below.

> Jason is 19 years old and has just moved to Middle City. He dropped out of high school when he was 15 and has never worked. Jason has located a place to live, but he is now looking for a job and is not having much luck. He comes to the welfare agency and meets Seth, an intake worker. Jason reacts angrily to Seth's suggestions that he see another worker about the possibility of enrolling in a youth employment program.

Jason is not yet prepared to receive assistance with his job search. Suggest at least two ways in which Seth might prepare Jason to take a more positive approach.

    1.

    2.

Turn to Answer 22 on page 601

FRAME

6

Read the following passage, then answer the question below.

> George M. is 68 years old and has been in a state prison for the past 20 years. It has been determined that George is now ready to be released. But in talking with George, you discover that he has no relatives, no means of support other than Social Security, and no place to live when he is released. He makes it very clear that he does not wish to go into a boarding home. He would like to live by himself and find some way of meeting older citizens in his community.

How would you help George? Number the actions you would take in the correct sequence. The first action you should take is already marked for you.

_____ Get an appointment for George with some of the resources that can help him and make sure George has this information.

_____ Spend time helping George to keep his appointments, possibly escorting him for his first visits.

_____ Talk with George directly about his situation, explaining the resources you might refer him to for assistance.

_____ Contact the resources you and George have agreed might offer him assistance with his needs.

Turn to Answer 23 on page 601

FRAME

7

> ***Where to refer.*** Where you will refer a consumer depends on the resources that are available in your community and your own ability to discover undeveloped or unused community resources. You have already examined some of the ways to identify the resource systems in your community (Lesson 1). However, you will frequently dis-

cover that even your active efforts to meet a consumer's unmet need may not result in locating a service to fill this need. This is because there are gaps in service in most communities. Gaps in service can occur because the needed services do not exist and because of the ways various resources limit their services by setting specific parameters for who will be served and how. The following case illustrates how specialization can create gaps in services:[3]

> Two boys, 10 and 11, are bedridden and paralyzed with muscular dystrophy. Prognosis is death within five years. Previous aid through the Crippled Children Commission has been terminated upon diagnosis, owing to the poor prognosis and the unavailability of hospital care for purely custodial cases. After full investigation by welfare, educational, judicial, and private agency personnel, no aid was given. At last contact, the mother was caring for these boys together with her other children, in a house with no plumbing, and with no help other than that supplied by an occasional visit from a physical therapist and a volunteer neighbor who read to the boys one afternoon a week. The judge of the juvenile court reported that the marriage of the parents appeared to be in jeopardy, as a result of long physical and mental strain. Reasons given by various agencies for not extending aid were:
>
> 1. Juvenile court: no neglect or other basis for jurisdiction.
> 2. Health department: no local health department.
> 3. Welfare and relief authorities (state and county): father is employed and thus ineligible for financial assistance; suggest foster care through special education services.
> 4. Crippled Children Commission: statute interpreted not to authorize home care.
> 5. Local school: insufficient personnel to furnish home tutoring.
> 6. State department of public instruction, special services division: locality not eligible for state-furnished special services.
> 7. Society for Crippled Children and Adults, Inc.: public agencies could help if they saw fit; private agency should not invade public agency field.

You can see from this example that referring a consumer to a resource will not always be a simple procedure. However, since many resources are highly specialized, gaps in services are a common occurrence in many communities. The important thing to remember is *not to give up!* When you discover a service gap in trying to meet an individual's need, there are at least two initial steps to take in trying to fill this gap: (1) You can *actively explore* your community for specific services and goods; and (2) you can *analyze your community* to determine whether any of its existing resources might be interested in providing an individual service. (For example, the Lions Club or other social clubs may have an interest in providing help to a consumer.)

You will be learning more about service gaps in your community and how to fill these gaps in Chapter 6, which deals with the process of mobilizing. Before you continue, stop for a minute and see if you can think of a consumer you have known who

---

[3]Harold Wilensky and Charles Lebeaux, *Industrial Society and Social Welfare* (New York: Free Press, 1965), pp. 250–251.

had an unmet need that could not be filled. See if you can think of any ways you might now try to meet that consumer's need. Then continue with Frame 8.

FRAME 8

THE IMPORTANCE OF FOLLOW-UP IN BROKERING

Don't forget consumers after you have referred them to another resource! Meeting service goals through a public welfare agency, a health department, an employment service, or a mental health center is no simple matter. Increasingly, if people are to get help from these resources, they need an informed guide who can help them to get what they need. Since consumers may find it difficult to get what they need, even after you have prepared them for help and have gone with them, you need to keep in touch with them to find out if they need your assistance and if the referral has been successful. If consumers need your assistance, there are several ways you can be of help:

1. Actively represent the consumer. When delays are unreasonable, you may have to telephone on behalf of the consumer to speed up the process. If you call a number of times and still cannot get any action, you may need to call someone with more authority.

2. Discuss problems. If the consumer did not get the service, what went wrong? This needs to be discussed, with you asking, for example, "How did it happen?" and "What do you want from this resource?" Any problems that have occurred should be discussed with the consumer.

3. Prepare the consumer. Make sure the consumer was adequately prepared for the referral, and if she or he was not, find out why and then help the person try again.

4. Straighten out difficulties. Did the consumer have trouble filling out forms? Was there difficulty in meeting all the eligibility requirements for the service? Is there another, more appropriate resource? You need to try to straighten out such difficulties either by communicating directly with the resource or by going to your own supervisor and asking for help.

When you are dealing with other resources on behalf of a consumer, remember to be very clear about what is needed. Try to be courteous and pleasant. Do not lose control of your own emotions, but act with and on behalf of consumers to help them get the services they need.

FRAME 9

Eric, a patient in a mental hospital, has been complaining of chest pains. You have referred him to the nurse for medical attention and possible X-rays. A few days later you contact Eric to find out the results of his visit. He tells you that the nurse was very busy and was not able to set up an appointment with the doctor. Eric did not know what to do, so he gave up.

If you were the worker in this situation, what would you do?

Turn to Answer 24 on page 601

Reaching Out to People in Your Community

In all communities there are people with unmet needs who do not know about the resources that are available to meet these needs. There are also people with unmet needs who know about available resources but, for various reasons, do not contact the resources that can help them. In this lesson you will learn what is meant by reaching out to your community to identify and help people with unmet needs.

Goal

Given a community or a description of a community, you will be able to demonstrate your brokering skills by explaining the techniques you would use to reach out to identify and assist individuals with unmet needs.

Learning Activities

To accomplish this goal, we will:

1. Examine the meaning and purpose of reaching out.
2. Explore the significance of the "hard-to-reach" agency or consumer.
3. Identify helpful ways of initiating a first contact with an individual, given a set of sample situations.
4. Consider four techniques for reaching out in your community.
5. Consider the importance of follow-up in reaching out.

FRAME
1

REACHING OUT—WHAT IS IT?

All human service agencies and organizations have an obligation to review their programs regularly so that services to consumers can be improved. Agencies must also work and plan to reach people who are not receiving services and who may already, or shortly, be in need and entitled to help and assistance. When you use your brokering skills to reach out to individuals in your community, you are helping your agency plan what services are needed and how they can be delivered to reach consumers in need.

Reaching out means *locating* the people who may need assistance, *identifying* the unmet needs of individuals in your community, and seeing that these individuals have *information* about and are *linked* with the appropriate resources that will meet their needs. The purpose of reaching out is to *identify* unmet individual needs and *prevent* these needs from getting worse. For example, by reaching out you may be preventing a young child from an illness by helping him to get a shot he needs; or you may be identifying a patient or resident who would like to participate in some kind of recreational program but does not know how to join.

Thus when you are reaching out in a community you will be assisting in identifying the problems affecting the individuals in that community and helping them make use of the appropriate community resources as aids in solving their problems. In so doing, you are making sure that the services your agency provides are known to the people for whom they were developed. In addition, you are providing a service that emphasizes the prevention of more serious problems.

FRAME

2

HARD-TO-REACH AGENCIES OR CONSUMERS

In the human services, you will frequently hear about people who are mentally ill, physically disabled, or poor or have other problems but do not use the services and resources that are available to help them. Often individuals who are blamed for not recognizing their problems and seeking assistance are characterized as hard to reach or unmotivated. But, more often, the problem of service availability rests with the hard-to-reach agency.

Many human service agencies are large and understaffed. Although people sometimes just do not know what help is available in their community, frequently potential consumers have tried to get help but have lost their self-confidence and patience because of repeated failures and frustrations in getting help. So some of the people with unmet needs in your community will be resentful, suspicious, angry, depressed, and hopeless. Others will be interested in listening to what you have to say.

To many people, human service agencies seem large, cold, and unfriendly. Therefore, human service workers should remember that the agency, the consumer, or both can be hard to reach.

FRAME

3

MAKING THE FIRST CONTACT

One of the most important tasks in effective outreach is establishing the first contact with an individual. This is sometimes assumed to be a difficult task since it usually means beginning a relationship with an individual you have not met before. However, establishing contact with an individual you do not know does not need to be difficult or complicated. Your success will depend on your ability to communicate clearly, impress the consumer with your wish to help, and ensure that the other person understands your intentions.

Keep the following helpful hints in mind when you are approaching an individual for the first time:[1]

---

[1]Adapted from Janet Rosenberg, *Breakfast: Two Jars of Paste* (Cleveland: Case Western Reserve University Press, 1972), pp. 63–65.

1. Understand yourself and your feelings. It is important to understand your own prejudices and feelings toward individuals in your community. Remember that it is easy to like and help someone who is similar to you, but it is much harder to understand someone who is different. We all have prejudices and feelings. When you are reaching out, you need to be aware of yourself and to understand what makes another person behave differently from the way you or others behave.

2. Approach the individual openly. Explain who you are and your reason for being available to help. Try to approach a person at a time when nothing much is going on so that other activities will not be distracting.

3. Try to understand people, their behavior, and their unmet needs. Show that you accept individuals as they are. Show that you care about their problems and are interested in helping.

4. Do not offer help too quickly. Take the time to try to understand the individual's unmet need before you rush to offer solutions. Help individuals to discover their own solutions to their problems. Make an effort to get to know individuals by encouraging them to talk about their needs.

5. Know what you can and cannot do. Be aware of what you can do to help an individual and of when you should go to other resources for help. Do not feel that you must do everything yourself!

F R A M E

Which of the following are examples of helpful ways of initiating a first contact with an individual consumer who may have an unmet need? After each example, circle your answer.

A. Telling a person who needs welfare that you think people on welfare are basically lazy.	Helpful	Not helpful
B. Finding out about a patient's need for recreation and telling her you cannot guarantee she will get what she needs, but that you will do as much as you can to help.	Helpful	Not helpful
C. Trying to start a conversation with a juvenile offender while he is playing cards with a fellow offender.	Helpful	Not helpful
D. Yawning when a young unwed mother expresses her feelings about putting her child up for adoption.	Helpful	Not helpful
E. Noticing that a consumer is getting very angry with the receptionist and taking time to talk with the consumer to try to understand the reasons for her anger.	Helpful	Not helpful

Turn to Answer 25 on page 602

F R A M E

OUTREACH TECHNIQUES

You will recall from the previous lesson that the basic steps involved in identifying an individual's unmet needs are to (1) find out as much as possible about the exact need, (2) find out what the person wants to do about the need or problem, and (3) begin to determine who can help and what information will be most successful in solving this need. These steps are usually followed when an individual comes to you for assistance; however, when you are reaching out, you are the one trying to find people who need assistance. While you will still be using these basic principles once you have located an individual with an unmet need, the key skill in reaching out is *finding* those individuals who need assistance. This process is also called *case finding*.

The following are four examples of techniques used to locate and engage individuals who cannot express or accept their need for help, those who have given up their efforts to get help, and those who do not know about the available resources for help.

1. Informal discussion with community residents. Be active in your community. Get to know as many people as you can so that they in turn can get acquainted with you. You may spend only a few minutes with people, telling them who you are and just getting to know them. Some people may at first be hesitant to discuss their problems with you. A good way to help them get to know you and what you are doing is by showing you are interested. Then they will be more willing to share their problems with you and receive your assistance. Do not try to force yourself on people, but do try to demonstrate your sincerity in wanting to help.

2. Observation. Be a good observer while you are working in your community. What do residents say to other residents? Do you notice any individuals who seem to have unmet needs that they may not recognize? By just watching individuals in their daily activities, you may be able to identify those who have problems or needs with which you may be able to help.

3. Interviews and questionnaires. Your agency or your supervisor may ask you to interview various people in your community to find out what their problems are. They may also provide you with a set of specific questions they would like community residents to answer. By interviewing various individuals and asking them specific questions on behalf of your agency, you will be able to discover what problems and needs are affecting people and to begin providing them with information that will help them in handling these problems.

4. Contacts with staff in your own agency and other agencies. When you see other workers in meetings or even while you are working, you might make it a habit to inquire whether they know of any individuals who may be having some problems. Other workers, including volunteers, clerical staff, your co-workers, or your supervisor, may know of individuals who have problems and may suggest that you make an effort to offer assistance.

FRAME
6

Read the following example and then answer the question below.

> Art is a worker in the state welfare department. While visiting the home of Mrs. Lane, a Food Stamp recipient, he asked if she knew of anyone who needed the services of a new program that provided meals and transportation for elderly citizens. Art learned that Mrs. Lane's parents and great aunts were in need of such services.

Circle the technique for reaching out that Art was using in this example.

a. Observation
b. Interviews and questionnaires

c. Informal discussion with a community resident

d. Contacts with staff in his own agency

Turn to Answer 26 on page 602

Turn to Answer 26 on page 602

FRAME

7

Read the following passage and then answer the question below.

Marty is an aide at a local clinic of the state health department. Although he is not assigned to work in the reception area, he passes through it several times a day. One day he noticed a woman he remembered seeing in the waiting area for the past few days. He also noticed that she was wandering around looking dazed and bewildered. Even though Marty did not work in the waiting area, he began to think about going over to the woman to see if there was anything he could do to help.

Check the statement that best describes what Marty should do in this situation.

_____ a. Marty has observed an individual who probably feels lost and confused. Even though he does not work in the waiting area, he should reach out and offer to help this individual.

Turn to Answer 27 on page 602

_____ b. Marty has observed an individual who is lost and confused. But Marty is not assigned to work in the waiting area of the clinic and should get back to his assigned duties.

Turn to Answer 28 on page 602

FRAME

8

THE IMPORTANCE OF FOLLOW-UP IN REACHING OUT

Remember our discussion of the importance of follow-up as a part of the referral process? Follow-up is also very important when reaching out. After initiating a contact with an individual, it is important to follow up on your initial contact. Follow-up is also used when individuals show no interest, hold back, or express anger at your attempts to contact them. You need to pursue and visit individuals again, even if they show no interest, especially if you think they have an unmet need that requires assistance.

Remember that it takes time for trust to develop and for an individual to engage in receiving assistance. So try to maintain your contacts with individuals by talking with them when and where you can. Assure them that you are interested in them and want to understand them. Express conviction about what you have to offer. Make it known that you regard the individual's feelings and problems as real and important. And stick to presenting the facts; do not make promises you cannot keep.

CHAPTER 4
Summary and Further Study

Chapter Summary

Chapter 4 described some of the basic principles of brokering, the process used to connect people with the services that will meet their needs. Lesson 1 described the resource systems found in most communities. These include the *informal resource system,* consisting of family, friends, and co-workers; the *formal resource system,* consisting of membership organizations or formal associations that exist to promote the mutual benefits and common interest of their members; and the *societal resource system,* which has been established through social legislation and voluntary citizen action to deliver services. Lesson 1 also recognized the inadequacies of each resource system relative to the problems people may encounter in trying to receive help. Finally, we reviewed some of the procedures that can be used to identify the resource systems in your community (such as consulting various directories).

In Lesson 2, special attention was given to two of the primary activities in brokering—*giving information* and *referring.* The steps and skills used in identifying an individual's unmet needs were first described to assist you in identifying whether a consumer needs information and/or a referral. Referrals occur when an individual's unmet needs require the provision of an appropriate community resource. The referral process involves preparing the consumer to receive assistance, discussing the purpose of the referral, assessing the consumer's knowledge and skills, contacting the appropriate resource, helping the consumer make an appointment, providing any support the consumer may need to get services, and following up to make sure the consumer has received the services he needs. The lesson concluded with a discussion of service gaps that may occur because the needed services do not exist or because of the ways various resources may limit their services to consumers. In this regard, we stressed the importance of actively exploring your community to fill service gaps and representing and assisting those consumers who may be having trouble getting help from existing resources.

Lesson 3 was concerned with the activity of *reaching out* to locate people who may need assistance and to prevent their problems and needs from getting worse. We noted that agencies and other resource systems frequently seem large and cold to the consumer and may be hard to reach. We also noted that consumers can be hard to reach. Attention was given to ways of making an initial contact with a community resident with such guidelines as understanding yourself, approaching individuals openly, trying to understand them, not rushing to offer help, and being aware of your limitations in helping. Examples of techniques to use in outreach included informal discussions with community residents, observations, interviews, questionnaires, and contacts with staff in your own and other agencies. The lesson concluded with a discussion of the importance of follow-up in reaching out.

Suggestions for Further Study

If you are interested in further study of the basic principles of brokering, you should investigate alternative schemes for categorizing and analyzing community resource systems. Making distinctions among informal, formal, and societal types is only one way of analyzing resource systems and may not prove useful from your perspective. Further study will also be necessary for a full understanding of the various resource systems and the inadequacies of each.

Expanding your knowledge of brokering should also include attention to communication skills, since these are basic to the process. It may be helpful to locate various case studies that illustrate the process of reaching out to help consumers meet their needs. (Some of these can be found in the book by Riessman et al., listed below.) Additional study will develop your ability to diagnose the unmet needs of consumers and thereby improve your skills in the brokering process. Remember, brokering is a specialty of human service workers; therefore, it is especially important that you become an expert broker!

The following readings can support further study and development of expanded knowledge and skills in human service brokering:

Ballew, Julius R., and George Mink. *Case Management in Social Work: Developing the Professional Skills Needed for Work with Multiproblem Clients.* Springfield, Ill.: Charles C. Thomas, 1996.

Collins, Alice H., and Diane L. Pancoast, *Natural Helping Networks: A Strategy for Prevention.* Silver Spring, Md.: National Association of Social Workers, 1976.

Connaway, Ronda S. and Martha E. Gentry. *Social Work Practice.* Englewood Cliffs, N.J.: Prentice-Hall, 1988.

Cox, Fred M., John L. Evlich, Jack Rothman, and John E. Tropman, eds. *Tactics and Techniques of Community Practice,* 2d ed. Itasca, Ill.: F. E. Peacock, 1984.

Cox, Fred M., John L. Evlich, Jack Rothman, and John E. Tropman, eds. *Strategies of Community Organization,* 4th ed. Itasca, Ill.: F. E. Peacock, 1987.

Crimando, William, and Ted F. Riggar, eds. *Utilizing Community Resources: An Overview of Human Services.* Delray Beach, Fla.: St. Lucie Press, 1995.

Fellin, Phillip. *The Community and the Social Welfare.* Itasca, Ill.: F. E. Peacock, 1987.

Fine, Sara F., and Paul H. Glasser. *The First Helping Interview: Engaging the Client and Building Trust.* Thousand Oaks, Calif.: Sage, 1996.

Froland, Charles, Diane L. Pancoast, Nancy J. Chapman, and Priscilla J. Kimboke. *Helping Networks and Human Services.* Beverly Hills, Calif.: Sage, 1981.

Hepworth, Dean H., and Jo Ann Larsen, *Direct Social Work Practice,* 4th ed. Pacific Grove, Calif.: Brooks/Cole, 1993.

Johnson, David W. *Reaching Out: Interpersonal Effectiveness and Self-Actualization,* 5th ed. Boston, MA: Allyn & Bacon, 1993.

Lauffer, Armand. *Getting the Resources You Need.* Beverly Hills, Calif.: Sage, 1982.

McMahon, Maria O'Neil. *Advanced Generalist Practice with an International Perspective.* Englewood Cliffs, N.J.: Prentice-Hall, 1994.

Pincus, Allen, and Anne Minahan. *Social Work Practice: Model and Method*. Itasca, Ill.: F. E. Peacock, 1973.

Reissman, Frank, Jerome Cohen, and Arthur Pearl. *Mental Health of the Poor*. New York: Free Press, 1964.

Rosenberg, Janet. *Breakfast: Two Jars of Paste*. Cleveland: Case Western Reserve University Press, 1972.

Weissman, Harold. *Individual and Group Experiences in the Mobilization for Youth Experience*. New York: Association Press, 1969.

Wilensky, Harold, and Charles Lebeaux. *Industrial Society and Social Welfare*. New York: Free Press, 1965.

Chapter 5

Consumer Advocating

Workers in the human services sometimes find it necessary to intervene on behalf of consumers in order to make sure they are provided with the resources to which they are entitled. When consumers are denied a service that they need, *and* when you *know* that they are entitled to that service, you are faced with a difficult decision. Should you try to defend the consumers' right to service, or should you keep quiet and accept things as they are? Even though there are risks involved, workers have a responsibility to defend and fight for the rights of consumers. This is part of a growing recognition on the part of the courts, legislators, and professionals themselves that the rights of consumers, as well as those of any other group, should be protected.

An advocate is one who pleads the cause of another, one who argues for a cause or a proposal. Lawyers are advocates when they fight for their clients and defend their legal rights before courts of law. In this chapter you will learn some basic concepts and principles of advocating as a human service worker. However, this chapter is only an introduction to a complex process.

In the human services, advocating is a special kind of pleading—standing up for an individual, a family, a group or a community. Advocating means standing up for individuals and being willing to do what is necessary to uphold their rights. While advocating does not mean making unreasonable demands on human service agencies, it does emphasize protecting and defending the rights of individuals by using recognized legitimate means on their behalf. Advocating is a challenging activity for any human service worker. In fact, it is so challenging that many workers are afraid of this activity, since it means they must speak out and confront human service agencies and institutions, sometimes even at the risk of losing their jobs.

When advocating, you may expect differences of opinion. This chapter introduces you to some of the basic skills involved in persuading and applying appropriate kinds of pressure on behalf of a consumer. Lesson 1 examines some basic techniques of advocating, such as pressuring and utilizing consumer grievance procedures. Since the protection of consumer rights is an important part of understanding advocating, Lesson 2 introduces some of the legal and human rights that are being defined and recognized for human service consumers. The overall objectives of this chapter are (1) to introduce you to some of the basic issues and principles involved in defending a consumer's rights to service, and (2) to illustrate some of the basic legal and human rights of human service consumers.

The following are some consumer advocating tasks that might appear in a human service job description:

1. Help out in a problem situation or dispute between consumers or between consumers and a service provider in order to achieve a satisfactory resolution.
2. Assist consumers to find or obtain supportive papers (e.g., birth records, licenses, Social Security numbers, and naturalization papers) in order to establish eligibility for services.
3. Plan or participate in organized campaigns or demonstrations in order to persuade officials or other decision makers to establish or change laws or policies on behalf of consumers.
4. Review service plans and procedures in order to assure that consumers' human rights are protected.
5. Describe community needs to decision makers (legislators, board members, and community officials) in order to persuade them to initiate, maintain, or restore programs.
6. Participate in legislative forums or hearings as a representative of the profession and consumers in order to explain and advocate a position on pending social welfare legislation.
7. Suggest or propose a plan to workers (or superiors) in order to gather needed support for a change in services, guidelines, or procedures.
8. Intercede on behalf of consumers in order to persuade others that the consumers qualify for services or financial assistance.

Advocating Techniques

When consumers are confronted with a situation in which they are denied services to which they are entitled, it may be necessary for the human service worker to consider the process of advocating. In this lesson you will review some of the techniques of advocating that are used in efforts to settle grievances or disputes between consumers and the human service system.

Goal

Given a description of a consumer in need of an advocate, you will be able to identify and describe two techniques that could be used with other agencies or other individuals in defending the consumer's rights to service.

Learning Activities

To accomplish this goal, we will:

1. Examine three reasons why human service consumers sometimes need advocates.
2. Study three factors to be considered in making the decision to assume an advocacy role.
3. Consider guidelines for overcoming fears of advocating.
4. Identify components of the technique of persuasion.
5. Explore three methods of persuasion, using examples.
6. Review five helpful hints to remember when persuading.
7. Distinguish between persuading and pressuring.
8. Explore two methods of pressuring.

FRAME
1

THE NEED FOR CONSUMER ADVOCATING

In their efforts to get services to people in need, workers sometimes discover a conflict between a consumer's needs and what an institution or agency is willing or able to do to meet that need. Usually there are three reasons why these situations can occur in delivering human services:

   1. The attitude of human service agencies and institutions. Often, the institutions and agencies with which individual consumers must deal are far from willing to provide services or even consider grievances brought to their attention. In fact, they are sometimes overtly negative, hostile, or secretive in concealing or distorting information about rules, procedures, and even office hours.[1]

2. What consumers know and feel about human services. Many people who need help from human service agencies and institutions are too uninformed, too apathetic, or feel too powerless to do anything when services are denied them or when they are not being served satisfactorily. Many will not exercise their rights, press for their needs, or appeal actions against them unless someone acts as their advocate. And if human service workers do not assume this role (or find someone who will), likely no one will.[2]

3. The wrongs suffered by consumers. In addition to being denied and uninformed about the services, consumers suffer other "wrongs" in the process of receiving services that they cannot "right" themselves. For example, some are harassed, some are "spied on," some are in institutions where they do not belong.

You can see from these situations, and probably from your own experience, that individuals who need help from the human services cannot always get this help on their own. They need someone to take their side and advocate for them.

F R A M E

2

In the human services it is sometimes necessary for workers to assume the role of advocates on behalf of consumers who are not being served satisfactorily. Check the reasons listed below that contribute to the importance of advocating.

_____ a. Many people with unmet needs are not familiar with human service agencies and feel too powerless to do anything when services are denied or delivered unsatisfactorily.

_____ b. Some human service agencies are, for various reasons, reluctant to provide services to "just anyone" who may need them, and these agencies can make it difficult for some people to get the help they need.

_____ c. Even though most human service agencies seek to make services available for anyone in need, consumers come in contact with agency workers who either refuse to help or do not know how to help.

_____ d. Consumers sometimes suffer "wrongs" in order to receive services, and they are not always aware of ways in which they can right these injustices.

Turn to Answer 29 on page 603

---

[1]Charles Grosser, *New Directions in Community Organization: From Enabling to Advocacy* (New York: Praeger, 1973), p. 197.
[2]Scott Briar, "The Current Crisis in Social Casework," *Social Work Practice 1967* (New York: Columbia University Press, 1967).

DECIDING TO ADVOCATE

Advocating is only one of many processes used to make sure that services are delivered to people in need. Making the decision to advocate on behalf of an individual consumer requires careful consideration of several factors.

First, you need to make certain that the complaint, action, or decision involves a legitimate grievance; you should not make unreasonable or unjustified demands on behalf of the consumer. If you are unsure about the merits of a consumer grievance, it is wise to check with a supervisor or other workers familiar with the situation before starting to advocate.

Second, you must decide whether advocacy is necessary. Have other means of solving the problem been tried? Is the need sufficiently important that strong measures are warranted? Is advocating the most useful process that can be applied in this situation? Before advocating, always explore other means of resolving the problem because it may be a result of a misunderstanding or lack of information.

Third, before advocating, discuss the problem thoroughly with the consumer and get his or her consent. This is especially important if advocating will require identifying the consumer by name to other sources. Of course, in some instances, getting a consumer's consent may be hard to do either because of the difficulty the consumer is having or because the consumer is simply unable to understand the situation. Whenever possible, it is critical to discuss future actions with the consumer and receive his or her support, understanding, approval, and participation; in order for worker and consumer to engage in the activity of advocating collaboratively.

You should always take the three steps outlined above before advocating. If the advocacy process is initiated as soon as the consumer encounters difficulty, then you run the risk of pursuing an unjustified complaint and alienating agency representatives who may be innocent of any wrongdoing.

Read the following example and then check the correct answer below.

Marcy's 8-year-old daughter is not feeling well, so Marcy takes her to the county health clinic. She is told that her daughter needs to be admitted to the hospital immediately for extensive tests. Marcy wants to stay with her daughter in the hospital since the child is very upset, but the head nurse refuses her request. When Marcy comes to you for help:

_____ a. Tell Marcy not to worry and immediately call the head of the nursing department at the hospital to complain about the situation.

Turn to Answer 30 on page 603

_____ b. Find out if the hospital allows parents to stay with their children. Discuss this with Marcy and decide that together you should try to discuss the situation again with the head nurse.

Turn to Answer 31 on page 603

_____ **c.** Tell Marcy not to worry and that you will check on the child to make sure she is okay.

Turn to Answer 32 on page 603

FRAME 5

You can see that making the decision to advocate on behalf of a consumer requires careful thought on your part. Before you learn some of the techniques of advocating, see if you can write in the spaces provided the three factors you need to consider before making the decision to be an advocate:

1.
2.
3.

If you have any trouble recalling these three factors, return to Frame 3 for a quick review.

FRAME 6

ADVOCACY GUIDELINES

One of the biggest difficulties for many workers to overcome in advocating is their fear that they will be refused when they confront any agency with a problem situation. An important guideline for overcoming this fear is to make it easy for the agency to say yes to your request. If you make an effort to practice the following three guidelines when advocating, you will have a better chance of getting a positive response to your request from the agency:[3]

1. Know the agency or resource well. Know who to contact and how. In most advocating situations, the first person to contact would be the one who was responsible for the unfavorable situation or decision. If satisfactory results are not obtained from this person, his or her supervisor may be able to help. If the situation is still unsatisfactory, you may need to contact other administrators and officials who may be in a position to help. The important thing to remember is to know as much as possible about the resource involved.

---

[3]Adapted from Janet Rosenberg, *Breakfast: Two Jars of Paste* (Cleveland: Case Western Reserve University Press, 1972), p. 83. Also see Roger Fisher and William Ury, *Getting to Yes* (New York: Penguin Books, 1981).

2. Be clear about the complaint or grievance. This is important no matter what advocating technique is being employed. State the complaint or grievance clearly so that the person who is receiving the complaint will understand the problem fully.

3. Be clear about what is being requested for the consumer. Finally, in any advocating situation it is important to state clearly what actions are needed for the consumer. Maximize consumer participation whenever possible.

F R A M E

7

Eric is a patient in a state mental hospital. Mike, an aide assigned to Eric's ward, has been talking with Eric about his complaint that the doctors and other staff have been cruel to him and treat him unjustly.

Mike is immediately outraged that a patient feels this way. He notices a doctor walking down the hall and rushes up to her saying, "I am going to be forced to go to the superintendent unless you and the rest of this staff start showing Eric that you care about him and respect him as an individual." Mike is stunned when the doctor says she does not have time to discuss this right now and walks away.

Can you think of reasons why Mike's attempt at advocating on Eric's behalf failed? Write them in the spaces below.

Turn to Answer 33 on page 603

F R A M E

8

THE TECHNIQUE OF PERSUASION

Several techniques are employed in advocating. One common technique is persuasion, something with which you are already familiar. For example, when a son begs his father for a new CD, or a woman urges her neighbors to work together to establish a recreation center for young people, or a dormitory supervisor urges students to keep the noise down so others can study, they are engaged in persuasion. Thus, when a worker seeks to influence someone to carry out a particular action or a decision by pleading or appealing to their reason or emotion, the technique of persuasion is being employed.

Before we discuss the components of persuasion,[4] we should note that these components apply to both oral and written persuasion, although our discussion emphasizes oral persuasion.

1. State the problem. When trying to persuade someone to change a decision or take an action, you must first state the problem clearly. The problem is the unsatisfactory

---

[4]See Elton Abernathy, *The Advocate: A Manual of Persuasion* (New York: McKay, 1964).

condition or difficulty that needs to be changed. It is important to plan carefully what will be said and to be certain the listener has an accurate understanding of the problem.

2. Discuss the problem. When discussing the problem, present all the important facts. This will help the other person understand more about the situation and why it needs to be changed. The facts about the problem include your observations of the situation, discussions with the consumer, discussions with other staff, and letters that may have been written about the situation. When discussing the problem, it is also important to try to keep your emotions under control and to show other people that you understand their position or why they may have acted as they did.

3. State the action desired. After discussing the problem situation, state the solution to the problem or the action desired. The solution to the problem should be one that you and the consumer have discussed. It should also be one that can be reasonably expected to win support, without sacrificing the rights of the consumer. When stating the proposed solution to the problem, you should also make a few comments regarding what will happen if the other person does not agree to the solution.

4. Summarize and restate. Finally, briefly summarize everything that has been discussed and agreed on. Restate the problem, the major facts, and the suggested or agreed on solution. It is also helpful to involve the other person in finding a solution to the problem situation that is mutually agreeable.

Now that you have reviewed the four components of the technique of persuasion it is important to remember that they should be applied in the proper order. *First,* state the problem; *second,* discuss the problem; *third,* state the proposed solution; and *fourth,* summarize the agreement, if any.

F R A M E

9

Read the following narrative, then answer the question below.

Roy is a welfare aide at the public welfare office. Doris, one of Roy's clients, called him telling him she was about to be evicted from her apartment because she was a month behind in her rent. Doris explained that she has been unable to get past the landlord's secretary to try to explain her situation.

Roy called Mr. Mann, Doris's landlord. He said, "Mr. Mann, I am calling you regarding one of your tenants, Doris S. I understand Doris is about to be evicted from her apartment, and I think if you were fully aware of her situation, you would find that eviction is not necessary." Roy then explained to Mr. Mann that Doris was no longer employed, but would receive within the next week a public assistance check that she intended to use to pay her rent. They then discussed some of the details relating to Doris's situation.

Roy tried to persuade Mr. Mann to change his decision to evict Doris from her apartment. Do you think Roy clearly stated the problem situation to Mr. Mann? Circle your answer. (Yes/No)

Turn to Answer 34 on page 604

Roy clearly stated the problem to Mr. Mann when he said, "I understand Doris is about to be evicted from her apartment, and I think if you were fully aware of her situation, you would find that eviction is not necessary." Roy started with the second part of his persuading effort by discussing Doris's situation with Mr. Mann so that he would be able to understand why Doris should not be evicted. Let's continue to follow Roy's efforts at persuading Mr. Mann.

During their discussion, Roy explained to Mr. Mann that Doris was behind in her rent payments because her past public assistance payments would not cover all of her recent expenses. However, she would be receiving her check within the week. Roy concluded their discussion saying, "I have discussed this situation with Doris, and we both feel that she should not be evicted since she will be paying her past due rent by the end of this week. We would like you to allow Doris to stay in her apartment, and we assure you the rent will be paid."

Mr. Mann assured Roy that an exception would be made now that he was aware of Doris's situation. Roy thanked Mr. Mann for his time and understanding but did not hang up before he restated their agreement regarding Doris's situation.

Underline the statement in Frame 10 that shows how Roy employed the third part of persuasion—stating his solution to the problem or stating the action he wanted Mr. Mann to take.

Turn to Answer 35 on page 604

Is the following statement true or false? Circle your answer. You may wish to refer back to Frame 10.

Although Roy was successful in persuading Mr. Mann to change his decision about evicting Doris, he forgot to make use of the fourth part of persuading, that is, to summarize briefly what they had discussed and agreed to regarding Doris.

a. True   **b.** False

Turn to Answer 36 on page 604   *Turn to Answer 37 on page 604*

FRAME
13

THREE METHODS OF PERSUASION[5]

Using the four components of persuasion, there are a number of ways to swing people to accept the proposed solution to an unsatisfactory situation. Three methods of persuasion are outlined below. You will probably be able to think of others based on your own experience and observations.

1. Common ground. This method begins by finding out where the worker and the other person agree. For example, both might find out that they agree, first, that the consumer has a problem and, second, that they want to find some way to remedy the situation. After both have agreed on something, the worker begins slowly to reveal the facts about the problem and to describe the situation. For example, the worker might say, "But here is something I'd like you to think about" or "Here is a good example of what we have been discussing." If the person doesn't want to listen or shows signs of discomfort, wait for another time to try again.

2. Cards on the table. In situations that are obviously not going to be remedied by finding a common ground or when the worker feels more comfortable being straightforward and honest, showing his or her true feelings can be very useful and persuasive. The worker might say, for example, "I know you disagree with me, but I want you to know exactly where I stand."

3. The blunt assault. This method is really an extension of the cards-on-the-table strategy. It is a very difficult procedure and does *not* work in most situations. In fact, it should be used only when other ways of persuasion have been tried and when the problem is an outright denial of a consumer's rights to service. The worker might say, for example, "I'm going to be blunt with you. I'm opposed to your decision in every way. I'll do everything I can to change it. Here's why I'm going to fight."

FRAME
14

Let's review the three methods of persuasion by examining three sample advocating situations. Read each situation, then check which persuasion technique is being used.

Situation 1. A consumer who is clearly eligible to receive health care has been denied treatment at the county health clinic. The worker goes directly to the supervisor responsible for this action and says the following:

> I'm not going to waste any time. You have denied Mrs. Haney services she is entitled to, and I am going to do whatever is necessary to see that she receives the treatment she is supposed to get.

---

[5]Adapted from Lynn Surles and W. A. Stanbury, *The Art of Persuasive Talking* (New York: McGraw Hill, 1960), pp. 49–63.

In this situation the worker is using the persuasion technique of

_____ **a.** common ground.

_____ **b.** cards on the table.

_____ **c.** blunt assault.

Situation 2. A worker calls another agency to try to get some information that has been denied to one of his consumers. The receptionist answering the phone says that obtaining this information is impossible. The worker says the following:

I sympathize with you. I run into many of the same problems where I work. We've got so many consumers and so many records that it gets pretty difficult to keep up with all the details somebody wants about a particular consumer.

In this situation, the worker is using the persuasion technique of

_____ **a.** common ground.

_____ **b.** cards on the table.

_____ **c.** blunt assault.

Situation 3. A worker calls a representative of another agency about a consumer who has been denied the opportunity to visit his young son, who is being detained by the juvenile authorities. The worker says to this representative:

I'm going to be very frank with you. Mr. Blink has been trying to visit his son for the past three days, and his requests have been repeatedly refused. I'd like you to understand that I am calling to see that Mr. Blink is granted the opportunity to see his son as soon as possible.

In this situation, the worker is using the persuasion technique of

_____ **a.** common ground.

_____ **b.** cards on the table.

_____ **c.** blunt assault.

Turn to Answer 38 on page 604

FRAME

15

General Hints on Persuasion

You should now have a good understanding of how the technique of persuasion is employed in advocating on behalf of a consumer. In addition, it may be helpful to remember the following hints when persuading someone to change an action or a decision:[6]

1. Always try to be sincere and speak with conviction.
2. Look the other person in the eye.
3. Avoid negative appeals; do not start out by telling people you know they are not interested in the problem or you know that the only reason they are listening to you is because they are being forced to.
4. Do not do all the talking; let the other person tell you how she sees the problem and what she thinks is an acceptable solution. Request the person's advice.
5. Control your emotions—try not to show anger or irritation.

FRAME

16

THE TECHNIQUE OF PRESSURING

There are times when efforts at persuasion will not be successful in correcting or changing a consumer's situation. When this happens, workers can use the alternative technique of pressuring. Pressuring involves the use of some kind of *forceful action* on behalf of the consumer and implies bold and vigorous efforts. Pressuring is a powerful technique, and considerable caution should be exercised in using it, since it can create hostility and resistance in the people involved. Pressuring should be used only when

1. Other means of advocating, such as persuasion, have been tried and have failed to get the actions desired.
2. There is considerable evidence that an injustice has occurred.
3. It appears reasonable to assume that there is a chance of succeeding with this advocating technique.

Before we discuss some of the different ways that pressuring can be used in advocating, it is important to note that your use of pressuring will require strong support and a great deal of assistance from your supervisor and other workers. If your supervisor is unwilling to give you the support needed to use the pressuring technique, then you should carefully reconsider the consequences of proceeding with this technique, since your job within the agency will be less secure without the supervisor's support.

---

[6]Surles and Stanbury, *The Art of Persuasive Talking,* pp. 49–63.

Grievance Procedures

One example of a pressuring method is making use of any formal procedures that your agency has adopted for handling consumer grievances. Some human service agencies, such as welfare and mental health agencies, provide the opportunity for consumers who are dissatisfied with the actions of the agency to make a formal appeal to agency officials asking that conditions or decisions affecting them be changed. When agency officials receive notice of this appeal, they usually give the consumer a chance to present his case at a hearing before representatives of the agency or other designated officials. Many consumers are not even aware of their right to appeal or challenge decisions affecting them, so if your agency has any consumer grievance procedures, you should be sure consumers know and understand that they have this right.

What are the usual steps in utilizing consumer grievance procedures?[7] Consumers and/or their workers may decide to appeal an action when consumers are dissatisfied with the services they are receiving or are denied services to which they are entitled. After the decision is made to appeal, the consumer, the human service worker, or both make a verbal or written request for a hearing. Usually a request for a hearing is accompanied by a written summary that gives all the necessary information relating to the consumer's challenge. This summary generally includes the following information:

1. Consumer's name and address
2. Statement of the specific action or decision being challenged
3. Statement of the consumer's current situation and how this relates to the challenge being made
4. Concluding statement describing why the challenge should be accepted

The consumer will then be notified of the time and place of the hearing. Most procedures give consumers the right to represent themselves or have someone else (e.g., a worker or an attorney) represent them, and the right to bring any additional people they need for support. When the hearing is held, all the information and facts relating to the claim will be examined by the agency representatives and the consumer. The consumer will then be notified of the decision reached as a result of the hearing. Should the consumer not be satisfied with this decision, there is usually some provision for making one other appeal to a higher level official.

F R A M E

17

Check the correct response. Pressuring differs from persuasion in that it involves

_____ **a.** understanding the other side's position.

Turn to Answer 39 on page 605

---

[7]Adapted from Department of Health and Rehabilitative Services, Florida Division of Family Services, *Fair Hearing Manual* (Tallahassee, October 15, 1971); and Joel F. Handler, "Justice for the Welfare Recipient: Fair Hearings in AFDC—The Wisconsin Experience," *Social Service Review* 43, 1 (Mar. 1969): 12–34.

_____ **b.** forceful action.

Turn to Answer 40 on page 605

_____ **c.** an appeal to reason.

Turn to Answer 41 on page 605

FRAME

18

Check the correct response. Pressuring is an advocating technique that should be used

_____ **a.** whenever you see any situation where it might be tried.

Turn to Answer 42 on page 605

_____ **b.** with a great deal of caution.

Turn to Answer 43 on page 605

_____ **c.** with strong support and a great deal of assistance from your supervisor.

Turn to Answer 44 on page 606

_____ **d.** when a consumer is dissatisfied with agency decisions affecting him.

Turn to Answer 45 on page 606

_____ **e.** B and C are correct.

Turn to Answer 46 on page 606

_____ **f.** A and D are correct.

Turn to Answer 47 on page 606

FRAME

19

A request for a hearing is usually accompanied by a written summary. Check which of the following are *not* typically included in this summary.

_____ **1.** Consumer's name and address
_____ **2.** Copy of all the consumer's records the agency has on file
_____ **3.** Statement of the specific action or decision being challenged
_____ **4.** Picture of the consumer

_____ **5.** Statement of the consumer's current situation and how this relates to the challenge being made

_____ **6.** Detailed description of all your contacts with and observations of the consumer

_____ **7.** Concluding statement describing why the challenge should be accepted

Turn to Answer 48 on page 606

FRAME

20

The Last Resort

Community resources—individuals or groups—may be used to bring pressure to bear on the consumer's behalf. For example, a lawyer could be contacted for the consumer if the person's rights are being violated. Often just a telephone call from a lawyer expressing interest in a particular case will be enough to convince someone that they are acting without respect for a consumer's rights. Other uses of resources include contacting city or county officials and state legislators. As with other pressuring techniques, these methods also require that you work closely with your supervisor and other workers to make certain you are using the most effective means of assisting the consumer in getting the services he or she needs.

Having now completed Lesson 1, you can see that there are a number of ways to defend and fight for the rights of consumers and that making the decision to advocate requires careful consideration and preparation.

Rights Issues in the Human Services

This lesson provides a very basic introduction to a vast area of knowledge and skills—legal and human rights—that underpins efforts of human service workers to advocate effectively on a consumer's behalf. Before the 1960s, consumers routinely lost or were deprived of some basic rights if they received certain kinds of human services (e.g., corrections, treatment in psychiatric hospitals, welfare). Since the 1960s, an increasingly complex and ever-changing body of law, regulation, and principles to define the rights of human service consumers has taken shape. This is due primarily to the work and determination of legal and public policy advocates.

Human service advocacy efforts are undertaken to change existing laws and policies and to propose new ones to help the consumer access the benefits to which he or she is entitled. Legal and human rights can be invoked as an argument to gain access where services have been denied or to create positive change in the framework of legal and human rights that legitimates delivering human services.

Because the body of knowledge governing "rights" of human service consumers changes continually and is impossible to cover in the limited space we have in this book, this lesson is a starting point. In very general terms, it describes some of the laws and basic rights relevant to human service consumers. The suggestions for further reading at the end of the chapter offer examples of literature you can consult for contemporary documentation of the rights of particular human service populations with whom you are working. The "issue scanning" skills you developed in Chapter 2 are relevant to how you should approach the material in this lesson. That is, we hope you will be strongly motivated to pursue, independently, a deeper understanding of legal and other rights as they apply to the consumers with whom you work. This kind of knowledge is absolutely essential to the effective practice of advocacy in the human services.

Goals

When you finish this lesson, you will be able to explain two kinds of rights, discuss the evolution of legal rights in America, and identify at least six basic rights that should be guaranteed to all human service consumers.

Amy Rebecca Olk, a freelance writer and volunteer with local and international humanitarian organizations, took the lead in reconceptualizing and rewriting this lesson for the fourth edition.

Learning Activities

To accomplish these goals, we will:

1. Discuss the meaning of *rights*.
2. Distinguish between legal rights and natural or human rights.
3. Consider the historical and philosophical basis for American legal rights and the evolution of legal rights of women in America as an example of how rights change over time.
4. Consider some "rights issues" pertaining to three groups of human service consumers.
5. Reflect on examples of human rights that some people believe should be guaranteed to all human service consumers.

FRAME

1

WHAT ARE RIGHTS?

> Government is a contrivance of human wisdom to provide for human wants. Men have a right that these wants should be provided for by this wisdom.
> —Edmund Burke (1729–1797)

> Wherever there is a human being, I see God-given rights inherent in that being, whatever may be the sex or complexion.
> —William Lord Garrison (1805–1879)

What does it mean when we say that human service consumers have rights? What does it mean to say that all people have rights? Webster's defines "right" as "a just claim or title," or "that which is due to anyone by just claim, legal guarantees, moral principles, etc." The ongoing, heated—and sometimes violent—debates over such issues as "civil rights," "gay rights," "welfare rights," "abortion rights," and, quite recently, the "right to die" are indications that the meaning of "just—defined as "guided by truth, reason, justice, and fairness"—is subject to continuous reinterpretation. The purpose of this lesson is not to explore such issues in depth, but rather to provide you with a basic introduction to the notion of rights in historical and philosophical context, followed by some examples of contemporary legal and human rights issues, particularly as they pertain to human service consumers.

To gain a better understanding of what rights are, it is necessary to examine in turn two major types of rights: *legal rights* and *natural or human rights*. A legal right belongs to a person because it has been established by the government, the legislature, the courts, or some other policy-making organization. The most important thing to remember about legal rights is that they are theoretically *enforceable* and recognized by a law or policy. "Human rights" is essentially a twentieth-century term for "natural rights" or "the rights of man."[1] A *human* or *natural right* is a right that belongs to people simply because they are human beings. Not all human rights are recognized or upheld by laws. Some human rights are also legal—that is, they are recog-

---

[1]Maurice Cranston, *What Are Human Rights?* (London: Bodley Head, 1973), p. 1.

nized by law and enforceable—but many that are not recognized by law are not enforceable even when they are denied or violated.

Human or natural rights are derived from the concept of *natural law,* which holds that there is a law higher and more powerful than that of man, whose authority is human reason, Justice, God, morality, etc. *Natural rights,* then, are the rights derived from natural law—the inborn rights of every human being as they exist in the state of nature. Throughout history, philosophers have disagreed about the very existence of natural law, some claiming it to be nothing but an illusion, an unreal metaphysical entity. Many moral and philosophical arguments, both supporting and challenging the existence of natural law, as well as different interpretations of what natural law is or may be, have traditionally influenced the way that societies and governments in the West define, enforce, or deny rights to their citizens.

Legal rights and natural or human rights are only two of the many types of rights. A discussion of all of the different rights that can be identified goes far beyond the scope of this book and into the realms of philosophy, political science, law, history, and theology. However, a familiarity with these two types of rights forms the basis for understanding the document that sets forth the nation's fundamental laws and form of government and defines the rights and liberties of the American people and therefore the framework in which human services are created and delivered: The United States Constitution.

FRAME 2

Provide answers to the two exercises below.

Legal rights (check the correct response):

_____ **a.** Belong to people simply because they are human beings.

_____ **b.** Are not enforceable.

_____ **c.** Are recognized by a law or policy.

_____ **d.** Belong to a person as a favor.

_____ **e.** Are the inborn rights of every human being.

Turn to Answer 49 on page 607

The belief in the existence of natural law is universal, having been upheld by all philosophers throughout history. (True/False)

Turn to Answer 50 on page 607

RIGHTS IN HISTORY

> The republican is the only form of government which is not eternally at open or
> secret war with the rights of mankind.
>
> —Thomas Jefferson (1743–1805)

During the European historical period referred to as the Enlightenment (or the Age of Reason), the concept of natural rights was at the forefront of political and philosophical discourse. John Locke, an extremely influential seventeenth-century English philosopher and natural rights theorist, wrote in his *Two Treatises of Government* that:

> The state of nature has a law of nature to govern it, which obliges every one; and
> reason, which is that law, teaches all mankind who will but consult it, that, being
> all equal and independent, no one ought to harm another in his life, health, lib-
> erty, or possessions.

Locke, however, realized that the state of nature was in practice unstable, because people tended to violate the natural rights of others. For all human beings to enjoy their natural rights, then, it was necessary for them to join together by means of a *social contract:* the willful surrender of some personal liberties in exchange for a government designed to enforce laws protecting these rights. These and other key elements of Locke's political philosophy, such as the concept of majority rule, were influential in shaping the American Revolution. After the confederate states won independence in the Revolutionary War (1775–1783), it became necessary to establish a strong national government that would promote unity among the states and establish protection for the rights of states and individuals. On July 4, 1776, the American colonies borrowed the words of John Locke to declare their freedom from British rule with the adoption of the Declaration of Independence, which states under the "Declaration of Rights" that:

> We hold these truths to be self-evident, that all men are created equal, that they
> are endowed by their Creator with certain unalienable Rights, that among these
> are Life, Liberty, and the Pursuit of Happiness.

The purpose of the United States Constitution and the Bill of Rights was to define the rights set forth in the Declaration of Independence in greater detail. The Constitution was drafted with the aim of translating moral rights into enforceable legal rights. Thus, the document that sets forth the nation's fundamental laws, defines the rights and liberties of the American people, and lists the aims of the government, has its roots in the concept of natural law.

As you reflect on the rights issues mentioned in the upcoming frames of this lesson and their significance with respect to particular groups of human service consumers and society as a whole, you will realize that the laws evolve as our search for truth and justice—that which is right, good, and reasonable—continues. As a human service advocate, or supporting another human service advocate, you will play an active role in this search. For example, consider the evolution of women's rights in America described in the box below.

An Example of How Rights Evolve: The Evolution of Women's Rights in America

Throughout most of history, women have been denied many of the legal rights and opportunities guaranteed to men. In addition to the rights denied them because of their gender, African American women have suffered a long history of slavery, racial oppression, and discrimination which has amounted to a further restriction of their rights and liberties. Although much has changed over the course of the twentieth century, racial and gender discrimination, as well as measures taken to combat it, continue to play a significant role in the shaping of policy pertaining to female human service consumers.

> Men, their rights and nothing more; women, their rights and nothing less . . .
> Failure is impossible.
> —Susan B. Anthony (1820–1906)
> American Suffragist

- St. Jerome, a fourth-century Latin father of the Christian church said, "Woman is the gate of the devil, the path of wickedness, the sting of the serpent, in a word a perilous object."
- Thomas Aquinas, the thirteenth-century Christian theologian, said that woman was "created to be man's helpmeet, but her unique role is in conception. . . . Since for other purposes men would be better assisted by other men."
- During colonial times, only boys were given a formal education. Girls were sometimes permitted to attend school during the summertime, when the young men were working.
- In the early 1830s, married women had no legal right to do as they wished with their own earnings.
- In 1839, Mississippi passed a law allowing married women to own property separate from their husbands.
- In 1868 and 1870, the 14th and 15th amendments to the U.S. Constitution guaranteed suffrage (the right to vote) to all men. It was not until 1920, with the passage of the 19th amendment, that women were granted full suffrage.
- During the nineteenth century, women worked up to 12 hours a day in cramped, poorly ventilated mills and factories—the only jobs deemed acceptable for them. It was not until the 1910s that the states began to pass laws to improve the working conditions of women and children and limit working hours.
- Women were not permitted to attend colleges with men until 1920.
- In 1948, the first women's rights convention took place in New York. Written by Elizabeth Cady Stanton, the convention's declaration read that "all men and women are created equal" and that "the history of mankind is a history of repeated injuries and usurpations on the part of men toward woman."
- In 1963, the Equal Pay Act guaranteed equal wages to men and women doing equal work.
- In 1968, Shirley Chisholm of New York was the first black woman elected to the House of Representatives.
- In 1971, the Supreme Court ruled that unequal treatment based on gender was a violation of the 14th amendment to the Constitution.
- In 1972, the Senate approved the Equal Rights Amendment (ERA), which stated that "Equality of rights under the law shall not be denied or abridged by the United States or any state on account of sex."

- In 1973, the United States Supreme Court ruled that a woman could not be denied the right to a legal abortion during the first three months of pregnancy.
- In 1984, a major political party chose Geraldine Ferraro to run for vice president, the first woman ever nominated for this position.
- In 1995, the Fourth Annual World Conference on Women was held in Beijing, China.

FRAME
4

A REFLECTION ON RIGHTS

1. Discussion and debate surrounding legal, human, and other types of rights appear frequently in the media. As mentioned above, rights issues can lead to heated debate and even violence. When reading, watching television, or surfing the Internet, try paying particular attention when rights are mentioned. What kinds of rights are being discussed? Whose interests are at stake? What clues does the issue provide you about individual or societal values, beliefs, and fears? Perhaps you come across a discussion or debate concerning the rights of a terminally ill person with AIDS (acquired immune deficiency syndrome) to commit doctor-assisted suicide rather than endure prolonged suffering. What types of rights—or ideas about rights—might be involved in this or some other rights issue?

2. How do you think that the rights issues you identified might be viewed in the year 2060? Do you think that today's debates will seem silly or outdated by future standards? Describe your thinking to a group of your colleagues and to a group of human service consumers, and then engage each group in a discussion and report the results.

FRAME
5

EXAMPLE OF RIGHTS ISSUES PERTAINING TO THE MENTALLY DISABLED

The term "mentally disabled" refers to a person with a developmental disability—typically mental retardation—or a psychiatric disability, also called a *mental illness* or a *mental disorder*. Only when a person's mental condition has an impact on his or her place in society do legal rights become an issue. For example, if a woman who is being successfully treated for bipolar disorder (manic-depressive illness) is rejected for an employment position solely on the basis of her psychiatric history, a legal response is in order.

As a group, the mentally disabled have suffered a long history of discrimination, exclusion from community life, stigmatization, mistreatment, and dehumanization. Until the 1960s, the constitutional rights of the mentally disabled, particularly those confined to institutions, were regularly violated. Thousands of involuntarily confined residents daily performed institution-maintaining labor—without any compensation—that would otherwise have required the hiring of regular employees. Inadequate or no treatment, routinized staff beatings, and unsanitary conditions prevailed in state institutions, to which over half a million people were confined. Not until the 1970s, when media exposure of apalling conditions in state institutions sparked public outrage, was the legal rights movement for people with mental disabilities set in motion.

A first wave of reform resulted in the formal recognition of some important rights of the institutionalized mentally disabled, such as the right to due process in the decision to institutionalize them; the right to freedom from abuse; payment for labor; nutritious food; a clean, sanitary environment; medical care; and appropriate habilitative treatment. The next stage of reform focused on the right to informed consent and freedom from exploitation, the right to be free from experimental or dangerous treatments and the rights to be paid for labor within the institution, to avoid involuntary sterilization, to refuse certain forms of treatment, and more.[2] Other important developments during this time were the community health movement in mental health and the growing recognition of the ability of many developmentally disabled individuals to learn and to lead productive lives outside the institutional setting.

Since the mid-1980s, new ideas about the place of the mentally disabled in society have emerged. Professionals and self-advocacy groups have argued that consumers of mental health and mental retardation services should play a more active, collaborative role in their own recovery and treatment. Rather than viewing mentally disabled people as flawed beings to be "fixed" by the system, the system should be driven by consumers' individual goals, needs, and preferences.[3] If inclusion and integration into the community are to be achieved, people with mental disabilities must be guaranteed the right to nondiscrimination, a right that is ensured by the Americans with Disabilities Act passed by Congress in 1991.

The following are some examples of rights issues, with descriptions of laws that have been recognized and defined for people with mental disabilities over the last several decades. While most of these rights have been firmly established, bear in mind that provisions vary from state to state and that statutes and regulations change frequently.

Involuntary commitment. Involuntary commitment is by far the most controversial and troubling issue in mental disability law. Here, the constitutional rights to individual liberty and protection from harm come into direct conflict. While the purpose of involuntary commitment is to provide treatment to an individual judged to be dangerous to himself or others, commitment represents a major infringement of the right to liberty.[4] Because of the controversial nature of this issue, state courts and legislatures have established stringent standards for involuntary institutionalization which contain procedural safeguards designed to protect the rights of the committed individual. While the right to a judicial hearing to contest involuntary confinement is guaranteed, the right to a hearing *before* commitment is not. The individual has a right to notice before a commitment hearing, as well as the right to attend and participate in the hearing.

Right to treatment. In *Wyatt v. Stickney,* a 1971 case, an Alabama federal court ruled that people involuntarily institutionalized for a mental illness have a constitutional right to treatment in exchange for their loss of liberty. A similar ruling was later issued for people with mental retardation. There are many variations in state and federal law and policy regarding this right, but the standards governing care and treatment of the involuntarily committed mentally disabled generally contain the same basic elements, such as the right to a professionally acceptable treatment plan tailored to individual needs, the right of the individual to participate in the development and revision of the

---

[2]Robert M. Levy and Leonard S. Rubenstein. *The Rights of People With Mental Disabilities* (Carbondale: Southern Illinois University Press, 1996), p. 3.

[3]Levy and Rubenstein, *The Rights of People With Mental Disabilities,* p. 7.

[4]Levy and Rubenstein, p. 15.

treatment plan, and the right to the least restrictive alternative. However, people with mental disabilities who do *not* live in an institution, and therefore are not in state custody, generally have no rights to community-based services under the Constitution.[5]

Right to the least restrictive alternative. The doctrine of the least restrictive alternative, incorporated into the legislation of virtually every state, guarantees individuals the right to treatment under the least restrictive conditions possible. For example, numerous court decisions have held that the states may not involuntarily institutionalize people with mental disabilities if services and programs in the community can provide them with adequate habilitation.

Right to education. Under Section 504 of the 1973 Rehabilitation Act, the 1975 Individuals with Disabilities Education Act or IDEA (formally called the Education for All Handicapped Children Act), and the 1990 Americans with Disabilities Act, all children and young adults with mental disabilities between the ages of three and twenty-one have the right to a free and appropriate public education. Many associated entitlements vary from state to state and, at this writing, are being revised.[6]

Right to payment for working. Thirty years ago, forcing the institutionalized mentally disabled to work without pay was recognized as a violation of the 13th Amendment of the Constitution.[7] Today, most state laws and regulations require that residents receive financial compensation for any work performed for the upkeep of the institution. Additionally, residents cannot be forced to work if they do not want to.

Sterilization. Sterilization is a surgical method used to prevent a person from having children. From the late 1800s until the 1960s, this practice was promoted as part of the now-discredited eugenics movement, which sought to improve the quality of the nation's gene pool by forcibly sterilizing people with mental disabilities as well as certain felons.[8] Today, most states have either repealed or rewritten their sterilization laws, so that involuntary sterilization is subject to very stringent standards. People with mental disabilities must be given the right to a hearing, the right to be represented by an attorney, and the right to appeal the decision before sterilization is authorized.

FRAME
6

The right to the least restrictive alternative means that (check the correct response):

_____ **a.** A developmentally disabled person should not be institutionalized if there are other services and programs in the community that can meet his or her needs

Turn to Answer 51 on page 607

---

[5]DeShaney v. Winnebago County Department of Social Services, 489 U.S. 189 (1989).
[6]Levy and Rubenstein, p. 252.
[7]Johnson v. Henne, 355 F.2d 129 (2nd Cir. 1966); Johnson v. Ciccone, 260 F. Supp. 553 (W.D. Mo. 1966).
[8]Levy and Rubenstein, p. 131.

_____ **b.** When a developmentally disabled person is institutionalized, she has the right to a judicial hearing, notice before the hearing, and the right to participate in it.

Turn to Answer 52 on page 607

FRAME

7

Read the example below and then indicate the correct response.

Alice is a resident in an institution for the developmentally disabled. She is required to see that all beds are made and floors are swept in her unit each day.

In most states, is Alice entitled to a fair wage for this responsbility?

_____ **a.** Yes

_____ **b.** No

Turn to Answer 53 on page 607

FRAME

8

Check which of the following statements is true. The right to treatment means that:

_____ **a.** People who are involuntarily institutionalized for a mental illness generally have the right to a professionally acceptable treatment plan.

_____ **b.** People with mental disabilities who do not live in an institution generally have rights to community-based services and treatment.

Turn to Answer 54 on page 607

FRAME

9

Reflection on the Rights of the Mentally Disabled. In recent years, the term "mental disability" has been expanded to include difficulties such as alcoholism and drug addiction. How do you think this broader conception of mental disability will change the way that rights of those individuals traditionally labled "mentally disabled" are perceived? Discuss this in a small group or write a short paper describing what you think and what you feel.

EXAMPLE OF RIGHTS ISSUES PERTAINING TO INMATES IN CORRECTIONAL INSTITUTIONS

As an institution, our penal and "correctional" system is an abject failure. The conditions in America's jails and prisons virtually ensure psychological impairment and physical deterioriation for thousands of men and women each year. Reformation and rehabilitation is the rhetoric; systematic dehumanization is the reality. Public attention is directed only sporadically toward the subhuman conditions that prevail in these institutions, and usually only because the prisoners themselves have risked many more years in confinement, and in some cases even their lives, to dramatize their situation by protest.[9]

The following are some of the basic rights of inmates that have been recognized in various parts of the United States.

Freedom from cruel and unusual punishment. Inmates have an absolute right to be free from cruel and unusual punishment; however, this is a right that is easy to state but often difficult to enforce because different standards are used to define what constitutes such punishment. Generally, three tests are applied to determine whether a punishment is cruel and unusual: (1) Does the punishment shock the conscience of a civilized society? (2) Is the punishment unnecessarily cruel? and (3) Does it go beyond what is necessary to achieve a legitimate aim of the correctional institution? Using these three tests, various states have decided that inmates have the right not to be confined in solitary for an excessive period of time, the right to a reasonable opportunity for physical exercise, and the right to be free from any physical or corporal punishment.

Right to communication. Most states have established for inmates the right to communication with the outside world, especially with attorneys, courts, and government officials. However, there are still limitations in most states regarding the free flow of written correspondence and reading materials. Most states give prison officials the right to read all nonlegal materials and personal correspondence of an inmate and to withhold or censor these materials if they feel it is necessary. Often, inmates are not informed that their communication has been withheld or censored, and they are thus denied any opportunity to challenge these actions.

Right to medical treatment. Lack of adequate medical, dental, and psychiatric care is usual in many correctional institutions. However, the general rule today is that inmates have a right to be provided with medical treatment. It should be noted that in most instances, the inmate is not considered the final judge of what medical treatment is necessary. The courts will usually accept the testimony of prison officials and doctors that treatment was adequate. Inmates should also have the right to be protected

---

[9]David Rudovsky. *The Rights of Prisoners* (Carbondale, Ill: Southern Illinois University Press, 1988), p. xi.

from sexual assault and to receive education and training while in the prison, but these rights are guaranteed in very few states.

Right to use available procedures for review of complaints. Inmates have a right to use available administrative procedures for review of their complaints. For example, many prisons provide for an internal review of the complaints registered by inmates. Inmates also have the right to challenge prison conditions in the courts.

Notice of rights. Some states have recognized the right of inmates to receive adequate advance notice concerning the kind of conduct that will result in discipline and/or punishment. Regarding prison disciplinary hearings, very few courts or states have been willing to specify an inmate's rights; however, some have held that the inmate is entitled to a written notice of the charges against him, a record of the hearing, the right to cross-examine witnesses, the right to call witnesses in his own behalf, the right to counsel, and the right to receive in writing the list of reasons that led to a decision.

Right to organize. The right of inmates to organize and to present their collective demands for changes in prision practices is still being tested in the courts. Most states will not tolerate political organizing, petitioning, or group meetings of inmates if the purpose of these meetings poses a danger to the security and discipline of the prison.

FRAME 11

In discussing inmates' rights it is important to keep in mind that an inmate, because (s)he has been convicted of a crime, must expect to lose certain liberties. But an inmate does *not* lose his citizenship, nor should he be deprived of any rights that are not expressly (or necessarily) taken from him by law.[10] Keeping this in mind, test your understanding of the rights to which inmates are or should be entitled.

Excluding the rights issues and controversies associated with capital punishment, inmates have an absolute right to freedom from cruel and unusual punishment. Check which rights would be included in the right to freedom from cruel and unusual punishment.

_____ **a.** The right to receive education and training

_____ **b.** The right to a reasonable opportunity for physical exercise

_____ **c.** The right to be free from physical abuse and punishment

_____ **d.** The right to adequate medical treatment

---

[10]Steven Wisotsky, "Equal Justice under Law." *The Florida Bar Journal* 47, 7 (July 1973): 464–466.

_____ **e.** The right not to be confined in solitary for an excessive period of time

Turn to Answer 55 on page 608

Turn to Answer 55 on page 608

F R A M E

12

Suppose you are a correctional guard working in a prison in a state that clearly recognizes the right of an inmate to receive adequate medical treatment. Joe, an inmate in your tier (cell block), comes to you complaining of severe stomach pains. You are busy doing a report at the time and scheduled to go off duty in a few hours, so you tell Joe to wait until the next shift comes on and tell the night guard, since you do not have time to be concerned about it. Have you violated or denied Joe his right to receive adequate medical treatment? (Yes/No)

Turn to Answer 56 on page 608

F R A M E

13

Check the correct response. "Notice of rights" means:

_____ **a.** An inmate receives advance notice of what conduct will result in discipline or punishment.

_____ **b.** An inmate receives written notices of any charges against him.

_____ **c.** An inmate is entitled to organize a group meeting for political purposes.

_____ **d.** A and B are correct.

Turn to Answer 57 on page 608

F R A M E

14

Reflection on the Rights of Prisoners. The "rehabilitative ideal" in correctional policy is the idea that the primary goal of correctional policy should be to reform criminals with a combination of therapeutic programs such as psychological counseling, remedial education, and job training. During the first half of the twentieth century, this ideal was embraced by many scholars, legislators, and prison administrators, but since the 1950s, the goal of rehabilitation in correctional policy has been largely abandoned.[11] Do you think

---

[11]Robert A. Burt, "Cruelty, Hypocrisy, and the Rehabilitative Ideal in Corrections," *International Journal of Law and Psychiatry* 16 (1993): 359.

that interest in the rehabilitative ideal can or will be reviewed? Do you believe that access to rehabilitative programs should be a right guaranteed to prisoners? Why or why not?

FRAME
15

EXAMPLE OF RIGHTS ISSUES PERTAINING TO THE HOMELESS

You will recall from Chapter 2, Lesson 3 that the term "homeless" gained widespread use in the 1980s as poor families and individuals unable to afford decent housing began appearing on the streets in record numbers. As private shelters and soup kitchens sprang up around the country to respond to this growing crisis, complex and contradictory perceptions of homeless people began to emerge. The image of the homeless as docile, grateful recipients of hot meals and blankets clashed with negative images of dirty, dangerous "lunatics" who posed a threat to public health and safety. The body of law and litigation pertaining to the rights of homeless people is equally as complicated, and continues to change as advocates for the homeless strive to ensure reasonable measures of personal freedom and civil protection for this group. However, these efforts are hampered by the growing hostility of politicians and community residents, who have tried to obstruct the placement of homeless shelters in their community and to "crack down" on the homeless with the passage of ordinances against begging, loitering, and sleeping in public places, among others.

Many homeless advocates have denounced emergency food and shelter responses to the needs of homeless people as "band-aid" solutions. Indeed, in the absence of a permanent solution to this growing problem, experimental approaches and shifting public sentiment will undoubtedly continue to shape legislation in this area.

Below are some rights issues that have emerged as cities and communities struggle to define the rights of the homeless.

The right to shelter. As of 1995, New York and West Virginia are the only two states that identify the right to shelter within their constitutions.[12] Most cities rely on nonprofit organizations and charitable groups to provide emergency shelter and services, and no city has succeeded in developing long-term housing solutions.

Voting rights. The right to vote is intrinsic to any democracy. Because homeless people lack the financial resources which can translate into political power, it is particularly important that this right be guaranteed to them.[13] The main obstacle to securing this right has traditionally revolved around residence requirements, as a mailing address is needed for voter registration. Policy advocates and organizers have legally challenged these restrictions, and many have succeeded in establishing the entitlement of homeless persons to register to vote by expanding the definition of residence to include specific locations to which the homeless person returns regularly, such as a shelter or a park bench.[14]

---

[12]Madeleine R. Stoner, *The Civil Rights of Homeless People* (New York: Aldine de Gruyter, 1995), p. 29.
[13]Madeleine R. Stoner, *The Civil Rights of Homeless People*, p. 120.
[14]Pitts v. Black, 608 F. Supp. 696 (S.D.N.Y., 1984) (Clearinghouse No. 38, 514); National Housing Law Project. Annotated Bibliography, 125–126.

Squatting and housing rehabilitation rights. The term "squatting" refers to the taking over of condemned or abandoned properties by homeless people seeking shelter. In 1974, a federal law called the Federal Homesteading Demonstration Program of the Community and Redevelopment Act was passed. It granted homeless people, and later low-income families in danger of becoming homeless, the right to take over condemned or abandoned properties and rehabilitate them with their own labor. Thanks to these federal provisions, most squatters have not been evicted, but many have met with opposition and harassment from unhappy neighborhood residents.[15]

Right to public assistance. While homeless people do have the right to public assistance in the form of food stamps, disability and veteran's benefits, medical care, Social Security Disability Insurance for disabled persons, and Supplemental Security Income for persons over the age of 65, there are frequently barriers to assistance, which deny homeless people access to these services. However, the laws are changing.

The right to a free public education. Forty-nine of the fifty U.S. states include provisions in their constitutions or statutes that guarantee children and youth the right to a free public education. However, this right has remained largely symbolic for the many homeless children who are unable to furnish required documentation, such as immunization records and proof of residence. Recent legislation, notably the decision in *Phyler v. Doe* and the 1987 Stewart B. McKinney Homeless Assistance Act, has succeeded in removing many of the barriers that prevent homeless children from attending schools, but it has been estimated that nearly half of all homeless children and youth in the United States still do not have access to education.[16]

Sleeping and loitering in public. This issue reflects the tension between governmental concerns about public health and safety and the protection of the right of homeless people to freedom of movement. Most local governments have laws or ordinances targeting vagrancy and camping, sleeping, and loitering in public places. Some cities have constructed pavilions or open shelters large enough to seat or sleep several hundred people at a time.

FRAME

Read each of the statements below and indicate whether each is true or false with respect to rights issues of the homeless.

_____ **a.** Few homeless children and youth experience difficulty accessing public education.

_____ True   _____ False

Turn to Answer 58 on page 608

---

[15]Madeleine R. Stoner, *The Civil Rights of Homeless People,* p. 115.
[16]Madeleine R. Stoner, *The Civil Rights of Homeless People,* p. 133.

_____ **b.** Most states guarantee their residents the right to adequate shelter.

_____ True   _____ False

Turn to Answer 59 on page 608

_____ **c.** Some states have expanded how they defne a resident of the state in order to ensure that the homeless can exercise their right to vote.

_____ True   _____ False

Turn to Answer 60 on page 608

_____ **d.** Homeless people have the right to take over certain condemned properties and rehabilitate them with their own labor.

_____ True   _____ False

Turn to Answer 61 on page 609

FRAME
17
_____

Reflection on the Rights of the Homeless. As indicated above, no city in the nation has succeeded thus far in developing a long-term solution to the growing problem of homelessness. Some believe that the institutionalization of emergency responses to homelessness, such as shelters and soup kitchens, undermines efforts to find long-term solutions. They feel that financial resources needed to sustain these structures would be better spent on the construction of low-income housing and alternative permanent housing arrangements. What do you think can—and should—be done now and in the future?

FRAME
18
_____

HUMAN RIGHTS OF ALL HUMAN SERVICE CONSUMERS

As discussed in Frame 1, the concept of natural law holds that there is law which transcends the law of states, whose authority is God, morality, or human reason. In the aftermath of the horrors of World War II, the idea of natural law as guided by a universal moral code, as opposed to the nineteenth-century emphasis on human reason, came back into vogue. During the trials of Nazi war criminals at Nuremberg in 1945, natural law was invoked as the legal basis for condemning the actions of the Nazi leaders. In 1948, the United Nations Commission on Human Rights was instructed to draft a convention on human rights and measures of implementation that would be enforced by law. The result was the 1948 Universal Declaration of Human Rights.[17]

_____

[17]See Appendix A, Universal Declaration of Human Rights, in Maurice Cranston, *What Are Human Rights?* pp. 87–93.

You will recall from Frame 1 that a human right is one that belongs to people simply because they are human beings. Some of these rights are enforceable by law, but many that are not recognized by law are not enforceable. While the courts and legislatures recognize many rights of consumers of various kinds of human services, many rights are still regularly denied or violated. The following are some of the rights that some believe *should* be guaranteed to all consumers of human services, regardless of the setting in which they are receiving services. Below are some of the articles from the Universal Declaration. Italicized text beneath the articles describe how each set might pertain to groups of human service consumers.

Articles 1, 2, and 3

- All human beings are born free and equal in dignity and rights. They are endowed with reason and conscience and should act towards one another in a spirit of brotherhood.
- Everyone is entitled to all the rights and freedoms set forth in this Declaration, without distinction of race, colour, sex, language, religion, political or other opinion, national or social origin, property, birth or other status.
- Everyone has the right to life, liberty and security of person.

Application to Human Service Consumers: The right to be free from discrimination based on race, religion, or sex should be guaranteed to all human service consumers. They should also have the right to be free from discrimination based on their status as human service consumers (e.g., when applying for a job or trying to get an education). Currently, these rights are greatly restricted in settings concerned with corrections, mental health, and mental retardation.

Articles 5 and 6

- No one shall be subjected to torture or to cruel, inhuman or degrading treatment or punishment.
- Everyone has the right to recognition everywhere as a person before the law.

Application to Human Service Consumers: Consumers of human services should have the right to be treated with respect as individuals. They should not be treated as objects of pity or hopeless burdens on society.

Articles 7, 8, 9, and 10

- All are equal before the law and are entitled without any discrimination to equal protection of the law. All are entitled to equal protection against any discrimination in violation of this Declaration and against any incitement to such discrimination.
- Everyone has the right to an effective remedy by the competent national tribunals for acts violating the fundamental rights granted him by the constitution or by law.
- No one shall be subjected to arbitrary arrest, detention, or exile.
- Everyone is entitled in full equality to a fair and public hearing by an independent and impartial tribunal, in the determination of his rights and obligations and of any criminal charge against him.

Application to Human Service Consumers: The above rights are sometimes collectively referred to as due process. *This right would assure consumers protection in their efforts to defend themselves in any area of human service. It would require that the fate of consumers not be decided in closed chambers and that consumers be advised of any charges or actions agains them. It would also require that consumers have the right to challenge any evidence against them, introduce witnesses on their behalf, and be provided with counsel (an attorney).*

Article 12

- No one shall be subjected to arbitrary interference with his privacy, family, home or correspondence, nor to attacks upon his honour and reputation. Everyone has the right to the protection of law against such interference or attacks.

Application to Human Service Consumers: All human service consumers should have the right to be treated in a way that does not invade their privacy. They should have the right to receive assistance without having to answer personal questions, such as being required to give the names of their friends. This right may be restricted in some settings, such as correctional situations, but should be recognized as much as possible in human service settings.

Article 18

- Everyone has the right to freedom of thought, conscience and religion; this right includes freedom to change his religion or belief, and freedom, either alone or in community with others and in public or private, to manifest his religion or belief in teaching, practice, worship and observance.

Application to Human Service Consumers: This is a right that needs to be recognized for all human service consumers, but especially for those in institutional settings. Consumers should be guaranteed the right to practice their own religion, unless the institution can show that it would be seriously threatened by the practice.

Article 29

- Everyone has duties to the community in which alone the free and full development of his personality is possible.
- In the exercise of his rights and freedoms, everyone shall be subject only to such limitations as are determined by law solely for the purpose of securing due recognition and respect for the rights and freedoms of others and of meeting the just requirements of morality, public order and the general welfare in a democratic society.
- These rights and freedoms may in no case be exercised contrary to the purposes and principles of the United Nations.

Application to Human Service Consumers: All consumers of human service programs should enjoy certain of the same privileges as any other citizen, such as the right to adequate food and nutritional care; the right to enjoy the community through intellectual, recreational, and cultural activities; and the right to be trained to have a job, earn an adequate living, and receive equal pay for equal work. Generally speaking, these rights are not guaranteed to many consumers of human services.

FRAME
19

The right to due process requires that all human service consumers:

_____ **a.** Have their privacy respected and protected.

     _____ True   _____ False

Turn to Answer 62 on page 609

_____ **b.** Have the right to challenge any evidence against them.

     _____ True   _____ False

Turn to Answer 63 on page 609

_____ **c.** Be treated with dignity.

     _____ True   _____ False

Turn to Answer 64 on page 609

_____ **d.** Be advised of any charges or actions against them.

     _____ True   _____ False

Turn to Answer 65 on page 609

_____ **e.** Be able to introduce witnesses on their behalf.

     _____ True   _____ False

Turn to Answer 66 on page 609

FRAME
20

Reflection on Human Rights. An interesting activity might be to compare the human rights listed above with the legal rights of a particular group of human service consumers. What are the legal rights guaranteed to this group? Which rights are typically denied and where (give examples)? What do you think are the reasons or circumstances for these discrepancies? A wealth of information about human and legal rights can be found on the Internet, as well as in books and journal articles (see Suggestions for Further Reading).

Some believe that if there are to be any rights, a legal procedure must exist to uphold them and that a declaration of human rights must be more than just a utopian ideal. Do you think this is possible? Why or why not?

CHAPTER 5
Summary and Further Study

Chapter Summary

This chapter addressed the need for consumer advocacy, techniques of advocating, and rights issues in the human services.

Lesson 1. Two specific techniques of advocating—persuasion and pressuring—were discussed. Different methods of applying the techniques were described, along with advantages and disadvantages. We gave special attention to basic principles of the advocating process, for example, thoroughly understanding the situation, gaining support of the supervisor, choosing the appropriate technique, and applying the technique properly.

We considered the factors that are important in deciding whether advocating is an appropriate intervention. For example, human service workers must consider the particular agency involved in the grievance, the grievance itself, and the consumer's needs.

Lesson 2. Rights issues in the human services were illustrated in Lesson 2. We distinguished between legal rights and human or natural rights and considered the historical and philosophical basis for American legal rights and the evolution of legal rights of women in America as an example of how rights develop. Examples of rights issues for three groups of human service consumers were described, followed by examples of human rights that some experts believe should be guaranteed to all human service consumers.

The chapter emphasized the complexity of the advocating process and encouraged further discussion, study, reflection, and exploration along with written assignments designed to relate the contents of the chapter to specific situations.

Suggestions for Further Study

To fully understand the process of effective advocating, you need further study of such subjects as how to determine the need for the advocating process in specific case situations, how to gather support from various sources in applying advocating techniques, and how to ensure the most protection for both the consumer and the worker in the process.

You will also need further study to be able to identify situations in which discrimination or denial of services is being directed not at individual consumers, but at entire groups or populations of consumers. This is generally described as "class discrimination," and the process of advocacy takes on broader dimensions in such situations.

When a worker identifies a situation in which a number of consumers with similar characteristics (e.g., unwed mothers) are being denied services, advocacy techniques can be used most effectively by helping the entire group rather than working case by case. Advocacy techniques are one of several avenues that workers pursue, usually after careful investigation and preparation. We discussed some of the conceptual foundations in Chapter 2. In that overview, we explained that active advocacy on behalf of consumer populations—generally called *systems advocacy*—usually lies beyond the responsibility of the entry-level worker because it involves actually negotiating for dramatic changes in agency policies and procedures or even in laws. The worker can and does lay the foundation for such changes, however, and can learn, through further study, how to direct the attention of agency administrators and others to class discrimination, if this is where they need to take appropriate action.

Further study will be especially needed in the area of consumer rights, *since this area is constantly changing with new laws being made, court cases being decided, and policies that affect the rights of consumers being revised*. The professional journals in human service practice areas, the readings below, and the information pamphlets and newsletters of state, local, and federal human service agencies should provide a rich resource.

Advocacy—General

Blackburn, R., and Busuttil, J. *Understanding Human Rights for the 21st Century*. Herndon, Va.: Cassell Academic, 1996.

Cloward, R. A., and R. M. Elman. "Advocacy in the Ghetto." *Transaction* 14 (Apr. 1969): 27–35.

Cranston, M. *What Are Human Rights?* London: Bodley Head, 1973.

Doniger, A. "The Role of the Private Bar in the Defense of Civil Rights and Civil Liberties." *Boston Bar Journal* 34 (Nov.-Dec. 1993): 5.

Duncan, C., D. Rivlin, and M. Willliams. *An Advocate's Guide to the Media*. Washington, D.C.: Children's Defense Fund, 1990.

Ezell, M. "The Advocacy Practice of Social Workers." *Families in Society* (Jan. 1994): 36–46.

Frankel, O. K. *The Rights We Have*. New York: Crowell, 1974.

Gibson, J. S. *Dictionary of International Human Rights Law*. Lanham, Md.: Scarecrow Press, 1996.

Henkin, Louis. *The Age of Rights*. New York: Columbia University Press, 1990.

Sunley, R. *Advocating Today: A Human Service Practicioners Handbook*. New York: Family Service Association of America, 1983.

Rights Issues: Mentally Disabled

Children's Defense Fund. *94–142 and 504: Numbers That Add Up to Educational Rights for Children With Disabilities: A Guide for Parents and Advocates*. Washington, D.C.: Children's Defense Fund, 1989.

Cornwall, J. K. "CRIPA: The Failure of Federal Intervention for Mentally Retarded People (Civil Rights of Institutionalized Persons Act)." *Yale Law Journal* 97 (Apr. 1988): 843–862.

Costello, J. C. and J. J. Preis. "Beyond Least Restrictive Alternative: A Constitutional Right to Treatment for Mentally Disabled Persons in the Community." *Loyola of Los Angeles Law Review* 20 (June 1987): 1527–1557.

Dicker, S. "Developmental Disabilities and the Law: A Symposium." *University of Little Rock Law Journal* 4 (1981): 395–509.

Durham, M. L. "The Impact of Deinstitutionalization on the Current Treatment of the Mentally Ill." *International Journal of Law and Psychiatry* 12 (Spring-Summer 1989): 117–131.

Ennis, B. J. *Prisoners of Psychiatry: Mental Patients, Psychiatrists, and the Law.* New York: Harcourt Brace Jovanovich, 1972.

Gallo, L. V. "*Youngberg v. Romeo:* The Right to Treatment Dilemma and the Mentally Retarded." *Albany Law Review* 47, 1 (1982): 179–213.

Guthiel, T. G., D. B. Appelbaum, and B. Wexler. "The Inappropriateness of 'Least Restrictive Alternative' Analysis for Involuntary Procedures with the Institutionalized Mentally Ill." *Journal of Psychiatry and Law* 11 (Spring 1983): 7–17.

Levy, R. M., and L. S. Rubenstein. *The Rights of People with Mental Disabilities.* Carbondale, Ill.: Southern Illinois University Press, 1996.

Schwartz, S. J. "Protecting the Rights and Enhancing the Dignity of People with Mental Disabilities: Standards for Effective Legal Advocacy." *Rutgers Law Journal* 14 (Spring 1983): 541–593.

Strobes, J. "The Constitution and the Rights of the Mentally Ill." *Journal of Legal Medicine* 10 (Dec. 1989): 661–702.

Sunderman, L. M. "The Constitution and the Rights of the Mentally Ill." *Journal of Legal Medicine* 10 (Dec. 1989): 661–702.

Twarty, S., and S. S. Sanbar. "Recent Trends in Mental Health Law." *Medical Trial Techniques Quarterly* 30 (1983): 1–13.

Yudof, M. G. "Education for the Handicapped: *Rowley* in Perspective." *American Journal of Education* 92 (Feb. 1984): 165.

Rights Issues: Housing /Rights of the Homeless

Children's Defense Fund. *Your Family's Rights under the New Fair Housing Law: Protecting Families with Children from Housing Discrimination.* Washington, D.C.: Children's Defense Fund, 1989.

Coates, Robert C. Legal Rights of Homeless Americans. *University of San Francisco Law Review* 24 (Winter 1990): 297–362.

Collin, R. W. "Homelessness: The Policy and the Law." *Urban Law* 16 (1984): 317–329.

Crosland, David W. Can Lawyers Really Help the Homeless? *Human Rights* 14 (Spring 1987): 16–19.

Stolove, Evan S. Pursuing the Educational Rights of Homeless Children: An Overview for Advocates. *Maryland Law Review* 53 (1994): 1344–1370.

Stoner, M. R. *The Civil Rights of Homeless People.* New York: Aldine de Gruyter, 1995.

Tye, Kirk A. Voting Rights of Homeless Residents. *Clearinghouse Review* 20 (July 1986): 227–235.

Rights Issues: Prisoners / Inmates in Correctional Facilities

Abramovsky, A. "First Amendment Rights of Jewish Prisoners: Kosher Food, Skullcaps and Beards." *American Journal of Criminal Law* 21 (Winter 1994) 241–272.

Burt, R. A. "Cruelty, Hypocrisy, and the Rehabilitative Ideal in Corrections." *International Journal of Law and Psychiatry* 16 (Summer-Fall 1993): 359–370.

Call, J. E. "The Supreme Court and Prisoners' Rights." *Federal Probation* 59 (March 1995): 36–46.

Eisenberg, H. B. "Rethinking Prisoner Civil Rights Cases and the Provision of Counsel." *Southern Illinois University Law Journal* 17 (Spring 1993): 417–490.

Fahey, S. D. "Jailhouse Suicides: Where is the Abuse of Power?" *Mississippi College Law Review* 14 (Fall 1993): 77–96.

Gardner, E. "The Legal Rights of Inmates with Physical Disabilities." *Saint Louis University Public Law Review* 14 (Fall 1994): 174–216.

Gardner, M. R. "The Right of Juvenile Offenders to Be Punished: Some Implications of Treating Kids as Persons." *Nebraska Law Review* 68 (Winter-Spring 1989): 182–213.

Parrott, L. A. Jr. "Prisoners' Rights in the 1990s: Is the Supreme Court Now More Responsive to 'Contemporaneous Standards of Decency'? (Case Note)" *University of Richmond Law Review*

27 (Fall 1992): 151–170.

Roth, A. D. "An Examination of Whether Incarcerated Juveniles Are Entitled by the Constitution to Rehabilitative Treatment." *Michigan Law Review* 84 (Nov. 1985): 286–307.

Rudovsky, D., A. J. Bronstein, E. I. Koren, and J. D. Cade. *The Rights of Prisoners: The Basic ACLU Guide to Prisoners' Rights,* 4th ed. Carbondale, Ill.: Southern Illinois University Press, 1988.

Schlam, P. R, and H. M. Stone. "Prisoners' Rights and Religious Freedom." *New York Law Journal* 214, 29 (Aug. 11, 1995): 3.

Stollman, D. J. "Female Prisoners' Rights to Be Free from Random, Cross-Gender Clothed Body Searches (Case Note)." *Fordham Law Review* 62, 6 (Apr. 1994)" 1877–1910.

Rights Issues: Welfare Recipients

Collin, R. W., and W. M. Hemmons. "Equal Protection Problems with Welfare Fraud Prosecuting." *Loyola Law Review* 33 (Spring 1987): 17–49.

Davis, M. F. *Brutal Need: Lawyers and the Welfare Rights Movement,* 1960–1973. New Haven, Conn.: Yale University Press, 1993.

Epstein, Richard Allen. "The Uncertain Quest for Welfare Rights." *Brigham Young University Law Review* 1985 (1985): p. 201–229.

Handler, J. F. "Justice for the Welfare Recipient: Fair Hearings in AFDC—The Wisconsin Experience." *Social Service Review* 43, 1 (Mar. 1969): 12–34.

Melnick, R. S. *Between the Lines: Interpreting Welfare Rights.* Washington, D.C.: The Brookings Institution, 1994.

Roberts, P., and M. Allen. "An AFDC Mother's Right to Counsel: Custody Issues in Proceedings Instigated by the IV-D Agency." *Clearinghouse Review* 19 (July 1985): 278–286.

Schulman, J. "Women and Poverty: Women's Issues in Legal Services Practice." *Clearinghouse Review* 14 (1981): 1035–1074.

Weinstein, J. B. "Poor's Right to Equal Access to the Courts." *Connecticut Law Review* 13 (1980): 848–857.

Additional Resources

American Civil Liberties Union Guides, for example:

Annas, G. J. *The Rights of Patients: The Basic ACLU Guide to Patient Rights,* 2nd ed. Carbondale: Southern Illinois University Press, 1989.

Brown, Robert N. *The Rights of Older Persons: The Basic ACLU Guide to the Legal Rights of Older Persons Under Current Law,* 2nd ed. Carbondale: Southern Illinois University Press, 1989.

Carliner, D., L. Guttentag, A. C. Helton, and W. J. Henderson. *The Rights of Aliens and Refugees: The Basic ACLU Guide to Alien and Refugee Rights,* 2nd ed. Carbondale: Southern Illinois University Press, 1990.

Guggenheim, Martin, Alexandra Lowe, and Diane Curtis. *The Rights of Families: The Basic ACLU Guide to the Rights of Today's Family Members.* Carbondale: Southern Illinois University Press, 1996.

Hunter, Nan D., Sherryl Michaelson, and Thomas Stoddard. *The Rights of Lesbians and Gay Men: The Basic ACLU Guide to a Gay Person's Rights,* 3rd ed. Carbondale: Southern Illinois University Press, 1992.

Pevar, Stephen L. *The Rights of Indians and Tribes: The Basic ACLU Guide to Indian and Tribal Rights,* 2nd ed. Carbondale: Southern Illinois University Press, 1991.

Rubenstein, William B., Ruth Eisenberg, and Lawrence Gostin. *The Rights of People Who Are HIV Positive: The Basic ACLU Guide to the Rights of People Living with HIV Disease and AIDS.* Carbondale: Southern Illinois University Press, 1996.

Freedom Forum First Amendment Center (1993). *Freedom of Religion, Speech, Press, Assembly & Petition: The First Amendment.* Nashville, Tenn.: 1207 18th Avenue South, Vanderbilt University.

Hawes, Joseph. *The Childrens' Rights Movement: A History of Advocacy and Protection.* Boston, Mass.: Twayne Publishers, 1991.

Southern Poverty Law Center Publications (400 Washington Avenue, P.O. Box 548, Montgomery, Alabama 36101. Phone: 334–264–0286). Examples:

Hate Violence and White Supremacy: A Decade Review, 1980–1990. A 46-page review of the major events, leaders, and developments in the white supremacist movement during the 1980s.

The Klan: A Legacy of Hate in America. A 28-minute documentary film portraying the violent history of the Ku Klux Klan in the United States. Nominated for an Academy Award in 1983.

The Shadow of Hate: A History of Intolerance in America. A free video and text kit for secondary schools. Includes a 40-minute video documenting episodes of intolerance in U.S. history; a 128-page illustrated text, *Us and Them;* and a 32-page teacher's guide.

Teaching Tolerance. A free semiannual magazine providing teachers with resources for promoting interracial and intercultural understanding.

Watson, A. S. "Children, Families, and Courts: Before the Best Interest of the Child." *Virginia Law Review* 66 (Apr. 1980): 653–679.

Chapter 6

Mobilizing

Mobilizing is work in which the people or organizations in the community become or are motivated and organized to effect changes for the better. Mobilizing emphasizes *community* unmet needs and activates responses to these problems.

Workers who engage in mobilizing try to help residents make their communities better places to live. We all know that the resources and services currently available in our communities are not completely responsive to all needs of all people. For example, residents may need day care, recreational outlets, better housing, or additional help for youthful offenders. Mobilizing is the process of encouraging existing service agencies to work together or collaborate in resolving community problems, or of creating new resources responsive to community-identified needs.

In this chapter you will learn about the organizing skills that are essential to effective community work, including how workers get to know a community and its problems. You will also examine the basic steps of organizing used to help community groups address issues. The overall objective of the chapter is to provide you with principles and practices used to mobilize a community in an effort to resolve its problems.

These are examples of mobilizing tasks that might appear in a human service job description:

1. Discovering gaps within the service delivery system and recommending services to modify them.
2. Defining and communicating specific community needs by acting as a catalyst for the formation of self-help groups.
3. Describing an unmet service need and proposing a plan to a policy maker, using the telephone, personal visits, or written communication, in order to marshal support.
4. Discussing plans or ideas for new services with colleagues or lay individuals and encouraging support of the plans.
5. Reading local newspapers in order to determine issues facing current or potential consumer groups.
6. Participating in existing community groups, serving as a resource and discussing human services.

LESSON 1

Identifying Unmet Community Needs and Taking Action

In this lesson you will gain beginning knowledge about how to identify unmet community needs. You will also learn the basic steps of mobilizing and how they are used to gather community support for changing or modifying services.

Goal

Given an actual community situation or a description of a possible community situation, you will be able to explain how you would begin to identify the unmet needs of the community.

Learning Activities

To accomplish this goal, we will:

1. Clarify what is meant by unmet community needs.
2. Examine structures common to all communities.
3. Review the meaning of *mobilizing*.
4. Define the major objectives of mobilizing.
5. Identify the major types of community groups that may serve as mechanisms for mobilizing.
6. Consider five basic steps to follow in mobilizing for change.

FRAME 1

WHAT IS AN UNMET COMMUNITY NEED?

Optimally, a need involves a problem that can be solved. When we talk about unmet needs in community work, we are talking about needs or problems in the community that are not being adequately addressed by existing community resources (e.g., no recreational program to keep potentially delinquent teenagers off the streets or no program to help idle patients in a hospital keep physically fit). We know that individuals in our communities have many needs that often can be met by existing or newly developed services. In mobilizing, we are looking beyond individual needs and trying to examine needs or problems at the local community level. The statement of a need by a single consumer, community resident, or worker does not necessarily mean that a real unmet community need exists.

How are unmet community needs identified? Learning about any community (its people, organizations, and problems) is a continuous process. To gain knowledge of a community, it is usually important to contact organized groups in the community who are interested in problems your agency wishes you to address. For example, a civic group may be concerned about the lack of recreational facilities. Or it may be necessary to recruit persons not affiliated with groups who can play an important role in seeking change (e.g., parents of children with special learning disabilities whom the local school system has ignored).

Whatever the community's unmet needs may be, it is important to know something about established groups in the community. It is also important to be *out in the community*—which includes talking with residents and human service consumers and their friends and observing their activities. There are five questions to keep in mind when trying to identify unmet community needs:

1. What do the residents say the issues are?
2. What do the residents talk about with one another?
3. Do the stated problems and the conversations reflect the same concerns?
4. How do nonresidents in the community—merchants, professionals, and so on— see the problems?
5. What are the different points of view regarding the issues, and is there any common ground?

Remember that different groups or individuals may view or define the same problem in different ways. For example, the merchant whose windows are regularly broken may speak of "young hoodlums"; the school social worker may be concerned about "teenage gangs"; and parents may talk about their kids having "no place to play." All these people are talking about the same *general* problem in different ways. The worker will want to find out, in such a case, what is happening in the community that results in juvenile delinquency. Is it lack of parental control, lack of recreation facilities, or what? Only by being in the community and finding out more about the real nature of the problem and the needs can a worker begin to discover what can and should be done.

FRAME

2

Underline the correct word from each pair in parentheses.

Mrs. Betty R. needs day care services for her children in order to hold a job. There are a number of day care services but none that she can afford given the salary she will earn. Mrs. R. is experiencing an individual need that is being (met/unmet). The provision of day care services is a community need that is (met/unmet).

Turn to Answer 67 on page 610

FRAME

3

We have said that there are five key questions to remember in pinpointing unmet community needs. Read the following paragraph, then answer the questions below.

> Hank is a human service worker who makes it a habit to "hang out" in the places frequented by community residents. When he does so, he listens carefully to conversations to find out what the residents seem to be most concerned about. He also engages many of them in conversations, asking them how they see the problems in the community, making mental notes as to whether statements of the problems are the same things they talk about in their conversations. From this Hank sizes up what he thinks the unmet needs of the community are.

Hank has remembered to keep only some of the five key questions in mind as he goes about searching for unmet community needs. Beside each question below, place a check mark if Hank has remembered the question and an *X* if he has forgotten it.

_____ **1.** What do the residents say the issues are?

_____ **2.** What do the residents talk about with one another?

_____ **3.** Do the stated problems and the conversations reflect the same concerns?

_____ **4.** How do nonresidents in the community—merchants, professionals, and so on—see the problem?

_____ **5.** What are the different points of view regarding the issues, and is there any common ground?

Turn to Answer 68 on page 610

FRAME

4

COMMUNITY STRUCTURES

Learning about a community is an important first step in finding out what unmet community needs exist. Whether the community in which you work is a town or a neighborhood, you should be familiar with its structures (such as social service agencies, educational agencies, and consumer groups), as these can be valuable resources for seeking new approaches to solving community problems. You should know *how* to contact them and *who* to contact. If your community is a hospital, a prison, or another kind of institution, you should be familiar with its comparable structures (such as social services, volunteer services, and recreation services).

To acquire a better idea of these various community structures, carefully study Figures 6.1 and 6.2 in Frames 5 and 6. Place a check mark beside the organizations or services that you are familiar with in your own community, whether it is a neighborhood or an institution.

Local, State and National Governments:

City courts
Sanitation boards
Social Security offices
Local health departments
Departments of public safety
Community recreation
  centers
Political organizations
County extension service
Public health service units
City planning boards
U.S. Employment Service

Consumer Groups:

Cooperatives
Consumers leagues
Credit unions
AFL local unions
Farm Bureau Federation
National Grange
Tax Payers League
Neighborhood improvement
  associations
American Home Economic
  Association
Urban League
NAACP
American Civil Liberties
  Union
Property owners
  associations

Civic Groups:

Mental health associations
Safety councils
Cancer Society
Heart Association
American Red Cross
Infantile Paralysis
  Foundation
League of Women Voters
Junior League
Citizens Council
Lions, Kiwanis, Rotary
Optimist, Exchange Clubs

Other Community Subgroups:

(Ways must be found for
reaching the people not
identified with existing
community organizations.)

Informal social groups
Newspapers, radio, TV
  stations
Garden, current events
  clubs
Adult study groups

Business and Industrial Groups:

Wholesalers groups
Trade associations
Chambers of commerce
Better Business Bureaus
American Institute of
  Banking
Manufacturers associations
Business women's clubs
Merchant associations

Your
Community

Religious Groups:

Protestant welfare agencies
Ministerial associations
Churches
Synagogues
Knights of Columbus
YMCA—YWCA
YMHA—YWHA
B'nai B'rith
National Conference on
  Christians and Jews

Educational Agencies and Groups:

Colleges and universities
AAUW
Local education associations
School citizens committees
Alumni groups
Adult education councils
Boards of education
Parent-teacher associations
Libraries

Professional and Fraternal Groups:

Disabled American Veterans
American Veterans Committee
Veterans of Foreign Wars
American Legion
Eagles, Elks
Women's auxiliaries
Masons, Oddfellows, Moose
Engineers and architects
  associations
Social workers associations
Teachers associations
Hospital associations
Nursing associations
Medical associations
Bar associations

Social Service Agencies:

State and county public
  human service programs
Family service bureaus
Child day care centers
Child welfare services
Settlement houses
Jewish community centers
Travelers Aid Society
Planned Parenthood Bureau
Visiting nurse associations
Council of Social Agencies
Community Chest
Campfire Girls
Girl Scouts and Boy Scouts
Salvation Army

FIGURE 6.1.   Neighborhood Structures [*Source:* Edwin F. Hallenbeck, "Who Does What in Your Town?" *Adult Leadership* 4, 1 (May 1955): pp. 22–23.]

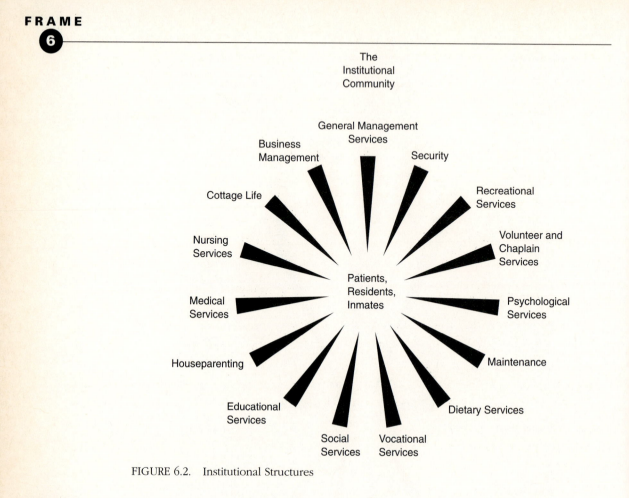

FIGURE 6.2.   Institutional Structures

INSTITUTIONAL STRUCTURES

Sometimes it is difficult to view an institution (mental hospital, prison, or halfway house for delinquent youths) as a community. However, institutions are like total communities in that they provide life-supporting services for consumers and such necessities as food, shelter, clothing, recreation, and safety.[1] Total institutional communities were established to meet the needs of consumers in terms of rehabilitation and the needs of society in terms of socially controlling people who cannot cope with the pressures of life, or who do not conform to social expectations and legal limits.

Unmet needs may exist if there are no rooms or lounge areas where an individual can be alone or meet others. The same can be noted if the consumers are not allowed to have

---

[1]Erving Goffman, *Asylums: Essays on the Social Situation of Mental Patients and Other Inmates* (Garden City, N.Y.: Doubleday, 1961).

their own personal clothing but are forced to wear prison uniforms or hospital clothes. Unmet needs in an institution may also relate to improving the quality of treatment, creating or expanding recreational and occupational programs, and improving the level of staff skills.

Resources available to the institutional community include volunteer services, occupational therapy, recreational therapy, social services, and psychological services. These resources are as important to an institutional community as religious, educational, and social service resources are to a neighborhood or geographic community.

You can see the large and challenging task that any worker would have in trying to identify actual unmet needs in a community. There is no simple method for performing this task. Now that you have some understanding of the components of a community and how unmet community needs are identified, continue with Frame 8 to learn how mobilizing is used to deal with unmet community needs.

FRAME

8

WHAT IS MOBILIZING?
WHAT SHOULD IT ACCOMPLISH?

Mobilizing means assembling community resources and making them responsive to unmet community needs. We begin by identifying the unmet needs; then our goal is to do something about these needs. Mobilizing is designed to *link resources with unmet community needs*. But this is not always easy.

Many groups in our communities do not make their needs known (e.g., children in need of health care), and some occasionally resist help when it is offered (e.g., alcoholics). It can also be difficult to get community resources to work together to deal with a need (e.g., getting a prison staff to develop an inmate rehabilitation program). Some resources need help in working with others (e.g., schools and police), and some are resistant to changing policies or services. Also, in the human services, we are always searching for better ways to find out who needs services and where and why services are needed.

In addition to helping existing agencies work together, mobilizing involves activities related to developing a new service. For example, the development of a new day care center for children might involve mobilizing the support of parents, churches, fund-raisers, the welfare and health departments, merchants, and other resources in the community. Mobilizing for community support requires attention to all aspects of community life.

Mobilizing activities are designed to accomplish one or more of the following objectives:

1. Making existing community resources known and easily *accessible* to the community (e.g., finding recreational equipment for use on hospital wards to help patients relate to one another).

2. Getting existing community resources either to *change* their present services or to *work together* in dealing with the unmet need (e.g., encouraging schools to develop teenage counseling programs before students are expelled).

3. Bringing existing needs *to the community's attention* in an effort to gather support and acceptance (e.g., elderly residents in need of a "meals on wheels" program).

4. Working for the *establishment of new services* when all other alternatives have been exhausted (e.g., developing a new Big Brother program for delinquent youths).

You can see that trying to bring community resources and people together may mean either supporting and working with existing community resources or creating a new service to meet the need.

FRAME
9

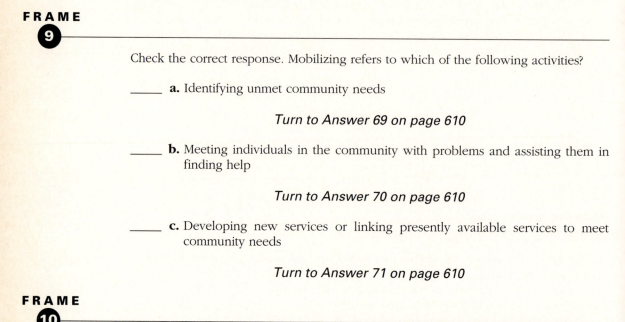

Check the correct response. Mobilizing refers to which of the following activities?

_____ **a.** Identifying unmet community needs

Turn to Answer 69 on page 610

_____ **b.** Meeting individuals in the community with problems and assisting them in finding help

Turn to Answer 70 on page 610

_____ **c.** Developing new services or linking presently available services to meet community needs

Turn to Answer 71 on page 610

FRAME
10

Place a check mark beside the explanations for why it is often difficult to bring community resources to bear on fulfilling unmet community needs.

_____ **1.** Too many community groups make their needs known.
_____ **2.** Some community groups resist help when it is offered.
_____ **3.** Community resources often change the types of services they offer.
_____ **4.** Community resources often wish to work alone.
_____ **5.** Few community groups make their needs known.

Turn to Answer 72 on page 610

FRAME
11

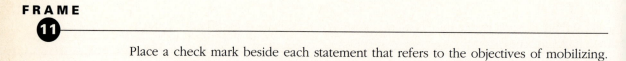

Place a check mark beside each statement that refers to the objectives of mobilizing.

_____ **1.** To bring a need to the attention of the community in order to obtain acceptance of and support for fulfilling the need.
_____ **2.** To help families and groups learn how to obtain services to meet their needs.
_____ **3.** To gather and give information to consumers and agencies about unmet needs.
_____ **4.** To convince existing community resources to change their services or work together in addressing an unmet need.

_____ **5.** To publicize existing community resources and make them more easily accessible to community residents.

_____ **6.** To help organize welfare rights groups, protest movements, etc.

_____ **7.** To encourage the development and establishment of new services needed in the community.

Turn to Answer 73 on page 611

FRAME

12

As a human service worker in a community halfway house for delinquent girls, you are amazed to find that there are no job preparation and training courses offered in your community. Since many of the girls in your halfway house have no experience in finding or keeping a job, you have decided to mobilize some of the community leaders and seek out some of the relevant resources to promote a new program of job training for youths in the community. Answer the following questions as a way of indicating how you would proceed.

1. How would you determine the need?
2. How would you bring existing resources together?
3. How would you gather community support and acceptance?

Turn to Answer 74 on page 611

FRAME

13

MECHANISMS FOR MOBILIZING GROUPS

A number of mechanisms are used to mobilize support in the community, most of which involve working with some kind of *community group.* Organizing community residents to solve a community problem is the main activity in mobilizing. When a worker brings two or more people together, he is using group work activities.

There are many kinds of community groups, some already formed, others organized for the purpose of solving a particular community problem. The typical kinds of groups a worker may encounter include:

1. Councils of representatives from existing community organizations
2. Committees of interested individuals not necessarily affiliated with any organized group, operating permanently or formed for the specific purpose of solving a specific unmet community need
3. Existing organizations in the community, such as school boards, city commissions, and neighborhood organizations
4. Existing consumer groups, such as welfare rights organizations, patient or inmate councils, and parent of retarded or delinquent youths

All these groups may be involved in a number of activities related to the community, such as making decisions or recommendations, giving advice, studying problems, and effecting changes in the community. So the *group* is an important mechanism used in mobilization efforts.

Steps in mobilizing. We know that no two communities are alike in their unmet needs and how they deal with them. But there is a basic plan workers can keep in mind when mobilizing for change. When attempting to deal with an unmet community need by bringing together fragmented and isolated services or creating new services, it is important to plan activities in the community. Not all workers follow these exact steps in their community work, but the steps do show you one approach to planning and organizing certain work activities related to the community. Once a worker has identified an unmet community need, some of the steps in mobilizing for change might include the following:

1. First find out whether there is an existing service that can meet the need (e.g., a local community action agency may have a free transportation service to the Food Stamp office of which community residents are unaware).

2. If there is an appropriate service or program, find out if the need can be met through an existing service organization by making the organization aware of the need (e.g., a number of patients in a mental hospital may request that a basic reading program be started, and the volunteer coordinator, once aware of the need, can start one).

3. If there is no existing service and no organization immediately capable of providing the service, help get one started by recruiting a group of interested people to work on solving the problem.

4. If a group of interested people is organized to work on the problem of meeting a community need, make sure the group represents the largest possible number of community organizations and interested parties related to the problem at hand.

5. Whether working with an existing organization or organizing a group, help develop a plan of action by gathering support in the community and involve the largest possible number of people and groups in the community who might make a contribution.

FRAME
14

Check the correct response. Which of the following groups would probably be formed for or involved in the purpose of addressing a specific unmet community need?

_____ **a.** A city commission

Turn to Answer 75 on page 611

_____ **b.** A committee

Turn to Answer 76 on page 612

_____ **c.** A club

Turn to Answer 77 on page 612

Wanda P. is a psychiatric aide in a mental health hospital. She is concerned about the lack of opportunities for patients on her ward to take trips outside the hospital. Within the hospital, there is a patient activity group that was established by the hospital superintendent some time ago to act in an advisory capacity to hospital staff regarding patient activities (e.g., recreation, home visits). Wanda goes to this group and discusses the problem with them, hoping they may be interested in requesting a field-visit program for patients.

What type of group is Wanda working with?

Turn to Answer 78 on page 612

Check the correct response. In order to help get a service or program started to meet a need, which of the following should you do?

_____ **a.** Develop a plan of action.
_____ **b.** Recruit residents to form a group that will work toward solving the problem.
_____ **c.** Gather support in the community.
_____ **d.** A and B.
_____ **e.** A, B, and C.

Turn to Answer 79 on page 612

In conclusion, if you find an existing service or an organization capable of providing the service in your community that can meet a need, your task is to gather support in the community for this service. If, however, there is no organization in the community capable of filling or willing to fill the need, your task is to help such a service get established. Community support is needed, and a group could be formed to plan ways to meet the need or solve the problem.

LESSON 2

Helping Community Groups Solve Problems

A distinguishing feature of the mobilizing process is group problem solving. This requires organizing the group and then encouraging its members to attend meetings where the problem will be discussed and solutions will emerge. In this lesson, you will be introduced to basic principles of problem solving, particularly as they apply to the group situation. You will also examine the skills and roles that workers should assume in order to create and maintain effective problem-solving groups.

Goal

Given a description of an unmet need (problem) in your community, you will be able to describe the steps that you would take to organize and support a group of people who would work on solving the problem.

Learning Activities

To accomplish this goal, we will:

1. Distinguish between a formal and an informal meeting.
2. Identify important skills of group meetings.
3. Review different roles that people can play when working with community groups.
4. Examine six stages of group problem solving.

FRAME

PREPARING FOR AND PARTICIPATING EFFECTIVELY IN COMMUNITY MEETINGS

Most community work requires a familiarity with the skills needed to prepare and participate in both formal and informal meetings.

Formal meetings are those in which the transaction of business proceeds according to set ground rules—for example, only one person will talk at a time; anyone may submit a proposal or make a motion; the proposal must be discussed; and the majority rules when a vote is taken. *Informal meetings* are those in which the transaction of business proceeds by casual group discussion, usually involving three or more persons. Informal meetings involve a face-to-face meeting of the group, and discussion is carried out without fixed rules. All group members are expected to participate in the discussion, and one person usually assumes the role of discussion leader. Informal meetings have a definite subject for discussion—that is, the group does not simply engage in casual conversation.

Many of you have already developed some of the skills used to participate in these meetings in your roles as parents or other active participants in your community. Since it is impossible for us to cover all the skills needed, we will talk about five of the more important ones: (1) getting people to come to a meeting, (2) setting up a meeting, (3) achieving major goals at the first meeting, (4) developing and distributing an agenda, and (5) keeping a group moving toward its goals.[1]

Getting people to come to a meeting.

This can be a difficult job. You may be asked to recruit people and get them interested. First you should visit each person you are trying to involve, explain the purpose of the meeting, and tell the person why it is important that she attend. This is particularly important if it is the person's first meeting or if you have never met the person before. Talking with people to persuade them to come to a meeting can be time consuming. Once the group is established, one way to cut down on the time involved is to appoint a committee to recruit people for subsequent meetings. Another way is to ask each group member to bring a friend who has a contribution to offer. People are more likely to attend if a friend asks them to come.

Here are some helpful hints to remember in trying to get people to attend a meeting:

1. Explain the purpose of the meeting and why it is important for the person to attend; do this in person if at all possible.
2. Make your request far enough ahead of time to allow the person to make arrangements to attend.
3. Follow up with a note or phone call just prior to the meeting.
4. Thank each person who attends and acknowledge their contribution.
5. Do not "write off" a person you have invited who doesn't show up. Try again—there may have been a good reason why the person could not attend.

Setting up a meeting.

If you are asked to set up a meeting or help others to set up a meeting, you should have a checklist of things to do, based on questions such as the following:

1. Does everyone know where and when the meeting is being held? Have reminders been sent out?
2. Are there enough seats for everyone?
3. Are there name tags or cards identifying each person? If there are no tags, is there another way for people to be introduced to one another?

---

[1]These skills may be found in Gertrude S. Goldberg, Alvin B. Kogut, Seymour Lesh, and Dorothy Yates, *New Careers: The Social Service Aide: A Manual for Trainees* (Washington, D.C.: University Research Corporation, 1968).

4. Are there copies of the agenda for everyone? If not, can the agenda be put on a big poster, chalkboard, or newsprint pad?

5. Has someone been selected to take notes at the meeting so decisions and discussions are not lost?

6. Will a report of the meeting be sent both to people who attended and to those who could not come?

7. Do you have printed material from your agency to hand out? If not, are you prepared to tell the group something about yourself and your agency's services?

8. Have other people been encouraged to participate in the meeting and been given the necessary help?

Obviously, there will be some things you will want to add to this list or change, depending on the particular meeting you are setting up. The important thing is to make sure these questions are taken care of when you are setting up a meeting.

Achieving major goals at the first meeting.

Certain things have to happen at the first meeting of a group if it is to have a chance for success in launching a program. Participants need to experience some accomplishments early in the process, and it is important to set realistic goals that can be easily achieved. The following six goals for group members relate to the meeting process itself and are therefore good ones to start out with:

1. People should get acquainted and exchange points of view.
2. Group members should agree on what they will tackle first.
3. The group should agree on how it will tackle the problem.
4. People should be given responsibilities for working on the problem.
5. The group should agree on the time and place for the next meeting.
6. The members should make plans for involving other interested people in the next meeting.

FRAME
2

For the following list of meeting activities, put an *F* next to those that are more commonly found in formal meetings and an *I* next to those more often found in informal meetings.

_____ **1.** A chairperson is chosen to preserve order and help keep the meeting moving.

_____ **2.** The group conducts its conversation without fixed rules.

_____ **3.** There is usually a discussion leader.

_____ **4.** When a vote is taken, the majority rules.

_____ **5.** Only one person will talk at a time.

_____ **6.** All group members are expected to participate in the discussion.

Turn to Answer 80 on page 613

F R A M E

Circle the correct answers in parentheses.

A regular membership meeting of a committee of community residents to discuss past progress and future actions would be (informal/formal) while a luncheon meeting of agency executives with a mutual interest would probably be (informal/formal).

Turn to Answer 81 on page 613

F R A M E

Check the correct response. If you were responsible for getting ten specific persons to come to the first meeting of a newly formed committee on developing day care services, the best way for you to proceed would probably be to

_____ **1.** send personalized letters explaining the purpose of the meeting.

Turn to Answer 82 on page 613

_____ **2.** visit each person to explain why he or she is needed.

Turn to Answer 83 on page 613

_____ **3.** call each person to explain his or her potential role.

Turn to Answer 84 on page 613

F R A M E

Suppose one of the persons you contacted for the meeting mentioned in the previous frame is Mr. Cranston, who, even after indicating his interest and promising to attend, did not show up. As time for the next meeting approaches, you could either go by and see Mr. Cranston again and invite him to the meeting or assume he is really not interested, as indicated by his absence from the first meeting, and spend your time working with people you know you can depend on. Which do you think is the best course of action?

Turn to Answer 85 on page 613

F R A M E

When setting up a meeting, you should be sure to perform certain activities, eight of which we have noted. In the space provided, state the two activities that will inform everyone at the meeting of what is going to happen and will help people who did not attend the meeting.

1.

2.

Turn to Answer 86 on page 614

FRAME

If a group is to be successful in launching its program or project, which of the following should occur at the first meeting? Check those that apply.

_____ **1.** Group members should agree on the problem that has first priority.

_____ **2.** Members should get acquainted and exchange points of view.

_____ **3.** The group should agree on how it will tackle the first problem.

_____ **4.** Members should identify other persons who should be involved in the next meeting and plan how to bring them in.

_____ **5.** Members should be given responsibilities for working on the problem with the first priority.

_____ **6.** The group should agree on the time and place for the next meeting.

Turn to Answer 87 on page 614

FRAME

8

There are two additional skills used in planning and participating in group meetings:

Developing and distributing an agenda.

It is important to develop and distribute an agenda for each meeting. The written agenda usually includes a list of things to be discussed by the group. You can make up the agenda before the meeting, or a committee of group members can make it up. If everyone has a copy of the agenda at the meeting, it will help people stick to the topics and know what is going to happen next. Topics that are not on the agenda can also be discussed, but the agenda will give the group an idea of where it is going. Avoid making the agenda too long because this can result in too little time being spent on important topics.

Keeping the group moving toward its goals.

Some things to remember for keeping a group going in its efforts to solve community problems are listed below:

1. The more people are involved in the planning and leadership of the group, the more likely you are to have an ongoing, active group.

2. Seeing a problem through and then moving on to another one not only maintains interest but also increases involvement in community affairs.

3. Taking time at the end of the meeting to plan for the next one is a good way to get people interested in participating in it and in coming again.

4. Bringing new people into the group helps members feel that it is worth being part of the group.

5. Time should be allowed for all members to take part in discussions.

6. Members should take increasing amounts of responsibility for the group as time goes on. You should be available for advice and direction, but leadership should usually be assumed by the members as soon as it is feasible.

F R A M E
9

An agenda, or list of topics to be discussed at a meeting, is useful in which of the following ways? Check the correct response.

_____ **a.** It helps participants know what will happen during the meeting.

_____ **b.** It eliminates nonproductive discussion, since only topics on the agenda may be discussed at the meeting.

_____ **c.** It helps give direction to the meeting.

_____ **d.** A and C.

_____ **e.** A, B, and C.

Turn to Answer 88 on page 614

F R A M E
10

Mrs. Pope is the leader of a local committee aimed at trying to provide services for unmarried mothers. She has been successful in leading this committee in the accomplishment of many tasks. She has delegated many of her responsibilities to other members and has involved many of them in planning and directing projects. She also sees to it that new people continue to be invited to join the group.

Name *at least* two other ways in which Mrs. Pope is probably helping to keep this committee active and moving forward in solving the problems of unwed mothers.

1.

2.

3.

Turn to Answer 89 on page 614

F R A M E
11

YOUR VARIOUS ROLES IN COMMUNITY WORK

In working with different community groups, you may have to play a number of different roles, depending on the type of group, your style of working, how you handle groups, and what assignment your agency has given you to work on with the group.

You will probably even play different roles with the same group. It is important to decide which of the following roles will be most useful to the community group in achieving its goals:

Organizer. If you are trying to recruit community residents or establish a pressure group to work for quicker action on some community problem, you will be organizing. You will have an active role and will be persuading, urging, and convincing. You may also need to lead the first group meeting until the group has selected its own leader.

Enabler. Enabling involves helping a group to function better by encouraging the development of leadership within the group. You may give the group information, offer suggestions and examples, keep minutes for the group by recording actions and decisions, and help the group acquire information and consider different plans of action; however, your objective is to encourage the group to be independent of you, to develop its own leadership, and to make its own decisions and plans.

Gatekeeper. The gatekeeper attempts to keep communication channels open by encouraging the participation of others or by proposing limits on the flow of communication so that others will have a chance to participate. The gatekeeper may also praise, agree with, and accept the contribution of others.

Tension reliever. When conflict arise within the group, you may try to resolve differences between members and relieve tension. Good ways of doing this are by using humor and by temporarily changing the topic of discussion.

Follower. The follower goes along with the movement of the group, more or less passively, accepting the ideas of others and serving as an audience for group discussion and decisions.

FRAME
12

Which of the following roles attempts to keep communication open among group members? Check the correct response.

_____ **a.** Enabler

Turn to Answer 90 on page 614

_____ **b.** Organizer

Turn to Answer 91 on page 615

_____ **c.** Gatekeeper

Turn to Answer 92 on page 615

_____ **d.** None of the above

Turn to Answer 93 on page 615

FRAME

13

Check the correct response. If you are giving group members information or suggesting methods of action with the goal of helping the group become independent by developing its own leadership and making its own decisions and plans, you are acting as

_____ **a.** Enabler.

> *Turn to Answer 94 on page 615*

_____ **b.** Organizer.

> *Turn to Answer 95 on page 615*

_____ **c.** Gatekeeper.

> *Turn to Answer 96 on page 615*

_____ **d.** Follower.

> *Turn to Answer 97 on page 615*

FRAME

14

MAJOR STAGES OF GROUP PROBLEM SOLVING

As you work with groups to solve community problems, you should try to follow some steps that will assist you in helping such groups to function effectively. The following are some basic steps.

1. Clarify the problem and obtain information. Help the group spell out the problem by getting complaints, preferences, and facts from the people experiencing the problem. Make sure everyone has a clear understanding of the problem. Decide what information is needed to clarify the problem and determine ways to get this information.

2. Set goals. Help group members decide what result they want, what is to be done, and what change needs to be made.

3. Find alternative solutions. Think of at least three viable options for solving the problem and discuss different possibilities. Check each possible solution by identifying the pros and cons, then decide which is the best.

4. Plan and organize for action. Putting the plan into action involves gaining approval from those in authority, overcoming resistance, and using resources. Keep lines of communication open, since people must understand what has been done, what is being done, and what is going to be done. Encourage the group to perform their tasks with as little of your assistance as possible.

5. Evaluate progress as you go along. Based on what steps should be taken according to the plan of action, determine what steps have been taken and what the results have been. If something did not work, find out why. Decide what changes in plans have to be made as a result of what has happened thus far.

6. Follow up on the action. Are people carrying out their responsibilities on time? If the community said it would act, has it done so? What did the group learn about getting things done? What should be done differently next time? By gaining information from all those involved in the mobilizing effort about the success of the plan and unmet needs, the group is led into another problem-solving process in which new problems and needs are defined.

The most difficult aspect of these problem-solving stages is the first one, clarifying the problem. Since participants may identify different problems or may see similar problems from different perspectives, workers carrying out the mobilizer role usually need to devote more time and energy to the first stage than to any other stage.

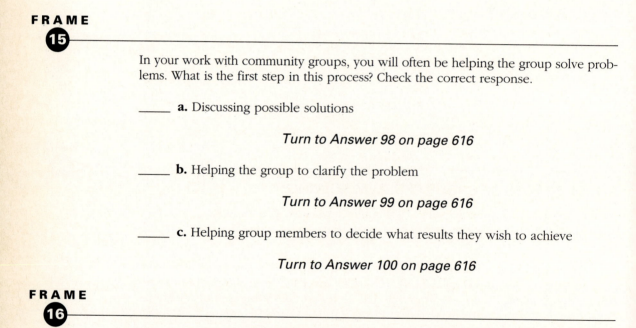

FRAME 15

In your work with community groups, you will often be helping the group solve problems. What is the first step in this process? Check the correct response.

_____ **a.** Discussing possible solutions

Turn to Answer 98 on page 616

_____ **b.** Helping the group to clarify the problem

Turn to Answer 99 on page 616

_____ **c.** Helping group members to decide what results they wish to achieve

Turn to Answer 100 on page 616

FRAME 16

Once you are sure that all group members clearly understand the problem, what is the next task in the problem-solving process? Check the correct response.

_____ **a.** Deciding what result is desired

Turn to Answer 101 on page 616

_____ **b.** Identifying ways to solve the problem and deciding which is best

Turn to Answer 102 on page 616

_____ **c.** Acting on solving the problem

Turn to Answer 103 on page 616

Turn to Answer 103 on page 616

F R A M E

17

Assume that you have proceeded through the first four phases in the problem-solving process with a group working on the development of a recreational program in your institution. You have helped the group spell out the problem so that they all under-stand it clearly; they have decided on the results they want and the best ways to solve the problem; and they have put a plan into action. What two things remain for the group to do to complete their plan of action?

1.

2.

Turn to Answer 104 on page 617

Turn to Answer 104 on page 617

CHAPTER 6
Summary and Further Study

Chapter Summary

This chapter described the major tasks and strategies of mobilizing within the community. We discussed the process of identifying unmet community needs and taking effective action to meet those needs along with strategies involved in organizing and working with community groups.

The important first step of mobilizing is the identification of unmet community needs, whether the community is a neighborhood or an institution. Once an unmet need has been identified, the process of mobilizing begins with specific steps to be taken in order to link resources with unmet community needs. We emphasized that the primary task in mobilizing, whether working to make an existing service more accessible or working to create a new service, is to develop a plan of action by gathering community support and involving as many people and groups as possible who can make a contribution.

Human service workers who engage in the mobilizing process usually work with formal and informal community or staff groups, and they need to understand the different kinds of meetings, the skills necessary for working with groups, and the common mobilizing roles assumed by workers engaged in the process. Workers need to be aware of the six stages of problem solving with groups, beginning with helping the group define the problem and concluding with what is involved in following up on the action.

Suggestions for Further Study

Most of the literature available on mobilizing comes from the field of social work related to community organization and from the areas of sociology concerned with the structure of communities and the process of community development. Further study is needed in order to refine your skills. For example, the activity of identifying unmet community needs should receive further study, especially in terms of consumer analysis and needs assessment. You should also explore the area of developing information sources in the community and the area of identifying and utilizing indigenous leadership in the community.

Understanding community power structures is also important. There is a wealth of literature in this area, largely from the fields of sociology and political science. The works of such authorities as Roland Warren will provide helpful perspectives on community power structures. This is an important area of further study for human service workers who carry out mobilizing activities, since decisions are often made through a political process involving tradeoffs between various power groups and not always in the humanitarian tradition of the "common good."

Further study also is indicated in the area of effective work with groups, specifically the process of group dynamics. Much attention is given to this area in the disciplines of psychology and sociology. Another important area relates to working with community groups that require particular organizing strategies. In organizing some groups, you may have to concentrate on short-term, problem-focused activities, for example, in starting a Boy's Club; other groups can be organized around some ongoing community issue, such as an organization for neighborhood improvement. The role of the mobilizer will differ, and the strategies employed will vary, depending on the nature of the group.

The readings below are a resource for pursuing the suggestions for further study in mobilizing:

Alinsky, Saul. *Reveille for Radicals*. New York: Random House, 1969.

Bennis, Warren, Kenneth D. Benne, and Robert Chin. *The Planning of Change,* 2d ed. New York: Holt, Rinehart & Winston, 1969.

Brager, George, and Harry Specht. *Community Organizing*. New York: Columbia University Press, 1973.

Brody, Ralph. *Problem Solving: Concepts and Methods for Community Organizations*. New York: Human Sciences Press, 1982.

Goffman, Erving. *Asylums: Essays on the Social Situation of Mental Patients and Other Inmates*. Garden City, N.Y.: Doubleday, 1961.

Kramer, Ralph M., and Harry Specht. *Readings in Community Organization Practice*. 3d ed. Englewood Cliffs, N.J.: Prentice-Hall, 1983.

Lauffer, Armand. *Getting the Resources You Need*. Beverly Hills, Calif.: Sage, 1982.

Lauffer, Armand. *Social Planning at the Community Level*. Beverly Hills, Calif.: Sage, 1978.

Naparstek, Arthur J., David E. Biegel, and Herzl R. Spiro. *Neighborhood Networks for Human Mental Health Care*. New York: Plenum Press, 1982.

Rothman, Jack, John L. Ehrlich, and Joseph G. Teresa. *Changing Organizations and Communities*. Beverly Hills, Calif.: Sage, 1981.

Tropman, John E. *Effective Meetings: Improving Group Decision-Making*. Beverly Hills, Calif.: Sage, 1980.

Tropman, John E., John L. Ehrlich, and Jack Rothman, eds. *Strategies of Community Intervention: Macro Practice,* 5th ed. Itasca, Ill.: F. E. Peacock, 1995.

Tropman, John E., John L. Ehrlich, and Jack Rothman. *Tactics and Techniques of Community Intervention,* 3rd ed. Itasca, Ill.: F. E. Peacock, 1995.

Warren, Roland. *The Community in America*. Chicago: Rand McNally, 1972.

Weissman, Harold. *Community Development in the Mobilization for Youth Experience*. New York: Association Press, 1969.

UNIT THREE

HELPING CONSUMERS TO FUNCTION MORE EFFECTIVELY

Preview of Unit

Everyone has difficulty at times in coping with the problems and frustrations of daily living, especially individuals, families, and groups who have resource, information, and power deficits. At times the difficulties are so great that people need special assistance with their behavioral, emotional, and/or resource problems. Such assistance ranges from provision of concrete resources or short-term help in problem solving to ongoing long-term services that may include occasional in-patient or institutional settings.

The core theme of Unit Three is the helping process, a general and systematic approach human service workers use to facilitate changes in, for, and by consumers. The helping process includes the following six steps, which will be useful to keep in mind as you work through the lessons: (1) developing a helping relationship; (2) identifying the presenting problems and issues; (3) assessing the total situation; (4) defining and specifying goals or desired outcomes; (5) working to achieve the consumer's desired outcomes; and (6) evaluating the extent to which the outcomes were achieved. Chapter 7 introduces the core skills required throughout systematic helping efforts: interviewing, relationship building, and mapping the system with ethnic competence. Chapter 8 provides a comprehensive overview of the stages of the helping process, starting with initial meetings, then moving through assessment, goal setting, service planning, contracting, service delivery, and evaluation. Chapter 8 also discusses some approaches to helping used during service delivery: case management, using natural helping networks, and working effectively with groups of consumers. Chapter 9 includes descriptions of more advanced intervention models and case materials.

All of the services you deliver are part of "a helping process." Thus, the roles and methods presented in Units Two and Three are part of the general framework of helping that we develop in this unit. For example, brokering, advocating, and mobilizing described in Unit Two are three of many services available within the helping process to address consumer needs. Additional choices are discussed in Unit Three: supporting, counseling, using natural helping networks, and educating. These options occur within helping interactions and throughout the general and systematic six-step process of helping. Achieving integrated helping skills and insights is a lifelong process for any human service worker.

Approaches presented in Units Two and Three help consumers cope more effectively by changing themselves, their situations, their environments, or all three. Even when individual and family problems stem from external, environmental problems, workers may intervene with the individual or family because help is needed now; the consumer cannot wait for long-term external changes, such as a more equal distribution of resources. As human service workers, we help people function more effectively while working for change on multiple levels (e.g., individual, group, community, state, federal government, and society). At the same time, we strive to empower consumers to cope with current problems and handle future problems. Indeed, the empowerment of consumers, discussed throughout this book, is a central goal of human service work.[1]

In practice, the helping process is highly integrated, and it is not always clear what "step" is being taken at a particular moment. We will illustrate this dynamic through the use of case materials that provide increasingly rich opportunities to integrate the concepts. The goals of the unit are: (1) to introduce a framework of knowledge and skills for using the helping process as a disciplined approach to delivering services and (2) to emphasize how to use the helping process for the empowerment of consumers, facilitating their efforts to define and effectively address the problems they face.

---

[1]See Barbara Solomon, *Black Empowerment: Social Work in Oppressed Communities* (New York: Columbia University Press, 1976).

Chapter 7

Relating to Consumers

Irrespective of the type of agency or the presenting problem, relationship-building and communication skills are central to the process of interacting with consumers during service delivery. In this chapter we describe three skill areas that are the foundation for communicating effectively in building helping relationships: (1) interviewing skills, (2) relationship-building skills needed throughout the service delivery process, and (3) general assessment skills that enable problem identification and service planning in a systems framework.

The roles and skills described in this text—brokering, advocating, mobilizing, relating, collaborating, intervening, managing the transition to the new service delivery systems, information managing, and integrating—depend on the development of relationships with people who are consumers, workers, or other agency or community members. This chapter is principally concerned with developing relationships with consumers, although the basic skills apply in general to all relationships. As indicated in the preview to this unit, the broad framework within which we typically conceive of our service delivery relationships with consumers is the helping process. Helping is fundamentally a process of skillful communication that requires abilities in (1) developing a helping relationship, (2) defining the presenting problems and issues, (3) assessing the total situation, (4) defining desired outcomes, (5) working to achieve the designated goals, and (6) evaluating the extent to which the goals were achieved. Workers use the human relations skills developed in this chapter to move through these stages of the helping process.

Three themes are emphasized throughout this chapter. One is that forming human relationships, especially helping relationships, requires the *ability and desire to assume a learner's role* in approaching consumers and to use interviewing and relationship-building skills to encourage consumers to share their perspectives and life experiences. A second theme is the notion of *empowerment*. Empowering involves emphasizing consumer strengths and reframing problems as opportunities for consumers to develop the skills and knowledge needed to handle their worlds effectively. Empowering consumers means maximizing consumer involvement and choice at each stage of the relationship, thus enabling consumers to select and achieve *their* objectives by building on personal strengths, family strengths, and community resources. A third, critical theme is *ethnic competence*. The ethnically competent approach to helping is based on the worker's ability to appreciate human differences in culture, social status, presenting problem, emotions and how they are interpreted, beliefs, or race, to name a few, and to form relationships with consumers within this context.

In this chapter we seek to build the foundation for competence in helping interactions. You will learn about the components of effective interviews; how to develop relationships with consumers; a systems approach for assessing consumers and their environments; and the attributes of an ethnically competent human service worker. You will discover that human service workers who are ethnically competent apply the empowerment model through their emphasis on respect, on working within the consumers' cultural framework, and on building on consumers' natural helping networks and individual resources. Our overall objective is to create a core set of skills you can use in all aspects of the service delivery process, especially in establishing helping relationships with consumers.

A wide variety of tasks appearing in human service job descriptions will require competence in the core skills introduced in this chapter. The tasks introduced in the chapter introductions for brokering, advocating, and mobilizing certainly require the ability to interview, build relationships (Lesson 2) and map systems (Lesson 3). A few additional examples of tasks are highlighted below. More will be presented in the chapters that follow.

1. Discuss options with consumers in order to help them understand choices and resolve a particular problem.
2. Talk with consumers or relatives about problems in order to reassure, provide support, or reduce anxiety.
3. Encourage and help consumers to discuss their points of view, feelings, and needs in order to increase their insight into the motives for their decisions and actions.
4. Express and demonstrate understanding of consumers' points of view, feelings, and needs in order to establish open and trusting relationships.
5. Participate in leisure activities with consumers in order to provide new skills or recreation or to reduce loneliness.

Interviewing

Interviewing is the central tool used for collecting information and formulating and implementing service plans with consumers. In this lesson you will learn about the interviewing process, how interviewing skills can help in your work with consumers, and how to acquire interviewing skills. The basic communication skills are described here in the context of interviews with individuals or families, but they are applicable in all helping interactions with systems of all sizes. Development of good interviewing skills will serve you well in all aspects of your practice, whether you are working with consumers (individuals, small groups, or communities) or with other helpers.

Goals

To learn interviewing skills that are important in helping others; to learn the functions of these skills and when to use them; and to acquire and develop proficiency in using the skills.

Learning Activities

To accomplish these goals, we will:

1. Define and identify basic verbal and nonverbal interviewing skills.
2. Understand the functions of specific interviewing skills in working with consumers.
3. Examine common errors in interviewing.
4. Identify ways of learning the skills in order to use them with consumers.
5. Suggest ways to practice the skills and to critique your performance.

FRAME
1

COMMUNICATION SKILLS

The understanding and use of nonverbal and verbal skills are important in all interactions with consumers if you are to develop a positive working relationship, understand the consumer's needs and goals, plan what to do, achieve positive outcomes, and evaluate the plan with the consumer. The first objective of good interviewing is to help consumers *explore* their situations.[1] Thus, self-exploration is the primary goal at the beginning of the helping process. A second objective is to increase consumer *understanding*.[2]

Let's begin with the essential communication skills needed for effective helping. Communication is much more than using words; it is based on common meanings and shared experiences. For example, when a consumer uses a term that could have different meanings to different people, ask the consumer to explain his experience. Some terms are unique to particular cultures. Do not assume that you understand a term that you do not use commonly. Such a word may be a key concept to understanding the consumer's experience. People quickly form impressions of the person with whom they are communicating. What you say and how you say it are very important in establishing relationships. Thus, it is necessary to develop your verbal and nonverbal communication skills.

Successful verbal communication in a helping relationship includes the following skills:[3]

1. Using a shared language base (standard language, dialect, slang, jargon) and stating things simply.
2. Listening to and understanding what is being said as well as what is not being said.
3. Asking open-ended questions and giving clarification and feedback.
4. Being aware of the use of intonation, inflection, and volume of voice.
5. Detecting whether the verbal messages are consistent with the nonverbal messages.

FRAME

2

Attending and Nonverbal Behaviors

We speak to one another in many ways—through the way we are dressed; our facial expressions; where and how we sit; our body movements (hand or foot motions); the direction and intensity of our gaze; and all nonlanguage sounds, such as voice tone, cries, throat clearing, groans, and "Mm-hmms."[4] Communication theorists call these sounds paralinguistic communication. There may be a big difference between a person's words and her nonverbal communications. Nonverbal communication is speaking without words. Identifying nonverbal communications may be one of the most important approaches to understanding consumers and uncovering their pressing concerns.[5]

---

[1] Gerald Egan, *The Skilled Helper, A Problem Management Approach to Helping,* 5th ed. (Pacific Grove, Calif.: Brooks/Cole, 1994).

[2] Egan, *The Skilled Helper.*

[3] Leon Ginsburg, Margaret Emery, and John Isaacson, *Syllabus on Orientation and Training of Beginning Workers to Provide Social and Rehabilitation Services* (West Virginia University School of Social Work, 1971).

[4] Robert G. Harper, Arthur N. Wiens, and Joseph D. Matarazzo, *Nonverbal Communication: The State of the Art* (New York: John Wiley, 1978).

[5] Joseph Simons and Jeanne Reidy, *The Human Art of Counseling* (New York: Heider and Heider, 1971), p. 53.

The single most important interviewer behavior is to follow carefully what is being said.[6] This process is called *active listening,* or simply verbal following. Active listeners usually have good interviewing skills. Active listening is important whether you are talking with a depressed consumer or with a neighborhood group interested in getting an additional traffic sign placed in their community.

Nonverbal interviewing skills are sometimes referred to as *attending behaviors* and include culturally appropriate eye contact, body language, facial expressions, and gestures. Good attending behaviors include the following:[7]

1. Maintaining good eye contact.
2. Sitting in a position facing the consumer.
3. Assuming a relaxed posture with a slightly forward lean.
4. Sitting in an open position (uncrossed arms and legs).

These attending behaviors indicate liking, respect, and a positive attitude on the part of the interviewer toward the consumer.[8]

The demonstration of attending behaviors helps to reinforce verbal skills and promote a climate of mutual support and encouragement. Good attending behaviors may increase consumer comfort and thereby the ability to share thoughts and feelings. Skillfull attending also communicates to the consumer that the interviewer is interested and listening.

One approach to helping the consumer feel at ease is to use *minimal prompts*. Minimal prompts are "Mm-hmms," head nods, and one or two words, such as "Yes" or "Go on." Repetition of the consumer's last word or few words also communicates that you are listening and stimulates the consumer to continue talking about the same topic. Since the goal is to gain the maximum amount of information from the consumer, especially in the beginning when you are trying to get to know and understand the consumer, nonverbal behaviors and minimal prompts are important tools. If you wait three to five seconds after a consumer stops talking, the consumer will usually begin talking again, continuing to discuss the same topic. Thus, silence or a pause is also a way to encourage the consumer to continue talking.

Generally, the worker's rate or pace of speech should be similar to that of the consumer in order to create a comfortable climate for sharing thoughts and feelings. It is usually helpful to match tone of voice, use of familiar words, volume, and body position with that of the consumer. If the consumer is depressed and speaking quite softly and slowly, however, it may be necessary to help improve the consumer's mood by being more upbeat in speech. While you do not want to speak more rapidly than the consumer, at times it may be helpful to increase your pace and have more lift in your voice than the consumer does, especially since you want the consumer to leave the interview feeling better than when the interview began.

---

[6]David Katz, "Laboratory Training to Enhance Interviewing Skills," in F. W. Clark and M. L. Arkava, eds. *The Pursuit of Competence in Social Work* (San Francisco: Jossey-Bass, 1979).

[7]Allen Ivey and Jerry Authier, *Microcounseling,* 2d ed. (Springfield, Ill.: Charles C. Thomas, 1978); Allen Ivey, *Intentional Interviewing and Counseling,* 3rd ed. (Pacific Grove, Calif.: Brooks/Cole, 1994).

[8]A. Mehrabian, *Nonverbal Communication* (Chicago: Aldine & Atherton, 1972).

FRAME

Assume that you have just completed a videotaped conversation with a colleague in which you demonstrated good attending behaviors. What four aspects of "good attending" behaviors can be observed?

1.

2.

3.

4.

Turn to Answer 105 on page 618

FRAME

4

Asking Questions

Both open and closed questions are valuable tools for interviewers. Most of us ask closed questions in everyday conversations. These are questions that can be answered with a yes or no or with a simply one- or two-word response. Closed questions help the consumer focus and can be used to confirm or reject the interviewer's understanding of an issue. Such questions can help the interviewer obtain specific information and may be used to control the direction and focus of the interview.[9] Since closed questions tend to reflect the interviewer's way of seeing the world, however, you should try to avoid using them when you want to hear the consumer's own story. Closed questions usually reduce the amount of consumer response[10] and require more work from the interviewer if they relate to complex issues, as the interviewer has to formulate what she or he thinks is going on. For example, "Are you having trouble sleeping because you are worried about final exams?" instead of, "Tell me what you think may be happening that is making it difficult for you to sleep." If the consumer is shy or very quiet, you may need to use closed questions initially to stimulate the flow of information. Then use open questions to elicit more information.

Open-ended questions usually begin with *what, when, how,* or *why* and encourage the consumer to define a situation, experience, or feeling. In addition, they permit the interviewer to focus on consumer concerns and encourage self-exploration within the consumer's frame of reference.[11] Since most people do not use naturally open questions in informal conversations, it is important to practice using open-ended probes. As you talk with your friends, note whether your questions are closed or open. If they are closed, restate them in an open form. For example, rather than asking, "Was your day lousy?" which concludes with an adjective describing the day, ask, "How was your day?" We generally recommend avoiding *why* questions because they are more difficult to answer than *what* questions (e.g., "What happened last week?"). In order to understand what happened or how someone felt, use brief, open-ended

[9]Egan, *The Skilled Helper;* Ivey and Authier, *Microcounseling.*

[10]A. Siegman and B. Pope, eds. *Studies in Dyadic Communication* (Elmsford, N.Y.: Pergamon, 1972).

[11]Egan, *The Skilled Helper.*

questions. Requests for information or clarification (e.g., "Describe your day.") are like open questions, despite the fact that they are not phrased in question form.

At worst, a series of closed questions feels like an inquisition or an investigation; the consumer begins to feel as if he or she is being interrogated by the police rather than being offered help. While there may be a long intake form to complete in connection with your first interview with a consumer, it is important not to let the form structure the interview. Much of the information will come out naturally, and you can request any information that does not surface as part of the interview at the end. Review the form at the end of the interview, show it to the consumer, state its purpose, and go through the questions and complete it with the consumer. Some agencies now give forms to consumers at the beginning of service that request concrete information such as income, employment, and address.

FRAME

List four words or phrases that you might use to ask open-ended questions:

1.

2.

3.

4.

Which of the four is *least* desirable to use? _____

Turn to Answer 106 on page 618

FRAME
6

Paraphrasing and Reflecting

Paraphrases are restatements of the content just expressed by the consumer. A paraphrase is not a verbatim statement but a summary, or shortened version, of what was heard. However, a paraphrase does not change, or add to, the meaning of what was expressed. Paraphrases are within and consistent with the consumer's frame of reference and include critical and unique words used by the consumer. Paraphrases tell consumers that you heard them correctly and stimulate consumers to continue exploring the issue. Paraphrases also give consumers opportunities to hear and think about what they are saying.

Paraphrases and reflections of feelings require using the consumer's frame of reference and giving the consumer full responsibility for exploring issues. Reflections of feelings, however, are statements of feelings that are expressed or alluded to by the consumer but not explicitly labeled. The interviewer's statement contains feeling words that refer to implicitly expressed affect. A consumer may come into the office with downcast eyes and a sad face, yet she may not state that she is feeling sad. The interviewer might then reflect that the consumer appears sad, or "down." (If the woman explicitly labels her feeling and the interviewer restates the same feeling, the interviewer has paraphrased.) Through the use of reflection of feeling, the interviewer can convey to the consumer the understanding not only of the content being expressed, but also of the feelings that the consumer is experiencing. Reflections of feelings are ways to express empathy with the consumer.

Reflection, like paraphrase, offers you an opportunity to check whether you accurately heard and understood what was said. Sometimes paraphrases and reflections are expressed in question form or as statements followed by "Is that correct?" Paraphrases and reflections allow the interviewer to be more active without inserting new ideas or changing the direction of the consumer's communication. Minimal prompts serve the same function, for they reinforce what is being said and encourage the consumer to continue exploring the topic. However, minimal prompts are a more passive tool. There is some evidence that active interviewers are more successful in sustaining consumer verbalization rates than are passive interviewers.[12] Reflections may also stimulate "deeper" exploration of a topic.[13]

Paraphrases are thought to encourage consumers to talk about experiences, whereas reflections encourage discussion of feelings. One study found that reflection of feeling resulted in significantly more words about emotions than did advice, open-ended questions, or statements that attempt to change consumer attitudes.[14] In addition, interviewers who used reflection were seen as more trustworthy and more expert than were workers who used closed questions, open questions, paraphrases, or influencing statements. There is evidence that reflections and questions about the consumer's feelings stimulate statements about emotions.[15] However, if a consumer is feeling "down," you might want to focus on experience, since focusing on feelings may result in the consumer's feeling more depressed.

FRAME
7

Complete the following exercises by first paraphrasing the consumer's statement and then reflecting feelings. (The first one is completed for you as an example.)

1. Female college student

I am not certain what happened, but suddenly things are going well for me, especially at school. I am finding it easier to concentrate and to get my work done. I even got an A on my last exam. Everything is going so well I can hardly believe it. I don't have to worry so much about things. I can relax and do my work and enjoy other parts of my life.

a. You said (paraphrase): *Everything is going so well for you with school work that your grades are high and you can enjoy other parts of your life.* Or, *your school work is going so well that you can relax and enjoy your life.*

---

[12]K. Heller, J. D. Davis, and R. A. Myers. "The Effects of Interviewer Style in a Standardized Interview." *Journal of Consulting Psychology* 30 (1966): 501–508.
[13]Egan, *The Skilled Helper.*
[14]P. S. Highlen and G. K. Baccus, "Effect of Reflection of Feeling and Probe on Client Self-Referenced Affect," *Journal of Counseling Psychology* 24 (1977): 440–443.
[15]R. P. Ehrlich, A. R. D'Augelli, and S. J. Danish, "Comparative Effectiveness of Six Counselor Verbal Responses," *Journal of Counseling Psychology* 26 (1979): 390–398.

b. You feel (reflecting feelings): *happy and relaxed that all parts of your life are going well!*

2. Male college student

I have a lot of trouble talking with my parents. Every time I try to tell them about something that is bothering me, they don't seem to listen. Instead of reacting to what I say, they ask if I need more money. Why don't they want to listen to me?

a. You said:

b. You feel:

3. 40-year-old man

Since my wife has been in the hospital, my whole life has changed. I have full responsibility for our four children. I have never cooked or taken care of household things. I'm not sure how to handle all this new responsibility. I don't miss my wife, since things were such a mess before she went to the hospital. I do miss female company and find it very difficult to work full time and take care of the house.

a. You said:

b. You feel:

4. Male college student

I have been dating a girl for several months. I really like her and thought she felt the same way. The other day I saw her with someone else. I asked around and found out she has been dating this other guy while she's been seeing me. I felt like yelling at her but was afraid she would tell me to get lost. I don't know what to do.

a. You said:

b. You feel:

5. 10-year-old girl in foster care

I miss my mother and father, and I know they miss me. Why can't I see them? This new place is not my home, and I don't belong here. The other kids don't like me. I have to clean my room and help with chores around the house. I have to do homework. I haven't made friends in my new school. I know my mother wants me to come home. Why aren't you helping me?

a. You said:

b. You feel:

6. 30-year-old woman

I have been seeing you now for two months, and there is no change in my life. My husband is still drinking. My children are still in foster care. Why haven't you done anything to help me? What's the sense of my paying bus fare and taking my time to come and see you?

a. You said:

b. You feel:

7. 21-year-old woman

I went to a weight-control class at school. The group was supposed to help us lose weight. I was one of the heaviest people in the group. I lost weight with the others during the four weeks of the group, and now I have gained back everything I lost plus some. I don't know why I can't stay on my diet. What's wrong with me? Can you help me?

a. You said:

b. You feel:

8. 15-year-old in juvenile corrections facility

I have done everything I was asked to do. When can I get out of here? My mother is sick and has all the other kids to take care of. She keeps asking me when I'll be coming home. What can I do to get out of here? Will talking with you help?

a. You said:

b. You feel:

9. 50-year-old alcoholic man in treatment center

I know that I'm an alcoholic and I'm glad I came here to dry out, but now I'm ready to leave and I don't want to go to AA meetings. I know I can handle my liquor now. I didn't have a problem for the past ten years. The problem started when I had stress at work and at home. I know that I can leave here now and be a social drinker and be fine.

a. You said:

b. You feel:

Turn to Answer 107 on page 618

FRAME

Summarizing

It is important to periodically summarize what the consumer has been saying. A summary usually combines paraphrases and reflections of feelings. A summary may also include information shared by the consumer at any time. In contrast, a paraphrase or a reflection refers to material just shared by the consumer in his preceding statement. A summary statement of a consumer's experiences and feelings may be used to

   1. begin an interview (summarizing past material),
   2. close an interview, or
   3. help the consumer focus during an interview.

Summaries are especially helpful if the consumer has talked about a number of issues. A summary of the major issues may help a consumer focus without leading him.

By hearing a summary of all his topics, the consumer has the opportunity to select a focus for the next part of the interview. An interviewer might summarize what was heard and then ask the consumer which issue he would like to explore in more depth. Summaries may be used to encourage consumers to look at a problem or situation in a new way because they may perceive facts and feelings in a different way.[16] A summary can help to move the interview forward by avoiding repetition, eliciting new information, helping reach a decision, and/or providing a bridge to a new topic.

Sometimes it is difficult to avoid giving advice within the process of summarizing. Advice must be used carefully if interviewers are to help consumers determine what they wish to do. Advice is thought to prod the consumer toward decision making or action outside the interview situation. The worker's aim in using advice is to gain the consumer's acceptance and implementation of the advice. The consumer may reject advice that is not helpful or that is inappropriately timed. Some consumers will nod agreement in response to a worker's advice but will not follow through on the suggestion. Beginning interviewers often overuse advice in their efforts to be helpful. Additional suggestions and warnings about the use of advice are included at the end of this lesson in the section on common errors in interviewing (Frame 11).

Like other relationship-building and interviewing skills, advice is used differently in various cultural contexts. For example, among Native Americans (Indians), advice is expected and is more acceptable than it is among other cultural groups. A Native American client will consider the advice carefully, discuss it with family members, and then independently decide whether to follow it. Other differences would emerge for Asian Americans or African Americans, and other ethnic groups. The important theme of cross-cultural skills is addressed in more depth in Lesson 3 of this chapter.

FRAME

9

Interpretation, Confrontation, and Information Giving

Interpretation, confrontation, and information giving are used to reach the second objective of interviewing: to increase consumer understanding. They are the interviewing skills used after the worker and consumer have thoroughly explored the presenting problem.

The interviewer makes *interpretations* based on meanings attached to the consumer's verbal and nonverbal communications. These interpretations are made within the interviewer's frame of reference, knowledge, and experience. Unlike reflecting, in making an interpretation the interviewer adds something to what the consumer has said. An interpretation may involve suggesting an alternative frame of reference.[17] Appropriately timed and accurate interpretations may stimulate an in-depth discussion of central issues and the development of new insights. However, inaccurate or premature interpretations may result in misconceptions about the consumer's behavior or situation and may prevent thoughtful exploration.[18] Interpretation should be used only when the consumer is able to accept and understand its meaning. Ideally, through exploration, consumers will begin to interpret and confront their own thoughts and behaviors.

---

[16]Ivey, *Intentional Interviewing and Counseling*.
[17]Egan, *The Skilled Helper*.
[18]Ivey, *Intentional Interviewing and Counseling*.

Confrontation means pointing out distortions, inconsistencies, games, and discrepancies among the consumer's behaviors, statements, and values. Confrontation is thought of as negative, combative, or argumentative. Confrontation differs from reflections and interpretations, pointing out the discrepancies in what the consumer has just expressed.

A consumer's immediate response to confrontation may be disorganization or rejection of the confrontation. A consumer may try to discredit the confronter, attack the confronter's words, persuade the confronter that she or he is incorrect, devalue the topic, seek support elsewhere for his or her position, or change his or her mind in order to correspond with the confronter's observation.[19] If the confrontation is appropriately timed and accurate, however, a consumer may accept it and move toward action.[20] If consumers check the accuracy of their understanding of your statement, it is an indication that they may be open to a different, more objective view of their behavior.[21]

Directions and *information giving* are frequently part of discussions between an interviewer and a consumer. Giving directions that seek to influence consumer action or behavior can lead to consumer agreement, no response, or rejection of the directions. Information giving may be used to help the consumer feel at ease, such as in a precounseling meeting to clarify consumer expectations. Directions and information giving may include direct guidance, expert information, information about resources, or a description of agency rules. Information giving is sharing information about agency services, arrangements, and resources, as well as information about common problems and illnesses and about helpful change plans or treatments.

At times, the most appropriate and helpful response to a consumer's statement is simple *support* and/or *genuine praise*. When a consumer describes success in working toward a goal, praise is appropriate. When a consumer describes feeling wonderful, an expression of support, such as "I'm so happy to hear you are doing well," is usually appropriate. We sometimes forget to notice and reinforce positive actions, even though we know that recognition and praise of positive behaviors is important for maintaining the behaviors. Remember to use praise in initial contacts with consumers.

As you learn to identify and comfortably use interviewing skills, remember that you will also need to incorporate relationship-building skills, described in the next lesson, in your interviewing style in order to become an effective interviewer and helper.

FRAME 10

As a review of the material covered so far, take a close look at the following segment from an actual termination interview and then answer the questions.

WORKER: (1) Ray, when you first came in, you had recently experienced an assault.
(2) Why don't you just briefly describe some of the problems you were having then.

[19]Egan, *The Skilled Helper*.
[20]Egan, *The Skilled Helper*.
[21]Egan, *The Skilled Helper*.

RAY: Umm. I had a lot of feelings I didn't understand, like hate and—ah—shyness in public. Mmm, I think I'd lost my masculinity almost and I don't know, I think, I was just uncomfortable with the way my life was going.

WORKER: (3) Where are you now?

RAY: I think things have changed a lot in my life and probably won't ever be the same, but I'm back to a point where I like the way I am now.

WORKER: (4) How are things different now?

RAY: Umm. I'm a lot less uneasy about making friends, and it seems like I don't have as many close friends as I once did and that really doesn't bother me. I used to think that, if I did not have friends, there was probably something wrong with me, and now it doesn't seem to matter. I really think it's good because in the past I put too much trust in people, in friends, and as a result I had a lot of people that were not really friends.

WORKER: (5) Fair-weather friends?

RAY: Yeah. And now I think people I deal with are more honest and more sincere with their friendship and don't try to take advantage. I used to have several friends who would take advantage; I think now I'm comfortable with what I've got, and my family is interested in the things that I do, and I think that's helped a lot.

WORKER: (6) Well, I think that gets into a value judgment, but that would be my feeling too, and that's okay. (7) If you don't have any real feelings of bitterness toward other people, I think it's okay not to have lots of friends.

RAY: I don't feel like I have a need for a lot of friends right now. I'm comfortable with what I've got, and my family has taken an interest in the things I do, and I think that's helped a lot.

WORKER: (8) What about feelings of depression. Are they there?

RAY: Once in a while I have a little trouble. On the boat I almost got to the point of crying for a few days, yet there was really nothing to be concerned about.

WORKER: (9) You seem more subdued today.

RAY: Yeah, I don't know. Had the pants scared off me yesterday—I think that might be part of it.

WORKER: (10) What happened?

RAY: Oh, I was climbing on a ladder up to the top of the house. At the same time a guy was on a ladder next door and fell off and hurt himself real bad. It scared me badly.

WORKER: (11) He was hurt; he fell.

RAY: Yeah. He broke both legs and probably his back, and it scared me. It was the first time in a long time that I had been around anybody that was hurt, and it shook me up pretty bad.

WORKER: (12) I bet it did. And perhaps you experienced some feelings of depression because of your earlier experience. I think after what you went through some periods of depression are expected. (13) To get upset when you see somebody else hurt is normal. Do you think you handled it well?

RAY: Yeah, I think I handled myself pretty well. There were several other people around the accident when it happened, and no one seemed to want to do anything, so I called the ambulance and moved the man's truck out of the driveway and took his ladder down, and my partner covered him up with a blanket and kept everybody away from him so he could—so as not to move him any. And I think I handled myself pretty well, but I was real shaky the whole time.

WORKER: (14) That's wonderful! You handled yourself in the immediate crisis. You really have come a long way. (15) How do you think you are going to do in similar situations in the future?

RAY: Well, it was a little shaky to get back up on the ladder that afternoon, but I think I did all right. Ah, I shook it off pretty well.

WORKER: (16) Mmmm.

RAY: It's still with me a little bit, and it still makes me a little nervous when I think about it, but as far as going on with climbing ladders and working high, I think I can do it.

WORKER: (17) Well, you feel you can handle difficult situations, yet you said you almost cried on the boat—

RAY: I don't know what that was about; it was strange. I just suddenly got depressed, and I was depressed for, oh, two days, three days, I guess.

WORKER: (18) Okay, what did you do to bring yourself out of it?

RAY: I just kicked myself in the butt and said there's no reason for this, no reason to be depressed, because there wasn't. Everything was going fine.

WORKER: (19) Did you change any activities; were you doing anything differently?

RAY: No. I tried to go on with what I was doing. I think that those feelings came from being real tired.

WORKER: (20) You were tired?

RAY: Yeah, I was real tired. I'd been sick.

WORKER: (21) Did you have flu, or do you think this was because you were feeling depressed?

RAY: I think that when things aren't going well and I have pressures and allow myself to get tired, I tend to get depressed.

WORKER: (22) So it sounds like you had a lot of stress.

RAY: Yes, It was piled up at that time.

WORKER: (23) Again, that's not uncommon to have these feelings after having a lot of stress. Usually you can hold up while the work has to be done. What I'm glad to hear is that you came out of it.

1. Identify the two skills used by the worker in sentences (1) and (2):

a.

b.

2. a. Identify the skill used by the worker in response to Ray's first statement (3): _____

b. What other skill might have been appropriate to use here?_____

c. Give the numbers of additional worker's statements that are examples of the same skill. _____

3. If this had been the worker's initial interview with Ray, list some of the words used by the worker that would need clearer definition. _____

4. Identify the skills used in the following statements:

a. (5) _____   d. (9) _____

b. (6) _____   e. (12) _____

c. (7) _____   f. (14) _____

5. What effect or outcome did the use of a confrontation have? How did the consumer respond to this confrontation (e.g., what was the consumer's response to worker statement 17 and then to worker statements 18–21)?

Turn to Answer 108 on page 619

Turn to Answer 108 on page 619

FRAME

11

COMMON ERRORS IN INTERVIEWING

What follows are some tendencies that are important for interviewers to avoid. They spring from a desire to be helpful or from anxiety about being helpful in the first meeting with a consumer. The desire to help the consumer solve problems quickly may lead to premature problem solving, that is, to suggesting a change before you fully understand the situation and before consumers have had time to explore their situation fully with you. A critical aspect of helping is providing opportunities for consumers to step back and look at their thoughts, feelings, and behaviors in order to assess their situations before acting. You need to be patient, to show respect, and to allow consumers to determine their first steps.

Premature problem solving involves giving advice as soon as the consumer mentions a problem. Advice can be helpful when it takes the form of offering a resource, but telling a consumer what to do can be harmful. The following advice is an example of how an interviewer can close off problem solving prematurely: "If I were you, I would call my mother-in-law and tell her not to come this week, since she is interfering with your schedule." The consumer may agree, but we know that solutions do not occur quickly or easily. As a general rule, by the time you see a consumer, the problem behavior or situation has been around for a long time. In most cases, if a simple solution existed, the consumer would have found it and would not be talking with you. The most common consumer responses to inappropriate or premature advice are:

1. *Superficial agreement,* with no intention to follow through. This occurs when the consumer is trying to be polite, is not assertive enough to disagree, is uncomfortable discussing the situation, or is convinced that you have solved the problem.
2. *Anger,* expressed or unexpressed.
3. *Feeling misunderstood* by the interviewer.
4. *Feeling that the interviewer is not interested* in getting to know or really understand the consumer.

Advice based on your perceptions and experiences may be seen as imposing your ideas on the consumer and ignoring the consumer's uniqueness. A consumer may describe a situation or a feeling, such as depression, which is similar to something you have experienced; you may assume that it is the same and tell the consumer what you did in that situation. But depression, like most human experiences and feelings, affects different individuals in different ways and emerges from diverse sources. It is important not to accept the consumer's label of depression and, instead, to ask for examples from the consumer's own experiences. Once you clearly understand the consumer's situation, your response may be different. In fact, human service workers generally encourage consumers to develop their own advice or solution (with interviewer guidance) without direct suggestions.

When people do not know how to solve a problem, they tend to give advice based on their own experiences or on something they have heard about but have not tried. For example, if the consumer's problem involves too many school absences and you know nothing about school phobia, you may assume that you are helping by telling the child she must return to school or face expulsion. However, if you had reviewed the literature on school phobia, you would have found creative, effective techniques for helping the child return to school. Interviewers sometimes mistake giving advice for appearing competent and attempt to prove their knowledge and helpfulness through advice giving. True competence is helping consumers explore and understand their situations so that they can make their own choices.

Another common error is asking series of closed questions. For example, if a consumer tells you that he wants to run away from home, you might assume that there is a problem in his relationship with a new stepparent. You might then ask closed questions about the relationship between the consumer and the stepparent and thereby miss the real reasons for the consumer wanting to run away and what he hopes to accomplish from this choice.

FRAME
12

ACQUIRING INTERVIEWING SKILLS

Now that we have clearly defined the basic nonverbal and verbal interviewing skills and noted common errors, we will explore ways to acquire these skills so that they will become part of your helping behaviors. Several structured training programs have been designed to enable human service personnel to develop interviewing skills. In one of the major training programs, developed by Allen Ivey and his associates, each skill is presented and practiced separately; then the skills are combined in interviewing situations. This approach to learning helping skills is called microcounseling.[22]

First, the skill is clearly defined, verbally and in written form, and the learner is given an opportunity to discuss and ask questions about the skill. The second step is to watch the skill modeled, preferably on videotape. In the microcounseling training model, the trainee tries using the skill, and this practice attempt is recorded. If videotape equipment is not available, audiotape recorders may be used; however,

---

[22]Ivey and Authier, *Microcounseling*. When this approach is used in skill training with consumers, Ivey calls it the psychoeducation model.

videotape is much preferred as you can see nonverbal behaviors, and the performance is more realistic. The trainee practices the new skill in an interview with one of the other trainees or with someone who plays the role of the consumer.

Initially, it is important to practice one skill at a time in very brief (two-minute) interviews. For example, the skill may be to practice developing open-ended questions. If you find yourself asking a closed question, try to restate the question in open-ended form.

The interviewer-trainee then looks at the tape, makes a self-assessment, and is given feedback by other trainees and the trainer. Guidelines for giving feedback are outlined below. It is crucial to follow these guidelines as you practice each skill and help your colleagues perfect their skills. Once each skill is acquired, it is practiced with others in simulated interviews.

There is considerable evidence that students can acquire the skills described in this lesson by using a structured skill training model. However, the research shows that students do not necessarily transfer their newly acquired skills to their work with actual consumers. In fact, graduate social work students were found not to transfer to the field the interviewing skills they demonstrated in simulated interviews with their peers.[23] Thus, it is important to continue to work on maintaining and developing your interviewing skills as you interact with consumers in work settings.

Guidelines for Giving Feedback

1. Sources of feedback. The most important sources of feedback on your performance are you and the person you interviewed. Additional sources of feedback are your peers and your supervisor. Periodically assess yourself and seek feedback from consumers and others. Ask the consumer how she experienced the interview, what was helpful, and how the interview could have been more helpful.

2. Be concrete or behaviorally specific. Generally, global comments do not help us know what to do differently. Make specific suggestions, such as "It might have been useful to have stated the question as follows. . . ."

3. Be reinforcing, be positive. We learn best from positive feedback. Do not assume that others know when they have done something well. Sometimes we are not aware of the strengths in our performance and may not continue to use the skill unless we are told that it is helpful to do so.

4. Limit feedback. Limit your feedback to one, two, or three things that might be improved in any one session. It is difficult, if not impossible, to learn several new things at once. Save some feedback for the next time if you have many comments or suggestions.

5. Stress the helpful things. Seek to identify what would have been more helpful rather than just pointing out weaknesses.

In this lesson, you have learned nonverbal and verbal skills. The verbal skills included open-ended questions, paraphrases, and reflections, which are nondirective interviewing techniques. These verbal skills are designed to maximize consumer input and minimize both interviewer input and the tendency to lead the consumer.

---

[23]J. Kopp, "The Transfer of Interviewing Skills to Practicum by Students with High and Low Pre-Training Skill Levels," *Journal of Teaching in Social Work* 4 (1990): 31–51.

Relationship Building

In Lesson 1 of this chapter you learned some of the communication skills needed in order to become an effective helper. This lesson describes how these and other skills contribute to building helping relationships and emphasizes the importance of relationship throughout the helping process.

Goals

Given a description of a worker who is attempting to develop a helping relationship with a consumer, you will be able to identify whether the necessary characteristics of a helping relationship are present, which skills are being used, and what practice principles are being applied.

Learning Activities

To accomplish these goals, we will:

1. Define the basic characteristics important for developing effective helping relationships.
2. Examine four long-range purposes of the helping relationship.
3. Identify and describe five characteristics of a helping relationship.
4. Review three factors of helping that are used in building relationships.
5. Explain three ways of working within the helping process.
6. Consider practice principles that are useful in building relationships.

FRAME 1

THE HELPING RELATIONSHIP

Building an open and supportive relationship between consumers and helpers is an important part of successful practice in a human service agency. While there are numerous components of good relationships, this lesson focuses on those aspects that are critical in the development of good helping relationships.

The helping relationship is unique: Help is offered to meet the needs of the consumer, not the needs of the helper. In other relationships, this is not true. For example, friendships are generally equal relationships in terms of what participants give and receive. Helping may occur among friends and relatives, but in these relationships there is the expectation of mutual help and reciprocity. In a helper–consumer relationship the giving is in one direction (from the helper to the consumer) without the expectation of something in return. Further, good helping relationships have clear objectives and are time limited.

We talk about certain individuals being "natural" helpers. What does this mean? Several human qualities, such as warmth, empathy, and genuineness, are characteristics of "natural" helpers and can be taught to paraprofessional and professional helpers.[1] You can communicate warmth, genuineness, and empathy through the nonverbal attending behaviors described in the preceding lesson. Additional ways to communicate these qualities will be introduced in this lesson.

F R A M E

2

WARMTH AND EMPATHY

Most of us like to experience "warmth" from another person. When some other person, especially someone whom we do not know well, treats us warmly, we feel better about ourselves and more comfortable with that person. A consumer may feel uncomfortable or afraid during his first encounter with you. If you treat the consumer warmly, it will ease the tension and shorten the time required for the consumer to feel comfortable enough to speak openly with you.

The concept of warmth is familiar to most of us, whereas *empathy* is a term that is not usually a part of everyday speech. Empathy is the ability to understand another person by seeing the world through the other person's eyes; it means being able to understand the consumer's unique experiences and feelings from the consumer's perspective. Seeing things from the consumer's perspective is important for establishing a relationship and helping the consumer develop trust, openness, and ease in talking with you. Thus, empathy is both a means of building relationships and a means of gathering information.

Gerald Egan describes two levels of empathy. Basic empathy is being able to get inside the consumer's world by getting a feeling for what this world is like, looking at the world from the consumer's frame of reference.[2] Empathic workers can communicate this understanding in a way that shows that they have some understanding of the consumer's feelings, experiences, and behaviors.[3] Empathy means communicating basic, initial understanding as expressed by the consumer. Empathy is used from the outset to build a relationship and develop an understanding of the consumer's situation. Advanced empathy corresponds to interpretation; it means expressing for the consumer what the consumer is only half saying or implying. Advanced empathy is generally used later in the counseling process to help consumers develop new perspectives on themselves and their situations. On both levels, the empathic helper must *accurately* understand the consumer's experiences and feelings.

---

[1]Robert R. Carkhuff, *Helping and Human Relations: A Primer for Lay and Professional Helpers,* vols. 1 and 2 (New York: Holt, Rinehart & Winston, 1969).
[2]Gerald Egan, *The Skilled Helper: A Problem Management Approach to Helping,* 4th ed. (Pacific Grove, Calif.: Brooks/Cole, 1990).
[3]Egan, *The Skilled Helper.*

Empathy is expressed nonverbally through good attending behaviors and appropriate facial expressions, such as smiling at the right time. Empathy is a complex concept that is difficult to pinpoint. The best way to express empathy is through accurate reflections of feelings. A consumer may come into your office, sit down, look at the floor, and tell you that his father has just left home, he has lost his job, and his girlfriend has broken up with him. An empathic response would be, "You are feeling miserable; it seems like your whole world is falling apart."

There's a difference between restating content and reflecting feelings, as shown in the following example:

CONSUMER: The other students in my class just seem brighter and better prepared than I am. It seems that they are learning empathy faster than I am. I'm wondering whether this field is right for me.

HELPER 1: You think the other students are brighter and will be better human service workers than you will be.

HELPER 2: You are feeling discouraged in comparison with your classmates and questioning whether this is the right field for you.

The first helper responded by paraphrasing the consumer's words, whereas the second helper reflected the expressed, yet not labeled, feelings. The second response is an empathic response. To communicate empathy, it is important to communicate both the content and the feelings in the consumer's communication. This is done by careful listening, by seeing things through the consumer's eyes, and by not imposing your ideas and experiences on what you are hearing. If a consumer is uncomfortable talking about feelings, however, it is advisable to focus on content and engage in paraphrasing rather than reflection.

Accuracy is important. Accurate empathy is a way of telling the consumer you are interested—you are listening and seeking to understand what is being expressed. Allow yourself time to think about what was just said in order to respond accurately. Learn to wait as the consumer pauses; use this time to think about what feelings the consumer has just expressed. Sometimes helpers make errors by trying too hard and talking too much. It is best to think about what you are going to say and to respond briefly. Try to reflect the kernel of what is being expressed. Avoid the tendency to continue talking in order to correctly express what you think you heard. The goal of an empathic reflection is simply to let the consumer know that you heard and that you understand what was said in order to encourage the consumer to continue talking. Therefore, it is important to be brief—obviously, much briefer than the consumer. If you are uncertain about the consumer's feelings, you may state the reflection in the form of a question: "Is that correct?" This gives the consumer a chance to clarify for you, and it gives you an opportunity to check whether you heard correctly and understood accurately.

Empathy is also expressed by matching your tone of voice and pace of speaking to those of the consumer. If a consumer speaks rapidly in an animated, excited tone, and your response is flat and slow, your response is not fully empathic, though your words may be accurate. Remember, you can help a depressed consumer change moods by modeling positive attitudes and by speaking as rapidly as the consumer (or more so). At the same time, you do not want to be fully animated when the consumer is barely getting words out. It is easy to express empathy when someone is feeling low. It is equally important to show understanding and empathy when feelings are high. For example:

CONSUMER (*in animated voice*):   I just heard that I got the job I wanted and that my closest friend is coming to visit this weekend.

HELPER: I haven't seen you happier! It's wonderful that things are going so well for you.

Your language or choice of words can help communicate that you are assuming the consumer's frame of reference. Here is another example:

CONSUMER (*a 10-year-old*):   My teacher thinks I'm crazy. Whenever someone is fooling around in class, she thinks it's me. She doesn't yell at some of the other kids, even though they started it all.

HELPER 1:   You are confused. You wonder why your teacher singles you out for discipline.

HELPER 2:   You're mad because she picks on you and doesn't seem to see the real troublemakers.

The second helper's response will communicate more to a 10-year-old. The first helper is accurate, but the response sounds too adult. It is not within the consumer's frame of reference.

At the same time, it is important to be yourself and not take on a way of talking that is not your own and that may sound like you are pretending to adopt the consumer's frame of reference. For example, using a word such as *bread* for *money* may do more harm than good if this is not part of your usual vocabulary. You *can* use informal words that are understandable to the consumer without completely altering your language; however, it must be natural for you. Workers who come from backgrounds similar to those of the consumers may have some advantage in communicating understanding and empathy for the consumer's plight. When there are shared experiences, values, and social class, the consumer may have increased confidence in the worker's ability to understand what is being said. This is why skilled helpers sometimes train former addicts, former prisoners, or persons from a particular neighborhood to work with consumers with similar life experiences.

The suggestions that follow provide ways for you to express empathy:[4]

1. *Attend* carefully, physically and psychologically, to the messages transmitted.
2. *Listen* especially for the key issues or problems.
3. *Respond* fairly *frequently, but briefly,* to core issues.
4. Be *flexible* and *tentative* enough so that the consumer has room to move (to affirm, deny, explain, clarify, or shift emphasis).
5. Be *gentle, but firm,* helping the consumer focus on important issues.
6. *Respond* to both *feeling* and *content* unless there is some reason for emphasizing one or the other.
7. Move *gradually toward* the exploration of *sensitive topics* and *feelings.*

---

[4]Gerald Egan, *The Skilled Helper,* 4th ed. (Pacific Grove, Calif.: Brooks/Cole, 1994), p. 98.

8. After you have responded, *attend* carefully to *verbal* and *nonverbal clues* that either confirm or deny the accuracy of your response.

9. *Note signs of consumer stress or resistance* and try to judge whether these arise because you have been inaccurate or perhaps have been too accurate.

10. Remember that the skill of empathy is a tool to help consumers see *themselves* and *their situations* more clearly with a view to more effective management.

FRAME
3

Testing for Empathy

Two consumer statements are written below. Each statement is followed by a range of responses. Check the most appropriate empathic response to the feelings and content expressed by each consumer.

1. A 15-year-old female in a group home is talking to the houseparent:

I can't stand this place. I need a new place to live. I have tried to get along here and to make friends, but no one talks to me. It seems I'm constantly in arguments and in trouble here. No one understands me; no one is interested in me. You don't let me go anywhere or do anything and you constantly nag at me.

_____ **a.** You do not seem to like it here or to get along with anyone; you want to move to a different house.

_____ **b.** I think it would be good if you tried to get along here. There's really nowhere else to put you, and I'm certain that you can learn to get along with the other girls and with the staff.

_____ **c.** You feel you don't fit in here. You are trying to make it, but feel left out and probably pretty alone. It sounds like you are feeling this home is a hopeless situation for you.

_____ **d.** You are feeling sorry for yourself and sound like you want to leave.

2. A 19-year-old female student is talking to a peer counselor at the college counseling center:

I'm feeling lousy. I met someone I really like, and we dated for six months. I really care about him. His brother recently became ill, and he left school to help out at home. I didn't hear from him and called to see why he wasn't back in school. Then this past weekend, when he came back for his things, he said he didn't want to see me again. Now I can't seem to get to work, and I keep avoiding my friends. There's nothing I want to do except get away and be alone.

_____ **a.** You became dependent on someone during the past six months and now you can't function on your own.

_____ **b.** You are feeling really down and rejected; it's such a sudden change, and you feel so lousy that it's difficult to do any of the things you used to enjoy.

_____ **c.** It sounds like you're feeling sorry for yourself when it's really your boyfriend who is in the difficult situation—having to drop out of school to help his family.

_____ **d.** You are embarrassed that your boyfriend no longer wants to see you, so you are staying away from your friends.

Turn to Answer 109 on page 621

FRAME

4

COMBINING RELATIONSHIP BUILDING WITH INTERVIEWING

In the following example, the consumer's presenting problem was physical abuse by her spouse. The excerpt is from the first interview with the consumer. Read the excerpt and then answer the questions that follow.

WORKER: (1) So what I'm trying to get at, are you satisfied with your marriage?

ALICE: No, I don't feel satisfied; that's why I am here.

WORKER: (2) What's missing? What isn't right?

ALICE: Well, it's boring and occasionally he beats up on me—not often like my first husband, but still every now and then he'll go out and come home drunk and start a fight with me.

WORKER: (3) Boring. How long have you been married to him now?

ALICE: Five years.

WORKER: (4) Five years together.

ALICE: Being bored is better than getting smashed, which is how it was with my first husband.

WORKER: (5) Do you go out at all?

ALICE: Rarely.

WORKER: (6) Does he dance?

ALICE: A little; usually he just sits around if we go out to a place with music. I guess he doesn't like to dance or doesn't like to dance with me.

WORKER: (7) Do you have any couples you go out with? Any pretty good friends to be with?

ALICE: We have a few friends. I have a couple of female friends I knew before I met him, but he doesn't like them and doesn't like me to spend time with them.

WORKER: (8) Do you feel that your marriage is boring or that your life is boring?

ALICE: Both. Well, we didn't even do anything for my birthday, and I didn't care. My birthday was last weekend, and we just stayed home.

WORKER: (9) Oh, happy birthday.

ALICE: Thanks. Anyway, maybe we're just going through a difficult time, or maybe it's hopeless.

WORKER: (10) How old are you?

ALICE: I'm thirty-seven.

WORKER: (11) Have you thought about, well, maybe not trying to make him do everything with you, just starting to do things on your own? Maybe join a women's league? Like you got into selling for Avon, and that's a way to get out of the house more.

ALICE:		Well, I get out some now.
WORKER:	(12)	How often?
ALICE:		Oh, once or twice a week.
WORKER:	(13)	There are pretty good programs at the YWCA.
ALICE:		Like what?
WORKER:	(14)	I think they have bowling there and an aerobics class. I'm in an aerobics class. It's fun.
ALICE:		Where is your class?
WORKER:	(15)	Well, I go to the class in Breming, but the Clarksville one offers many more different classes.
ALICE:		Yeah.
WORKER:	(16)	I think the thing to do is for you to get out more. Start doing more activities, like at the "Y" and selling Avon and other things.
ALICE:		I do like getting out and talking to people.
WORKER:	(17)	How do you think your husband would feel if you started going out more? Do you think he would mind?

1. What common errors did this worker make in responses 11 and 16?
2. Which skill did this worker use most often?
3. Rephrase questions 5 and 8 to convert them to open-ended questions or requests for more information or clarification, making certain your rephrased questions are relevant in the context of the interview.

Question 5:

Question 8:

4. Does this worker seem to follow the consumer's statements and relate to what the consumer is saying? _____ Yes _____ Sometimes _____ No _____
5. What skill is missing in this interview? (For example, look at response 3 and consider what skill might have been used there.)
Missing skill:

Turn to Answer 110 on page 622

F R A M E

5

GENUINENESS AND RESPECT

Warmth, empathy, and genuineness are considered important characteristics for building positive helping relationships. To be *genuine* means to be yourself. Some of the issues discussed under the section on empathy also relate to genuineness, such as using words that the consumer understands yet not using street jargon that is not part of your usual speaking pattern. When you know yourself and are comfortable with who you are, it is possible to be yourself and be appropriately spontaneous even in formal helping situations.

Genuine helpers avoid defensiveness. When a consumer is being critical, the worker listens and tries to understand why the consumer is feeling this way. For example:

CONSUMER: I don't see the point in my continuing to see you; nothing has changed at school. These talks seem to be a waste of time.

WORKER 1: You are wasting our time by not wanting to deal with the issues.

WORKER 2: You see no benefit to yourself from coming here; it seems like a lot of time and energy with nothing to show for it.

The first worker blamed the consumer for not gaining from counseling, whereas the second worker listened and paraphrased the consumer's concerns.

Genuine people also seek consistency between their values and their behaviors. Genuine helpers reflect openness to people and ideas and are able to share their own ideas and feelings. Here are some suggestions for ways to express genuineness in working with consumers:

1. Avoid emphasizing your formal helping role and avoid professional jargon and stereotyped helping behaviors.
2. Allow yourself to be spontaneous without being haphazard or unpredictable.
3. Remain open and nondefensive even when you are questioned.
4. Be consistent and avoid discrepancies between your values and your behavior and between what you think and feel and what you say while remaining tactful.
5. Share yourself and your experiences with consumers if this is appropriate and will be helpful.
6. Over time become comfortable with behaviors that are helpful to consumers but are not a part of your style of communicating.[5]

Respect for consumers is also important for developing helping relationships and for successful helping. Respect is expressed in your attitudes toward consumers and in how you work with them. Your attitude is respectful if you are oriented toward, and work *with,* the consumer.[6] The important issue is how to express this respect in your behavior so that it is communicated to the consumer. You can express respect in several ways, including the following:[7]

1. Having positive expectations of consumers; expecting that consumers can change and can achieve their goals.
2. Being willing to work with the consumer; being available to the consumer.
3. Regarding the consumer as a unique person, supporting the consumer's individuality, withholding critical judgment, and offering unconditional regard.
4. Having regard for consumer self-determination; allowing consumers to select their own areas for change by helping them assess their own resources in order to use them and cultivate new resources.
5. Being honest with consumers; avoiding manipulation and duping clients into changing or into a different lifestyle.
6. Being "for" consumers, taking their interests seriously even if this means challenging their actions and placing realistic demands on them.
7. Understanding consumers and communicating your understanding.
8. Assuming that consumers want to live more effectively.

---

[5]Egan, *The Skilled Helper*
[6]Egan, *The Skilled Helper*
[7]Egan, *The Skilled Helper*

9. Communicating appropriate warmth as well as competence; avoiding a cold, aloof stance (warmth is not simply friendliness; in a professional relationship warmth is expressed differently than it is in a friendship; expressing warmth should be geared to the needs and comfort of the consumer).

10. Helping consumers unlock and access their own resources and participate fully.

Respect means expecting consumers to make functional, reasonable decisions based on an honest, realistic assessment of their resources. The worker may need to help the consumer be realistic about resources and goals. Further, consumers' resources may be blocked in a variety of ways, challenging the worker to help consumers to use and further develop their own resources freely. Helping a consumer formulate alternatives and discussing the potential consequences—positive and negative—of each option is a central function throughout the helping process. You can also express respect by (1) using good attending behaviors, (2) communicating accurate empathy, (3) expressing warmth, (4) using appropriate reinforcement, and (5) being genuine.[8]

FRAME 6

Checking Your Understanding of Genuineness and Respect

1. List three of the ways suggested to communicate genuineness.

    a.

    b.

    c.

2. Identify four behaviors for expressing your respect for consumers.

    a.

    b.

    c.

    d.

Turn to Answer 111 on page 622

FRAME 7

SELF-PRESENTATION AS A RELATIONAL SKILL

How attractive you appear to the consumer is important, especially in the initial stages of developing a relationship that provides comfort and rapport. *Attractiveness,* as used here, does not mean physical beauty. Your attractiveness, as perceived by the consumer, is affected by a number of factors. For example, similarity in dress, ethnicity,

---

[8]Egan, *The Skilled Helper*.

and age between you and the consumer may cause you to appear more attractive to the consumer. If a consumer is experiencing difficulties with her children, she may feel more comfortable initially talking with a worker who also has children. People may feel more comfortable with others of the same or similar social class, education, interests, values, language, perhaps even personality characteristics. Some of these factors you cannot change at will. To pretend to be similar to a consumer only harms the relationship; real differences need to be acknowledged. For example, you do not want to use street language with a black youth gang when this is not your language. This lack of genuineness will harm your attempts to build a relationship. On the other hand, you do not want to use sophisticated language that the consumer will not understand or that will cause the consumer discomfort and increase the distance between you.

We have focused on characteristics and qualities that you can change. Age, sex, and ethnicity, which cannot be changed, can, when possible, be matched to those of the consumer or acknowledged and discussed with the consumer. These differences may increase the time it takes to develop an effective helping relationship, but they will not make developing such a relationship impossible. The key issue is communicating qualities that will let the consumer know that you are with them, you are listening and understanding, and you can be trusted to offer meaningful help and support.

The appearance of expertness is also considered important for building relationships and engaging the consumer in the change process. Competence is communicated through your appearance and your role (the consumer assumes that because you have a helping position or job, you are competent), by your training, by your reputation, and, most important, by your behavior. When you actually help a consumer, you are perceived as competent. Consumers may see you as competent before actual help is offered or before their goals are accomplished; however, their final assessment will emerge from their actual experience of working with you.

FRAME

8

LONG-RANGE PURPOSES OF THE HELPING RELATIONSHIP

Generally, the overall purposes in any helping relationship are to enable a person, group, community, or institution to make choices about a problem or situation and to change or maintain their situation. Thus, specific goals are defined by the consumer or by the consumer and worker jointly. If the consumer is not meeting with you by choice, your first goal is to develop a helper–consumer relationship based on agreed-on goals. Until the consumer agrees to work with you toward such goals, she or he is simply an applicant or a resister, not a consumer.[9]

Contained within the overall purposes are at least three fundamental purposes that can be used as guidelines for helping others make decisions and choices:

1. Help the consumer increase self-awareness. This means helping the consumer understand himself and others better and function in a manner consistent with this knowledge.

---

[9]Eileen Gambrill, *Casework: A Competency-Based Approach* (Englewood Cliffs, N.J.: Prentice-Hall, 1983).

2. Help the consumer feel more confident and able. This means helping the consumer feel "I can" and "I am." It also means helping the consumer feel "I am good" and "I am important." A theory called "self-efficacy" tells us that if people *expect* to succeed in change efforts, they are more likely to participate.[10]

3. Help the consumer become more self-directing and competent. This means helping consumers increase their skills in decision making, problem solving, taking action, and accepting the consequences of their actions and decisions. Optimally, consumers will acquire new skills from their work with you, which will help them better handle future problems.

FRAME
9

CHARACTERISTICS OF A HELPING RELATIONSHIP

Helping relationships are special ones. They differ from the kinds of relationships people encounter in most of their daily lives and are distinguished by the following characteristics:

Mutuality. The helping relationship is a mutual, not a one-way relationship. The consumer and the worker both bring themselves to the helping relationship, and so the success or failure of the relationship depends as much on the worker as it does on the consumer. This is especially important for you, as the worker, to recognize, since some agency workers tend to blame the consumer if a relationship is not established.

Honesty. The helping relationship is not necessarily pleasant and friendly. Any worker who attempts to always keep interactions on a pleasant and friendly level, regardless of the circumstances, has not developed a true helping relationship with a consumer. For example, many workers fear that their relationship with a consumer will be irreparably damaged if they have to do anything that the person will not like or if they have to tell the consumer something that she does not want to hear. Pure helping relationships are characterized by a sincere interest in the consumer and by honesty.

Feelings. The helping relationship involves feelings as well as knowledge. In addition to having the knowledge and skills required for helping, in a true helping relationship the worker is committed to working *with* the consumer. This means that the worker treats the consumer as someone who, in spite of having problems, has feelings and opinions. The worker recognizes these as important and empathizes with the consumer.

Immediacy. The helping relationship takes place in the here and now. Since the helping relationship is limited in time and scope, the worker must be concerned with what is happening in the present. The worker must be aware, not only of *what* is said, but also of *why, when,* and *how* it is said, both by himself and by the consumer.

Being nonjudgmental. The helping relationship must be nonjudgmental. The worker in a helping relationship is not there to judge, to approve or disapprove. In a true helping relationship, the worker demonstrates to the consumer that they are both human beings and capable of making mistakes. Thus, the worker is not superior to the consumer but is there to provide help.

---

[10]Albert Bandura, "Self-Efficacy: Toward a Unifying Theory of Behavior Change," *Psychological Review,* 84 (1977): 191.

FRAME

10

Sue has just received a memo from her supervisor informing her that Rose Martin, a consumer whom she has been helping, has failed to report her salary increase and that the agency is considering cutting off her assistance grant, since she has violated agency regulations.

Sue has made it a point to have a very pleasant and friendly relationship with Rose and has never had to deny her any assistance she needed. But she now decides that her relationship with Rose will be seriously damaged if she tells her this news in person, so she writes Rose a letter instead.

Do you think that Sue has built an effective helping relationship with Rose? Circle the correct response. (Yes/No)

Turn to Answer 112 on page 623

FRAME

11

APPLYING YOUR KNOWLEDGE OF RELATIONSHIP BUILDING

This final exercise frame is an opportunity to review some of the important knowledge included in this lesson and some major difficulties in building good helping relationships.[11] Before beginning the exercises, let's review some of the common mistakes workers make:

1. Premature advice, interpretation, confrontation, problem solving
2. Manipulative responses
3. Responses showing a lack of respect or absence of genuineness
4. Absence of empathy or use of inaccurate reflections of feelings
5. Minimizing consumer feelings or using placating statements such as "Everyone has that problem at some time" or "Everything will be all right"
6. Use of clichés
7. Use of language that is not familiar to the consumer
8. Inadequate responses, such as a minimal prompt (head nod or "uh-huh") when empathy is needed
9. Responses that change the topic focus or ignore the problem
10. Asking irrelevant questions
11. Judgmental remarks
12. Inappropriate self-disclosures
13. Asking a series of closed questions
14. Ignoring feelings

Several consumer statements are used in this exercise. Each statement is followed by four possible worker responses. Designate in the parentheses preceding each worker response whether it shows appropriate empathy. If the response is empathic,

---

[11]Adapted from Gerald Egan, *The Skilled Helper: A Workbook* (Monterey, Calif.: Brooks/Cole, 1982), p. 38.

place a plus sign (+) in the parentheses; if the response is inappropriate or poor, give it a minus (–). Then write the reason for your choice in the blank space as in the following example:

Example: High school student to school counselor:

Mr. Jones doesn't like me. I'm no different from the other guys, but whenever there's trouble I get blamed.

Counselor's response:

a. (–) You ought to settle down in class. Why get thrown out for something stupid?

Reason: premature advice

1. Hospital patient, 58, to a nurse's aide:

They've been taking tests for three days now. I don't know what's going on. They don't tell me what they're for or what they find. The doctor comes in for a moment every now and then, but she doesn't tell me anything either. And I still feel so weak and listless.

Aide's response:

a. (   ) Well, tests take time, you know. It's always a while before they tell you the results.

Reason:

b. (   ) Is this your first time in this hospital?

Reason:

c. (   ) Why don't you ask your nurse to call the doctor and ask her what's going on.

Reason:

d. (   ) Well, now, perhaps a little more patience would help everyone, including you.

Reason:

2. Girl, 22, to job counselor:

Every time people ask me about my education and I say "high school," I see their minds turn off. I feel that I'm as educated as any college grad. I read quite a bit, and I deal well with people. I think I've got whatever you're supposed to get from college—except the degree. College isn't the only way to learn!

Counselor's response:

a. (   ) Uh-huh.

Reason:

b. (   ) You feel good because you've directed your own education.

Reason:

c. (   ) You're not angry only at potential employers. You feel resentful of the whole system, and you'd like to show people they are wrong.

Reason:

d. (   ) You resent being categorized when you say "high school." You know you're an educated person.

Reason:

3. High school senior to peer counselor:

I graduate at the end of the first semester. I wonder what to do next. I could go right downstate to college so I could get away from home sooner. But that means leaving my friends here, and all the freshmen probably have their own friends in cliques by now. Maybe I should just do nothing for a semester.

Counselor's response:

a. (   ) It's a tough decision. It would be exciting to get away from home and start college, but you're worried you might not have any friends.
Reason:

b. (   ) It seems that you fear loneliness in your life.
Reason:

c. (   ) It's good for us to have to face these decisions. It builds maturity.
Reason:

d. (   ) I wish I had the luxury of having that kind of decision to make.
Reason:

4. 58-year-old resident of a halfway house to a caseworker:

You always hang around with the younger residents, playing pool and Ping-Pong and listening to that awful music. I have to sit in the dining room alone. When you do talk to me, I get the feeling you think you're wasting your time.

Caseworker's response:

a. (   ) You're jealous of the younger people living here.
Reason:

b. (   ) Come sit with me now, and we'll have a nice chat.
Reason:

c. (   ) I really don't like the young people at all. I have to force myself to be with them.
Reason:

d. (   ) Do the other caseworkers deal with you like I do?
Reason:

5. 24-year-old mental health center inpatient to aide:

Do you know what happened last night? I went to see that stupid psychiatrist. And all he did was spend ten minutes with me, and he didn't say anything.

Aide's response:

a. (   ) You have difficulty dealing with doctors.
Reason:

b. (   ) Talk to me about something new; you've complained about this before.
Reason:

c. (   ) I can see that you're scared by that kind of treatment.
Reason:

d. (   ) You feel irritated with him because he doesn't give you enough time.
Reason:

Turn to Answer 113 on page 623

FRAME

12

Helping others to become increasingly empowered and gain new confidence and skills is not easy, and it is never simple. It requires you to use yourself in ways that benefit others. How effective you will be in helping others will depend largely on how successful you yourself are in becoming realistic, self-confident, self-directing, self-actualizing, and rejoiceful of life. A positive, hope-inspiring model is a powerful tool.

If you feel that you have a good understanding of some of the principles used in building helping relationships, proceed to Lesson 3 to learn about assessment skills and ethnic competence. If you need a review, return to Frame 1 on page 298.

Mapping the System with Ethnic Competence

Working with persons whose cultures, lifestyles, and life experiences are different from our own is a privilege and a unique learning experience. Often, however, we minimize the differences, assuming that all of us are basically alike. When we make this assumption, we greatly limit the possibilities for forming helpful relationships with consumers and limit our opportunities for personal growth. Ignoring cultural differences can lead to failure of the helping process.

As described in the preceding lesson, the development of a good helping relationship depends on the worker's communication of interest, empathy, warmth, respect, and genuineness. These characteristics cannot be communicated to others, especially consumers who are culturally different from the worker, unless the worker acquires cross-cultural skills, knowledge, and understanding. Through the application of the suggestions in this lesson for developing ethnic competence, you can communicate the characteristics that are important for building effective relationships. For example, by expressing interest in the consumer's culture and placing yourself in a learner's role, you communicate interest and respect, and through the information shared by the consumer, you develop the basis for the expression of empathy. Of course, it is essential to be genuinely interested in the other person's culture and life experiences. You will see that some of the interviewing skills described in Lesson 1 and the relationship-building characteristics described in Lesson 2 will help you perform as an ethnically competent worker.

Assessing the consumer's situation is essential in order to develop an appropriate and effective helping plan. There are a number of ways to assess a situation. While some workers may have considerable time to assess a consumer's total situation (past and present, including many sources of information), most workers do not have the luxury of time and are required to assess situations quickly. This lesson presents a broad perspective on assessment designed to be relevant in different settings with different sizes of systems—individuals, small groups, and communities. Depending on the presenting situation and the consumers with whom you are working, it is important to assess individuals within their total environment, by considering their unique histories and surroundings.

Goal

Using a systems approach to assessment, to increase your sensitivity to differences among individuals in order to deliver services that meet the needs of consumers from diverse cultures.

Learning Activities

To accomplish this goal, we will:

1. Identify issues related to cross-cultural practice and cultural differences.
2. Demonstrate how knowledge of race or religion does not necessarily tell you how people are unique.
3. Describe ways of working effectively with persons of different cultures without having specialized knowledge about the consumer's cultural background.
4. Demonstrate how environmental factors may affect human behavior and the behavior of consumers in particular situations.
5. Identify ways of viewing consumers within a broad social context and within their family context.
6. Demonstrate the process of designing and using ecosystem maps to facilitate assessment.

FRAME

1

AN ECOLOGICAL SYSTEMS APPROACH TO ASSESSMENT

An ecological approach to assessment emphasizes not only the consumer and the consumer as part of a family but also the total context in which the family functions—the consumer's total environment.[1] Thus, an ecological systems approach extends the unit of attention beyond the consumer and her immediate family to all the elements of the family's environment. A systems perspective helps us look at the complexity of a consumer's situation through the analysis of interrelated systems.

An *ecosystem map* (ecomap) is a diagram of the important people, institutions, and resources in a person's or a family's environment. It is a pictorial description of the important factors in a given situation and the relationships among these factors. When an ecomap is filled out jointly with a family, it becomes a tool that stimulates discussions about the family's activities and interactions and their feelings about these activities and interactions. For example, to complete the employment circle of their ecomap, employed family members need to describe their jobs and what these jobs mean to them. The ecomap is shorthand for describing a large amount of complex information in a few words, on a single page.

Basically, the ecomap was designed to reflect two types of information: (1) *the systems and people that affect the consumer's life,* such as primary and extended family members, neighbors, and economic, social, and cultural institutions (e.g., a church, school, or social welfare organization); and (2) *the relationships* between the consumer and the systems or persons affecting the consumer's life. A circle is used to show each of the systems or organizations of people that are important in the consumer's life. Included as circles to be filled in are the following categories: extended family, church, recreation, social welfare, neighborhood, school, work, culture,

---

[1]Ann Hartman, *Finding Families: An Ecological Approach to Family Assessment in Adoption* (Beverly Hills, Calif.: Sage, 1979).

friends, and health care. Additional, unlabeled circles are included for designating other influences that a consumer may see as important.

Relationships between the systems or people and the consumer are communicated through two symbols. Lines are drawn to designate whether the relationship between the consumer and the system is strong, tenuous, or stressful. Arrows are used along these lines to designate the direction of the relationship. For example, a consumer may feel a strong relationship with a place of employment, so a straight line would be drawn with arrows pointing away from the consumer and toward the employer. Yet the employing agency may not value the consumer or may be planning to lay off workers; thus a dotted line may be drawn designating a tenuous relationship, with arrows pointing away from the employer and toward the consumer. As the consumer identifies important influences in his or her everyday life, and as you discuss relationships with these influences, important information is shared. You begin to gain an overall picture of the consumer's life situation.

Completed ecomaps can be useful in helping consumers see their situation and their relationships in new ways. You might review the ecomap with the consumer as a basis for discussing situations and persons that are important to the consumer and as a basis for beginning to identify areas for change.

Frames 2 and 3 demonstrate how to complete an ecomap by mapping a case for you. The case describes a family in a crisis situation.

FRAME

2

A CHILD WELFARE CASE RECORD

Presenting Problem: Placement of Maria Rael, a 2-week-old referred by St. Mary's Hospital, New York City. Child was born in July 1996.

Mother: Clara Rael, a 22-year-old Hispanic who became critically ill the evening before she and her infant daughter were to leave the hospital. Mrs. Rael was married in March 1996.

Father: Robert Rael, a 25-year-old Hispanic who is currently in New York City on emergency leave from the Navy; he is stationed in California.

Background Information from Hospital Social Worker's Chart: Mrs. R. had a normal delivery and was preparing to return to the home of the T.'s, friends who live in New York City and with whom she had been living since her husband's departure for California a month and a half ago. On the evening before she was to leave the hospital, Mrs. R. had a stroke and was in intensive care when her husband arrived.

Mr. R. is a trim man with much poise and dignity. He is soft-spoken and extremely polite and appears intelligent. It is evident that he is in love with Mrs. R.

Mr. R. was very upset the day he arrived but thought his wife looked better the next day. The doctor advised him that things were hopeful. Mr. R. assured the worker that he had faith in the doctors and thanked her and the hospital for the fine care his wife was receiving. When asked if he had seen his new daughter, he said he had been too worried about his wife to ask about Maria. The worker suggested they visit the nursery the next day.

Mr. R. planned to go to the Red Cross to request an extension of his leave. The worker was concerned that the father might blame the infant for his wife's illness and develop feelings of resentment toward his daughter. The history indicated that there were no relatives to care for the infant.

The next day, Mr. R. came in with his brother, who lives in New York City with his wife and four young children. Mr. R.'s parents still reside in a small town in northern New Mexico, as do Mrs. R.'s parents. Mr. R. said he had known Mrs. R. for three years prior to their marriage. They were married in March 1996 just before he was transferred to New York. They moved to New York; however, three months later, he was again transferred, this time to California. Mrs. R. remained in New York and moved in with friends.

The worker said that she recognized his concern for his wife but that they needed to discuss plans for Maria's care. The worker said she thought there were no relatives who could care for the child, and she would make a referral to a worker in the state child welfare agency, who would assume responsibility for seeing that the child was cared for.

Mr. R. confirmed the worker's impression that there were no relatives or friends who could help. Mr. R.'s brother said he and his wife would care for the child except his wife had so much to do caring for their own four children. Mr. R. looked directly at the worker and said that whatever plan could be made would meet his approval because he felt the worker liked his wife and baby.

The worker, Mr. R., and his brother went to the nursery to see Maria. The nurse described her as a good baby in excellent health.

More preparation is needed before Mr. R. will be able to face the responsibility of planning for his child's care. A foster home seems the only feasible plan, as there are no relatives who can assume responsibility. Mrs. R.'s doctor said the patient appears improved and is alert; however, paralysis is severe, and the prognosis is not known. The doctor agreed that foster care was a good plan, and he saw no reason why the worker could not discuss plans with Mrs. R.

The R.'s friend, with whom Mrs. R. lived prior to her hospitalization, called the hospital. The Red Cross worker also called.

The next day, Mr. R. said his wife is improving. The worker explained that sometimes people appear better when in fact their condition is worse. Mr. R. acknowledged the severity of his wife's condition, and with tears in his eyes he expressed how nice everyone at the hospital has been to them.

Now that he felt some relief about his wife, Mr. R. wanted to discuss his child's care and the lack of help from relatives to care for her. He said he had held the baby this morning and was struck by how much she looks like her mother. He quoted the nurses' praises of his baby and seemed pleased.

The worker explained the advantages of the baby's being cared for in a home rather than in the hospital and explained foster care. The worker said that even if Mrs. R. recovered, she would need special care for at least six months before she could care for the baby.

Mr. R. asked a number of questions about the homes and the care they give. He indicated an understanding of the program and gave the impression that such a plan would meet with his approval.

The worker told Mr. R. that he could meet with the state worker in order to apply for foster care services. Mr. R. noted how difficult the separation would be for his wife. He went to the ward to see his wife. She asked about the baby.

The worker talked with the doctor, who agreed that Mrs. R. could see her baby briefly. The worker contacted Children's Services the next day; they will send a worker to the hospital to talk with Mr. R.

FRAME

3

The ecomap in Figure 7.1. has been completed as the *hospital worker* might have filled it out. Remember that these are *her perceptions* as ascertained from the hospital record. Look at the ecomap as you read the explanations that follow it.

The ecomap reflects the hospital worker's case summary; it shows how this particular worker probably perceived relationships and resources. The worker may not have perceived relationships accurately or may not have found out the actual quality of certain relationships.

To complete the ecomap, we first filled in the large circle in the center. Usually this circle contains the names of the primary or nuclear family members, as they generally reside in the same house. In this case, however, Mr. R. was stationed across the country, and Mrs. R. was living with friends before her hospitalization. Since she is not at present living with anyone, and since the worker does not see the friends' home as a place where Mrs. R. can go after her release from the hospital or as a placement for Maria, we placed Mrs. R. in the center circle with Maria. Mr. R. was placed between the household center circle and the work circle in order to show that he has a separate residence.

After the names were put in the appropriate circles, lines were drawn to show the strength of the relationships between one person and another and between people and institutions. Since each family member may have a different quality of relationship with another person or institution, lines are drawn directly to each individual's name. If all household members have a similar relationship to a person or institution, lines can be drawn from the household circle to the person or institution. The solid line between Mrs. and Mr. R. symbolizes a strong and supportive relationship. A broken line was used between Mrs. R. and her parents and parents-in-law because the worker did not explore this relationship and did not seem to consider it a strong resource. A broken line stands for a tenuous or nonexistent relationship; however, it means there is the potential for a strong relationship. Though not shown in the figure, a crossed line (xxx) symbolizes a conflicted, stressful, or confused relationship.

Arrows are used to designate the direction of influence in a relationship. In this ecomap, the hospital is influencing the R. family, so arrows are pointed away from the hospital and toward the family. In some cases, influence flows in both directions, which would be shown by arrows pointing toward both circles.

The record did not include information about cultural or religious systems. Thus, a broken line is used; if the worker thought these systems were strong relationships, she probably would have explored them with Mr. and Mrs. R.

The completed ecomap presents information about the consumer's culture. Using a broad definition, culture is the total environment, all the things that have affected a person's life since birth. Culture, then, is our total experience, all that we have learned through interacting with people, ideas, values, institutions, and traditions outside ourselves. As human service workers, we may define culture more narrowly, using it to describe ethnicity or "cultural group." However, in order to understand the consumer's

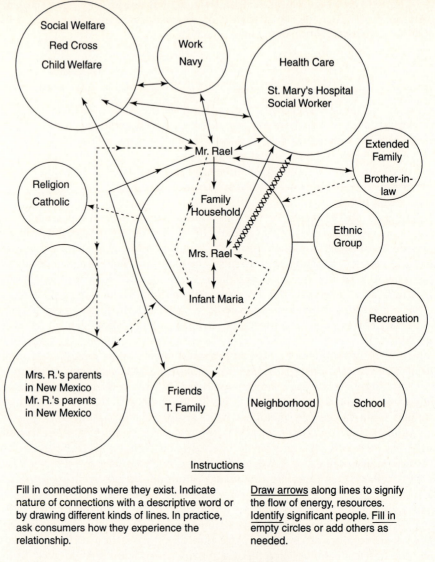

Instructions

Fill in connections where they exist. Indicate nature of connections with a descriptive word or by drawing different kinds of lines. In practice, ask consumers how they experience the relationship.

Draw arrows along lines to signify the flow of energy, resources. Identify significant people. Fill in empty circles or add others as needed.

——— Strong relationship
------- Tenuous relationship
XXXXX Stressful relationship
No line means that there is no relationship.

FIGURE 7.1. The Ecomap: An Ecological Framework for Assessment and Intervention [*Source:* Ann Hartman, D.S.W., University of Michigan School of Social Work.]

total culture we must understand the consumer, the consumer's experiences, and the consumer's resources.

Since the consumer's culture includes all the systems and people shown in an ecomap, and since understanding the consumer's ethnic-group identification as part of the consumer's culture is so important, we will discuss ethnic competence in conjunction with the ecomap. Consideration of the cultural issues and developing cross-cultural or ethnic competence in working with consumers are keys for developing effective helping relationships, for understanding the consumer, and for developing effective helping plans.

FRAME

4

ETHNIC COMPETENCE

Americans have begun to acknowledge that the United States cannot accurately be described as a "melting pot." Those who most successfully "melted," or were assimilated, into the U.S. culture in the past were European immigrants whose goal was integration and acculturation and whose skin color was similar to that of the majority group. Some Americans cannot "melt" into the dominant society or capture the trappings of the "good" life; others do not wish to do so because they feel that the "price" of joining is too great. We, as a society, can gain much from Americans' diverse lifestyles and differences in values, ideas, and approaches to problems. Yet, we tend to be more concerned with helping minorities adjust to dominant societal values and customs than with helping society at large gain from understanding diverse cultures. For example, we do not offer mainstream Americans opportunities to learn the rituals, traditions, and coping styles of Native Americans. At the same time that differences have not long been tolerated, keeping racial groups out of the mainstream serves the economic interests of the dominant society because it provides an inexpensive, seasonal labor force. We refer to this phenomenon as *institutional racism*.

An awareness of real differences across cultures is critical for effective helping. In interviewing someone who is culturally different from you, you want to maximize the consumer's input, minimize your input, and eliminate, to the extent possible, your preconceptions and assumptions. This is especially true when you are not well informed regarding the individual's culture. Case records may reflect the prejudices of others; therefore, it is wise to read them with caution and openness. Collect your own data and form your own impressions.

It is possible to productively interview persons who have life experiences, values, and ways of thinking that are different from your own. Since the goal of the human service worker is to understand the other person, you need to be open to new perspectives and different ways of thinking. One approach to maintaining openness is *ethnographic interviewing*.[2]

The use of ethnographic information in the planning, delivery, and evaluation of human services for minority- and ethnic-group consumers means much more than simply making contact with consumers who are culturally or racially different from you and your peers. "It means adequate preparation for an alertness to those cultural features of the client's background which influence the outcome of a social service encounter."[3]

Through ethnographic interviewing, you put yourself in the role of a *learner* and place the consumer in the role of the authority. In order to provide assistance you

---

[2]James W. Green, *Cultural Awareness in the Human Services* (Englewood Cliffs, N.J.: Prentice-Hall, 1982).
[3]Green, *Cultural Awareness*, p. 49.

need to *learn* about the community in which the consumer lives and you need to understand the consumer's ways of thinking. Ask your new authority (the consumer) to teach you about his or her ways, to lead you through his or her perspectives. As you learn about the experiences, hopes, and desires for a change of consumers who are different from you, you learn about a different way of life and a different way of perceiving. To do this, it is necessary to avoid assumptions, to seek out relevant data, and to ask questions before drawing conclusions.

The ethnographic approach usually begins with learning about experiences and issues that are not necessarily linked to the consumer's major problems or the agency's goals. Thus, you first present yourself as a learner rather than a human service worker with your own agenda. This approach will be new to consumers who are accustomed to being asked bureaucratic questions by human service workers. Since consumers are not accustomed to being in the teaching role in relation to human service workers, it is important to indicate that you have no special goal or underlying motive for talking with the consumer in this manner except to understand him better.

Techniques used by the ethnographic interviewer include noting the special words a consumer uses and asking what these terms mean. One way to encourage consumers to explain how they really experience different aspects of their lives is to ask if the explanation given to you is the same explanation they would give to a friend. If it is not, encourage them to use the same words in talking with you as they would use with friends. Using this approach tells consumers that you are different from past workers they have experienced and that you want to build a culturally sensitive relationship.

Addressing cross-cultural practice raises two questions: (1) What distinguishes cross-cultural interactions? and (2) What makes some people successful cross-cultural practitioners? A distinguishing characteristic of cross-cultural practice is that we cannot assume shared meanings, a shared language, shared jargon, or shared understandings. This is why we begin differently. We must first understand and then perhaps we can help. The qualities that distinguish a person who is successful in cross-cultural practice include the following:

1. The ability and desire to stand back and wait before finding ways to be helpful
2. The ability and desire to learn from others
3. The belief that others have ways that are different from yours
4. The belief that the ways of others may be preferable to your own ways
5. Respect for different ways of doing things, though they are not how you would handle similar situations
6. Respect for the choices of others
7. Respect for the values of others
8. An assumption that the ways or lifestyles that other people have developed for coping with life are of equal value to your own coping styles and tactics

Cross-cultural practice means questioning ourselves, our perceptions, and our values.

FRAME
5

List four qualities that distinguish people who are successful as cross-cultural practitioners.

1.

2.

3.

4.

Turn to Answer 114 on page 625

CROSS-CULTURAL ENCOUNTERS

How do "Anglo," or Caucasian, workers successfully handle cross-cultural situations? How do they relate to consumers whose culture is different from their own? Let's look at one Anglo worker's approach to a Navajo family living on the reservation in northern Arizona:

> When the worker arrives at the home (called a *hogan*) for a visit, she waits in her car or stands outside, close to the car, until her presence is acknowledged. When she proceeds to the door, she is prepared to wait patiently. She does not assume that she is welcome. Once her presence is acknowledged, she explains her reason for coming and waits to see if she is invited inside. The family may elect to come outside to talk with her. If invited inside, she waits until offered a seat and then takes the seat she is motioned to take. The family thus is in charge. Once the worker is seated, she briefly states her reason for being there and then once again waits. This time the wait may be longer, as a decision is being made whether or not to accept her presence in the home.

Many Navajos are accustomed to meeting non-Native Americans who believe and act as if Navajo ways are inferior to theirs. Therefore, Navajos appreciate acknowledgments of the beauty of their land and welcome an interest in their way of living. A worker might begin to develop a relationship by expressing interest in the Navajo way of living. She might also describe her way of living and what meaning that holds for her.

The worker presents options to the family and avoids proposing a final plan. She may include her opinions regarding each option, such as her personal advice and why she would recommend a particular option. But the family unit is left to make its own decision. Actually, the worker probably carries out the following actions: (1) She presents who she is and why she is there; (2) she listens; (3) she lists alternatives; (4) she leaves; (5) she returns at a later time for the decision or waits to hear from the family.

Lists of do's and don'ts are not critical. Making an error, such as entering a hogan and walking in the wrong direction, is not the critical issue. What is critical are attitudes of openness and respect. A major difference in cross-cultural work is the amount of time spent listening and watching and waiting. Waiting for directions is more important when you do not understand how things are handled in a given community. Place less emphasis on setting goals and more emphasis on the process of relationship building. Among Native Americans, advice is usually received openly. You may simply state what your agency can offer and advise the consumer as to how he or she can take advantage of your services. At this point the traditional helping system—the extended family—decides whether to accept or reject the offer. In any case, it is essential to listen and determine cultural relevance and variance.

An openness to learning, based on respect for other cultures and different ways of interacting with others and with the environment, is important for effective cross-cultural practice. As in all transactions, the interview and verbal exchanges are important. However, the pace of talking, the timing of questions, and the observation of nonverbal behavior take on special significance if the consumer's primary language is different from the worker's. Ethnic diversity is expressed and continued through language. Through "learning a new language one enters into a different world, wherein the thought and behavioral responses are significantly different from one's own culture."[4] Common concepts in your culture may not have words in another language. To fully understand the culture of others, you must understand the culture through the concepts used by its members. Observing and interpreting the behavior of others while using your concepts is a source of error. If you do not know the language and distinct concepts of others, you must depend on representatives of the other culture to interpret meanings and behaviors. Again, cross-cultural practice means becoming a learner and using experts as resources.

Most of the literature on cross-cultural helping appears to be focused on Caucasian helpers working with people of color. What is the experience for the worker when these roles are reversed, when the consumer is Caucasian and the worker is a person of color? It is not unusual for workers in this situation to be faced with prejudiced, racist attitudes.

In one case a female, African American student was assigned to a female, Caucasian consumer living in a residential center for mental health patients. This consumer grew up in an upper- or upper-middle-class family on the east coast. As she grew up she enjoyed many advantages and her self-image was supported by her feeling that this made her special. She married an uneducated man and was disinherited by her family. They moved to another part of the country and when she developed mental health problems her husband hospitalized her and kept all their economic resources. The consumer seemed to be developing a relationship with the worker and had agreed to work on specific goals, yet made racist comments during their sessions. How would you handle such a situation? Do you ignore the comments, confront the consumer, or refuse to work with the consumer?

This was a painful experience for the worker, yet she decided to focus her energies on building a relationship and on helping the consumer meet her goals and not to confront the consumer or immediately attempt to change the consumer's attitudes. As the relationship developed and the worker provided real help, she began to correct the consumer when she made racist comments. In addition, she pointed out how making such comments was affecting her relationships with others in the residential setting, resulting in painful conflicts. Slowly the consumer ceased making prejudiced comments. She was also able to express her appreciation to the worker. We often work with consumers whose values are different from ours. It took considerable patience and understanding on the worker's part to continue providing services to the consumer.

Value conflicts also occur when women who are attending college and are career-oriented work with women who assume traditional female roles. Should the worker help the consumer see that she has other options or work with the consumer without attempt-

---

[4]Green, *Cultural Awareness,* p. 69.

ing to modify her values? When a worker feels that the consumer's values are getting in her way, should she still respect her values in their work together? These are extremely challenging, difficult situations for which there are no easy answers. It is important to consider and discuss such practice situations with your classmates and colleagues.

The key components of cross-cultural practice are summarized in the following five characteristics of ethnic competence:[5]

1. Awareness of the limitations of your own culture. Our service approach—as manifest in our educational systems (e.g., the human service program in which you are currently enrolled), our agencies' culture, and the culture of our helping process (values, frame of reference, experiences, and goals)—*may* have limited relevance for persons involved in a daily struggle for basic survival or for persons who are members of a traditional community that emphasizes continuance of traditional values and lifestyles.

2. Openness to cultural differences. Our recognition of consumers' human needs must be balanced with a respect for and understanding of cultural differences. The opportunity to live in a society that supports cultural pluralism is the opportunity to be open to cultural differences.

3. Openness to learning from consumers. Our ability to approach those of other cultures as potential sources for new knowledge will create opportunities for new learning experiences.

4. Using existing cultural resources. Encourage consumers to draw on the natural strengths and resources in their societies, and thus to be less dependent on social services. (This is discussed further in the lesson on natural helping networks.)

5. Acknowledging cultural integrity. All cultures are affected in some way by societal change, but it is important to recognize that while cultures are constantly in flux and are affected by exposure to other cultures, they still maintain their differences and distinct characteristics. Differences may be present without being apparent; differences may be shared within cultural groups but not cross-culturally and thus may not often be observed by persons from other cultures. We need to identify and respect the unique differences and values among different cultural groups and thereby build respect for the cultural integrity of each group.

FRAME

7

Considering what you now know about cross-cultural practice and ethnic competence, complete the ecomap in Figure 7.2 for the Rael family, this time from the perspective of a culturally competent worker. As you fill in the ecomap, assume that, as a culturally competent practitioner, you asked the Raels and others relevant questions for understanding the roles and relationships of family members, friends, and professionals. For example, on this second map you will probably draw solid lines between Mr. and Mrs. Rael and their parents because you have explored this relationship among Hispanics in New Mexico. Of course it may be the case that relationships between Mr. and Mrs. Rael and their parents are strained or distant at this time; however, it is still likely that there are strong bonds between them. One of the sur-

[5]Green, *Cultural Awareness,* p. 69.

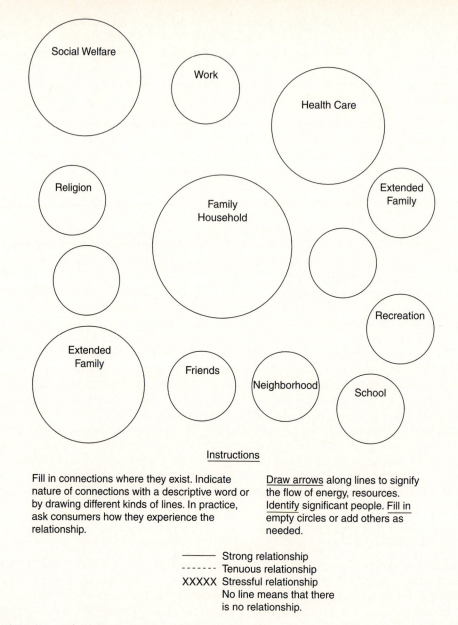

Instructions

Fill in connections where they exist. Indicate nature of connections with a descriptive word or by drawing different kinds of lines. In practice, ask consumers how they experience the relationship.

Draw arrows along lines to signify the flow of energy, resources. Identify significant people. Fill in empty circles or add others as needed.

——— Strong relationship
- - - - Tenuous relationship
XXXXX Stressful relationship
No line means that there is no relationship.

FIGURE 7.2.   Ethnically Competent Ecomap

prises in the Rael case record is that the relationships between extended and immediate family members were not explored adequately by the worker. The worker in the Rael case was not culturally competent. How would *you* answer the following questions?

1. What are the cultural variables to consider in assessing this case?

2. How might these variables affect the worker's service plan?

3. If this were your case, what would you do that the Raels' service worker did not do?

4. How might you get more information about the consumers' culture and related issues and resources?

5. What is most surprising about what the worker *did* and *did not* do?

The following points are intended to stimulate your thinking about the preceding questions. First, a surprising aspect of this case is that the family did not insist on caring for the infant, Maria. Second, the worker did not explore family resources for caring for the child. She seemed to simply ignore the close family relationships and strong natural helping network in Hispanic communities. She accepted Mr. Rael's statement that there were no family resources. For example, she did not raise the question of approaching grandparents to care for the child, nor did she explore the situation with Mr. Rael and his brother when they visited the hospital together. The worker also did not discuss options or plans with the mother. Third, the worker did not explore religious ties or the church as a resource. Additional cultural variables she might have explored include the roles of mother and father and the father's perceptions about the child (rather than assume that the father felt distant from the child or that the father's initial reaction to the infant suggested there might be a problem).

Compare your completed ecomap with the one in **Answer 115 on page 625.**

Chapter Summary

This chapter covered three basic skills that are essential to service delivery: (1) interpersonal skills needed for effective interviewing; (2) relationship building; and (3) assessment skills with cross-cultural sensitivity, or ethnic competence. Interpersonal skills and characteristics such as warmth and empathy may be a part of a person's natural communication repertoire, but we also know that people can develop these skills. Being ethnically competent comes from knowledge and from a new way of seeing the world, as well as from skill in communicating respect and understanding. Demonstrating the ability to assess a consumer's total situation using an ecomap that reflects awareness of possible cultural differences is a skill critical to delivering help that is relevant and understandable within the consumer's framework.

These three skill areas are essential for people working with individuals, families, or communities. When you are in a counseling role, you will spend more time listening and learning from the consumer. If you are in an advocate role or working with a community group, you may be as verbally active as others around you; nevertheless, you will still be relating to consumers through your interpersonal and cross-cultural skills.

The development of interviewing and relationship-building skills is a continuing process throughout your career. You can always become more skilled in these areas. To continue to grow in these areas, remember to use the resources around you and within you, such as the use of taping and feedback from yourself, your peers, your supervisor, and the consumers with whom you work.

Suggestions for Further Study

Relationship building and interviewing are fascinating skills to develop. You may be interested in looking at issues of the *Journal of Counseling Psychology,* which publishes current research on the effects of specified interviewing skills, how best to teach and learn these skills, and research on other variables that are important in effective counseling. There are a number of other journals in social work, education, and psychology that publish articles on relationship building and interviewing. Moreover, new books are constantly being written and new training formats are being developed that are applicable for human service workers and for teaching new skills to consumers. Many of the consumers that you will work with lack good interpersonal and communication skills. The development of such skills may increase their chances for securing employment, maintaining a marriage, building positive relationships with their children, meeting others, and forming friendships. Consumers also need new skills to survive in institutional settings and make the changes that are necessary for them to develop new ways of coping.

We have learned the importance of a systems perspective in developing human service workers who can work effectively in diverse settings with diverse groups. You may want to read *The Skilled Helper,* by Gerald Egan, *Intentional Interviewing and Counseling,* by Allen Ivey, and *Cultural Awareness in the Human Services,* by James Green. All three books include excellent bibliographies that will direct you to stimulating readings in these areas. Also, see the readings below:

Acuna, R. *Occupied America: The Chicano Struggle toward Liberation.* San Francisco: Canfield Press, 1972.

Atkinson, D. "Ethnic Similarity in Counseling Psychology: A Review of Research." *The Counseling Psychologist* 11 (1983): 79–92.

Bestman, E. W., "Cross-Cultural Approaches to Service Delivery for Ethnic Minorities: The Miami Model." In Miranda and Kitano, eds. *Mental Health Research and Practice in Minority Communities: Development of Culturally Sensitive Training Programs.* Washington, DC: Department of Health and Human Services, 1986.

Blanchard, E., and S. Unger. "Destruction of American Indian Families." *Social Casework* 58 (1977): 312–314.

Bricker-Jenkins, M., N. Hooyman, and N. Gottlieb, eds. *Feminist Social Work Practice in Clinical Settings.* New York: Sage, 1991.

Carkhuff, R. *Helping and Human Relations,* vol. 1, *Selection and Training.* New York: Holt, Rinehart & Winston, 1969.

Carkhuff, R. *The Art of Helping: A Guide for Developing Helping Skills for Parents, Teachers, and Counselors.* Amherst, Mass.: Human Resources Press, 1972.

Cormier, W., and S. Cormier. *Interviewing Strategies for Helpers,* 3d ed. Pacific Grove, Calif.: Brooks/Cole, 1991.

Cournoyer, B. *The Social Work Skills Workbook,* 2d ed., Pacific Grove, Calif.: Brooks/Cole, 1996.

Davis, Larry E., and Enola K. Proctor. *Race, Gender, and Class: Guidelines for Practice with Individuals, Families, and Groups.* Englewood Cliffs, N.J.: Prentice-Hall, 1989.

Egan, G. *Exercises in Helping Skills: A Manual to Accompany the Skilled Helper.* Monterey, Calif.: Brooks/Cole, 1994.

Egan, G. *Interpersonal Living: A Skills-Contract Approach to Human Relations Training in Groups.* Monterey, Calif.: Brooks/Cole, 1976.

Egan, G. *The Skilled Helper: A Problem-Management Approach to Helping,* 5th ed. Pacific Grove, Calif.: Brooks/Cole, 1994.

Evans, D. R., M. T. Hearn, M. R. Uhlemann, and A. E. Ivey. *Essential Interviewing: A Programmed Approach to Effective Communication,* 3d ed. Pacific Grove, Calif.: Brooks/Cole, 1989.

Goldfried, M. R., and A. P. Goldfried. "Cognitive Change Methods." *In Helping People Change: A Textbook of Methods,* edited by F. H. Kanfer and A. P. Goldfried. 2d ed. Elmsford, N.Y.: Pergamon, 1980.

Hartman, A., and J. Laird. *Family-Centered Social Work Practice.* New York: Free Press, 1983.

Hinde, R. A. *Nonverbal Communication.* London: Cambridge University Press, 1972.

Iglehart, A. P., and R. M. Becerra. *Social Services and the Ethnic Community.* Boston, Mass.: Allyn & Bacon, 1995.

Ivey, A. E. *Intentional Interviewing and Counseling: Facilitating Client Development in a Multicultural Society,* 3d ed. Pacific Grove, Calif.: Brooks/Cole, 1994.

Ivey, A. E., and J. Authier. *Microcounseling,* 2d ed. Springfield, Ill.: Charles C. Thomas, 1978.

Logan, Sadye, Edith Freeman, and Ruth McRoy, eds. *Social Work Practice with Black Families: A Culturally Specific Perspective.* New York: Longman, 1990.

Lum, D. *Social Work Practice and People of Color: A Process-Stage Approach,* 3rd ed. Pacific Grove, Calif.: Brooks/Cole, 1996.

McAdoo, H. "Black Kinship." *Psychology Today* 12 (May 1979): 64ff.

Maluccio, A. N. *Learning from Clients.* New York: Free Press, 1979.

Meier, M. S., and R. Rivera. *The Chicanos: A History of Mexican Americans.* New York: Hill & Wang, 1972.

Miller, N. "Cultural Beliefs and Institutional Barriers: Issues in Service Utilization among Urban Indians." In *Proceedings, Health and Education Systems: Coordinating Social Work Services for Handicapped Children,* edited by J. Karkalits. Washington, D.C.: MCH Training Project No. 2031, PHS/HSA, Department of Health and Human Services, 1980.

Padilla, A. M., R. A. Ruiz, and A. Alvarez. "Community Mental Health Services for the Spanish Speaking/Surnamed Population." *American Psychologist* 30 (1975): 892–905.

Pedersen, Paul B., and Allen Ivey. *Culture-Centered Counseling and Interviewing Skills: A Practical Guide.* Westport, Colo.: Praeger, 1993.

Perlman, H. H. *Relationship: The Heart of Helping.* Chicago: University of Chicago Press, 1979.

Pinderhughes, E. *Understanding Race, Ethnicity and Power.* New York: Free Press, 1989.

Red House, J., et al. "Family Behavior of Urban American Indians." *Social Casework* 59 (1978): 67–72.

Robinson, J. "Clinical Treatment of Black Families: Issues and Strategies." *Social Work* 34 (1989): 323–329.

Rogers, C. *Client-Centered Therapy.* Boston: Houghton Mifflin, 1951.

Rogers, C. R. "The Necessary and Sufficient Conditions of Therapeutic Personality Change." *Journal of Consulting Psychology* 21 (1957): 95–103.

Shulman, L. *The Skills of Helping: Individuals, Families and Groups,* 3rd ed., Itasca, Ill.: Peacock, 1992.

Spicer, E. H., ed. *Ethnic Medicine in the Southwest,* 241–270. Tucson: University of Arizona Press, 1977.

Solomon, B. B. *Black Empowerment: Social Work in Oppressed Communities.* New York: Columbia University Press, 1976.

Stack, C. B. "The Kindred of Viola Jackson: Residence and Family Organization of an Urban Black Family." In *Afro-American Anthropology: Contemporary Perspectives,* edited by N. E. Whitten and John F. Szwed, 303–312. New York: Free Press, 1970.

Sue, D. W. *Counseling the Culturally Different: Theory and Practice.* New York: Wiley, 1981.

Taft, R. "Coping with Unfamiliar Cultures." In *Studies in Cross-Cultural Psychology,* edited by N. Warren, 121–153. New York: Academic Press, 1977.

Valle, R., and W. Vega, eds. *Hispanic Natural Support Systems: Mental Health Promotion Perspectives.* Sacramento: State of California Department of Mental Health, 1980.

Chapter 8

Collaborating with Consumers: Stages and Approaches of the Helping Process

All human service workers share at least one main goal in their work with consumers: They want to understand consumers' problems and how they can be most helpful to consumers. Workers engage in a systematic process in their efforts to reach this goal. This process is known generally as the *helping process,* or the *problem-solving process,* and it is the subject of this chapter. The core helping skills developed in Chapter 7— interviewing, relationship building, and mapping the system—are a foundation for competent performance as a helper. Thus, these skills must be integrated throughout the helping process. In addition to using these core skills in all of your interactions with consumers, you will discover that the helping process underlies your performance of all the direct service delivery roles we develop in this text: brokering, advocating, mobilizing, relating, collaborating, and intervening. But before you try to make all of these connections, it is important to study the helping process by itself and in some depth.

The helping process is systematic. It follows a certain *sequence, or set, of stages.* These stages of helping correspond to how events typically unfold in your interactions with consumers: starting from initial meetings and then moving through assessment, goal setting, service planning, contracting, service delivery or implementation, and evaluating your change efforts. The reason that you can discern such a sequence is because you are the one who is seeking to make it happen.

The helping process is also systematic because certain *models, or approaches, for effective helping* have been developed in human service professions. These approaches include case management, using natural helping networks, educating and working with consumer groups. They are typically considered to be part of service delivery. Other helping approaches and models of intervention are introduced in Chapter 9. The helping approaches are applied, in depth, during the intervention stage of the helping process that follows the assessment, goal setting, and contracting stages. Case management is a model for practice that emphasizes the worker's role as the coordinator of services. Using case management skills, the worker executes all the helping phases described in this chapter, including the possibility of referring the consumer to other workers for more in-depth counseling or other services. The involvement of natural helping networks is suggested as an effective approach to drawing on resources already existing within the consumer's environment and to maintaining changes without formal help. Educating is used frequently, as many consumers wish to improve their skills in communication, job seeking, assertive behavior, and other areas. Group work is expanding across the country and is a good way for consumers to help one another as they help themselves.

You can see there is a great deal to cover in explaining the helping process. While we cannot hope to achieve full understanding of all the models and approaches in the scope of this book, we will aim for a comprehensive introduction. The table below shows how we organized the lessons in this chapter using the distinctions of *stages* of helping and *approaches* of delivering helping or human services. It may be useful to keep this "big picture" in mind as you work through the individual lessons.

Organization of Chapter 8 Lessons

Stages of the Helping Process		*Corresponding Lessons*	
Stage One	From initial meetings to assessment	Lesson 1:	Assessment
Stage Two	Goal setting, service planning, and contracting	Lesson 2:	Goal Setting, Contracting, and Service Planning
Stage Three	Service delivery approaches/interventions (or implementation of the service plan)	Lesson 4: Lesson 5: Lesson 6: Lesson 7: (Chapter IX:	Case Management Using Natural Helping Networks Educating Working with Consumer Groups Advanced Intervention Models)
Stage Four	Evaluation	Lesson 3:	Evaluating the Helping Process

The overall objectives of this chapter are to provide you with a framework for understanding the stages of the helping process and to introduce the knowledge and skills required to perform in each stage throughout the entire process. In this chapter you are plunging into the center of your work with consumers. We hope you will be especially attuned to applying the learning, language, and systems thinking themes we developed in Chapter 1 as you explore the content, raise questions, and practice the critical skills of helping.

Examples of the helping process that might appear in a human service job description fall into at least three areas: consumer status assessment, service planning, and implementation and evaluation. These are highlighted below as concrete examples of what workers might be accountable for in carrying out the helping process. Case management, collaborating, with natural networks, and educating aid in intervention or augment the core elements of the helping process.

Consumer status assessment. Assess the nature and severity of consumer needs and problems.

1. Observe consumers and gather information from appropriate sources, looking for signs (bruises, burns, cuts, unusual thinness, and excessive dirt) in order to assess the possibility of physical abuse or neglect in children or adults.
2. Observe consumers and gather information from appropriate sources, looking for signs (withdrawal, flat affect, and depression) in order to assess the possibility of neglect or sexual or psychological abuse in children or adults.
3. Observe consumers and gather information from appropriate sources in order to make preliminary judgment about the need for special counseling or mental health treatment.
4. Observe consumers and gather information from appropriate sources in order to determine whether an emergency situation exists (potential suicide or overdose) and immediate intervention is required.
5. Observe consumers and gather information from appropriate sources in order to establish existence of substance (e.g., alcohol or drugs) abuse problem(s).
6. Determine urgency of consumers' situation and emotional state in order to decide whether consumers need emergency services or routine handling and referral.
7. Interview consumers or review applications and complete paperwork, as required, in order to determine initial or continued eligibility.

Service planning (specific). Develop, implement, and modify a service plan for a consumer.

1. Analyze case history and consult with consumers and with the other workers involved to arrive at a mutual decision and a plan for termination of services and/or assistance.
2. Work with reluctant or involuntary consumers in order to gain their cooperation in achieving service goals.
3. Discuss the overall situation with consumers, including limitations and advantages of possible approaches in order to arrive at a plan for service.
4. Review and analyze case records and other information sources and consult with consumers and with the other workers involved to evaluate consumers' progress and to alter service plans if needed.
5. Coordinate the service plans with others (co-workers, other providers, and family) in order to facilitate delivery of effective services.

Evaluation. Collect baseline information and information on consumer progress.

1. Observe consumers (if possible) in their natural settings and record their behavior and/or ask consumers to monitor themselves to determine the extent of an issue.
2. Develop with consumers ways (such as charts and calendars) to monitor consumer progress daily.
3. Discuss past results with consumers as a basis for modifying the intervention plan.

Assessment

This lesson begins with a five-step process for meeting consumers and introducing them to relevant services. The major thrust of the lesson is the process of assessment. Some workers believe that assessment is the most difficult and yet the most important step in the helping process. Clearly, the worker who does not identify the right problem, situation, or issue for change may find it impossible to help the consumer. In this lesson we identify how important information is gained through the assessment process.

Goals

To introduce the assessment process as the basis for goal setting and developing helping plans; to develop skills in collecting important assessment information from consumers.

Learning Activities

To accomplish these goals, we will:

1. Identify the five steps related to the attitudes, environmental arrangements, information, and emotional climate needed to begin an assessment process.
2. Differentiate between information based on inference and information drawn from behavioral observation.
3. Identify and define the component parts of an assessment.
4. Identify appropriate assessment resources.
5. Identify assessment information in written records.

FRAME
1

VIEWING CONSUMERS' SITUATIONS: WHERE AND HOW TO BEGIN

The goals of a first encounter with consumers are to begin to form a helping relationship, to understand the consumers' issues and situation, and to begin the assessment process. Assessment starts with the first contact. Every interaction with consumers provides information that is helpful in getting to know them and assessing their needs and options. This lesson describes five steps that are useful in the initial contact with consumers, and these steps provide a beginning for viewing consumers' situations through their own perspectives.

Before Your First Encounter

A consumer's first contact with an agency is usually with a receptionist or secretary, either by phone or in person. These contacts are critical; they can shape the consumer's perceptions, attitudes, and expectations of the organization. It is important to learn through direct observation and by asking consumers what they experienced when they entered the agency. In some settings receptionists need special training in order to be open and supportive. Some consumers are angry when they get to the agency and may express this anger in the way they treat the first person they encounter. Some agencies subject consumers to long waits. Some receptionists act as if they do not care about consumers, as if consumers are unimportant annoyances rather than the reason the agency exists. In these situations it is especially important to try to create a welcoming environment for the consumer. Agencies need to consider ways that consumers can be treated with respect. It is important to train and monitor receptionists. When long waits cannot be avoided, receptionists can express concern over a long wait and can let consumers know approximately when they will see a worker. Consider what the consumers you work with experience even before they meet you.

Step 1: Anticipatory Empathy

Before your first meeting with a consumer, if you have some information about his or her situation, it is helpful to begin thinking about the situation and how the consumer may be feeling. This is called *anticipatory empathy*.[1] It is especially helpful to use anticipatory empathy before meeting a consumer whose behavior you do not condone and who is being required by law to meet with you. For example, you may have a great deal of difficulty working with consumers who have abused others. By considering the situation in which the behavior may have occurred and the consumer's feelings, you can prepare yourself for more open communication.

Several techniques can help you to use anticipatory empathy. One technique is to read descriptions written by consumers in similar situations. For example, child welfare workers were given a statement written by a natural mother describing her feelings about her child's placement in a foster home. The statement gave the workers an opportunity to think about how someone in this situation might feel. If a worker assumes that a child was placed in a foster home because the parent did not meet the child's needs, the worker may simply blame the parent. Without looking at the parent's perspective, it may be difficult to develop a good working relationship with the parent, to make the necessary changes that would make it possible for the child to return home.

If material is not readily available that describes the perspective of a consumer group, such as alcoholics, child abusers, parents who lack parenting skills, prisoners,

---

[1]Adapted from Eileen Gambrill, *Casework: A Competency-Based Approach* (Englewood Cliffs, N.Y.: Prentice-Hall, 1983).

or mental health patients, you can develop empathy by asking yourself the following questions:[2]

1. What might it be like to be in this person's situation?
2. How would I feel if I had committed an illegal or a harmful act and was required to discuss what I had done with a human service worker?
3. Do I have any stereotypes about this person?
4. What coping mechanisms might this person use, such as placing blame elsewhere for the situation or acting indifferent and apathetic to a difficult home environment?
5. What concerns might the consumer have about me and about the agency?
6. What cultural, ethnic, sex, age, and economic differences should I be sensitive to?
7. What might this consumer expect me to do or think about him or her?

These questions help workers separate the consumer from the consumer's negative or destructive behaviors and provide an important basis for the belief that change is possible.

Step 2: Creating a Comfortable Environment

Just before meeting with the consumer, it is important to create a comfortable environment in which to talk and help the person to be physically at ease. You might want to arrange the chairs in your work area in such a way that you can look directly at the consumer, 3 to 4 feet apart, which is usually a good distance for maximum comfort and informality. Eliminating a desk or other furniture between you and the consumer also communicates that your full attention is focused on the consumer and is less formal. If you do not have a private office in which to talk and must see the consumer in a large room, try to arrange two chairs in a part of the room that seems separate and semiprivate. Planning for a quiet place to talk will eliminate searching for a place during the initial few minutes of your meeting. A corner in a park or a bench in the front yard of an institution may also offer privacy and quiet.

Step 3: Initial Greeting

The first few minutes are important. The initial contact with the receptionist is also important in welcoming the consumer into the agency. What is conveyed in these first few minutes may affect the consumer's comfort and therefore his or her willingness and ability to talk with you during the rest of your meeting.

When the consumer enters the agency or the room where you are going to meet, get up and greet the visitor by name, ask to take his coat or offer a place to put it, and suggest a place to sit down. The gesture of going toward the consumer increases the consumer's comfort and promotes a feeling of being accepted. It also conveys that your attention is focused 100 percent on the consumer. The degree of friendliness and informality you communicate should be geared to your perceptions of what will be most comfortable for the consumer.

---

[2]Gambrill, *Casework*.

Step 4: Orienting the Consumer

Once you are each reasonably comfortable and the initial introductions are complete, it is important to describe for the consumer what services you can offer. This orientation process includes such critical information as describing fees, defining confidentiality and its limits, and defining agency services and their limits. Sharing information provides the groundwork for working together and gives the consumer an opportunity to begin to know you. It is like a preliminary contract; it offers a beginning base for determining whether you can work well together. This orientation process is especially important for persons who have not had earlier experiences as consumers. Anticipate how it must feel to ask for help. Consumers may be unclear about what will happen; some consumers may be ashamed or embarrassed that they need help; others may be frightened; and still others may expect poor treatment. Building positive expectations will increase consumers' willingness to work with you.

It is also important to be careful about what you say during this phase. If you promise things that cannot be delivered, you reduce trust. Do not say things that you do not mean. For example, you may not be able to promise total confidentiality to an adolescent, and yet you know that adolescents may want what they say to be secret from their parents. Be clear about the limits of confidentiality. If an adolescent tells you that he or she is about to run away from home, or to injure him- or herself or others, you need to make it known that you will share this information with parents or with the authorities.

Through the orientation process, consumers who are not requesting service voluntarily may become actual consumers. A person is not a consumer until she or he accepts working with you toward announced, shared goals. Once goals are agreed to, a contract can be developed and your work together can begin. There is considerable evidence that consumers who are not willing partners, and who do not have expectations that your work together will be helpful, are less likely to experience success. They are also less likely to carry out the service plan and continue coming to meet with you (unless appointments with you are required). Many consumers begin as nonvoluntary and then agree to work with you. For example, a parent who is abusing a child may see you because the courts have required that the parent contact you. You clarify that in order to have the child home again or in order for the child to remain at home, the parent must agree to work with you to change the home situation. If this is a shared goal, the consumer will usually agree to work with you.

Step 5: Opening Statements

You may wonder what to say after the hellos, name exchanges, and handshakes. It is helpful to begin your contact with a consumer by offering him an opportunity to talk. Several common openers are:

1. "What can I do for you today?"
2. "How can I help today?"
3. "What's on your mind?"
4. "What brings you here today?"

These open-ended questions are designed to help consumers describe in their own words their reasons for seeking assistance. We suggest that you practice and develop "openers" that you feel comfortable saying, using language that is familiar to the consumers. It is important to avoid jargon and clichés. The first statement above is used so frequently that it sounds like a professional cliché. Which words might you choose? Practice some "openers" using your own words.

FRAME

2

APPLYING THE FIVE-STEP PROCESS

The following interaction describes a worker who is meeting a consumer for the first time. The setting is a state child welfare office.

The receptionist calls to tell the worker, Ms. Aquilar, that the consumer, Mr. Berg, is waiting to see her. (1) Ms. A. walks to the waiting area. (2) The receptionist unobtrusively directs Ms. Aquilar to Mr. Berg. (Note that Mr. Berg's name was not announced from the front desk.) (3) The worker walks over to Mr. Berg, introduces herself by name, expresses her appreciation that he came in, and extends her hand. (4) Mr. B. stands when the worker addresses him and nods acknowledgment but does not offer his hand. (5) Ms. A. invites Mr. B. to go with her to her office. (6) Mr. B. follows Ms. A. to her office, where Ms. A., opening the door to the office, invites him to enter in front of her. (7) Ms. A. offers Mr. B. a chair and stands in front of another chair about 4 feet from his, placed so they can easily look at each other. Mr. B. and Ms. A. sit down.

MS. A: (8) Mr. Berg, I appreciate your coming here today. May I take your coat?

MR. B: (9) No, I'll just wear it.

MS. A: (10) Okay. Well, feel free to put your coat on another chair if it gets too warm in here.

MR. B: (11) (*Nods and looks around the office.*)

MS. A: (12) I want to say again that I appreciate your coming in today. I know it isn't convenient for you to get to the office. I also know this is not a trip you wanted to make. You are probably feeling that we are all against you. I understand how you might see me as an enemy. I want to say that I asked you to come in today to find out how you see the situation and to find out what you think actually happened to Kim. I am also hoping to learn more about you and your family situation in general. As you know, I have talked with Kim and with your wife in your home. I have looked forward to this opportunity to learn how you see things at home and what you might want to do about the situation.

MR. B: (*Looks up and then gazes past Ms. A.*)

MS. A: (13) It is important to say that the agency is concerned about the situation and that I want to learn all I can. Our interest is in helping improve the situation and keeping your family together. I am hopeful you will work with us toward that goal. It is true, however, that if Kim is actually in danger and if your family is not willing to work with us, we will do whatever is necessary to protect Kim and your other children, including placing them in another home. Do you have any questions at this point about the agency or why I asked you to come in today?

MR. B: (14) Yes, I'd like to know why you are interfering and why you came to our home and talked with my wife.

MS. A: (15) As I told Mrs. B., a call was made to our 24-hour emergency hotline from an unidentified person who said there were screams in your home and that they thought someone was beating your daughter. According to law, we must follow up immediately on all hotline calls. When Kim was seen in your home, she had a number of bruises on her arms and legs. My goal is to determine the source of those bruises, the extent of the problem, and to begin to look at what can be done to make things better for you and the other members of your family.

Using the numerals in the dialogue, indicate which sentences demonstrate each step in the five-step process in the space provided below.

Step 1: *Anticipation empathy.* Found in sentences _____
Step 2: *Creating comfortable environment.* Found in sentences _____
Step 3: *Initial greeting.* Found in sentences _____
Step 4: *Orientation.* Found in sentences _____
Step 5: *Opening statements.* Found in sentences _____

Turn to Answer 116 on page 627

FRAME
3

THE DIFFICULTY IN GETTING STARTED

What if consumers are still having trouble describing their situation and do not seem to be responding to your efforts to make them feel at ease? This happens in any human service setting, and overcoming this difficulty means an extra effort on your part. For example, if you work in an institution such as a prison or mental hospital, inmates or residents may show some resistance to being interviewed. If the interview makes them late for a meal, they may approach the interview in an irritated frame of mind. Or they may be unwilling to talk because they are afraid of what other residents or inmates will think of them. In these situations you need to help the consumers identify whatever is bothering them about talking to you. Address this issue directly. If the consumer will not disclose reservations, anticipate and state the possibilities, such as "You may feel talking with me will not help or being honest with me will get you into trouble." Also, beginning with neutral questions may help the consumer begin talking. Show your interest in the consumer.

FRAME
4

COMPONENTS OF AN ASSESSMENT

Now that you have some ideas about what to do when you meet a consumer for the first time and are aware of the importance of listening, you are ready to learn assessment skills. Assessment is a complex process. The assessment components outlined here represent a comprehensive approach, and it is important to remember that all the components may not be covered when assessing a situation. Part of the skill in doing an assessment is determining which components to discuss thoroughly, which to cover briefly, and which to ignore. Time limitations may demand taking immediate action before the assessment is completed. When this occurs, it is critical to evaluate the thoroughness of your data collection and observations in order to be clear about what you do not yet know about the consumer's situation and the bases for your initial judgments. To what extent is your assessment based on actual observations and factual information, and to what extent did you make inferences from whatever the consumer said?

A behavioral description is a precise description of actions you observed or a description of what someone else observed in their words. Behavioral descriptions involve presenting information as objectively as possible without adding your impressions or interpretations. When you make an assumption about what you think may have happened, you are making an inference. Inferring means adding your impressions; an inference is a guess about what exists. Based on an inference, you may make a statement about a situation. Inferences may be drawn from what you see or hear by using your own experience to interpret your behavioral observations.

Distinguishing inferences from behavioral descriptions is important if you are to objectively assess another person's situation. Being aware of what an inference is and your basis for it means being aware of conclusions or assumptions that come from yourself and that ultimately may or may not be correct. It is important to make inferences from what you observe and experience, and although all your observations are influenced by your own ways of seeing and thinking, inferences, more than behavioral descriptions, reflect your own frame of reference. Moreover, a record with behavioral descriptions as well as inferences provides information that can be used by other workers. If you take over a case and the existing record contains all inferences, you almost need to begin anew collecting information, for you cannot be certain whether the worker's inferences reflect the consumer's situation or whether they are a reflection of the worker's inaccurate perceptions. On the other hand, when the record includes behavioral descriptions, you have the material to begin to formulate your own inferences and assessment.

FRAME
5

See if you can distinguish behavioral descriptions from inferences. In the case summary below, underline the words that are inferences and circle the words that are behavioral descriptions. For example, the word *disoriented* would be underlined. The worker concluded that the consumer was "disoriented." A behavioral description would describe exactly what the worker observed that led to the conclusion that the consumer was "disoriented."

Case summary. Robert was disoriented, wandering aimlessly through the downtown area. He was seen stopping individuals, asking them for money to buy food. He was abusive and angry. The police brought him into the mental health center. Robert was messy and poorly dressed and had not bathed for days. He was wearing a jacket that was two sizes too big for him; it had tears in the sleeves and was covered with dirt and spots.

Robert did not know the day of the week or the year. He looked away from the worker when he talked and did not answer questions; rather, he described situations that did not relate to the worker's questions. He was disturbed and disconnected, and he rambled.

Turn to Answer 117 on page 627

F R A M E
6

BUILDING ON THE CONSUMER'S STRENGTHS

Given the emphasis on, and commitment to, the empowerment of consumers, and given what we know about how to achieve successful outcomes in human service work, workers continuously focus on consumer strengths, resources, and skills. We want to increase individual power and build on strengths. If you do not know the extent of a consumer's strengths and skills, you may find yourself doing things for consumers that they can do for themselves. This results in undermining the consumer's strengths instead of building on them. The goal is to expand what consumers can handle, not take over tasks that the consumer can already do. An exception to this rule is when consumers are experiencing an unusual crisis, such as a death in the family or a sudden illness. There are times when consumers cannot handle everyday tasks, and at these times it is important to offer special help and support by taking care of things for them.

Emphasizing strengths and giving positive feedback and praise help to build self-esteem and confidence. As consumers feel better about themselves, they are better able to take on the job of changing or improving their situation. One way to promote this goal is to give honest praise.

It is important to identify strengths in each individual and in his or her situation. Sometimes it is difficult to find even one strength. However, it *is* possible to find positives in every individual, and to find some strengths even in a very problematic situation. One strength you can point out to consumers is the fact that they are talking with you. Praise consumers for this act. Let consumers know that you understand that their role is a difficult one. Other sources of strength may be found in such resources as a school counselor, family members, friends, neighbors, and other human service providers. In looking for strengths, consider all the systems included in the ecomap in Chapter 7.

In addition to strengths, it is important to distinguish between the consumer's thoughts, feelings, and behaviors. At times, all three need your attention; at other times, only one of these areas is problematic. Workers sometimes assume that change in one area will result in change in the other two. You *cannot assume* that changing a thought will change behavior or that changing a behavior will necessarily change feelings. For example, a consumer might decide to stop seeing an abusive boyfriend, yet continue to think about him. In this case, the behavior changed (seeing the boyfriend), but old thoughts (and probably feelings) persisted. It might be important to devise a plan to decrease the frequency with which or the amount of time that the consumer thinks about the boyfriend and possibly devise a third plan to address her feelings. Different, separate plans may be needed to address thoughts, feelings, and behaviors.

Other factors that workers generally explore with consumers before completing an assessment are physiological factors, such as drugs, alcohol, hormonal changes, and nutrition. If there is a serious alcohol problem within a family, working on communication among family members will be difficult and probably unproductive. There are at least two problems you should always screen for even when there is no indication that there is a problem in either area: drug abuse and sexual abuse, past or present. These are not easy issues to explore with a consumer. It may be helpful to tell the consumer that you routinely ask all consumers about these two issues because they can significantly affect people's lives and daily functioning. Human service providers are also concerned about issues or situations that limit their work, such as the maturational level of the consumer, family conditions, community and social factors, and the physical environment.

Ethnic, cultural, and religious factors are critical, too, especially for understanding the problem and for designing a plan that is likely to be carried out without challenging traditional ways of handling similar situations. It is not necessary to have extensive knowledge about a consumer's culture in order to consider cultural variables. It is critical to explore these issues and to learn about the consumer's culture from the consumer, as explained in Chapter 7, Lesson 3.

In general, the focus of concern is the consumer's present situation, but it is useful to spend some time exploring important aspects of the consumer's past. One example of information from the past that is relevant in the present is how the consumer handled similar situations in the past. This information can tell you about the family's methods of coping. Information on how problems were handled in the past can help you identify the potential for change within the consumer and the consumer's current situation. Potential for change is evaluated for individuals as well as for situations and resources. Other previous experiences that should be identified are medical histories, earlier experiences with helpers or helping systems, and previous attempts to handle the problem. These factors will help you understand the situation, identify points for change and possible interventions, and assess how difficult change may be.

Focus on the current situation. Even if you can learn the original cause of a problem, this knowledge may not help you to change the current situation because what prompted the first occurrence of a problem may be very different from what is currently maintaining it. To understand a problem/issue/situation better, and to obtain clues about what to modify in order to achieve the desired outcomes, it is helpful to look at the context of the problem. For example, what happens just before an argument occurs, and what follows it? What are the events surrounding the problem or situation? Consumer self-recordings are often the best source of information about these events.

A helpful approach to assessment is to identify behavioral excesses (things consumers do too much of) and behavioral deficits (things consumers do not do enough of, or do not do at all). It is important to know whether the desired behavior is something the person can do, or whether it is something the person needs to learn how to do. For example, look at an individual who does not relate well to members of the opposite sex. Does the individual not have the skills needed to talk with persons of the opposite sex, or does the individual have the verbal–social skills but simply does not have opportunities to use these skills?

SUMMARY OF ASSESSMENT COMPONENTS

There are many factors to consider in completing an assessment. Nine components of a comprehensive assessment are summarized below.

1. Consumer strengths, resources, and skills. Examples may be educational resources and personal resources and strengths such as social skills, self-care skills, and household management skills.

Note: Remember to build on consumer strengths and to avoid doing tasks for consumers that they can do for themselves. Supporting strengths and giving positive feedback help develop good relationships with consumers and help consumers to feel good enough about themselves to begin to work on their problems. Remember, one strength is that the person is here with you at this time, creating an opportunity for change.

2. Situational strengths and resources. Examples are family, neighbors, friends, institutions (e.g., churches), natural helping networks, and material resources (e.g., housing and income).

3. Family and community factors. Includes family interactional patterns and relationships and the physical environment in which the consumer lives and works, such as an economically depressed neighborhood.

4. Physiological, medical, and psychiatric factors. This category includes drug and alcohol abuse, as well as medical problems; physical complications, such as hormonal changes or nutritional deficits or factors; developmental stage; and developmental disabilities based on reports from professionals who assess these areas. There may also be a psychiatric diagnosis; however, such labeling presents problems that can result in categorizing persons mistakenly or lead to assumptions that change cannot occur.

5. Cultural, ethnic, and religious factors. It is important to understand the consumer's cultural experience and attachments; a consumer's ethnicity or race does not indicate what factors in his or her experience affect relationships and behaviors. Values, choices, beliefs, and perceptions need to be individualized and learned from the consumer.

6. Past history—social history. An overview of medical, education, work histories; social skills; family constellation; and sexual and other forms of abuse. These factors may help you to understand the current situation, identify change points, and assess the potential for change. Past information should be requested only if it is helpful in dealing with the present. The focus of an assessment is the current situation.

7. Potential for change—motivation. Prior experiences with helpers; earlier attempts to change the situation and the results of those attempts will help you understand the consumer's current motivation and potential for change. It is important to look at ways in which the consumer handles situations by exploring how similar problems were handled in the past. How does the consumer see the problem? Does the person see the problem as others see it? Is the consumer engaging in denial?

8. Behavioral excesses. Identification of behaviors, thoughts, and feelings that create difficulties for the consumer and need to be reduced.

9. Behavioral deficits. Identification of behaviors that the consumer can display but does not use, does not use frequently enough, or does not use in particular situations, and behaviors that the consumer cannot display. If the behavior is not part of the person's repertoire, is it a knowledge/skill deficit, or are there emotional reactions that inhibit the consumer's performance of the behavior? These distinctions are critical for developing a case plan.

FRAME
8

Now that you know the key parts of an assessment, see if you can complete the assessment form that follows the presentation of the Coe family.

Mrs. Coe recently called the local center for the elderly to request services for her mother. The center provides hot lunches five days a week and activities following lunch. Your job includes helping with the activities and arranging transportation for senior citizens who come to the center as well as working with some of their families. You are also the first contact person for people who call the center to request information about the center's services. Your responsibilities are to find out whether consumers have needs in addition to a hot meal and opportunities to meet others. In this role you get to know some members, interview them when they first come to the center, and make a home visit to observe their functioning at home.

The Coe household consists of Mr. and Mrs. Coe, Mrs. Coe's mother, and the Coes' three children. The Coe family lives in a medium-size midwestern city. They moved to the city from a farm ten years ago because Mr. Coe could not make enough money farming to support his family. Mrs. Coe has one sibling, a brother who is currently living in a state mental hospital in a smaller town about 50 miles from the Coe home.

Mrs. Coe's mother, who used to be a great help to the family, has deteriorated physically and mentally. Currently, the mother is more of a burden than a help to the family. She seems more and more withdrawn. She does not go out and spends long periods of time in her room. She does, however, continue setting the table for dinner. She eats erratically, and the Coes are worried about her physical health and mental status.

Johnny, the Coes' oldest child, just turned 16 and has become difficult to handle. He refuses to observe a curfew imposed by Mr. Coe, sometimes staying out all night. The Coes blame his disobedient behavior on the group of boys he hangs out with. Sally Coe is 13 and is her father's pride and joy. She helps her mother with household chores and with the care of Jimmy, the Coes' 4-year-old son. The Coes do not think Jimmy is normal. According to Mrs. Coe, the child constantly causes trouble around the house. The two older children were never a problem when they were young. Mrs. Coe asserts that Jimmy cannot do anything right.

Mr. and Mrs. Coe have been married 18 years. Mrs. Coe is 38 years old and Mr. Coe is 41. They began dating in high school and married soon after Mr. Coe inherited the family farm from his father. Mr. Coe is an unskilled laborer. Work is sporadic. The family frequently has financial difficulties, especially during periods when Mr. Coe is laid off. Construction work has been slow during the past two years. For this reason, Mrs. Coe took a job as a hostess/waitress in a small all-night diner. She works a variable schedule, depending on when she is needed. Generally she is home from the time the children return from school through dinner. She has tried to work the morning shift, but she does not always have this choice and fills in when she is called to work, especially during periods when Mr. Coe is unemployed.

The Coes own a small house in a middle-income neighborhood. Most of their neighbors are close to their age and have children. The children like the city, but the adjustment has been difficult for Mr. Coe and for Mrs. Coe's mother. They both enjoyed living in the country and miss the farm, their lifestyle, and their old neighbors.

Two months after your first home visit to the Coe house, Mrs. Coe calls to say that Johnny is using drugs and getting into frequent fights with his father. She insists that Johnny needs to be placed somewhere else for a while. She feels that the family cannot handle him and that he is a bad example for the younger children, especially their daughter. You suggest a home visit to talk about the situation.

When you arrive, Johnny is sitting on the front steps. His parents seem upset. Mrs. Coe is convinced that the only solution is for Johnny to be sent somewhere where he will learn to obey his father, stop using drugs, and be separated from his friends. Johnny agrees that he wants to leave home.

You tell Mrs. Coe about foster placement services through the state child welfare office. Mrs. Coe calls the local state welfare office and makes an appointment to see a worker there. Mrs. Coe also wonders if something more can be done for her mother. Mr. Coe wonders if there is a place for his mother-in-law to go or if she can live alone.

Now that you have read about the Coe family, write the assessment components in the spaces below, considering the whole family. If more information is needed about the case in order to fill in a component, note this and mention the area that you would explore to get the information.

1. Consumer strengths:

2. Situational strengths:

3. Family and community factors:

4. Physiological and medical factors:

5. Cultural, ethnic, and religious factors:

6. Past history:

7. Potential for change (include any information on coping patterns):

8. Behavioral excesses:

9. Behavioral deficits:

Turn to Answer 118 on page 628

FRAME

9

The goal of an assessment is to give the worker and the consumer a better understanding of the situation as a basis for setting goals and developing a list of potential interventions. Thoroughness is especially important when the situation is unclear, when involved persons see the problem differently, and when information is needed to devise an effective service plan.

It is important to be concrete in written and verbal communication with and about consumers. Concreteness is reflected in specific definitions of consumer statements (what does that mean in concrete, actual terms?); clarification of the problem or situation in terms of the individual; descriptions of behaviors, thoughts, and feelings; and clear descriptions of issues and their related outcomes. If the consumer wants a specific, concrete service, such as information about Food Stamps, clothes, or temporary help with utility bills, it is not necessary to explore all the topics described above as part of an assessment. Also, if the consumer is very clear about what the problem is, less information is needed in order to define goals.

FRAME

10

FROM THE PRESENTING PROBLEM TO THE DESIRED OUTCOME

In an assessment interview, the focus is on the current situation. Past information is requested only to help the worker understand the current situation, especially learning how long the problem has existed and what has been tried to alleviate it. The primary focus of the assessment process is to move from the presenting problems as expressed by the consumer to specific definitions of the problems, and finally, to the desired outcomes as reflected in the following examples, based on the Coe family.

Presenting Problem	Specific Direction	Desired Outcome
Johnny is difficult to handle.	He sometimes stays out all night.	Tell us what time he will be home.
	He ignores his father's curfew.	Do not stay out past midnight.
Mrs. Coe's mother is withdrawn.	She spends long periods of time alone in her room.	Spend time with the family.
	She does not go out.	Go to the senior center for lunch twice a week.

The assessment process helps the consumer specify the issues. When problems are clearly specified, it is easier to move on to defining the consumer's goals or desired outcomes. This process of goal setting is discussed in the next lesson. The link, however, between presenting problem and desired outcome is a natural one. A good assessment leads directly to the definition of goals.

Problems to avoid and preferred ways to express presenting problems are summarized below:[3]

Weaknesses That Occur When You Are Learning to Specify Problems	Preferred Ways to Express Presenting Problems
Vague problem	Specific terms differentiate problems experienced by the consumer
Problem expressed in negative terms (something to stop or get rid of)	Positive changes specified
Goals and plan suggested by the worker	Consumer states desired outcomes and selects the final plan

The Case Assessment Summary (Figure 8.1) can serve as a guide and as a reminder of information to collect in completing an assessment.[4] It is important to find out *who* identifies the problem, as well as who has the problem. A problem may not be recognized as such by the person who reportedly has the problem. For example, something that a child does may be a problem for a parent, but may not be a problem from the child's perspective. Thus, on the Case Assessment Summary (Figure 8.1) it is important first, to describe the problem, then to identify who labeled this a problem (for whom is this a problem?), and then to state who has the problem. It is helpful in tracking the progress of a case to write down the date that the problem was first noted.

---

[3]Gambrill, *Casework*.
[4]Format developed by Gambrill, *Casework*.

Problem checklist (clear description of problem)	Who labeled it a problem?	Who has the problem?	Date noted	Examples of the problem	Situation (where, when, with whom)	Desired outcome
"Johnny ignores his father's curfew and sometimes stays out all night."	Parents	Johnny Coe, 16-year-old son	10/13/97	He was out past midnight three nights last week	Two school nights; one weekend night; was with male school friends; did not say where he was going or when he would be home	Tell parents what time he will be home; be home by 10 P.M. on school nights and by midnight on weekends
"Jimmy is not normal." (Clear description of problem not given.)	Parents	Jimmy Coe, 4-year-old son	10/13/97	"He causes trouble around the house." (Specific examples needed.)	Home observation would be helpful	Not specified
"Grandmother has deteriorated physically and mentally."	Mrs. Coe	Grandmother	10/13/97	Spends hours alone in her room; does not go out; often skips supper	At home	Spend more time with family; make friends; spend time outside the home with other elderly; eat regularly
Financial difficulties	Mr. & Mrs. Coe	Mr. Coe	10/13/97	An unskilled construction worker, he is frequently laid off	Work/home	Stable employment
		Mrs. Coe		She had to begin working; at times works during hours children are home; un-	Work/home	Daytime hours

Problem checklist (clear description of problem)	Who labeled it a problem?	Who has the problem?	Date noted	Examples of the problem	Situation (where, when, with whom)	Desired outcome
				satisfying work; ir-regular income		More satis-fying job
Move from farm to small city	Mr. & Mrs. Coe	Mr. Coe	10/13/97	No friends; accustomed to rural lifestyle		Increase in-come
		Grandmother		Role change		
Use of il-legal drugs	Mr. & Mrs. Coe	Johnny Coe	12/14/97	(More infor-mation needed)		Stop drug use
Fights with father	Mr. & Mrs. Coe	Johnny Coe	12/14/97	Mrs. Coe calls case-worker, wants Johhny placed elsewhere	At home	Cease fights; resolve dis-agreements
Grand-mother is a burden on the family when she used to be a help	Mrs. Coe	Coe family	12/14/97	Needs care; only contri-bution she now makes is setting the table (Specify type of care needed)	At home	Alternative living arrange-ment

FIGURE 8.1.   Case Assessment Summary for the Coe Family

It is of primary importance to give concrete examples of the problem. Examples may change over time, but they help specify and individualize the consumer's prob-lem in order to set goals and plan services. Specifying the situation in which the prob-lem occurs will provide information about the context of the problem that can help determine where to direct change efforts. Some problems may occur in all situations, and this would simply be noted. Some problems may occur only in certain situations, and some problems may occur more frequently in certain situations, around certain people, or at a particular time of day. When the consumers can give you the informa-tion, also note the situation in which the problem generally occurs. Consumers may assist by describing the problem in writing as it occurs. The last column in the Case Assessment Summary asks for the consumer's desired outcome.

LESSON2

Goal Setting, Contracting, and Service Planning

This lesson reflects the strong belief that consumers are the key factor in defining their goals or desired outcomes, that they must be involved in the development of plans for modifying their situation, and that written contracts developed between consumers and workers must be agreeable to all parties involved.

Goal

To learn to develop achievable goals with consumers and incorporate these goals into workable contracts and plans that are likely to succeed.

Learning Activities

To accomplish this goal, we will:

1. Explore ways to help consumers define goals or desired outcomes in clear, concrete terms.
2. Explain how to prioritize goals.
3. Discuss how to pinpoint or operationalize problems.
4. List the components of a good helping plan.
5. Discuss the importance of clear contracts in the helping process.
6. Describe how to develop written contracts.

FRAME

1

GOAL SETTING

Goals define the aims of the helping relationship and the desired outcomes that consumers want to reach. Clear definitions of goals provide a standard for evaluating your progress with consumers. Thus, you will always be working toward changes that are desired by, and important to, the consumer. Consumers are more likely to work on goals that they have selected. Consumers learn new skills when they successfully make a change, they can then apply these skills to work on subsequent goals. At times, goals may be imposed by legal authorities, parents, or institutions. When this occurs, it is important to include additional goals selected by the consumer.

You and the consumer will generally begin defining goals in your first session together. As part of the assessment, you will compile a list of problems and desired outcomes expressed by the consumer. By the end of the first session you should have compiled an overview of the consumer's primary concerns. Through the assessment process you should also have gained a total picture of the consumer's situation, including information about important components of the consumer's life. These components may not relate directly to the presenting problems, but should help you to define relevant goals and develop a service plan. Consumers usually present their problems and concerns in general terms. With your help, consumers can define their concerns specifically so that objectives become clear. The consumer, with your help, needs to select one or more areas of concern on which to focus.

Once you have an overview of the consumer's concerns and the contexts in which they occur, you begin to define them further, and the consumer selects the concerns on which to focus attention. During your sessions with the consumer, it is important to prioritize goals, decide where to begin, and develop a plan. There are several questions to consider when focusing on concerns and assigning priorities:

1. How important is the concern to the consumer?
2. How serious is the concern, and what are the consequences if it remains unchanged?
3. How difficult will change be?
4. How can the concern be expressed as a positive goal?

Whenever possible, you want to begin working on the consumer's primary concerns. Consumers are more likely to carry out plans that they have helped to develop and are motivated to follow. In addition, a motivation for change increases the chances of success and, if at all possible, you want the consumer to experience success in the initial change effort. Consumer expectations of success also increase the possibility that they will carry out the plan and that the plan will succeed. You can increase consumers' positive expectations by expressing your own expectations of success. For all these reasons, initial change efforts generally revolve around the concerns that are of primary importance to the consumer, even if you think another area is more important. The Noel case, described in more detail in Frame 7, is a good example. The consumer, Mrs. Noel, was concerned about her child's behavior. The worker assessed that changes were needed in Mrs. Noel's interactions with her son; however, initially attention was focused on the child's behaviors. With the worker's help, Mrs. Noel was later able to identify and assess her own behavior.

Nevertheless, there are two situations in which you are obligated to address concerns that are not of primary importance to the consumer. The first is when judicial authorities have ordered specific changes. The court may have intervened because the consumer was arrested for child abuse, stealing, or property damage. Or an adolescent may be taken to the juvenile authorities for not attending school. The adolescent may not express interest in increasing his school attendance, yet he must attend school in order to stay out of trouble with authorities. In such cases, the human service worker attempts to negotiate with the consumer—to identify and work on the consumer's goals as well as the authorities' goals.

The second situation in which workers are obligated to act is when a crisis is occurring or is likely to occur. In crisis situations the human service worker may have to direct the consumer's attention to change involving problems that are not of primary concern to the consumer. If, for example, a consumer will be expelled from school if she does not stop using foul language in class, change efforts are indicated to avoid a worse problem—namely, expulsion. This second situation is more critical to address if the crisis will affect persons in addition to the consumer. While the consumer may elect to take the consequences of ignoring problems, you will need to use all your skills to convince consumers to address a crisis situation that, if not handled, may harm others. For example, you may know that a consumer plans to kidnap his daughter, who is in the custody of his estranged wife. Such an act would be potentially damaging to both the daughter and the mother and have legal consequences for the father. The process in such situations involves helping the consumer to identify goals that have personal meaning beyond the legally mandated goals or the crisis situation. Sometimes, when you help consumers understand the consequences of not addressing a particular problem, they will decide to address the problem and include relevant goals in the planning process. Even if there is a legal mandate that the consumer is supposed to follow, the consumer may want to work on other issues. In this circumstance, encourage the consumer to select a problem to address in addition to the legally mandated problem.

Beyond legal mandates and crises, the first criterion for problem solving is the *importance of the problem to the consumer*. If you work in an institutional setting, such as a group home for adolescent boys, you may see the staff defining goals that help them work with the consumer. Some of the goals that make consumers "better" residents might not be appropriate if the consumer lived outside the institution. Consumers often select goals that will improve their chances for success outside the institution, and these are usually the most important goals to work on.

The second consideration is the *severity of the problem*. The consumer needs to identify how severe the problem is, determined by measuring how frequently the problem occurs and/or its duration and intensity. For example, a college-age female might present the problem of relating with males. Does this person want relationships with men? Has she ever had satisfying relationships? How often does she interact with men? If the consumer has never had a satisfying relationship with a man and has no relationships with men now, the problem would be more severe than if the consumer had relationships with men, has had satisfying relationships in the past, yet currently does not have a regular relationship with a male. The number of men that she comes in contact with and the frequency with which she interacts with them may be helpful information to determine problem severity as well as to specify the problem and illuminate potential change targets and strategies. It may be that she has relationships but has difficulty initiating conversations with men or meeting men. Her current communication skills may be excellent, except in initial meetings with men. Depending on the consequences, you may encourage the consumer to begin work on less severe problems in order to provide an initial experience of success.

The third consideration is *selecting goals that have a high potential for achievement*. We generally want consumers to experience success early in the helping relationship. Initial success encourages consumers to continue working for improvement. To ensure success, divide a goal into smaller components so that the initial step is something more attainable than the long-range goal. The terms of short-range and long-range goals define how long it will take to achieve a goal. Steps toward a long-range goal may be called short-range goals. For example, a long-range goal may be for a consumer to develop satisfying relationships with persons of the opposite sex. There may be a number of short-range, or immediate, goals. One would be to increase the consumer's skill in talking with persons of the opposite sex. Another may be to teach the consumer the skills needed to initiate contacts with those of the opposite sex.

The definition of positive goals (desired outcomes) is essential for effective human service work. Consumers tend to express their concerns in terms of problems that are behaviors or thoughts or situations they want to change. In fact, most of us think in negative terms when we think about getting help. We are problem oriented. Therefore it is necessary to work with the consumer to move from defining problems to describing how the consumer would like things to be. Consumers often need help in thinking about how they would like their lives to be. They also need help in considering alternative behaviors, things they would like to be doing in place of things that they feel are not good for them. Making preliminary statements about desired outcomes is a useful step in defining goals and moving away from being preoccupied with problems.[1] By helping consumers explore what they would like to do differently, workers gain additional information about what needs to be changed in order for the consumer to experience improvement.

In general, the primary consideration is to begin working with consumers to achieve goals of importance to them. In addition, we help consumers define attainable goals and consider problem severity, how difficult change will be, and how goals may be defined in small steps. Since we know that people are more encouraged to work for positive goals than to eliminate negative behaviors, we help consumers define their concerns as desired outcomes. An example of moving from the consumer's presenting problems to defining desired outcomes is shown in Figure 8.1 on page 346.

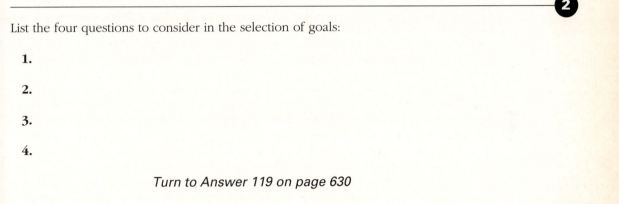

FRAME 2

List the four questions to consider in the selection of goals:

1.

2.

3.

4.

Turn to Answer 119 on page 630

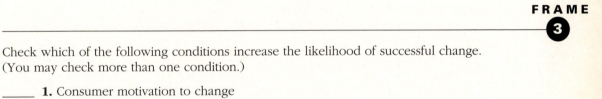

FRAME 3

Check which of the following conditions increase the likelihood of successful change. (You may check more than one condition.)

_____ **1.** Consumer motivation to change

---

[1] Eileen Gambrill, *Casework: A Competency-Based Approach* (Englewood Cliffs, N.J.: Prentice-Hall, 1983), p. 95.

_____ **2.** A behavior rather than a thought or feeling

_____ **3.** When change is ordered by a legal authority, such as a court judge

_____ **4.** When consumers expect they can and will change

_____ **5.** When the consumer selects the change targets

Turn to Answer 120 on page 630

FRAME

PINPOINTING THOUGHTS, FEELINGS, AND BEHAVIORS

For an effective helping plan to be developed and positive change to occur, we need a considerable amount of information about the problem. The more specifically we define the goal and the more we know about the context in which a problem occurs, the better chance we have for developing a plan that will be successful. A helpful tool for learning to be specific is *pinpointing* targets for change.[2]

Pinpointing is one way to become more specific in defining behaviors to be changed. The importance of being specific cannot be overemphasized. The more specific you help the consumer to be, the better your chances are for developing a service plan that will be successful. Often the helping process is unsuccessful simply because the wrong behavior was pinpointed for change. For example, many people talk about wanting to lose weight and pinpoint losing pounds as the target behavior. However, the behavior to be addressed is the quantity and quality of food consumption and exercise, and the specific problem will vary from one person to another. One person's problem may be eating too much at mealtimes and another person's problem may be eating between meals. You want to pinpoint the problem as close to the source as possible, not the result, and pounds gained are the result of a behavior. It may even be that to get closer to the source of the problem, thoughts about food need to be pinpointed, so the goal is to decrease the number of times the consumer thinks about or talks about eating.

The consumer, with your help, may target the problem behavior of eating (between-meal snacks, sweets, starches, second helpings, bites, depending on the consumer's particular eating problem) or may target conditions that lead to and/or support overeating. For example, a consumer may be living in a new community where she does not know anyone and does not go out. She is bored and lonely and at home most of the time. Given these conditions, she begins to eat and, consequently, gains weight. You may help her to change the long hours alone and the loneliness by developing positive goals, such as identifying ways to meet people and pinpoint participation in activities outside the home.

In addition, consumers may present something as a problem that is not the actual problem. Consider the following case:

> Parents sought help for their 3-year-old son. The parents went to an agency that provided assessment and services for children with special problems. The presenting problems was tantrums. When the worker asked how frequently the

---

[2]The term *pinpointing* and the material that follows are based on the work of O. R. Lindsley, University of Kansas, Lawrence.

child had tantrums, the parents said "all the time." When asked how severe the tantrums were, they described the child banging his head against a wall while screaming. The worker asked the parents to record the number of tantrums the child had each day during the next week. The worker explained that this information was critical for a complete assessment. The child was being seen by a psychologist, a medical doctor, a teacher, and a speech therapist, and the parents were being seen by a social worker. Each professional would present a written evaluation in a case staffing. Then the professionals would jointly discuss the case and make recommendations to the parents. The social worker explained to the parents that they knew more about their child than anyone else, and that the data collected during the coming week would be an integral part of the worker's case assessment presented in the staffing. The parents agreed. They returned a week later saying that tantrums were not a problem. The parents then began to discuss the real issues.

If the parents had not carefully observed and recorded the frequency of their child's tantrums at home and discovered that tantrums were not a central problem, the social worker would have recommended focusing on the child's tantrums. In effect, agency staff would have spent time addressing an issue that was not the central problem.

Clarity about the target also provides a basis for evaluation. The more specific you are about change goals, the easier it will be to determine whether the goals were achieved. Following the pinpointing principles will help you become more specific in defining problems and desired outcomes. A well-specified target is defined clearly enough to measure it. Apply the following four rules to pinpoint behaviors, thoughts, and feelings:

1. Define a movement cycle as one full occurrence of the behavior, thought, or feeling so that the number of times the behavior occurs can be counted. You have one movement cycle or a count of one when the person is in a position to begin the behavior over again. Given this rule, if you are counting the number of times you go up the stairs, a full movement cycle has occurred (a count of one) when you have descended the stairs and thus are in a position to climb them again. You are interested in counting and therefore need to define the beginning and end points of each occurrence of the behavior. The specificity and information required to count how often a behavior, thought, or feeling occurs demands a thorough exploration of the problem. When you have met the pinpointing requirements through interviewing and/or observing a consumer, you will know considerably more about the behavior and how it is uniquely experienced by the individual.

2. If the pinpointed behavior involves sitting, staying home, or doing nothing, your pinpoint does not pass the "dead man's test." While some "dead man" behaviors have been changed successfully, it is more meaningful to increase a desired behavior than to reward do-nothing behaviors. For example, if you reward a child for staying in his seat at school, it is not clear what the child is being rewarded for, except sitting there. It is important to pinpoint specific outcomes. It is preferable to reward desired behaviors, such as completing school assignments.

3. Take small steps whenever possible so that the consumer experiences success and the goal does not seem too large at the outset. Desired outcomes can sometimes be more easily attained by dividing the behavior into smaller steps. The smaller the unit of behavior, the more precision and information will be available for you and the consumer to assess.

4. Whenever possible, target a positive goal that the consumer wants to increase rather than something to decrease. Generally, people are more motivated to work for positive goals, thus increasing the likelihood for follow through and success. By focusing on one behavior at a time and selecting the behavior that is most important to the consumer, the consumer is more likely to experience success. However, it is difficult to allow such freedom in a crisis situation involving a behavior that is troublesome to others, or when serious consequences will ensue if a behavior is not altered rapidly.

FRAME 5

Read the following examples of poor pinpoints, then judge the additional examples below:

	Poor Pinpoint	*Problem with the Pinpoint*
OTHERS' BEHAVIOR	Fighting	The -*ing* form implies ongoing behavior rather than discrete episodes that can be counted
OWN WORK BEHAVIOR	Better interviewing skills	Too general; specify which skills
CONSUMER	Anxiety	Too abstract

Which of the following examples are clearly pinpointed? Which are not? Why are they poor pinpoints? Which rules were broken? Place a check after the well-pinpointed behaviors. State the reason why other behaviors are not well pinpointed or suggest better pinpoints.

Self-Behaviors

- number of pages read
- eliminating number of minutes over conference time period
- yelling at home
- calories consumed
- nail biting
- promptness
- focusing on the topic during conferences
- hanging up clothes
- patience
- percentage of verbal participation in class
- turning in records on time
- omitting inferences in written records
- interruptions in interviews

Consumer Behaviors

- self-esteem
- anxiety in groups
- percentage of verbal participation
- truancy
- obsessive talking
- leaving child unattended
- positive comments to child
- going to bed on time
- improve self-functioning
- clean house
- staying home
- alcohol consumed
- compliments to spouse
- activities with children

Turn to Answer 121 on page 630

Now try pinpointing some behaviors of your own, of consumers you have worked with or are currently working with, and of friends or relatives.

Pinpoint Practice Form

	Target Behaviors to Be Increased	*Target Behaviors to Be Decreased*
Own work behaviors	1. 2.	1. 2.
Consumer behaviors	1. 2.	1. 2.
Others' (spouse, friend, parent, child, instructor, etc.) behaviors	1. 2.	1. 2.

Examine your pinpoints. Do they begin and end so that you could count one, two, three, etc.? If they are observable behaviors, are they defined clearly enough so you know what to count? Are you clear about what you will count each day? Sometimes you can define a pinpoint more specifically after you try counting it and seeing whether the target is pinpointed clearly.

MONITORING BEHAVIORS

Recording the frequency of a behavior, thought, or feeling can provide important information for setting goals and developing service plans. The following case describes the role of monitoring behaviors in assessment, in helping a mother better understand the problem, and in implementing a service plan. Giving the consumers the tools to assess their own situations by monitoring themselves can be an empowering experience for the consumer.[3] Also, self-monitoring often changes the monitoring target in the desired direction.[4]

> Mrs. Noel, a mother of three, came to a multidisciplinary center requesting an evaluation of her youngest child, James. The parents thought James was developmentally disabled. This preschool child seemed slow; however, he was found not to be developmentally disabled. The mother said James did nothing right.

---

[3]J. Kopp. "Self-Observation: An Empowerment Strategy in Assessment," *Social Casework* (1989): 276–284.
[4]J. Kopp, "Self-Monitoring: A Literature Review of Research and Practice," *Social Work Research and Abstracts* 24 (1988): 8–20.

During a 2-hour home visit, the worker asked Mrs. Noel to go on with her normal activities. The worker observed that Mrs. Noel blamed her youngest child for every disturbance and misbehavior, and yet he tried to do things that would please her. Often the disturbance was initiated by the eldest child, out of the mother's sight, yet the mother automatically reprimanded James without having observed any of the children's behaviors. She gave him no positive attention or feedback, although she was positive in her communications with her other two children. During an interview in the agency she said that this child was not wanted and was seen as deviant from birth. Thus, the mother's pinpoint was the child's negative behaviors, but the actual problems were the mother's interactions and interpretations and, at times, the other two children. The mother was asked to record the positive things James did during the day as a way for her to perceive and think about this child differently. (Her list for two days is included below.) This information not only aided in assessment but also changed the mother's perceptions and prepared her to begin to be open to discussion about the actual problems.

Thursday

1. Got my purse for me.
2. Emptied ashtrays.
3. Picked up living room.
4. Emptied water.
5. Fed dog.
6. Polished his and Robert's shoes.

Friday

1. Emptied ashtrays.
2. Scraped lunch dishes.
3. Stripped bed.
4. Got ashtray for Daddy (without being asked).
5. Put up bowl.

FRAME

8

DEVELOPING CLEAR GOAL STATEMENTS

Describing problems clearly (clearly enough so that their frequencies can be recorded), simplifies the specification of desired outcomes or goals. It is necessary to specify the presenting problems in order to determine the range of problems for each consumer. For example, depression can mean different things to different individuals. Clearly defined presenting problems help the consumer identify desired outcomes. Outcomes are developed by asking consumers how they would like things to be or what they would like to be different.

The consumer defines the problem and describes the desired outcomes from her own perspective. Even when there are legally mandated changes in behavior, workers must attempt to (1) understand the problem from the consumer's perspective; (2) identify how the consumer might like things to be; and (3) design goals that meet the consumer's needs as well as the demands of the court. Thus, in Mrs. Noel's case the initial focus was on her son's behavior rather than her own. If a goal is specified clearly, it is possible to measure its achievement. A goal statement seeks to answer the following questions: Who? What? When? Where?

Once Mrs. Noel was able to recognize that James did some good things, and in fact was trying hard to please her, as is reflected in the list of things he did for her during only two days, she slowly became open to the idea of looking at her interactions with her son. Since she did not know he did good things, it seemed likely that she was not praising him for the good things he did. This deficit was also observed by the worker. During a 2-hour home visit, the worker observed that all of Mrs. Noel's statements to James were negative and scolding comments. He was sometimes even blamed for things he did not do. The important thing was for the consumer to recognize her lack of positive statements addressed to her son. After recording the good things he did, Mrs. Noel agreed to look at how often she was scolding him or saying no to him. Later, Mrs. Noel also recorded the number of compliments and positive comments she made to James. In some cases it would be preferable to focus only on positive statements because increasing positive comments is the goal and gives a positive behavior to work toward. In this case, since there were no positive statements to build on, the use of negatives was extreme, and an intermediate goal was to help Mrs. Noel become aware of her many negative interactions with her son, the worker began with her record of "No's" and "Stop its" to James each day. Her record for nine days follows and is further explained below:

Saying "No" or "Stop It" to James

Date	Time	Number of Negatives	Rate per day
Fri. Oct. 20	7:00–9:00 a.m.	7	.03
	11:00–3:45 p.m.	6	
Sat. Oct. 21	7:00–12:00 noon	12	___
Sun. Oct. 22	10:00–12:00 noon	27[a]	___
Mon. Oct. 23	7:00–9:00 a.m.	9	___
	11:00–3:45 p.m.	5	
Tues. Oct. 24	7:00–9:00 a.m.	1	___
	11:00–3:45 p.m.	10	
Wed. Oct. 25	7:00–9:00 a.m.	4	___
	11:00–3:45 p.m.	7	
Thurs. Oct. 26	7:00–9:00 a.m.	5	___
	11:00–3:45 p.m.	4	
Tues. Oct. 31	7:00–9:00 a.m.	6	___
	11:00–3:45 p.m.	9	
Wed. Nov. 1	7:00–9:00 a.m.	10	___
	11:00–3:45 p.m.	15	

[a]This was the worst period. It was rainy, and James kept wanting to go trick-or-treating right away; then he'd want to play outside; next he'd want to know if Aunt Dee was coming yet. (The children had stayed at Aunt Dee's for vacation.)

Mrs. Noel and the worker charted her behavior so that Mrs. Noel could clearly see her interactions with James. It is fascinating to look at daily behavior on a chart because the chart provides a picture across time. Consumers often experience insight simply from the opportunity to observe a record of their behavior. The worker taught Mrs. Noel to record the time period during which she observed herself so that they could compute a rate of her behavior each day (the number of "No's" and "Stop its" divided by the period of time she recorded her behavior), rather than a simple number of "No's" and "Stop it's" per day. By using a rate, a consumer can record behavior for a different period of time each day and still be able to compare the behavior across days. Mrs. Noel used minutes rather than hours in case she decided to record for brief periods of time such as for 10- or 20-minute time samples.

The worker changed the data into daily rates by *dividing the number of "No's" by the number of minutes* that Mrs. Noel recorded her behavior. Try doing this yourself. Write the daily rate for each day in the rate column above. Look at the first day's record. Mrs. Noel kept track of her behavior for two time periods on the first day: from 7:00 A.M. to 9:00 A.M. and from 11:00 A.M. to 3:45 P.M. That's a total of 6 hours and 45 minutes. To convert the hours to minutes, multiply 60 minutes by 6, giving a total of 360 minutes, plus 45 minutes, or 405 minutes. She said "No" or "Stop it" 13 times during both time periods, so divide 13 by 405. Her rate for the first day was .03 times per minute. Compute her daily rate of "No's" for the remaining eight days and check your division.

Turn to Answer 122 on page 631

Because Mrs. Noel kept a record during two time periods, the worker could see whether her behavior varied from morning to evening. Since there did not appear to be important differences between these two time periods, they were added to get one overall rate per day. Next, her daily rates were charted on graph paper so that she and the worker could observe patterns and change across time.

What can be learned from the chart of Mrs. Noel's "No's" (see Figure 8.2). Rates for nine days are charted. Just "eyeballing" the chart, what can you say about these nine days? One way to determine a trend is to draw an imaginary straight line between the dots—run the line through the middle of the data points, not connecting all the points but approximating their "average." This cannot be done with these nine data points because the data are variable. Looking at the first three data points, it appears that the behavior is increasing. Yet the next four days show a steady decrease in her "No's." The middle data point for the nine days is .034. This is easily found by simply counting up on the graph to the fifth data point beginning with the lowest point. The fifth data point is the midpoint of the nine days. The midpoint for the first three days is .04. This was determined by looking for the middle point between the first and the third days, again counting up from the lowest day. The midpoint for the last six days is .034. Considering the last three days, you might conclude that the rate is again going up. However, the variability of the rate during the nine days and the fact that her rate went up and then decreased again suggest that more information is needed—at least an additional week—to determine whether the behavior is consistently increasing or whether the behavior continues to vary.

You might practice your graphing skill by converting Mrs. Noel's "No's" and "Stop its" into movements per hour, instead of movements per minute. The first rate would

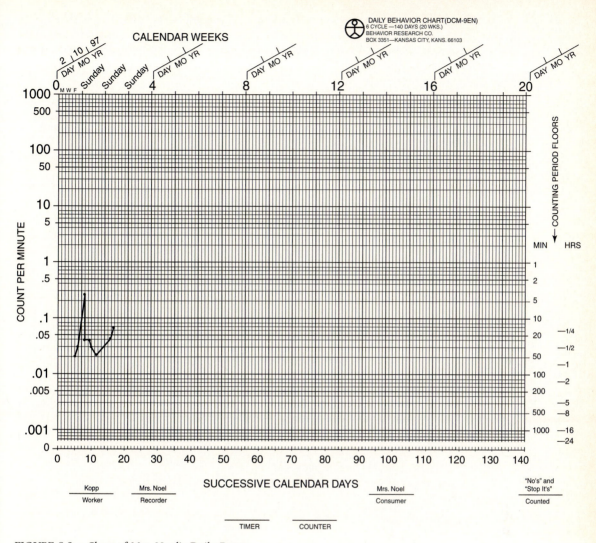

FIGURE 8.2.   Chart of Mrs. Noel's Daily Rates

be 1.85 negatives per hour. This number is obtained by rounding off the number of hours she recorded her behavior to seven and dividing her 13 movements by seven hours. The number of negatives can be rounded off to 2. You can see that this is not quite as precise as dividing by minutes, but you will have whole numbers. Try making your own graph with Mrs. Noel's negatives per hour on the vertical axis and the days she recorded on the horizontal axis.

Looking at the trends in the data can tell you whether a special service plan is needed. In this example it appears that the behavior will not decrease without special change efforts. One plan might be to record positive comments as well as to work toward increasing the positives while continuing to monitor negatives to see if one decreases as the other increases. However, you cannot assume that negatives will decrease as positives increase; Mrs. Noel could increase positive comments *and* continue her "No's." If a service plan is initiated, the data will show whether it is working. Now that you know how to define problems clearly enough to measure them and have some new recording skills, let's take one last look at the differences between clear and unclear goal statements.

Goal Statements

To understand how to develop clear goals, or desired outcomes, we will critique the following commonly used, yet unclear, service plan goals:

1. Improve parenting skills.
2. Establish a stable environment.
3. Stop abusive behavior.
4. Improve attitude toward children.

These statements describe vague goals that could mean very different things to different people. Given these broad goals, it is impossible to develop an effective plan, since we do not even know where change is needed. For example, what specific skills in parenting are lacking? Is it that the consumer does not have positive contacts with the child? If so, what types of contacts are missing? On a separate piece of paper, write examples of at least three clear, behaviorally specific goals for each of the preceding vague goal statements.

Turn to Answer 123 on page 631

Human service workers sometimes distinguish between long-term and short-term goals. Improving parenting skills might be defined as a long-term goal, or objective. In this case a number of short-term goals, or steps, might be defined as ways to achieve improved parenting skills, such as (1) talking with the child each evening about his day at school; (2) enforcing a consistent bedtime; and (3) praising the child for completing specified chores and homework.

These are other examples of equally unsatisfactory statements of goals:

1. Attend parent education classes.
2. Obtain safe house for children.
3. Look for a job.
4. Deal successfully with drinking problem.
5. Obtain services from mental health center.

The first unsatisfactory statement confuses the means with the ends. Attending parent education classes is a possible means toward achieving parenting skills. However, parents could attend classes daily for months and still not provide a minimum level of care for their child. What do you want the parent to be able to do that the parent now either does not do or cannot do?

The same criticism can be made of statement 5. What is supposed to happen as a result of receiving mental health services? Many workers seem to think that simply the willingness to receive such services and the act of going to sessions are evidence of change.

The word *safe* in statement 2 lacks definition. What interpretation could be made of this word? What is needed is a definition of a "safe house." Do specific changes need to be made in the physical environment? Would the final criterion be health department approval of the home environment?

Statement 3 has a similar problem because "look for a job" can mean different things to different people. One way to define this as a goal would be to specify the number of job applications to be filled out and the number of interviews; in other words, how many jobs will the consumer actually apply for? For example, Mrs. X may apply in person for three jobs as a waitress during the coming week (or by a week from today).

Statement 4 does not define *success*. It does not give the consumer any direction. In defining desired outcomes, it is important to help the consumer define what will be different when the goal is achieved. This will provide you and the consumer with more information and with a basis for determining when your work is done, as well as a basis for evaluating success.

Once the desired outcomes are defined, you are ready to help the consumer decide where and how to begin. Often the consumer will know how best to approach a goal. It is important to involve the consumer in each step. The consumer not only selects the goals but also defines how to achieve them. You may offer suggestions, but whenever possible, let the consumer make the choice. The consumer's assets and strengths, which were specified during the assessment phase, will be useful in developing a helping plan. A careful review of both personal and situational assets will guide you in helping the consumer determine what needs to be done to accomplish desired outcomes and what resources can be used.

F R A M E
9

INVOLVING THE CONSUMER IN DEVELOPING ALTERNATIVES

The more thorough your information about the problem, the easier it will be to develop a plan for helping. If you know what precedes a problem, what follows it, what attempts have been made to solve it, how the consumer and significant others feel about the problem, and what the consumer's desired outcomes are, the helping plan will become clear. For example, if you learn from a consumer that when her 3-year-old daughter is not given what she wants, she cries until she gets what she wants and that when she starts to cry, she gets hugs and attention from her mother, you have clues about what to change in order to eliminate the child's cries. In this case, the plan might be to ignore the crying, and if this does not work, to ask the child to go into another room until she stops crying. If crying gets the mother's attention, the child is smart to continue crying in these situations.

Remember that the consumer knows the problem or situation better than anyone else does. Consumers often have good ideas about what needs to be changed, what is likely to work, and how to implement it. All too often, professionals ignore consumers' ideas about the origins of a problem or situation and how to bring about change. If the plan for helping requires assistance from others, the others need to understand what you will be doing.

Thus, consumer involvement in the development of a plan is the first rule. If others are needed to implement the plan, you may want to include them in the planning process. We know that if people are included in developing the plan, they are more likely to carry out their role in its implementation. The second important rule is to develop and discuss a number of alternative plans. If alternatives are developed from the outset and consumers know there are several possible tactics, they will be less discouraged should their initial attempt fail. Part of your job is to encourage the definition of alternative solutions and to stimulate the listing of ideas about how to change a situation. Sometimes you will need to consult books and journals and/or your supervisor to locate specific information about effective interventions for particular problems. In other cases, there may be no information about how best to help with a particular problem or situation; then, you and the consumer must use your ingenuity to develop a helping plan.

As alternative plans are presented and discussed, it is important to analyze the possible positive and negative consequences of each plan. Consideration of the possible consequences of alternative intervention plans is important in determining which plan to try first. Encourage the consumer to decide which plan to try first. Have alternative plans ready in case the first attempt is not successful.

A service plan includes the following component parts:

1. The desired outcomes
2. The change strategies and how they will be implemented
3. Who will be responsible for implementing each part of the plan
4. Who will evaluate whether the plan is working
5. The timetable for the implementation and completion of the plan

What should a service plan look like? Consider the Coe family. The Case Assessment Summary in the preceding lesson is a good tool from which to develop a service plan. Note that the Coes' major concerns are included in the summary. However, you probably would not begin working on all these issues at the same time. Given the three criteria discussed earlier in this lesson for prioritizing problems—importance to consumer, severity of the problem, and possibility for successful change—the first decision that needs to be made is which problem to begin working on. In the last contact with the Coe family, the worker learned that Johnny's relationship with the family had reached a crisis situation. Had the family not already decided to place Johnny outside the home and sought services from a child welfare worker, this probably would be the problem you would focus on first. However, the family is now receiving services for this issue through a child welfare worker, and Johnny is currently not living in the home.

Mrs. Coe expressed concern about her mother, Mrs. Johnson, and the family's need for help with her. This situation is of importance to the whole family and may be nearing a crisis in that the family feels they can no longer care for Mrs. Coe's mother at home. Further, placement outside the home would be a major change, one that would be very difficult for the grandmother. Thus, based on discussions with the family and weighing possible places to begin, you and the Coes decide to direct your energies initially toward services for Mrs. Johnson.

A Service Plan for Mrs. Johnson

Consumers: Mr. and Mrs. Coe.

Presenting Problem: Mrs. Coe's mother, Mrs. Johnson, who lives with the Coes, has recently deteriorated physically and mentally; she has become a burden on the family instead of the helpful participant in the household that she used to be. The family is currently experiencing other sources of stress (difficulties with two of the three children and financial problems). There is also stress on the marriage and family system caused by Mr. Coe's periodic unemployment and Mrs. Coe's need to work. Until recently, Mr. Coe had provided the family's income.

Initial Service Plan:

1. Collect additional, specific information about Mrs. Johnson's current condition, abilities, and rate of deterioration.
2. Resources for Mrs. Johnson need to be explored by worker and by Mr. and Mrs. Coe.
3. Develop a helping relationship with Mrs. Johnson.
4. Explore the alternatives with each member or with the whole family: (1) Slow down Mrs. Johnson's rate of deterioration through the use of medicine (if indicated), self-help skills, and physical therapy; (2) place Mrs. Johnson in a retirement center or nursing home; (3) get help in the home (e.g., homemaker) to aid in caring for Mrs. Johnson; and (4) develop activities for Mrs. Johnson outside the home (e.g., day care or senior center).
5. Finalize the plan with Mrs. Johnson and the family as a whole.

The first four tasks are further assessment, the exploration of resources, and the exploration of alternative actions with the Coes and Mrs. Johnson to determine the best plan for Mrs. Johnson. Since Mrs. Johnson has not identified herself as a consumer, the worker's task is to develop a helping relationship with Mrs. Johnson and then to involve Mrs. Johnson in planning for herself.

In order to demonstrate the use of written contracts, let's *assume* that the plan is to mobilize resources so that Mrs. Johnson can continue to live with the Coes without being a burden on the family. The initial plan with the Coes will be written into contract form, considering the material in the next four frames on developing written contracts.

F R A M E

10

DEVELOPING CONTRACTS

It is advisable to write the service plan in the form of a contract. Written agreements are used in many human service settings. Contracts are tools to involve and protect both the worker and the consumer. A contract may seem legalistic, rigid, and unfeeling. Depending on how they are used, however, contracts are one way to ensure the consumer's rights, to free the consumer, and to increase consumer control in developing and implementing the plan. Such contracts are not legal documents; rather, they are a way to involve interested persons and to identify each person's roles in the achievement of the desired outcomes. Contracts help to document who does what and when. Thus, contracts explain to the consumer what the worker and the agency will do, clarify what is expected of the consumer and significant others, and provide a basis for tracking progress.

Four advantages of written contracts are: (1) Consumers are recognized as integral participants in the process designed to bring about change; (2) the expectations of consumers are specified; (3) a time limit for accomplishing changes is established;

and (4) signing the contract can strengthen the consumer's commitment to participate in change efforts.[5]

FRAME

11

Contract Suggestions

1. Develop the agreement *with* consumers, not *for* them.
2. Include consumers' goals in the contract.
3. Agree to support the consumers' goals as long as they carry out the responsibilities defined in the contract.
4. Make a copy of the contract for consumers.
5. Consider drawing up a separate contract for each person even when consumers live together (e.g., a husband and wife).

What two major themes are reflected in the five suggestions for drawing up contracts?

　a.

　b.

Turn to Answer 124 on page 632

FRAME

12

Additional Contract Suggestions

6. Write the agreement in language that the consumer is comfortable with, using plain, concise, clear, understandable terms. Specify each party's (e.g., worker and consumer) responsibilities.
7. Limit the number of items expected of consumers so as not to overwhelm them.
8. Develop realistic plans that you and the consumer can carry out in the time available.
9. Establish specific target dates.
10. Specify consequences for failure to fulfill a contract and when they will occur.

What three arrangements should be specified in a contract?

　a.

　b.

　c.

Turn to Answer 125 on page 632

---

[5]Ted Stein, Eileen Gambrill, and K. T. Wiltse, *Children in Foster Homes: Achieving Continuity of Care* (New York: Praeger Special Studies, 1978).

WORKING WITH A SAMPLE CONTRACT

Contracts should be evaluated on an ongoing basis and changed as needed. It is important to date the original contract when it is signed, and to date any subsequent deletions or additions. Clearly specified contracts help consumers by reflecting concise plans, agreement on a course of action, and the obligations of each participant (including the agency). With these written expectations, distortions and confusion are less likely to occur. Also, there is a framework for further action should the initial plan not work. Contracts provide an objective record of agreed-on goals, responsibilities of each person involved, and agreed-on tactics. In this way, contracts provide a basis for checking progress and evaluating change. You may need to alter the original agreement based on the consumer's experience with the plan. The following initial contract is designed to accomplish tasks that must be achieved *before* the final goals are specified and a second contract is developed.

Initial Contract for the Coes

This agreement is a contract between <u>Mr. and Mrs. Coe</u> and <u>Judy Kopp</u>
                                         (consumer)   (worker)

of the <u>Family Service Agency</u>. The purpose of this agreement is <u>to develop a plan for</u> <u>the Coes and Mrs. Johnson that will be in the best interests of all family members</u>.

    In order to accomplish the above goal, the following arrangements will be carried out:

Arrangement	*Who Is Responsible?*
1. Worker will meet with Mrs. Johnson to begin to develop a helping relationship with her, to assess her assets and deficits further, and to help her identify her goals.	Judy Kopp
2. The Coes and the worker will meet with Mrs. Johnson to begin to discuss their perspectives of the problem. Thus far, no expectations have been expressed by the Coes to Mrs. Johnson.	Mr. & Mrs. Coe; Judy Kopp
3. The Coes will explore living resources outside the home.	Mrs. Coe
4. The worker will explore resources to give help to Mrs. Johnson in the home.	Judy Kopp
5. Explore resources for activities for Mrs. Johnson outside the home and for additional financial help. Observation of such resources that sound promising.	Judy Kopp will locate resources; Mrs. Coe will make follow-up contacts and visits to identified resources
6. Arrangements will be made for Mrs. Johnson to see a physician and to be assessed by a physical therapist to determine the extent of deterioration and what steps can be taken to retard deterioration and/or restore higher levels of functioning.	Mrs. Coe; Judy Kopp

Arrangement	*Who Is Responsible?*
7. A family meeting will be held to discuss whether Mrs. Johnson should remain in the Coe home and to improve family communication, understanding, and higher support.	Family members; Judy Kopp

   This agreement will be reviewed on <u>Nov. 11 (2 weeks from now)</u> in
   (date)

order to plan the next steps. A new contract will be written to reflect the next goal, which will relate to whether services will be sought for Mrs. Johnson to make it possible for her to continue living with the Coes without disrupting the family or whether placement outside the home will be pursued.

Date <u>Oct. 28, 1997</u>   Signatures   *Judy Kopp*

                                               Mrs J Coe

                                               Mr J Coe

F R A M E
14

WRITING A CONTRACT

Through implementation of the initial contract with the Coes, the worker learned a considerable amount about the services, and the lack of services, for the elderly in their community. This information is summarized below. After reading the information, write a second contract. The second contract should include both the Coes and Mrs. Johnson as active participants. Think carefully about the information summarized. Recall the roles you could play if you were the worker and consider where changes are needed before completing the second contract. Also, consider the contents of the first contract. Write your contract on a separate piece of paper, following the model contract (see Figure 8.3) in Frame 15. Feel free to make changes in the model contract to fit the needs of this particular situation. You might want to develop two separate contracts: one between the worker and Mrs. Johnson and another between the worker and Mr. and Mrs. Coe.

Information and Activities Following First Contract

The worker met twice with Mrs. Johnson; the worker also observed her in the home just before and during dinner (the times when Mrs. Johnson is not in her room). Mrs. Johnson was willing to talk with the worker and seemed to enjoy and appreciate the worker's attention and interest. The worker talked with Mrs. Johnson about her past and current situation. Mrs. Johnson enjoyed reminiscing; she told the worker about her family, their struggles and joys living on a farm, her friends, and the kinds of things she used to enjoy doing. The worker learned that one reason Mrs. Johnson spends increasing amounts of time in her room is the tension among other family members and her sense that she is in the way. Although it is true that she has regressed, she also tries not to get in the family's way and wants to avoid becoming involved in their conflicts. It will be important for the worker to meet jointly with the Coes and Mrs. Johnson to give them an opportunity to express their feelings.

Mrs. Johnson agreed to see a doctor. The doctor confirmed that there seemed to be some deterioration in her mental functioning; however, she is alert most of the time and is able to care for herself. She has some chronic medical problems, such as arthritis, stomach pains, and dizziness. She is losing some of her hearing and needs stronger glasses. She needs to see a doctor regularly. Because of dizziness and her advanced age, she does need some help getting in and out of the bathtub and in exercising her hands and fingers, where the arthritis is worsening. Thus, a health aide would be helpful for 1 to 2 hours, five days a week. Arrangements were made with the doctor for a referral to the Visiting Nurses Association. Visiting Nurses made a home visit but said they could not provide service because this was a chronic case; they cannot handle additional long-term cases because of a shortage of home health aides. The agency that has a health aide said their caseload was too large to accept a new consumer right now. The best they could do was to place Mrs. Johnson on the waiting list; however, the list is quite long.

The worker also contacted the Senior Citizens Center for a volunteer to drive Mrs. Johnson to the doctor and make arrangements for Mrs. Johnson to participate in their daily lunch and afternoon program. Transportation services were cut drastically as a result of funding cuts, and it does not appear likely they will be able to transport Mrs. Johnson. The worker tried two other agencies but could not arrange regular transportation for Mrs. Johnson. The worker also contacted a local church of the denomination Mrs. Johnson used to attend. Church officials agreed to send a representative to meet Mrs. Johnson and see if they could arrange transportation for her so that she could attend church on Sundays.

Mrs. Johnson is not currently covered by health insurance, so the worker investigated the possibility of her receiving medical insurance coverage through the state Medicaid program. The program is complex and follow-up will be needed.

There seems to be a shortage of persons available to serve the elderly in their own homes. If this gap in services continues, a number of persons will be forced to enter nursing or boarding homes who could otherwise remain in their own homes if limited help were available. Also, there are no regular transportation services for the elderly.

Mrs. Coe looked into local nursing homes. She was surprised to find out how expensive they are. She visited the least expensive home and was shocked at the lack of attention and care, the offensive odor, and the general dilapidation and poor maintenance of the home. Even this home is beyond the Coes' budget. Mrs. Coe is contacting the state welfare office and Social Security to see if Mrs. Johnson is eligible for any state or federal assistance. At this time, Mrs. Coe is discouraged yet open to exploring the possibilities for services within their home so that Mrs. Johnson will not have to move to a nursing home or boarding home. The worker thought of other tasks that Mrs. Johnson could do around the house to help the family, such as keeping kitchen cabinets in order and preparing part of the family's dinner before the other family members return from work and school.

Turn to Answer 126 on page 632 after completing your contracts

F R A M E

15

This agreement is a contract between _____ and _____
                                              (consumer)   (worker)

of the _____.
                    (agency)

The purpose of this agreement is _____

_____

_____

In order to accomplish the above goal(s), the following objectives/arrangements will be met/made/carried out by the persons specified below:

         Arrangements   *Who Is Responsible?*

1. _____   _____

2. _____   _____

3. _____   _____

This agreement shall be reviewed on _____ in order to plan the next steps in
                                                   (date)

the completion of the goal. The total period of time for the accomplishment of the goal is from _____to _____.

Upon successful completion of this agreement, _____

_____

_____

Date _____   Signatures _____

                                               _____

                                             _____

FIGURE 8.3.   A Sample Contract Form

F R A M E

16

ENCOURAGING CONSUMER PARTICIPATION

Since many of you will work with consumers who are not voluntarily seeking help, we want to include some suggestions for working with involuntary consumers. Consumers who are not requesting help are not actually consumers; rather, they are *resisters,* meaning that they do not want to work with you or the system that employs you, or they are *applicants,* which means that they are open to working with you but are not yet committed to a joint helping effort.[6] Given these definitions, a person is

_____
[6]Gambrill, *Casework.*

not a consumer until he and the worker have agreed on goals. One definition of a resistant consumer is a consumer who does not respond as we would like him to respond. When you are working with a consumer who is not committed to changing, does not seek help, or has had negative experiences with past helpers, it is a challenge to understand why there is resistance to change and to develop ways to involve such a person in working with you. The ideas that follow are relevant for "motivating" and increasing the participation of all consumers, including those who voluntarily seek help.

Too often, we think of motivation as a characteristic. Motivation is not a given personality trait but a transactional state regulated by the worker, the consumer, and the consumer's environment.[7] Thus the challenge is to build interactions and an environment that support consumer motivation. Resistance may be a way of dealing with anxiety arising from threats to personal autonomy experienced in asking for, or being required to receive, help. Further, consumers may feel that change will create more problems than it alleviates. Apparent resistance may also reflect confusion caused by ambiguous goals or an absence of agreement between worker and consumer goals. The level of motivation as conceived here depends on the consumer's desire for an outcome.

Clear, agreed-on goals are an important component of motivation to change. The goals must promise a reward that exceeds the cost of change. Changing long-established patterns or making changes not supported by persons close to the consumer is difficult. Initial resistance to change is common even when consumers intellectually agree that they want to change. Remember, for most consumers, interaction with human service workers is a novel experience. Moreover, noncompliance with treatment plans is a problem in all fields. Many patients of physicians, for instance, do not carry out recommended treatment plans. Thus, motivating consumer participation is a challenge in all helping roles. The suggestions presented here may prove helpful and may stimulate you to develop additional ideas as you work with resistant consumers.

Factors that affect motivation and consumer participation include cultural variables, prior experiences with helping systems, support from and attitudes of family members and significant others, attitudes about receiving help, economic constraints, and the consumer's perception of the problem and its resolution. Too often, workers fail to consider obstacles to service—the costs to consumers, especially those with limited material resources. These costs include long waits for service, transportation difficulties, child care, and work commitments. For some consumers, receiving service requires the investment of a whole day. Providing concrete services such as food, housing, child care, and transportation not only allows the consumer to receive needed services but also frees the consumer to focus attention on less urgent problem areas.

We suggest that workers ask themselves the following questions about consumers and their life situations when assessing consumer motivation and resistance:[8]

1. What is the consumer's level of anxiety regarding the problem(s), the services, or the relationship with the worker? What are the specific sources of anxiety or lack of anxiety?

---

[7] Janet Moore-Kirkland, "Mobilizing Motivation: From Theory to Practice," in *Promoting Competence in Clients,* Anthony Maluccio, ed. (New York: Free Press, 1981).
[8] Moore-Kirkland, "Mobilizing Motivation."

2. How does the consumer perceive the consequences of achieving the goals of the change effort?

3. What are the effective motivators in the consumer's life at this time?

4. What practical factors might impede change?

The initial goals in all helping situations are consumer involvement and worker understanding of the consumer's perception of the situation. The relationship-building skills and interviewing skills described in previous lessons are designed to help achieve these initial goals. Building positive expectations on the part of the consumer is important for engaging the consumer in positive change efforts. You can do this by describing successes with other consumers, expressing your positive expectations that the consumer can change the situation, encouraging the consumer to describe past successes, and pointing out factors that predict successful outcomes. One such factor is the consumer's belief that he or she will be successful.

A key factor in ensuring participation is consumer involvement in determining goals and service plans. The more that consumers feel that they have selected the goal and the plan, the more committed they will be to implementing them. Other suggestions for increasing consumer participation include defining small, achievable goals, including clear goal definitions, and clarifying mutual expectations, as described in this lesson. In addition, it is helpful to give the consumer rationales for each step in the service plan and opportunities to practice new behaviors with you.

Developing incentives and opportunities for positive feedback is also important. For example, it is helpful to call the consumer a day or two after the plan is to be initiated to ask how things are going and to praise the consumer for initial efforts. If the consumer has encountered problems, you may be able to help resolve them over the phone. Otherwise, if a consumer runs into a problem, the consumer may drop the plan, at least until the next contact is made with you. The consumer may also cease contact with you, feeling embarrassed about the initial "failure." Once a change has occurred, assuming it is a positive change, you can expect natural rewards or reinforcers for continuing the new behavior. Initially, though, when change is most difficult, planned support is indicated. When possible, involve family members and friends in supporting change efforts. Natural support groups and/or support from other consumers with similar problems are effective in encouraging change efforts. When consumers report back to others, they are likely to carry out the service plan to which they are committed.

One consumer who was preparing for release from prison decided that in order to survive outside he needed to reduce his negative, angry reactions to authority figures such as police. He kept a diary of his reactions (thoughts, feelings, and behaviors) to prison guards, and when a change tactic was introduced to reduce his "hate thoughts," he put his daily diary under the worker's office door every morning. This was an opportunity to confirm his carrying out his plan and for indirect, daily feedback from the worker on his progress, for the worker highly commended the consumer for the diary and the changes he was reporting.

Before initiating the plan, it is important to describe to consumers any potential negative outcomes or roadblocks in order to prepare them for possible setbacks and reduce feelings of discouragement. You might predict, for example, that the first few steps of a plan, and especially the first few days, will be the most difficult. While change may be slow initially, the pace of change will increase over time. For example, a child may initially respond to structured expectations with more negative behaviors to test the new arrangement before accepting and adapting to it.

Another way to motivate consumers is to describe others who have experienced and overcome similar problems. Consumer support groups can also be helpful motivators in providing positive models of consumers who achieved their goals. You can describe such models, arrange for a consumer to talk with a successful model, or show videotapes of persons describing how they handled a similar situation. It may also be helpful to provide written instructions and a checklist to keep track of accomplishments and problems and to serve as a reminder to consumers to carry out their plans.

Without the consumer's commitment to the plan, there is little chance of its success. The consumer should be comfortable with the plan and feel some confidence in being able to carry it out. Plans that are effective for some consumers may not be helpful for others, especially if they include activities that the consumer has not agreed to. It is important to engage consumers in developing creative approaches to change.

Evaluating the Helping Process

This lesson is designed to provide you with an understanding of how to evaluate the helping process. Evaluation is usually described as the final component in a helping framework, but evaluation begins when you first meet a consumer. You evaluate the effects of helping all the time and use preliminary results to develop new plans with a consumer. Evaluation serves as a basis to determine problem severity, when to change interventions and when to terminate the helping process, to demonstrate your effectiveness to the general public, and to improve your practice.

Goal

To provide human service workers with a method of evaluating their practice with consumers that will increase their helpfulness and provide a guide for what steps to take next.

Learning Activities

To accomplish this goal, we will:

1. Examine the role of evaluation in the helping process.
2. Apply an approach to evaluation that you can use as a basis for assessing your work with consumers.
3. Demonstrate how to record and graph data about consumer progress.
4. Explore several applications of this process and conduct and evaluate the outcome of your own self-change project.

FRAME

1

EVALUATION IS HELPING; HELPING IS EVALUATION

Continual evaluation is an integral part of the helping process. It is possible to evaluate your efforts to promote change with each consumer as long as you specify desired outcomes and monitor movement toward the achievement of the outcomes. Through monitoring, you should know whether the service plan is working or whether the plan needs modification.

Evaluation has different meanings for different human service workers.[1] The evaluative information of interest to you may depend on your role in an agency. As an agency director, you may be interested in the number of consumers served each month, the number of hours worked, and the cost of providing services. As a human service worker, you will be more interested in measuring the effectiveness of services. At times, you use your best guess by asking the consumer how things are going or asking your supervisor for an estimate of your progress. While workers may rely, in part, on intuition and consumer estimates of progress, it is possible to measure the effects of service plans on a day-to-day basis. This approach will provide additional help and information to the consumer.

Without ongoing evaluation, it is difficult to know whether you are helping. If change seems to be occurring, you may not know what actually *is* helping the consumer. At times your work is frustrating and difficult. Frustration is increased when it is not clear *what* work makes a difference to those you are helping. The use of data to determine the achievement of desired outcomes can change your experience as a practitioner. You will find that it is encouraging and reinforcing for consumers to see change from day to day. Consumers are excited by the opportunity to see the results of their efforts. As a worker, you will find that your plan does make a difference, and that is a positive experience. If desired changes are not occurring, it is possible to realize this within a couple of days after the plan is initiated. If you estimate how the helping process is progressing according to the consumer's verbalized impressions, it generally takes longer to know whether change is actually occurring.

Monitoring change needs to be integrated with the case plan, ensuring continual feedback on progress. Consumers are asked to keep records of their progress through diaries, self-anchored rating scales, or counting the frequency of a behavior. Change may also be measured by using standardized tests and scales. Monitoring their own behavior, thoughts, or feelings may become part of the consumer's responsibility and part of the contract. Some consumers will change through the use of self-monitoring alone.[2] Numerous studies have shown that observing their own behavior closely enough to monitor its frequency provides consumers and workers with new information and insights about the behavior.

For example, a consumer whose presenting problem was feelings of depression, lack of assertive behavior with parents, and feelings of anger toward her parents was able to keep many records. She kept a diary in which she wrote what happened just before and after she experienced angry feelings. She also kept track of the times she was not assertive with her parents. In addition to the diary, she rated her feelings of depression on a scale ranging from 1 (which represented her lowest feelings) to 5 (symbolizing her highest or best feelings). This case is included in Chapter 9 as an example of cognitive behavior therapy.

---

[1] M. J. Austin et al., *Evaluating Your Agency's Programs* (Beverly Hills, Calif.: Sage, 1982).

[2] Judy Kopp, "Self-Monitoring: A Literature Review of Research and Practice," *Social Work Research and Abstracts* 24, 4 (Winter 1988): 8–20.

FRAME

2

SPECIFYING BEHAVIORS AND OUTCOMES

The process of evaluating the results of service plans begins with how well the target behaviors and desired outcomes are specified. If you and the consumer are clear about what is to be changed and the expected outcome, it is not difficult to evaluate change in the targeted behavior, thought, feeling, or situation. Your criteria for successful helping are your defined goals or desired outcomes. Ideally, these criteria should be written down as part of a clear contract. In fact, you should consider evaluation criteria before you draft the contract, in order to build into the contract the criteria for success and the bases for determining the attainment of the goals.

Recall Mrs. Noel and her son (described in Lesson 2). The initial goal was to change Mrs. Noel's perception of her youngest child. Therefore, the specified and measurable target was to increase her awareness of the good things he did by asking her to observe and record them. If your goals were also to improve the relationship between mother and son and to ensure that his mother praised him for positive behavior, the specified target would be the number of positive responses the mother gave to the son. You would help Mrs. Noel increase her compliments, positive statements, and attention to her son. By asking her to record the number of compliments and "Thank you's" to her son, you would have a record at the end of the intervention period that would tell you the extent to which the goal of positive interactions was achieved.

You and the consumer define the degree of change, as well as the change target. In some instances, the mother might want to eliminate all "No's" or perhaps cut the "No's" in half and increase the positive statements. It is important to be clear about the degree or level of change desired so that the consumer has a criterion for success and so that both parties know when the change process is successful. The criterion or goal may be changed once the helping plan is initiated; however, be specific and clearly operationalize each change.

The consumer is empowered in the assessment and change process by collecting the information—the data—herself. Monitoring as an empowerment process is explained more fully in Frame 4.

FRAME

3

SOURCES FOR MEASURING OUTCOMES

In evaluating outcomes with consumers, there are different sources of measurement:

1. Worker determination of change.
   a. The worker may simply review case notes and, with the consumer, estimate goal achievement.
   b. The worker may verify the extent of change with others who work or live with the consumer.
   c. The worker may observe change by observing consumers in their natural environments.

d. The worker may discuss estimated change with his or her supervisor.

2. Actual measurement of target and change over time by worker and/or consumer.

Actual measurement of changes or outcome by the consumer and/or worker is the preferred way to determine effectiveness. Single-case design is useful for assessing and measuring change.[3] When using a single-case design, it is necessary to measure the target behavior before intervention. This is called a *baseline.* How often is Mrs. Noel complimenting her child or saying "No" *before* attempts are made to change these interactions? The baseline is used as a means of assessing whether the service plan is working. If the first plan is not working in that no measurable change in the number of positive and negative statements can be found, it is time to try another plan. There are times when a change is initiated without first measuring the extent of the problem (without a baseline). In such cases, you cannot be as certain whether the change that was initiated had an effect on the problem, but you can, with data, follow whether the goal is reached. You can also periodically collect follow-up data to determine whether the consumer maintains the change.

F R A M E

4

MONITORING PROCEDURES

The record of the target behavior, thought, or feeling is continued after the plan begins. Usually the *record is kept by the consumer,* since the primary interest is changing behaviors in the consumer's natural environment. Parents may monitor themselves (keep a record of their behaviors), a child may record his own behavior, or each may keep a separate record of the same behavior. If both parent and child monitor the child's behavior, you have a check on the accuracy of the child's record. But be careful not to allow monitoring another's behavior to be a way for one family member to impose additional control over another. In general, it is preferable for the person who needs to change to monitor herself. In fact, a review of the literature reveals that self-monitored data overall is reliable and accurate.[4] If someone else is going to monitor a consumer, be certain there is agreement to and clear understanding of the arrangement, and, after monitoring begins, check with the consumer to be certain the monitoring arrangement is not creating a problem.

The following example illustrates an evaluation format that can be used by consumers and helpers:

> An African American mother who was supporting her children on a small public assistance grant asked to join a parent group being held at the public assistance and child welfare office. The group was created to teach innovative approaches to providing parental support. Each group member pinpointed their concerns.
>
> Mothers with little formal education can keep excellent records of their children's progress in changing targeted behaviors. This mother wanted her teenage daughter to pick up the clothes she consistently left strewn around the house.

---

[3]Martin Bloom and Joel Fischer, *Evaluating Practice: Guidelines for the Accountable Professional* (Englewood Cliffs, N.J.: Prentice-Hall, 1982).

[4]Kopp, "Self-Monitoring."

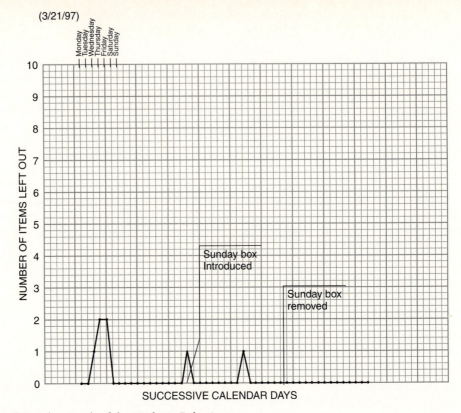

FIGURE 8.4. Graph of the Mother's Behavior

First, the mother recorded the number of items of clothing left around the house each day. Thus she had a daily record of how frequent or serious the problem was (how often clothes were left out each day) before she tried to change the behavior. This baseline provided the basis for determining whether change efforts were working. The change procedure used in this case was the Sunday Box.5 (A "Sunday Box" is a cardboard box positioned in a convenient place in the house.) Every time an item of clothing was left out, it was placed in the Sunday Box, presumably by the first person who found it. Usually the mother noticed the strewn items and placed them in the box. Each Sunday, the box was opened and the clothes were returned to the owner. Items that found their way into the Sunday Box could not be claimed until the following Sunday. The mother recorded and charted the number of items she left out each day, as well as the items left around the house by her daughter. She charted the daily records on graphs designed to show daily frequencies of behaviors.

---

[5]O. R. Lindsley, Educational Administration, University of Kansas, Lawrence, Kansas. Personal communication.

As you can see from the graph in Figure 8.4, the problem persisted during the baseline period (before the Sunday Box was introduced). The problem was solved one week after introducing the Sunday Box. When asked what happened that week, the mother said her daughter had left out a pair of slacks that she wanted to wear to a high school football game on Friday night. Since the slacks were left out on a Thursday and were in the Sunday Box on Friday, she could not wear the slacks to the game. The mother thought that this experience made an impression that led her daughter to put her clothes away on a regular basis. While leaving clothes out is an objective, observable behavior, it is also possible to monitor and record thoughts and feelings.

The record kept by this mother is shown in the table on page 379. The mother computed the rate by recording during an eight-hour period on weekends (when her daughter was home for more hours) and a four-hour period on weekdays (when her daughter was in school). Thus, by converting hours to minutes she recorded the behavior for 240 minutes on weekdays and 480 minutes on weekends. To convert the record into a rate, she divided the number of items left around the house by the number of minutes she recorded or observed the behavior. Since the data are converted into a rate, you can compare different time periods.

If the behavior occurs frequently and fairly consistently throughout the day, a time sample can be used, such as an hour each day. This makes recording less demanding yet gives accurate information. Initially it is wise to record for a longer period of time to be certain that the behavior occurs throughout the day. A one-hour time sample would provide a fairly accurate picture if the behavior occurs consistently throughout the day.

This mother actually converted the number of items left out each day into a rate by dividing the number of items by the number of minutes in the observation period. The rate is included on the table. She also used the standardized daily graph paper shown in Frame 7, page 383. The standardized paper was used because the mother was a member of a mothers' group. Each member was monitoring her children's behaviors. Using the same graph paper made it easy for group members to share their data. This paper is unique because it includes 20 calendar weeks and therefore is useful for records kept over several months. However, because the behavior of leaving clothes out was not a high frequency behavior and because we are mainly interested in the total number of items left out each day, converting the data to a daily rate does not give us additional information. Therefore, the graphs included here are less complex. They are designed to show the total number of items left out each day for mother and daughter (columns 3 and 5 on the table). The mother's behavior is graphed for you (Figure 8.4). A blank graph is included to give you an opportunity to graph the number of items the daughter left out each day (Figure 8.5).

Take the number of times the daughter left clothes out each day and place a dot on the blank graph. The first day, she left out four items of clothing, so place a dot for the first day at 4 on the vertical axis on the first Monday. At the top of the graph, the first week at the left end of the graph is marked with Monday, Tuesday, Wednesday, Thursday, Friday, Saturday, and Sunday representing the days of the week. Find the day of the week on which the record begins and place a 4 on the perpendicular line for that day. The first day was a Monday, March 21, 1997, so find the Monday line. Each perpendicular line represents a day of the week. Each horizontal line represents the number of times the behavior occurred per day.

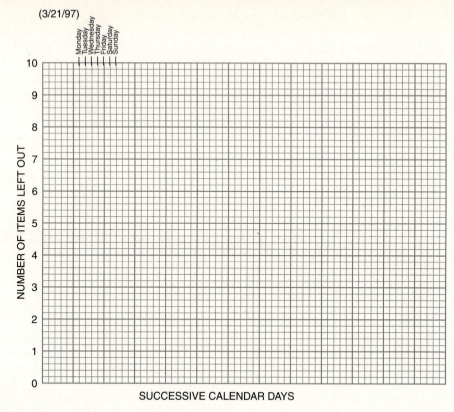

FIGURE 8.5.   Graphing the Daughter's Behavior

This mother actually recorded items left out by her three daughters. One daughter left items out every day until the Sunday Box was introduced and she experienced losing items she wanted. The mother decided to include herself so that each family member had the same expectations placed on them to follow a household rule. The mother kept a baseline for 18 days. Usually we recommend a baseline for a week to two weeks, depending on how variable the behavior is and on how quickly the consumer wants to begin the modification plan. You can see that the Sunday Box was an effective plan for changing the family members' behavior. Once the plan was used consistently and the daughters knew they would lose an item for a week, they changed their behavior fairly rapidly. The mother removed the Sunday Box and continued the record for two additional weeks to make certain the change was maintained. The last two weeks are a follow-up stage. Since our main concern is the continuance or maintenance of desired changes, follow-up is important. Sometimes maintenance is more lasting if the plan or procedure is removed slowly or phased out. For example, clothes might have been returned every other day for a while before the box was completely removed. In this situation, however, the change was maintained without slowly fading out the planned arrangement or consequence.

When you have finished charting the daughter's behavior, turn to **Answer 127 on page 633** and compare your graph to see if you charted the data correctly. Correct any errors you made—use a pencil so that you can erase.

| | | ———— Mother ———— | | ——— Daughter——— | |
Date	Time in Minutes*	Clothes Out	Rate	Clothes Out	Rate
3/21	240	0	0	4	.017
3/22	480	0	0	0	0
3/23	480	1	.002	1	.002
3/24	240	2	.008	1	.004
3/25	240	2	.008	1	.004
3/26	240	0	0	0	0
3/27	240	0	0	2	.008
3/28	240	0	0	1	.004
3/29	480	0	0	0	0
3/30	480	0	0	0	0
3/31	240	0	0	0	0
4/1	240	0	0	1	.004
4/2	240	0	0	0	0
4/3	240	0	0	0	0
4/4	240	0	0	0	0
4/5	480	0	0	0	0
4/6	480	0	0	1	.002
4/7	240	1	.004	1	.004
4/8	240	0	0	1	.004
4/9	240	0	0	0	0
4/10	240	0	0	1	.004
4/11	240	0	0	3	.012
4/12	480	0	0	2	.004
4/13	480	0	0	2	.004
4/14	240	0	0	0	0
4/15	240	0	0	0	0
4/16	240	1	.004	0	0
4/17	240	0	0	0	0
4/18	240	0	0	0	0
4/19	480	0	0	0	0
4/20	480	0	0	0	0
4/21	240	0	0	0	0
4/22	240	0	0	0	0

Note: Data were collected for two more weeks through 5/6 with continued use of the Sunday Box. Box was then discontinued, and mother continued to monitor the behavior. On 5/24 client reported that all rates had remained zero during the past two weeks.
*4 hr = 240 min; 8 hr = 480 min.

Records such as this are kept by helpers, parents, friends, and spouses. Most frequently, however, consumers keep their own records of their behaviors. This is called *self-monitoring* or *self-recording*. One important reason for using self-monitoring in evaluation is that many behaviors, thoughts, and feelings can be monitored regularly only by the individuals themselves. Since most of the behaviors of concern occur when the worker is not present, and since workers cannot reliably measure the thoughts and feelings of others, often only the consumer can keep the daily record.

Another important reason for using self-monitoring is that it can be empowering. Self-monitoring gives the consumers an active, important role in the assessment and service plan stages. It also provides information needed to evaluate how well an intervention is working and when an intervention needs to be changed to accomplish the desired outcome.[6]

Asking clients to record information about themselves increases their activity and sense of control in the assessment process while decreasing the aura of professional authority.[7] As the consumer and worker discuss information collected by the consumer, they become collaborators in assessment and intervention planning, with the worker acting as a consultant rather than as a decision maker or advice giver. This transfer of responsibility to the consumer is an important step toward empowerment. Relatively powerless consumers who are initially suspicious of the worker's commitment to help them are not dependent on the "expert's" assessment of their situation. Instead, consumers become experts about themselves—the sources of the data on which the intervention plan is based.

The overall goal of empowerment is to help consumers who have been subjected to negative valuations and limited by barriers they had no role in creating (e.g., barriers created by racism) to perceive themselves as causal forces capable of bringing about a desired effect. Rather than giving aid to the consumer, the worker forms a collaborative, complementary relationship with the consumer that helps prevent the reinforcement or extension of the consumer's feelings of powerlessness.[8]

Commonly, workers make their assessment of a consumer's situation based solely on the consumer's verbal report. Consumers' verbal reports are indirect sources of information because they are based on recall that is vulnerable to error.[9] On the other hand, self-observation or self-monitoring is a direct information source that can increase the accuracy of assessment information. Clearly, information recorded while an event is experienced complements self-exploration during counseling sessions. Knowledge is a source of power; the new knowledge and heightened insight that consumers experience through focusing their attention on a particular dimension of their lives is unquestionably empowering. Through close observation, consumers acquire new information about themselves, their relationships with others, and the relationships between their behavior and their environment.

FRAME
5

RECORDING FOR EVALUATION

To record, we need a clearly pinpointed or defined target. The target must be clear to the recorder in order for the record to be consistent across time (day to day) and across situations so that the same phenomenon is recorded each time it occurs. It is important to decide who will record occurrences and how the record will be kept.

---

[6]Kopp, "Self-Observation."

[7]Kopp, "Self-Observation."

[8]Barbara Solomon, *Black Empowerment: Social Work in Oppressed Communities* (New York: Columbia University Press, 1976).

[9]Dean Hepworth and Joann Larsen, *Direct Social Work Practice: Theory and Skills,* 2d ed. (Chicago, Dorsey Press, 1986).

The simpler the recording approach, the more likely that the record will be kept. Minimal time should be expended in recording. Recording can be simplified by using golf wrist counters, armbands with beads for counting, masking tape attached to the hand, or knitting-needle counters attached to pencils. The proximity of the recording device to the place where the behavior generally occurs can simplify the task and serve as a reminder to record the target behavior. The data are helpful only if they are used to assess change. Thus, *data must be graphed daily in order to analyze progress.*

The Sunday Box is a simple, clear example of a change project. The results were helpful in improving family interactions by removing a source of annoyance and tension. Further, the consumer learned some new skills for helping herself and her children. She experienced a sense of accomplishment by carrying out the project, seeing the change charted, and sharing the information with the helper and other group members.

FRAME

6

SELF-MONITORING

The following data, collected by a student, offers another opportunity to practice charting as part of a self-monitoring project. A good way to learn more about self-monitoring and changing behaviors is to select a target you would like to modify. For example, you might try counting your open and closed questions in conversations with friends in order to meet the personal goal of using more open-ended questions.

The student who kept the following record was a quiet person in class and was concerned that she would not be able to speak out effectively and advocate for consumers with her colleagues in staff and community meetings. She decided to begin learning to talk in groups by increasing her verbal participation in classes.

Date	Time	Class	Number of Times Talked in Class	Rate
11/19	9:30–10:20	H.S 330	0	
11/21	"	"	1	
11/23	Thanksgiving Holiday			
11/26	9:30–10:20	H.S. 330	0	
11/28	"	"	0	
11/30	"	"	0	
12/3	"	"	1	
12/5	"	"	0	
12/7	"	"	0	
12/10	"	"	1	
12/12	"	"	2	
12/14	"	"	3	

The student kept the record for five class days (through November 30) without attempting to change her behavior. She then decided to set a goal of saying one thing during each class; she tried to plan what she would say the night before. This worked the first day, but it was not a strong enough plan, for she returned to her silence on December 5 and 7. She then approached the instructor and asked her to look in her direction more often during class and to call on her at least once. This seemed to help, and she was able to practice talking in class. (This is the portion of the table included here.) After one week of being called on, she changed her plan. This time, she announced to two friends in her class that she was committed to speaking in class. She asked them to help remind her by glancing in her direction. This commitment to her peers was a strong incentive for the student, who wanted to show that she could succeed with her personal change plan. Once she gained experience speaking in class and confidence that she had something to contribute, it was not difficult for her to continue participating in class discussions. She then worked on talking to supervisors and speaking out in other groups.

In order to test your understanding of the monitoring process, convert the number of times that the student talked into rates and chart them on the sample graph (see Figure 8.6). Compare your rates and your graph to those in the answer.

Turn to Answer 128 on page 634

FRAME

7

A SELF-MONITORED PROJECT

The best way to know what it feels like to be a consumer is to experience some of the situations that consumers experience, such as applying for Food Stamps or public assistance. Some writers have conducted in-depth studies of consumers, and these accounts have been most informative.[10]

If you want to experience the sense of discovery that comes from learning about yourself and you want to see how difficult it is to maintain consistent records, try self-monitoring. You will learn not only the positives and problems of monitoring but also more about yourself, and you will have an opportunity to change something in your life that is important to you.

For example, one woman wanted a male friend to phone her more often. She felt that she was always calling him, which perhaps decreased his reasons for calling her. So she monitored her calls to him and his calls to her and found that her "hunch" was true. In an effort to increase his calls to her, she decreased the number of calls she made to him.

A man who had recently stopped seeing his girlfriend reported that his frequent thoughts about her were interfering with his work. He counted the number of "Susan thoughts" he had each day for a week and then initiated a plan. Every time he thought about Susan, he wrote her name 50 times. This became so bothersome that he quickly gave up his "Susan thoughts." And his work productivity increased.

---

[10]Susan Sheehan, *Is There No Place on Earth for Me?* (New York: Vintage, 1982); Sharon R. Curtin, *Nobody Ever Died of Old Age* (Boston: Little, Brown, 1972); and Jonathan Kozal, *Rachael and Her Children: Homeless Families in America* (New York: Fawcett Columbine, 1988).

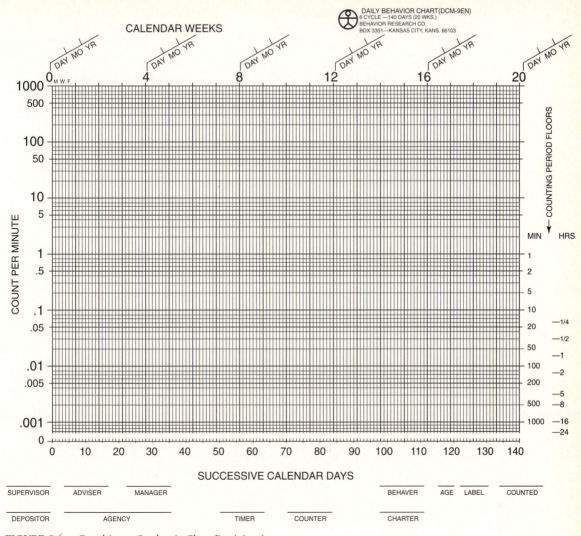

FIGURE 8.6. Graphing a Student's Class Participation

We suggest that you try monitoring a behavior that you would like to change. You might consider a work-related behavior, such as using more open-ended questions. It is not necessary to monitor every conversation. Decide to monitor your questions (open and closed) for an hour or two at the same time every day. If you select a time when you generally engage in conversation, this time span will give you a substantial amount of data.

A table of work-related behaviors and consumer behaviors selected by human service students is shown below. Perhaps these examples will give you some ideas for your self-monitoring project; at any rate, they illustrate what others have chosen to monitor.

Consumer and Student Behaviors Pinpointed by Interns

	Consumer		Student	
	Behaviors to Increase	*Behaviors to Decrease*	*Behaviors to Increase*	*Behaviors to Decrease*
Academic	Relevant comments in class Classes attended	Comments without being called on Classes missed	Pages read Pages written	TV time Misspelled words
Tasks at home	Items of clothes washed Grocery shopping	Children left alone in house Unpaid bills	Take out garbage Cook dinner	Items of clothes left out Meals out
Job related	On time for appointments Appointments for job interviews	Minutes late Losses of temper	Praise to other workers Number of home visits Consumer contacts Clear desk each evening	Late written reports
Behaviors during interviews	Positive comments about self Express feelings New information Discuss sexual abuse	Complaints Excuses for not carrying out goals Deny sexual abuse	Open-ended questions Reflections Eye contact	Fidgets/pencil taps Interruptions Questions off the topic
Interpersonal behaviors	Compliments, kisses, invitations to spouse to share activities Verbal comments in group meetings Smiles Number of activities participated in	Critical comments to spouse (e.g., bed unmade) Nags to spouse and children False accusations	Compliments to others Phone calls to friends Initiate conversations in groups	Negative comments about friends Mumbles
Physical behaviors	Put on makeup Steps in dressing	Beers consumed Calories consumed	Miles jogged Positive self thoughts	Sweets eaten Negative thoughts (e.g., "I can't do that")

You have the basic information about recording. Determine the behavior, thought, or feeling you want to monitor. Clarify your definition of the target behavior to ensure that you count the same thing each time it occurs. Sometimes you need to try monitor-

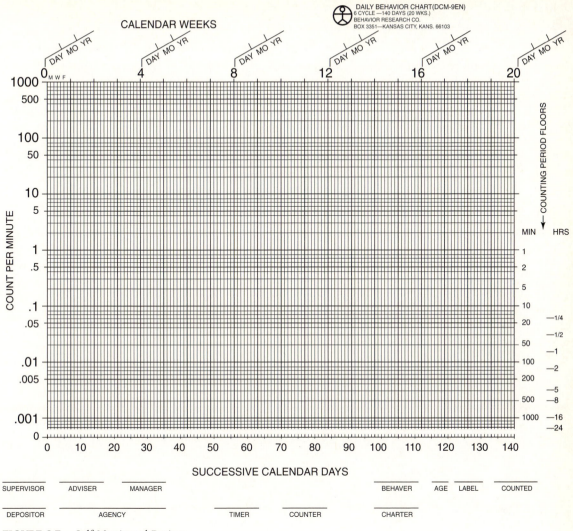

FIGURE 8.7.   Self-Monitored Project

ing to refine the definition. Devise a convenient form to record your information and make sure it includes a place for the date, the time period, the number of times the behavior occurred, and the rate. Try to think of a simple reminder to help you record information. Some people leave a piece of paper on the refrigerator if they are recording eating behaviors. Others put a piece of masking tape on one arm each morning on which they can make a hatch mark each time the behavior occurs. At the end of the day, transfer the data to the record sheet and place your daily rate on a graph. Use Figure 8.7 for your self-monitored project, or create your own graph. Share your personal change projects with classmates to increase your knowledge of practice evaluation.

FRAME

8

You now know how to monitor and graph data about your behavior, thoughts, and feelings or about the behavior of others. As you have learned, it is not difficult to evaluate your practice. In this lesson you used a single-case design. The particular design is called an *AB design: A* stands for the before phase, or the frequency with which a behavior occurs before a change plan is initiated, also called the *baseline; B* stands for the period during which a service plan is in effect. In the student's project there were four phases, since she tried three different change plans. Thus, her design was *ABCD*. Each time you change the plan, you begin a new phase. When one plan is not working, try something else until the consumer's goal is reached. If the first change plan works, you have a two-phase, or an *AB,* design. Whenever possible, include a third, or *C,* phase. This is a follow-up phase for when the change plan is discontinued, and you continue monitoring the behavior to be certain the change is maintained without special change tactics. Since you hope that changes will continue or that appropriate behavior will be maintained, you want to be certain that improvement does not stop when the intervention is discontinued.

Case Management

Case management is an approach to helping consumers receive a variety of services and resources. Specifically, the case manager is knowledgeable about a wide array of resources, is familiar with a number of service providers, ensures that the consumers actually receive the services, follows up to ensure that the services are meeting the consumer's needs, and helps consumers maximize their benefits from diverse services and systems.

Goal

To describe the case management approach to helping consumers maximize their use of services and resources in a community.

Learning Activities

To accomplish this goal, we will:

1. Define *case management*.
2. Identify how case management can be helpful in working with consumers.
3. Explain the important components of the case management approach.
4. Describe the common tasks performed by effective case managers.
5. Specify the purposes of case conferences.
6. Identify the relevant information and steps to follow for presentations in case conferences.

FRAME
1

DEFINING CASE MANAGEMENT

Rarely can one worker or one agency provide all the services a family needs. Providing effective services may involve a number of agencies. For example, an immigrant family without basic financial resources may require services from one agency for emergency food, another agency for housing, a third for monthly income, a fourth for clothing and furniture, a fifth to arrange for English-language classes, a sixth to meet the family's social and recreational needs, and a seventh for employment. Someone is needed to explain all these resources to the family, to see that the referrals are made, to coordinate among the services, and to follow up to see that the family's needs are met.

The service coordination component of case management is not new to the human service field. In fact, many of the skills needed were described in the lessons on brokering and advocacy. However, the emphasis of case management is the coordination of a number of services, rather than the direct provision of services.

Working with consumers, case managers are responsible for assessing needs and specifying desired outcomes, as well as arranging for others to provide the needed services. The role of a case manager is similar to that of a symphony conductor; the case manager orchestrates the delivery of diverse services from different agencies.

Case management includes at least six basic activities:[1]

1. Consumer identification and outreach
2. Assessment
3. Service planning
4. Linkages with needed services
5. Monitoring service delivery
6. Consumer advocacy

The first activity, consumer identification and outreach, includes the possibility of identifying consumers in need. For example, consumers may be found where people in need of help tend to congregate, such as soup kitchens. Outreach means reaching people who do not seek formal help. Although individual assessment is the same in all human service work, the case management approach emphasizes the use of community resources to meet the diverse needs of consumers.

Service planning is critical, for the case manager may be working with a number of different service providers and agencies. The manager must clearly define needs and desired outcomes, and must plan services to meet them. Additionally, the case manager must evaluate whether the services rendered are meeting the consumer's needs. Linkages with services are developed and maintained as a basis for assuring that the consumer's needs are met. The case manager may convene meetings of all the service providers to assess progress and ensure coordinated efforts. Monitoring service delivery is also important for ensuring that consumers' needs are met, that the appropriate services have been found, and that consumers are taking advantage of the services. It is the case manager who sees that consumers use and follow through with services. The use of written contracts to clarify which services will be provided and to offer a basis for evaluation is recommended.[2]

Thus a case manager is an evaluator (to assess the family's needs), a facilitator (to get needed services to a family), and a coordinator (to see that all operates smoothly and to serve as a central contact person for what may be a confused and weary consumer). The case manager is the main link with the consumer, assuring coordination, eliminating duplication of services, and making sure the consumer does not get caught in the gaps between services. Simply telling a consumer about a needed resource or making one referral phone call often is not enough. The more complex the

---

[1]Irene Shiffren Levine and Mary Fleming, *Human Resource Development: Issues in Case Management* (College Park: University of Maryland, Center of Rehabilitation and Manpower Services, 1984).
[2]Eileen Gambrill, *Casework: A Competency-Based Approach* (Englewood Cliffs, N.J.: Prentice-Hall, 1983).

social welfare system, the more facilitation, coordination, negotiation, and follow-up are needed. The scarcer the resources, the more advocacy is needed.

MODELS OF CASE MANAGEMENT

There are two general case management models: (1) the case manager who provides general counseling services plus other needed services available through her own agency and arranges for specialized services from other organizations and (2) the case manager who arranges, coordinates, and evaluates services provided but does not offer direct counseling services. Therefore the case manager may need both managerial and therapeutic skills.[3] Workers who are providing services may meet at the request of the case manager. Thus, skills in group process and communication, which are central to effective teamwork, also are central to the case management approach.[4]

Six case management models are used in the mental health field in working with mentally ill persons in the community.[5] Through these case management models, persons who are chronically mentally ill are able to live in their own communities rather than in institutions. In the *generalist model,* one case manager is responsible for all case management functions. The case manager provides all the services needed by one consumer, thus giving the consumer only one person to relate to and giving the worker an opportunity to practice a variety of skills and to function relatively autonomously. This model is useful in areas where varied services and large numbers of resources are not available. The *specialist model,* on the other hand, is a team operation in which each team member offers a specialized service to the same consumer.

Using the *therapist–case manager model,* the case manager serves as the consumer's counselor *and* provides the other case management functions. The consumer receives formal counseling and auxiliary services. This model may be appropriate in areas where resources are limited, such as in rural communities. A limitation of this model is that the worker may focus time and energy on the provision of counseling at the expense of case management services.

The *family model* of case management recognizes that families are often the major resource for the mentally ill. When there is no formal case manager, families find or provide the needed services in order for a consumer to remain in the community and out of institutional placement. The case manager may help such families by providing information and support so that the family can more effectively serve as a major resource to the ill member.

The *psychosocial rehabilitation-center model* describes special facilities and services that an extended family might provide. These centers, such as Fountainhouse in New York and Independence Center in St. Louis, provide social support, housing, recreation, work, and opportunities to learn the skills needed to live successfully in the community.

---

[3]Anne V. Bertsche and Charles R. Horeji, "Coordination of Client Services," in Weisman, Epstein, and Savage, *Agency-Based Social Work.*
[4]Gambrill, *Casework.*
[5]Levine and Fleming, *Human Resource Development.*

The *supportive-care model* assumes that the support needed to maintain consumers in the community is available through neighbors. Citizens are given support for providing direct services to a consumer and for linking the consumer with other service. This model is used primarily in rural areas, though it has been used successfully in urban neighborhoods. Community members selected as supportive-care workers are assigned to consumers on a one-to-one basis. Their services are contracted through local human service programs, and they receive monthly supervision. There are also programs that use a *volunteer model*. Volunteers are given brief training and monthly group supervision. Committed volunteers may give consumers the support and attention they need to function in the community.

These six models of case management include functions carried out by individuals or teams, by counselors or case management specialists, by paid staff or volunteers, and by professional staff or indigenous, paraprofessional workers.

In child welfare settings, the worker using a case manager approach first assesses the home situation, especially the child's safety, to determine whether the child and his or her parents will receive services in their own home or whether a temporary out-of-home placement is required. If services are given in the home, the case manager defines goals with the parents and the child, identifies the activities to achieve each goal, and specifies a time frame in which each goal will be accomplished. The plan is written into a contract, which is signed by all participants. If the child is in an out-of-home placement, goals and tasks are also defined for the child and the foster care providers. All the participants are considered members of a case management team, which meets periodically to assess progress and modify the plan and the tasks as needed. The case manager arranges for needed services, such as a specialized assessment for a child with special problems, counseling services for the whole family, a parent support group, and tangible services such as Food Stamps and clothing. The worker arranges for all the services needed in order for the family to remain together or to be reunited and evaluates the family's progress.

FRAME
3

A team organization is used in the child welfare case management model and in the specialist model of case management; however, team members differ depending on which model is used. The child welfare model team consists of the worker, parents, other relatives if involved, foster care persons, and the child: the specialist team is composed solely of human service workers, each offering a specialized service.

Is this true or false? Circle the correct response. (True/False)

Turn to Answer 129 on page 635

FRAME
4

TASKS OF A CASE MANAGER

As coordinator, supervisor, manager, facilitator, and evaluator, the case manager keeps the process going. The manager helps the consumer negotiate complex systems. Consumers should be encouraged to handle as many tasks as they possibly can. This may include making direct contact with other service providers. It is always important to build on the consumer's strengths and to ensure that consumers do not rely on the worker to do tasks that they are capable of doing themselves. At the same time, when people experience crises, they may need special help until they can assume full responsibility for coordinating their daily lives. Case management is designed to (1) ensure timely delivery of needed services and (2) develop with consumers an overall service plan.

As a review and summary of the tasks of a case manager, listed below are 12 tasks, defined by a group of case coordinators:[6]

1. Complete the initial interviews with the client and his family to assess the consumer's eligibility for services.
2. Gather relevant and useful data from the consumer, family, and other agencies to formulate a psychosocial assessment of the consumer and his family.
3. Guide group discussions and decision-making sessions among relevant program representatives, the consumer, the family, and significant others to formulate goals and design an integrated intervention plan.
4. Monitor adherence to the plan and manage the flow of accurate information within the action system to maintain a goal orientation and coordination momentum.
5. Provide follow-up to the consumers and their families to speed identification of unexpected problems in service delivery and to serve as a general troubleshooter on behalf of the consumer.
6. Provide counseling and information to help the consumer and family in situations of crisis and conflict with service providers.
7. Provide ongoing emotional support to the consumer and family so that they can cope with problems and utilize complex services.
8. Document consumer progress and adherence to the plan.
9. Act as a liaison between consumer and family professionals, programs and informal resources involved with the plan, helping consumers express preferences and secure needed services.
10. Act as a liaison between programs to ensure the smooth flow of information and minimize conflict between subsystems.
11. Establish and maintain good public relations with resource systems and with persons in authority positions to mobilize resources for current and future consumers.
12. Perform effectively within your organization to be in a position to develop and modify policies and procedures affecting consumers.

It is clear that many of the skills presented earlier in this book—such as assessment, goal specification and planning, the use of written contracts, evaluation, advocacy, brokering and mediating, and working with groups—are important for effective case management. As a case manager, you will be a consultant to consumers, to their significant others, and to other workers through your help in designing and implementing service plans and through your input in evaluating the outcome of services and recommending next steps. It is important for case managers to understand how organizations function, how decisions are made, and how agency resources affect services and policies. Thus, knowledge of organizations as well as direct-service skills are important in carrying out the case management role.

---

[6]Gambrill, *Casework.*

For positive case management outcomes, it is necessary to respond quickly to requests for service; to develop strong relationships with consumers; to provide clear, feasible goals that are understood by all parties concerned; to make appropriate referrals; to respond quickly to service providers; to make frequent contacts with consumers; to provide service continuity from intake to follow-up; and to plan and conduct case conferences and consultations.

Most of these activities were described earlier. Before we describe case conferences and consultation, the following checklist provides a review of the key issues in carrying out the case management role.

Checklist for Reviewing Quality of Case Management[7]

_____ **1.** Clear objectives have been identified.

_____ **2.** A time limit has been established with each resource person.

_____ **3.** Each involved resource person has agreed to pursue specific objectives within the agreed-on time frame.

_____ **4.** Clear criteria are agreed on to evaluate progress.

_____ **5.** Each resource person has agreed to share needed data according to an agreed-on schedule.

_____ **6.** Each resource person has agreed to meet with you as necessary.

_____ **7.** A written agreement between each resource person and the social worker has been formed, signed, and distributed to other involved parties (as appropriate).

_____ **8.** Resources are selected that are most likely to offer effective services related to presenting concerns.

_____ **9.** Resources are selected that will complement one another in terms of reaching desired outcomes.

_____**10.** Each resource involved serves a needed function; that is, services do not duplicate one another.

_____**11.** Arrangements are made between the social worker and client to review and integrate activities and outcomes of involved resources as necessary.

_____**12.** Resources selected are those most accessible to clients and significant others (in terms of money and transportation) as well as most likely to offer effective service.

_____**13.** Steps are taken as necessary to encourage clients to seek out needed resources and to facilitate use of these resources.

FRAME
5

CASE CONFERENCES

As a worker in the human services, you are probably familiar with the activity of meeting with other workers and with your supervisor to discuss consumer problems and/or service plans. This kind of meeting, called a *case conference,* is one situation in

---

[7]Gambrill, *Casework,* p. 297.

which workers use their recording and reporting skills to share and manage information. These skills are described in Unit Four.

Case conferences involve workers, either within an agency or between different agencies, and provide opportunities for working together and sharing information on consumer-related problems. A case conference can serve one or more of the following purposes:

1. It may help clarify the consumer's situation and the behavior of a given consumer.
2. It may help in determining the best service plan.
3. It may help in setting up new service plans and in gaining support for effective plans.
4. It is a mechanism for coordinating services.

A case conference is called when a worker or a supervisor, working to clarify and evaluate a consumer's problem, sees the need to share information related to the assessment, the goal, or the service plan. The case conference in human service agencies provides an opportunity for workers to work together on consumer issues. If a young boy has been in trouble with the law and is not doing well in school, a case conference could be called between the probation office, the school social worker, and the teacher to clarify the boy's problem and seek to understand his behavior. Case conferences within agencies can also be used for peer supervision and feedback so that workers can acquire new ideas and support from colleagues in dealing with difficult situations. Periodic case conferences may be called by case managers to coordinate services, share information, and assess progress toward achievement of the consumer's desired outcomes.

A case conference may include service providers representing multiple disciplines or multiple services throughout your own agency or within a single unit of your agency. For example, if you work on a ward in a psychiatric hospital, a multidisciplinary case conference might be held including a nurse, a psychiatrist, the director of the unit, you, and a member of the consumer's family. Whenever possible, the conference should also include the consumer, whose cooperation is clearly important for achieving real change. Case conferences may also involve workers from other settings. For example, if you work in youth services, a case conference might include the school counselor or a teacher. If you work in a child welfare setting, a case conference may include you, the natural parents, the natural parents' counselor, and the child. If the child is in a placement outside her own home, the foster care providers would also participate in the conference. All participants are seen as a team working together to achieve the child's, the parents', and the agency's goals.

FRAME

List two activities that occur in case conference.

1.

2.

Turn to Answer 130 on page 635

FRAME

Summarizing Information at a Case Conference

At a case conference, you will have to (1) keep a record of the discussion; and (2) share information orally and in writing with other workers and with consumers. If you are working on a case that has been selected for discussion at a case conference, you will need to prepare a presentation. Whether you are asked to present your case orally or in writing, you will need to *review* the case, *summarize* the consumer's background, *explain* the problem, and present your *recommendations* for the case plan. Your summary should include the following items:

1. A statement of the consumer's problem
2. Your observations of the consumer
3. How you have been working with the consumer—the service plan to date
4. A summary of the results of any service delivered
5. The reasons this information is being shared with other workers and specific questions highlighting the problem areas that you would like others in the conference to help you in answering

When preparing the case summary, include only information that is important and necessary to an understanding of the situation. Give clear, specific, objective information, as well as relevant feelings and inferences. Do not be afraid to admit the problem areas. Other workers need to understand the problems you experienced so that the group can work together on solutions. As a case manager, your summary includes the goals and plans for other workers. If the other workers are present, they would share their own goals and progress; however, as the case manager, you would present the overall plan.

FRAME

8

Read the case summary below, then answer the questions in Frames 8–12.

Name of worker: Ms. Anne Harper

Date of report: April 5, 1996

1. Ms. Harold is totally disabled due to several mild strokes and an extremely disoriented mental condition. She is gentle and well meaning, but the least little thing puts her in a panic. At the present time, her condition seems to have worsened, and her train of thought wanders so rapidly that she cannot even complete one sentence without changing the subject. She continues to live alone, and while she keeps her house very neat and orderly, she continuously needs help in managing her affairs.

2. Ms. Harold needs adult protective services, health services, home-management services, and, sometimes, housing improvement services.

3. At the present time, Ms. Harold has been in a dither because her glasses have broken and she can hardly see to walk across the room without them. It is only the frames that are broken; however, she feels she needs her lenses changed, since they haven't been changed in many years and the lenses are inadequate. Since Ms. Harold has only her assistance grant to live on and has no friends or relatives able or willing to help her, it is difficult for her to pay for glasses, especially since the optometrist requires at least half the payment in advance. Ms. Harold also needs help in getting Food Stamps and getting her marketing done.

4. I cannot see any possibility of Ms. Harold's being completely able to function on her own. Mainly, we need to enlist the help of volunteers and various aides and assistants to help her to continue to function on a basic level.

5. We have been working toward getting her glasses and have made an appointment for July 10 with Dr. Jarrod Williams. Ms. Harold preferred to wait for this appointment, rather than go to a different eye doctor. We were able to get a $10 donation from the United Methodist Church toward the purchase of the glasses, and we have been promised $10 from our own emergency fund. I will also see if I can get another $10 from somewhere when the time comes for her to go to the doctor.

Check which of the following components of an effective case summary is included in the preceding summary.

_____ **a.** The worker's observation of the consumer

Turn to Answer 131 on page 635

_____ **b.** A clear statement of the consumer's problem

Turn to Answer 132 on page 635

_____ **c.** An explanation of the reasons for sharing this information with other workers

Turn to Answer 133 on page 635

FRAME

9

Does the case summary presented in Frame 8 include a summary of the results of any services provided by the worker? Check the correct response.

_____ **a.** Yes, in paragraph 2

Turn to Answer 134 on page 636

_____ **b.** Yes, in paragraph 3

Turn to Answer 135 on page 636

_____ **c.** Yes, in paragraph 4

Turn to Answer 136 on page 636

_____ **d.** Yes, in paragraph 5

Turn to Answer 137 on page 636

_____ **e.** No

Turn to Answer 138 on page 636

FRAME
10

Is there a tentative service plan (that is, one not fully worked out) included in the case summary presented in Frame 8? Check the correct response.

_____ Yes

Turn to Answer 139 on page 636

_____ No

Turn to Answer 140 on page 636

FRAME
11

Assuming that Ms. Harold's major problem is her inability to manage her affairs effectively, state below at least one question that the worker could use to gain help from other workers.

Turn to Answer 141 on page 636

FRAME
12

You should now have some ideas for rewriting this case summary to make it more effective for presentation at a case conference. In the space below, identify the five major components of a case presentation. You will need to invent some identifying information about Ms. Harold—for example, her address, age, race, and marital status. Such information is usually included in a written summary and is also appropriate in an oral report. Then write a more effective summary of this case.

1.

2.

3.

4.

5.

Turn to Answer 142 on page 637

Effective Case Conferences

In a case conference the focus is on what the workers, consumers, and significant others need to know in order to improve services to consumers. The meeting usually proceeds in the following steps:

1. The worker presents a summary of the case and the problem and raises specific questions.
2. The group discusses the case, asks questions, and makes observations and suggestions.
3. A member of the group sums up the discussion. The case presenter is asked whether the discussion provided any help in solving the problem or in thinking of new ways to help the consumer.
4. The meeting either ends or goes on to discuss another case. Usually, the worker who presented the case writes a short report of the session and enters it in the case record.

Remember, the case conference is really a formal way of managing and sharing information with other workers. Information is managed informally when you share it with other workers over the phone or talk to other workers during the course of the day. It is your responsibility to make sure that you share the information you collect with other human service workers at the appropriate times in order to gain new perspectives and thereby guarantee consumers the best services possible.

Case conferences with your supervisor and other workers are also common activities for planning and evaluating your work with consumers. In the case management model, when you are coordinating services from several agencies, conferences are essential. Through joint meetings, workers have opportunities to help one another, to put together the pieces of a common puzzle, and to compare and evaluate the outcomes of service plans.

CASE CONSULTATIONS

In the process of presenting material about a case, workers identify problems for which they seek consultation. The difference between a case conference and a meeting with a consultant is that case conference participants usually share the responsibility for the case, whereas a consultant is neither responsible for service provision nor an active participant in implementing the plan. The consultant is more like a knowledgeable visitor to the case. The consultant listens to the problem, gains an understanding of the total situation, and offers suggestions based on expertise.

In a sense, a case conference is similar to a joint consultation where several workers put their heads together to come up with ideas for helping. Sometimes workers confront difficult situations in which nothing they try seems to help. You may be able to resolve such difficult situations through outside advice or consultation. A consultant is generally a person who has considerable experience dealing with complex problems but does not know the consumer with whom you are working and does not have responsibility for providing direct services to the consumer.

Consultation may be given free through other workers, or an agency may pay someone to serve as a consultant. Consultation is probably not used often enough in the human services. Requesting help is a sign of strength and requires recognizing that there will be some situations in which you would benefit from assistance. Being too proud to request help only limits your potential success with a consumer. There may be instances in which you could handle the problem yourself, but a fresh opinion may give you new ideas and make your job easier. Moreover, consultations are stimulating learning experiences during which new ideas help to spark your own thinking.

Asking and answering the following questions may help you determine when a consultant would be helpful:

1. What does the consumer need and what am I trying to do?
2. What skills and resources are missing to do this job?
3. What problems are blocking the program?
4. What people might help most in this service situation?

Answering these questions helps you clarify your actions and the nature of the consumer's problem and may lead to seeking the help of another worker or an outside consultant. In many agencies, your supervisor will be the first person to contact. Together, you will discuss the problem and then decide which persons can further help.

If you determine that a consultant would be helpful, the following guidelines are useful for setting up meetings in a logical sequence:

1. Present the problem. In your first meeting, outline the problem. Describe the consumer's background, how the consumer sees the situation, how you see the problem, how you have tried to help the consumer, and where you have been having trouble.

2. Make your needs known. After stating the problem, tell the consultant what you want him to do. Be specific so that you and the consultant are clear about what the problem is. The consultant will ask questions in order to better understand the situation.

3. Wait for the consultant to accept or decline. The consultant will determine whether he can handle the job you outline.

4. Work together to problem solve. This means answering questions and being willing to expose all the difficulties you are encountering in working with the consumer. Do not hesitate to share what you have tried and how you feel it worked or did not work.

5. Listen to suggestions from the consultant. The consultant will not tell you what to do but will make suggestions and offer possible solutions. It is your decision, or yours and your supervisor's, as to what will actually be done.

You are free to use any or all of the suggestions in the way that you and your supervisor think will help solve the problem. Given the consultant's perspective and your new perspective, take a new look at the problem. Review the suggestions and decide whether to use any of them. If you decide to use one or more of the suggestions, ask yourself how you can best use the new information. Based on newly acquired perspectives, work with the consumer to try to resolve the problem.

FRAME
15

Check the correct response. Before a consultant can determine whether she can be of help, she should have

_____ **a.** a clear idea of the problem.

Turn to Answer 143 on page 637

_____ **b.** knowledge of what the consultee wants him to do.

Turn to Answer 144 on page 637

_____ **c.** direct exposure to the consumer.

Turn to Answer 145 on page 637

_____ **d.** A and B above.

Turn to Answer 146 on page 637

_____ **e.** all of the above.

Turn to Answer 147 on page 637

FRAME
16

Below are four steps involved in a successful consultation. Place them in the order in which they should be accomplished for maximum results by numbering them 1 through 4.

_____ **a.** Give the consultant an opportunity to assess her ability to help.

_____ **b.** Outline the problem for the potential consultant.

_____ **c.** Work with the consultant on possible solutions.

_____ **d.** Specify what you are asking of the consultant.

Turn to Answer 148 on page 638

Using Natural Helping Networks

Using natural helping networks means using all available human resources to help consumers. Natural networks can include nuclear families; extended families; friends or acquaintances; and various clubs, groups, and organizations. When conducting assessments it is important to explore all relevant resources if you are to maximize the helping process and build on the strengths inherent in the lifestyles and values of consumers.

Goal

To understand the concept of natural helping networks so that you, as a human service worker, can use these resources to help consumers more effectively.

Learning Activities

To accomplish this goal, we will:

1. Ask you to identify your own natural helping networks and their importance in your lives.
2. Consider ways to work with natural helpers to enhance change.
3. Explain how to work with natural networks to increase the possibility that changes are maintained.
4. Explore additional ways to strengthen consumers by building on the resources that they already have when they first come for help.

FRAME
1

DEFINING A NETWORK

A *network* is an anthropological term that describes close and loosely knit groupings of people. A network may be a primary family, an extended family, or a neighborhood block organization. The term *network* allows us to describe diverse natural groupings of persons that go beyond family groups. Natural helping networks usually function without the use of professional or formal arrangements. Natural helpers are friends, family members, neighbors, and church members who have helped one another for centuries. These ways of helping are still present, though less so in contemporary urban centers, or at least less apparently than in traditional cultures, small communities, and rural areas.

For example, the Navajo live in extended family groups of three or more hogans in close proximity and generally quite a distance from other neighbors. If a Navajo woman decides to seek help from a non-Navajo formal agency, she is likely to journey to the nearest Indian Health Service or Bureau of Indian Affairs service unit with her family members. This natural group will present the problem to a health worker. The worker will listen, describe options and alternatives, and give advice. Then the family members will return home and together decide whether they want formal help and, if so, in what form. Essentially, they continue to help and support one another, yet at times they may seek external resources, such as Anglo health services. The Navajo extended family group is an example of a close natural network *through which* the human service worker should communicate and work.

The H'mong, who are recent immigrants to this country from Thailand, were resettled throughout the United States, usually at great distances from one another. In their homeland, they lived in clans with a leader who helped families make important decisions. Since their relocation in the United States, some H'mong people have located their clan leader and have developed a long-distance communication system with him. This is clearly a helping network, though it is loosely knit in the sense that communication is infrequent.

Networks may be small and have considerable interaction among all members, such as Navajo extended families; or they may be large, more loosely knit networks, such as H'mong clans whose members live in different parts of the United States. Loosely knit networks generally do not have daily contact with one another and may be sources of more tangible resources; small, tightly knit networks are usually sources of intangible, emotional resources.[1]

Informal help occurs so frequently that it often goes unnoticed. Formal human service agencies were developed to fill gaps in aid and to compensate for breakdowns in informal helping systems. As formal helpers, we may become so absorbed in organizing and maintaining formal helping systems that we ignore the natural, informal ones. Moreover, we generally think that effective informal systems exist in small communities or traditional societies but not in large, urban areas. This is not necessarily the case; linkages developed in rural areas are still visible, though perhaps in different forms, and other sorts of helping systems may also be developed by urban residents.[2] Natural helping networks developed by groups such as the H'mong and the Navajo provide us with models of effective helping from which we can draw ideas for improving our approaches and services. Additionally, when providing services to persons who are members of groups that have established ways of providing help and support to one another, it is wise to work within or be supportive of the consumer's natural helping network in order to offer services that are useful, not destructive.

---

[1] Paul Craven and Barry Wellman, "The Network City," *Sociological Inquiry* 43 (1973): 73–74, cited in Alice H. Collins and Diane L. Pancoast, *Natural Helping Networks: A Strategy for Prevention* (Washington, D.C.: NASW, 1976), p. 29.

[2] Collins and Pancoast, *Natural Helping Networks*.

FRAME

2

Think about and then list the natural helpers and natural helping systems that have been available to you over the past ten years:

Where and from whom did you receive help and support?

1.   4.

2.   5.

3.   6.

In a crisis, where would you turn now?

Are there situations in which you would contact a formal service system for help? If so, what are they?

Think about all the resources that are currently available to you (include those not used, but potentially available to you). Use an ecomap (Figure 8.8) to chart your resource network. Place yourself in the large center circle. If others live with you, include them in the center circle, and fill out the other circles as appropriate. Blank circles can be labeled to symbolize categories of natural systems available to you for which no circle was designated. Include friends whom you depend on emotionally and with whom you interact frequently (more often than once a month); include resources that you do not depend on emotionally but that provide support, such as an employer. (The sort of support asked for here is not only economic support but also psychological support.) You may not receive emotional support from your employer, but the employer may be a source of positive feedback and a resource that you can turn to should a crisis occur in your life. If you are employed but your employer is not a positive source of support, designate this with a minus sign (–) in front of the name.

Through discussing your resources with other students, you will increase your awareness of the diversity of natural helping networks along with the positive and negative aspects of support. Some persons with whom you interact regularly may be sources of stress rather than positive sources of support. Designate sources of support with a plus sign (+).

Think about the fact that in some cultures the natural helping resources are not selected by individuals but are a given; whereas, if you are a Caucasian American, most of the natural helpers you identified may be relationships you choose.

FRAME

3

HELPING NETWORKS AS MUTUAL-AID SYSTEMS

Human service workers have become increasingly aware of the power and importance of natural helping networks. We have come to realize that if we provide formal services without involving the informal systems, we may weaken the natural systems. Rather than promote increased reliance on formal systems, it is important, first, to explore the natural helping systems and encourage their use to the extent possible, building service plans around

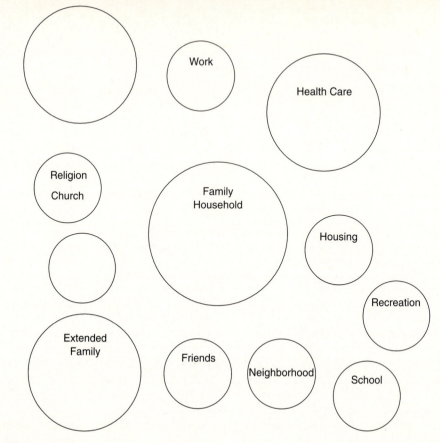

FIGURE 8.8. Ecomap

the consumer's natural strengths, aids, and resources. We are also aware that natural networks may be able to provide services when formal service systems are not available.

This means that human service workers need to support natural helping networks in the same way that they support individual strengths and resources. This requires learning from the consumer or others which resources are available and encouraging their use. It is a mistake to assume that professional or formal services are superior to informal and indigenous helping. An example of using natural helpers can again be seen among the Navajo. A Navajo who is ill seeks the consultation and help of a medicine man (a traditional healer). Most Navajos assume that non-Native Americans look down on, and even laugh at, their use of traditional healers. It is helpful to learn about the success of these traditional helpers. You will then be better able to encourage consumers, who know that traditional helpers are effective, to take advantage of their aid. You, in turn, need to provide services in ways that enhance rather than hinder the natural systems and, if appropriate, develop collaborative models.

Helping networks are mutual-aid networks. There may be a central figure in a neighborhood who is a natural helper—a woman who is closely tied to the neighborhood and enjoys the trust of others who share their problems with her. Such people have natural helping capacities and have demonstrated the ability to handle problems effectively. Other natural helpers, such as pharmacists, bartenders, and cooks in group homes, provide assistance through their formal work roles. For example, a gas-meter reader who served rural families isolated from one another looked after the needs of aged residents.[3] He helped an injured resident get to a hospital and welcomed new Black families into a predominantly White neighborhood. Another interesting example of natural helping was a female custodian at a community college to whom students went with their "love" problems. College administrators recognized her contribution and transferred this custodian to the school cafeteria so that she would have more contact with students. Moreover, the college deans were instructed to respond to her requests to help students. It is noteworthy that the administration was aware of, and supported, this natural helping system. You may notice that some cooks or other employees in group homes or institutions are of special importance to residents. At times, adolescents will trust and talk openly to such employees when they will not be open with persons designated as their formal helpers.

The natural helping system or network with which most of us are familiar is the immediate family. Families remain the major service providers to the elderly, the mentally ill, and the disabled. Social service providers may be needed to provide families with information about services and sometimes with special skills and knowledge in order for them to serve as effective helpers.[4] As helpers, we have learned that chances for improvement are great if the whole household unit is involved in helping. Individual change within a family unit is difficult without simultaneous support for change by family members. Moreover, change may not be possible unless all family members change in the way they interact with one another.

It is important to understand how others perceive the consumer. You can learn a lot from interviewing family members and from observing interactions in their home. This knowledge and understanding can help in developing effective plans with a consumer. For example, it will tell you whether family members are likely to help or hinder change efforts. Observing the family as a whole and understanding the individual within the family context offer a different perspective from understanding individuals as isolated human beings. In other words, to understand an individual, you need to understand the person within his or her natural environment.

Working with the family as a unit requires a different perspective and some different skills than does working with individuals. Family members are mutual helpers, and the worker becomes simply one person in the helping network rather than the sole source of help. Recent approaches in child welfare emphasize working as a team with the natural parents, the foster parents, and the child. Working with natural systems eases the worker's burden, reinforces natural helping resources, increases chances for success with the present problem, and provides a model for handling future problems.

A worker in an Indian Health Service hospital saw a woman in her 30s accompanied by six members of her extended family. She was depressed and confused by the fact that her husband had left home. She sought help for her physical symptoms and advice in handling her situation. The worker listened to the problems and described

---

[3]Collins and Pancoast, *Natural Helping Networks.*

[4]Irene Shiffren Levine and Mary Fleming, *Human Resource Development: Issues in Case Management* (College Park: University of Maryland, Center of Rehabilitation and Manpower Services, 1984).

several options, including searching for a job and other activities to divert her attention from her loss, a healing ceremony, and alternative ways she might approach her husband. The family decided to return home to discuss the options presented and then decide whether to accept formal help or resolve the problems through their own network, which included a traditional healer. In this case, the worker helped the family clarify the issues and see their options: however, the family members decided to define their own goals and develop their own plan by seeing the traditional healer. The worker supported this approach and thereby strengthened the existing family network.

It sometimes seems more expedient to intervene and provide the service directly to consumers rather than to utilize a natural helping network. The worker who served the Rael family (described in Chapter 7, Lesson 3) found it easier to refer the father to a child welfare worker who would place the infant in a foster home than to explore natural resources and possibly develop a placement in the home of a relative. Sometimes, in our rush to provide needed services, we overlook natural resources.

The worker's first job is to determine the characteristics of the consumer's social networks and family interactions. By exploring the membership of the consumer's networks, the worker can identify the persons whom the consumer sees as significant and with whom there is regular, face-to-face contact.[5] Contacts can be categorized into the spheres found on an ecomap (Chapter 7, Lesson 3). These include church, extended family, persons with whom the consumer lives, recreational resources, school, work, and social welfare organizations. Detailed information about relationships can be gained by asking the consumer to define the roles each of these resources plays in his life. It is also important to determine whether the consumer sees each resource as supportive or as a source of stress. One approach is to ask the consumer how many supportive contacts he had with the individual during the past month; then ask whether the consumer would like more contacts with this resource. Next, find out if the relationship is more burdensome or conflicting than it is supportive. Additionally, ask the consumer how the natural resource feels about contacts with formal helping systems.[6] Based on the information obtained, the worker may elect to encourage the use of natural resources, to strengthen natural resources, or to provide services without involving the consumer's natural helping networks.

Psychologist Carolyn Attneave describes this excellent example of helping an extended family clan network:[7]

A mental health center referred an abused Indian child to a psychologist. The child had lived with her grandmother from 3 months to the age of 5 years and then had been sent to her mother's. Since giving birth to this daughter, the mother had moved to another state, had married a man from another tribe and had had four children with her husband. She lived two states away from where her mother and first daughter lived. The grandmother was an alcoholic and a local court had ordered the daughter taken from the grandmother's home and placed with the mother and new stepfather. The child was placed in the mother's home without preparation. Abuse occurred and the child was in foster care at the point the psychologist was contacted.

---

[5]Benjamin H. Gottlieb, *Social Support Strategies: Guidelines for Mental Health Practice* (Beverly Hills, Calif.: Sage, 1983).
[6]Gottlieb, *Social Support Strategies*.
[7]Collins and Pancoast, *Natural Helping Networks*.

The extended kinship clan of the stepfather was concerned about the child and the family. They planned a weekend meeting to discuss the situation and invited the psychologist to join them. They met from sundown one evening to sundown the next day. Approximately 50 persons were involved. After a large supper the first evening, 20 of the most involved adults spent the night in a ceremonial meeting. During the all-night meeting, the psychologist was inducted into the network clan for helping the child, details of the situation were described, and participants were able to share their helplessness in a nonjudgmental, mutually supportive situation. At some point during the meeting, the psychologist said it might help their understanding if more was known about the grandmother. The mother looked away. There was silence, no response and much tension. The psychologist dropped the subject.

Several weeks later when the psychologist brought the child to the family for a planned visit, the grandmother was there. The psychologist was surprised and the child was overjoyed. The network had thought about the psychologist's comment and had brought the grandmother across two states to spend two weeks with the extended family. During the next 24 hours there were rituals of receiving the child into the clan, ceremonies which included her mother, stepfather and grandmother. The eldest member of the clan later stood next to the therapist as she was watching the children play together. He said it was a good idea to get to know the grandmother better. The clan had decided among themselves to include the grandmother in order to ease the child's transition to her home.

FRAME

4

NEIGHBORHOOD HELPING NETWORKS

It may be easier to work with a network that is well defined and has clear kinship boundaries than with the more loosely knit networks in a neighborhood or rural community. Nevertheless, there are excellent examples of effective natural helping network projects in neighborhoods. Agencies sometimes look toward "natural neighbors" when they realize that a neighborhood has unmet needs and that formal services are not available to meet the existing needs. For example, a worker was aware that a particular neighborhood needed more day care services and had a high incidence of child abuse. The worker began to get to know the neighborhood and its needs and resources by observation and through informal conversations with neighbors, ministers, and businesspeople. Through this process the worker identified the invisible boundaries of a neighborhood, the natural helpers, and those who needed help. Once natural helpers were identified, the worker arranged to talk with them, asking for an opportunity to learn about the neighborhood. The interview was informal and general. A project called the Day Care Neighbor Service was developed to explore the potential of natural networks to prevent abuse and neglect of neighborhood children.[8]

The worker discovered that neighbors knew about neglected or abused children and were concerned about them. Neighbors were aware of family problems and poor child care before such cases came to the attention of agencies. As a result, assistance could be provided before situations deteriorated to the point that children

---

[8]Collins and Pancoast, *Natural Helping Networks.*

had to be removed from their homes, causing much damage to the child and the family. Two neighborhood leaders were identified. Each of these women managed rental units located next to a housing project. In addition to managing the rental units, they each helped their renters when they had problems and needed resources. The women knew the public and private social welfare resources and therefore were valuable information sources. The agency worker asked each woman to accept a role as a neighborhood helper, with the agency worker serving as a consultant. Within this arrangement, the worker was contacted when the neighborhood helper encountered problems that she was uncertain about handling, needed additional information about resources, or had a crisis for which professional intervention was needed immediately.

The worker assessed the strengths of the neighborhood helpers and gave them support. In one case, one of the helpers saw herself as less effective than she was. The worker, through talks with this woman, was able to help her gain confidence and offer more help. The worker also gave the support needed to enable neighborhood women to continue their support–leadership roles with less skilled and less strong neighbors. The worker empowered the natural helpers. The service was preventive in that problems could be identified before they were so severe that they were brought to the attention of professionals or authorities. Thus, the natural helping network of two neighborhood women continued as it had functioned before but with support and consultation services from someone attached to a formal agency.

In some cases, therefore, human service workers can refer consumers to natural helpers or give services to natural helpers who in turn serve consumers. If a natural helping system is intact, there may not be a need for formal human services. If there is a natural system available that needs strengthening in order to be more helpful, the human service role may be to provide support to the natural helper or helping system rather than to the consumer. There are, however, consumers who do not have access to natural helping networks, either because they are not aware of such resources or because they are in a new environment, such as an institution. There are also consumers who have lost or are separated from natural helping networks, such as children removed from natural families and placed in foster care. In these situations, substitute natural helpers may be needed. Children who are in institutions may need parent figures to supply needs that would generally be met by parents.

Human service workers are rediscovering the importance of natural helping networks and finding ways to work with natural helping networks and strengthen such resources to decrease the need for formal human services. In the next lesson we describe educating, another helping tool used by human service staff that strengthens consumers and their ongoing personal resources.

Educating

In addition to case management and using natural helping networks, human service workers are involved in helping individuals and groups acquire information and learn the skills they need to improve their daily functioning. Educating through the teaching role is a central approach human service workers use to empower individuals, families, and community groups to solve problems. In the process of educating, workers use a wide range of tools to facilitate knowledge and skill acquisition in consumers. For example, one tool is to model the skills or behaviors that the consumer is lacking; another is to offer the consumer an opportunity to practice new behaviors and responses. In this lesson we will consider key aspects of the relationship that must be created in order to help consumers to learn.

Goal

Given a description of consumers who need to acquire basic skills to improve their daily living, you will be able to describe how you would use educating to help them learn the skill.

Learning Activities

To accomplish this goal, we will:

1. Identify four characteristics of a learner.
2. Review the basic steps of educating.
3. List helpful guidelines for effective educating.
4. Identify two reasons for using evaluation in educating.

FRAME
1

EDUCATING: UNDERSTANDING THE CONSUMER AS A LEARNER

Educating can be defined as training by instruction, demonstration, and practice. As a human service worker, you will need to develop good teaching skills if you are to help consumers learn how to cope with the problems they encounter in daily living, such as accessing resources, creating a family budget, finding a job, preventing health problems, or staying out of trouble with the law.

It is important to note that, in teaching, you must respect the consumers' past experiences. In addition, consumers learn best when the skills taught have an immediate usefulness to them. Therefore, you should give consumers a chance to decide what skills they need to know and help them relate these skills to their present experiences. Consumers as learners have four main characteristics:

1. Consumers have *experience* in living.
2. Consumers have a *readiness* to learn different things because they are facing new and different challenges and tasks.
3. Consumers are *sensitive to failure* and may have to overcome personal doubts and fears about their ability to learn.
4. Consumers are interested in the *immediate usefulness* of new knowledge.

When teaching consumers, it is important to remember the special characteristics of a learner. It is also important to note that educating involves imitation. In an earlier lesson, we mentioned the importance of the consumer's determining her own approach to solving problems; in this lesson we emphasize the consumer as a learner and thereby indicate that teaching involves the process of modeling behaviors for consumers so that they may learn how to cope with problems of daily living.

When you are educating, you are dealing with the world of *information*. You are trying to help the consumer discover how to use information—about jobs, child rearing, and homemaking—in order to function more effectively. When you teach a consumer new ways of doing things, you build a special kind of helping relationship, conveying warmth, genuineness, empathy, and respect, as defined in Lesson 2 of Chapter 7. Support for the consumer and expectations that the consumer can achieve the learning goals are important when using the educating approach.

We all learn best by *doing* and *practicing,* as well as by drawing on our own experiences. For example, do not expect a delinquent youth to learn how to occupy his time constructively by reading a book on the subject. A more effective approach is to show the youth how to plan free time and to provide opportunities for him to practice various recreational activities. Be available to answer questions, but give the youth a chance to try it on his own. Once he has acquired new skills, encourage him to practice them in everyday situations.

Research shows the power of modeling for imparting new behaviors and new ways of handling situations effectively. *Modeling* means to demonstrate, or act out, the desired behavior. Just as we know much about training human service workers in interviewing skills, we know how to teach consumers new skills, such as communication skills, parenting skills, and assertive behaviors. Effective training programs have been developed and tested. Modeling is an important component of these programs. In fact, modeling alone is an effective training tool. Training formats used for consumers are similar to those used in training human service workers.

Learning will also be easier for consumers when new skills or ideas are presented in terms of their past experiences. For example, if you are helping a woman who has been out of work learn how to find a job, you might talk with her about her previous job and how she found it. Then, based on her past experiences, you can help her decide what type of job she would like and then teach her how to find such a job and how to handle job interviews.

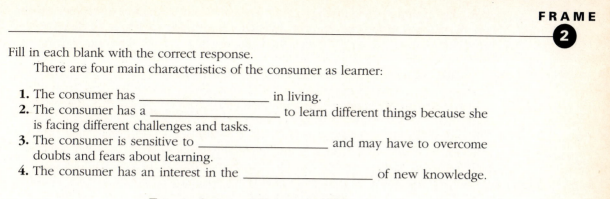

FRAME
2

Fill in each blank with the correct response.

There are four main characteristics of the consumer as learner:

1. The consumer has _____ in living.
2. The consumer has a _____ to learn different things because she is facing different challenges and tasks.
3. The consumer is sensitive to _____ and may have to overcome doubts and fears about learning.
4. The consumer has an interest in the _____ of new knowledge.

Turn to Answer 149 on page 639

FRAME
3

BASIC STEPS IN EDUCATING

Consumers learn best by doing and by having new skills presented in terms of their own experiences, but it is also important to remember that learning needs to be focused on immediate *problems*. For example, do not try to show someone how to plan well-balanced meals if he is out of work and has no money to buy groceries. Help the person deal with the problem at hand—in this case, getting some food and finding a job—and then focus on teaching additional skills that may be useful.

The same steps used in effective interviewing training are applied to the process of teaching or training consumers:[1]

1. Present a clear definition and description of the skill to be learned. It is best to give consumers a verbal definition and a written description plus the opportunity to discuss the skill.
2. Show a positive model of the skill.
3. Give consumers an opportunity to practice the skill.
4. Give consumers positive feedback on their use of the skill.
5. Provide opportunity for consumers to see and hear themselves performing the skill, preferably through the use of videotapes or audiotapes. Use the tapes as bases for feedback.
6. Give additional practice opportunities until the skill is performed at the desired level.

Such structured learning formats are used extensively to teach children to interact with one another in new ways, to teach parents new skills in relating to children, and to teach adults how to avoid being passive or aggressive, yet to express their needs and wishes assertively. Specifically, this approach may be used to teach alcoholics how to refuse a drink and to teach adolescents the interpersonal skills needed in de-

---

[1]Allen Ivey and Jerry Authier, *Microcounseling,* 2d ed. (Springfield, Ill.: Charles C. Thomas, 1978).

veloping meaningful relationships. You may teach a consumer to express feelings simply by expressing feelings in your interactions with the consumer (in other words, teach the desired behavior through modeling it), or you may develop a training program following the six steps listed above.

One way to educate consumers is through *assertiveness training*.[2] There are several approaches to teaching people to be more assertive. Most follow the general steps outlined above, beginning with definitions and examples of assertive, nonassertive, and aggressive behaviors. Next, the consumer describes a particular situation in which she was not assertive. Training is then individualized and focuses on teaching the consumer to behave more assertively in this specific situation. The consumer is asked to describe a recent situation and exactly how she responded. The worker then discusses with the consumer how she would like to act in similar situations and specifically in this situation. With the worker's help, the consumer describes what she wished she had done in the situation. The worker can demonstrate how the consumer might have behaved by asking the consumer to role play the other person while the worker enacts the consumer's role.

Once the goals are defined, the consumer practices the new behaviors by role playing with the worker or a peer. These practice sessions can be videotaped, with the consumer's signed permission, so that the consumer can see and critique her performance. The role playing is then repeated to give the consumer additional opportunities to practice the skill until the desired level of performance is attained. Then the consumer is asked to practice the new skill outside the helping session in a real-life situation. The consumer reports on the experiences and, if needed, is assisted in modifying behavior through additional role-playing activities with the worker. Role playing is only a first step. The goal is always to acquire successful behaviors for everyday situations. We cannot assume that a behavior learned in a practice situation will transfer to a real-life situation; therefore, we must make efforts to ensure the transfer of learning through assignments in natural settings and follow-up sessions.

FRAME
4

If you were going to teach a group of consumers basic homemaking skills, which of the following things would you do? Check the correct response.

_____ **a.** Tell them to read a basic home economics textbook.

Turn to Answer 150 on page 639

_____ **b.** Tell them what the ideal home should be like so that they can learn to run a home properly.

Turn to Answer 151 on page 639

---

[2]Eileen Gambrill and Cheryl Richey, *Shy or Sociable: It's Up to You,* 2d ed. (New York: Harper & Row, 1984).

_____ **c.** Find out their experiences in homemaking and what problems they are having now. Then define and model the new behaviors and give them opportunities to discuss and practice the behaviors.

Turn to Answer 152 on page 639

Turn to Answer 152 on page 639

FRAME
5

TESTING YOUR UNDERSTANDING OF TEACHING

Read the following paragraphs, then complete the sentence below.

Wayne is a worker in a community correctional center for adult male offenders. Hank, one of the offenders Wayne supervises, is now eligible for parole. But Hank is terrified at the thought of leaving the center. He doesn't know how to get a job, where to look for one, or how to conduct himself during a job interview.

Wayne decides to try to assist Hank by teaching him various ways of securing a job. In their first session, Wayne demonstrates to Hank some of the procedures and skills he will need during a job interview. Wayne gives a lengthy, detailed description of the job interview and then ends the teaching session, feeling confident that he has provided Hank with most of the skills he will need for a successful job interview. Wayne is surprised when he learns that Hank has had more than four opportunities for job interviews but has turned them all down.

Check all the probable reasons that Wayne's efforts at teaching have not been very successful.

_____ **a.** Wayne has not given Hank enough practice or rehearsal for a job interview.

_____ **b.** Hank is not very intelligent and will probably never be able to handle himself in a job interview.

_____ **c.** Wayne has shown interest in Hank but has failed to adapt his demonstration to Hank's individual needs.

_____ **d.** Wayne has neglected to follow the basic training steps.

_____ **e.** Hank is not interested in getting a job.

Turn to Answer 153 on page 639

FRAME
6

EVALUATING THE EDUCATING PROCESS

How do you know if the teaching process is helping the consumer? How do you know if the consumer will have any additional learning needs? Evaluating your educating activities is an important part of educating because it enables you to assess (1) your own efforts, (2) the progress that the consumer is making, and (3) what additional teaching is needed.

The best way to use evaluation in educating is to *actively involve consumers* in the process. For example, you might ask consumers for their reactions to what you have been doing. Have they understood what you have been demonstrating? Was anything unclear? Do they feel confident in what they have learned? Are there any other skills that they can identify that will help them perform better?

Other criteria can also be used. Did the consumer's performance improve in practice sessions? Did the consumer get a job after the training experience? Did the consumer save money after lessons in family budgeting? Did the potentially delinquent young man plan his time sufficiently to stay out of trouble over the past year? These and other criteria can be used to evaluate your teaching effectiveness. Review Lesson 3, Chapter 8 as a basis for evaluating the educating process.

Good educating requires that special attention be given to following the basic principles of helping and educating:

1. Follow the rules for problem specification and goal selection described in detail in Lessons 1 and 2 of Chapter 8.

   a. To the extent possible, have the consumer select the problem and goal; work on the target problem of most concern to the consumer.

   b. Work on a goal that you and the consumer predict a chance of success in learning.

   c. When appropriate, divide the goal into smaller steps and work on one step at a time.

   d. Show your interest in the goal and express your expectation that the goal will be achieved.

2. Specify the problem and measure where the consumer is before teaching begins.

3. Be specific about the desired goal or outcome: What would the consumer like to know and be able to do at the end of training: What will the consumer do differently at the end of training?

4. Once you have selected the target, try an information search to find the best techniques to use in teaching and learning the skill and the materials that may help. Use your agency as a resource; then check resources in your college library or libraries of neighboring academic institutions and your local public libraries. Other resources for information and training materials are other agencies and local businesses.

5. Give directions clearly and concisely.

FRAME

7

Check the correct response. Why should you make an active effort to evaluate your educating activities?

_____ **a.** You need to find out what progress, if any, you and the consumer are making.

Turn to Answer 154 on page 640

_____ **b.** You need to know if the consumer likes you.

Turn to Answer 155 on page 640

_____ **c.** You need to determine if the consumer needs additional coaching.

Turn to Answer 156 on page 640

_____ **d.** You need to make certain that the consumer is following your instructions accurately.

Turn to Answer 157 on page 640

_____ **e.** A and C.

Turn to Answer 158 on page 640

_____ **f.** A, C, and D.

Turn to Answer 159 on page 640

FRAME

8

POINTS TO REMEMBER IN EDUCATING

Successful educators base their teaching style on their experiences and their observations of others. Although no one source has identified all the skills and knowledge a good teacher needs, we offer the following list. Examine it, organize the items in your own way, then apply them when you think they are appropriate. Add your own ideas to this list and make necessary changes based on your experiences in educating human service consumers.

1. Do not put too much pressure on a consumer to learn faster than his abilities will allow, and do not hesitate to repeat and repeat again.
2. Be generous with praise. It is possible to give only positive feedback by praising approximations of the goal, ignoring areas that need improvement.
3. Develop special learning exercises that will motivate the consumer to work hard at learning the new behaviors.
4. Work with the consumer in whatever way is best for that individual.
5. When a consumer has established his own best way of dealing with a problem, interfere as little as possible.
6. Remember that the consumer needs to recognize the practical value of what you are teaching.

FRAME

9

Check which of the following would *not* be helpful in teaching:

_____ **a.** Pressure a consumer to learn as fast as possible.

_____ **b.** Be generous with praise.

_____ **c.** Once a consumer has established his own best way of dealing with a problem, make sure it is exactly what you have taught.

_____ **d.** Remember that a consumer needs to recognize the practical value of your teaching.

_____ **e.** Motivate the consumer and work *with* him in a way most suited to that individual.

Turn to Answer 160 on page 640

Working with Consumer Groups

Quite often, the problems experienced by human service consumers can be handled successfully in groups. This allows consumers to share similar problems with one another and to help one another in resolving problems. In this lesson you will learn how to organize and work with groups.

Goal

Given a description of consumers with similar problems, you will be able to explain (1) how to organize consumers into an activity group and (2) how to help group members solve their problems so they can live and work together more effectively.

Learning Activities

To accomplish this goal, we will:

1. Define *group*.
2. Describe two different kinds of groups and two different kinds of settings in which you might organize groups.
3. Examine five guidelines that will help you in getting to know a group of people.
4. Discuss two elements that are basic to organizing a new group and five hints to remember in planning an activity with a group.
5. Examine four basic principles to remember when you are working with an activity group.
6. Explain three ways of helping a group meet its needs.

FRAME
1

WHAT IS A GROUP?

People tend to form groups naturally to satisfy their needs for belonging and for interacting with others. Thus, we might think of our family and friends as different groups.

As a human service worker, you may organize groups to help people solve their common problems. In the human services, the term *group* means more than just any collection of individuals, such as those in a waiting room. A group that you might be working with in the human services is a collection of individuals participating to accomplish a *shared* specific objective together. Group members may also share similar problems and interests. For example, you might help organize and work with a group of consumers that has resource deficits, or you might work with a group of consumers that is trying to develop recreational activities for themselves. Working with groups in institutions and in the community could include groups in hospitals, schools, prisons, halfway houses, and community centers. Groups of community residents who are welfare recipients are examples of community groups in which consumers share a variety of everyday living issues. Whether you work in an institutional or a community setting, your job will be to identify consumers who share similar problems and help them to develop shared objectives and to use the group to deal with their problems.

Specially trained psychiatrists, psychologists, and social workers often use groups to help treat people who are suffering from psychological problems. Such a group, usually referred to as a *therapy group,* tends to focus more on the growth and/or change of its individual members. Therapy groups are formed to provide play therapy for children, geriatric remotivation or resocialization therapy, marital counseling, and so forth. Professionals also organize groups to help people with problems such as eating, smoking, and social skill deficits. Although you may be assisting a mental health specialist in such areas, as a human service worker you are more likely to be working with *task groups* and *activity groups.*

In a task group, consumers are helped to solve a common problem related to everyday living. A group of consumers, for example, may need child care services while the group members are enrolled in a work-training program. The members of an activity group may be healthy or may be seriously disturbed. For example, you may be working with a group of patients or inmates in an institution, or you may be working with a group of neighborhood residents concerned about common community problems. No matter what kind of group you are working with, you will be trying to help the group identify and solve common problems. Even when working with a group of seriously disturbed consumers, you will be helping group members solve common problems, such as handling the frustration that may accompany the process of learning how to weave a basket. Task groups are organized to perform certain tasks or achieve certain goals, either for themselves or for others. Staff committees are task groups. Citizen action organizations form task groups to offer support to consumers or to solve social welfare problems. Members of task groups are not necessarily experiencing the problem they organized to solve.

You may also have opportunities to work with *self-help groups* or with consumers who are receiving help through self-help groups, such as mental patients' rights groups, Alcoholics Anonymous, and Parents Anonymous (for parents who abuse their children). These self-help groups have grown in popularity over the past ten years. Some of these groups are organized by persons who have mastered the problem other group members are experiencing, while other groups consist of persons who are experiencing the problem and meet to give one another mutual support. Support groups have been organized for parents of children with terminal illnesses, for recently divorced persons, for wives whose husbands are in prison. These groups help people who are going through a crisis or a life transition that causes unusual stress and requires a readjustment on the part of the person experiencing the change.

F R A M E

2

Write in the blank whether each statement below is *true* or *false*.

_____ **1.** Using our definition of a group, neighbors within the community constitute a group.

_____ **2.** Any collection of individuals, such as people watching a movie, would be considered a group in human services.

_____ **3.** The term *group* carries a special meaning in human services.

_____ **4.** In human services we think of a group as being a collection of individuals working together to achieve a specific objective.

Turn to Answer 161 on page 641

F R A M E

3

GETTING TO KNOW A GROUP

If you recognize that a problem is common to a number of consumers with whom you are working, you may wish to help these consumers form a group in which they can work together toward solving the problem. Or there may be a group in existence that needs your help in focusing their energies to solve their problems. Establishing contact with potential group members or with groups that are already formed requires planning. In either case, some basic principles will help you to make contact with these consumers and to build relationships.[1]

1. Approach potential group members or an existing group of consumers *openly,* explaining who you are and what your purpose is. You also need to have potential goals in mind, such as improved climate on the ward, improved neighborhood appearance, or greater participation in health department services.
2. Do your *homework.* Know what to look for and what to expect by finding out important information about the consumers, both before you meet with the group and during the first few meetings.
3. Approach the consumers when they can give you enough *time* and attention, so you can explain your interest.
4. Have a sense of *humor,* especially if you are met with a hostile silence. You will also need to have considerable patience, particularly if the group decides to "test you out" to see if you are really committed to helping them.

---

[1]See Frank J. Carney, Hans W. Mattick, and John D. Callaway, *Action on the Streets* (New York: Association Press, 1969); and Irving Spergel, *Street Gang Work: Theory and Practice* (Reading, Mass.: Addison-Wesley, 1966).

5. Remember that group members will respond positively to you only if you consistently demonstrate through *word and deed* what you can do to help them.

6. Be a *good observer* of the group. Try to learn as much as you can about each group member and about the group, what they do, what activities seem to interest them most, and what their needs and aspirations are.

7. As group members and potential group members begin to identify their problems and goals, gather information about how to accomplish their goals, at least initial information regarding the steps that must be taken in order to accomplish the goals.

FRAME 4

Alex is a psychiatric aide in a hospital. He has noticed that several patients in his ward have complained about the lack of recreational activities at the hospital. He would like these patients to get together to form an activity group and, perhaps, to plan some recreational activities.

Check the step that Alex should take to make contact with potential group members.

_____1. Go to each patient who has complained and tell the patient that he has heard the patient complaining about the lack of recreational activities.

_____2. Go to each patient and openly seek his or her thoughts about forming a new recreational group.

_____3. Post a notice on the bulletin board telling patients that he is organizing a group.

Turn to Answer 162 on page 641

FRAME 5

Sherrie is a family service aide. She is aware of a group of welfare recipients in a local housing project who are meeting regularly to try to develop child care resources so they can attend a training program. One of the group members gives Sherrie permission to attend one of their meetings. When she arrives and begins to explain who she is and why she is there, the group members are sullen and hostile toward her.

Of the three choices below, check the best response for Sherrie to make.

_____1. Sherrie should maintain a sense of humor and not show that she is upset or angry as she tries to win the group over.

_____2. Sherrie should tell the group that they are being rude and unappreciative of her help.

_____3. Sherrie should leave immediately and forget about helping this group.

Turn to Answer 163 on page 641

ORGANIZING GROUPS

In organizing and working with activity and task groups, it is important to remember that while you are helping the group resolve problems, you are also helping the members develop a sense of belonging and offering them an opportunity to improve their skills in getting along with one another. Therefore, it is important for each group member to participate fully. To accomplish this, you need to look for (1) the *individual* interests and problems of each group member and (2) the *common* interests and problems of most of the group.[2] Once you have focused attention on the problems facing the group, joint participation can begin.

As a human service worker, you will find that engaging in an *activity* is a useful means of communicating with the group. Through activities, group members can have fun, seek companionship, find relief from boredom and fatigue, and develop better ways of working and living together. The following five guidelines may help when you are organizing group activities or working with an activity group:

1. If the activity is to be conducted successfully, both the planning for it and the performance of it should be done *with* the group rather than *for* them.
2. Use an activity that will promote personal reactions among the group members.
3. If you show anxiety about the necessity for controls on the range of allowable group activities, individuals will begin to test your limits. Be firm and fair.
4. Be imaginative and flexible in your planning with the group.
5. Be sure to obtain the necessary facilities, staff approval, and advice before promising an activity.

Leon is a cottage parent in a halfway house for youth offenders. Several boys in his cottage are having problems getting along with one another, and Leon would like to get them involved in an activity group. After identifying the group members, Leon decides that he will take them on a camping trip because he enjoys camping and believes that all boys enjoy outdoor activities.

Do you think this is a wise decision? _____Yes _____ No
Why?

Turn to Answer 164 on page 641

Josie works in a training center for developmentally delayed children. She is working with a group of children to help them plan field trips outside the institu-

---

[2]George M. Beal, Joe M. Bohlen, and T. Neil Raudabaugh, *Leadership and Dynamic Group Action* (Ames, Iowa: Iowa State University Press, 1962).

tion. In one of the group meetings, the children ask Josie to take them on a trip to the library the next day. Josie quickly agrees to do so.

Do you think this is a wise decision on Josie's part? _____Yes _____ No
Why?

Turn to Answer 165 on page 641

FRAME
9

Working with Groups

Working with groups of consumers to help them solve common problems requires the development of certain skills. To be an effective group worker, it is important for you to build and maintain a positive relationship with the group. The following are some basic techniques and guidelines that may be useful:[3]

1. Be on time. Try to arrive early. Being on time sets an example of responsibility and provides you with the opportunity to greet and observe group members as they arrive.

2. Relax, but act interested. A relaxed posture and a pleasant speaking voice help create a nonthreatening climate. Try not to slouch or gaze out the window. Instead, make an effort to show an interest in the group, frequently looking around the group at each member.

3. Identify the activity. Introduce, explain, demonstrate, and participate in the activity. Try to involve all group members as rapidly as possible. Clarify terms and words by asking for definitions and explanations. Encourage group members to select and plan activities.

4. Enforce the rules. Rules must be enforced, but do this without bossing or demanding a level of precision that destroys group enjoyment. Also, remember to be generous with praise and encouragement.

5. Maintain interest. Try to stop an activity while group interest is still high. The members will then look forward to their next meeting.

6. Request feedback. Find out why the group liked the activity. Begin to identify leadership within the group so that future direction may come more from the group itself.

7. End on time. A partial function of groups is to assist members to plan their time better. Prompt conclusions to meetings help members carry over what they are learning into their daily routines.

FRAME
10

Marilyn is a correctional officer in an institution for women. She works with a group of inmates that was organized so that members could plan and participate

---

[3]See Janet P. Murray and Clyde E. Murray, *Guidelines for Group Leaders* (New York: Whiteside and Morrow, 1954); Henry Swift and Elizabeth Swift, *Community Groups and You* (New York: John Day, 1964); and Charles F. Tarr, *Group Counseling: Models and Methods* (New York: State Division for Youth, n.d.).

in leisure activities. A local counselor consented to meet with the group to teach assertiveness skills, which will increase members' abilities to plan effectively together. Marilyn arrives early for the meeting to make certain that the room is ready for the evening's activity. After the meeting starts, she explains that everyone will have an opportunity to practice their skills and helps members choose partners to work with. During the meeting, Marilyn goes around the room complimenting the group members on what a good job they are doing. At the end of the scheduled time, Marilyn reminds the group that it is time to quit for the evening, even though several group members complain. Marilyn quickly points out that group meetings must be limited to two hours, but perhaps their guest could return for a future meeting. As everyone leaves, Marilyn checks with the group members informally to determine if they enjoyed the meeting.

Identify which of the seven principles of being a good group leader Marilyn applied by checking the appropriate items.

_____ **a.** She arrived early.

_____ **b.** She acted interested.

_____ **c.** She involved everyone as soon as possible.

_____ **d.** She enforced the rules without being bossy, and she also gave praise.

_____ **e.** She stopped the activity while the group interest was still high.

_____ **f.** She checked to see if everyone enjoyed the meeting.

_____ **g.** She ended on time.

Turn to Answer 166 on page 642

F R A M E

11

Helping Groups Meet Their Needs

It is important when planning and participating in activities with a group to be sensitive at all times to helping both the individual members and the group as a whole to solve problems and meet their needs. Whether a group is problem focused or concentrates more on activities, you can help solve problems and meet needs by remembering to do the following:

1. Be available and accessible to the group.
2. Ask the group questions that show you are interested and want to help. ("Who has a problem?" "What can I do to help?" "What do you think we should do now?")

3. Provide information and guidance to the group on matters where they may need help or support, for example, finding jobs, family problems, needs that are not being met in the institution, and helping an individual prepare to leave the institution.

4. Help members assume more and more responsibility for the direction and activities of the group.

Working with groups is different from working with individuals because group members have one another as helping resources, as well as you. It is your job to mobilize group members to help and work with one another. Group process and interaction are important. The group as a whole is your client, in addition to each group member. As a result, your goal is to minimize relating to each group member on an individual basis by helping each group member address others individually and directly. The goal is to help group members interact with one another as much as or more than they interact with you. Often you will simply be like a member of the group, especially once the group has been together for a while. In some cases you may simply serve as a consultant or special aide to the group. Your role will depend on the group's goals and the group members' skills. As the group develops, members assume identifiable roles within the group. One member may assume some leadership functions by being good in expressing the shared feelings and needs of group members. Some group members will tend to be quiet and to follow, while others may talk frequently and be directive. As a group leader, aide, or facilitator, you need to help group members participate as equally as possible and to develop improved ways of interacting with one another.

It is also important to be aware of whether you need the assistance of other staff members or professionals. In addition, the knowledge and skills needed for effectively helping groups meet their needs will require learning about communication patterns within the group and studying group process. This lesson serves only as a preliminary introduction to working with groups, and we hope that you will use the bibliography at the end of this chapter to expand your knowledge and understanding of this important activity.

When you are working with groups, you will make mistakes, but do not be discouraged! By making mistakes, you will learn more about yourself and about the group. Group members want a worker who is interested in them, who likes them, and who enjoys doing what they are doing. A case example of a group ("A Resocialization Group") is provided in Chapter 9.

CHAPTER 8
Summary and Further Study

Chapter Summary

This chapter was planned to provide you with the basis for doing human service work with individuals and families. The chapter covered all the phases of helping from initial meetings through assessment, goal setting, service planning, contracting, and evaluating your change efforts. It also discussed different approaches of helping, including case management, using natural helping networks, strategies for educating consumers, and working with consumer groups.

Lesson 1. The first contact with a consumer—it may be a phone call, a direct contact at the agency, or a community meeting—is critical. Five steps were defined as guides for the initial contact: (1) anticipatory empathy (anticipating the consumer's perspective); (2) creating a comfortable environment; (3) handling the initial greeting in a way that will help the consumer feel comfortable; (4) the orientation process, which involves describing your role and responsibilities, the agency's services, and mutual expectations; and (5) suggested opening statements for beginning an interview.

Once the initial contact is made, the worker's primary goals are to listen and observe accurately and to remember what is said. This lesson illustrated how to differentiate between inference and behavioral observation and how to pinpoint, which are important skills in gathering assessment material. It also defined the components of a good assessment and applied them in the analysis of written case material. Assessment components are consumer strengths and resources, including family, neighborhood, and community; as well as personal resources, such as education, interests, and commitment to family relationships; physiological variables; cultural, ethnic, and religious factors; past history; coping styles; potential for, and motivation to, change; and behavioral excesses and deficits. Assessment focuses on the current situation. Through the assessment/interviewing process, the worker helps the consumer move toward defining presenting problems in specific terms and defining desired outcomes as the basis for developing a service plan.

Like interviewing and relationship building, the process of assessment through evaluation involves skills that you will work on and perfect throughout your career as a human service worker. Assessment, of course, is the most challenging of these and forms the base for the others, beginning with goal setting. If the worker fails to make an accurate assessment, he will not likely be able to help. However, remember that assessment is a changing reality and continues to be checked and possibly modified throughout numerous contacts. Further, a wise helper knows that the consumer's *first* presenting issue may not be the primary concern. Thus, workers must be prepared to modify goals/desired outcomes and follow consumers. Good assessment skills develop over time, through experiences with consumers, continued observation of others, continued reading, and continued supervision and feedback.

Be careful not to impose your own experiences and ideas on the consumer. After working with a number of consumers with similar problems or with consumers whose problems are similar to ones you have worked through, it is easy to make assumptions about the consumer's situation or jump to conclusions too quickly. Always remember that every individual is unique, and two different people may experience a similar event quite differently. Approach each consumer and each situation as new and unique, build a relationship, and carefully explore the context of the problem and the consumer's individual needs *before* working *together* to develop a service plan.

It is also important to be aware that the person who labels something as a problem in most instances is not the person who has the problem. While this is not always true, it clearly demonstrates the need to learn the perspectives of each person who has identified a problem. Development of desired outcomes requires family decision making. Thus, the worker would need to work with the family as a group to identify the desired outcomes as well as the interventions and interventive approach to achieve each outcome.

Lesson 2. The second lesson, on goal setting, contracting, and service planning, emphasized specification of goals so that an effective, highly individualized service plan can be developed. Lesson 2 showed you how to record or monitor target issues in order to assess problem severity and frequency as a basis for service planning and evaluation. The lesson described written contracts as helpful tools for service implementation and evaluation.

Asking consumers to observe their own situations carefully through the use of diaries or descriptions of events and what occurs just before and after the events will help in understanding the situation and in giving consumers insight about what needs to be changed and how this change might be accomplished. The information that comes from careful observation will also help you and the consumer develop the best change plan.

This lesson discussed how to pinpoint thoughts, behaviors, and feelings; how to define goals and prioritize problems and goals as a basis for determining where to begin working with consumers; how to observe and record behaviors; and how to develop service plans and contracts with consumers. It also introduced some ideas for "motivating" all consumers, including those who initially do not want to work with you. You now have some tools for beginning the effective delivery of services and for monitoring your progress with consumers. Remember, however, that you and the consumer will develop the service plan together, including goals for change and change techniques. It is your job to provide alternatives to consumers and to define possible consequences of each alternative; it is their job to tell you what they wish to do and what they think will work best for them.

Lesson 3. Lesson 3 described ways in which workers can evaluate their service plan for each consumer. The evaluation process includes monitoring and recording the frequency of the presenting problem before, during, and after the service has been introduced, so that the worker and consumer can determine whether the plan is effective. Evaluation continues throughout the service phase. If the behavior is not changing in the expected direction or as rapidly as hoped, a different plan can be introduced. Seeing change can be reinforcing for consumers and workers, as well as a basis for evaluating the helpfulness of services.

Lesson 4. In Lesson 4, case management was defined as a model for helping that emphasizes the worker's role as a service coordinator or facilitator in the use of diverse agencies, services, and roles (including brokering, mobilizing, and advocating). Case managers carry primary responsibility for their cases, but may not provide all the services. Rather, the case manager uses the assessment to help consumers obtain services and monitors the process to ensure that their needs are actually met. The use of case management in the fields of child welfare and mental health was discussed. This lesson described case conferences and consultation, two helping processes used by case managers. Case conferences are meetings of all the involved persons focused on a particular case. Case conferences may include workers from other agencies, the consumer, and members of the consumer's natural helping network. They are useful for sharing ideas and information and for developing and evaluating service plans. The primary worker may need to develop a written case summary for the case conference that would include a statement of the consumer's desired outcomes and most immediate concerns, the worker's observations of the consumer, the service plan to date (what the worker and the consumer have been doing), a summary of the results of delivered services, the reasons for the conference, and key questions that the worker wants addressed in the case conference.

Consultations, like case conferences, are ways to seek additional help. The worker determines the help that is wanted from a consultant. Consultants may be other workers in the agency, specialists from other agencies, or private practitioners. A general guide for meeting with consultants was suggested: Present the problem clearly; clarify the help wanted; allow the consultant to accept or decline the request; and, if the consultant agrees to help, work together to problem solve and listen to the consultant's suggestions. The worker is free to use or reject the consultant's suggestions and will likely make this decision jointly with a supervisor.

Lesson 5. Lesson 5 described working with natural helping networks (natural groupings of people including, but not limited to, family groups). People often receive the help they need from these networks. However, at times they may need additional help from more formal networks. Whenever possible, formal help should be given within the context of natural helping systems. When consumers are members of natural helping networks—either large, loosely organized networks or small, closely knit ones—the natural resources need to be explored and included in any helping plan. It is important not to usurp the help naturally available to consumers but to strengthen and build on their natural resources. The ultimate goal of human service workers is to empower consumers so that workers are no longer needed. This goal cannot be achieved if natural resources are ignored and thereby weakened, or if they are seen as inadequate to meet consumers' needs.

Lesson 6. Educating consumers, described in Lesson 6, is an additional technique for helping and can be implemented by workers or natural helpers. Modeling a behavior or skill that the consumer wants to acquire is an effective educating technique. Educating includes instruction, demonstration or modeling, and practice. Structured training approaches used in teaching consumers new behaviors and new skills are similar to the steps used to teach human service workers interviewing skills. In teaching consumers, workers follow the processes recommended for problem specification and goal selection, and measure where the consumer is before training begins as a basis for evaluation. An effective training program can be developed through goal specification—What would the consumer like to know or be able to do at the end of training?—and consulting with outside resources for the best teaching approach for the specified goal.

Lesson 7. Lesson 7 presented information that is needed to work with groups of consumers. We identified four kinds of groups: therapy groups, activity groups, self-help groups, and task groups. Special attention was given to the skills needed in contacting consumers for the purpose of forming a group, including openly approaching the group, doing your homework, having a sense of humor, and identifying the individual and common interests of group members. A few principles were noted related to the effective functioning of a group worker, such as being on time, giving praise, and enforcing rules. The lesson concluded with a discussion of how the worker assists the group in solving its problems, with special emphasis on the role of the worker in helping members of the group assume more and more responsibility for the direction and activities of the group.

Suggestions for Further Study

It would be helpful to read introductory practice texts, especially those using a systems perspective, such as Pincus and Minahan and Compton and Galaway, referenced below. The problem-solving framework Compton and Galaway describe is similar to the framework presented here. The authors take you through the steps involved in helping, but do so in more detail than here and include brief readings from a number of resources in each area. Pincus and Minahan offer a framework that is relevant whether you work with an individual or a large community group. Their description of practice using a systems framework is relevant for human service workers across consumer groups and practice settings. You may also want to spend time considering attitudes, ethics, and values in working with people. These are issues that you will struggle with as long as you are a human service worker. An excellent resource in this area is *Ethical Decisions for Social Work Practice* by Lowenberg and Dolgoff, cited below. They present value dilemmas that human service workers confront.

There are useful readings on case management and natural helping networks referenced in the lessons on these topics. You may want to augment your knowledge of different techniques used in human service work by reviewing materials on educating consumers and on working with groups. Some excellent materials are included in the references below, as well as the references to service evaluation.

Assessment, Goal Setting, and Contracting

Ciminero, A. R., H. E. Adams, and K. S. Calhoun, eds. *Handbook of Behavioral Assessment,* 2d ed. New York: Wiley, 1986.

Compton, B. R., and B. Galaway. *Social Work Processes,* 5th ed. Pacific Grove, Calif.: Brooks/ Cole, 1994.

Corey, G., M. S. Corey, and P. Callahan. *Issues and Ethics in the Helping Professions,* 4th ed. Pacific Grove, Calif.: Brooks/Cole, 1993.

Gambrill, E. *Casework: A Competency-Based Approach.* Englewood Cliffs, N.J.: Prentice-Hall, 1983.

Hartman, A., and J. Laird. *Family-Centered Social Work Practice.* New York: Free Press, 1983.

Haynes, S. N., and C. C. Wilson. *Behavioral Assessment*. San Francisco: Jossey-Bass, 1979.

Hepworth, D. H., and J. A. Larsen. *Direct Social Work Practice: Theory and Skills,* 4th ed. Pacific Grove, Calif.: Brooks/Cole, 1993.

Ivey, A. *Intentional Interviewing and Counseling: Facilitating Client Development in a Multicultural Society,* 3d ed. Pacific Grove, Calif.: Brooks/Cole, 1994.

Morales, A., and B. W. Sheafor. *Social Work: A Profession of Many Faces,* 3d ed. Boston: Allyn & Bacon, 1983.

Pincus, A., and A. Minahan. *Social Work Practice: Model and Method*. Itasca, Ill.: F. E. Peacock, 1973.

Rauch, J. B., ed. *Assessment: A Sourcebook for Social Work Practice*. Milwaukee, Wis.: Families International, 1993.

Shulman, L. *The Skills of Helping: Individuals, Families, and Groups,* 3d. ed. Itasca, Ill.: F. E. Peacock, 1992.

Case Management, Natural Helping Networks, and Educating

Addams, Jane. *Twenty Years at Hull-House*. New York: Macmillan, 1982.

Austin, M. J., and W. E. Hershey, eds. *Handbook on Mental Health Administration*. San Francisco: Jossey-Bass, 1982.

Collins, A. H., and D. L. Pancoast. *Natural Helping Networks: A Strategy for Prevention*. Washington, D.C.: National Association of Social Workers, 1976.

Gottlieb, B. H. *Social Support Strategies: Guidelines for Mental Health Practice*. Beverly Hills, Calif.: Sage, 1983.

Harris, M., and H. C. Bergman. "Case Management with the Chronically Mentally Ill: A Clinical Perspective." *American Journal of Orthopsychiatry*, 57 (1987): 296–302.

Lowenberg, F., and R. Dolgoff, *Ethical Decisions for Social Work Practice,* 5th ed. Itasca, Ill.: F. E. Peacock, 1996.

Manoleas, P., ed. *The Cross-Cultural Practice of Clinical Case Management in Mental Health*. New York: Haworth Press, 1996.

Raiff, N. R., with B. K. Shore. *Advanced Case Management: New Strategies for the Nineties*. Newbury Park, Calif.: Sage, 1993.

Rose, Stephen M. *Case Management and Social Work Practice*. White Plains, N.Y.: Longman, 1992.

Rothman, J. *Guidelines for Case Management: Putting Research to Professional Use*. Itasca, Ill.: F. E. Peacock, 1992.

Rothman, J. *Practice with Highly Vulnerable Clients: Case Management and Community-Based Service*. Englewood Cliffs, N.J.: Prentice-Hall, 1993.

Vourlekis, B. S., and R. R. Freene, (eds.) *Social Work Case Management*. Hawthorne, N.Y.: 1992.

Whittaker, J. K., and J. Garbarino. *Social Support Networks: Informal Helping in the Human Services*. New York: Aldine de Gruyter, 1983.

Whittaker, J. K., J. Kinney, E. M. Tracy, and C. Booth, eds. *Reaching High-Risk Families: Intensive Family Preservation in Human Services*. New York: Aldine de Gruyter, 1990.

Evaluation

Austin, M. J. *Evaluating Your Agency's Programs*. Beverly Hills, Calif.: Sage, 1982.

Barlow, D. H., and M. Hersen. *Single Case Experimental Designs: Strategies for Studying Behavior Change,* 2d ed. Elmsford, N.Y.: Pergamon, 1984.

Bingham, R. D., and C. L. Felbinger. *Evaluation in Practice: A Methodological Approach,* New York: Longman, 1989.

Bloom, M., J. Fischer and J. G. Orme. *Evaluating Practice: Guidelines for the Accountable Professional,* 2d ed. Boston: Allyn & Bacon, 1995.

Briar, S. "Effective Social Work Intervention in Direct Practice: Implications for Education." In *Facing the Challenge,* edited by CSWE, New York: CSWE, 1973.

Ciminero, A. R., K. S. Calhoun, and H. E. Adams. "Self-Monitoring Procedures." In *Handbook of Behavioral Assessment,* 2d ed., edited by A. R. Ciminero, H. E. Adams, and K. S. Calhoun, 195–232. New York: Wiley, 1987.

Concoran, K., and J. Fischer. *Measures for Clinical Practice.* New York: Free Press, 1995.

Fischer, J. "Is Casework Effective? A Review." *Social Work,* 18, 1 (1973): 5–20.

Fischer, J. "Does Anything Work?" *Journal of Social Service Research* 1 (1978): 215–243.

Gabor, P., and R. M. Grinnell. *Evaluation and Quality Improvement in the Human Services.* Boston: Allyn & Bacon, 1994.

Grinnell, R. M. *Social Work Research and Evaluation.* 3d ed. Itasca, Ill.: F. E. Peacock, 1988.

Grinnell, R., Jr. and M. Williams. *Research in Social Work: A Primer.* Itasca, Ill: F. E. Peacock, 1990.

Kratochwill, T. R., ed. *Single Subject Research: Strategies for Evaluating Change.* New York: Academic Press, 1978.

Maluccio, A. N., ed. *Promoting Competence in Clients: A New/Old Approach to Social Work Practice.* New York: Free Press, 1981.

National Association of Social Workers, *1980 Code of Ethics.* New York: National Association of Social Workers, 1981.

Patterson, G. R., J. B. Reid, R. R. Jones, and R. F. Conger. *A Social Learning Approach in Family Intervention,* vol. 1, *Families wtih Aggressive Children.* Eugene, Ore.: Castalia, 1975.

Reid, W. J., and P. Hanrahan. "Recent Evaluations of Social Work: Grounds for Optimism." *Social Work,* 27 (1982): 328–340.

Rubin, A. "Practice Effectiveness: More Grounds for Optimism." *Social Work,* 30, 6 (1985): 469–476.

Rubin, A., and E. Babie. *Research Methods for Social Work.* Belmont, Calif.: Wadsworth, 1989.

Videka-Sherman, L., and W. J. Reid, eds. *Advances in Clinical Social Work Research.* Silver Springs, Md.: NASW Press, 1990.

Wood, K. M. "Casework Effectiveness: A New Look at the Research Evidence." *Social Work,* 23 (1978): 437–458.

Groups

Ball, S. "A Group Model for Gay and Lesbian Clients with Chronic Mental Illness." *Social Work,* 39 (1994): 109–115.

Berman-Rossi, T., and Cohen, M. "Group Development and Shared Decision Making: Working with Homeless Mentally Ill Women." *Social Work with Groups,* 11, 4 (1989): 138–153.

Brown, L. *Groups for Growth and Change.* New York: Longman, 1991.

Cox, E. "The Critical Role of Social Action in Empowerment-Oriented Groups." *Social Work with Groups,* 14, 3/4 (1991): 77–90.

Henry, S. *Group Skills in Social Work: A Four-Dimensional Approach,* 2d ed. Pacific Grove, Calif.: Brooks/Cole, 1992.

Knight, C. "Use of Support Groups with Adult Female Survivors of Child Sexual Abuse." *Social Work,* (May 1990): 202–205.

Middleman, R., and Wood, G. *Skills for Direct Practice in Social Work,* 91–151. New York: Columbia University Press, 1990.

Shulman, L. "The Group as a Mutual Aid System." in *The Skills of Helping: Individuals, Families, and Groups,* 3d ed. Itasca, Ill.: F. E. Peacock Publishers, 1992.

Toseland, R. W. *Group Work with the Elderly and Family Caregivers.* New York: Springer Publishing Co., 1995.

Toseland, R. W., and R. F. Rivas. *An Introduction to Group Work Practice,* 2d ed. Boston: Allyn & Bacon, 1995.

Yalom, I. *The Theory and Practice of Group Psychotherapy.* New York: Basic Books, 1985.

Chapter 9

Advanced Intervention Models and Case Material

Unlike the other chapters in Unit Three that are designed to facilitate your direct acquisition of knowledge and skills to aid you in accomplishing your goal of working effectively with consumers, Chapter 9 is an auxiliary resource. Chapter 9 has two goals: (1) to broaden your familiarity with advanced intervention techniques, and (2) to provide case materials to aid in extending your acquisition of the skills and knowledge described in Unit Three.

Numerous theories have been developed to explain human behavior, and a variety of intervention models have been designed for use in delivering services to individuals, families, and small groups. Theories describe relationships among phenomena and predict events. In addition to the generic helping approaches described in Chapter 8 (e.g., using natural helping networks), a number of interventive approaches and models are used by the helping professions. Since it would be impossible to cover all of these strategies in this text, we have chosen to illustrate some frequently used advanced treatment models, each based on one or more theoretical orientations.

The approaches described in Lesson 1 emphasize intervention as a learning process. The change target and goal may predict which intervention will be used, because some intervention models are designed to change behaviors, others to modify feelings, and still others to bring about changes in people's thoughts or cognitions.

In doing an assessment, the worker and consumer together determine which area is causing the most difficulty—the consumer's behavior, thoughts, or feelings—in order to focus change efforts and select appropriate intervention techniques. Yet, we cannot assume that change in one area will automatically result in change in the other two. Depending on the consumer and the problem, it may be necessary to plan different change efforts for thoughts, feelings, and behavior. We generally begin with the area that is most problematic for the consumer. The selection of the most important problem provides the skilled worker with the foundation for selecting the most appropriate helping approach. If change is directed toward one area and the other areas are carefully monitored, it is possible to determine whether change also is occurring in the other areas. Change in behavior may result in changes in how others respond to the consumer, which in turn may change the consumer's perceptions of self (thoughts) and the consumer's self-esteem (feelings).

Our knowledge about ways to help others has increased dramatically, yet we continue to search for more effective ways of changing problem behaviors, thoughts, and feelings. The emphasis on practice evaluation and clinical research is a response to the need for more effective interventions. Practitioners, through measuring the outcomes of their work with consumers, can contribute significantly to the knowledge base.

Several case studies are presented in Lesson 2 to illustrate the approaches described in Lesson 1. The cases can provide additional learning opportunities, and can be used to extend the ideas introduced in Units Two and Three.

As you read the lessons in this chapter, recall the general steps used in the helping process. The following ten steps, described in previous lessons, are also built into the approaches described throughout this chapter:

1. Building a helping relationship
2. Exploring the consumer's total situation
3. Defining presenting problems, issues, and situations; identifying the range of problems seen by the consumer and the helping person
4. Assessing the situation
5. Identifying conditions controlling the problem; specifying behaviors, thoughts, feelings, and environmental elements that determine the frequency and severity of problems
6. Selecting targets for intervention and setting goals; defining desired outcomes
7. Identifying natural strengths and resources and selecting appropriate change tactics or interventions
8. Developing a helping plan and a contract
9. Assessing the effectiveness of the plan throughout its implementation using pre-, during, and postchange measures
10. Ending the helping process

In addition to offering consumers concrete help and support, human service workers engage in activities designed to bring about a change in the behavior patterns, feelings, and perceptions of individuals and groups. We think familiarity with a few of the advanced techniques widely used in human service agencies will be helpful to you in your work. This chapter provides only an *overview* of selected approaches. Those who want to use these techniques will need to consult additional readings and receive specialized training and supervision to acquire the skills necessary for effective actual clinical applications.

Models of Intervention as a Learning Process: Some Examples

This lesson describes five widely used models emphasizing intervention as a learning process. These models are used frequently in diverse human service settings.

Goal

To attain beginning understanding of reality therapy, behavior therapy, cognitive or cognitive-behavior therapy, time-limited intervention, and crisis intervention.

Learning Activities

To accomplish the goal, we will:

1. Identify the aims and basic assumptions of each model of intervention.
2. Describe some of the procedures used to carry out these approaches.

FRAME

1

REALITY THERAPY[1]

Reality therapy was developed by Dr. William Glasser as an intervention approach to help individuals and groups change their responses to their environments, and their perceptions of reality. The primary aim of reality therapy is to help people develop new modes of behavior by accepting responsibility for their actions and by learning how to fulfill their needs appropriately. Reality therapy is used most frequently with youth offenders, adult legal offenders, mental patients, and disturbed children. In institutional settings, where people may have similar kinds of problems, reality therapy is usually applied in group sessions.

---

[1]See William Glasser, *Reality Therapy: A New Approach to Psychiatry,* Reprint ed. (New York: Harper Collins, 1975); William Glasser, *Stations of the Mind: New Directions for Reality Therapy* (New York: Harper Collins, 1981).

Four major principles underlie reality therapy. The first principle is that *everyone is viewed as having two basic emotional needs:* (1) the need to love and be loved, and (2) the need to feel worthwhile about self and others. When working with consumers, the key to fulfilling these basic needs is the consumer's involvement with someone for whom he or she cares and who (the consumer feels) cares in return. When people have not learned an acceptable range of methods for fulfilling these needs early in life, they may be driven to unrealistic and unacceptable actions to fulfill their needs. If consumers continue these unacceptable actions, they may become increasingly unable to behave realistically or responsibly. The reality therapist hopes to teach people how to recognize their needs and, subsequently, how to change their behavior in order to fulfill their needs with realistic, acceptable behavior.

The second principle of reality therapy is that *only present or future behavior can be changed*. Thus, in reality therapy sessions the focus is on what the person is doing now. Of course, present behavior can also include activities closely preceding the time of the session. The reality therapist asks *what,* not why, in focusing on current behavior.

A third principle of reality behavior is that it *deals only with reality*. This means that attention is directed to actions and events as they exist in fact, not as they should have been.

The fourth principle is *responsibility*. Responsibility is the ability to fulfill one's needs and to do so in a way that does not deprive others of the opportunity to fulfill their needs. A responsible person can give and receive love, and behaves in ways that support feelings of self-worth and the worth of others. Thus, consumers learn to accept responsibility for their behavior and the consequences associated with it. Consumers must accept these realities in order to change unacceptable behavior.

Procedures of Reality Therapy

The specialized learning promoted through reality therapy is made up of three separate yet related procedures.

1. Involvement. Through the worker's involvement with the consumer, a trusting relationship develops that gives the consumer the strength and confidence to begin to face reality and see how his or her behavior is unrealistic. It is important for the worker to be strong enough to reject the consumer's requests for sympathy and to model responsible behavior by being a responsible person.

2. Rejection of unreality. The worker *rejects* unrealistic behaviors while *accepting the consumer* and *maintaining involvement*. The worker helps consumers realize that they are responsible for their behavior. In reality therapy, the concern is with consumers' behavior, not necessarily with their attitudes or feelings. Along with this, the worker freely gives praise when consumers act responsibly and shows disapproval of irresponsible behavior.

3. Learning. The worker teaches consumers better ways to fulfill their needs within the limits of reality. When consumers admit that their behavior is irresponsible, the final phase of learning begins. Here consumers can rely on the worker's experiences to help them learn more effective ways of behaving. When consumers can express their behavior in responsible ways, therapy is nearing an end.

In practice, these three basic procedures are woven together to form the process of re-ality therapy.

These three procedures can now be translated into the basic steps generally fol-lowed in reality therapy. First, the worker helps the consumer *identify* his unrealistic, nonproductive behavior. Once identification has occurred, the worker helps the con-sumer to do one or both of the following:

1. Make a judgment about his behavior, such as saying, "I'm not supposed to do that."
2. Identify the consequences of his behavior, for example, saying, "When people do that, they usually get into trouble."

At this phase in the therapeutic process, the worker helps the consumer formulate alternative plans for developing behaviors that the consumer judges to be appropriate. Throughout the entire process, the worker is warm, supportive, and personal with the consumer.

When the therapy reaches the final stage of planning, the worker will be open and honest with the consumer. Should the consumer select a plan for behavioral change that the worker considers inappropriate, the worker will share this observation with the consumer and assist in formulating more appropriate alternatives. The dia-logue below illustrates these procedures.

An 8-year-old boy (Bob) who lives in a group foster home stole some cherries; he has the following conversation with his house parent (H.P.) on the way home:

H.P.: Bob, what do you have in your pocket?
BOB: Just some cherries.
H.P.: Where did you get the cherries?
BOB: Down in Mr. Miller's orchard.
H.P.: Did he give them to you?
BOB: No.
H.P.: How did you get them?
BOB: Well, I sort of took them. [Identifies his behavior.]
H.P.: What do we call that, Bob?
BOB: I guess it's kind of stealing. [Identifies his behavior.]
H.P.: Is that what you are supposed to do?
BOB: No. [Makes a value of judgment of his behavior.]
H.P.: What happens when boys take things that don't belong to them?
BOB: They get into trouble. [Identifies the consequences of his behavior.]
H.P.: What else?
BOB: People get mad at them and then they don't trust them anymore. [Identifies consequences.]
H.P. Is that what you want, Bob?
BOB: No. [Makes a value judgment of the consequences of his behavior.]
H.P.: Well, what do you think you could do?
BOB: Not steal any more cherries. [Begins to formulate an alternative plan.]
H.P.: What about the ones in your pocket?
BOB: I guess I ought to take them back. [Formulates alternative plan.]
H.P.: Is that all?
BOB: Yeah, I could throw them over the fence. [Formulates alternative plan.]

H.P.: Would that make it right?

BOB: No.

H.P.: Well, then, what are you going to do?

BOB: I guess I ought to give them back to Mr. Miller and say I'm sorry. [Formulates a plan.]

H.P.: That's a good idea, Bob. When are you going to do it?

BOB: I guess I could do it now. [Formulates a plan.]

H.P.: Is there any way I can help you?

BOB: Sort of. I'm afraid of Mr. Miller. Will you go with me and just be there beside me? [Formulates a plan.]

H.P.: Of course, Bob. Let's go.

This introduction to reality therapy will help you when you are working with a reality therapist. To gain further insights and skills in this therapeutic process, it is important to seek the supervision of an expert.

F R A M E

BEHAVIOR THERAPY

Behavioral interventions emphasize the relationship between the consumer's environment and behavior. Behavior is seen as the outcome of learning experiences in response to the environment including people, situations, and events. The primary goal of behavior therapy is to teach consumers new modes of behavior and, when appropriate, change their environment to facilitate their learning. Behavior therapy specifies behavior—either observable, overt behavior or nonobservable, covert behavior (thoughts) and verbal expressions. Thus, the behavior therapist is concerned about thoughts and verbal expressions as well as observable behaviors. Moreover, interviewing and relationship-building skills are important building blocks for effective behavioral techniques. Behavioral techniques are taught to consumers, and service plans are controlled and implemented by consumers, whenever possible.

The behavioral approach, based on learning theory, assumes that the principles of human behavior that explain adaptive, or "normal," behavior also explain the development of maladaptive, or "abnormal," behavior. Consumers are responsive to their environments, including important people in their lives. They learn from observing people, from interacting with people, and from human reactions to their behavior. Based on observations of human learning, behavioral techniques have been developed and applied to a wide range of human problems from implementation of consistent exercise programs to family interactions. Behavioral techniques and procedures have been developed to treat alcohol and other substance abuse, children's behavior in their homes and at school, work behavior, depression, phobias and fears, sexual functioning, anger, eating problems, speech issues and problems, and communication problems. Behavior therapy is applied with all age groups, in outpatient as well as inpatient settings. A number of self-help programs have been developed based on behavioral procedures. Behavioral procedures are often used in institutional settings where the principles and techniques described here can be taught to consumers for use in their own environment.

In summary, behavior therapy emphasizes the following points:

1. Individualizing consumers, their issues, and their situations
2. Building positive behavior
3. Promoting active consumer involvement in problem specification, determining goals and a service plan, and selecting and implementing change procedures
4. Focusing on present problems and current conditions
5. Focusing on the interaction of individuals within their environment, rather than on intrapsychic phenomena
6. Bringing about specificity of behaviors from vague statements to measurable targets
7. Monitoring change and measurement of intervention outcomes
8. Maintaining change and generalizing change from the setting where the behavior was learned to other settings

Behavioral interventions are based on learning theories, such as respondent learning and operant learning. Some behavior is triggered by the events that precede it or stimulate a particular response. This is called *respondent behavior*. Other behavior is controlled by the events that follow it, by rewards or punishments, and this is called *operant behavior*. A raised hand in a classroom is a stimulus to the teacher. If you are called on, the teacher has responded to your stimulus, and the teacher's response is a stimulus for you.

Some responses are automatic or involuntary. When an eyelash (a stimulus) is caught in your eye, tearing (the response) occurs. But most responses are not automatic; they are learned behavior. And we now know that through special learning we can control even some responses, such as breathing, that we generally think of as automatic. The learning may be so complete that we respond without stopping to think about whether to respond. In other situations we may pause and think about the response, in which case our thinking may be a mediator between the stimulus and the response. This mediating factor, our thoughts, has promoted some behaviorally oriented therapists to become interested in the cognitive-behavioral approach, which applies principles of behavior therapy to covert behaviors such as thoughts and feelings.

Operant behavior is responsive to events that follow the behavior, such as the tangible reward of a salary increase or the social reward of praise and attention from others. Reinforcement usually increases the occurrence of a behavior. Thus, many events may follow the occurrence of a particular behavior. The events that cause the behavior to continue or increase are called *reinforcers*. We learn both positive and negative consequences of our behavior and are free to respond to them or not. At the same time, we display common behavior over long periods of time that seems almost automatic. We describe such behavior as *habit*. At times it is difficult to understand why people do certain things. Behavior and our learning histories are complex. Special assessment skills are required to understand the variety of factors that may control or predict the occurrence of certain behavior, especially behavior that appears undesirable and unproductive.

Behavior Modification Procedures

Behavior therapy deals with respondent and operant behavior using different procedures for each. For example, procedures for modifying respondent behavior are most commonly used with such problems as *excessive fear* and *anxiety*. Many of the procedures are based on a method called *counterconditioning*. Among respondent emotional reactions, certain responses do not "go together." For example, you cannot simultaneously be anxious and relaxed. Using this latter concept, *counterconditioning means replacing an existing response, such as anxiety, with a response that will not go with it, such as relaxation.* The following is a familiar example that illustrates this concept:

> *Example:* Most children do not like bad-tasting medicine, and their parents have a difficult time getting them to take it. But when a parent accompanies the medicine with candy or verbal praise, the anxiety is reduced or overcome, and the child takes the bad-tasting medicine. A parent who does this is using basic principles of counterconditioning.

Most procedures for modifying operant behavior, such as making a bed or throwing a temper tantrum, apply the basic rule that undesirable behavior is weakened by not being rewarded and desirable behavior is strengthened by being followed with a reward. Two such procedures used in human service institutions are *reinforcement* and *extinction*.

Reinforcement

Reinforcement is the introduction or removal of any event following the occurrence of a behavior in order to maintain or increase the frequency of that behavior. There are two basic types of reinforcement: *positive* and *negative*. Positive reinforcement uses any event that, when it follows a response, increases the strength or maintains the occurrence of that response. Positive reinforcers may be different for each individual. However, items that serve as reinforcers for many of us are food, money, and attention. Positive reinforcers must be identified for the individual consumer. When this technique is used, a treatment plan is developed that will strengthen or maintain specified desirable behavior by presenting a positive reinforcer immediately following the occurrence of the desired behavior.

> *Example:* Approval (positive reinforcer) was repeatedly shown to a mental patient who had just made his bed (desired behavior) with the result that in the future he made his bed without the need for reinforcement.

Negative reinforcement is an attempt to maintain or strengthen desired behavior (response) by the removal of a stimulus (negative reinforcer) that a person wishes to avoid and that may cause pain or discomfort to that person. When this technique is used, a treatment plan is developed where specified desirable responses will be strengthened by removing the negative reinforcers.

> *Example:* Self-feeding was increased among developmentally disabled children who were previously regarded as unwilling to feed themselves. The aide discovered many of the children actually did not like it when the food server spilled food on their trays (which happened frequently) in the course of feeding and thus served as a negative reinforcer. When the aide eliminated the source of food spilling by placing the food on a buffet table directly accessible to the children, many were able to feed themselves—they did not have to experience the discomfort that occurred with the food server spilling the food on a tray.

Token economies are systems of reinforcement that have been used effectively in institutional settings to modify residents' behavior. Tokens are objects that symbolize various units of value to a consumer because they can be exchanged for something the consumer wants. Token reinforcers may be coins or chips or simply points earned for performing certain behaviors. Token economies are useful because the reinforcer is flexible (i.e., tokens can be exchanged for any number of diverse rewards, and thus the rewards can be individualized) and can be given as soon as the behavior occurs. Reinforcers that immediately follow each occurrence of a desired behavior are more effective in building behaviors than reinforcers received a week later. The relationship of the reinforcer to the behavior in time and in frequency (also called the contingency arrangement) can control whether or not change occurs.

Tokens are also useful because their value can be changed. For example, if a desired behavior has been learned and the consumer has received a token for each occurrence of the behavior, the worker may slowly "fade out" the reinforcer. This can be done easily with tokens by increasing the number of times the behavior must occur in order to receive a token.

Money is the most common example of a token because its value comes from what it can be exchanged for. Tokens are secondary reinforcers, and what they buy are primary reinforcers. If points are recorded publicly, however, the earning of points itself may become reinforcing for the consumer. Points on a test are a form of token; they are more immediate reinforcers than grades, and, added together, they represent the grade. Thus, token economies are flexible systems and therefore helpful in working with consumers in groups within and outside of institutional settings.

Extinction

A second technique for modifying operant behavior is called extinction. When a reinforcement for maintaining certain behavior is removed, the behavior slowly disappears. When the behavior no longer occurs, or occurs at a very low rate, it is said to be extinguished. This procedure is used to weaken or eliminate a response.

Example: If it has been determined that a child's tantrum behavior is sustained by parental attention, tantrums may be reduced or eliminated by withholding parental attention (ignoring child) during tantrum behavior.

Behavior modification is typically most successful with consumers who have very observable problems. It is therefore criticized because it does not try to encompass thoughts and feelings. Behavior modification is also criticized as being manipulative (e.g., a way of controlling behavior) and as limited to being most effective in institutional settings where consumers are not free to come and go at will. So before using behavior modification (or any other advanced intervention), it is important to understand the scope of the consumer's problem and to assess whether the setting in which the consumer functions is amenable to the requirements of this intervention technique.

F R A M E

3

COGNITIVE THERAPY

Over the past 20 years, there has been increasing interest in cognitive techniques for dealing with the problems of depression, fear, pain, anxiety, and self-esteem. More recently, cognitive therapy has been applied to substance abuse, personality disorders, panic disorders, and schizophrenia. Cognitive therapy emphasizes identifying and changing distorted thinking. The cognitive therapist works to change the way consumers conceive of the world around them, the way in which they structure reality. Cognitions, or thoughts, are verbal or pictorial "events" in the person's consciousness that are based on attitudes or assumptions developed through prior experiences.[2] The cognitive approach is a structured, time-limited approach that uses both cognitive and behavioral interventions in treatment.[3] In fact, a number of studies have been conducted comparing cognitive to behavioral treatments for depression. The most successful outcomes come from combining cognitive and behavioral interventions.[4]

Cognitive therapy is based on the assumption that changing a consumer's cognitions, or thoughts, about a particular issue will result in changes in the consumer's feelings and behavior as well. Some people develop distorted thinking about themselves and assume the distortion is correct. As a result, they never question the distortion or attempt the task that they are certain they cannot perform. For example, a depressed woman may walk into another person's home and say to herself, "This person works and keeps a perfect house, and my home never looks like this." The consumer *assumes* that she cannot keep a clean house, and so she never attempts to do so. No matter what family members may say to dissuade her of this self-evaluation, the depressed woman insists she is worthless as a housekeeper.

A common thought pattern among depressed persons is that "I am no good," "I am a constant source of problems for my family and friends," and "I cannot do anything well." The cognitive therapist works with the consumer to change such thought patterns so that the person will cease feeling depressed. If the person stops thinking she is worthless at keeping house, she may attempt to clean the house, experience success, receive compliments from others, and continue keeping the house orderly. An alternative, equally positive cognitive change would be for her to change her expectations of herself in relation to housecleaning—to realize that her performance in this area is satisfactory and that a "perfect" house is not her primary goal, nor is it a measure of her value as a family member.

Distorted thoughts often seem to occur automatically without an identifiable cause. It may be difficult or impossible to identify the *origins* of the distorted thought. For example, it is possible that in the example above the negative thoughts were not actually related to the experience of housecleaning. Consumers may exaggerate one experience, assume they are worthless at completing a task, and not attempt it again. Thus, the distorted thoughts may seem to occur automatically and are seen as beyond the consumer's control. Such distorted thoughts continue, and somehow they seem plausible to the consumer. The more plausible the distortion seems to others, the less it is questioned and the stronger it becomes. Generally, the consumer will interpret a wide range of experiences based on a few stereotyped ideas. Cognitive theory suggests that the unpleasant thought precedes the unpleasant feeling. Several types of cognitive distortions have been identified:[5]

---

[2]Aaron T. Beck et al., *Cognitive Therapy of Depression* (New York: Guilford Press, 1979), p. 3.
[3]Beck et al., *Cognitive Therapy*, p. 3.
[4]Paul Blaney, *The Effectiveness of Cognitive and Behavioral Therapies* (New York: Academic Press, 1984).
[5]Beck et al., *Cognitive Therapy*, p. 14.

1. *Arbitrary inference* (wrong conclusion) means a consumer makes an inference without factual evidence or reaches a conclusion based solely on inference that is actually contrary to the evidence.
2. *Selective abstraction* (out of context) involves focusing on a detail taken out of context and conceptualizing a whole experience around the fragment.
3. *Overgeneralization* (everything is wrong) occurs when a consumer draws a general conclusion about his or her ability, performance, or worth based on a single incident (e.g., if the lawn is not mowed regularly, the homeowner concludes that he is a lousy neighbor).
4. *Magnification* and *minimization* of events (it's a catastrophe or it's nothing) are examples of errors in evaluating events; an unpleasant event becomes a catastrophe.
5. *Inexact labeling* of feelings (wrong connections) means that the emotional reaction tends to be inappropriately linked to a descriptive label created by the consumer rather than to an actual experience.
6. *Personalization* (it's my fault) occurs when a consumer relates external events to him- or herself when there is no basis for drawing such a connection.
7. *Absolutistic, dichotomous thinking* (it's either right or wrong) is the tendency to place all experiences in one of two opposite categories (e.g., saint or sinner, flawless or defective).

Cognitive Therapy Procedures

In using cognitive therapy, the worker and the consumer explore the consumer's situation to find out whether the consumer is having dysfunctional, irrational, or distorted thoughts. Next, the therapist and the consumer discover the origin of the distorted and inaccurate thought patterns. The therapeutic techniques are designed to identify and correct distorted thoughts and the dysfunctional beliefs underlying them. The approach includes specific learning experiences designed to teach the consumer to

1. Monitor negative thoughts.
2. Recognize connections between thoughts, feelings, and behavior.
3. Examine the evidence for and against negative thoughts.
4. Substitute reality-oriented interpretations for distorted ones.
5. Learn to identify and alter distorted beliefs that can distort experiences.[6]

After the distorted thoughts are explored, the therapist explains the rationale for cognitive therapy and the process of identifying and recording negative thoughts on a daily monitoring form. Using this record, the consumer's cognitions and underlying assumptions are discussed, and the logic and validity of each are explored. The absence of identification of successful actions is also discussed. Negative thoughts (e.g., suicidal thoughts) are identified along with the thoughts that support them (e.g., "I am worthless and I cannot change"). Using the therapist as a model, the consumer learns to question assumptions. Behavioral techniques are used to encourage consumers to try certain tasks and thereby to look at situations in new ways. Also, in working with depressed consumers, behavioral interventions may be used

---

[6]Beck et al., *Cognitive Therapy*, p. 4.

first to get the person activated and overcome inertia. Behavioral interventions may be helpful in overcoming distorted beliefs, and cognitive therapy may be instrumental if consumers are to cease making incorrect inferences regarding future events. The new skills of identifying and questioning distorted thoughts should be transferred from the counseling situation to the person's natural environment. Thus, cognitive therapy involves educating the consumer and helping the consumer develop new skills.

Let's apply these cognitive therapy ideas to a hypothetical situation. Perhaps you once did not prepare for an exam and therefore received a low grade. All your friends received high grades on this exam. Your first thought might have been, "This professor doesn't like me" or "I'm not as bright as my friends" or "I can't learn the material in this course." If one such thought had persisted, it might have affected your performance in the course for the rest of the semester. You might, for example, have decided that the situation was hopeless and fulfilled your negative expectations by seeing yourself as unliked, dumb, or simply unable to absorb the course material. You then would not have done the work and therefore would have done poorly in the course. On the other hand, you might have had such thoughts for a moment but then recalled that, in fact, you were not prepared for the exam and could receive a good grade if you prepared the next time. A consumer who needs help does not process his first impression but accepts the distorted thought as reality. In these situations cognitive therapy is indicated and can be helpful in reordering thinking to match more closely what actually did occur.

FRAME
4

TIME-LIMITED INTERVENTION

Many helpers representing varied theoretical orientations and intervention approaches have become increasingly interested in time-limited, brief, short-term intervention. Twenty-five years ago Bill Reid, a social work educator who created the Task Centered model for helping consumers, conducted a study at the Family Service Society of New York comparing long-term therapy without time limits to short-term, time-limited intervention.[7] At that time, in the late 1960s, most counselors and social workers agreed that intervention that continued until the worker and client (generally, the worker) agreed it was time to discontinue intervention was preferred. In addition, in general, long-term treatment was perceived as higher-status, higher-quality service than time-limited contacts. Reid's research found that there were more positive changes when brief treatment (8 sessions) compared to extended treatment (18 months) was used, that consumers were more satisfied with the services they received, and that the changes were more durable six months post intervention. The consumers in the study were relatively healthy, middle-class persons receiving voluntary, client-requested treatment.

Actually, many providers do brief treatment but not by plan, as consumers may discontinue before the worker feels they are ready to do so. Intervention termination may

---

[7]W. J. Reid and A. Shyne, *Brief and Extended Casework* (New York: Columbia University Press, 1969).

occur with or without planning. Time-limited intervention is distinguished by defining the time limit at the first meeting with an individual consumer or family or group.

There are a number of short-term or time-limited intervention models: I. K. Berg's[8] Solution-Focused Approach, W. J. Reid's[9] Task Centered Strategies, and Jay Haley's[10] Problem-Solving Therapy, for example.

As Reid points out, the dynamic of change does not lie simply in the life measure we call time; it is not the time span itself, but its psychological effects on both the consumer and the worker. Time limits encourage early mobilization of worker and consumer and focus on the central issues. Time limits force partialization of the issue to be worked on and of the goal to be reached. There is likely to be some change, and even small changes are rewarding. Small changes and the consumer's knowledge that the worker believes change is possible relatively soon, as is implicit in setting time limits during their first contact, motivates and encourages consumers. Time-limited intervention affects both the scope and the pace of the helping process. Once a time limit is defined—say eight sessions—the worker realizes she or he must strive to define the issues and formulate a contract with a change strategy that will have a clear impact. Most consumers appear to be positively affected by a time limit, frequently finding the notion of a foreseeable endpoint as hopeful and encouraging. Data show that the greatest changes occur early in worker–consumer relationships. This may be because consumers are hurting the most at the beginning of the helping process and are therefore the most motivated to work toward change.

Generic components of time-limited or brief intervention include: (1) defining the time limit before or during the first contact (at the end of the assessment); (2) focusing attention on the present and on the presenting issue; (3) giving consumers task assignments to carry out between sessions; (4) the worker focusing on building consumer hope for positive outcomes; (5) the worker enhancing and encouraging consumer involvement throughout the relationship; (6) designing the intervention plan to achieve at least one of the consumer's desired outcomes; (7) planning one follow-up session, generally one to three months after the last scheduled session; and (8) an option to renegotiate a new time-limited contract, but this option should be used infrequently (with less than 20 percent of cases).

The initial interview is critical and should involve the following components: (1) building hope through examples of other consumer successes, emphasizing consumer strengths, (2) demonstrating empathy (worker identifies and clearly expresses the consumer's major feelings); (3) defining only one or two central issues; (4) worker and consumer agreeing to work together to accomplish a clearly identified goal and creating a contract for goal accomplishment; (5) setting the time limit (total number of sessions and weeks); and (6) assigning a task (a homework assignment) for the consumer to carry out between the first and the second session. As in all helping, goals are best when they are specific, explicit, realistic, attainable, consider constraints, can be modified, can be measured, are prioritized, are stated in terms of consumer's desired outcomes, and, of course, are developed collaboratively.

---

[8]I. K. Berg, *Family-Based Services: A Solution-Focused Approach* (New York: W. W. Norton, 1994).

[9]W. J. Reid, *Task Strategies: An Empirical Approach to Clinical Social Work* (New York: Columbia University Press, 1992).

[10]Jay Haley, *Problem-Solving Therapy,* 2nd ed. (San Francisco: Calif.: Jossey-Bass, 1989).

In brief intervention models the focus is on the here and now. The worker emphasizes the chief complaint: Who is doing what that presents a problem to whom and how does the behavior or issue constitute a problem.

In all intervention efforts the worker wants to increase the consumer's hope and positive expectations. Some ways to do this include:

- avoiding assumptions about where the consumer is
- breaking goal into small steps
- being clear about each step
- anticipating with the consumer the consumer's reservations and hesitations
- generating alternative ideas for interventions
- exploring the potential consequences of each intervention
- helping clients identify their concerns about the agency and the helping process
- discussing past successes of this consumer and of other consumers
- clarifying what the consumer hopes to accomplish
- *involving the consumer in planning*

Assignments and Tasks

Task assignments, to be completed by the consumer in his or her natural environment between contacts, are important in change efforts. Reid's definition of tasks in Task-Centered or Task Strategy Intervention is generic among short-term intervention advocates: a task is something that consumers can do themselves outside the formal helping session. Tasks serve at least two functions: (1) they emphasize the active nature of the intervention and change process and the consumer's role in the process, and (2) they emphasize the need for change to take place in real-life situations.

Often the first task assigned at the end of the first session with a consumer is for consumers to observe themselves alone or in interactions with others by keeping a diary, daily notes, or counting the specified thoughts, feelings and/or behaviors of concern. Self-monitoring was described in Chapter 8. Ideally, as described in the evaluation lesson of Chapter 8, monitoring continues as a means of determining whether the consumer is moving toward his or her desired outcome. Self-monitoring can be empowering because it tells the consumer that he or she knows the most about themselves and that the information they collect is critical to the intervention process; also, it gives consumers information with which to assess themselves and a tool they can use to modify future issues.

In brief models the focus of intervention is a direct response to the consumer's immediate request. Although the worker may recognize other areas needing intervention, no attempts are made to intervene in other areas unless such intervention is needed in order to address the consumer's central concern. A key tenet of the task focused model is to focus on the consumer's goals. Design the intervention to directly address this central concern. Offer alternative procedures and encourage the consumer to suggest interventions. Review with the consumer the potential pluses and minuses that might be related to each potential intervention. Brief intervention models generally focus on one issue rather than attempting to address all the identified issues.

Although the issue may not be completely resolved at the end of the specified number of sessions, if the consumer is making progress toward resolution at a good pace, termination may be appropriate. Termination at this point reflects your confidence that the consumer can continue to change without you.

CRISIS INTERVENTION

The process by which the human service worker helps families deal with emergencies is called *crisis intervention*. Crisis intervention is a set of techniques developed to help individuals, families and communities handle periods of unusual stress in order to end the painful reaction to a stressful event as rapidly as possible and to ensure that permanent damage does not occur.

All of us experience stressful events throughout our lives, and many of us experience crises. Crises may occur when a family member dies or becomes critically ill, when an employed family member loses their job, or when other radical changes or external hardships occur. There may be one event, a series of events, or a number of simultaneous events. Crises are usually unanticipated or unusual events during which the consumer generally experiences unfamiliar feelings of helplessness and vulnerability.

Studies of mourning and loss, separation, acute physical disability, and chronic illness show that most people respond to a crisis in similar ways. A crisis creates disequilibrium; healthy individuals strive to restore the equilibrium. We all have different ways of doing this. The active crisis is time limited; a new equilibrium is usually reached within four to six weeks. However, people who experience a series of stresses within a short period of time are vulnerable to mental disturbance.[11] The helping process is designed to assist the consumer in reaching a new equilibrium, a healthy adjustment to the new condition.

Numerous sources of stress have been identified in the mental health literature. They are not all negative events. They represent major decision-making points in life or major changes, such as moving to a new area, marriage, or a new job. These can be as stressful as the loss of a loved one. We do not know why some people handle crises well and come through them without scars, while others experience crises as debilitating. We all experience crises somewhat differently. More fortunate persons, those with natural resources—social, family, work, and economic—are more likely to handle crises without continuing problems. Crisis situations are usually managed successfully when extended family and friends gather to support the person. For example, when the spouse of a relative dies, friends and family members usually gather around so that the person is not alone; they provide companionship and perform everyday tasks during the critical days.

While a number of techniques are used in crisis intervention, several distinct activities are recommended when working with persons in crises:

1. Focus attention on the present crisis, the current surrounding situation, and, possibly, on the precipitating events.
2. Examine how a family or an individual handled crises in the past.
3. Offer support and assistance to relieve the immediate situation.

---

[11]LeNora Mundt, "Mental Health Treatment Methods," in *Handbook on Mental Health Administration,* Michael Austin and William Hershey, eds. (San Francisco: Jossey-Bass, 1982), p. 48.

4. Provide brief, intensive services until some equilibrium is restored and consumers are able to resume their usual level of functioning.
5. Screen for suicide risk.

As you interview a consumer, it is important to find out how many changes have occurred in the preceding six months. Such data may be a cue as to whether the person needs additional help to get through the next six months. If you think that suicide is a possibility, consult with others and involve your supervisor. If the person has attempted suicide in the past, is thinking about suicide, or has a suicide plan, it is critical to develop a plan to protect the consumer. Further, if the consumer does not have a natural support system, intervention to prevent suicide is even more critical. Some agencies use a contract whereby the consumer agrees to call the worker or another designated person if he or she is considering suicide. Protections may also be developed through neighbors and local clinics.

Assessment also focuses on the events preceding the stressful event and the person's attempts to alleviate the stress. Common symptoms found in persons experiencing stress or a crisis are depression, despair, lethargy, emotional instability, difficulty concentrating and carrying out usual life tasks, changes in social relationships or activities and interests, changes in sleeping and eating patterns, and (sometimes) thoughts of suicide. Psychological effects of crises may include disorganized thinking, reduced effective functioning, hostility and emotional distance, impulsivity, and dependency.[12]

An important point to explore with a consumer in crisis is the identification of a similar experience in the past and how the experience was handled. This will help the consumer to feel more in control and hopeful about the present. It will also provide ideas for relieving the current feelings of anxiety and hopelessness. By focusing on a past success in handling a difficult situation (even just getting through it), the consumer acquires perspective on the current situation and an opportunity to feel better. One goal of the initial crisis interview is for the consumer to feel somewhat better than when the interview began. A consumer may appear confused and helpless; exploring recent events will help the consumer see some aspects of the problems as temporary or situational. By identifying the problem as situational, the consumer may get a handle on the situation and see the possibility for change.

The goals of the treatment process are to relieve the symptoms as soon as possible, restore the person to his or her former level of functioning, facilitate an understanding of the precipitating event, identify the way in which the person restored balance, recognize the current state of equilibrium, anticipate any recurrence, and reinforce the ability to cope. It is important that the client understand what happened in order to prevent recurrence of the symptoms and to allow the client to become aware of new behaviors and coping abilities that he or she can call upon when anxiety or stress recurs. According to crisis theory, this process involves four to six weeks of intense work with the client because of the acute nature of the anxiety and the client's sense of inadequacy to cope with the situation.[13]

Conducting Interviews in a Crisis Situation

Crisis intervention is intense, short-term help. It is a preventive approach in that help given at the time of the crisis may prevent long-term dysfunctioning or men-

---

[12]William Getz, *Brief Counseling with Suicidal Persons* (Lexington, Mass.: Lexington Books, 1983).
[13]Mundt, "Mental Health Treatment Methods."

tal illness. If natural helping networks are unavailable, formal help may be critical. You may need to give direct advice, since people in crisis tend to think less clearly and have difficulty handling daily responsibilities such as paying bills and preparing meals. It is important to provide assurance that these abilities will return. By helping a person recognize the source of the crisis and understand that the symptoms they are experiencing are "normal" and time limited, the worker can provide the consumer with an opportunity to develop realistic expectations and increased hope.

Given the goals and activities of crisis intervention, the following questions are recommended as a guide for conducting initial crisis interviews:[14]

1. What prompted the consumer to seek help now? Who referred the consumer?
2. In the consumer's words, what happened that precipitated the crisis?
3. How is the consumer trying to solve this crisis? What has been tried? How has it worked?
4. How was the consumer functioning before the crisis?
5. What has changed; what is different between how the consumer functioned before the crisis compared with how she is functioning now?
6. Has anything like this happened before? If so, what were the outcomes?
7. Has the consumer experienced similar situations or different situations that were also difficult? What did she do then? What worked and what did not work?
8. What are the consumer's environmental supports (family, friends, neighbors, church, organizations, work, recreation)?
9. Is this a *chronic* (has continued or is expected to continue over a long period of time) or *acute* (severe, short-term) situation?
10. From the consumer's perspective, what is the most important problem to work on?
11. What do you as the worker think are the most important issues?
12. If you and the consumer have different perspectives, how can your goals be combined? What can be done to resolve the difference?
13. Can you and the consumer work together? Do you have the support of the consumer's family and friends?
14. What is the consumer's suicide status? Has the consumer ever considered suicide? Has the consumer ever attempted suicide? Does the consumer think about suicide now? Does the consumer have a suicide plan?
15. How stable is this consumer?
16. Are there community resources available?

These questions are intended to serve as suggestions. They may not all be used in an interview; however, they include the main themes in crisis work. It is critical to ask consumers about suicide (question 14), especially a consumer who does not have a natural support system. If the consumer's answers to the questions are "yes," especially regarding prior suicide attempts and concrete plans, consult an expert immediately and make arrangements so that the consumer is not alone or at least has someone checking on her. Some of these questions may be difficult to ask. We suggest that you practice conducting crisis interviews to increase your skill and comfort in working with persons in crisis.

---

[14]Getz, *Brief Counseling,* pp. 81–82.

LESSON2

Case Material

This lesson contains four actual cases selected to illustrate beginning and advanced interventions designed to help consumers function more effectively. The cases provide examples of individual and group interventions described in the chapters of Unit Three. Consumers' names have been changed to maintain confidentiality.

Goal

Using case examples, to be able to describe application of an intervention approach intended to help consumers to function more effectively.

Learning Activities

To accomplish this goal, we will:

1. Present case material and identify the intervention model being illustrated in the case.
2. Ask you to personalize these examples by identifying questions for group discussion, and by using the cases as models for building your own illustrations.

FRAME
1

CASE EXAMPLES: REALITY THERAPY/BEHAVIOR THERAPY

What aspects of reality therapy and/or behavior therapy could be applied to the Robert Miles and Mrs. Walter cases that follow?

Case 1: Robert Miles

Robert Miles, a 15-year-old placed in a state correctional facility for juveniles, was sent to the facility a year ago, after his third arrest for shoplifting. He has been held in juvenile detention for possession of drugs. He was adopted at age 5 by a family that lived in a large metropolitan area. According to his adoptive parents, his natural mother was a prostitute. Robert's parents had difficulty managing him throughout elementary school; however, there were no major problems until high school. He dropped out in the ninth grade and spent most of his time in the downtown area with friends his age and older.

Robert is an attractive, slim, white youth who expresses himself well and has formed a few relationships with other residents. He spends most of his time alone. He has been seen by a counselor for two months but has not shared information about the activities that resulted in his arrest. He talks about his family and the school he attended and some of his old friends, but he does not acknowledge stealing or any involvement with drugs. (According to the record, Robert served as a liaison between an older male and some friends his own age in arranging drug purchases.) He is friendly and pleasant to talk with, presenting himself as well-behaved. He has learned to survive in an institutional setting and is considered a leader. When discrepancies between how he presents himself and his illegal behavior are pointed out, he denies the behavior. If facts are presented, he becomes angry. When specifically asked why he was sent to reform school, he states that it was a mistake, that he took the rap for others, and that his parents wanted to get him out of the house.

At the same time, he claims to have a good relationship with his adoptive parents. When asked if he has heard from them, he attempts to hide the fact that his parents do not call or write. He insists that they want him to return home, and he describes his friends and what he will do when he does return home. Robert talks about missing his parents and friends. He states that he wants to finish high school and learn skills that will enable him to obtain a job. He expresses an interest in mechanics.

When questioned about drug activity, he claims to have no experience with drugs. He talks about how difficult it is to be in an institution, away from home. And yet he manipulates the environment on his behalf whenever possible. For example, he talked houseparents into giving him permission for evening leaves. One evening, while on leave, he was picked up by the local police and returned to the school. He appeared detached and incoherent, as if he had consumed drugs. The police found him with an older man who was known to be a cocaine dealer. Robert was placed on restriction, but he still refused to talk openly about what had occurred that evening. He denied using cocaine, claiming to have had only a couple of beers while he was out.

Case 2: Mrs. Walter[15]

Born into an upper-middle-class family in a small New England community, Mrs. Walter was married at age 23 to the man her father employed as a caretaker. They remained married for 46 years. Now 70 years old, she has a 43-year-old son, a 40-year-old daughter-in-law, and four grandchildren ranging in age from 11 to 20. She attended college for a year and a half, following what she described as a very comfortable childhood and adolescence. She then held several jobs before and during her marriage. She worked for a publishing company, a theater, and a state employment agency. Mrs. W. and her husband lived with her parents

---

[15]Adapted from a case conducted by Trinidad Arguello, MSW, director, Home Health Care Project and associate instructor, College of Nursing, University of Utah.

for the first seven years of their marriage, until her husband's tree business produced enough income for them to buy their own home. When they moved, she felt alienated from her friends and her social class. She found the transition to a lower social class and a lower standard of living to be very difficult.

Mrs. W. perceives her early years of marriage as very stressful. She was bothered by the fact that her husband did not have a job and that her parents supported them. Their move from the country to the city was a stressful event. Her father's death at age 56 was another stressful event. Her mother then lived with them until she died 10 years later. Other stressful events included several miscarriages and vaginal surgeries. After her father's death, Mrs. W. inherited a large sum of money and a trust fund. She paid for the house and contributed to her husband's business. It was shortly after her father's death that Mrs. W. began to experience periods of depression.

Mrs. W. has been in and out of treatment for the past 40 years. Her records are not complete; however, she was hospitalized in an eastern city where she received numerous treatments including psychoanalysis, electroconvulsive therapy (shock treatment), and chemotherapy. In 1952 she was given a lobotomy. She currently experiences some periods of depression but has had no psychotic symptoms since 1979. She takes antidepressant medication. According to Mrs. W., the lobotomy helped her function better; she held several jobs, cared for her family, and participated in community activities after the operation.

Around 1974 Mr. W. retired. The couple moved to the Southwest where their son owned an investment company. Shortly after this move, Mrs. W. started to deteriorate. Approximately seven years ago, she was committed to the state hospital and has not returned home except for brief visits. Five years ago, she was placed in a boarding home. Mrs. W. recently moved from the boarding home to a transitional living unit run by the community mental health center. Her psychiatric diagnosis is Chronic Depressive Disorder.[16]

The town in which Mrs. W. now lives is a small, primarily Hispanic community. Mrs. W. finds living in this town very difficult. She is unable to relate to the people or the culture. Most of the people prefer to speak Spanish, and her lack of fluency in Spanish limits her communication. The food does not agree with her. She has a distaste for "Mexicans and Mexican food."

When she is surrounded by things that are culturally significant to her, she changes from being depressed and negative and feeling rejected to a more positive attitude. She views her situation as that of being alone in a foreign land without hope of returning home. The cultural variables impinging on this woman are environmental stressors that contribute to her mental illness. She strongly identifies with her English heritage. Her physical appearance and mannerisms are suggestive of someone who has been raised in an upper-middle-class environment. She states that she can trace her mother's family history back to the queen of England. When she talks about her family and its past, her face is radiant. When she talks about her husband, there is an immediate transformation. Her facial expression hardens, she appears angry, and her body becomes rigid. She clenches her fists, and her voice be-

---

[16]Diagnostic label is defined in *Diagnostic and Statistical Manual of Mental Disorders*, 4th ed. Washington, D.C.: American Psychiatric Association, 1994.

comes harsh. Her disappointment in her marriage is evident when she talks about its hardships.

It appears that her family has totally disengaged from her. Her son refuses to have anything to do with her, and her husband wants her cared for by the state in a hospital or boarding home for the rest of her life. Family contacts are lessening. Two years ago, members of her family visited her twice, on her birthday and at Christmas. There were no family visits in the past year. Contacts now are limited to letters and presents from her daughter-in-law. Once in a while, Mrs. W. becomes assertive and phones her family. Following these phone contacts, Mr. W. complains to the staff that "Mrs. W. is harrassing the family." Mrs. W. expresses a great deal of anger, including aggressive and hostile feelings toward her husband, whenever the subject of finding a place to live is discussed. She views him as the one who is responsible for her "illness" and "isolation" and as the one who needs help. Her current income is her Social Security benefit and $30 a month from her husband.

In the worker's opinion, as long as Mrs. W. is in this geographic location she will continue to feel helpless, hopeless, and alienated. This environment continues to stimulate and exacerbate her hostility, her aggressiveness, and her hatred toward those around her, making it more difficult for her to work toward changing offensive behavior. Mrs. W. has difficulty allowing others to get close to her, though she is lonely and seeks acceptance. She expresses feelings of living within a vacuum: "There is nothing here for me; no one appreciates me; they don't know what good things are; they don't appreciate good food; they don't know what being a Christian is; they lie and steal and sin." Mrs. W. focuses on the negative aspects of others. Frequently, she is nonspecific in her accusations and has erroneous perceptions about her relationships with others. She becomes angry with other residents for no apparent reason, and when she misplaces something, she accuses others of stealing whatever it is.

At times she is a cooperative, friendly, and pleasant person. In this mood she tends to be helpful and easily shares her possessions with others. She is an intelligent person, but her memory shows marked deficits. There seems to be impairment in her short-term memory. However, she is well oriented most of the time, and her speech is clear and normal.

When the atmosphere in the transitional living unit (TLU) becomes tense, Mrs. W.'s difficult behavior increases: Her voice volume escalates; she talks about the harm her husband had done to her and her overwhelming unhappiness; she paces throughout the house; she is intrusive and demands attention; she functions at the limits of appropriate behavior required for living in the TLU and strains the patience of staff and residents.

Although her husband has made it clear to her and to the staff that under no circumstances will she live with or near her family, Mrs. W. refuses to acknowledge that she will never return home. When the matter is brought up, she changes the subject, usually by verbally attacking her husband and those around her. Her reactions become distorted. She talks about her desire to go home and the things she needs to do there. She attacks the other residents with such comments as, "They are of low intelligence; they are alcoholics; they can't speak English; they're sicker than I am; they have no culture." She is in a continuous state of "culture shock," which overwhelms her.

Mrs. W. is aging, and her physical capabilities are diminishing. She is rejected by her family, and totally independent living is an unrealistic goal. She will probably end up in a boarding or nursing home. As she grows older and realizes that she will never return home, further deterioration is expected.

When asked what she wants to do, she says, "I want to return home; take a vacation to California to see my granddaughter; visit my son and grandchildren; go to a play or a symphony; eat lobster in a nice restaurant." While she is able to verbalize these desires, she does not have the foresight to change her behavior to obtain these goals, nor is she always aware of what behavior she needs to change. Her primary goal is to return home, and she expects the agency to help her achieve this. The aim of the program and the agency, on the other hand, since her family refuses to have her live with them, is to assist her toward acquiring more independent living skills and to find her a more pleasant living environment in a larger community closer to her husband.

Goals. When asked what immediate goals she can identify, Mrs. W. says that she wants to (1) return home, (2) visit her granddaughter in California, and (3) see her family more often. Her worker identified areas that she needed to work on in order to meet her goals. She must (1) develop positive attitudes about herself and those around her, (2) learn more appropriate ways to interact with others, and (3) accept the reality of her living situation. The worker's long-term goals for Mrs. W. were (1) to reintegrate her in a community, (2) to locate a suitable place for her to live after she leaves the TLU, and (3) to help her stabilize her physical and mental condition.

Service plan. Mrs. W.'s goals were developed through individual discussions with her. For example, in dealing with the probability of her not returning home, she was encouraged to discuss with other residents the reality of never returning home and of moving to a more independent living situation. At first her attention span when dealing with this topic was 5 minutes, ending in a rage. After two months, the discussion lasted 30 minutes, and her anger was more controlled. She could separate her negative perceptions of residents from her feelings about going home.

Mrs. W. was encouraged to initiate contact with her granddaughter and to begin saving money for the trip to California, if it became a mutually agreed on decision, although discussion did cover the possibility that the trip might not occur. Discussions included how to handle rejection if the trip did not materialize and to think about other ways to spend her savings. Mrs. W. wrote a letter to her granddaughter exploring the possibility of a visit. She was cheerful while talking about plans. She was also encouraged to invite her family to visit her at the TLU and to arrange visits to where her family lives, which is over two hours away. However, her family responded negatively to both requests.

One-to-one sessions focused on her perceptions about what caused her illness and on specific thoughts that maintain her depressed state. Her ability to sustain discussion on these topics improved. Low-frequency, positive behavior, such as assertiveness, was reinforced through praise and positive attention; high-frequency negative statements, such as hostile comments about other residents, were ignored.

The worker observed her interactions with staff and other residents. When her hostile talk was ignored or confronted, it increased (at least initially). She was then taught to talk about her feelings rather than express her general hostility, and she was given praise when she did this. She slowly decreased the hostile comments. After many discussions with TLU staff members, the worker was able to gain their support in the implementation of tactics to help Mrs. W. change her behavior. To learn more appropriate ways of interacting with others, she was not reinforced for negative interactions and was given relaxation training to use when she felt angry or experienced stress. Negative behavior was corrected through role playing.

Mrs. W. also participated in drama and discussion groups. Through the use of drama she expressed some of her pent-up feelings and raised her self-esteem. In group discussions she practiced assertiveness, expressed her feelings about living with others, and got feedback on her behavior from other residents. She frequently chaired the discussion group. In this role she had an opportunity to assert herself in a group and to express feelings appropriately.

She also kept a daily log of her activities, thoughts, and feelings. The dual purpose of the log was to provide another medium of expression and a written resource for recall. The record reduced her frustration when she could not recall conversations or events. She needed some reminding, but she wrote the log fairly consistently.

Several tactics were used to try to integrate her into the community and increase her socializing with persons outside the TLU. Shopping trips for clothes and food, hairdresser appointments, and attendance at community social events were arranged. On a few occasions she visited TLU staff members in their homes. She became a member and worker in the Foster Grandparent Program. It was hoped that this program would meet some of her needs by giving her opportunities to relate to children who need love and acceptance. It also provided opportunities to interact with other elderly persons.

Another part of treatment was performing daily chores in the home. Like other residents, she had assigned tasks including cooking, cleaning her room, cleaning the kitchen, and washing her clothes. The completion of these tasks would prepare her for the household duties required in a more independent living situation. At first she expressed negative feelings toward all activities. Then she became more receptive and at times looked forward to the activities, especially cooking.

She was encouraged to take daily walks to the stores in the area, to participate in church activities, and to practice the organ in the church. Every other week she was assigned to teach residents to cook a particular dish. This assignment was made to increase her self-esteem and minimize her feelings of helplessness. Her real talent for cooking made this an enjoyable assignment.

Recently, the worker began contacting residential facilities in nearby cities, looking for another placement for Mrs. W., but her limited income eliminated most placements. Those she could afford would not be acceptable to her. Nursing and boarding homes were rejected by Mrs. W. and by staff members because the goal of the TLU is a more independent living situation. The search for a residence included advertising in a city newspaper, applying for low-income housing for senior citizens, and asking her husband to investigate resources in the city where he was living.

Because of her age, her medical history, and the stress of living in an unfamiliar environment, Mrs. W.'s prognosis was questionable. Her primary goal continued to be to return home. If a residential home, such as a room in a family's home, was not found, she would likely be placed in a nursing home.

Future interventions need to focus on exploring her family's relationships and her legal status and rights. It is unclear what happened to the money in her trust fund, for example, and what her legal rights are. Mrs. W. talked about divorcing her husband at times. It is questionable whether she really wants a divorce, but this needs to be explored further.

Follow-up summary. An aftercare worker from the local community mental health center in a city near where Mrs. W. was living in the TLU found a placement for her in a private boarding home. This city is an hour from the city where Mrs. W.'s family lived. Mrs. W. would have a private room and live in a semi-independent situation. She would buy her own food and cook in the owner's kitchen. It was arranged for her to spend her days at the Foster Grandparent Program. The local mental health agency would provide follow-up services to Mrs. W. to help with psychological and medical problems.

Mrs. W. agreed to the move, and arrangements were made for her departure. She was asked to notify her husband, which she did. Mr. W. accepted the plan and offered to drive her to her new home. However, later the same day Mr. W. called the agency to say the placement was not acceptable because the residents spoke Spanish and the home was located in the old part of the city (Mr. W. had called the home). This news upset Mrs. W., and she began to show her old patterns of behavior. Once the worker explained to Mr. W. that there would be ongoing follow-up with the mental health agency, he agreed to the placement.

Next, the son called requesting a better placement. The worker gave him a detailed account of the placement search and explained that Mrs. W. did not have the financial resources for the placements he thought more suitable. He agreed to the original plan but stated that the family would search for additional financial resources to find Mrs. W. a more suitable placement. Mr. W. and his daughter-in-law picked up Mrs. W. the next day and drove her to her new placement.

The following is a summary of Mrs. W.'s major problems and the techniques used to help her:

Problems

Behavior Problems	*Helping Techniques*
Blames others for missing items	Correcting misconception
Talks negatively about Mexican Americans	Nonreinforcement
Rejects others	Focusing on positive behavior of others
Outbursts of rage	Relaxation training
Refuses to listen to others	Focusing attention
	Relaxation training

Affective Problems	
Anger	Anxiety-management training
Loneliness	Identification of feelings
Discouragement/self-pity/depression	Recording thoughts/feelings

Thought Problems	
No one is any good/people are sinners	Positive imagery
Not wanted by family	Positive imagery and thought stopping
Living without family	Coping imagery
I have no purpose in living	Correcting misconceptions
Thoughts about dying	Thought stopping and positive imagery

CASE EXAMPLE: COGNITIVE THERAPY

The Alice Swift case below demonstrates the application of some cognitive-behavioral procedures.

Case 3: Alice Swift[17]

Alice Swift is a 25-year-old Caucasian female. She referred herself to our agency and stated that her problem was the "need to find out my feelings and to be able to communicate."

Ms. S. recently moved back to her parents' home. She dropped out of high school in the 10th grade, when she was 16 years old. She recently lost her job and could no longer afford her apartment. Therefore, she is temporarily staying with her parents and looking for full-time employment. She lived in another state for the past six years. During this time she held a variety of part-time and full-time jobs. Also, she accumulated a number of debts. She recently ended a year-long relationship with a male friend, which was another reason she wanted to return home. Her friends went to lots of parties, and she felt overwhelmed by a number of personal obligations because she had difficulty saying no. She thought that she could escape personal and economic pressures by returning home.

She has difficulty expressing her thoughts and feelings openly with her parents. She also experiences some discomfort expressing thoughts and feelings in some situations with peers and older persons. Ms. S. has difficulty saying no to her parents and friends and other adults. Ms. S. typically "goes along" with plans made by her mother for daily activities (e.g., going grocery shopping), though she does not want to participate in the activities.

CONSUMER GOALS

Long-term

1. To improve relationships with parents and old friends.
2. To improve communication with parents and friends.

Short-term

1. To increase expression of thoughts and feelings.
2. To increase comfort level and skill level in expressing thoughts and feelings.

The steps that Alice can take to achieve her goals include:

---

[17]Adapted from a case completed by Cynthia Nowowiejski, graduate student, School of Social Work, University of Washington, Seattle.

1. Expressing thoughts and feelings when they occur.
2. Acting assertively in all relationships.
3. Clarifying situations to enhance communication.

WORKER GOALS

1. To assist Ms. S. in exploration of thoughts and feelings—identification and expression of thoughts and feelings.
2. To increase Ms. S.'s comfort level and skill level in being assertive, in expressing her thoughts and feelings.
3. To provide support and encouragement.

The steps that the worker can take to achieve her goals include:

1. Assessing situations in which the consumer cannot identify or express thoughts or feelings.
2. Exploring typical patterns of communication and identifying dysfunctional patterns.
3. Exploring deficits in skill or inhibition behavior with regard to consumer assertiveness.
4. Reviewing literature and resources on assertiveness in order to teach assertiveness skills, if needed.

Ms. S.'s problem in communicating effectively, specifically in identifying and expressing thoughts and feelings, was selected as the target problem. She selected this problem on the assumption that improvement in this area would have an impact on the other identified problem areas: unemployment and family communication problems (e.g., improved communication could affect behavior in the job search process and in the family unit).

MEASURES/DATA OBTAINED

The data were obtained through the use of several measures: consumer log, consumer log with self-anchored scale, assertion questionnaire, assertion problem list, and role playing.

Incident _____
Date _____
Time _____

	EVENTS BEFORE	DURING	EVENTS AFTER
Behavior	_____	_____	_____
Thoughts	_____	_____	_____
Feelings	_____	_____	_____

FIGURE 9.1. Sample Format for Consumer Log

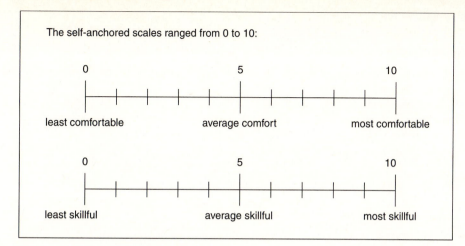

FIGURE 9.2.   Two Self-Anchored Scales

Consumer logs are journals in which consumers make notes about situations or events that they think are relevant to the problem area. Alice Swift kept a target-problem log, which included daily situations that were opportunities for assertive behavior. The log included the specific incident; the events preceding and following the incident; and her behaviors, thoughts, and feelings during the incident.

The table below consists of sample excerpts from Alice's log, and Figure 9.1 shows the format the worker helped her develop for keeping her log. The log was helpful in obtaining enough information about the problem situation to develop, implement, and evaluate the service plan adequately. The log aided in specifying and defining the problem and its antecedents and consequences.

Consumer logs can be combined with other measures to add to their utility and accuracy. After two weeks of keeping a log, Alice added two self-anchored scales (Figure 9.2) to rate her skill and comfort in situations in which she wanted to be assertive. Her self-ratings follow each entry in her log (see the table).

Sample Entries in Alice Swift's Log

Before Opportunity to Be Assertive	*During*	*Immediately After*
Thursday, April 26		
8:00 a.m.: As I was leaving for work, Mother asked me what I was doing that day, for we needed to go shopping.	*Thoughts:* Why does she need me to go shopping with her? Why can't she go alone? *Feelings:* Angry at her for assuming I'd go with her and at myself for letting her assume this. *Behavior:* Said we could go.	*Thoughts:* She likes to control my behavior, which in turn upsets me. Then I'm not sure what to do because I feel guilty if she gets upset with my behavior.

(continued)

Before Opportunity to Be Assertive	*During*	*Immediately After*
Comfort level: 1 *Skill level: 0*		
Friday, April 27 *7:00 a.m.:* A friend called and asked for a ride to work.	*Thoughts:* I'll be late if I take her. *Feelings:* Angry that she uses me in this way. *Behavior:* Said I would pick her up.	Wished I'd said I could not pick her up without more notice because it made me late for work. Fumed all the way to work.
Comfort level: 4 *Skill level: 1*		
Wednesday, May 2 Wanted to talk with an old acquaintance from high school.	*Thoughts:* Maybe he won't want to talk to me. *Feelings:* Afraid. *Behavior:* Said hello and that I was back in town; talked for a minute.	I felt good that at least I said hello; next time it may be easier.
Comfort level: 3 *Skill level: 3*		
Tuesday, May 8 Mother was slamming doors. I asked her if she was upset. She started yelling at me for being out so often.	*Thoughts:* I'm really screwing this up. I'm too emotional to talk with her. *Feelings:* Angry; guilty. *Behavior:* I said, "Can't you find friends?" She carried on about how awful her life is and how terrible everyone treats her. I said maybe she ought to disappear, and we'd all be better off.	Mother did not talk to me the rest of the day. She spent most of the day in her room. I went out.
Comfort level: 2 *Skill level: 2*		
Sunday, May 13 Went out with friends, and it got later and later.	*Thoughts:* I need to get home. *Feelings:* Afraid they won't invite me again. *Behavior:* Said thanks but that I had to get up early the next day.	Felt a little guilty but was glad to get some sleep.
Comfort level: 5 *Skill level: 0*		

The self-anchored scale is flexible and easy to use. It is useful in measuring the intensity of a problem, can be individualized for use by a particular consumer, and can provide a measurement of consumer change over time.

Reviewed: Session 4

Rating frequency of assertion

Indicate how often each of these events occurred by marking Column A, using the following scale:
>   1 . . . This has *not* happened in the past 30 days.
>   2 . . . This has happened *a few times* (1 to 6 times) in the past 30 days.
>   3 . . . This has happened *often* (7 times or more) in the past 30 days.

Rating how you feel about assertion

Indicate how you feel about each of these events by marking Column B, using the following scale:
>   1 . . . I felt *very uncomfortable or upset* when this happened.
>   2 . . . I felt *somewhat uncomfortable or upset* when this happened.
>   3 . . . I felt *neutral* when this happened (neither comfortable nor uncomfortable: neither good nor upset).
>   4 . . . I felt *fairly comfortable or good* when this happened.
>   5 . . . I felt *very comfortable or good* when this happened.

Important: If an event has not happened during the past month, then rate it according to how you *think you would feel if it happened.* If an event happened more than once in the past month, rate roughly how you felt about it *on the average.*

	A (Frequency)	B (Comfort)
1. Turning down a person's request to borrow my car	1*	2*
2. Asking a favor of someone	2	3
3. Resisting sales pressure	2	2
4. Admitting fear and requesting consideration	1	2
5. Telling a person I am intimately involved with that he/she has said or done something that bothers me	1	1
6. Admitting ignorance in an area being discussed	2	3
7. Turning down a friend's request to borrow money	1	2
8. Turning off a talkative friend	1	2
9. Asking for constructive criticism	1	2
10. Asking for clarification when I am confused about what someone has said	3	4
11. Asking whether I have offended someone	1	3
12. Telling a person of the opposite sex that I like him/her	2	2
13. Telling a person of the same sex that I like him/her	2	2
14. Requesting expected service when it hasn't been offered (e.g., in a restaurant)	1	2
15. Discussing openly with a person his/her criticism of my behavior	1	3
16. Returning defective items (e.g., at a store or restaurant)	1	3
17. Expressing an opinion that differs from that of a person I am talking with	3	4

	A (Frequency)	B (Comfort)
18. Resisting sexual overtures when I am not interested	1	3
19. Telling someone how I feel if he/she has done something that is unfair to me	1	4
20. Turning down a social invitation from someone I don't particularly like	1	2
21. Resisting pressure to drink	2	4
22. Resisting an unfair demand from a person who is important to me	2	2
23. Requesting the return of borrowed items	1	2
24. Telling a friend or co-worker when he/she says or does something that bothers me	1	2
25. Asking a person who is annoying me in a public situation to stop (e.g., smoking on a bus)	1	2
26. Criticizing a friend	1	2
27. Criticizing my spouse	1	2
28. Asking someone for help or advice	2	2
29. Expressing my love to someone	2	1
30. Asking to borrow something	1	2
31. Giving my opinion when a group is discussing an important matter	1	3
32. Taking a definite stand on a controversial issue	1	3
33. When two friends are arguing, supporting the one I agree with	2	2
34. Expressing my opinion to someone I don't know very well	2	3
35. Interrupting someone to ask him/her to repeat something I didn't hear clearly	2	4
36. Contradicting someone when I think I might hurt him/her by doing so	1	1
37. Telling someone that he/she has disappointed me or let me down	1	1
38. Asking someone to leave me alone	1	1
39. Telling a friend or co-worker that he/she has done a good job	2	4
40. Telling someone he/she has made a good point in a discussion	1	4
41. Telling someone I have enjoyed talking with him/her	1	4
42. Complimenting someone on his/her skill or creativity	1	4
TOTALS	60	106

*Alice's Scores: Frequency and Comfort Ratings

Frequency	60
Comfort	106

FIGURE 9.3.   An Assertion Questionnaire [*Source:* Peter Lewinsohn, Richardo Muñoz, Mary Ann Youngren, and Antonette Zeiss. *Control Your Depression* (Englewood Cliffs, N.J.: Prentice-Hall, 1978).]

The assertion questionnaire (Figure 9.3) and assertion problem list (Figure 9.4) are examples of written measures. These measures were used in the assessment phase for identifying specific problem areas. Like the self-anchored scale, they are self-report measures and reflect the consumer's perceptions of the problem. In addition to these measures, there are written measures in the form of tests or questionnaires that have been developed to measure consumers' perceptions of critical relationships, attitudes,

---

The personal problem list is developed as a basis for setting goals related to being more assertive. The list can be used as an assessment tool and a guide for developing a service plan. (The consumer did the checklist during session 5.)

To use this tool, ask the consumer to list 5 to 10 problematic situations that meet all of the following criteria:

1. Situations you are currently handling in a nonassertive way.
2. Situations that occur regularly (at least once a month).
3. Situations that are troubling you.
4. The situation should not be so specific that it is unlikely to occur again, such as, "My mother complaining about the pot roast I cooked last night," or so general that it would be difficult to specify a way of dealing with it, such as, "Anyone complaining to me about anything."
5. The situations on the list should be reasonably different: merge similar items.
6. The situations should represent diverse settings (school, home, work, eating out, etc.) and diverse types of behavior (resisting pressure, expressing warmth, making requests, handling disagreements, etc.), unless you have difficulty in only one area.

Alice wrote the following problem list:

1. Telling my mother I won't take her shopping.
2. Initiating conversations with people I'd like to get to know better.
3. Being able to say no to friends when they want to stay out late on a work night.
4. Asking for help in a store.
5. Returning an item to a store.
6. Asking the doctor to explain what is wrong in simple terms.

FIGURE 9.4. Personal Problem List [*Source:* Peter Lewinsohn, Ricardo Muñoz, Ann Youngren, and Antonette Zeiss. *Control Your Depression* (Englewood Cliffs, N.J.: Prentice-Hall, 1978).]

---

and feelings. Some of these questionnaires have been tested for consistency (reliability) and for accuracy (validity) across individuals and across time. A set of measures developed by Walter Hudson, called *The Clinical Measurement Package,* is one example of reliable and valid tests, and includes measures of self-esteem and marital satisfaction. These measures, like self-anchored scales, can be completed by consumers repeatedly across time— before, during, and after interventions—to determine whether there was change. They require minimal time and expense and can be useful in the initial data collection process.

Measures of the target behavior based on direct observations are usually the best measures of change. In Alice Swift's case, role playing provided an opportunity for observation of the consumer during the intervention phase. Role playing was selected as the method for practicing skills in assertive behavior. This is a convenient, efficient method. Verbal and nonverbal behavior can be identified through role playing. The utility of role playing can be increased by using videotape or audiotape to record interactions for review and feedback for the consumer. This method raises questions of validity: Are the role plays representative of consumer's behavior in real situations? Are the situations selected related to desired outcomes?

Intervention occurred in two areas: behavior and feelings, with anger being defined as the predominant feeling. The intervention selected was role playing. Role playing was used for three sessions. During the first session, the worker reviewed information about assertive, nonassertive, and aggressive behavior, and the step-by-step process of becoming more assertive. A guide to assertive living, *Your Perfect Right,* by Robert Alberti and Michael Emmons, was used as the resource for this information.

In each of the three sessions, the consumer selected a situation from her log that she wanted to role play. The situations were selected on the basis of her lack of assertiveness in handling the actual experiences.

The steps used in the weekly role-playing sessions were as follows:

1. The worker and consumer reviewed the consumer log.
2. The consumer selected a situation to role play.
3. The consumer and worker role played the situation as it happened. The consumer chose to play herself, and the worker played the other person.
4. Both the worker and the consumer reviewed the situation, looking carefully at components of the consumer's response (eye contact, body posture, gestures, facial expression, voice, message content).
5. Alternative responses were generated as steps for handling the incident. The worker modeled other responses.
6. The consumer was asked to close her eyes and imagine herself handling the situation, using an alternative response.
7. The consumer and worker then role played the situation again.

During all phases of the role plays, the worker pointed out consumer strengths in handling situations. Role playing was used to increase the consumer's skill and comfort in behaving assertively. After the consumer became more confident in behaving assertively and had received positive feedback for her behavior from the worker and friends, the sessions were designed to work on her feelings.

The worker planned the same approach for addressing the consumer's anger, such as defining anger, describing constructive expression of anger, and the use of anger in assertiveness. Role playing was used to demonstrate constructive expression of anger. The consumer selected situations from her daily log to use in role playing situations. The worker and the consumer generated alternative responses in situations involving feelings of anger and replayed the situations using these responses.

RESULTS

Six sessions were held in Alice Swift's case before an intervention plan was implemented. The total duration of the intervention period was three one-hour sessions (sessions 7, 8, and 9). Part of session 9 and all of session 10 were spent on the termination process—reviewing progress and setting goals for counseling with another worker. The worker did not have an opportunity to spend enough time on the consumer's angry feelings due to time limitations.

The consumer was motivated and cooperative in all aspects of the counseling process. The worker thought the consumer might find the log tedious and burdensome and was prepared to change this part of the service plan; however, the consumer kept the log until the last session. A collaborative relationship was developed in the beginning of the counseling process, and decisions were made jointly.

Evaluation

Baseline data were collected for five weeks preceding intervention on the target problem of assertiveness and on the consumer's feelings of anger. Baseline data were collected for three weeks on her feelings of comfort and skill levels in situations that presented opportunities for assertive behavior; the scales were added to the log after the consumer had been recording for two weeks. All data were put onto graphs and evaluated with the consumer.

FRAME

3

CASE EXAMPLE: WORKING WITH CONSUMER GROUPS

The next case illustrates a group intervention. In the midwestern metropolitan community mental health worker case, the nursing home admissions and human service workers are working to "resocialize" consumers released from state mental hospitals and placed in nursing homes.

Case 4: A Resocialization Group[18]

Some groups are organized to help consumers resolve their own problems and/or build their skills and to increase their options, while other groups are organized to bring about change outside the group members. The resocialization group case that follows has both goals: (1) to change the behavior and feelings of group members and (2) to bring about changes in the nursing home environment. In this case, the nursing home administrators and the human service workers had different goals for the group. Thus, this case exemplifies beginning advocacy efforts as well as goals to enhance the individual and interpersonal lives of the group members.

> In a midwestern metropolitan community mental health center, workers were given the task of placing consumers released from state mental health hospitals into nursing homes or boarding homes in the community. Given this assignment, the workers visited a number of nursing homes looking for potential placements. They were shocked by what they found. Many of the nursing and boarding homes that these consumers could afford were located in old, poorly maintained facilities. The homes were crowded and understaffed. Residents had no privacy and no group activities, and often waited hours when they needed staff assistance. The only activity seemed to be watching television. Residents rarely interacted with one another. Typically, they sat in the same spot each day doing nothing.
>
> The workers asked the administrators of several homes if they could conduct activity groups for the consumers they placed in the homes. Some administrators agreed to this arrangement, others did not. At the same time, the workers' goals included not just providing activities for residents for an hour or two a week but also

---

[18]Adapted from a group case written by Nancy Suave, graduate student, School of Social Work, University of Washington.

helping residents take an interest in their environment and in one another. In other words, the workers hoped to empower the consumers. They thought that if the consumers began interacting and improving their communication skills, they could begin to be assertive about having their needs met. Through working together, it was hoped that the residents could begin to bring about change and improvements in the nursing homes. The initial process involved resocializing the residents.

Resocialization groups include teaching consumers new skills in relating to one another or stimulating the use of the members' existing skills. With the nursing home residents, the first step was working with them in small groups toward building relationships among group members. The residents not only did not have anything to do and did not interact with one another but also had no control over meeting their basic needs. They were expected to simply sit, not cause trouble, eat meals when they were served, and comply with the rules and schedules of the homes. By stimulating group interaction and responsiveness to their environment, workers helped residents develop the motivation and skills to become more cohesive and to modify their environment.

Description of One Resocialization Group

Eight residents were recruited to participate in the first resocialization group. In general they were a representative sample of the resident population; however, they were placed in the nursing home by the mental health center workers and were people whom the workers assessed could participate in group activities and express themselves verbally in a group.

Mr. Paul is an 83-year-old bachelor who moved to the Midwest as a young man in order to work in his uncle's paint store. He and his uncle had difficulty working together, and after 5 years he left his uncle's business and did a variety of odd jobs. He began to show some paranoid symptoms around 40 years ago but continued to function on his own until he suffered a stroke 10 years ago. He recovered most of his physical functioning but felt someone had caused his stroke; he has had periods of disorientation since the stroke. After he recovered from the stroke, he was referred to a community mental health center and subsequently placed in a state hospital. He was moved to the nursing home 2 years ago. He seems alert and oriented most of the time. He speaks in a soft voice, often with his head down. He interacts with some residents. He has no visitors. His only living relative is a niece who lives in the area but with whom he has no contact.

Mr. Abramo is 72 years old and has been in the nursing home for 8 years. He spent most of his life in a small town in the Midwest. In 1952 he was diagnosed as schizophrenic. He received shock treatments, which had little positive effect. He was then placed on medication, which he continues to take. He was in and out of psychiatric hospitals until his move to the nursing home. He has no physical limitations; however, his affect is very flat and he rarely smiles. He is alert and oriented and able to make his own choice about group participation, but he needs to be encouraged to attend. He sometimes leaves early and says that he is "nervous." He has one brother in the area who maintains contact with him. He was married once for 3 years and has one daughter, who does not visit him.

Mrs. Quinn was hospitalized for early senility by her children when they determined she could no longer live alone. Before her admission to the hospital, she had become demanding of their time and was not eating regularly. She was hospitalized when she was 70 years old and came to the nursing home 2 years ago. She is able to converse about the present, but spends much time alone in her room ruminating about past events. During these times she sometimes does not seem to know where she is. She is oriented enough, however, to interact with others in a group situation. Her husband died when she was 60, and this apparently was when she began to deteriorate mentally. Her two daughters contact her occasionally and visit her on holidays. She had an active community life before her husband's death, but not the financial resources to be cared for in her home or to pay for a nursing home; thus, her daughters had her committed to a state hospital.

Mrs. Elton is now 83. She was diagnosed as depressed when she was in her 50s and has been in and out of the state hospital since that time. She was treated with shock therapy and drugs. She developed rheumatoid arthritis and is now confined to a wheelchair. Mrs. Elton is alert and talks with other residents but is forgetful and fabricates stories about her past. She often sits in her wheelchair, just outside her room, and watching people seems to be her favorite activity. In general she tends to be a passive observer. She has no family in the area. Although she was married at one time, there is no information about her husband or whether they had children. She has one long-time friend who visits her.

Mrs. Afton was also diagnosed as depressed. She comes from a large family. She spends long periods of time alone, rarely interacting with residents or staff. She worked as a domestic most of her life and was seen as an outpatient at a community mental health center where she received medication during periods of depression. She frequently stopped taking the medication and at times was hospitalized. Her depression worsened as she grew older until she was hospitalized 3 years ago when she was 65. She came to the nursing home 6 months ago. She has six children who visit her fairly regularly.

Mrs. Dupont has a borderline IQ—her IQ is low, but not low enough to be labeled retarded. She also has a temper. Her husband took her to the hospital after she threatened to kill him. She was hospitalized and given tranquilizers to control her angry outbursts. He divorced her shortly after she was hospitalized, and she remained in the hospital until she was placed in the nursing home a year ago. Mrs. Dupont is now 58 years old; she was 55 when she was first hospitalized. She has two grown children and several grandchildren. Her husband remarried and has no contact with her; the children visit infrequently.

Two members, Mrs. Allen and Mrs. Jones, were institutionalized for over 20 years before placement in the nursing home. Each was diagnosed as schizophrenic and treated with drugs for years. The drugs contribute to their low activity levels and absence of mood changes; they tend to sit and stare with blank faces. They do not take care of themselves. Their hair is uncombed, they do not use makeup, and their clothes are like sack dresses. Very little is known about their histories prior to their hospitalization. They have no visitors and no contacts outside the nursing home.

Group goals were initially defined by the worker. The worker ultimately wanted the group members to define their own goals and plan the activities, but the worker initially set the following short-term goals:

1. To stimulate group members to talk with one another.
2. To stimulate group members to observe and talk about their immediate environment and the community in which the home is located.

3. To reach a point where group members express what they want to do during group meetings and ways their immediate environment could be changed to meet their needs better, such as curtains, additional radios, more variety in the food they eat, and things to do in the home.
4. Teach skills, such as verbalizing opinions and feelings, making eye contact with others in the group, asking how others are feeling, inquiring about the past lives of other members, and discussing news events that occur outside the home.
5. Teach self-help skills, such as fixing hair and putting on makeup, and learning to do things with their hands, such as simple sewing and crafts.

What follows is a brief summary of four meetings of the resocialization group.

First Meeting

Present: Mr. Paul, Mr. Abramo, Mrs. Quinn, Mrs. Elton, Mrs. Afton, Mrs. Dupont, Mrs. Allen, and Mrs. Jones
Topic: Hats

Each member was invited to the first meeting by a large, hand-printed invitation as well as by a personal verbal invitation. The worker went around and reminded members about the meeting and escorted most of them to the meeting room. Members were told that the group would talk about a special topic of interest each week. For the first meeting the worker brought a number of different hats, some quite old. Members were encouraged to try on the hats and talk about how they looked. The hats were used to stimulate group members to talk about things they were doing when the hat styles were popular. Refreshments were served at the meeting. Special treats were of interest to most members and were an incentive to attend meetings, especially initially, when members took little interest in one another.

Mrs. Jones smiled several times when people tried on hats and laughed aloud when a farmer's hat was placed on her head. Mrs. Allen also smiled several times and answered questions appropriately, although she repeated one answer numerous times. Mr. Paul and Mr. Abramo sat next to each other and conversed while exchanging a cowboy and a panama hat. Mrs. Afton responded appropriately when addressed and made a couple of comments to others about the hats they tried on. Mrs. Elton, though quiet, gave brief responses when addressed and seemed interested in the activity. Mrs. Quinn's responses were not consistent—at times she responded appropriately and at times her responses were inappropriate. Mrs. Dupont participated in trying on the hats but interrupted others frequently. Her behavior was somewhat disruptive but was generally ignored and decreased in the last half of the meeting. The residents were thanked for attending the meeting and invited to the next meeting. In general they appeared to enjoy the activity and the refreshments. Each member participated and, though most did not talk directly to one another, responded to questions from the worker. This first meeting lasted only an hour so that members would not lose interest. It was decided that meetings would slowly be increased to two hours.

Second Meeting

Present: All members except Mrs. Dupont, who was not feeling well
Topic: Shoes

Each member was reminded about the meeting on the day it was planned. Again the worker went around "picking up" members just before the meeting. Several styles of shoes were brought to the meeting for group discussion. Each member picked out a shoe to discuss. They were asked to name the footgear, to describe its function, and to recall experiences related to similar shoes.

Mrs. Elton reminisced about high-heeled shoes and dancing when she was young. Mr. Paul responded when asked questions, but did not initiate conversation. Mr. Abramo contributed to the discussion when asked, but he left the group early, stating that he was "nervous." Mrs. Quinn also responded when asked questions, but several of her responses were inappropriate. Mrs. Jones initiated conversation on one occasion and otherwise responded appropriately, as did Mrs. Allen. Mrs. Allen was not repetitive at this meeting. Mrs. Afton was quieter than she had been during the first meeting. She appeared somewhat withdrawn but did talk about one type of shoe. Mrs. Quinn talked about her husband's work shoes. She initiated a conversation with Mrs. Elton, who was sitting next to her when refreshments were served. Mr. Paul was asked to help serve the refreshments. He enjoyed this role.

Again, members were thanked for their participation. This time, plans for the third meeting were discussed with group members. The worker mentioned several possible activities. There was no general discussion about what the members would like to do during the next meeting; however, when flowers were mentioned, Mrs. Elton said how much she liked flowers, and Mr. Paul mentioned that he liked to garden. Thus, flowers were selected as the topic for the next meeting.

Third Meeting

Present: All members
Topic: Flowers and gardening

The meeting started 15 minutes late because Mr. Paul had been moved to a new room and the worker had difficulty finding him, and Mrs. Allen was sleeping. Staff had not awakened her. The late start meant that some members were in the meeting room for a while together without the worker. When the worker returned, several group members were interacting with one another; others were sitting quietly, yet seemed to be listening.

The worker brought several kinds of flowers. They were distributed to group members to touch, smell, and see. Subjects involving flowers were discussed, including various kinds of flowers, members' favorite kinds and colors, occasions for giving and receiving flowers, gardening and tools, and conditions necessary for plants to grow. The worker brought empty jars and bottles so that members could keep the flowers in their rooms after the meeting.

Mrs. Quinn talked about the flowers she had received when her husband died but seemed not to be present for most of the meeting. Mrs. Elton and Mrs. Afton talked more often during this meeting, and each initiated some interactions with other members. Mr. Paul talked about gardening, and Mrs. Jones reminisced about her experiences gardening. Mrs. Allen responded to questions. Mr. Abramo talked about raising vegetables in the rural area where he had lived. He participated more than he had in previous meetings, and he smiled on several occasions. Mrs. Afton talked about preserving vegetables, and Mrs. Quinn talked about drying and pressing fresh flowers. She was encouraged to demonstrate this with a couple of flowers. She agreed to make a dried flower arrangement before the next meeting. The conversation drifted to the appearance of the home and how flowers improved the environment. So much interest was expressed in flowers and gardening that the worker asked if members would like small plants to care for. Several members wanted plants. The worker asked if they would begin caring for more than one plant in case other members decided later that they also wanted plants in their rooms. (The worker had some difficulty with staff regarding giving residents plants to care for in their rooms. However, the staff finally agreed, and the plants were delivered to members who had requested them before the fourth meeting. The worker wrote instructions for two members as reminders for them and placed the instructions next to their plants.) Mrs. Allen talked about wearing flowers as a child, and this prompted some discussion about personal appearance and self-care. The worker followed up on this issue at the next meeting by suggesting they talk about hair- and dress styles. Members agreed to this topic, although Mr. Abramo voiced some opposition. The worker pointed out that styles also change for men.

The worker asked the group to plan the refreshments for the next meeting as a way to increase group interaction and discussion and give members one joint decision to make on their own. One purpose of the meetings was to stimulate members to take initiative and begin to plan for themselves. The members could not agree on refreshments, so refreshments were planned for the next two meetings as a way of including everyone's ideas. Mrs. Dupont became angry at one point, but she calmed down when her ideas were included. The worker asked for two volunteers to help prepare refreshments before the next meeting. With a little coaxing, Mr. Paul and Mrs. Quinn agreed to help the worker before the next meeting. It was also agreed that this job would be rotated among group members for future meetings.

Members were asked to bring old pictures, if possible, to the next meeting as examples of dress and hairstyles.

Fourth Meeting

Present: All members
Topic: Hair- and dress styles

The worker brought magazines, including men's magazines, and photographs to the meeting and distributed them for discussion. Each member was asked to pick at least one picture to talk about. Several members brought their own pictures. Each member said something about the picture he or she had selected and passed the pictures to the other members. There was more interaction between group members during this meeting than there had been during the first three meetings. The worker asked questions about prices and stores to encourage members to think about what was going on outside the nursing home. They also talked about wearing different clothes in different roles and the meaning of appearances. Mrs. Elton complained about the lack of help from staff in fixing her hair. Mrs. Afton agreed to help Mrs. Elton with her hair. The worker encouraged Mrs. Allen and Mrs. Jones to meet with them as a way to help them acquire more interest and skill in fixing their own hair.

Members laughed about some of the old pictures and talked about how styles had changed. Mr. Abramo and Mr. Paul talked together about some of the pictures, and Mr. Abramo smiled several times about the styles. Mrs. Quinn talked about an old picture she had and the way she used to dress. Mrs. Elton talked about recent styles and how she missed going shopping. Mrs. Dupont also talked about shopping and the stores she used to go to. Mrs. Elton talked about making her own clothes. Her knowledge and skill could be helpful in future meetings to help others who lack skill in mending clothes.

Time was spent at the end of the meeting talking about topics for future meetings. A couple of members suggested topics. It was agreed that at the next meeting they would talk about an experience they had before entering the nursing home and the state hospital and that they would do a simple craft activity. At the following meeting they would talk about some things they would like to do in the nursing home. The worker decided to give them some simple role-playing situations for practice in talking with staff and with one another outside the group meetings. The group would continue meeting, and at subsequent meetings the worker hoped to include skill-training activities and activities that the members found stimulating and enjoyable.

Evaluation of Group Meetings

Members increased their verbal participation in general, began to talk more with one another, became involved in planning group activities, and took some limited responsibilities through helping with refreshments. The worker talked informally with nursing home staff about any changes they had observed in group members' behaviors. She learned that Mrs. Quinn was spending less time alone in her room, that Mrs. Elton talked with some residents as she sat in her wheelchair at the door of her room, that Mrs. Afton had helped Mrs. Allen and Mrs. Jones with their hair on a couple of occasions, that Mrs. Dupont smiled more often, and that Mr. Paul and Mr. Abramo spent some time talking together. If this nursing home kept daily logs of patient activities, the logs would be a good baseline for determining if group members increased their activities outside group meetings. However, this home was not recording patient activities and did not offer regular group activities, so that this kind of information was not available. The worker did come early the day of the group meetings, which gave her some time to observe members outside the meetings.

The worker recorded her summary impressions of each person's participation following each group meeting on a scale (see Figure 9.5). A numerical score was assigned to each participant for each session, indicating the level of group participation. The worker also kept track of group members' interactions and showed them in a sociogram that depicted the seating arrangement of participants as well as the direction and frequency of interaction between individuals (see Figure 9.6). The arrows are used to show the direction of interactions. The number of responses by each member are represented by the slash marks on each arrow. This information is a check on the accuracy of the worker's impressions recorded on the modified remotivation scale. It is difficult to conduct a meeting and record interactions. Therefore, the worker did not complete a sociogram for every meeting. She arranged for an assistant leader to attend some meetings and keep track of the members' interactions for the sociogram. The sociogram in Figure 9.6 includes the leader and four of the eight group members.

Impressions and Future Plans

After four meetings, the worker could assess the progress of each individual in order to begin defining goals for individuals in addition to the group goals. The worker observed, for example, that Mr. Abramo, who was initially reluctant to attend the group,

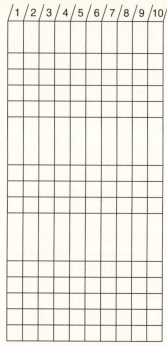

Interest

0   Refuses to come to meeting

1   Attends, shows little interest

2   Shows some interest

3   Interested

4   Interested and appreciative

Awareness

0   Usually unaware of what is going on

1   Sometimes unaware of what is going on

2   Usually aware of proceedings

3   Always aware of proceedings

Participation

0   Does not talk

1   Sometimes answers direct questions

2   Usually answers direct questions

3   Sometimes volunteers comments or answers

4   Usually volunteers comments or answers

5   Talks too much

FIGURE 9.5.   A Modified Scale for Recording Individual Participation in a Remotivation Group [Adapted from the *Remotivation Progress Report* developed by the National Remotivation Technique Organization.]

now initiates attendance on his own and is always on time for the meetings. He may become "nervous" and leave the meeting early, but he contributes verbally when asked questions and sometimes initiates conversations, especially with Mr. Paul. Mr. Abramo now knows the worker's name and greets her by name when they pass in the hallway of the nursing home. A goal for Mr. Abramo is to try to understand what environmental events may affect his "nervous" reactions and to work toward decreasing these responses. The worker encourages his interactions with Mr. Paul outside the group meetings and looks forward to increasing his initiation of conversations with additional group members.

During the first four meetings, the worker saw progress made in relation to all five of the original goals, especially the first goal of stimulating group members to talk with one another. Stimulating members to observe and talk about their immediate environment and the community in which the home (the second goal) is located is expected to be facilitated through the plan for the fifth meeting. Members began to achieve the third goal of expressing what they want to do during meetings at the fourth meeting. Additional progress is needed toward members addressing changes in their immediate environment. The worker will focus on skill development (goal 4) in subsequent meetings, once members feel more comfortable with one another. Some progress was made toward goal 5, teaching self-help skills, through one member's

Participants

Week No.	1	2	3	4	5	6	7	8	9	10

Comprehension

- 0 Unable to comprehend
- 2 Usually comprehends
- 4 Always comprehends

Knowledge

- 1 Has very little knowledge of topics
- 2 Answers usually incorrect/not on topic
- 3 Answers occasionally incorrect/not on topic
- 4 Has fair knowledge of most topics
- 5 Has good knowledge of topics

Speech

- 1 Difficult to understand
- 2 Sometimes difficult to understand
- 3 Fair speech
- 4 Good speech

Group Relations

- Participates in intergroup comments
- Good relationships with others in group
- Does not resent being interrupted
- Resents being interrupted
- Shy
- Interrupts others
- Argues with others
- Gets angry easily

TOTAL

helping two others with their hair, and additional progress will be made in doing things with their hands in future group meetings.

In addition to the difficulties encountered in achieving group goals, there are a number of problems in conducting a resocialization group in an institutional setting. These problems relate to institutional and staff hindrances to group attendance and interaction. Staff members at the nursing home were not open to helping support group attendance, nor to supporting the group goals outside group meetings. They are not encouraged to help residents achieve improved functioning. Rather, staff members serve a maintenance function. At times it appeared that they not only were not supportive but were sabotaging the group goals. The worker, however, defined these problems as obstacles that had to be addressed or worked around. At times, staff members were not willing to prepare members to attend the meeting by en-

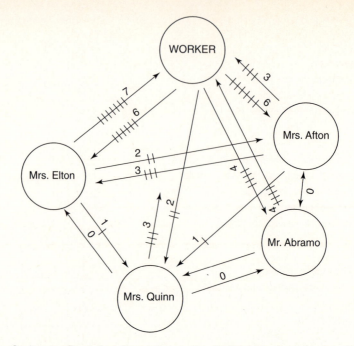

FIGURE 9.6. Sociogram Depicting Group Interaction in Remotivation Therapy Group. Session 3 *Date:* 3/5/84 *Topic:* Flowers

couraging them to dress before meetings. Illnesses and physical limitations can prevent or limit participation. The worker continued to attempt to gain staff member support through individual interactions with staff and through explaining how the group may help staff; for example, increasing member independence would decrease staff work.

Other problems came from group members: poor attention span, low comprehension level, short-term memory loss, and sensory deficits that hinder group communication. After a worker spends time preparing for group meetings, it can be discouraging when members do not show interest in an activity or are difficult to reach during meetings. It is important to modify expectations to fit the limitations of group members and at the same time to expect progress from each member in small steps.

The first four meetings were successful in providing stimulation to group members and in increasing their socialization. There is also evidence that the group meetings are affecting the behavior of participants outside the meetings in the daily functioning of the nursing home.

Summary and Further Study

Chapter Summary

This chapter is only an introduction to advanced intervention techniques used in the human services to help consumers modify their behavior in order to cope more effectively with the demands and challenges of everyday life. The aims and major principles of five advanced intervention models were described, along with case materials. The goal of the chapter was to assist you in broadening your understanding of advanced techniques so that you will be familiar with some approaches of professionals with whom you will be working and will be more effective in helping consumers.

Lesson 1. In dealing with consumers who have developed inappropriate, deviant, or counterproductive behavior and/or thoughts, or in dealing with consumers in crisis, human service workers try to bring about behavioral or cognitive change in the consumer or offer support and brief counseling in an effort to help consumers develop the basic skills needed to solve the personal problems encountered in daily living. Lesson 1 introduced you to some of these approaches.

Reality therapy includes procedures for involvement, for rejecting unrealistic behavior while maintaining supportiveness, and for teaching the consumer more realistic ways to fulfill basic needs. The four steps followed in therapy sessions usually include helping the consumer (1) identify behavior, (2) make a value judgment of behavior, (3) identify the consequences of behavior, and (4) formulate a plan for changing behavior.

The description of *behavior therapy* included the major types of behavior: respondent and operant. Behavior therapy emphasizes the interaction between the person and the environment, specificity of behaviors for change, and the consumer's involvement in bringing about desired changes. Behavior therapy includes a number of procedures to help consumers change their behavior, such as reinforcement and extinction.

Crisis intervention is a time-limited treatment that focuses on the crisis situation and helps the consumer to reestablish equilibrium and avoid permanent damage from the crisis experience. An interview outline was included consisting of 16 relevant questions to ask in an initial interview with someone experiencing a crisis. The questions represent a summary of the issues covered in crisis intervention.

Cognitive therapy is appropriate for consumers who have negative ideas about themselves and their environment and want to change their situation by addressing feelings of hopelessness and thoughts about situations perceived as being completely beyond their control. The approach involves exploring sources of distortion and helping consumers see that their perceptions are not consistent with reality.

Time-limited intervention models emphasize setting the total number of sessions in the first interview, consumer-selected and specifically defined problems and goals, the use of contracts, clearly defined interventions focused on the central goal, and between-session assignments. Strategies to motivate consumers are important and are generally enhanced by having time limits.

You may want to study the therapies included in Lesson 1 in more depth. Suggestions for further study are identified below.

Lesson 2. contained actual cases with individual consumers, and groups of consumers. The cases include applications of some of the approaches presented and provide opportunities to integrate the material presented throughout Chapters 7, 8, and 9.

Suggestions for Further Study

Ayllon, T., and N. Azrin. *The Token Economy: A Motivational System for Therapy and Rehabilitation.* Englewood Cliffs, N.J.: Prentice-Hall, 1968.

Bandura, A. *Principles of Behavior Modification.* New York: Holt, Rinehart & Winston, 1969.

Barlow, D. H., ed. *Clinical Handbook of Psychological Disorders: A Step-by-Step Treatment Manual,* 2d ed. New York: Guilford, 1993.

Beck, A., J. A. Rush, B. F. Shaw, and G. Emery. *Cognitive Therapy of Depression.* New York: Guilford Press, 1979.

Beck, A. T., F. D. Wright, C. F. Newman, and B. S. Liese, *Cognitive Therapy of Substance Abuse.* New York: Guilford, 1993.

Beck, J. S. *Cognitive Therapy Basics and Beyond.* New York: Guilford, 1995.

Blaney, P. *The Effectiveness of Cognitive and Behavioral Therapies.* New York: Academic Press, 1984.

Corey, G. *Theory and Practice of Counseling and Psychotherapy,* 5th ed. Pacific Grove, Calif.: Brooks/Cole, 1996.

Dixon, S. *Working with People in Crisis.* 2d ed. Columbus: Merrill, 1987.

Franks, C. M., G. T. Wilson, P. C. Kendall, and J. P. Foreyt. *Review of Behavior Therapy,* Vol. 12. New York: Guilford, 1990.

Gambrill, E. D., and Richey. *Taking Charge of Your Social Life.* Belmont, Calif.: Wadsworth, 1985.

Garvin, C. D. *Contemporary Group Work.* Englewood Cliffs, N.J.: Prentice-Hall, 1981.

Getz, W. *Brief Counseling with Suicidal Persons.* Lexington, Mass.: Lexington Books, 1983.

Glasser, W. *Schools without Failure.* New York: Harper & Row, 1969.

Green, J. K., and W. Morrow. "Precision Social Work." In *Behavior Modification Procedure: A Sourcebook,* edited by E. J. Thomas. Chicago: Aldine, 1974.

Kazdin, A. E. *Behavior Modification in Applied Settings.* Homewood, Ill.: Dorsey, 1975.

Kendall, P. D., and S. D. Hollon. *Cognitive-Behavioral Interventions: Theory, Research, and Procedures.* New York: Academic Press, 1979.

Konopka, G. *Social Group Work: A Helping Process,* 2d ed. Englewood Cliffs, N.J.: Prentice-Hall, 1971.

Meichenbaum, D. *Cognitive Behavior Modification: An Integrative Approach.* New York: Plenum, 1977.

Miller, L. K. *Principles of Everyday Behavior Analysis,* 2d ed. Monterey, Calif.: Brooks/Cole, 1979.

Mundt, L. "Mental Health Treatment Methods." In *Handbook of Mental Health Administration,* edited by Michael Austin and William Hershey. San Francisco: Jossey-Bass, 1982.

Prochaska, J. D. *Systems of Psychotherapy,* 3d ed. Pacific Grove, Calif.: Brooks/Cole, 1994.

Reid, W. J. *The Task Centered System.* New York: Columbia University Press, 1978.

Reid, W. J., and A. Shyne. *Brief and Extended Casework.* New York: Columbia University Press, 1969.

Rose, S., and J. Edleson. *Working with Children and Adolescents in Groups.* San Francisco: Jossey-Bass, 1987.

Spiegler, M. D., and D. C. Guevremont. *Contemporary Behavior Therapy,* 2d ed. Pacific Grove, Calif.: Brooks/Cole, 1993.

Sundel, M., and S. S. Sundel. *Behavior Modification in the Human Services,* 2d ed. Englewood Cliffs, N.J.: Prentice-Hall, 1982.

Thoresen, C. E., and M. J. Mahoney. *Behavioral Self-Control.* New York: Holt, Rinehart & Winston, 1974.

Watson, D. L., and R. E. Thorp. *Self-Directed Behavior: Self Modification for Personal Adjustment,* 6th ed. Pacific Grove, Calif.: Brooks/Cole, 1993.

Wright, J. H., M. E. Thase, A. T. Beck, and J. W. Ludgate. *Cognitive Therapy with Inpatients: Developing a Cognitive Milieu.* New York: Guilford Press, 1993.

UNIT FOUR

WORKING ACROSS BOUNDARIES FOR COMPETENT PRACTICE

Preview of Unit

Delivering human services in the information age requires an ability to work across—to span—boundaries created by numerous organizations, programs, professions, consumers, categories of need, cultures, levels of government, and sectors, as well as the boundaries of hierarchy (such as supervisor versus subordinate). A boundary divides, separates, sets limits, or is the limit itself. Sometimes it is a line, sometimes it is a region or a zone. Boundaries give shape and form to organizations, programs, water, political entities, groups, activities, ideas. But the defining feature of a boundary is separation.

Sometimes the boundary is clear, a line in the sand, or a border demarcating where one country begins and another ends. Other times boundaries are messier, precisely because we cannot know exactly when we have crossed the boundary and when we have not. For example, we all tend to be aware of major national cultures such as Latino, African American, and Native American. We tend to be less aware that the functional groupings of people, people who interact together for quite a while (as in an office or an organization), also develop a common language (conceptual categories) so that they begin to be understood better by each other than by other people. In short, they develop a cultural boundary. But how do we (and can we) draw exact lines between a consumer and a human service worker, between one culture and another, between health and welfare, or between supervisor and colleague?

There have always been boundaries among hierarchical levels, among human service programs, and among professions, but they become more serious as organizations get bigger and specialisms proliferate.[1] Though boundaries are less clear in the human services, there are many of them. In the human services, we divide categorical services from provided services, private charitable services from publicly funded ser-

---

[1]Colin Hastings, *The New Organization: Growing the Culture of Organizational Networking.* (London: McGraw-Hill, 1993), p. 4.

vices, and roles and services at the federal level of government from those at state and local levels.

In the human services, the expansion of boundaries (numerous programs, professions, consumer populations, regulations, funding streams, providers) creates calls for what is termed "service integration" or, more simply, the ability of human service workers to work across or to span the divisions (of category, geography, eligibility, access) to deliver the full array of services that a particular consumer might require. In Unit Four, you will learn three generic skills that will enable you to work across the burgeoning boundaries in the human services: managing information, managing the transition to new service delivery systems, and integrating.

Chapter 10 is concerned with managing information. All agencies must keep records documenting service delivery. These provide information about progress for supervisors and other workers to use in delivering services that will meet consumer needs. How information is managed and shared across program or worker–consumer boundaries can make the difference in the comprehensiveness and connection among services delivered. Chapter 11 introduces two skills essential to managing the transition to new service delivery systems underway in so many human services: supervising "up," how you cross the hierarchical boundary between you and your supervisor, and networking, how you work across the numerous boundaries and manage the new relationships created in emerging redesigned service systems. Chapter 12 discusses the skill of integrating, or finding ways to connect knowledge, skills, and values with the actual delivery of human services. Integrating addresses the question of competence in some depth. It seeks answers to questions such as these: Am I being effective in delivering human services? How do I know? As such, integrating facilitates learning about what you do and how well you are doing it. Integrating is a search for clarity and meaning with respect to your actions and results.

The goal of this unit is to assist you in developing your knowledge and skills in these work activities so that you will be more effective in working across boundaries to deliver human services. A key principle, emphasized especially in Chapter 12, is that gaining competence (or effectiveness) in working across boundaries is an ongoing process rather than something that is finally achieved. This applies whether you are managing information, using supervision, networking in or across organizations and programs, or integrating. Collectively, the three skills described in Unit Four enable you to account for your actions and contribute to the planning and management processes that are necessary for an agency to deliver services and achieve results effectively and efficiently.

As you begin this unit, think for a minute about a consumer who has needs that cut across programs you know about; or think about the large volume of consumer information that a human service agency collects in just one day; or consider the roles that supervisors play in relationship to your work; or imagine you are asked to make a presentation to a consumer group describing a typical work week. They want to know what you do, how you make decisions, how you involve consumers in making choices, and what kind of results you think you achieve. How would you respond to this opportunity? How skilled are you at crossing all the boundaries we encounter in our daily work? Would you, for example, feel comfortable walking into the executive director's office in your organization (whoever is in the highest position in the hierarchy) to chat about the needs of a particular consumer? We hope the introduction to the skills developed in Unit Four will be a foundation for increasing your skill in these areas.

Chapter 10

Managing Information

Information is increasingly recognized as a prime resource throughout the U.S. economy. The nation's service industries—including banking, financial services, retailing, and insurance—are driven by information to an extent that it is absolutely essential to function at the most basic level. The effective management and use of information are critical to the success of firms, not only in service industries but in the manufacturing sector as well.[1]

The value of information is also recognized in the human services. Information is the lifeblood of the human services because information feeds decision making about such things as what services are needed, how and where services can best be provided, and who will benefit from the services. Information also feeds decision making about the human service organization itself, for example, what skills and experience do the workers have and need; what equipment is required to perform tasks; what policies will guide service delivery and worker performance; and what should be preserved from the numerous meetings conducted to discuss agency matters. The human services are an information industry. Human service organizations collect, provide, and use information. Every agency, every consumer, and every worker depends on the timeliness and accuracy of information—which is essential to carrying out the mission of every human service organization by every human service worker for the benefit of the consumer.

Managing information is thus a key role in delivering human services. Managing information is the process of collecting, organizing, handling, storing, updating, and closing consumer, worker, and agency information. Earlier chapters described a variety of roles you perform while delivering human services. While engaged in each role—be it brokering, consumer advocating, mobilizing, relating to consumers, counseling through the formal helping process, or intervening—you are involved in a process of managing information—information about yourself, the consumer, and the agency context through which services are being provided.

In this chapter you will learn to manage information using the skills of recording and reporting. Since all human service agencies require that records be maintained, Lesson 1 addresses recordkeeping skills. Lesson 2 discusses how to prepare oral and written reports for other workers and for administrators to assist them in making decisions about consumers, services, and worker needs. The overall objective of the chapter is to introduce you to the process of information management through the skills of

---

[1]Paragraph from U.S. Department of Health and Human Services, *Information Resources Management: Long Range Plan FY 1991–1995*. Washington, D.C.: July 1990, p. 1.

recording and reporting. Information management is a clinical as well as an administrative function. Thus, a secondary objective is to suggest yet another way of viewing yourself as you deliver human services—namely, as a helper who is also a skillful and sensitive information manager.

Much of information management involves the use of standard forms and procedures to compile and record routine consumer and agency information. Examples of information management tasks that might appear in a human service job description include the following:

1. Record, dictate, or key in information about consumers, using prepared forms or narrative, in order to establish records, update case status, document services provided, or terminate and close the case.
2. Draft, dictate, and/or proofread correspondence to consumers, workers, or others in order to answer inquiries or request specific action or information.
3. Fill out standard forms or questionnaires in order to provide data for special studies about consumers or the agency (unit).
4. Use standard reporting forms or methods (e.g., work sampling, time study, and case sampling) in order to compile data for reimbursement, billing, cost analysis, or other purposes.
5. Collect or compile information about accidents and injuries to consumers and staff in order to process insurance reports and/or deal with lawsuits.
6. Calculate or record employee (including paid consumers) information (e.g., attendance, leave, travel status, and compensatory time) in order to report activities, prepare payrolls, or summarize employees' status.
7. Verify expenditures or record financial transactions in order to document expenditures and balance accounts for programs or units.
8. Fill out requisitions and/or vouchers in order to purchase supplies and other items.
9. Process payment invoices or vouchers in order to authorize or deny payment to vendors, suppliers, or other providers.

Recording Skills

All human service agencies require that some kind of written record be kept on each consumer. In this lesson you will learn why records are kept, and you will be given some guidelines to follow in writing information in these records.

Goal

Using information you have collected or been given about a human service consumer, you will be able to demonstrate your recording skills by writing the relevant and necessary information in the records.

Learning Activities

To accomplish this goal, we will:

1. Offer a definition of an agency record and discuss ten uses of records.
2. Consider seven items included in the records of most human service agencies.
3. Distinguish security, privacy, and confidentiality as three critical issues raised by recordkeeping practices.
4. Discuss three skills used in the recordkeeping process: observation, description, and note taking.
5. Review five helpful hints for effective recording.
6. Look at three examples of recording forms used in human service agencies.

F R A M E
1

DEFINITION AND USES OF AGENCY RECORDS

There is a certain amount of variation among agencies regarding the kinds of records maintained and the amount of detail required. Nevertheless, in general, consumer records are intended to document transactions and results of service delivery in a manner that:[1]

- Individualizes the consumer, the need, the situation, and the source
- Links goals, plans, and activities to the assessment of the consumer's need and to resources to address it

---

[1]Jill Doner Kagle, *Social Work Records*, 2d ed. (Belmont, Calif.: Wadsworth, 1991), p. 1.

- Facilitates appropriate communications about the case in and among authorized providers

The record has a number of uses, some of which are described below:[2]

1. Identifying the consumer and the need. Records contain information that identifies the consumer situation and the need for service. They contain descriptions and assessments of the consumer situation as well as statements about reasons for initiating service and problems that are the focus of attention. The record helps workers organize their thinking about a consumer and can help to uncover the need for additional information. Practitioners review the information in records to discover or recall basic details of a case.

2. Planning and documenting services. The record is both a descriptive and an evaluative document. It provides workers and agency management with a permanent, documented account of services given to a consumer and shows what happened from the time the individual first came to the agency's attention up to the present. The record is a repository of information about activities performed with and on behalf of the consumer, from opening to closing the case.

The information in the record is also needed to plan what will happen next; that is, the record is a useful tool in the ongoing evaluation of services. First, the worker and consumer identify the purpose, goals, and plan of service. Then, throughout the service delivery process, the worker documents progress in implementing the plan, achieving the goals, and accomplishing the purpose of service. Workers also use the record to document the process of service and cite factors that may be facilitating or impeding progress. Such systematic documentation can signal the need for changes in service goals and plans.

3. Sharing information with the consumer. The record may be used as a vehicle for communicating with the consumer. Some contemporary approaches to practice encourage the worker to share portions of the record or the recording process with the consumer. For example, a worker asks the consumer to document each time a specific target behavior occurs; these charts are reviewed during each meeting and become part of the case record.

4. Facilitating supervision, consultation, and peer communication. The record tells other workers who may be involved with the consumer what has already been done to date and what is in progress. Since supervisors and other workers do not always meet with the same individual consumers throughout the service delivery process, they use records to learn about how other workers have been involved and to plan further services and treatment. In interdisciplinary and team settings, the record facilitates collaboration among workers by creating a common source of information to which all members can refer. Supervisors often read consumer records to gain an appreciation of a particular case or group of cases. They use this information to assist the worker in planning and implementing further services. Supervisors also read records to assess the quality of a worker's performance and to discover the worker's strengths as well as areas needing change or further development.

---

[2]Kagle, *Social Work Records*, pp. 2–5.

5. Providing data for administrative tasks. Information about consumers and services is used to track consumers through the delivery system and inform broader administrative decisions about consumer needs, service patterns, workload management, personnel performance, and allocation of resources. Automated recordkeeping systems enable administrators to select and process information from records to help them in managing the agency and its resources. In addition, workers prepare other forms and reports for management purposes that can be linked to consumer records (e.g., daily logs of time).

6. Providing data for human service education and research. Records are used to teach the practice of human services in community colleges and universities. They are also used in in-service training programs in agencies. Records are also a resource for large-scale studies that are directed to formulating agency policies or inquiring about the effectiveness of specific practices.

F R A M E

Three reasons for keeping consumer records are listed below. First, see if you can add three additional reasons that may or may not have been discussed in Frame 1. Then consider arguments you might propose for not keeping consumer records.

1. Consumer records:

    a. Inform workers in other agencies about services being provided to a consumer.

    b. Help workers evaluate their progress with consumers.

    c. Enable workers to share information with consumers during the process of service delivery.

    d.

    e.

    f.

2. If you can think of any reasons for *not* keeping consumer records, list them here.

Turn to Answer 167 on page 643

F R A M E
3

WHAT ARE THE COMPONENTS OF MOST AGENCY RECORDS?

The records you would keep on a ward if you were working in a mental hospital would obviously be a little different from the records you would keep if you were working in a prison or a welfare department. However, in both situations your records would include some of the same basic items.

    Seven major items are included in most agency records.

1. The date of the activity
2. The identifying information about the consumer, such as name, age, address, and sex
3. The purpose of the activity (e.g., reason for interview) and a short statement of the major problem as identified by the consumer and clarified by the worker
4. Important facts surrounding the problem
5. How the problem was handled, the service plan, why it was handled that way, and the outcomes
6. What follow-up activities, if any, are being planned
7. Comments and questions to discuss with a supervisor or another worker

SECURITY, PRIVACY, AND CONFIDENTIALITY

Consumers are asked to share very personal information about their private lives through the recording process. This can be an emotional process: it also raises several critical issues to which workers must be sensitive: security, privacy, and confidentiality. *Security* refers to the agency's ability to maintain the safety and accuracy of records as well as control over who receives them. *Privacy* refers to the consumer's right to decide what information they wish to reveal and to whom. *Confidentiality* is the worker's implicit or explicit agreement to maintain the private nature of communications with consumers.[3]

> The consumer's obligation to share personal information is predicated upon a reciprocal obligation on the part of the worker and the organization: not to reveal this information except in specified, socially valued circumstances. The confidential nature of the relationship between consumer, worker, and organization is a fundamental social right of the consumer and an ethical and legal responsibility for the worker and the organization.[4]

Most individuals who are using human services take for granted that some sort of record will be made of their activities and requests. Your agency will have explicit policies and procedures addressing how you explain recording procedures to consumers. Typically these procedures will identify how the agency handles security, privacy, and confidentiality. In general, you should be able to explain to any consumer how your agency uses the record and what goes into it. Moreover, the consumer should know that the record will be shared with other workers, such as supervisors, but only because they need this information to provide services. A safe rule is to write the record in terms that you would be willing to have the consumer read if the occasion arose. As Jill Doner Kagle suggests, human service workers can learn a great deal by asking themselves, "Knowing how personal information is handled in this organization, would I want to be a consumer here?" We would add, "What information about myself would I be willing to have placed in this agency's record?"

Human service workers have an ethical commitment to protect the privacy, confidentiality, and security of consumer records. However, the subject of security, privacy,

---

[3]Jerry Finn, "Security, Privacy, and Confidentiality in Agency Microcomputer Use." *Families in Society* (May 1990): 283–290.
[4]Kagle, *Social Work Records,* p. 164.

and confidentiality is complex. We strongly encourage you to pursue the readings suggested at the end of this chapter to study these issues in more depth. The book by Jill Doner Kagle, especially Chapter 7, is a good place to start.

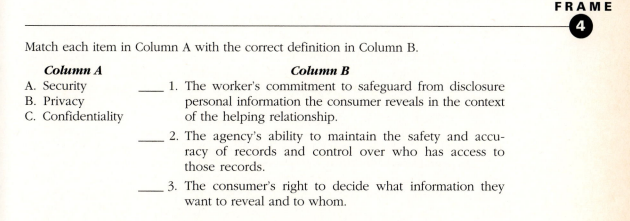

FRAME

4

Match each item in Column A with the correct definition in Column B.

Column A	***Column B***
A. Security	____ 1. The worker's commitment to safeguard from disclosure personal information the consumer reveals in the context of the helping relationship.
B. Privacy	
C. Confidentiality	

____ 2. The agency's ability to maintain the safety and accuracy of records and control over who has access to those records.

____ 3. The consumer's right to decide what information they want to reveal and to whom.

Turn to Answer 168 on page 643

FRAME

5

THREE SKILLS USED IN RECORDKEEPING

At least three skills are important to effective recordkeeping: observing, describing, and note taking.

Observing

In human service work, a large amount of information passes between consumers and workers. Observation can be defined as the act of obtaining or collecting information through the five senses (seeing, hearing, touching, tasting, and smelling). As you refine your observation skills, it is important to be able to answer three questions with regard to the information you are collecting:

1. *What is it for?* In order to answer this question, it is necessary to determine the purpose of your observation and the objectives you are seeking to accomplish.
2. *How will you get it?* Depending on the purpose of the observation, the observer must decide on the procedures and techniques to be used in gathering the facts.
3. *What can you find out?* The basic element of the observation process is a detectivelike observer who will search to make sure the necessary clues and facts are obtained and reported accurately and objectively.

The factors that influence the accuracy of observations are generally physical and psychoecological. Physical factors relate to the sharpness of the senses. For example, changes in voice tones may be missed if the observer has a slight hearing loss. Psychoecological factors relate to all the people, things, and physical surroundings affecting an individual's behavior. For example, the situation and location of the observation, the cultural background of the individual being observed, and the individual characteristics of the observer all may affect the thoroughness and objectivity of observations.

There are at least four general observational procedures commonly used in the human services to gather and update consumer information.

1. Using secondary sources. Secondary sources include records and reports about the consumer as well as comments made by others who have been in contact with the consumer. Using secondary sources is a way of observing the consumer indirectly. This procedure can provide such information as an identification of the consumer's problem as presented and described when he first came to your agency's attention; an indication of the original service plans that were made by your agency, and a summary of the actions taken to date to assist the consumer.

2. Spectator observation. As a spectator, the observer tries to position herself outside the focus of the observed person's attention, for example, by sitting beyond the observed person's immediate visual range or by talking with someone else out of the observed person's immediate hearing range. In spectator observation, the observer usually attempts to minimize the effect of her presence on the observed person.

3. Participant observation. In this procedure, the observer actively participates in the treatment or rehabilitation of the observed person, while mentally noting what the observed person says and does and his interactions with other people and things in the setting.

4. Interviews. Chapter 7 discussed the interview as a means of collecting consumer information. Obviously, observation is a critical element in any interview. In fact, Kadushin has suggested that "one can observe without interviewing, but one cannot interview without observing."[5] Thus, the interview may be used both to collect and to update consumer information.

When you are engaged in the process of observation to update consumer information using any of these general procedures, it is important to determine (1) whether there is any new information that your agency needs to know in order to help the consumer more effectively and (2) whether the consumer is functioning better or worse than noted earlier.

FRAME 6

Match each observational procedure on the left with the appropriate example on the right.

_____ 1. Using secondary sources   A. The observer reads a story to the observed person, noting what the observed person is doing.

---

[5]Alfred Kadushin, *The Social Work Interview: A Guide for Human Service Professionals*, 3d ed. (New York: Columbia University Press, 1990), p. 45.

_____2. Interviewing

_____3. Spectator observation

_____4. Participant observation

B. The observer consults records and reports about the observed person to obtain background information.

C. The observer tries to place himself outside the observed person's immediate focus of attention.

D. The observer conducts and directs a purposeful conversation with the observed person.

Turn to Answer 169 on page 643

FRAME

7

Describing

How do workers organize nonverbal clues and other information gained from observing a consumer? Information, such as clues about a person's level of functioning, needs to be transferred from memory to a written description. The process of describing involves a mental summing up of all that has been learned about a consumer through direct contact.[6] In the human services, describing is the step taken before further decisions are made regarding consumer problems and how they can be resolved. To be skillful in describing, you have to (1) make an effort to mentally review each bit of information you have received from or about the individual; (2) match these clues to previous information; and (3) sum up the problems. The key to the skill of describing is to detect clues during your observation that can be written down at a later time. This is a mental, not a verbal, process. You will be making mental notes. You will not be telling the consumer, for example, "I see you are frowning, and that is a nonverbal clue that tells me you are angry."

Four considerations are basic to making mental notes about clues or pieces of information related to consumers:

1. Individuality. Make sure you understand what the consumer is saying both verbally and nonverbally. It is difficult to make definitive rules that will tell you in advance what different verbal and nonverbal signals mean. This is because consumers are individuals. People may use words and gestures differently in communicating. Before you mentally catalog any clues, make sure you understand what they mean to that individual consumer. In addition, if consumers are from a culture that is different from yours, remember that they may intend a different message from the one you think their actions are communicating.

2. Frequency. Consider how often the clue occurs. If people are rigid and tense for only a fleeting instant, you cannot automatically assume that they are anxious or nervous. However, if they send this signal repeatedly throughout your contact with them, you would probably then have a basis for making a mental note of this as a clue to understanding the consumer's behavior.

[6]Alice H. Collins, *The Human Services: An Introduction* (New York: Odyssey Press, 1973).

3. Quality and context. You should consider the way in which you got the clue. Was the consumer in a crisis situation? Was he at home? Was he on a ward? Was the clue more nonverbal (e.g., a hesitant manner, or a deliberate and open manner)?

4. Past behavior. You need to have some understanding of the way the consumer acted in the first contact with you or your agency. If you do not know how the consumer talked and acted during the first contact, you may have a hard time figuring out what clues the person is sending you. For example, suppose an individual spoke loudly and quickly when first coming to your agency and was therefore thought to be very angry. Knowing this, you now observe this individual and note that while the person is still talking loudly and quickly, she is also smiling and sitting in a very relaxed position. At this point you might mentally make a note that although this individual has a tendency to talk loudly and quickly, this does not necessarily indicate anger.

FRAME 8

Read the following passage, then answer the question below.

> Margaret was a psychiatric technician in a state mental hospital. One day, Allen, a patient who had made remarkable progress and was about to be released, became involved in a noisy and violent fight with one of the attendants on the ward. Margaret and several other technicians heard what was happening and stepped in to break it up. Afterward, the other technicians wanted to fill out a report on Allen's behavior and felt the report should state that Allen might not really be ready to be released. Margaret, having had considerable contact with Allen during his stay at that hospital, was sure that there was some reason for his unusual behavior. She persuaded the other technicians to help her explore the reasons for Allen's behavior before they filled out any reports.

Check which of the following things Margaret considered before she decided to take the step of describing Allen's behavior:

_____1. What Allen was saying both verbally and nonverbally

_____2. How often this clue had occurred

_____3. The way in which she had received the clue

_____4. Her prior knowledge of Allen during his stay at the hospital

_____5. All of the above

Turn to Answer 170 on page 644

FRAME 9

Note Taking: An Aid in Effective Recording

Since you are probably in contact with many individual consumers during your daily activities, it is important that you remember what happened with each consumer. With all the activities you are involved in every day, how can you improve your ability to remember specific information about an individual you have observed or talked with? One method is to keep your own personal log or notebook for jotting down important information about an individual. You can then refer to this when you start to write in the record.

While you should try to complete agency records as quickly as you can after you have seen an individual, many times you simply will not have the time to do this right away. This is why many workers keep their own logs or notebooks and jot down the important information they need to remember about each individual. The most important items to include in a log are (1) the date of activity, (2) the name of the individual, (3) a description of your involvement, (4) what happened, and (5) your observations and impressions.

The log can be a short, simple account of your activity. In keeping a personal log, it is important that the time between your contact with the individual and your note taking be as short as possible. The longer you wait to write down important information, the more likely you will be to forget or change it. It should be pointed out, however, that although it is a good idea to write down facts such as name, address, and age during an interview, it can be very distracting to the consumer if you spend a lot of time writing. The best thing to do is to set aside a few minutes immediately after each contact to jot down your notes—and try to make them as brief as you can. Remember, you only need the most important information in a log.

FRAME
10

GUIDELINES FOR EFFECTIVE RECORDING

Now that you understand why records are necessary and how notes may aid in writing records, it is helpful to examine some tips on how to write effective records.[7]

1. Select pertinent information to record. Some records will require simple facts, while others will require that you summarize or give a brief description of what happened. You cannot record everything that happened, but if you write enough, another worker will not repeat what you have already done.

2. Write clearly and legibly so that other people can read what you have written. Remember that one reason agencies keep forms and records is to make sure that services can be offered in a continuous fashion, regardless of whether the same worker is always available to see the consumer. If others cannot read your writing, this goal will be difficult to achieve.

3. Do not try to use technical language unless you are very sure of what you are saying.

---

[7]Rose C. Thomas, *Public Service Careers Program: Manual for Case Aide Trainees* (New York: City of New York Department of Social Services, March, 1968); also see Gertrude S. Goldberg, et al., *New Careers: The Social Service Aide: A Manual for Trainees* (Washington, D.C.: University Research Corporation, October, 1968).

4. Avoid making entries that tell only how hard you are working. This fools no one, is annoying, and is not particularly helpful to other workers who use the records.

5. From time to time look at your old records, see how you are doing, and decide whether there are any areas that need improvement (e.g., incomplete descriptions of consumer's behavior, missing dates, and missing notes on consumer successes).

F R A M E

11

EXAMPLE OF FORMS

Three examples of recording forms used by human service agencies are shown below. Most human service organizations will use a number of different forms in their record-keeping systems. These examples include the following forms:[8]

Form 1: A personal and service data form for an individual consumer
Form 2: A form outlining a service agreement between a consumer and an agency
Form 3: A form authorizing the release of information about a consumer

_____

[8]Forms taken from Kagle, *Social Work Records,* pp. 119–20, 138, 139.

Form 1

FACE SHEET <adult, individual>
Side 1: Personal Data
Print or type. Mark as many as apply.

(case number)

(service)

(date opened/reopened)

Client name

(last)   (first)   (middle)

Address

(number)   (street)

(city)   (county/state)   (zip)   (census track)

Sex
M (   )
F (   )

Birth Date ____ ____ ____
(month) (day) (year)

Phone (day) ____
(area)

Religion
(   ) Cath.
(   ) Prot.
(   ) Jew
(   ) None
(   ) Other
_____
(specify)

Ethnicity
(   ) Afric. Am.
(   ) Asian Am.
(   ) Nat. Am.
(   ) White
(   ) Other
_____
(specify)

Language
(   ) English
(   ) Spanish
(   ) Polish
(   ) Yiddish
(   ) Other
_____
(specify)

Marital Status
(   ) Never married
(   ) Married
(   ) Separated
(   ) Divorced
(   ) Widowed

Veteran Status
(   ) None
(   ) Veteran
(   ) Child of
(   ) Parent of
(   ) Spouse of
(   ) Widow(er) of

Lives
(   ) Alone
(   ) Parent(s)
(   ) Spouse
(   ) Child(ren)
(   ) Other relative(s)
(   ) Nonrelative(s)
(   ) Nursing home
(   ) Foster home
(   ) Institution
(   ) Community group home

Family Income
(   ) Less than $5,000
(   ) 5–10,000
(   ) 10–15,000
(   ) 15–20,000
(   ) 20,000+

Source of Income
(   ) Wage/salary/investments
(   ) Soc. Security/pension
(   ) SSI
(   ) AFDC
(   ) County
(   ) Other _____
(specify)

Education (highest level)
(   ) Preschool
(   ) Special education
(   ) K–8
(   ) 9–11
(   ) High school
(   ) Some college
(   ) College degree
(   ) Postgraduate

Occupation
(   ) Student
(   ) Homemaker
(   ) Professional/ managerial
(   ) Clerical/sales
(   ) Skilled/tech.
(   ) Unskilled

Disabled
(   ) Yes
(   ) No

Employment Status
(   ) Unemployed
(   ) Retired
(   ) Employed—part time
(   ) Employed—temporary
(   ) Employed—full time
(   ) Self-employed

Seeking Change
(   ) Yes
(   ) No

Form 1 *(continued)*

FACE SHEET <adult, individual>
Side 2: Service Data <mental health>
Print or type. Mark as many as apply.

1. Diagnosis—DSM–IIIR

2. _____

3. _____

4. _____

Source of Referral/Request

( ) Self   ( ) Attorney   ( ) School
( ) Personal network   ( ) Court   ( ) Employer
( ) Physician   ( ) Police   ( ) Clergy
( ) Psychologist   ( ) Social worker   ( ) Other
( ) Outreach

_____   _____
(specify agent)   (specify)

Contact with Referral Source
( ) Yes, they initiated
( ) Yes, we initiated
( ) No

Reason for Referral/Request

( ) Depression/suicidal   ( ) Developmental disability
( ) Anxiety/stress   ( ) Mental retardation
( ) CMI/thought disorder   ( ) Education problems
( ) Antisocial behavior   ( ) Employment problems
( ) Substance use/abuse   ( ) Physical disease/disability
( ) Situational crisis   ( ) Financial difficulties
( ) Information/referral   ( ) Interpersonal difficulties
( ) Medication   ( ) Other _____
                                        (specify)

Services Planned

( ) Information/referral   ( ) Individual counseling
( ) Assessment   ( ) Family counseling
( ) Medication   ( ) Couple counseling
( ) Education   ( ) Group counseling
( ) Inpatient/milieu   ( ) Crisis intervention
( ) Day care—sustaining care   ( ) Residential placement
( ) Detox/substance program   ( ) Early childhood stimulation
( ) Sheltered workshop   ( ) Employment placement
( ) Other _____
       (specify)

Service Review

_____
(case opened/reopened)

_____
(dates of previous service)

_____
(previous primary provider)

Plan Approval

_____   _____
(signature, recipient)   (date)

_____   _____
(signature, guardian)   (date)

_____   _____
(signature, primary provider) (date)

Form 2

Service Agreement

INSTRUCTIONS: This form is to be completed by worker and client by the end of the third interview. One copy is to be retained by the agency and placed in the client's record. One copy is to be retained by each client.

We have agreed to the following:

1. Purpose(s) or Goal(s) of Service:_____

_____

_____

2. Plan of Service: _____

_____

_____

3. _____ agrees to undertake the following responsibilities:
   (client name)

_____

_____

4. On behalf of the agency, _____ agrees to undertake the following
   responsibilities: (worker name)

_____

_____

_____

This Agreement covers the period from _____ to _____
                                    (date)   (date)

Signed _____   _____
       (client)   (worker)

_____   _____

Authorization for the Release of Information

INSTRUCTIONS: This form is to be prepared in triplicate. These copies are to be distributed: 1. To the client or the client's guardian
2. To the party that releases information
3. To the party that receives information

1. _____, hereby give consent
   (full name)

to _____
   (name of party to release information)

of _____
   (address of party to release information)

to release the following information: _____

_____
(description of information to be released)

to _____
   (name of party to receive information)

of _____
   (address of party to receive information)

for_____

_____
(description of how information will be used)

My signature means that:
1. I have read the authorization or have had this authorization read to me. I understand and agree to its contents.
2. I have been informed that no other information may be released without my written consent.
3. I have been informed that I may revoke this authorization by written statement at any time and that this authorization will be automatically revoked on _____
   (date)

Signed:

_____   _____
(client)   (date)

_____   _____
(guardian)   (date)

_____   _____
(witness)   (date)

Reporting Skills

In this lesson you will learn about the activity of reporting, another skill in the information management process. You will be using your reporting skills whenever you are called on to summarize your observations and contacts with consumers. For example, you may need to summarize all important information about a consumer by reading her files, or you may be asked to complete a consumer service report summarizing the services that have been delivered to a number of consumers.

Goal

To be able to prepare an oral or written report on information that you have submitted or gathered regarding an agency consumer or service.

Learning Activities

To accomplish this goal, we will:

1. Identify three reasons for preparing reports.
2. Review the four basic steps of report preparation.
3. Consider four guidelines that will help you in organizing and presenting an oral report.
4. Examine the purpose of a memo and four principles that will help you in writing effective memos.
5. Review the three steps followed in summarizing information.
6. Consider three guidelines useful in writing reports.

FRAME

1

WHY PREPARE REPORTS?

A report should communicate information to someone who wants or needs it in the most convenient and usable form. This is true of a student's book report, the news report of the day on television, or a mother's report on her child's behavior. In the human services, oral reports are used, for example, to convey information about consumers to supervisors or to other workers in case conferences. Written reports, such as letters and memos, may be used to inform administrators about consumer services and about your needs as a human service worker. There are three main reasons for preparing agency reports:

1. To identify and explain worker and consumer needs
2. To communicate information about consumer progress to supervisors and administrators
3. To share problems, impressions, and information with workers in your own and other agencies

FRAME

2

Check which of the following could be considered a report.

_____ A. A memo to a co-worker concerning your impressions of one of your consumers
_____ B. An oral presentation at a case conference
_____ C. An explanation of consumer progress to the director of your agency
_____ D. An agency budget
_____ E. All of the above

Turn to Answer 171 on page 645

FRAME

3

Check each item that is a reason for preparing an agency report.

_____ 1. To tell a friend about your job
_____ 2. To explain to the director that you are in need of more clerical support
_____ 3. To relate to your supervisor the problems you have been working on with a consumer
_____ 4. To explain your feelings to a fellow worker
_____ 5. To confirm a meeting with a worker in another agency
_____ 6. To describe problems you are having to fellow workers at an agency conference
_____ 7. To outline consumer needs not being fulfilled by the community at a local conference

Turn to Answer 172 on page 645

FRAME

4

STEPS IN PREPARING REPORTS

Whether you are preparing an oral or a written report, there are certain steps you can follow that will help to make your report easily understood.

1. Be clear about the purpose of the report.

2. *Identify* the consumer, the problem, and/or the information you will be reporting on.

3. *Collect* current information that is relevant to the purpose of your report.

4. *Organize* your information so that you can present the report in a coherent manner.

FRAME
5

PRESENTING REPORTS

Oral Reports

There will be many occasions in your work in the human services on which you will orally report information to other workers. For example, you may share your information regarding a consumer with your supervisor, or you may share your observations and problems about one or more consumers with other workers in staff meetings or in case conferences. No matter where you are reporting orally, the following guidelines should help you in presenting your report:

1. Remember that you give an oral report primarily to share useful information with others. Be careful not to ramble on. You need to be well organized and keep to the point.

2. Know what you are going to say and how you are going to say it. If you follow the basic steps of preparing reports, this should be easy.

3. Jot down some short notes of your main points so you will be able to keep on track, and remember your main purpose.

4. Stand up and speak up. Stand or sit straight, be friendly, and do not start out by apologizing ("I don't know if I can say what I mean"). Listen carefully to any comments or suggestions you receive and concentrate on the issues and information—not on personalities.

FRAME
6

Oral reports are used in agencies mainly to share information with supervisors and co-workers regarding one or more consumers. Check the items below that you should try to accomplish when presenting a report.

_____ 1. Avoid using notes since this will detract from your presentation.

_____ 2. Use impressive words and statements that will show your hard work in preparing the report.

_____ 3. Be sure you know what you are going to say and how you are going to say it.

_____ 4. Stick to the purpose of your report.

_____ 5. Prepare a few notes to help you remember the major points you want to cover.

_____ 6. Concentrate on personalities not issues.

_____ 7. Avoid making apologies, especially at the start of your presentation.

Turn to Answer 173 on page 645

FRAME

Written Reports

The memo. A common type of written report is the memorandum, or memo, which is generally used to announce information or to remind someone about a service that is needed or about an important event. You will probably be using memos to report to administrators in your agency, and you may sometimes use a memo to communicate with other service workers, especially in a large agency. Each agency usually has a set form for memos, and you should be familiar with yours. To make your memos effective, you should try to do the following:[1]

1. Keep them brief. Give all the necessary information by answering the questions Who? What? When? Where? How? and Why? If you have several thoughts on a single subject, put each thought into a separate paragraph. Above all, keep it short—a short memo is much more likely to be read than a long one.

2. Send the memo out *early enough* so that others have time to comply with your request. Generally, you should allow at least a week so that people have time to plan their response and their work accordingly.

3. Use words that everyone will understand. Be as specific as possible in your wording—*be clear.*

4. State the general *purpose* of the memo very near the beginning so that the receiver will be clear about what he or she is expected to do.

FRAME

8

Check the situations in which it would be best to send a memo.

_____1. To report to your supervisor on a difficult problem you are having with a consumer

_____2. To make an announcement to co-workers about an article that you found useful

_____3. To remind fellow workers of a staff conference

_____4. To describe your impressions of a consumer to a fellow worker

_____5. To advise your agency director about a needed resource

_____6. To report the services already received by a consumer to a worker in another agency

_____7. To submit a request for additional services to your administrator

Turn to Answer 174 on page 645

---

[1]See Thora Kron, *Communication in Nursing* (Philadelphia: Saunders, 1972).

Read the following memo, then answer the questions that follow.

11–15–97

Memo
To: Joan Wright, Director
From: Phillis Bright, Service Worker
     Please excuse my delay in fulfilling your request. I was unable to understand some of the tasks you expected me to accomplish as stated in your memo. Since you had stated a completion date of November 20th for all tasks, I would appreciate it if we could meet sometime during the next two days to discuss these tasks.
PB/pm

1. Check which of the following are true.

_____ A. Mrs. Wright, it can be assumed, is not an effective memo writer.
_____ B. Mrs. Bright, the service worker, is a very effective memo writer.
_____ C. Both Mrs. Wright and Mrs. Bright could benefit from a lesson on effective memo writing.
_____ D. There is a strong possibility that the tasks requested of Mrs. Bright will be completed on time.
_____ E. Mrs. Bright's request for a meeting within two days is reasonable.

Turn to Answer 175 on page 645

2. Check which of the following helpful hints for effective memo writing Mrs. Bright applied in her memo.

_____ A. She used easily understood terms.

Turn to Answer 176 on page 646

_____ B. She allowed sufficient time for a reply.

Turn to Answer 177 on page 646

_____ C. She provided sufficient information to allow Mrs. Wright to prepare for the meeting.

Turn to Answer 178 on page 646

3. Explain below or on a separate sheet of paper what Mrs. Bright could have written at the beginning of her memo to help identify its purpose immediately.

Turn to Answer 179 on page 646

FRAME

On a separate piece of paper, rewrite Mrs. Bright's memo as if it were from you. Use the ways identified above to make it more effective.

Turn to Answer 180 on page 646

FRAME

11

The summary. Another kind of written report involves writing a summary of information and observations from one or more sources. For example, you may be asked to read agency reports concerning consumers' needs and progress and to submit your observations in writing; or the personnel office of your agency may ask you to write a short summary of the kind of training you would like. In all such situations, you need to be able to write a short report summarizing the important facts that are being requested.

Writing is putting thoughts on paper, and speaking is saying thoughts out loud. However, many people find it much harder to write than to speak. The problem is that many of us are unable to write the way we talk. We talk easily, but when we have to write, we do not know where to begin. Nevertheless, writing a summary report is not too difficult. Just remember that the key to writing a report is *planning* what you are going to say. If you follow three basic steps when you are summarizing information, you should not have any trouble.

1. Get your facts together. If you need to read agency files or other agency papers involving consumers and/or services, read them with the purpose of your report in mind. Look for ideas and main activities instead of concentrating on single words. Also, try to see the difference between someone's personal opinion and the facts.

2. Organize your facts. In organizing ideas and facts, many workers find that listing all the facts on a single sheet of paper helps in deciding what needs to be reported. After they have chosen the main facts, they expand the list into an outline by going back and filling in additional information they will need under each fact. It is also important to organize ideas by placing them in a logical order or progression.

3. Remember the purpose. Once you have gathered and organized your facts and ideas, you are ready to summarize. When you are writing your summary, always keep asking yourself, "What is my purpose in writing this report?" and "Who am I writing it for?" Asking these questions will serve as a constant reminder to you to include only the most important information in your report.

FRAME

The first step in planning a summary report is to gather the relevant facts and ideas. Check which of the following would be helpful to follow when performing this task.

_____ A. Look for description of all activities.
_____ B. Keep the purpose of your report in mind.

_____ C. Search for key words.

Turn to Answer 181 on page 647

F R A M E
13

Suppose a service worker from another agency has requested information on a consumer who had previously obtained services from your agency, and your supervisor has requested that you write a report and send it to the service worker. After you have obtained the relevant facts on the consumer, what would your next step be? Check the correct response.

_____ A. Organize your facts.
_____ B. Summarize the relevant facts.

Turn to Answer 182 on page 647

F R A M E
14

Guidelines for writing. When writing your summary report, expand on the main ideas and facts you have put in your outline. Some people have a personal organizing method that works best for them. Whatever method you use, once you have planned your summary by gathering and organizing your facts and ideas, you are ready to write your summary report. You may find the following guidelines helpful to you in writing your reports:

1. **Purpose.** At the beginning of your report, explain why you are writing the report.
2. **Clarity.** Use specific, concrete, familiar words and write short sentences, which are easier for you to write and easier for the reader to understand.
3. **Brevity.** Most of your reports should be short—usually no more than one page. Remember to stop writing once your message is finished.

F R A M E
15

Remember the report concerning the consumer who had previously obtained services from your agency and is now requesting services from another agency? The following report, in letter form, concerns a similar situation. Read the letter, then answer the questions below.

July 1, 1997

Mr. Arthur Davis
Regional Rehabilitation

Dear Mr. Davis:

Rebecca Holmes has been in our program for two years. She appeared to be the most deprived child in the class according to our first report. She was often absent and sometimes upset when arriving for school.

In 1988, Rebecca had a speech screening test at age 3. At that time she was functioning verbally at an age level of 2.1 years. During the first year in our program, both her parents were in the home. Her attention span was short, but she seemed to be well adjusted and happy during the second year.

In 1990, Rebecca had a second speech screening test, and she had increased only to 2 years 3 months. During the second school year, Rebecca's mother was out of the home. Because of her father's difficulty in running the household, Rebecca was bathed and dressed at school, and her clothing was provided and cleaned by volunteers and staff. She was picked up daily by the director. Rebecca's father was always waiting for her at the end of the day, and the two expressed much affection for each other.

At the beginning of this year, Rebecca left school for three months, and when she returned she was much more upset than in previous years. This behavior was still continuing when school closed this year.

Sincerely,

Arnold Armstead
Jones Elementary School

1. Was this an effective report? _____Yes _____ No

Turn to Answer 183 on page 647

2. What did Mr. Armstead fail to do when writing this report? Check the correct response.

_____ A. Make it brief.
_____ B. Organize the facts.
_____ C. Obtain the facts.

Turn to Answer 184 on page 647

3. In order to organize the facts better, Mr. Armstead could have used an outline, writing down the major facts and then filling them in with additional relevant information. Besides not organizing the report, what else did Mr. Armstead fail to do? Check the correct response.

_____ A. Write clearly.
_____ B. Stop writing once the message was finished.
_____ C. State the purpose and keep it in mind when writing the report.

Turn to Answer 185 on page 648

FRAME

On a separate piece of paper, rewrite the report presented in Frame 15. Remember to outline the facts first and then fill them in with additional information as you write the report.

Turn to Answer 186 on page 648

CHAPTER 10
Summary and Further Study

Chapter Summary

This chapter gave special attention to the process of managing information through the skills of recording and reporting.

Lesson 1. Lesson 1 presented some of the important issues and skills related to recording. Records, required in any human service agency, are used to (1) identify the consumer and the need; (2) plan and document services; (3) share information with the consumer, (4) facilitate supervision, consultation, and peer communication; (5) provide data for administrative tasks; and (6) provide data for human service education and research. Most agency records include the date of the activity, identifying consumer information, purpose of the activity, facts of the case, how the problem was handled and why, follow-up activities, and comments and questions to discuss with other workers. Security, privacy, and confidentiality are three critical issues human service workers and agencies protect through policies and professional standards.

Observation, description, and note taking were discussed as three skills used during the recordkeeping process. Observation, the act of obtaining information through the senses, is most effective when you are able to identify the purpose, procedures, facts, and clues for each situation. Physical and psychoecological factors influence the accuracy of these observations, so it is important to recognize when these factors are interfering with an accurate observation. We also emphasized some general observational procedures—using secondary sources (such as records and reports), spectator observation, participant observation, and interviewing. The skill of describing was presented as a process that involves mentally summing up all that has been learned about a given consumer. We suggested that keeping your own log regarding consumers may assist you in effective recording, especially if the time between your contract with the individual and your formal entries into the record is kept at a minimum. The lesson concluded with general guidelines for effective recording and examples of recordkeeping forms.

Lesson 2. Another major skill discussed in this chapter was reporting. As a means of summarizing observations, impressions, and facts, reports communicate information in the most convenient and useful form to someone who wants or needs it. In the human services, both oral and written reports are prepared (1) to identify and explain worker and consumer needs; (2) to communicate consumer progress to human service administrators, and (3) to share problems, impressions, and information with other workers.

Four basic steps to remember in preparing any kind of report are (1) identify the purpose of the report; (2) identify the consumer, the problem, and/or the information you will be reporting on; (3) collect the relevant information, and (4) organize the information. With regard to oral reports, we stressed the importance of planning what you are going to say and how you will say it and delivering the report in a confident, straightforward manner. We discussed two major kinds of written reports: the memo and the summary. The memo is used to communicate with other service workers, and we presented suggestions for its preparation. The summary involves a combination of facts, information, and observations from one or more sources. The key to effective summarizing is planning, that is, getting your facts together and organizing them, perhaps using an outline, before summarizing the material. In preparing any report, it is always helpful to identify the purpose and to be as clear, concise, and brief as possible.

Suggestions for Further Study

This chapter has been a brief introduction to the information management process in the human services. Although we presented the basic components, further study will be necessary for a comprehensive understanding and application of this process.

The Information Management Process

Most of the discussion and examples in this chapter were drawn from assessment or information-collecting situations. Expanding your knowledge of information collecting should include further attention to the process of observation and description. Note also that the skills and knowledge needed for effective recording and reporting of therapeutic information may differ somewhat from those described in this chapter (see Unit Three). Further study should include attention to recording and reporting therapeutic information, with particular emphasis on becoming more familiar with diagnostic labels and agency terminology. For example, particular terminologies are used in medical settings.

Study and reflection with respect to relevant legal and ethical issues raised in soliciting and maintaining information about consumers should also be explored (e.g., privacy, confidentiality, reporting of abuse). See the articles by Schrier and Bernstein and the book by Hepworth and Larson. Attention to expanding your knowledge of cultures other than your own will improve your effectiveness in managing information from and about consumers and workers. The next step after collecting and updating information involves testing your conclusions in order to determine whether there are enough observational facts to support them. This testing procedure was not discussed in this chapter, but it is important for you to become familiar with it.

Suggested readings are identified below:

Badding, Nancy C. "Client Involvement in Case Recording." *Social Casework* 70 (Nov. 1989): 539–549.

Benjamin, Alfred. *The Helping Interview with Case Illustrations*. Boston: Houghton Mifflin, 1987.

Bernstein, A. G. "Privileged Communications to the Social Worker." *Social Work* 22 (1977): 264–268.

Cwickel, Julia G., and Ram Cnaan. "Ethical Dilemmas in Applying Second Wave Information Technology to Social Work Practice." *Social Work* 36 (Mar. 1991): 114–120.

Franklin, Cynthia, Jack Nowicki, John Trapp, James Schwab, and Jerene Peterson. "A Computerized Assessment System for Brief, Crisis-Oriented Youth Services." *Families in Society: The Journal of Contemporary Human Services* 74 (Dec. 1993): 602–616.

Glastonbury, Bryan, and Walter LaMendola. *The Integrity of Intelligence: A Bill of Rights for the Information Age*. New York: St. Martins Press, 1992.

Hepworth, Dean H., and Jo Ann Larsen. *Direct Social Work Practice,* 4th ed. Pacific Grove, Calif.: Brooks/Cole, 1993.

Hutchinson, Elizabeth D. "Mandatory Reporting Laws: Child Protective Case Finding Gone Awry?" *Social Work* 38 (Jan. 1993): 56–63.

Kadushin, Alfred. *The Social Work Interview: A Guide for Human Service Professionals,* 3rd ed. New York: Columbia University Press, 1990.

Kagle, Jill Doner. "Recording." In *Encyclopedia of Social Work,* 19th ed., 2027–2033. Washington, D.C.: National Association of Social Work, 1995.

Kagle, Jill Doner. *Social Work Records,* 2d ed. Belmont, Calif.: Wadsworth, 1991.

Kessler, David A. "A Better Way to Report Adverse Events." *Nursing* 23 (Nov. 1993): 49–50.

Kron, Thora. *Communication in Nursing*. Philadelphia: Saunders, 1972.

Martin, David G., and Allan D. Moore. *First Steps in the Art of Intervention: A Guidebook for Trainees in the Helping Professions*. Pacific Grove, Calif.: Brooks/Cole, 1991.

Schrier, C. "Guidelines for Recordkeeping Under Privacy and Open-Access Laws." *Social Work* 25 (1980): 452–457.

Schubert, Margaret. *Interviewing in Social Work Practice: An Introduction,* rev. ed. New York: Council on Social Work Education, 1982.

Schuerman, John R., and Lynn Vogel. "Computer Support of Placement Planning: The Use of Expert Systems in Child Welfare." *Child Welfare* 65 (Nov. 1986): 531–543.

Schulman, Eveline D. *Intervention in Human Services,* 4th ed. New York: Macmillan, 1991. (See Part Two: Recording and Reporting)

Tebb, Susan. "Client Focused Recording: Linking Theory and Practice." *Families in Society: The Journal of Contemporary Human Services* 72 (Sept. 1991): 425–432.

Waldo, Willis H. *Better Report Writing*. New York: Van Nostrand Reinhold, 1965.

Wilson, Suanna J. *Recording Guidelines for Social Workers*. New York: Free Press, 1980.

Computers, Information Technology, Expert Systems, and Electronic Information Management in the Human Services

Further study is especially warranted in the explosive growth area of information technology and the human services. You may recall from Chapter 2 our discussion of the contemporary information age. Human service work is very much affected by those trends, especially the electronic aspects of the information management process. Study in this rapidly developing area might begin by understanding the language of information technology and exploring the relationship between information technology and helping. Information technology is the use of computer and communication technologies to receive, handle, store, retrieve, transmit, process, update, analyze, and present data for the purpose of deriving meaning from it. In other words, information technology supports the human acts that surround the activity of informing ourselves. Within the context of the human services, the information being handled is likely to be about actual or potential consumers (identity data, problems/needs, service links, etc.), agency resources, accessible external resources (facilities of other agencies), or agency procedures (e.g., child abuse regulations). Helpers—those who act to offer assistance to others—share several common bonds. One is the goal of improving the self; another, providing comfort or support to individuals and groups. But a third common bond, not typically recognized, is the need for information—about needs, strategies for helping, methods of helping, available resources, and so on. In this regard, information technology becomes a medium for helping that is becoming readily available to the helping professions. Especially see: B. Glastonbury, W. LaMendola, and S. Toole, *Information Technology and the Human Services* (New York: John Wiley, 1987), p. 3; and G. R. Geiss and N. Viswanathan, *The Human Edge: Information Technology and Helping People* (New York: Haworth Press, 1986), pp. 19–20.

Butterfield, William H. "Computer Utilization." In *Encyclopedia of Social Work*, 19th ed. Washington, D.C.: National Association of Social Workers, 1995.

Cnaan, Ram A., and Phyllida Parsloe, eds. *The Impact of Information Technology on Social Work Practice*. New York: Haworth Press, 1989.

Finholt, Tom, and Lee S. Sproull, "Electronic Groups at Work." *Organization Science* 11, 1 (1990): 41–64.

Frese, Michael, Eberhard Ulich, and Wolfgang Dzida. *Psychological Issues of Human–Computer Interaction in the Workplace*. New York: North-Holland, 1987.

Gailliers, Robert, ed. *Information Analysis: Selected Readings*. Reading, Mass.: Addison-Wesley, 1987.

Geiss, Gunther R., and Narayan Viswanathan, eds. *The Human Edge: Information Technology and Helping People*. New York: Haworth Press, 1986.

Gingerich, Wallace J. "Expert Systems." In *Encyclopedia of Social Work*, 19th ed., 917–925. Washington, D.C.: National Association of Social Workers, 1995.

Glastonbury, Bryan, Walter LaMendola, and Stuart Toole. *Information Technology and the Human Services*. New York: John Wiley, 1988.

Grebel, Harmen, and Jan Steyaert. "Social Informatics: Beyond Technology: A Research Project in Schools of Social Work within the European Community." *International Social Work* 38 (Apr. 1995): 151–164.

Grasso, Anthony, and Irwin Epstein. *Information Systems in Child, Youth, and Family Agencies: Planning, Implementation, and Service Enhancement*. New York: Haworth Press, 1993.

Kerslake, Andrew, and Nick Gould, eds. *Information Management in Social Services*. Brookfield, Vt.: Avebury, 1996.

LaMendola, Walter, Bryan Glastonbury, and Stuart Toole, eds. *A Casebook of Computer Applications in the Social and Human Services*. New York: Haworth Press, 1989.

Macarov, David. "Technology's Ongoing Development." In *Certain Change: Social Work Practice in the Future*. Silver Springs, Md.: National Association of Social Workers, 1991.

Pardeck, John W., and John W. Murphy, eds. *Computers in Human Services: An Overview for Clinical and Welfare Services*. New York: Harwood Publishers, 1990.

Phillips, David. *Human Services in the Age of New Technology: Harmonising Social Work and Computerisation*. UK: Ashgate Publishing Company, 1995.

Reinoehl, Richard, and Thomas Hanna, eds. *Computer Literacy in Human Services*. New York: Haworth Press, 1990.

Shoech, Dick. *Computer Use in Human Services: A Guide to Information Management*. New York: Human Sciences Press, 1982.

Shoech, Dick. "Information Systems." In *Encyclopedia of Social Work*, 19th ed., 1470–1479. Washington, D.C.: National Association of Social Work, 1995.

Steyaert, Jan, David Colombi, and Jackie Rafferty, eds. *Human Services and Information Technology: An International Perspective*. Brookfield, Vt.: Ashgate, 1996.

Chapter 11

Managing the Transitions to New Service Delivery Systems

As discussed in Chapter 2, the ability to manage change and transition is a hallmark of effective entry-level delivery of human services. Chapter 2 concentrated on the broad and rapid forces of social and technological changes that are under way, and how these forces can foster problems of living that engender the need for human service professions. We also noted the reforms or calls for reform that are under way in many areas of practice.

In the real world of service delivery, you will likely be asked to manage frequent transitions from one way of delivering services to another.[1] You may even participate in the effort to redesign the services. Many times, the changes from one kind of service system to another will reset or redefine familiar boundaries that demarcate where one element begins and another element ends. For example, there are boundaries of *place* (e.g., Florida ends at this marker and Georgia begins on the other side; the Department of Health is contained in this building and the Department of Family Services resides in this other building). These are boundaries of *program* (e.g., the Medicare program finances inpatient hospital, skilled nursing facility, home health, and other institutional services, and physicians services and hospital outpatient services for the elderly and disabled while the Medicaid program is the major source of funds for health care of the poor). There are boundaries of *role* (e.g., I am a human service worker, you are a consumer; or I am a supervisor, you are a subordinate). And there are boundaries of *access* (e.g., you are eligible for Medicare and Medicaid versus you are eligible only for Medicaid). Sometimes the boundaries are clear; more often, they are changing, fuzzy, and highly complex. Today and tomorrow, when we can see and anticipate continuing redefinition of human services (e.g., their place, programs, roles, and access), we can be sure that we will experience pressure on familiar work rela-

---

[1]Myron E. Weiner, *Human Services Management: Analysis and Applications,* 2nd ed. (Belmont, Calif.: Wadsworth Publishing Company, 1990), p. 421.

tionships "at key boundaries." We can also be sure that these pressures mean we will all need skill in creating new work relationships and redefining existing ones.

This trend of change and experimentation to create new service delivery systems (to redefine the boundaries of and in the human services) is likely to accelerate. So Chapter 11 introduces a set of skills developing two kinds of relationships that will be the cornerstones of effective practice under rapidly changing boundary conditions:

- supervising "up" or how you cross the "hierarchical boundary" created by the terms and roles of supervisor and subordinate; and
- "networking" or how you cross "organization and program boundaries" to link and connect with peers and counterparts in numerous settings relevant to the needs of consumers.

Supervising "up" and networking are boundary-spanning skills, and they are rarely, if ever, developed as such in courses and textbooks at the entry levels of practice. To say they are boundary-spanning skills means they are skills that you need to work at the edges of your role—skills you need to develop to be able to cross formal and informal boundaries that define where your role appears to "end" and some other role "begins." For example, think of the authority boundary between "boss" and "subordinate," or think of the organizational boundary between one human service organization and another. You might not be able to "see" these boundaries in the sense that you can see where one building begins and another building ends. But we all know such boundaries are there nonetheless. In today's complex world, we have developed so many "differentiations" that now it is a major skill to be able to weave skillfully among them.

Boundary-spanning skills move you "up," "across" and "out" from the focus on a particular consumer or consumer population. They require you to link, build "bridges" or make connections in perhaps unaccustomed social directions. For example, supervising "up" is a reversal of the familiar top-down connection between you and your supervisor. Rather than acting simply from the point of view of crossing the supervisor–subordinate boundary by the supervisor "looking down" to the subordinate (much as a parent to a child), the supervisor-subordinate boundary can also be crossed by "supervising up" (where the person being supervised develops skills in helping the supervisor do a better job (perhaps more a parent-to-parent relationship or simply adult-to-adult relationship). Adding this other side to supervising makes it much clearer that supervision is a two-way relationship, where both parties are responsible for effective interaction and results.

Supervising "up" is thus the skill you bring to communicating with your supervisor—to helping your supervisor do her or his job more effectively and to gaining the greatest personal, organizational, and societal benefit from the relationship. Supervisors, agency administrators, and workers have to keep in touch with each other. Some important reasons are to understand consumer needs and service delivery, to keep the agency operating, and to make sure that the overall work is getting done. Unless workers are as highly skilled at communicating with one another as they are with consumers, it is unlikely that services will be delivered effectively, efficiently, or accountably. Achieving skill and understanding in the supervisory relationship gives workers a better sense of the linking that must take place at many levels in order for services to be delivered.

Networking generally suggests a connecting or linking process that moves out, across, or sideways.

> People working in and toward new forms of organization will have to be very aware of the nature of different kinds of boundaries, and in particular, aware of their own reactions to such boundaries. They may not only have to cross physical boundaries (in the sense of new locations) but they will encounter also political boundaries within the organization, psychological boundaries, mental boundaries, status boundaries, and even historical boundaries. . . . Boundaries between hierarchical levels, between department functions and professional specialisms have always been there, but they become more serious as organizations get bigger and specialisms proliferate. . . . That means more impediments to communication both visible (physical distance) and invisible (the difficulties of understanding arising from different cultures). . . . *All of these need to be understood and strategies developed for moving across them with fluency and ease where necessary.*[2]

Networking is a process of crossing or spanning the formal and informal boundaries that separate one organization from another, or one program from another, so that the boundaries are no longer barriers. In networking, we seek to create quick, open person-to-person communications throughout the delivery system. In networks they create, human service workers can engage with consumers, providers, relatives, other workers (in their own and other settings), elected and appointed officials, businesses and nonprofit organizations, community organizations, and so on without being immobilized by differences. Though this is easier said than done, in the human services, communication and relationships among a network of people are the primary means of accomplishing the work. Networks and networking skills have to be developed and nurtured over a long period of time to encourage them to flower as one would tend any exotic plant to encourage it to flower.[3]

In this chapter, you will learn about supervising "up" and networking as communication processes essential to working across—or spanning—the numerous boundaries that separate and create divisions in the world of human service work. By supervising "up" to redefine the supervisor–supervisee relationship and by networking "out" and "across" organizations and programs, entry-level human service workers can participate in reshaping the connections and links in the human service delivery system. The overall objective of the chapter is to assist you in learning how to form effective partnerships "up," "over," and "out," and to suggest how these partnerships can lead to excellence in the process and results of delivering relevant human services to the consumers in your care.

---

[2]Colin Hastings, *The New Organization: Growing the Culture of Organizational Networking* (New York: McGraw-Hill, 1993), p. 74 and p. 4.

[3]Colin Hastings, *The New Organization: Growing the Culture of Organizational Networking,* p. 59.

LESSON 1

Supervising Up

How do you cross the boundary between you and your supervisor? How do you use supervision? What does your supervisor do? What is "supervising up" and how is it done? In this lesson you will learn about your relationship with your supervisor, the purpose of supervision, and how it can help you in delivering human services.

Goal

To be able to demonstrate your skill in supervising up as a means of using supervision for more effective and enriching individual and organizational results.

Learning Activities

To accomplish this goal, we will:

1. Examine the meaning, responsibilities, skills, and expectations of supervision.
2. Explore the processes of "supervising up."
3. Examine the primary elements of the communication process.
4. Identify and explain primary barriers and bridges to effective communication.
5. Reflect on some of the games played through the supervisory relationship.
6. Suggest how the supervisory relationship might contribute to organizational excellence.
7. Review several ways of helping your supervisor, challenging some common myths about the supervisory role.

FRAME
1

SUPERVISING "UP"

While most discussions of supervision focus on how supervisors relate to their subordinates, very little attention has been given to how subordinates can relate effectively with their supervisors. "Supervising up" is a different way to think about being on the receiving end of supervision. It involves risk taking and assertiveness to help your supervisor help you.

Supervising up may sound peculiar, even suspicious. It is an automatic reaction. When most of us think of supervising, what comes to mind immediately is managing *downward*—directing and coaching one's subordinates—not the other way around. . . . The concept of supervising up sounded suspicious to me when I first heard of it. Now, however, I wish I had heard of it much earlier in my career—it would have enabled me to have built better relationships with my superiors in days gone by. . . . Know that managing upward relationships is ethical and responsible behavior. It's good for you, your boss, and your organization.[1]

FRAME

2

WHAT IS SUPERVISION?

Not long ago, the supervisor was often viewed with suspicion and fear and was seen as someone who told workers what to do. Even today, many workers do not trust their supervisors or believe what they say. Effective supervision is a necessary function if we are to deliver human services to people who need them.

Supervision in general and in the human services is the art of getting work done through the efforts and abilities of other people. Supervision helps workers do a better job. The supervisor makes sure that the work gets done. Supervision promotes each worker's individual growth and capacity. The supervisor is there to help workers and to see that they learn about their job and their agency. Supervision is a means of communicating throughout the agency. The supervisor is the link between the top administrators of the agency and individual workers. Supervision keeps work moving toward carrying out the agency's objectives.

If you want to be able to use supervision, you need to know what a supervisor does. The responsibilities of supervisors include the following:

1. Planning and organizing the work to achieve results. Supervisors plan the work that must be done and how it should be done, then assign workers specific tasks and make sure the tasks are completed.

2. Instructing workers. Supervisors make sure that workers know how to do their jobs. They do not always do this training themselves, but they make sure that workers have the knowledge and skills needed to perform their jobs.

3. Communicating with workers. Supervisors see that the word gets through. They make sure communication is clear from administrators to workers, from workers to administrators, and from workers to other workers. They also make assignments, hold interviews, make phone calls, and talk with workers and consumers.

4. Evaluating performance and results. Supervisors find out if things need to be done differently. They look for problems that need attention, and they let a worker know how well he or she is doing.

How does a supervisor fulfill these duties? A basic rule about supervision is that a supervisor must be effective at getting results through the efforts of other people. The first thing a supervisor must know is what job has to be done and how to do it. Supervisors must also be secure in their own abilities and must be able to recognize talent in others.

Some of the ways a supervisor performs each of the four duties are:

---

[1]Wayne Baker, *Networking Smart: How to Build Relationships for Personal and Organizational Success* (New York: McGraw-Hill, 1994), pp. 84–85.

1. Achieving results.[2] To achieve results through employing people, supervisors must be able to plan and organize the work and lead workers so that the work will get done. Planning and organizing are the *thinking* supervisors do before taking action. Supervisors need answers to the following questions when they are planning:

What: Is the goal clear? What work is required to reach the goal?
When: How long will it take to do the job and each part of the job? When is the best time to start?
Where: Where will the work get done?
Who: Who will do the work? Who is best qualified?
How: How will the work get done? What methods will be used?

2. Instructing workers.[3] A supervisor uses many methods to make sure workers know how to do their jobs. Staff meetings serve the double purpose of giving information and helping workers understand various problem areas. To instruct individual workers, a supervisor may ask another worker or an agency trainer to teach a certain subject or skill area, or the supervisor may personally demonstrate specific skills and techniques. When doing this, the supervisor should be patient, prepare what will be said, avoid giving too many details at one time, and try to demonstrate as well as inform about the skills and techniques needed on the job.

3. Communicating with workers. The supervisor has a special responsibility to communicate with each of his or her workers. Supervisors should let workers know how they are getting along, make sure all workers understand what they are saying, listen to workers when they have problems, and tell workers in advance about changes that will affect them.

4. Evaluating performance. It is up to the supervisor to stimulate quality consciousness and pride in results in the workforce. Supervisors observe the work that is being done and find the problems that need attention. Supervisors should make sure their workers feel free to come up with ideas about how things could be done better. Supervisors should also involve their workers in efforts at making improvements. The supervisor is responsible for evaluating how workers are performing. Ratings tell the supervisor when workers need additional training, if they are misplaced in their jobs due to lack of some special abilities, and whether they are eligible for promotions and/or pay increases.

EXPECTATIONS

Now that you know what your supervisor does, it will be useful to think about what you can expect from your supervisor and how you can use supervision to help you do a better job. Your supervisor will or should provide the following:

1. Training. Your supervisor should see to it that you receive whatever on-the-job training is necessary for you to do your job. If you are not sure how to do some-

---

[2]Bradford B. Boyd, *Management-Minded Supervision,* 3d ed. (New York: McGraw-Hill, 1984), pp. 244–268.
[3]Boyd, *Management-Minded Supervision,* p. 173.

thing and you tell your supervisor, you can expect her to teach you or make sure someone else shows you how to do it.

2. Explanations. You can expect your supervisor to explain what she expects from you and also to explain any important policies, rules, and regulations of your agency that you should know.

3. Changes. You can expect your supervisor to tell you about any changes in your duties and responsibilities and about anything else that affects you and your work.

4. Evaluations. Your supervisor will evaluate your performance on the job by assessing your work and making suggestions on how you can improve.

5. Discipline. If you don't follow rules and regulations, or if you don't live up to what is expected of you, you may be disciplined by your supervisor.

6. Support. You can expect your supervisor to give you the opportunity to demonstrate your ability, to understand your viewpoints, to encourage you to improve your performance, and to try to help you when you request assistance with a problem.

In turn, this is what your supervisor expects from you:[4]

1. Cooperation. You will be expected to be cooperative with all your co-workers and to demonstrate a willingness to work and learn alongside them.

2. Initiative. Your supervisor will expect you to complete whatever duties you are given and then, if you haven't been told what to do next, to look around, see what needs to be done, and do it if you can.

3. Willingness to learn. Your supervisor expects you to learn about your job and agency and the way things are done in your agency. You should not be ashamed to say "I don't know" and to seek your supervisor's help when you need it.

4. Willingness to follow directions. Your supervisor will expect you to be able to follow directions and, after you have been working a while, to be able to work on well-established routines without direction.

5. Being knowledgeable and liking your work. Your supervisor expects you to know your job, to like your work, and to show that you like your work. You are also expected to be familiar with your agency's procedures and to be able to apply them in your daily activities.

6. Acceptance of criticism. Criticism is necessary, since it is the way your supervisor lets you know how he expects the job to be done. You should accept it with a smile and try to improve when it is justified and constructive.

FRAME

3

COMMUNICATING WITH YOUR SUPERVISOR

Supervising up requires effective communication between both parties. Communication is a two-way street; it is the creation of understanding. When you communicate with your supervisor, you are sending and receiving messages, and you want to be understood.

Delivering human services can involve large numbers of people with different skills and responsibilities doing certain tasks. If we did not communicate constantly

[4]See Gladys Kimbrell and Ben S. Vineyard, *Succeeding in the World of Work* (Bloomington, Ill.: McKnight and McKnight, 1975), p. 69.

and effectively with one another, it would impossible to perform our jobs effectively. There are guidelines and procedures that everyone in the organization needs to understand so that new and existing policies can be communicated to everyone concerned. Agency administrators must know what is happening at all levels, and the communication processes that provide this information are vital. If communication in either direction fails, the continued life of the organization is in danger.

It is deceptively simple and easy to define communication as the transferring of information from one person to another. This definition is basically correct; however, it leaves unstated some important characteristics of the communication process. Without going into great detail, let's take a closer look at some of the major aspects of successful communication.

The communication process starts with someone who wants to share information with someone else. This person, the *sender,* must decide exactly what he wants to communicate and assemble it in the form of a written or spoken *message.* The message must be prepared with the overall purpose of the communication in mind, and with an appreciation for the language generally used by the person receiving the message. The entire message must be carefully constructed to be as clear and concise as possible. The message goes to the *receiver,* the person or group for whom the message is intended. Unless the receiver gets the message, understands it as it was meant, and takes the intended action, the communication has failed.

The final stage of the communication process is concerned with determining whether the receiver has understood the message and was offered opportunities for clarification. The sender needs to be alert to *feedback* from the receiver so that he can make sure the receiver gets the correct message. By noting the effect of communication, the sender should be able to continually improve the quality and effectiveness of future communication. A diagram of the communication process generally looks like this:

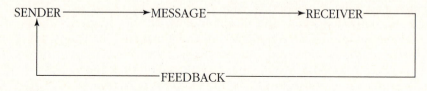

SENDER ⟶ MESSAGE ⟶ RECEIVER

FEEDBACK

FRAME
4

BARRIERS TO EFFECTIVE COMMUNICATION WITH YOUR SUPERVISOR

One of the main reasons you should learn about communication is so that you will understand how communication breaks down or is blocked. This happens because people do not always say what they mean and because they sometimes get the wrong idea about what is being said to them.

In most communication, the sender of a message hopes to get feedback from the receiver. But often, while the message is being sent, there are blocks or barriers that prevent the receiver from understanding the message. These barriers may be created by the sender, the receiver, or the message. Experts in communication have identified five such impediments to communication:[5]

---

[5]Boyd, *Management-Minded Supervision,* pp. 60–70.

1. The listening barrier. It is entirely possible for a person to hear every word that someone else says but to have none of it register. Senders or receivers may nod their heads and look as though they understand what is being said, but the sender cannot be sure.

2. The word barrier. Words mean different things to different people. If the message is confusing or technical, it may not be understood—and the communication will be blocked.

3. The self-interest barrier. People listen to what they want to hear and shut out what they do not want to hear. When people's personal interests and emotions become most important, understanding is nearly impossible.

4. The planning barrier. When the sender does not spend time planning the message with a specific purpose in mind, the communication is almost sure to be blocked.

5. The barrier of failing to see the need. This is the "sin of omission"—in which people fail to communicate when they need to. "I didn't think it was necessary to tell them" is a common response of people creating such a block to communication.

BRIDGES TO EFFECTIVE COMMUNICATION

Now that you know some of the ways that communication can be blocked, you need ways to remove these barriers in order to improve our communication. Let's look at each barrier to communication and talk about a bridge that you can use to make sure you are being understood.[6]

1. The feedback bridge to remove listening barriers. In any communication, it is up to the sender to make sure the receiver understands the message by using the feedback bridge. In face-to-face communication, the receiver is constantly sending reactions to what is being said and sending out signals that tell whether she is listening. These signals may be seen in a person's posture and facial expressions or heard in the voice. The sender can check if the message is getting across by saying, for example, "Let me see if I can put it another way," or by asking questions to see if the message has been understood.

2. Gearing to the receiver to remove word barriers. How do you remove the problem of having your words misunderstood? You bridge the gap by gearing your message to the receiver. You have to consider the receiver's vocabulary. If you are using words that she does not understand, you will have to put the message another way. As a message receiver you have to swallow your pride and admit it when you are not sure of a word's meaning. Asking what a word or term means shows your interest in understanding the message and tells the sender that he needs to make the message clearer.

3. The empathy bridge to remove self-interest barriers. How do you keep your personal interests and emotions from becoming all important? You use the empathy bridge. This means putting yourself in the other person's shoes and seeing things from her point of view. It means asking yourself, "Why is she saying that? Why does she feel that way? What would make her ask that?" It means trying to understand the message that the other person is sending.

---

[6]Boyd, *Management-Minded Supervision,* pp. 60–70.

4. The planning bridge to remove planning barriers. How can you plan your communication better? You can bridge the planning gap by trying to pinpoint the answers to the following six questions before you send the message: What am I trying to get across? Who will receive my communication? When is the best time to communicate? Where is the best place to communicate? How should I communicate? Why am I communicating?

5. The awareness bridge to remove barriers of failing to see the need. How do you prevent yourself from not communicating when it's really needed? You can use the awareness bridge. As a worker in the human services, you should be aware of your responsibility to communicate with other workers. You can do this by always striving for understanding, by working at listening to others, and by making sure others have the information they need. You can put communication on a positive basis when problems arise by finding ways to keep them from happening again instead of blaming someone else. Accept your responsibility to communicate with your co-workers and do everything you can to keep your agency operating smoothly as you help consumers. Develop an awareness of the importance of communication in performing your job.

FRAME
5

GAMES WE ALL PLAY

At some point in a supervisory relationship, workers and supervisors will "play games" with one another. These games reflect the irrational, but human, aspects of working together in frequently difficult and tense situations in which the demands and needs of consumers can overwhelm both worker and supervisor. Even in the most comfortable of working conditions, the personal needs of the worker and the supervisor can affect the supervisory relationship. For some workers, it is difficult to admit to their supervisor that they do not know something. Exposing vulnerability is also difficult for supervisors. Playing games can be viewed as protecting one's vulnerability in terms of power. The more the supervisor engages in power sharing, the less the need for a worker to play games in order to minimize losses and maximize rewards. The more the worker recognizes the ambiguous boundaries of the supervisory relationship, the less the potential for feeling inadequate about work performance or self.

In this frame, we identify some of the typical games that workers and supervisors play. By using the label "games," our goal is to highlight some of the more complex aspects of a supervisory relationship, *not* to suggest the cynical view that all human interaction is merely a game. Kadushin has identified some of the following games played by workers and supervisors:[7]

1. *Two against the agency*—a game in which the needs of consumers are seen as more important than completing the agency's paperwork, which takes time away from serving consumers. Both worker and supervisor conspire to let the paperwork become low priority.

2. *Be nice to me because I am nice to you*—a game in which flattery is used to avoid dealing with difficult issues, such as poor worker job performance or the inadequate quantity and quality of supervisory time.

[7]Adapted from Alfred Kadushin, "Games People Play in Supervision," *Social Work* 13, 3 (1968): 23–32.

3. *Help me but don't psychoanalyze me*—a game in which personal problems are addressed in the supervisory relationship and the boundaries between supervision and therapy are unclear.

4. *Job evaluation is not for friends*—a game in which the supervisory relationship is re-defined as a social relationship (coffee breaks, lunch dates, carpool companionship, etc.) in order to avoid engaging in the evaluation of worker and/or supervisor job performance.

5. *If you knew Freud like I know Freud*—a game of seeking to be one-up or to put someone down in which both parties in the relationship conspire not to expose the ignorance of the other person.

6. *So what do you know about it?*—a game in which the most experienced member of the supervisory relationship "pulls rank" by flaunting more experience (the worker is a mother of two children, and the supervisor is unmarried and without children).

7. *Heading them off at the pass*—a game in which either party to the relationship continuously admits his or her mistakes before anything else is said and does so in such detail as to elicit praise for whatever strengths exist ("Don't be so hard on yourself").

8. *Little old me*—a game in which a person seeks to gain strength by using dependence and weakness to unload responsibility for something on to the other person ("What would you do next?" or "I did it the way you told me to").

9. *What you don't know won't hurt me*—a game in which either party shares or distorts information, consciously or unconsciously, in order to present a more favorable picture. The behaviors can be passive and reticent or overwhelming in the sense of sharing endless trivia.

10. *I wonder why you said that*—a game in which honest disagreements are redefined and labeled as psychological resistance in order to shift the burden for accepting an idea or doing something that seems unusual to the other person.

11. *One good question deserves another*—a game in which an honest question raised by the worker or supervisor is met with yet another question in response, which is a device for avoiding the first question, especially when the answer is difficult to identify or is unknown.

While we have identified a few of the games that supervisors and workers play, it should be apparent that open and honest communication can frequently prevent the need to play such games. In playing these games, the worker or supervisor usually loses in the process of appearing to win. The loss reflects poor communication and the inability to build the strong supervisor–worker relationship needed to enhance the growth and development of both parties.

Now let's move from the cynical view of games played in supervisory relationships to a more positive and optimistic view of how the relationship might contribute to promoting excellence in the agency.

FRAME

6

ATTRIBUTES OF ORGANIZATIONAL EXCELLENCE

As noted in Frame 5, supervising up requires an understanding of the games that can be played in the supervisory relationship. Supervising up also requires an understanding of the attributes of organizational excellence. Peters and Waterman identified such attributes after looking at successful American corporations.[8] We apply their findings to the supervisory relationship in order to demonstrate how the worker and the supervisor can consciously use their relationship to promote excellence in serving consumers, promote supportive working conditions, and enhance their own effectiveness as agency staff members. Excellent supervisory relationships can be built by paying attention to the following principles:

1. Reflecting a bias for action. This is a process in which the worker and supervisor "get on with it," carrying out their respective job responsibilities using practical and immediate approaches to decision making (establishing standardized methods or procedures for handling difficult situations or problems) and thereby avoid getting "bogged down." This process can usually be accomplished by MBWA (management by walking about) in which supervisors drop into workers' offices and workers stop by supervisors' offices. This does not mean checking with one another every hour but rather maintaining frequent contact in busy work environments in order to gain feedback or monitor developments.

2. Staying close to the consumer. This is a process of remaining alert and open to hearing and seeing the changing needs of consumers by listening intently and regularly to the people you serve.

3. Promoting creativity and leadership. This is a process of fostering innovations in handling the agency's work and encouraging each other to provide leadership on issues of importance (supervisor encouraging a worker to try a new service approach, or worker encouraging a supervisor to advocate for the needs of the unit with top administration). This process is based on encouraging practical risk taking in order to generate a reasonable number of mistakes. Yes, mistakes!

4. Identifying productivity through people. This is a process of respecting each other whereby *both* the worker and the supervisor are seen as a source of ideas and the primary source of quality services and productivity in the agency. We are not machines or cogs in the agency's wheel but human beings with immense, usually untapped, ingenuity.

5. Recognizing the "hands on" and value base of our work. This is a process in which the basic philosophy of serving people in need has far more to do with achieving agency service objectives than our specific agency procedures or organization chart. The values and ethics that guide the work of supervisors and workers are important enough to be reflected in daily practice and are not simply "fluff" or "nice ideas."

6. Sticking to the knitting. This is a process of staying close to the things we do best (workers serving consumers, and supervisors helping workers) and staying away from activities that we know little about. In other words, we should not offer new services to consumers unless we have the capacity to do it well.

7. Keeping it simple. This is a process of keeping the supervisory relationship as simple and clear as possible and keeping top management posted and in touch with consumer issues. This process reflects the goal of minimizing the bureaucratic layers in an agency in order to create a streamlined, efficient, and effective organization.

---

[8]Thomas J. Peters and Robert H. Waterman, Jr., *In Search of Excellence: Lessons from America's Best-Run Companies* (New York: Harper & Row, 1983).

8. Keeping the relationship both loose and tight. This is a process by which a minimum of decisions are kept within the control of supervisors (tight) and a maximum number are made by the worker (loose). The underlying concept is the recognition that the tightest control maintained by the agency is in the area of organizational values, where everyone understands the rules for treating one another fairly and that the only reason the agency exists at all is to serve consumers.

Have you seen any of these attributes of excellence in the human service settings in which you have been a participant? If not, why not? They obviously reflect ideal working conditions and therefore represent important goals for workers *and* supervisors to pursue together. Few of these attributes can be achieved by working alone. Most of them can become realities if the supervisory relationship is viewed as a collaborative team of two or more persons. In the context of collaboration, it is important for workers to identify specific ways in which to help their supervisors do their supervisory work. This is the topic of the next frame.

FRAME

7

HELPING YOUR SUPERVISOR

The essence of supervising up is helping your supervisor do her job. The primary skills for the worker are advance planning and environmental monitoring. Advance planning requires the worker to think ahead by anticipating events and preparing for them. For example, workers can plan for an upcoming supervisory conference by preparing written memos for the supervisor to read in advance of the meeting or written notes for use at the meeting itself. These notes or memos might include descriptions of complex cases or difficult work relations with staff inside or outside the agency.

Written notes or memos might also address broader issues, such as problem statements and recommendations for changing the agency's services. Similarly, written materials might be generated in order to address a problem found throughout the agency with specific recommendations for changes in procedures or reporting structures. Most workers, unfortunately, define such activities as outside their job responsibilities and thereby miss another opportunity to contribute to excellence in the agency by supervising up. It goes without saying that not all suggestions will be accepted; some might even be viewed negatively by staff members who do not appreciate or understand the value of supervising up.

The second skill of environmental monitoring involves workers using their eyes and ears effectively. Workers are in a prime spot to monitor their caseload or the group of consumers with whom they are working. Such monitoring can lead to observations and suggestions for improving or changing services to meet changing needs. Similarly, workers are able to monitor changes in the community through the experiences of the consumers they serve. Such changes can be very important to the supervisor and the agency in ways that the worker may not fully see because persons higher up in the agency's administrative structure may have more information related to such changes. Therefore, it is important *not to assume* that the "higher ups" know how changes in the community are affecting consumers (e.g., changes in school busing patterns, shortages in food banks, and changes in consumer satisfaction with the institutional food service). Making such assumptions can ultimately hurt the interests of consumers.

Workers also need to explode some of the common myths about supervisors because worker expectations might be erroneously based on these myths. Here are just a few:

1. Myth: Supervisors prefer verbal messages to written messages.
2. Myth: Supervisors are usually more knowledgeable and competent than are workers.
3. Myth: Supervisors are proactive leaders, not reactive ones.
4. Myth: Supervisors do not want feedback on their supervisory skills.

As for the first myth, supervisors are constantly juggling the demands made by upper levels of administration with the demands of the workers in their unit. As a result, they become very busy and do not always manage their time as effectively as they would like. Therefore, verbal messages from staff members are sometimes heard and sometimes not. Workers can help their supervisors by using written messages to identify problems or make recommendations. This helps the supervisor, who is able to read and respond at a time convenient to the supervisor, not the worker. It is important to check out this myth with your supervisor so that your expectations are linked to supervisor's preferences.

The second myth is based on the perception that, in most cases, your supervisor is more knowledgeable and competent than you are. This view depends on the issue or topic at hand. There will be numerous situations where your knowledge might exceed that of your supervisor based on your continuous contact with consumers. Recognize that you and your supervisor have different areas of expertise and seek to blend them rather than view them in terms of "more or less" competence. Some workers tend to idolize their supervisor and mistakenly place her on a pedestal. This usually gets in the way of achieving mutual respect and support. Ascribing special qualities to a supervisor makes it difficult to see him or her as a human being who is vulnerable and can make mistakes.

The third myth is to see your supervisor primarily in the light of proactive leadership, fighting for the needs of staff with the "powers that be" or promoting innovations inside and outside the agency. It is also necessary to see supervisors as reactive leaders or managers, especially when they deal with you and your co-workers. Part of the process of supervising up is based on the premise that supervisors are reactive beings who can benefit from being pushed or reminded to act on an issue. Workers who recognize this reality and skillfully assist their supervisor by supervising up are able to see both the proactive and reactive elements of managerial leadership.

The fourth myth relates to giving your supervisor feedback on her supervisory skills. Most workers assume that supervisors do not want such feedback because they rarely ask for it. Clearly it is important to raise the issue with your supervisor to determine if, in fact, she does want feedback and in what form and frequency. Most supervisors are skilled staff members who are capable of receiving and processing feedback. Similarly, most workers are exceedingly adept at identifying the strengths and areas for improvement in the supervisor's management processes. A key ingredient of supervising up is to find the time and place where such feedback can best be processed. Again, this is a mutual exploration and needs to be guided by some of the following practices for making effective use of feedback:

1. Focus feedback on the person's behavior rather than on the person.
2. Focus feedback on observation rather than on inferences.
3. Focus feedback on description rather than on judgment.
4. Focus feedback on descriptions of behavior as part of a range of possible behaviors (e.g., more or less) rather than simply qualitative distinctions (e.g., good or bad).
5. Focus feedback on behavior related to a specific situation (e.g., preferably the "here and now" rather than the "there and then").
6. Focus feedback on sharing ideas and information rather than on giving advice.
7. Focus feedback on exploring of alternatives rather than on answers or solutions.
8. Focus feedback on the value it may have to the recipient, not on the value or release that it provides to the person giving the feedback.
9. Focus feedback on the amount of information that the person receiving it can use rather than on the amount that the worker might like to give.
10. Focus feedback on time and place so that personal data can be shared at appropriate times.
11. Focus feedback on *what* is said rather than *why* it is said.

FRAME

8

ASSESSING SOURCES OF WORKER SATISFACTION WITH SUPERVISION[9]

In this frame you have an opportunity to reflect on the sources of job satisfaction you derive from your relationship with your supervisor. The specific steps for this exercise follow:

Step 1: Rank the items below by placing a "1" next to the item that reflects your most important source of satisfaction, a "2" next to the second most important item, and so on until you have ranked them all.

Step 2: Write a sentence or two justifying the top three items in your rank order, explaining why you think they are so important.

Step 3: Ask your supervisor to rank the items according to his or her best guess about *your* sources of satisfaction.

Step 4: Compare your responses with those of your supervisor and discuss the similarities and differences.

_____ 1. Through supervision I share responsibility with, and obtain support from, somebody in administrative authority for case decisions.

_____ 2. My supervisor provides the help I need in dealing with problems I face with consumers.

_____ 3. My supervisor supports my development as a human service worker.

_____

[9]Adapted from Alfred Kadushin, *Supervision in Social Work,* 3d ed. (New York: Columbia University Press, 1992), p. 243.

_____ 4. My supervisor provides administrative access to the agency resources I need to help my consumers.

_____ 5. My supervisor provides stimulation in thinking about theory as it relates to the practice of delivering human services.

_____ 6. My supervisor provides me with the critical feedback about how I am doing as a human service worker and what I need to change.

_____ 7. My supervisor provides me with the emotional support I need to do my job more effectively.

_____ 8. My supervisor provides me with a real appreciation of the work I am doing.

_____ 9. My supervisor helps me feel a sense of belonging in the organization.

_____ 10. My supervisor helps me to grow toward greater maturity as a person.

FRAME
9

The art of supervising up is finding the best circumstances to help your supervisor do his job and thereby help you. Overdoing the process of supervising up can lead to resentment and annoyance. Failing to supervise up can lead to your own frustration and anger. The skills of advanced planning and environmental monitoring need to be refined at the same time as you confront some of the myths about supervisors.

As we conclude this lesson, it is important to remember that supervising up is not a well-understood concept, so it may take you some time to learn how to implement it effectively and gain appreciation for your efforts. Your patience should be rewarded in time by an appreciative and understanding supervisor. While you are struggling, remember that your supervisor is also struggling to acquire and refine the skills of supervisory management. You might use the references at the end of this chapter as a resource for conversations about the subject.

Networking Across Organizations and Programs

Many human needs require spanning the boundaries of numerous human services categories.[1] For example, at-risk children, school dropouts, the homeless, the frail elderly, and young people who get lost in the transition from high school to productive work all typically face multiple problems of living that defy a simple one-to-one match with any singular response. In addition to consumer needs, as we mature in a career, we grow from being accustomed to working with others who are trained similarly to us to being willing and able to teach and learn with service providers from many other disciplines. Increasingly, therefore, human service workers at all levels find themselves forced to think and act in systems terms—and to network or link a number of separate organizations, programs, and people.

What is networking across organizations and programs and how is it done? What are some of the pitfalls associated with networking or branching across organizations and programs in the human services? How is networking related to the development of your career—to your growth as a provider of human services? In this lesson, you will learn about networking as an important skill for creating the kinds of interconnections needed to help the consumers in your care. You will also develop a practical connection between networking and the discussion of systems thinking in Unit One, seeing networking as a key skill used to deliver human services in holistic terms.

Goal

To be able to demonstrate your skill in networking as a means to span the divisions that prevent consumers and human service workers from achieving full, self-sufficient solutions to complex problems of living.

---

[1]Myron E. Weiner, *Human Services Management: Analysis and Applications,* 2d ed. (Belmont, Calif.: Wadsworth, 1990), p. 432.

Learning Activities

To accomplish this goal, we will:

1. Define organizational networking.
2. Contrast organizational networking and teamwork.
3. Introduce a link between "service fragmentation" and networking across organizations and programs.
4. Suggest some kinds of networks and identify some issues in making the transition to working in them.
5. Discuss barriers to networking.
6. Reflect on the relationship between learning and networking.
7. Provide exercises to create, extend, and activate service delivery networks, and offer a caution in practicing the skill of networking to overcome the fragmentation of the human service delivery system.

FRAME

1

WHAT IS NETWORKING?

Networking is the active process of building and managing productive relationships—a vast web of personal and organizational relationships—within and between organizational units and programs.[2] It includes everyone you work with, and it includes external ties. Networking "smart," according to Wayne Baker, means building and managing a broad array of relationships in intelligent, resourceful, and ethical ways that are good for you and your career, good for the people you work with, good for your organization, and good for your consumers.

One of the many aims of redesigning human service delivery systems is to network "smart"—to improve service delivery through direct relationships and information sharing between people, irrespective of role, status, level, culture, program, or location—in short, to find ways to cross or break down and redefine traditional boundaries that divide human service practices (sometimes usefully, sometimes less so). We can think of these linking processes as *organizational networking,* which will be focused:[3]

- within the organizations and its programs (internally driven);
- between organizations and programs (externally driven);
- on connecting computers (hard networking); or
- on connecting people (soft networking).

Our "networking territory" is thus both inside and outside the places where we work and it includes individuals and groups (see Table 11.1). The internally driven mentality is about having your own wide range of resources and seeking to maximize their

---

[2]Adapted from Wayne E. Baker, *Networking Smart: How to Build Relationships for Personal and Organizational Success* (New York, McGraw-Hill, 1994), pp. xiii–xiv, 34.
[3]Colin Hastings, *The New Organization: Growing the Culture of Organizational Networking* (London: McGraw-Hill, 1993), pp. 15, 21.

use within and across your organization. The externally driven mentality is about recognizing what resources you or your organization lack and what connections with other organizations can fill in those gaps. Each worker's networking territory can be examined for how well it covers the areas needed to deliver human services and to meet career development needs.

TABLE 11.1. **Your Networking Territory**[4]

	Inside	*Outside*
Personal (individuals)	superiors peers subordinates team members directors	consumers government officials peers in related programs and agencies business officials community leaders

Group	work units
	teams
	departments
	divisions
	programs
	offices
		organizations:
		   consumer
		   educator
		   community
		   business
		   religious
		   volunteer

Beyond one-to-one relations, networking smart entails making self-conscious connections within your immediate work setting and beyond it. Only with a well-developed network territory can you deliver human services as collaboratively as possible to consumers.

ORGANIZATIONAL NETWORKING AND TEAMWORK

The terms networking and teamwork are sometimes used interchangeably. Today, however, there are some attempts both to distinguish and relate these concepts.

Networks form when disparate groups of people and groups "link" to work together for some common purpose. Teams are small groups of people who work with focus, motivation, and skill to achieve shared goals. Teams tend to be small, in the same place, and tightly coordinated. Networks tend to be large, spread out, and loosely linked. Lipnack and Stamps, who make these distinctions, also suggest that a concept like "TeamNet" can bring the best of both practices together.

TeamnNet applied to small groups means more networked teams.

---

[4]Baker, *Networking Smart,* p. 34.

> TeamNet applied to large groups means more teamlike networks. In an ideal TeamNet, people work in high performing teams at every level, and the network as a whole functions as though it were a highly skilled and motivated team.[5]

Not all networks are teams. In fact, some networks never even come together to work on a common task. In this sense, the distinction between a network and a team is important.

FRAME 2

REFLECTING ON PRACTICE[6]

As a way to anchor the concepts and skills developed in this lesson on networking across organizations and programs, we suggest you draw, on a large sheet of paper, a map of all the key groups and individuals with whom you have contact in order to get your work done. This includes people in your own organization, in other organizations and institutions, and social and personal support systems (e.g., mentors and sponsors, family) and leisure elements that are important to your job success.

Figure 11.1 is the beginning of a map to help you identify all those people who either have expectations of you in your role or contributions to make toward your success and the success of the consumers with whom you work. Please add to the figure to make it fit with your personal and professional situation.

FRAME 3

WHY NETWORK?

Networking is receiving more emphasis today because of rapid changes under way in the world of work. In the human services, networking has always been important, but it is more prominent today because of the ever increasing fragmentation—the almost bewildering array of categories of need, eligibility requirements, and services. As noted in the discussions of various other roles (e.g., brokering, advocating, and mobilizing), sometimes this mosaic of services contains a match with the problems of living facing a consumer; sometimes it does not.

This problem of fragmentation of services has long been recognized in the human services. Some regard it as a problem of duplication and waste, others regard it as the American way. It stems in part from a penchant for (a) inventing new programs that respond to identified problems from a provider rather than a consumer orientation, and (b) doing so without much regard for whether the new program duplicates or conflicts with existing programs.[7] A broader picture of the forces contributing to the need for networking is provided in Table 11.2.

---

[5]Jessica Lipnack and Jeffrey Stamps, *The TeamNet Factor: Bringing the Power of Boundary Crossing into the Heart of Your Business* (Essex Junction, Vt.: Oliver Wright Publications, 1994), p. 7.
[6]Exercise from Hastings, *The New Organization,* pp. 70–71.
[7]William A. Morrill et al., *Improving Outcomes for Children and Families at Risk: Collaborations Which Integrate Services, Next Steps* (Princeton, N.J.: MathTech, Inc., May 14, 1991).

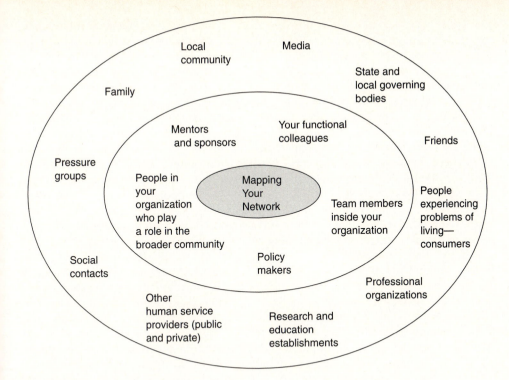

FIGURE 11.1.
Mapping Your Network [*Source:* Colin Hastings, *The New Organization: Growing the Culture of Organizational Networking,* p. 71.]

TABLE 11.2. **Forces for Networking Across Programs and Organizations**[8]

Individual Level	*Systems Level*
Multiple, diverse needs of individual	Multiple, diverse needs of system
Fragmented view of individual	Fragmented agency services
Lack of responsiveness to individual needs	Lack of responsiveness to consumer needs
Lack of parental voice	Lack of consumer voice
Uncoordinated services	Uncoordinated services
Inadequate services	Gaps/duplicated services
Multiple professionals	Multiple, overlapping planning bodies
Differing treatment modalities	Different program models
Multiple billing procedures	Multiple funding streams
Professional jargon	Agency jargon
Professional territoriality	Agency territoriality

[8]Vicki C. Pappas, "Interagency Collaboration: An Interdisciplinary Application." In Howard G. Garner and Fred P. Orelove, *Teamwork in Human Services: Models and Applications Across the Lifespan* (Boston, Mass.: Butterworth-Heinemann, 1994), p. 64.

Those who have sought to do something about service fragmentation have often described their aims in policies or initiatives that have the goal of "service integration." Service integration has a long and intricate history. According to Kagan and Neville, service integration is in part a fundamental approach to service delivery that demands an attitudinal conversion from competition to collaboration, from exclusion to inclusion, from involvement to empowerment, and from restricted to holistic human services.[9]

Because the average consumer has to navigate a complicated, fragmented, and often confusing "nonsystem" of separate, isolated agencies, each providing their own services from their own disciplinary perspective, the human service worker's skill in building service delivery networks—and imparting that skill to consumers so that they can build their own—can be invaluable to consumers. In addition, human service workers are increasingly likely to find themselves working in a variety of temporary and permanent service delivery networks pulled together to be responsive to people as they seek a set of services that will meet their needs. Thus, human service workers must also be skilled at participating in, as well as creating and abandoning, when appropriate, such delivery networks.

Networking can also be thought of as the activity of crossing conventional boundaries for mutual benefit.[10] Some boundaries are organizational, such as the role boundary between a supervisor and subordinate. Other boundaries are more visible, such as the identification badge you may have to wear to enter your workplace or to visit some other workplace. Other boundaries are more fuzzy, for example, where one program begins and another ends, or, in the work setting, how long lunch breaks occur, or how part-time employees or consultants relate to full-time employees and inside employees. The point is that human service problems cross the boundaries of programs, organizations, sectors, and funding streams. With a big enough view, a big enough network, you can ultimately tie together many human service problems facing consumers.

FRAME 4

REFLECTING ON PRACTICE

Use the exercise below to assess the current state of your personal intelligence system—the network or networks that support you and your consumers in the world of delivering human services.[11] Answer yes or no to each question, depending on which answer best describes your current situation.

1. Do you feel you are generally in the know and typically find out about key decisions, events, and activities inside your organization?
2. Do you have personal contacts in most other groups, programs, or divisions in your organization?
3. Do you prefer to talk face to face to define and discuss complex problems and changing priorities?
4. Do you usually accept contact-building opportunities, such as transfers, temporary assignments, committee assignments, or relocations?
5. Do you actively share information with your peers and superiors?

---

[9]Sharon Lynn Kagan with Peter R. Neville, *Integrating Services for Children and Families: Understanding the Past to Shape the Future* (New Haven, Conn.: Yale University Press, 1993), p. 196.
[10]Lipnack and Stamps, *The TeamNet Factor,* p. 13.
[11] Adapted from Baker, *Networking Smart,* pp. 66–67.

6. Do you maintain contacts with people who provide human services in areas different from your own (e.g., teachers, public health nurses, eligibility workers at the welfare office, volunteers in homeless shelters, physicians, therapists in private practice)?
7. Do you stay in close touch with your consumers?
8. Do you regularly wander around in the outside world, attending meetings, civic and charitable events and so on?
9. Do you know and talk with your peers in other organizations?
10. Do you have contacts who can serve as your "high-level" eyes and ears (e.g., board members, supervisors in other areas)?

If you answered yes to eight or more questions, your personal intelligence system is probably in good shape. If you answered yes to six but fewer than eight questions, you have room for improvement. If you answered yes to fewer than five questions, you have a great deal of work to do.

FRAME
5

REFLECTING ON PRACTICE

You are working in a city office of family services. You are one of ten full-time employees working exclusively as "utility disconnect caseworkers." Your task is to assess a family's utility situation and arrange, in hardship cases, for restoration of gas and electricity, canceled for failure to pay. Your mandate does not include responding to any family needs except those associated with inability to pay utility bills. As a result, these cases tend to reappear in your agency's offices with their utilities again disconnected or with other serious problems.[12]

How might you network "smart" across what organizations and programs to achieve what results in this situation? To answer this question, give an example of the "networking territories" for two different utility disconnect caseworkers:

- one caseworker, Anika, being of the view that "the most important thing is to focus on the utility situation and the individual family" and
- the other caseworker, Mohammed, being of the view that "the most important thing in assessing a family's utility situation is to be part of a diverse network of providers who share a focus on how best to deliver family-centered services."

FRAME
6

THE MIX, INDEPENDENCE, AND PERSONAL GROWTH OF WORKERS IN SERVICE DELIVERY NETWORKS

The service delivery settings created by networking across organizations and programs can involve a bewildering array of people from different human service disciplines working together, formally and informally, as some sort of service delivery system. Since many professionals regard themselves as independent practitioners, working in

---

[12]Case from Lisbeth Schorr, *Within Our Reach: Breaking the Cycle of Disadvantage* (New York: Anchor Press, Doubleday, 1988).

a service delivery network involves a significant change that can be frustrating as well as an opportunity for career growth.

What are some examples of different types of service delivery networks that you might create or in which you might otherwise participate? Many arrangements are possible. For example, consider the network in which *each human service provider stays independent and makes his or her own decisions about how best to serve the consumer.*

> *Example.* Providers working together but operating independently can be seen in the field of case management of child sexual abuse. Professionals who gather information regarding abuse cases, who prosecute perpetrators, and who treat the victims all need to be involved. The prosecutor from the district attorney's office could provide the leadership for the network, which might include a physician, a law enforcement officer, a social worker, and a mental health professional. The various disciplines represented would be distinctive, have specialized knowledge and skills, and very little overlap among their roles. The network would focus on information sharing and coordination.[13]

A second possibility is a network in which *service providers from very different backgrounds must agree on a common, integrated plan to deliver services to the same consumer.* This kind of network must achieve a group synthesis. Although each member has expertise in his or her own discipline, he or she is also familiar with that of the others.

> *Examples.* One example is when a team conducts a joint assessment—observing the child at the same time, assessing from their own area of expertise, and then writing a unified assessment report. Another example is the evaluation of children with developmental disabilities by an interdisciplinary network consisting of a pediatrician, speech pathologist, audiologist, social worker, and psychologist. At the end of the assessment process, they must present a set of common findings and recommendations.[14]

A third kind of network you might create or participate in is the network in which *service providers from different professional backgrounds begin to exchange some of their roles* (they begin to learn and share across boundaries that otherwise act to keep them separated).

> *Examples.* In this model, activities are planned and implemented by the entire network, rather than by each discipline. A manager may coordinate the activities of the various professionals and even carry out their recommendations. Members share knowledge and skills from their respective disciplines. An example is the occupational therapist or psychologist who instructs a teacher regarding specific behavior management or exercise routines. Another example is an infant assess-

---

[13]Howard G. Garner, "Multidisciplinary versus Interdisciplinary Teamwork." In Howard G. Garner and Fred P. Orelove, *Teamwork in Human Services: Models and Applications Across the Lifespan* (Boston, Mass.: Butterworth-Heinemann, 1994), pp. 23–24.

[14]Pappas, "Interagency Collaboration," and Maite deLamerens-Pratt and Gerald S. Golden, "Teamwork in Medical Settings—Hospitals, Clinics, and Communities." In Howard G. Garner and Fred P. Orelove, *Teamwork in Human Services: Models and Applications Across the Lifespan* (Boston, Mass.: Butterworth-Heinemann, 1994), pp. 69, 164.

ment clinic where a pediatrician, nurse, occupational therapist, a nutritionist conduct a joint evaluation (with some sharing of each other's roles) to be able to formulate program recommendations.[15]

Following the progression of the three network situations described above, you will see that there is a movement from a service provider operating quite independently to a service provider being more tightly connected in a hub of other service providers and increasingly sharing tasks of assessment, planning, and service delivery. This progression is essential in moving toward more integrated delivery of human services. As we share responsibility for the decisions we make, we will experience moving between specialization (of our organization or particular area of practice) and working with service providers from numerous other areas (see the diagram below).[16]

| Working alone; possessing a sound preparation and competency in your own discipline | → | Working with others in your organization/ discipline believing that you can contribute to the consumer group | → | Working with other providers (from different backgrounds, programs, organizations) who can also make important contributions to the consumer group | → | Being willing and able to work with other disciplines in providing joint services to the consumer group | → | Committing to teaching, learning, and working with other service providers across traditional disciplinary boundaries (roles among specialists become blurred) |

Choosing to move our "circles of connection" increasingly outward and making them more diverse can be an experience of career growth and development. As workers grow and mature in their careers, they make choices as to whether and how to deepen their expertise as specialists and whether and how to move toward developing skill in working across specialties. Not all workers will choose the latter career path, and certainly not all would be expected to. The point of this lesson, however, is that the pressure to develop skill in reaching out across human service specialties is likely to increase in the future. How each human service worker responds will be in part a matter of how each worker regards his or her career development, and then matches that to the expectations of the human service setting.

F R A M E

7

REFLECTING ON PRACTICE

Take some time to provide examples from your own experience where you have worked with a diverse group of human service providers. Identify and discuss some of the strengths and weaknesses you and others, workers and consumers, experienced.

---

[15]deLamerens-Pratt and Golden, "Teamwork in Medical Settings," p. 166.
[16]Weiner, *Human Services Management,* p. 434.

If you have never participated in such an activity, then find a human service worker who has and interview the person for a description of what the experience is like, how he or she got involved in the network, what impact the experience had on the worker's career, and what was most difficult and rewarding about the experience—from the point of view of the consumer and the worker.

FRAME
8

PARTICIPATING IN SERVICE DELIVERY NETWORKS

Some basic tenets of creating and participating effectively in a variety of service delivery networks include:[17]

1. Good communication among individuals serving the same consumer is fundamental and essential. Each discipline has important information to communicate, and somewhat different interpretations about the effects of various solutions.

2. Working in a service delivery network promotes personal and professional development, facilitates reliable feedback among colleagues, and provides emotional support for professionals working in demanding and stressful situations.

3. Creating a service delivery network will often entail creating a new setting or new set of relationships. There may be pressure to create the new setting quickly, but some time must be taken to appreciate the history of the new setting and the values that will guide it.

4. Service delivery networks go through some predictable stages of development including: formation (clarifying working relationships, goals, strategies, and mechanisms to maintain accountability); implementation (taking action to produce preliminary results and analyzing progress to determine next steps); maintenance (managing tensions between the network and its external environment and among network participants); and termination or transformation (the network may end its active life because it achieved its goal or failed to, it may change into something else, or it may continue indefinitely).

5. Creating and participating in a network can present many challenges. People will bring differences in philosophy and orientation that can create problems in working together, in finding a common basis for communication. Some individuals will also experience role conflict, or confusion between how they work within the network and how they work in their home base organization. Another challenge can be how comfortable workers will feel in sharing information with and accepting information from others.

The reality is that organizational networking is frequently difficult, makes considerable demands on individuals, requires balancing constant trade-offs and contradictions, creates stress, and requires individuals to embrace complexity, see the whole picture, and stretch their capabilities to the limit.[18]

---

[17]See Garner and Orelove, *Teamwork in Human Services,* pp. 4, 5, 52; Julie S. Abramson and Beth B. Rosenthal, "Interdisciplinary and Interorganizational Collaboration." In *Encyclopedia of Social Work,* 19th ed. (Washington, D.C.: National Association of Social Work, 1995), p. 1483, and Weiner, *Human Services Management,* p. 434.

[18]Hastings, *The New Organization,* p. 71.

BARRIERS TO NETWORKING

The human services disciplines may be called "the helping professions," but they can be extremely competitive and even vicious with one another under certain conditions."[19]

Formidable barriers exist to conducting the organizational networking described in this lesson, especially those networks that come together for a common task. These barriers include.[20]

1. Specialization in helping professions, which will continue;

2. Persistence of categorical boundaries that divide human services;

3. The needs of individuals and professions for autonomy, which conflicts with the need to share information and responsibility and to work with others;

4. The need individuals and professions have for recognition of their individual contributions;

5. The western culture of individualism, in which asking for help can be seen as a sign of weakness, an admission of failure;

6. A sense of loss occurs when a worker's organizational, program, or professional identity gets "merged" with that of other organizations, programs, and professions, or when the familiar relationship between a supervisor and a subordinate is removed and both are made equal partners at the table working on improving how services are delivered. Workers can also experience loss when their role as an "expert" in human services relative to the consumer is changed such that both worker and consumer are to be regarded as experts, and

7. The shadow of hierarchy, where crossing a boundary is met with rebuff or rejection if the person fails to act in a manner that fits with the higher level (e.g., senior managers being busy and always in a hurry, and putting off those who work at a different pace).

FRAME

9

LINKING LEARNING AND NETWORKING

Since human service delivery system designs are in a continual state of change, and since some of them may begin to take on characteristics with which we are presently unfamiliar, we will all need to learn to change how we work to deliver human services. Changing how we network, and learning to recognize and overcome barriers to networking, are skills that will likely gain even greater emphasis in the coming years.

In today's rapidly changing world, learning is no longer a choice but a necessity. Whatever kind of network you create or participate in, it will have to go through its own process of learning to develop a culture that is different from that

---

[19]Howard G. Garner, "Critical Issues in Teamwork." In Howard G. Garner and Fred P. Orelove, *Teamwork in Human Services: Models and Applications Across the Lifespan* (Boston, Mass.: Butterworth-Heinemann, 1994), p. 3.

[20]See Hastings, *The New Organization,* p. 66–70.

of any of the parent organizations or settings.[21] To successfully create and participate in the variety of service delivery networks likely to emerge in the coming decade, most workers will need new mental maps of how their organization functions, the nature of different actors within the delivery system, and the politics of that system. Human service workers will need to be self-conscious about the networks they already have, how to extend those networks, and how to activate them. In developing and leveraging your networks, five core personal networking processes will be important:[22]

1. Crossing boundaries. When networking, you will have to be aware of the nature of various boundaries and your reactions to them. You may be crossing program boundaries, state/county/township boundaries, public/private boundaries, ethnic boundaries, disciplinary boundaries, income boundaries, and the like. You will need to develop strategies for moving across these boundaries with fluency and ease.

2. Exchange and reciprocity. When networking, it will be important to understand the processes of cooperation—how you can trade with other people in the network, how you can exchange currencies of different values to different people; how you can work to the benefit of your consumer, your agency, your profession, and yourself.

3. Alliance building and conflict management. As services are increasingly delivered through networking arrangements, workers will need greater skill in negotiating and resolving conflicts that inevitably arise in a network, along with competence in joint problem solving.

4. Communication skills. In addition to verbal and written skills, greater skill will be needed in conducting meetings and conferencing over the telephone and computer.

5. Personal management. Unless well managed, networking can create overload and stress. So human service workers will also need to learn to understand their own reactions to new service delivery situations, and have positive ways to cope with what will often feel unfamiliar.

What all this adds up to is that networking across organizations and programs is a perpetual learning process, both for the individual and for human service organizations and professions. Networks really begin to matter when they affect patterns of relationships and change the results of service delivery.[23] People network naturally, but those who are going to be successful in the future will know how to network, in a wide variety of ways, throughout the human service delivery system.

FRAME 10

REFLECTING ON PRACTICE[24]

As a way to consider some of the implications of this lesson on networking across organizations and programs, we suggest you reconsider the network you drew in Frame 2 identifying all the key groups and individuals with whom you have contact

---

[21]Edgar H. Schein, "How Can Organizations Learn Faster? The Challenge of Entering the Green Room," *Sloan Management Review* (Winter, 1993): 85–92.

[22]From Hastings, *The New Organization,* pp. 74–75.

[23]Ram Charan, "How Networks Reshape Organizations—For Results." *Harvard Business Review* (September-October, 1991): 104–115.

[24]Exercise from Hastings, *The New Organization,* pp. 70–71.

in order to get your work done. This was to include people in your own organization, in other organizations and institutions, and social and personal support systems (e.g., mentors and sponsors, family) and leisure elements that are important to your job success.

Compare the map of your network to that of your classmates or colleagues. What would you change about your network? What relationships are missing in your network? What relationships are you not investing sufficient time in? What do you need to do to extend and activate your network(s)?

FRAME
11

THE LIMITS OF NETWORKING

The notion that networking, supervising up, or any particular skill will be "the" mechanism that will once and for all coordinate the delivery of human services in a more coherent manner for an individual consumer or population of consumers is a myth that we do not wish to support. As Stephen Moore points out, it is a fallacy to argue that if service providers would only work together, there would be enough resources or that the current fragmentation of the delivery system will finally be resolved.[25]

Clearly service providers need to work together differently and in more effective ways. But doing so is only one step in a much larger process of reform and redesign of service delivery systems, and it is important to keep this in mind. Reforms must occur in policies, in organizational systems, in governance systems, and even in the nature of local or civic communities in this country to improve how human services are delivered and with what results. An important skill, however, in contributing to that reform process and in working in what might feel like a fundamentally chaotic environment, is the skill of networking across organizations and programs. Networking clearly underpins many of the skills we have already described in this text (e.g., brokering, mobilizing, case management), but networking must be practiced in a much broader and more self-conscious way as human service workers engage in the numerous roles that define entry-level practice.

FRAME
12

LOOKING AHEAD: REFLECTING ON THE FUTURE

We have emphasized that the human service delivery systems you are entering now and in the next century will be undergoing major changes, not all of which can be forecast at the present time. Living and working effectively during these times of delivering human services will require that all human service workers alter who they work with and how. With so many practice settings and consumer populations undergoing rapid changes and the increasing pressure to provide coherent, integrated, and responsive care, care that crosses boundaries that are familiar to us today, is likely. Yet making a transition to new service delivery systems, including building

---

[25]Stephen Moore, "Case Management and the Integration of Services: How Service Delivery Systems Shape Case Management." *Social Work* 37 (September 1992): 418–423.

networks across delivery systems, will not be easy when providers from disparate human services find they must work together in new, perhaps unaccustomed ways.

What will happen when pressures mount for all the different human service providers to try to "link together"? In Frame 6 we introduced the idea of three different kinds of service delivery networks, starting with a network in which each provider stays independent to a network that is more of a "teamnet," in which providers are cross-trained in aspects of each other's work and can thus exchange some roles and tasks as they work directly with consumers. We hinted at, but did not really develop, the idea that as different human service providers participate in creating closer and closer work relationships among themselves and others who would be network members, problems of competition and confusion can develop.

In this closing frame, we would like to push these ideas one step further—to look ahead to some different ways in which this kind of "service networking" might play out among the human service professions. This exercise asks you to think at the level of human service professions as a way to imagine the variety of situations in which you might find yourself delivering human services in the future.

David Macarov is a professor who can help to stretch your imagination in practical ways. In setting forth his "outlook on aging," he provides a rich example of the range of relationships that might ensue from "all the networking across organizations and boundaries." He observes that the explosive growth in the aged population, coupled with efforts to meet their needs, has resulted in a proliferation of agencies and services dealing with the elderly population. This growth has led to battles for "turf" on the one hand and a blurring of professional boundaries on the other. Macarov thinks this growth of the elderly population may result in the following five relationships among the human services professions.[26]

1. The Free Market. One pattern that may develop would entail a sharpening of professional distinctions, such as those between social workers, geriatric nurses, therapists, psychologists, and others, with different professions offering core services to different populations, geographical areas, client groups, or individuals, using other professions as auxiliary help. This could be seen as the free market or "catch-as-catch-can" model.

2. The Divided Pie. The second possibility is that there will be a sharing of professional knowledge and skills—teamwork—with each profession staking out and keeping within its boundaries. This divided pie model will require clear definitions and protocols and a mechanism for resolving interprofessional disputes. Given the structure and nature of the various professions involved, this would require constant communication, negotiation, and agreement with the ever-present danger of the consumer's needs being forgotten or neglected in the process.

3. The Family Feud. In the absence of continuing communication and goodwill, disputes over professional perquisites and responsibilities may grow and continue, especially because everyone usually wants to be the coordinator and no one wants to be coordinated. Conversely, because of a lack of resources, or a desire to foist the responsibility for the service onto others, disputes may arise over whose responsibility it

---

[26]From David Macarov, *Certain Change: Social Work Practice in the Future* (Silver Springs, Md.: National Association of Social Workers, 1991), pp. 45–46. Statements are slightly edited from the original.

is to provide a given service. In either case, this situation might degenerate into what could be called the family feud model.

4. Guerilla Warfare. The fourth possibility involves professional boundaries becoming more permeable. In the profession's desire to give better service or to dominate the field, each profession would try to widen its competence. Nurses would engage in family counseling; social workers would take temperatures and blood pressures; doctors would help families prepare their homes to receive a hospitalized aged parent; and everyone would engage in diet planning, budgeting, and other heretofore excluded activities. Although it would be desirable that such blurring of professional boundaries, if it comes about, be done through agreement and cooperation, it will probably be done in a highly competitive manner, with each profession seeking dominance. This would be a guerilla warfare model.

5. Mutation. Finally, it is possible that the scope and variety of services demanded for good care of elderly people will require the emergence of a new profession—one that contains elements of many present disciplines and activities related to the aged. Such a model would face resistance by existing professions and would have to surmount the difficulties of education and licensure that would arise. Nor is it to be conceded a priori that such practitioners would be more effective than those in previously described models. However, were it to come into being, this would be called the mutation model.

How would you "network across human service organizations and programs" in each of these five models? For example, in the free market, divided pie, and family feud scenarios, we see a sharpening of distinctions among human service specialties and more of a focus on guarding professional turf, with perhaps less emphasis on a consumer focus. These three situations are similar to working in a network of highly independent human service professionals in which each profession retains its autonomy in working with a consumer. Attempts to develop "a synthesis service delivery plan for a consumer" (a more coherent or more integrated approach to service delivery) across the human service professions would be extremely difficult if the free market, divided pie, or family feud scenarios emerge.

In the guerilla warfare model, however, we see the human service professions starting to broaden how they define their roles and moving toward exchanging and linking roles with other human service professions. The process will likely be painful and confusing, as the boundaries among professions blur. The mutation pattern, however, suggests just one possibility that might emerge from that sort of murkiness, namely, the emergence of some new (not known at the present) human service profession. The latter would be a disturbing outcome to established human service professions (as yet another source of competition). And, as Macarov points out, a new profession may not be improvement over what we have today.

Why consider such possibilities? Macarov makes a compelling case that human service workers need to attempt to foresee what the situation of consumers and relevant others may be in the future, for solutions seen as helpful today may prove dysfunctional in the future. Thus, as a way to prepare to act effectively, it can be helpful to anticipate the possibilities for how human service providers might relate to each other as the restructuring and redesign of human services continues. If you have already thought about what is possible when linking or not linking the various providers of human services, you will recognize the pattern if it occurs and perhaps be better able to function effectively in a wider variety of situations.

Summary and Further Study

Chapter Summary

Chapter 11 focused on two skills that are important in managing the transition to new service delivery systems: supervising "up" and networking across organizations and programs.

Lesson 1. Supervising up was developed as a boundary-spanning skill for creating a partnership between you and your supervisor—helping your supervisor to help you carry out his or her and your job responsibilities. Suggestions were made for developing an appreciation of your job in relationship to that of your supervisor, peers, and administrators or superiors. The meaning, responsibilities, skills, and expectations of supervision were then examined.

Supervision is one of the major processes in delivering human services. It involves the art of getting work done through the efforts and abilities of other people. Thus, communication is the fundamental skill involved in giving and receiving supervision. To understand the role of a supervisor more fully, the purposes of supervision and the major tasks performed by a supervisor were examined. The four purposes included helping workers do a better job, promoting each worker's individual growth and capacity, facilitating communication throughout the agency, and keeping work moving toward agency objectives. The primary tasks were identified as planning and organizing the work, instructing workers, communicating with workers, and making improvements. Typical expectations supervisors hold for workers were briefly explored within this framework.

Communication skills are the essential element within the supervisory relationship. We reviewed the basic concepts of sender, receiver, message, and feedback, then discussed common blocks and bridges that can be helpful in building a "supervising up" relationship. Since the supervisory relationship is traditionally hierarchical, the games people play in supervisory relationships were outlined to illustrate how unchecked or uninformed expectations can block effective relationships. Finally, the eight attributes of organizational excellence and specific suggestions for helping your supervisor were introduced to further the idea that supervising "up" involves a "bias for action" between a supervisor and supervisee who stay "close to the consumer" and focused on the "results to be achieved."

Lesson 2. Networking across organizations and programs was defined as the active process of building and managing productive relationships within and between organizational units and programs. Networking includes everyone you work with, as well as external ties. Networking is receiving more emphasis today in many sectors of work. In the human services, organizational networking is important at the individual and system levels, because of the fragmentation of services, multiple and overlapping programs, gaps in service, differing treatment modalities and billing procedures, and professional and agency territoriality. In other words, networking is important because of the burgeoning boundaries in the human services.

Human service workers need to engage in a continual process of mapping the adequacy of their networking territories so they can deliver human services directed toward self-sufficiency and other goals as collaboratively and effectively as possible.

Organizational networking and teamwork are related but not identical. Networks tend to be large, spread out, and loosely linked. Teams tend to be small, in the same place, and tightly coordinated. The term *teamnet* applied to small groups can mean more networked teams; applied to large groups, it can mean more teamlike networks. Not all networks are teams, but all team members are certainly linked.

Lesson 2 introduced the fact that there are a variety of service delivery networks, based on how the providers work together. There are three kinds of service delivery networks: (1) networks in which providers operate independently but come together to exchange information; (2) networks in which decision making is shared and a team decision-making process is used to plan and deliver services to the same consumer or come to a judgment about some organizational matter; (3) highly integrated networks in which some roles among the human service professions are exchanged.

Some basic tenets of creating and participating in service delivery networks were suggested, and barriers to networking were identified. Since human service delivery systems are in a continual state of change, the ability to form and reform service delivery networks will be a necessity. Doing so will entail a perpetual process of learning on the part of individuals and organizations. Individuals in particular will need to build their core personal networking skills, including: crossing boundaries, exchange and reciprocity, alliance building and conflict management, communication, and personal management.

Lesson 2 concluded with a caution that neither networking across organizations and programs, nor supervising "up," nor any particular skill will in itself be sufficient to overcome the fragmentation in the service delivery system so as to provide comprehensive solutions to consumer's problems of living. However, these skills are necessary in making the numerous transitions under way now and in the future of delivering human services. Another skill that will be essential is the ability to "look ahead" to the various practice networks in which you might find yourself. David Macarov's five "scenarios" of how the restructuring among human service professions might play out (for professions serving the elderly, but his analysis can be generalized) were presented.

Suggestions for Further Study

This chapter should be viewed as a very basic introduction to the complex processes involved in managing the transitions to new service delivery systems.

Supervising Up

Further study is most important for those interested in achieving an in-depth understanding of supervising up. Supervisors need to have a comprehensive understanding of all the work performed in the agency. Thus, one area of further study should be directed toward reviewing the roles and functions performed by direct service workers, supervisors, and administrators, and toward identifying ways in which supervisors relate to all these workers. Additional study will be needed to fully understand each of the major tasks of the supervisor and how they may change in new service delivery systems. The ability to analyze work is also important for a supervisor. Functional job analysis is one method used, and a review of the work by Sidney Fine and Wretha Wiley provides a general introduction to this technique. Additional study should address the skills needed for using management information systems, using performance standards, and taking corrective action. By now it should be clear that supervision includes a vast amount of skill and knowledge that needs to be mastered for effective performance. We hope that this chapter has made you curious to learn more about this function and locate some of the suggested references.

Austin, Michael J. *Supervisory Management for the Human Services.* Englewood Cliffs, N.J.: Prentice-Hall, 1981.

Austin, Michael J. "Managing Up: Relationship Building Between Middle Management and Top Management." *Administration in Social Work* (Fall 1988).

Baker, Wayne. *Networking Smart: How to Build Relationships for Personal and Organizational Success.* New York: McGraw Hill, 1994.

DiMattia, Susan S. "Empowering the Work Force: Superior Supervision: The 10% Solution." *Library Journal* 120 (Mar. 1995): 38.

Farmer, Richard E., Lynn Hunt Monahan, and Reinhold W. Hekeler. *Stress Management for Human Services.* Beverly Hills, Calif.: Sage, 1984.

Fine, Sidney A., and Wretha W. Wiley. *An Introduction to Functional Job Analysis: A Scaling of Selected Tasks from the Social Welfare Field.* Kalamazoo, Mich.: W. E. Upjohn Institute for Employment Research, 1971.

Fine, Sidney A., and Maury Getkate. *Benchmark Tasks for Job Analysis: A Guide for Functional Job Analysis Scales.* Mahwah, N.J.: Erlbaum, 1995.

Fisher, Roger, and Scott Brown. *Getting Together: Building Relationships as We Negotiate.* New York: Penguin, 1988.

Gambrill, Eileen, and Theodore J. Stein. *Supervision: A Decision-Making Approach.* Beverly Hills, Calif.: Sage, 1983.

Harrison, Michael I. *Diagnosing Organizations: Methods, Models, and Processes,* 2d ed. Thousand Oaks, Calif.: Sage, 1994.

Hawkins, Peter. *Supervision in the Helping Professions: An Individual, Group, and Organizational Approach.* Philadelphia, Pa.: Open University Press, 1989.

Holloway, Stephen. *Supervising in the Human Services: The Politics of Practice.* New York: The Free Press, 1989.

Imundo, Louis V. *The Effective Supervisor's Handbook,* 2d ed. New York: American Management Association, 1991.

Kelley, Robert E. "In Praise of Followers." *Harvard Business Review* 66, 6 (1988): 142–148.

Lassey, William R. and Marshall Sashkin, eds. *Leadership and Social Change,* 3d ed. San Diego, California: University Associates Press, 1983.

Morrison, James H. *Human Factors in Supervising Minority Group Employees*. Chicago: Public Personnel Association, 1970.

Munson, Carlton E. *An Introduction to Clinical Social Work Supervision,* 2d ed. New York: Haworth Press, 1993.

Pecora, Peter J., and Michael J. Austin. *Managing Human Services Personnel*. Newbury Park, Calif.: Sage, 1987.

Porter, Natalie. "Empowering Supervisees to Empower Others: A Culturally Responsive Supervision Model." *Hispanic Journal of Behavioral Sciences* 16 (Feb. 1994): 43–56.

Shout, Howard F. *Start Supervising,* 3d ed. Washington, D.C.: Bureau of National Affairs, 1984.

Shulman, Lawrence. *Skills of Supervision and Staff Management*. Itasca, Ill.: F. E. Peacock, 1982.

Shulman, Lawrence. *Interactional Supervision*. Washington, D.C.: NASW Press, 1993.

Weissman, Harold H. *Overcoming Mismanagement in the Human Service Professions*. San Francisco: Jossey-Bass, 1973.

Organizational Networking

Networking, the activity, and networks, the structure, are the subject of increasing interest in a variety of human service and management areas. Related topics are the redesign of human services, collaborative leadership, self-directed teams, boundaryless organizations and careers, and boundary-spanning roles and boundary leadership and management behaviors. A few of the many readings in this rich area are identified below.

Adams, J. Stacey. "The Structure and Dynamics of Behavior in Organizational Boundary Roles." In Marvin Dunnette, ed. *Handbook of Industrial and Organizational Psychology*. New York: Wiley, 1983.

Adams, Paul, and Kristine Nelson. *Reinventing Human Services: Community and Family Centered Practice*. New York: Aldine deGruyter, 1995.

Barge, J. Kevin. *Leadership: Communication Skills for Organizations and Groups*. New York: St. Martins Press, 1994.

Beckhard, Richard, and Reuben T. Harris. *Organizational Transitions: Managing Complex Change,* 2d ed. Reading, Mass.: Addison-Wesley, 1987.

Charam, Ram. "How Networks Reshape Organizations—For Results," *Harvard Business Review* (Sept.-Oct., 1991), pp. 104–115.

Chrislip, David. *Collaborative Leadership: How Citizens and Civic Leaders Can Make a Difference*. San Francisco: Jossey-Bass, 1994.

Fisher, Kimball. *Leading Self-Directed Work Teams: A Guide to Developing New Team Leadership Skills*. New York: McGraw-Hill, 1993.

Fisher, Roger, Elizabeth Kopelman, and Andrea Schneider. *Beyond Machiavelli: Tools for Coping with Conflict*. Cambridge, Mass.: Harvard University Press, 1994.

Fraser, George C. *Success Runs in Our Race: The Complete Guide to Effective Networking in the African American Community*. New York: W. Morrow, 1994.

Gilmore, Thomas N., Larry Hirschhorn, and Mal O'Connor. "The Boundaryless Organization." *Healthcare Forum* 37 (1994): 68–72.

Gray, Barbara. *Collaborating: Finding Common Ground for Multiparty Problems*. San Francisco: Jossey-Bass, 1989.

Hastings, Colin. *The New Organization: Growing the Culture of Organizational Networking*. New York: McGraw-Hill, 1993.

Hirschhorn, Larry, and Thomas Gilmore. "The New Boundaries of the Boundaryless Company." *Harvard Business Review* 70 (May-June): 104–115.

Jennings, Jerry T. *Who's Helping Out? Support Networks Among American Families*. Washington, D.C.: U.S. Department of Commerce, 1992.

Kilmann, Ralph H., Ines Kilmann, and Associates. *Making Organizations Competitive: Enhancing Networks and Relationships Across Traditional Boundaries*. San Francisco: Jossey-Bass, 1991.

Kofman, Fred, and Peter M. Senge. "Communities of Commitment: The Heart of Learning Organizations. *Organizational Dynamics* (Autumn 1993): 5–23.

Maguire, Lambert. *Social Support Systems in Practice: A Generalist Approach*. Washington, D.C.: NASW Press, 1991.

Mahtesian, Charles. "The Human Services Nightmare." *Governing* 8 (Dec. 1994): 44–49.

McCann, Joseph E., and Barbara Gray. "Power and Collaboration in Human Service Domains." *The International Journal of Social Policy* 6 (1986): 58–67.

Miles, Raymond E., and Charles C. Snow. *Fit, Failure, and the Hall of Fame*. New York: Free Press, 1994.

Powell, William E. "The Relationship Between Feelings of Alienation and Burnout in Social Work." *Families in Society: The Journal of Contemporary Human Services* 75 (Apr. 1994): 229–235.

Scheurell, Robert P. *Introduction to Human Service Networks: History, Organizations, Professions*. Lanham, Md.: University Press of America, 1987.

Sproull, Lee, and Sara Kielser. *Connections: New Ways of Working in the Networked Organization*. Cambridge, Mass.: MIT Press, 1992.

Tracy, Elizabeth M., James K. Whittaker, Ann Pugh, Stephen Kapp, and Edward Overstreet. "Support Networks of Primary Caregivers Receiving Family Preservation Services: An Exploratory Study." *Families in Society: The Journal of Contemporary Human Services* 75 (Oct. 1994): 481–489.

Warren, Donald I. *Helping Networks of the Aging and Retired*. New York: Edwin Mellen Press, 1992.

Wenger, G. Clare, and Fred St. Leger. "Community Structure and Support Network Variations." *Aging and Society* 12 (June 1992): 213–236.

Chapter 12

Integrating

What has integrating to do with delivering human services? What, in fact, is integrating? One perhaps idealistic answer is that integrating is a sense of wholeness in which worker, consumer, agency, and service outcomes are linked and mutually fulfilled. A similar answer can be found in the following quotation:[1]

> Suppose the most successful, most spontaneous and alive form of helping depends on the integration of knowledge, values, and personal or inner understandings. Suppose this integration is the basis of charisma (power of influence), of creativity (helping as an art), and of self-esteem (personal power). Theory may not be the key to effective practice. It is far more likely the crucial factor is something highly personal—how a particular worker integrates what he or she knows about him or herself and the consumer, and the present happening between the two (the creative factor).

These ideas about integrating may sound unrealistic. However, there is fairly extensive accumulated wisdom in the helping professions indicating that effective service delivery requires a certain personal mastery that the term *integrating* is intended to convey.

There are two aspects to integrating: one internal and one external. Internally, workers must take responsibility for pulling things together—for developing a clear sense of self and for engaging in ongoing efforts to link knowledge, values, and skills. Although a clear, healthy, integrated sense of self is absolutely essential to effective service delivery, it is not enough. Workers must also look outside themselves. Externally, workers who are skilled at integrating are concerned with accounting to others for what they do. They are interested not only in attaining and maintaining a whole sense of self but also in the advice and views of others. This concern for the external can take many forms ranging from discussions with peers in their own and other agencies, to presentations to supervisors about accomplishments, to discussions and presentations to consumer groups.

Integrating, or the ability to be congruent—and competence, or a concern for effectiveness—are closely linked. Lesson 1 provides an opportunity to reflect on the meaning of "competent" delivery of human services. It develops a foundation for valuing competence as an ongoing process. Lesson 2 is different from all the other lessons in this book because it presents a menu of choices for practicing self-assessment. Self-

---

[1]Donald F. Krill, *Practice Wisdom: A Guide for Helping Professionals* (Newbury Park, Calif.: Sage, 1990), p. 14.

assessment is a way of integrating—of checking your internal perceptions of how you behave with how others perceive you behaving. Formal or documented self-assessments can also provide you with greater clarity about what you are doing, what results you are achieving, and what improvements you would like to make. Both lessons in this chapter challenge you to explore answers to three key questions: (1) How do I define being a competent entry-level practitioner? (2) What approach do I plan to use to ensure an ongoing emphasis on competence in my practice? and (3) If a consumer or consumer group asked me right now to explain what I was doing or why I made a particular choice, could I do so? The overall objectives of the chapter are to increase the quality of your attention to who you are and what you are doing, and to provide a rationale for taking ongoing responsibility for linking learning and doing.

Integrating for effective practice involves determining the adequacy of your own performance, seeking advice and consultation, and keeping up with technical and professional developments. Examples of "integrating" tasks that might appear in a human service job description include the following:

Self-assessment/development. Determining the adequacy of your own performance; seeking advice and consultation; keeping up with technical and professional developments.

1. Evaluate your competence, biases, possible conflicts of interest, availability, and feelings about consumers in order to decide whether another worker could better serve the consumer's interest.
2. Meet with or talk to your supervisor (or other superior) for advice on how to deal with problem situations.
3. Participate in discussions with co-workers, talking over events of the day, problems, or particular consumers, to learn about program operations or share experiences in dealing with consumers.
4. Read administrative literature (manuals, memos, circulars) to learn about or keep up with agency policies and procedures.
5. Read articles in professional (scientific) journals and magazines to keep up with developments related to your job responsibilities.
6. Attend workshops, seminars, or programs dealing with topics of interest or need to improve your job knowledge and skills.
7. Present and/or publish findings from studies or analyses to share your information with appropriate audiences.
8. Review and discuss your performance evaluations with your appropriate superiors to clarify their assessment of your work.
9. Evaluate your actions and decisions to determine whether your practice activities are meeting the standards, values, and ethics required for quality service provision.
10. Attend meetings, review information, and make other contacts to keep up to date on service resources and providers.

A Framework for Competent Practice

Am I being effective in delivering human services? If asked by a consumer, a peer, a supervisor, or a member of an advocacy group, could I explain my actions? What kind of responsibility do I feel for the tasks I perform? All these questions are concerned with competence. People who deliver human services generally aim to work competently on behalf of consumers, themselves, and their agencies. Competence is a critical issue in the helping professions. Consider the following excerpts from the codes of ethics of various helping professions.

"Competence" in Selected Helping Professions[1]

Social workers. "The social worker should strive to become and remain proficient in professional practice and the performance of professional functions (e.g., accept responsibility or employment only on the basis of existing competence or the intention to acquire the necessary competence)." (National Association of Social Workers, 1993)

Marriage and family therapists. "Marriage and family therapists do not diagnose, treat, or advise on problems outside the recognized boundaries of their competence." (American Association for Marriage and Family Therapy, 1991)

Psychologists. "Psychologists strive to maintain high standards of competence in their work. They recognize the boundaries of their particular competencies and the limitations of their expertise. They provide only those services and use only those techniques for which they are qualified by education, training, or experience. They are cognizant of the fact that the competencies required in serving, teaching, and/or studying groups of people vary with the distinctive characteristics of those groups." (American Psychological Association, 1992)

Physicians. "A physician shall be dedicated to providing competent medical service with compassion and respect for human dignity." (American Psychiatric Association, 1989)

---

[1]Gerald Corey, Marianne Schneider Corey, and Patrick Callanan, *Issues and Ethics in the Helping Professions,* 4th ed. (Pacific Grove, Calif.: Brooks/Cole, 1993), p. 172; and Eveline D. Schulman, *Intervention in Human Services: A Guide to Skills and Knowledge,* 4th ed. (New York: Merrill, Macmillan Publishing), pp. 387–428.

Counselors. "Professional growth is continuous throughout the member's career and is exemplified by the development of a philosophy that explains why and how the member functions in the helping relationship. Members must gather data on their effectiveness and be guided by the findings. Members recognize the need for continuing education to ensure competent service." (American Association for Counseling and Development, 1988)

Nurses. "The nurse maintains competence in nursing (e.g., the care of the client reflects and incorporates new techniques and knowledge in health care as these develop, especially as they relate to the nurse's particular field of practice; the nurse assumes personal responsibility for currency of knowledge and skills; nurses must be willing to have their practice reviewed and evaluated by their peers; and nurses refer clients to and consult with other nurses with expertise and recognized competencies in various fields of practice.)" (American Nurses Association, 1985).

Codes of ethics provide broad guidelines for worker conduct. Looking only at the question of competence, you can see some common themes across the helping professions. These include *issues* of responsibility, qualification, effectiveness, accountability, and service quality and *approaches* to ensuring competent practice (e.g., self-assessment and continuing education). In this lesson we will use these two perspectives—issues and approaches—to help you develop a personal understanding of competence in delivering human services. Like other human service skills (e.g., learning, language, systems thinking, brokering, mobilizing, advocating, relationship building, and information managing), competence is presented as an ongoing process rather than as something attained once and for all. In short, the question of competence is very much a question of an ongoing ability and interest in learning.

Goals

To develop a foundation for valuing competent entry-level delivery of human services. To provide a framework of ideas that will support completing Lesson 2 of this chapter.

Learning Activities

To accomplish these goals, we will:

1. Reflect on the meaning of the term *competence*.
2. Distinguish four key *issues* of competent practice: responsibility, accountability, service quality, and worker effectiveness.
3. Consider examples of *approaches* to competence as an ongoing process: self-assessment and the assessments of others.
4. Illustrate some tensions in delivering human services to convey the context of practicing competency.

5. Challenge you to develop a personal statement of the issues you believe are important to your ability to practice competent delivery of human services.

COMPETENCE: WHAT IS IT?

There are different ways of viewing competence. Competence is often used as a synonym for the ability or capacity to perform certain kinds of tasks. What does competent practice actually mean? Here are some examples:

Competence includes knowledge, performance, and consequence. It involves knowing what to do when working with particular consumers, actually performing, and finding out the consequences of one's actions.[2]

Competence is the capacity of a person to engage her full range of abilities appropriately in interaction with and by influencing her environment and the people in it in such a way as to achieve life tasks and goals fairly.[3]

Competence in practice embodies knowledge, values, skills, and attitudes essential to fulfill one's professional role skillfully. Ingredients essential to perform one's role adequately vary according to the demands of each situation. A practitioner may thus be competent in providing certain types of service, such as marital or family therapy, and not in others, such as correctional services or protective services to children who have been abused or neglected. The elements of competent practice are in a constant state of change as a result of expanding knowledge, emerging skills, and the changing demands of practice.[4]

Competent practitioners are able to transform knowledge into action.[5]

Competence means professionalism. It means practicing with the maximum application of professional skill . . . and continuously improving practice. It means being self-critical, self-correcting, and self-improving. It means engaging in self-assessment.[6]

Another approach to understanding competence is to examine different models. To do this, we will draw from two sources: Martin Morf's discussion of the types of workers that have served as role models in different cultures and over the centuries and also the contemporary literature on work. Three models of competent work are relevant to delivering human services: (1) *the worker as artist,* (2) *the worker as citi-*

---

[2]Frank W. Clark, Morton L. Arkava, and Associates. *The Pursuit of Competence in Social Work* (San Francisco: Jossey-Bass, 1979), pp. 37–39.

[3]Claude F. Wiegand, "Using a Social Competence Framework for both Client and Practitioner," in Clark, Arkava, and Associates, *The Pursuit of Competence in Social Work,* p. 77.

[4]Dean H. Hepworth and Jo Ann Larsen, *Direct Social Work Practice: Theory and Skills,* 3d ed. (Belmont, Calif.: Wadsworth, 1990), p. 14

[5]Hepworth and Larsen, *Direct Social Work Practice,* p. 15.

[6]Catherine Alter and Wayne Evens, *Evaluating Your Practice: A Guide to Self-Assessment* (New York: Springer, 1990), p. 9.

zen, and (3) *the worker as linker.*[7] These models are a starting point from which to develop ideas about competent practice in any field. In combination with the ideas presented earlier, they are alternative ways to open a discussion about what it means to be a competent human service practitioner. Discussion is a key endeavor when the subject is competence because there is no single approach to the issue.

Model 1: The worker as artist

Craftsmanship or artistry is characterized by taking one's time to develop competencies and to produce the goods, advice, and decisions that constitute the craft. The "craft" tradition links work and life—it integrates skills demanded and paid for by others with personal decision making and pride in what one is doing. The craft attitude and way of thinking are learned through experience. Historically this was through apprenticeship arrangements, which today would be considered "on-the-job training" with a mentor.

> Prehistorians admire the quality of the work of early Indians who fashioned the elegant Clovis point which, tied to wooden shafts, epitomized early hunting cultures of North America. Early bronze artifacts, the results of a complex metal-using technology dating back to perhaps 2000 B.C., have survived as examples of outstanding workmanship. Anthropologists tell us that not only in Europe, but also in China, Japan, and the Middle East, and many other parts of the world, craftsmen (and women) acquired a high status.[8]
>
> The early teachers of social work practice were agency based practitioners who formulated practice theory out of their firsthand experience in meeting clients and dealing with human need. The craft and art of social work were passed on through a kind of apprenticeship arrangement. There were dedicated master teachers and devoted learners. Skill development was a laborious, painstaking process that extended beyond the two years of graduate training and persisted through one's agency career.[9]

Model 2: The worker as citizen

This model of competence stresses responsibilities to the community or collectivity. Artists often work alone and are not primarily concerned with how others react to their work. The prototypical artists make pots, drawings, or writings that meet their own criteria above all, although they no doubt entertain secondary hopes that others will like and buy them. Workers functioning as citizens may also work alone, but they are more likely to be social creatures. For example, the collective rice culture of Japan is a culture of workers who see themselves as citizens cooperating for the good of the group and ultimately of the total community or state. Workers operating as citizens are keenly

[7]See Martin Morf, *The Work/Life Dichotomy: Prospects for Reintegrating People and Jobs* (New York: Quorum Books, 1989), chap. 11. The following discussions of worker as artist and worker as citizen are adapted from this book. Also see Bradford W. Sheafor, Charles R. Horejsi, and Gloria A. Horejsi, *Techniques and Guidelines for Social Work Practice,* 3d ed. (Boston, Mass.: Allyn & Bacon), chapter 3.
[8]Morf, *The Work/Life Dichotomy,* p. 158.
[9]Ruth R. Middleman and Gale Goldberg Wood, *Skills for Direct Practice in Social Work* (New York: Columbia University Press, 1990), pp. 1–2.

aware of the effects of their work on the community. They "hate waste, minimize pollution, stress quality of their output, be it goods or services, because such quality is an important contribution to the quality of life offered by their community."[10] Competent work is responsible citizenship or the awareness that work has societal effects.

Model 3: The worker as linker

Under this model of competence, the worker is a generalist who connects ideas and approaches from a variety of areas. The worker is an artist, a citizen, and a scientist. The competent worker is able to play a variety of roles; understands the wide applicability of the problem-solving process; is not imprisoned in a specialty; is challenged by variety; and is able to apply relevant but perhaps diverse knowledge and procedures to work situations. The worker as linker is also able to evaluate the contributions made by others and to adapt flexibly and intelligently to new situations. The worker as linker tends to reflect while acting—to question the definition of her task, the knowledge she brings to it, and other resources she might draw on to accomplish it.

> It becomes quite obvious that [the processes of practice just described] are the work of an artist as well as a scientist. One of Michaelangelo's biographers pictured the artist scientifically studying the potentials of a block of marble. When his artisan hands went to work with the chisel, Michaelangelo was described as having freed the sculpted form from the marble. There is a comparable balance of the scientist and artist found in the [human service] worker who recognizes the potential of the client and enables that person to achieve that potential.[11]

Conclusions

These three approaches to working competently are really ways of thinking or attitudes. Thus the issue is not choosing one or the other. A richer approach might be to ask how each attitude is relevant to an ongoing process of delivering competent human services.

A few themes do emerge from these considerations about the meaning of competence. If you are a practitioner engaged in a process of delivering human services competently, then you ought minimally to have a willingness and interest: (1) to continually question whether you are working as well as you might; (2) to search for ways of becoming a more effective person and helper; and (3) to be able to account to self and others for the process and the results of your efforts.[12] In short, a competent practitioner always has something new to learn and is interested in communicating to others what is discovered.

FRAME

ISSUES IN PRACTICING COMPETENTLY

Four issues are at the heart of an ongoing focus on competent practice: (1) *responsibility:* knowing what you are responsible for and what you feel responsible for; (2)

[10]Morf, *The Work/Life Dichotomy,* p. 167.

[11]Claude F. Wiegand, "Using a Social Competence Framework for both Client and Practitioner," in Clark, Arkava, and Associates, *The Pursuit of Competence in Social Work,* p. 95.

[12]In part from Corey, Corey, and Callanan, *Issues and Ethics in the Helping Professions,* pp. 187–189.

accountability: being able to account for your actions; (3) *quality:* having a sense of your own and others' standards of quality; and (4) *personal effectiveness:* being familiar with the characteristics of effective human service workers.

Issue 1: Responsibility[13]

Responsibility is the personal causal influence you have on a particular event. There are at least three ways to be responsible for some event.

1. *Direct choice.* You choose this act rather than that act. I choose this job versus another and am therefore responsible to perform it. I choose this action versus some other or no action with a consumer, and am therefore responsible for a result. For example, you are interviewing a consumer and you hear the consumer's complaint about a late child-support payment, but you do not handle child-support services in your unit. You can choose to be responsible for addressing the late payment by contacting the worker who could help or by taking some other action, including follow-up.

2. *Group membership.* When you choose to be a member of some group, you share in the collective responsibility of that group. You cannot control all the choices or all the decisions a group makes. But your choice to be a member of a group includes accepting responsibility for the choices of action that the group makes, even if the particular decisions or actions were not your direct choice.

3. *Role acceptance.* You are answerable for your actions by virtue of your role. When you make a choice to take on the role of an entry-level human service worker, you assume responsibility for the accompanying tasks. When you make a choice to take on the role of a parent, you assume responsibility for the child.

It is not enough to be responsible for an event by choosing it, being a member of some group, or agreeing to perform a particular role. These avenues of responsibility are overt or assigned and leave out how you feel. Perhaps the most important aspect of responsibility is the notion of *felt responsibility*—or the extent to which you actually feel, inside yourself, responsible. In a mature person, assigned responsibility and felt responsibility are the same thing; that is, the mature person feels responsible or accepts responsibility for the events for which he or she is in fact responsible. Society terms a person whose felt responsibility does not correspond to assigned responsibility as *irresponsible*.

FRAME

3

Discovering Responsibility Through Tasks

In this frame you have the opportunity to see how human service worker responsibilities can be defined in terms of specific tasks. Most current job descriptions in human service agencies do not reflect such task specificity, which is unfortunate. However, it is useful to compare existing job descriptions with the following description in order to identify similarities and differences. The specific steps for this exercise are:

---

[13]Discussion from L. L. Cummings and Ronald J. Anton, "The Logical and Appreciative Dimensions of Accountability," in Suresh Srivastva, David L. Cooperrider, and Associates, *Appreciative Management and Leadership: The Power of Positive Thought and Action in Organizations* (San Francisco: Jossey-Bass, 1990) pp. 257–286.

Step 1: Circle all the action verbs (first word) and the "in order to" phrases in each task statement.

Step 2: Compare the format of this job description with your existing or a similar job description in the agency and describe the differences. (If you are not currently working or completing a field placement in an agency, develop a task-based job description of your student work using a course as an area of responsibility and your studying activities as tasks.)

Step 3: Underline the six responsibility areas in this sample task profile and compare them with the responsibility areas in your current job description.

Step 4: Redesign your existing job description, or create one if one does not exist, using the same format as the sample task profile.

Sample Task Profile for a Direct Service Worker in a Youth Corrections Agency

A. Evaluating Consumer Need and Determining Eligibility (15%)

1. Discuss problem situation (emotional, medical, administrative, etc.) with present or potential service consumer, during office visit or conversation (phone or casual), using knowledge of service resources, advising consumers of availability of resources in order to refer same to appropriate resource.
2. Talks with consumer (or relation), exploring problems, answering questions when necessary, in order to calm same (allay fears, release anxiety, reassure, support).
3. Questions (interviews) consumer regarding status of particular aspect of case (school attendance, employment, transportation, address, etc.), using telephone or personal visit in order to determine current need or status, or to update case information.
4. Interviews consumer, gathering background information in order to compile social history.
5. Screens case file(s) or consumer records relative to specific information in order to determine individual status or compile list of consumers with certain characteristics.

B. Planning for the Provision of Services (25%)

6. Informs consumer of the result of medically related tests or problems explaining implications, in order to discuss (explore) indicated follow-up.
7. Discusses aspect of administration of treatment (or treatment plan or program) with consumer (and/or relation), informing, clarifying, briefing, debriefing, or answering questions in order to promote understanding (or to allay fears).
8. Explains rules (or program or agreement) to consumer(s), answering questions when asked, in order to orient (or reorient) same to a particular program.
9. Discusses case with relation of consumer, collecting specific information in order to monitor case status for case planning purposes.
10. Collects consumer-specific information from service system colleague in order to receive information necessary for service planning (monitoring, verifying, or service provision).

11. Discusses consumer situation with service system colleague in order to exchange information useful in service planning or service provision.
12. Reports consumer-specific information (orally or in writing) to service system colleague (judges included) in order to provide information for service planning (or service provision or case action).

C. Arranging for the Delivery of Services (15%)

13. Discusses case situation with service representative (initiating the linkage of a consumer with an appropriate resource) in order to arrange an appointment for services.
14. Transports consumer to specific destination(s), using public or private vehicle in order to link consumer with service or treatment resource.
15. Confers with colleagues in staff (team, court unit, or committee) meeting, providing and/or receiving information as required for understanding in order to reach decision regarding disposition of specific cases.
16. Discusses case situation with relative, using personal visit, written correspondence, or telephone, planning alternate care for consumer (foster home, return to home, home visit, respite care, hospitalization, etc.) in order to arrange suitable or appropriate environment.
17. Confers with service system colleague(s) on specific case(s), or specific consumer group, corresponding when appropriate, reaching mutual agreement on details of service (case actions) and individual responsibilities in order to coordinate or implement services.
18. Authorizes services by issuing ID cards, signing off, writing orders, etc., using personal authority according to standard operating procedures (SOP) in order to effect the receipt of particular services or treatment to a consumer.

D. Providing Services (20%)

19. Counsels with consumer(s) or relative, preventing undesirable behavior when necessary, in order to motivate same toward acceptable (responsible) behavior.
20. Counsels consumer (and/or members of family), using recognized intervention methods and operational knowledge of particular agencies, advising same of consequences when appropriate, in order to improve social functioning and/or reconcile relations.

E. Monitoring Service Delivery (15%)

21. Investigates breach of service plan (for aberrant behavior or complaint), discussing situation with consumer's relations or collaterals, in order to determine facts.
22. Reviews case with consumer, evaluating present status (or progress), discussing situation when appropriate, in order to recommend continued or appropriate treatment.
23. Reviews case records (or consumer reports or information), evaluating information in order to develop or change treatment plans.
24. Discusses administrative matters with colleague(s), reviewing relevant issues, operating procedures, policies, administrative problems, etc., with them, reporting relevant information and clarifying issues in order to inform, coordinate, plan, or decide.

F. Recording Progress Toward Service Goals (10%)

25. Drafts (dictates) consumer reports (progress, discipline, incident), using case records and knowledge of case situation, recommending plans when indicated, in order to compile written information for service planning.

26. Records personal travel, using standard reporting form, in order to summarize items for reimbursement.

FRAME

4

Issue 2: Accountability[14]

The second critical issue in competent practice is accountability, which is an external, social, public process. It is being able to demonstrate that what you do is worth supporting. It is being able to explain what you do in terms understandable to others. The key questions others may ask are: What are you doing? Why are you doing it? How are you doing it? How much is it costing? and What results are you achieving?

> One of the staggering problems which continue to confront professional social work and other human service staff is accountability for the quality of services provided to clients. In a world that increasingly demands proof of effectiveness of all goods and services for public consumption, the [human service] worker is challenged to demonstrate capability through the evaluation of practice activities. . . . [Increasingly, the worker must] . . . show that efforts on behalf of clients are beneficial, that interventions are effective, that clients are helped, that our work makes a difference.[15]
>
> Accountability in human services involves being responsible not only for what is actually being done but also for improving the quality of what is being done. Accountability in human services exists at three levels: (1) to the clients, users, or consumers of the service; (2) to colleagues and to organization or agency; and (3) to the society that sanctions the entire operation. Clients who use the services, laws authorizing the existence and support of programs, lay people who help to support and serve on boards and committees and as volunteers in the programs are all expressing sanction.[16]

Whereas responsibility is concerned with what is assigned to you and how you feel about the delegation (e.g., making sure this happens is "my" responsibility), accountability is concerned with letting others know about what you do. Responsibility and accountability are obviously connected: You are accountable to others for what you are responsible for. Those others might include consumers, fellow workers, supervisors, legislators or boards of directors, and yourself.

The diagram below links the discussion of responsibility and accountability. You can see that given an assigned responsibility (parent, human service worker, specific task, or member of a treatment team), two aspects are important in a framework of competence. One is private; one is public. Felt responsibility is private—it is how you feel personally about tasks and assignments. Accountability, by contrast, is public—it

---

[14]Cummings and Anton, "The Logical and Appreciable Dimensions of Accountability," pp. 257–286.

[15]William D. Eldridge, "Practitioners and Self-Evaluation," *Social Casework*, 64, 7 (1983): 426–430.

[16]Naomi Brill, *Working with People: The Helping Process*, 4th ed. (New York: Longman, 1990), p. 264.

is what others hold you responsible for when you take on those tasks. Full acceptance of assigned job responsibilities thus includes both feeling responsible and being able to account to others for what you do.

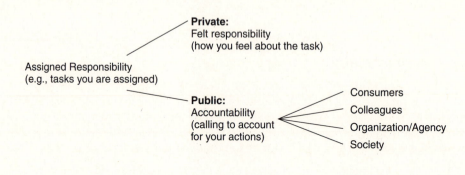

Issue 3: Service quality

The third critical issue to consider in maintaining a competent practice is service quality. The quality of service delivery is a contemporary issue in many human service (and other) organizations in the United States. One form of the quality movement you might experience is called TQM (total quality management). It is a set of tools, principles, and procedures concerned with involving everyone in an organization in controlling and continuously improving how work is done in order to meet customer expectations of quality. Customers of a human service agency might include citizens whose taxes or fees support services, legislators, boards of trustees, and the consumers actually receiving the services. In TQM, quality means everything of value to the organization and its customers. This includes the physical quality of the products and services, ethics, morale, safety, and wise use of resources.

> Quality means managers and employees continuously striving to meet customer expectations, to do the right thing right the first time, and to achieve ever higher standards of quality, timeliness, and efficiency.[17]

FRAME 5

Exploring Responsibility, Accountability, and Service Quality

This frame provides you with an opportunity to begin to apply the concepts of responsibility, accountability, and service quality.

---

[17]U.S. Office of Personnel Management, *Federal Total Quality Management Handbook: How to Get Started—Part I* (Washington, D.C.: Federal Quality Institute, 1990), p. 2.

Step 1: *Identify tasks.* Select at least two tasks from the task profile in Frame 3 or identify two tasks you are currently performing and for which you also feel responsible.

Example task: Interviews consumer regarding status of particular aspect of case using telephone or personal visit in order to determine current need or status or to update information.

Step 2: *Define quality requirements for each task.* Ask at least two different people you consider expert in their areas to describe how each task should be performed in order for them to recognize it as quality work. For example, you might interview a fellow worker, a supervisor, a consumer, a member of the consumer's family or network, or an instructor. An example of a completed form is provided after the blank form.

Task 1	Quality requirements as seen by _____ • • • Quality requirements as seen by _____ • • •
Task 2	Quality requirements as seen by _____ • • • Quality requirements as seen by _____ • • •

Step 3: *Report the results.* Accountability requires documentation of services, concern about the quality and responsiveness of services, and an ability and willingness to link with multiple customers. Use this exercise as an opportunity to engage in these kinds of discussions, to write down the results, and to share the report in an appropriate forum. Be sure you report the results of your interviews in the language of the people being interviewed.

| Task 1
Interviews consumer regarding status of particular aspect of case using telephone or personal visit to determine current need or status or to update case information. | Quality requirements as seen by *Supervisor*

• Encourages consumer to define situation by asking open-ended questions.
• Conducts the interview by the date specified in the plan.
• Records the results of the interview in the case record.
• Takes appropriate and timely action based on results of interview (e.g., referral and set next appointment).

Quality requirements as seen by *Consumer*

• Makes me feel comfortable in sharing information about my needs.
• Does not force herself into my life—seeks to listen to and understand the context of my life.
• Helps me to frame my options and strengthens my capacity to make the necessary choices.
• Answers my questions without sending me to 15 other places. |

Example of a Completed Form

FRAME

6

So far we have discussed three issues important in competent practice: (1) responsibility, or knowing what you are responsible for and what you feel responsible for; (2) accountability, or being able to account to others for how you handle your responsibilities; and (3) service quality, or the extent to which you focus on improvements based on customer expectations of quality. A fourth issue of competent practice is worker or personal effectiveness.

Issue 4: Worker effectiveness

What characteristics mark an effective human service worker? Human service workers are individuals with diverse personal characteristics. There are no homogeneous groups of helpers—within each organization, there are noticeable differences in lifestyles, aspirations, education, and abilities. Despite these differences, studies of effective helpers and change agents find that they share certain general competencies. Effective human service workers who think of themselves as helpers generally have one or more of the following competencies:[18]

1. Interpersonal competence. These skills include the abilities to support and nurture others and to confront difficult issues; to influence others and to listen well and empathize; to be highly aware and socially sensitive; and to facilitate interpersonal and group processes.

2. An ability to be in touch with self. One aspect of being in touch with yourself is to be aware of your knowledge, skills, and values as they apply to delivering human services. This includes the ability to recognize your own feelings and intuitions quickly and to have a clear understanding of your motivations. It involves knowing your skills and knowing when a situation requires the involvement of workers with other skills. It also includes the ability to avoid meeting your own needs through the helping relationship or acting self-indulgently with consumers. Workers who understand themselves and can understand others without losing sight of the agency's purpose are likely to be effective.

3. Sensitivity. Sensitivity is quite simply the use of all the senses (including intuition) to attend to whatever is happening: "That sensing is like a fine instrument, capable of picking up clues that the average person might not register: nuances of meaning, intonations of voice, subtle changes of facial expression or body posture; hesitations, slips of speech, and all the thousand and one subtle expressions of a person in the midst of life."[19] Sensitivity involves kindness and caring, and especially the ability to accurately read what is happening. Effective human service workers are excellent observers of behavior. They see, hear, and sense things that are not accessible to the untrained or unaware. They find patterns in chaos, structures in apparently unrelated events. They process information in distinctive ways that enable them and the consumers they work with to make sense of the patterns of life and to take actions.

4. An ability to link knowledge with problems in practice. These skills include the abilities to understand the knowledge you have about processes of problem solving and to link this knowledge with problems being experienced by consumers as well as dealing with your own problems in the workplace.

5. An ability to learn and to educate. These are skills concerned with teaching or creating learning experiences for yourself and consumers. One means of accomplishing this is by modeling effective behaviors. Other approaches include discussions, courses, readings, questioning, and tests.

6. A framework to guide their practice. Workers may not always be able to fully express it, but those who are considered effective by their peers, consumers, or other measures have one or more practice frameworks to guide their actions. One practice framework has been proposed in this text. It includes nine skill areas or competencies to achieve three specific service goals and is supported by a generic knowledge foundation.

---

[18]Characteristics drawn, in part, from Louise C. Johnson and Charles L. Schwartz, *Social Welfare: A Response to Human Need* (Boston: Allyn & Bacon, 1988); and Jerry L. Porras and Peter J. Robertson, "Organization Development Theory," in Richard W. Woodman and William A. Pasmore, *Research in Organizational Change and Development,* vol. 1 (Greenwich, Conn.: JAI Press), pp. 1–57, esp. 27–28.
[19]Jeffrey A. Kottler, *The Compleat Therapist* (San Francisco: Jossey-Bass, 1991), pp. 96–98.

7. An ability to integrate knowledge, skills, values, and self in practice. Practitioners must take responsibility for integrating within themselves all that they have acquired—the values, the knowledge, and the skill—with the total self in the practice of human services.[20] Integrating is a commitment to a psychological harmony of wholeness. Integrating is an ability to conform personal expression with psychological reality—of act with desire, or word with thought, of face with mind, of the outer with the inner self.[21]

How do these characteristics of effective human service workers strike you? What conclusions do you draw?

FRAME

7

APPROACHES TO ONGOING COMPETENCE

Professionals today must justify their decisions, compete for budgets, be explicit about what they do, and prove that what they do has some value. Consumer movements, clients' rights movements, and scarce financial resources all combine to make us all far more concerned with effectiveness and accountability than ever before. . . . [Human service] workers must engage in self-assessment.[22]

Several approaches are available to achieve an ongoing focus on competent practice. These approaches boil down to two: those you initiate (self-assessments) and those initiated by others.

Self-Assessment

The most basic level of responsibility for performance evaluation rests with the individual practitioner in the form of self-evaluation or self-assessment. Self-assessment means testing ourselves in a variety of ways, including using predesigned instruments, existing organizational processes (such as performance appraisal and case consultation conferences), and continuing education opportunities. A variety of self-assessment exercises have been included throughout this text; others will be the exclusive focus of the next lesson in this chapter.

Five questions can guide you in an ongoing process of self-assessment:[23]

1. What are the processes by which I make decisions about my competence on the job?
2. What do I do when I encounter a new or unexpected situation? (Consider specific examples when you were surprised by a turn of events and reflect on your responses.)

---

[20]Brill, *Working with People,* p. 257.

[21]Robert Grudin, *The Grace of Great Things: Creativity and Innovation* (New York: Ticknor and Fields, 1990), p. 73.

[22]Alter and Evens, *Evaluating Your Practice,* pp. 6, 9.

[23]Adapted from Eldridge, "Practitioners and Self-Evaluation," pp. 426–430.

3. What types and sources of information do I use for self-evaluation? Do I rely exclusively on my own perceptions of my performance, or do I actively seek out the perceptions of others?

4. What areas of personal and professional performance do I evaluate?

5. What procedures do I use to conduct self-evaluation? Do I conduct interviews? fill out preexisting forms? review case records? keep a journal? review past performance evaluations? involve peers and consumers as sources of feedback?

Assessment by Others

Human service agencies typically have a number of processes designed to evaluate worker performance. One is the performance appraisal process conducted by the immediate supervisor. Other mechanisms include training needs assessments and in-service training programs designed to address the needs; peer and consumer reviews; and program evaluations and audits conducted to assess the performance of groups of workers.

Licensing and certification offered through states, professional associations, colleges, and universities assure the public that licensees have completed minimum educational programs, have a certain number of hours of supervised training, and have gone through some type of evaluation and screening. Most professional organizations support efforts to make continuing education a mandatory condition of relicensure. Most observers would agree that it is essential for practitioners to keep current with new developments.

Conclusion

Most human service workers believe that they evaluate their practice and can be explicit about what they accomplish. However, much of what a competent human service worker does, from what is said to how it is said, from eye contact to body posture, is practitioner habit.[24] When this is the case, workers probably remain unreflective because their performance is achieving familiar and presumably desired results. Self-assessment requires active reflection—before, during, and after task performance. Self-assessment requires practitioners to explicitly evaluate their performance and to be able to show others the results. Commitment to self-assessment also increases the likelihood that workers will govern themselves as opposed to being governed by outside groups. That is, if the helping professions do not take steps to regulate themselves, it is quite likely other groups (such as the state or the federal government) will do it for them. Self-assessment in a variety of forms is the mark of a competent practitioner.

> Sidney Jourard has warned about the delusion that one has nothing new to learn. He maintains that contact at exciting workshops or with challenging colleagues can keep [workers] growing. He urges [workers] to find colleagues they can trust so that they can avoid becoming "smug, pompous, fat-bottomed and convinced that they have *the word*." Such colleagues can "prod one out of such smug pomposity and invite one back to the task."[25]

---

[24]Yosikazu S. DeRoos, "The Development of Practice Wisdom Through Human Problem-Solving Processes," *Social Service Review* (June 1990): 276–287.

[25]Corey, Corey, and Callanan, *Issues and Ethics in the Helping Professions,* p. 189.

FRAME
8

TENSIONS IN DELIVERING HUMAN SERVICES

All of the discussion about competence in delivering human services is not meant to suggest the work is simple, straightforward, or easy to assess. Although this text has presented many ideas and approaches that are critical to competent service delivery, no single text could ever presume to be complete or able to reduce human interaction to a mechanical sequence of steps.

Human service work is rarely straightforward. Service delivery—whether you are an entry-level or advanced practitioner—is full of tensions. The example below provides both a context for thinking about competence and an example of a worker clearly engaged in a process of self-assessment. This worker, Rhonda Buckner, pushed her self-assessment to the limits, however. She published it in a major newspaper, *The Washington Post*. We invite you to review her reflections and use them to discuss the issues being raised in this lesson. For example: How does Ms. Buckner define her responsibilities? How does she account for the results of her actions? What approaches does she use to assess her performance?

Helping the Mentally Disabled Live Independently: The Hard Part Is Deciding When Not to Intervene*

The apartment was indescribable: Waist-high piles of egg shells, containers and newspapers covered the floors, the bed, the stove and every other surface. The smell was even worse—a combination of mustiness, body odor and garbage.

For weeks, I had tried every method of persuasion I could think of to prod my mentally ill client, who was struggling to live on her own, to clean up or to let me hire a cleaning service. But she adamantly refused to part with even a single dirty rubber band. I was faced with a dilemma: Should I arrange a cleanup, alienating her and robbing her of the right to make her own decision, or should I do nothing and run the risk that she might be evicted?

As director of Personal Support Network, a nonprofit Northern Virginia program that helps people with mental disabilities live independently after their families die or can no longer take care of them, I must often make significant decisions that have a major impact on my clients' lives. While some are easy, others, such as this one, are not. Usually the choice is not clear-cut but a matter of degree and involves choosing an alternative that is "less bad" or one that is only slightly better.

The most difficult part of the job is determining how much control to exert. When making decisions like this—I decided to accede to my client's wishes—my staff and I ask ourselves a lot of questions. What would I do if I were a relative? Do we have the legal right to intervene? If so, should we? What will happen if we don't? Is that so terrible?

We're guided by a belief in the importance of empowerment, the notion that although our clients have disabilities, they are adults who have the right to make their own decisions, as long as they are not ruinous or clearly dangerous. Building trust with clients is essential and the relationship depends on allowing them autonomy, trying to help them take responsibility for their actions and to learn from their mistakes—as we all do.

Not all of our cases have happy endings. Sometimes, we are forced to step in and make decisions on behalf of our clients, over their objections. One of the most difficult

*Adapted from Rhonda Buckner, *The Washington Post Health* (Apr. 6, 1991): 9.

cases involved a 40-year-old man who had a history of manic depressive illness and was also a drug user and an alcoholic. He lived in a condominium his parents owned and received $320 per month in Social Security payments—his only source of funds, which we divided into weekly $80 installments to cover all his other expenses. He had no legal access to the account. Although he had not been found incompetent by a court, Social Security officials had decided he was incapable of managing his money and had awarded us financial responsibility.

One day, he went to a branch of the bank and told the teller his name—which was very common—and requested his account number and balance. The teller mistakenly gave him information about another customer and told him he had $23,000 in his account.

The bank discovered the error three weeks later, after our client had withdrawn $2,000. Bank officers immediately froze his Social Security account and threatened to prosecute him for fraud if he did not repay the money.

Because Personal Support Network was legally responsible for the account, it was my job to decide what to do. Without access to his account, he had no money and I worried that he might get into more trouble, possibly for stealing. A lawyer I consulted told me that if he were prosecuted, my client would probably go to jail because despite his mental illness, he could distinguish right from wrong and was therefore legally responsible for his actions.

"Let them prosecute me," he said defiantly, furious that I would consider paying the money back. "I want to go to court, I think I can beat this. It was the bank's mistake, not mine."

For days, I agonized about what to do. My client seemed to understand the consequences and, like many people, wanted to take his chances at a trial. Was it fair to deny him the right to self-determination? After all, I wasn't his legal guardian or judge.

But I was responsible for the account. And it seemed to me that paying the money back in weekly $5 installments would be a more effective lesson than sitting in jail. I agreed to the bank's terms, but I felt uneasy. My client remained angry, even though we had long discussions about the situation.

Six weeks later, his sister called to tell me he had been found dead in his condo, the victim of a heroin overdose. Although there is no way to tell for certain, the overdose appeared to be accidental; he left no note or other indication that he had planned to die.

I was shocked by the news and wondered often in the ensuing weeks whether my decision had contributed to his feelings of powerlessness, and ultimately to what might have been his suicide. Later, I decided that the two events were probably unrelated and there was nothing I could have done to prevent his tragic, premature death.

The thing I try not to forget is that the decisions we make on behalf of our clients can have a lasting impact on their lives.

FRAME
9

Lesson Summary

This lesson discussed issues involved in delivering human services *competently*. Competence was discussed as an ongoing process rather than as something that is achieved once and for all. We considered examples of how different helping professions address the question of competence in their codes of ethics. Then we examined the meaning of competence, including three alternative models of worker competence: the worker as artist, the worker as citizen, and the worker as linker. Treating competence as a process, we concluded that learning was at the heart of a focus on competent practice. Competence is a process of continually questioning whether you are working as well as you might, searching for ways of becoming a more effective person and helper, and being able to account to yourself and others for the process and the results of your efforts. Four issues that are critical to practicing competently were discussed: responsibility, accountability, service quality, and worker effectiveness. Self-assessment and assessments by others were discussed as the two basic approaches to ensuring competence. Self-assessment was emphasized as being critical—as the hallmark of an effective, competent practitioner.

LESSON2

Perception Checking

This lesson is different from all the other lessons in the book. It is composed of eight self-assessment exercises that relate to the issues of competence discussed in Lesson 1. As we stressed in that lesson, competence is an ongoing process. A critical skill that facilitates an ongoing focus on competence is the ability to conduct "perception checking." Perception checking is a process of collecting information that helps confirm or contradict your views of yourself or others. It also includes the ability to use the results to plan and experiment with future changes or consistencies in your behavior.

Goals

To be able to collect information about yourself based on your own perceptions and the perceptions of others. To use the results to identify actions to increase your competence.

Learning Activities

To accomplish these goals, you will:

1. Choose one or more of the eight self-assessment exercises described in Frame 1.
2. Use the results of the selected exercise(s) to identify at least one specific action you will take to increase or maintain your competence in the area assessed.

F R A M E

SELECTING FROM A SELF-ASSESSMENT MENU

Recent research shows that employers, including human service employers, want workers with a broad set of workplace skills.[1] Employees are also interested in these issues, primarily because they are being challenged as never before. The range of skills employees need to participate in today's economy is expanding. For example, workers are less supervised but more frequently called on to identify problems and make crucial decisions about their work.

---

[1]Anthony P. Carnevale, Leila J. Gainer, and Ann S. Meltzer, *Workplace Basics: The Essential Skills Employers Want* (San Francisco: Jossey-Bass, 1990).

As we discussed in Lesson 1, the push for demonstrated competence of human service workers is principally a drive for accountability and service quality. Scarce resources, demands for increased and new services, and the increasing pace of change are likely to continue through the next decades. Human service workers must therefore make it a habit to assess their competence on a regular basis, to be able to account to others for what they accomplish, and to manifest an ongoing concern for quality.

Self-assessment is one way of ensuring accountability and service quality. The eight exercises in this lesson are presented as tools to make self-assessment accessible to you. The exercises are presented in the form of a menu so that you can select those relevant to your needs. The specific exercises included in the lesson are listed below:

Self-Assessment Exercises in This Lesson

Exercise 1   Assessing Learning Skills
Exercise 2   Assessing Personal Management Skills
Exercise 3   Assessing Helping, Interviewing, and Relationship-Building Skills
Exercise 4   Assessing Group Effectiveness Skills
Exercise 5   Assessing Knowledge and Skills of an Entry-Level Worker
Exercise 6   Assessing Feelings and Actions at Work
Exercise 7   Assessing the Quality of Work Group Performance
Exercise 8   Considering Additional Readings About the Skill of Integrating

Although you can complete these exercises by yourself, their greatest value is often derived from asking your peers, your consumers, your supervisor, or your instructor to complete the same exercise. Then you can compare the results from multiple points of view and use the similarities and differences as a basis for discussion and further learning. Each exercise generally has specific instructions that clarify how to use it. The results of any exercise should provide you with a considerable amount of information. You should analyze all the results with the help of your supervisor or a colleague.

You may complete the exercises one after the other or you may skip around and do those that spark your interest. We also encourage you to develop your own exercises and to adapt existing exercises in ways that make them useful to you.

EXERCISE

1

ASSESSING LEARNING SKILLS[2]

Today your learning skills are critical success factors in delivering human services. Learning skills involve possessing or acquiring the knowledge and skill to learn effectively in whatever learning situation you encounter. Learning situations include much of what you encounter in a human service organization. Individuals who have learned how to learn (1) draw lessons from their previous experience, (2) observe others to discover models of effective practice, (3) experiment, and (4) question their own assumptions and norms.

---

[2]Patricia A. McLagan, *Models for HRD Practice: The Practitioner's Guide* (Alexandria, Va.: American Society for Training and Development, 1989), pp. 74–76.

Use the worksheet below to assess your learning skills. For each characteristic listed in the far left column, indicate with a check mark whether you think it is a real strength as it is now, acceptable as it is now (i.e., you are doing all right), needs some development, or needs major development. After you have assessed yourself, consider asking your supervisor and a fellow worker to complete the assessment. Then use the results (1) to discuss the different perceptions with those giving you feedback and (2) to develop a plan of action to strengthen how you learn while delivering human services.

Learning Characteristics	*A Real Strength as It Is Now*	*Doing All Right*	*Needs Some Development*	*Needs Major Development*
1. Understanding myself as a learner (e.g., learning style, learning preferences)	_____	_____	_____	_____
2. Reading skill	_____	_____	_____	_____
3. Listening skill	_____	_____	_____	_____
4. Note-taking skill	_____	_____	_____	_____
5. Openness to new ideas and ways of doing things	_____	_____	_____	_____
6. Willingness to be a learner and to be in a learning role with others	_____	_____	_____	_____
7. Finding good learning resources	_____	_____	_____	_____
8. Accurately assessing myself and using the results to plan future directions in my life and work	_____	_____	_____	_____
9. Getting candid feedback from others	_____	_____	_____	_____
10. Following through on learning plans	_____	_____	_____	_____
11. Remembering what I've learned	_____	_____	_____	_____
12. Recognizing and deliberately learning from mistakes and successes	_____	_____	_____	_____
13. Making theories applicable on the job and in life, even when connections are not obvious	_____	_____	_____	_____
14. Creating knowledge from experience to use deliberately when facing new experiences	_____	_____	_____	_____
15. Using library and other research and scanning services	_____	_____	_____	_____

Learning Characteristics	A Real Strength as It Is Now	Doing All Right	Needs Some Development	Needs Major Development
16. Learning as a team participant through group discussion and problem solving	_____	_____	_____	_____

What are the major areas for action to improve your learning capability for the future? What will you do to improve?

Areas for Action   **Actions to Take**

EXERCISE 2

ASSESSING PERSONAL MANAGEMENT SKILLS[3]

Personal management skills are the building blocks for good morale, a focused work life, and organizational productivity. They are also the foundation for carrying out the key roles in delivering human services described in this text. This exercise provides an opportunity to assess your capacities to demonstrate self-esteem, set goals, plan your career, manage relations with colleagues, and handle administrative matters. The specific steps for this exercise are as follows:

Step 1: Complete the inventory by checking one of the response categories for each item.

Step 2: Go back and circle three or four items that are the most important issues for you right now.

Step 3: Develop a one- or two-sentence rationale for the importance of each of the three to four items.

Step 4: Develop a plan of action to work on each of the three or four items over the next three months.

---

[3]Michael J. Austin, *Supervisory Management for the Human Services* (Englewood Cliffs, N.J.: Prentice-Hall, 1981); and Carnevale, Gainer, and Meltzer, *Workplace Basics.*

Demonstrating Self-Esteem/ Positive Self-Concept	*Doing All Right*	*Need to Do It More*	*Need to Do It Less*
1. Ability to take calculated and defensible risks	_____	_____	_____
2. Demonstrates leadership ability in a work group	_____	_____	_____
3. Demonstrates follow-through on tasks	_____	_____	_____
4. Shows capacity to deal with frustrations related to problem solving	_____	_____	_____
5. Shows capacity to feel good about self in spite of mistakes	_____	_____	_____
6. Demonstrates initiative in an effort to influence events	_____	_____	_____

Goal Setting

7. Shows ability to define personal and work-related goals	_____	_____	_____
8. Shows ability to identify potential problems and obstacles to reaching goals, and identifying how to overcome them	_____	_____	_____
9. Shows ability to measure progress toward goals	_____	_____	_____
10. Shows ability to identify resources necessary to reach goals	_____	_____	_____
11. Shows ability to revise goals when need be	_____	_____	_____
12. Shows ability to challenge self in setting personal goals	_____	_____	_____

Planning Career

13. Demonstrates ability to describe competencies or roles performed in current job	_____	_____	_____
14. Identifies three to five competencies of greatest strength and greatest weakness	_____	_____	_____
15. Links career needs with personal needs	_____	_____	_____
16. Is able to describe the work he or she would like to be doing in two to five years	_____	_____	_____
17. Is able to participate effectively in a learning community—the relationships in work/life in which he or she provides or receives development support	_____	_____	_____

Managing Relations with Colleagues

18. Demonstrates effective use of peer approval	_____	_____	_____

	Doing All Right	*Need to Do It More*	*Need to Do It Less*
19. Demonstrates appreciation and responsiveness to needs and peers	_____	_____	_____
20. Demonstrates tolerance for different peer approaches to problem solving	_____	_____	_____
21. Seriously considers suggestions from peers	_____	_____	_____
22. Promotes sufficient informality in work group to maintain morale and productivity	_____	_____	_____

Handling Administrative Matters

23. Demonstrates ability to plan and organize work	_____	_____	_____
24. Demonstrates ability to seek out and evaluate information	_____	_____	_____
25. Demonstrates ability to negotiate differences in opinion or approaches	_____	_____	_____
26. Demonstrates ability to foresee consequences of particular decisions	_____	_____	_____
27. Demonstrates decision-making abilities (defining goals, establishing procedures, etc.)	_____	_____	_____
28. Defers judgment and action until all data or opinions are determined	_____	_____	_____
29. Carries out tasks and work assignments in orderly fashion	_____	_____	_____
30. Demonstrates appreciation of need for controls and accountability (clients, staff, etc.)	_____	_____	_____

E X E R C I S E

3

ASSESSING HELPING, INTERVIEWING, AND RELATIONSHIP-BUILDING SKILLS[4]

In Unit Three we described the range of activities that are important for carrying out the counseling role. In this exercise you have an opportunity to assess your counseling behaviors in the areas of personal characteristics, counseling skills, case management skills, and professionalism. You can also involve others in this process by asking them to complete the exercise and then compare the results for similarities and differences. The specific steps for this exercise follow:

Step 1: Complete the checklist of interviewing behaviors.

---

[4]Adapted from "Marriage, Family and Child Counselor Agency Oriented Internship Assessment," San Francisco State University, 1976, Mimeo.

Step 2: Ask your supervisor or a co-worker to complete the checklist in terms of as-sessing *your* interviewing behaviors.

Step 3: Identify the similarities and differences and write a sentence or two explaining your reactions to each of the items where there was a difference.

Step 4: Develop a six-month action plan for improvement on the items you have se-lected as most important to you.

I. Personal Characteristics

A. *Relationships with others*

_____ Shows an exceptional ability to relate to others.

_____ Demonstrates a high degree of ability to relate to others.

_____ Relates adequately with most people.

_____ Has difficulty relating to some others.

_____ Often relates in a manner that "turns people off."

B. *Warmth and caring*

_____ Displays these qualities appropriately.

_____ Usually presents self as warm and caring.

_____ Displays some concern and support, but with some observable limits.

_____ Displays these qualities inappropriately or in a highly limited manner.

C. *Tolerance for ambiguity and stress*

_____ Recognizes a stressful situation; adjusts and tolerates accordingly.

_____ Sometimes behaves inappropriately under stress.

_____ Low tolerance for stress.

_____ "Falls apart" when under stress.

D. *Flexibility regarding environment and time commitment*

_____ Able to function effectively regardless of environment and, if necessary, is willing to devote more time than expected to complete the task.

_____ Able to function effectively regardless of environment, but reluctant to be flexible in time commitment.

_____ Needs a particular environment, but flexible in time commitment.

_____ Needs a particular environment to function and is not willing to be flex-ible in time commitment.

E. *Openness to and acceptance of others' values and lifestyles*

_____ Genuine and demonstrated acceptance of other values and lifestyles.

_____ Limited acceptance of other values and lifestyles.

_____ Closed to other values and lifestyles.

F. *Self-awareness and understanding*

_____ Has an awareness of personal stage of growth and shows continuance of this growth awareness.

_____ Generally seems aware of current growth process but appears ill equipped theoretically for inward probing.

_____ Sometimes seems unaware of feelings and motivation.

_____ Seems to have minimal awareness of feelings; does not seem to have accepted own problems; responds in stereotyped manner.

G. *Self-esteem*

_____ Self-directed and confident; accepts responsibilities; maintains sense of identity; functions independently.

_____ Good sense of identity and rootedness, needs only occasional reassurance.

_____ In frequent need of reassurance; lacks a significant degree of self-confidence.

_____ In constant need of reassurance; does not function well independently.

H. *Motivation toward continued learning*

_____ Shows openness and enthusiasm for learning new ideas, methods, and approaches.

_____ Can be encouraged to be open to some new ideas, methods, and approaches.

_____ Is generally uninterested in exploring new methods and ideas.

_____ Closed to new knowledge and techniques.

I. *Ability to relate to the population that the agency serves (if applicable):* ethnic, sexual, cultural, etc.

_____ Shows considerable ability along with some language familiarity, where applicable.

_____ Reflects an openness to cultural and lifestyle differences among consumer populations.

_____ Generally lacks cultural awareness.

_____ Resistant to people from different cultures and lifestyles.

II. Interviewing Skills

A. *Attending and listening:* Pays attention to the physical and psychological communication of the consumer, communicates attention to the consumer through verbal and physical action.

_____ Displays attentive listening to both verbal and nonverbal messages of consumer and self.

_____ Usually shows attentive listening as described above.

_____ Attentive listening is not commonly displayed.

B. *Empathy:* Responds to consumer in a way that shows an understanding of what the consumer experiences emotionally and intellectually and what the consumer is communicating verbally and nonverbally.

_____ Demonstrates understanding of consumer's thoughts and feelings enriched at a level deeper than consumer expressed verbally.

_____ Reflects accurately consumer's expressed surface feelings, but does not show understanding of consumer's deeper feelings.

_____ Shows awareness of consumer's thoughts and feelings, although responses are often mirror images and occasionally are "off base" from consumer's feelings.

_____ Displays little interest and understanding of consumer's thoughts and feelings.

C. *Process:* The awareness of, and the ability to work with, the dynamics that underlie the content of the helping relationship.

_____ Frequently aware of underlying process and, when aware, able to use it in a manner that facilitates the helping process.

_____ Frequently aware of underlying process, although has difficulty integrating it into the helping session.

_____ Seldom aware of underlying dynamics; slow to formulate understanding.

D. *Communication of respect:* Belief in the worth of the individual (i.e., respects each person's right and responsibility to make his or her own decisions and encourages the potential for change).

_____ Displays respect for consumer in a manner that enhances the consumer's self-esteem.

_____ Displays feelings of value for the consumer, but occasionally allows limitations in the feeling and communication.

_____ Frequently allows own prejudices to interfere with acceptance of consumer, detracting from consumer's feelings of self-worth and capabilities.

E. *Limit setting*

_____ Sets and maintains clear, consistent limits, appropriate to situation and dynamics, with the consumer.

_____ Experiences occasional difficulty with limit setting, maintains them well once set.

_____ Seldom sets realistic limits in the helping relationship.

F. *Clarity of expression:* Using clear language, within the consumer's frame of reference, to express thought, feelings, experience.

_____ Uses vocabulary appropriate to consumer.

_____ Occasionally speaks in vocabulary and terminology to which the consumer cannot relate.

_____ Frequently speaks at a different level from that of the consumer.

G. *Timing:* Use of intervention techniques, clarifications, interpretations, and self-disclosure at a time when most beneficial to the consumer's growth.

_____ Consistently displays an accurate sense of timing, which enhances the helping process.

_____ Usually displays a good sense of timing, only occasionally interrupting and disrupting the flow of the helping process.

_____ Frequently interrupts and redirects the consumer, preventing a smooth-flowing process.

H. *Confrontation:* Constructively challenging the consumer's discrepancies, distortions, and defensive behaviors.

_____ Frequently uses confrontation in a manner that enhances the consumer's self-awareness and moves toward growth.

_____ Occasionally confronts the consumer in a manner that enhances self-awareness; occasionally inappropriate.

_____ Seldom able to act confrontationally; inappropriately confrontational.

I. *Self-disclosure:* Willingness to tell the consumer something personal about self that is pertinent to the helping process and yet does not further burden the consumer.

_____ Possesses an ability to self-disclose when appropriate without changing the direction of the session.

_____ Shares self-disclosure when appropriate, although occasionally this information seems vaguely judgmental.

_____ Shares self in a way that takes up a significant part of the session; displays judgmental, superior, directing quality.

J. *Termination*

_____ Displays appropriate insight into, and is able to skillfully handle, the dynamics that are particular to ending a case.

_____ Usually shows the skills that are necessary for adequately dealing with termination; occasionally unable to sense and deal with termination issues.

_____ Displays inability to handle ending in an effective way.

K. *Variety of techniques*

_____ Can accurately use a variety of interviewing skills as needed.

_____ Is open to a variety of skills, but lacks expertise in more than one general area.

_____ Seems inappropriately limited in use of skills.

III. Case Management Skills

A. *Diagnostic evaluation*

_____ Is able to make knowledgeable, sound evaluations and communicate them to consumer and co-workers when necessary; evaluations are based on sound knowledge of consumer's themes and dynamics.

_____ Has adequate assessment knowledge and skills, occasional difficulty formulating and communicating.

_____ Seems unsure of evaluations of consumers; seldom formulates evaluations.

_____ Avoids evaluating consumers' functioning abilities.

B. *Intervention planning*

_____ Has ability to formulate, develop, and implement sound intervention plans that prove effective for consumers.

_____ Develops sound intervention plans, but finds implementation difficult.

_____ Develops intervention plans that are sometimes questionable.

_____ Formulates intervention plans that prove ineffective for consumers.

C. *Agency-specific skills:* Ability to learn to use specific skills appropriate to the agency, if any (e.g., reading and understanding medical records/charts, preparing court reports, being an effective advocate in the community, communicating the relevance and need for rules, use of milieu therapy).

_____ Considerable ability to learn and use agency-specific skills.

_____ Some ability to learn and use agency-specific skills.

_____ Limited ability to learn and use agency-specific skills.

D. *Crisis-intervention management*

_____ Consistently able to act effectively and swiftly at point of crisis.

_____ Action in crisis situation is usually effective and appropriate.

_____ Becomes flustered in an emergency situation; does not act swiftly or effectively.

E. *Identification of crisis*

_____ Usually able to identify the dynamic situation "beneath" the crisis.

_____ Aware that a crisis is occurring, but has trouble identifying the underlying issues.

_____ Cannot distinguish the crisis that is occurring.

F. *Intake interview skills*

_____ Gets necessary information and makes appropriate communication and referrals.

_____ Gives basic information, but lacks ability to provide a clear picture of the problem.

_____ Performance on intakes is unsatisfactory.

G. *Recognition of consultation needs*

_____ Is aware of need for abilities and limitations in seeking consultation with regard to effectiveness with different consumers.

_____ Is aware of limitations, but uncomfortable in seeking consultation.

_____ Is aware of personal limitations, but has difficulty in utilizing consultation.

_____ Unable to use consultation when in difficulty.

H. *Ability to write case summaries, reports, evaluations*

_____ Submits excellent reports that are current, orderly, and appropriate.

_____ Gives reports adequate to agency's needs; limited as to richness and appropriateness.

_____ Reports are disorganized and difficult to read.

I. *Presenting cases*

_____ Discusses feelings and events in some detail, showing relationships between the two.

_____ Includes detail but lacks relevant discussion.

_____ Speaks in generalities with small amount of supporting detail.

_____ Speaks in generalities.

IV. Professionalism

A. *Reliability*

_____ Communicates sense of enthusiasm and commitment (e.g., tries to be on the job on time, completes tasks).

_____ Occasionally late for appointments, meetings. Usually makes sure that breaks and leaves do not inconvenience other staff members. Tasks most often completed on time.

_____ Tends to be late; tasks sometimes not completed on time; takes unusual amount of time for breaks; leave privileges are used about the same as others, but with little concern for effect.

_____ Seldom on time; tasks often not completed on time; takes longer or more frequent breaks than others; tends to take advantage of leave privileges.

B. *Confidentiality*

_____ Always maintains consumer information in a confidential manner.

_____ Reveals consumer information in inappropriate ways.

C. *Judgment*

_____ Conveys exceptional professional judgment by conduct that is appropriate to the setting.

_____ Conduct is usually appropriate to the setting.

_____ Inappropriate conduct is often observable.

D. *Dealing with conflicting ideas*

_____ Displays an appropriate willingness to state opinions and initiates constructive dealing with opinions that conflict with other staff members.

_____ Sometimes states opinions, but only rarely becomes involved in discussions with others.

_____ Does not state opinions and therefore never becomes involved in discussion with those whose opinions may differ.

E. *Relationships with co-workers*

_____ Supportive of co-workers and willing to share related professional experiences.

_____ Usually seeks assistance and is supportive of co-workers.

_____ Available for assistance and meeting for the purpose of learning, but seldom initiates sharing.

_____ Will meet with co-workers for assistance when asked.

_____ Seems uneasy and distant with co-workers.

F. *Intrastaff decision*

_____ Actively participates in decision-making process.

_____ Occasionally involved in intrastaff decisions.

_____ Does not contribute to decision-making process.

EXERCISE

4

ASSESSING GROUP EFFECTIVENESS SKILLS[5]

In this exercise, you have the opportunity to assess your group effectiveness skills. Many of these skills require years of practice and additional study of group dynamics. However, this self-assessment should provide you with a foundation for identifying additional learning needs. The specific steps for this exercise are noted below:

Step 1: Complete the inventory by checking off your responses, then circle three or four items that are most important to you.

Step 2: Ask your supervisor or instructor to complete the same inventory in order to assess *your* group skills.

Step 3: Compare your responses, noting the similarities and differences.

Step 4: Which items were most reassuring to you? Which were most distressing? Develop a written statement explaining your reactions.

Step 5: Develop a six-month action plan describing how and where you plan to work on your three or four most important items.

Communication Skills	*Doing All Right*	*Need to Do It More*	*Need to Do It Less*
1. Amount of talking in group	_____	_____	_____
2. Being brief and concise	_____	_____	_____
3. Being forceful	_____	_____	_____
4. Listening alertly	_____	_____	_____
5. Drawing others out	_____	_____	_____
6. Thinking before I talk	_____	_____	_____
7. _____	_____	_____	_____
Observation Skills			
8. Noting tension in the group	_____	_____	_____
9. Noting who talks to whom	_____	_____	_____

[5]Adapted from Herman Resnick, "Group Process Skills," in Michael J. Austin, *Management Simulations in Mental Health and Human Service Administration* (New York: Haworth Press, 1978).

	Doing All Right	Need to Do It More	Need to Do It Less
10. Noting interest level of group	_____	_____	_____
11. Sensing feelings of individuals	_____	_____	_____
12. Noting who is being "left out"	_____	_____	_____
13. Noting reaction to my comments	_____	_____	_____
14. Noting when group avoids a topic	_____	_____	_____
15. _____	_____	_____	_____

Self-Disclosure

16. Telling others what I feel	_____	_____	_____
17. Hiding my emotions	_____	_____	_____
18. Disagreeing openly	_____	_____	_____
19. Expressing warm feelings	_____	_____	_____
20. Expressing gratitude	_____	_____	_____
21. Being humorous	_____	_____	_____
22. Being angry	_____	_____	_____
23. _____	_____	_____	_____

Tolerance for Emotional Situations

24. Being able to face conflict/anger	_____	_____	_____
25. Being able to face closeness and affection	_____	_____	_____
26. Being able to face disappointment	_____	_____	_____
27. Being able to stand silence	_____	_____	_____
28. Being able to stand tension	_____	_____	_____
29. _____			

Social Relationships

30. Competing to outdo others	_____	_____	_____
31. Acting dominant toward others	_____	_____	_____
32. Trusting others	_____	_____	_____
33. Being helpful	_____	_____	_____
34. Being protective	_____	_____	_____
35. Calling attention to myself	_____	_____	_____
36. Being able to stand up for myself	_____	_____	_____
37. Ability to be open with others	_____	_____	_____
38. _____			

General

39. Understanding why I do what I do (insight)	_____	_____	_____
40. Encouraging comments on my own behavior (feedback)	_____	_____	_____
41. Accepting help willingly	_____	_____	_____
42. Making my mind up firmly	_____	_____	_____
43. Criticizing myself	_____	_____	_____
44. Waiting patiently	_____	_____	_____

45. Allowing myself to have fun   _____   _____   _____
46. Allowing myself time alone   _____   _____   _____
47. _____

ASSESSING YOUR KNOWLEDGE AND SKILLS AS AN ENTRY-LEVEL WORKER[6]

One way to improve the delivery of services is through an assessment of personal knowledge and skill. The information gained can help you determine training or continuing education preferences that will in turn enhance your service delivery capacities. This exercise provides a self-assessment instrument as an aid in determining training needs. Each section of the inventory can be completed by you and/or a supervisor.

The self-assessment inventory is designed primarily for entry-level human service workers. The entry-level human service worker usually has responsibility for individuals and families. Entry-level workers generally are working toward or have completed an AA or BA degree, or have a high school education with human service experience.

Step 1: Complete the self-assessment inventory by circling a number in the response categories for both knowledge and skill.

Step 2: *After* you have answered each item, go back and see if you would change any of your responses.

Step 3: Ask your supervisor to assess *your* knowledge and skills independently.

Step 4: Compare the responses in order to identify similarities and differences.

Step 5: Make a list of the areas of greatest agreement and the areas of greatest disagreement.

Step 6: Secure your supervisor's reasons for his or her assessment in the areas of greatest disagreement.

Step 7: Develop an action plan for the next 12 months that reflects when and where you want to learn more about the areas that are most important to you.

---

[6]This section is based in part on Austin, *Supervisory Management for the Human Services,* pp. 317–323.

	Knowledge			Skill		
	Don't Know	Need to Know More	Know Enough	Can't Do It	Need More Practice	Can Do It
A. General Background of Human Service System						
1. Knowledge and skill in working in a wide variety of local social agencies or as part of a community human service system (e.g., mental health center, juvenile court, vocational rehabilitation agency, child welfare office, employment service, senior center, residential treatment center, youth service bureau, family service agency).	1	2	3	1	2	3
2. Knowledge and skill in working with a wide variety of consumer populations (e.g., young children, elderly, disabled, women, men, mentally ill, youth offenders, adult offenders, alcoholics, drug abusers, child abusers).	1	2	3	1	2	3
B. Human Growth and Development and the Social Environment						
3. Identifying basic concepts and developmental tasks related to the infancy phase of human growth and development.	1	2	3	1	2	3
4. Identifying basic principles regarding the early childhood or preschool stage of the life cycle.	1	2	3	1	2	3
5. Identifying concepts and developmental tasks related to the "latency" period of the life cycle.	1	2	3	1	2	3
6. Identifying developmental tasks and crises of adolescence as part of the life cycle.	1	2	3	1	2	3
7. Identifying adulthood developmental tasks and expectations as part of the life cycle.	1	2	3	1	2	3

	Knowledge			Skill		
	Don't Know	Need to Know More	Know Enough	Can't Do It	Need More Practice	Can Do It
8. Identifying the concepts and developmental tasks during the old-age phase of the life cycle.	1	2	3	1	2	3
9. Identifying key characteristics and concepts related to the impact of social environment on clients.	1	2	3	1	2	3

C. Getting Services to People in Need

10. *Social brokering*

—Identifying and using community resource system.	1	2	3	1	2	3
—Giving information, referring, and follow-up.	1	2	3	1	2	3
—Identifying and using outreach techniques.	1	2	3	1	2	3

11. *Consumer advocating*

—Identifying and using the advocacy technique of persuasion.	1	2	3	1	2	3
—Identifying and using the advocacy technique of pressuring.	1	2	3	1	2	3
—Identifying and promoting the legal and human rights of consumers.	1	2	3	1	2	3

12. *Mobilizing*

—Identifying community needs and organizing or locating appropriate services.	1	2	3	1	2	3
—Identifying and using mobilizing techniques (conducting meetings, organizing and working with groups, problem solving, etc.).	1	2	3	1	2	3

D. Helping People Function More Effectively: The Intervention– Treatment Process

13. *Relationship building*

—Identifying and making intake assessment of	1	2	3	1	2	3

	Knowledge			Skill		
	Don't Know	Need to Know More	Know Enough	Can't Do It	Need More Practice	Can Do It
consumer's social, emotional, physical, and familial condition.						
—Identifying presenting problem, the consumer's "problem to be worked."	1	2	3	1	2	3
—Identifying principles and using "helping" skills for better understanding (listening, leading, informing, interpreting, etc.).	1	2	3	1	2	3
—Identifying and gathering relevant consumer information (i.e., physical, psychological, social, and environmental functioning).	1	2	3	1	2	3
14. *Helping*						
—Identifying and using helping skills (communication skills, using the helping process, understanding/use of self, etc.).	1	2	3	1	2	3
—Identifying and building "helping" relationships (reality based, empathic, supportive, etc.).	1	2	3	1	2	3
—Identifying and using educating techniques in helping.	1	2	3	1	2	3
—Identifying and using group helping techniques (organizing, leading, etc.).	1	2	3	1	2	3
—Identifying principles and using reality therapy techniques.	1	2	3	1	2	3
—Identifying principles and using behavior therapy as a rehabilitative technique.	1	2	3	1	2	3
15. *Study and diagnosis*						
—Identifying and preparing assessment summary based on information from intake and initial contacts with consumer.	1	2	3	1	2	3

	Knowledge			Skill		
	Don't Know	Need to Know More	Know Enough	Can't Do It	Need More Practice	Can Do It
—Identifying case-specific intervention recommendations.	1	2	3	1	2	3
—Identifying components of total consumer problem constellation.	1	2	3	1	2	3
16. *Intervention plan*						
—Identifying and using an appropriate method of intervention.	1	2	3	1	2	3
—Identifying and using indirect helping procedures.	1	2	3	1	2	3
—Identifying and using ancillary and supportive services.	1	2	3	1	2	3
—Identifying components and formulating a working contract with consumer(s) (e.g., set goals, specify time and place for meeting).	1	2	3	1	2	3
—Identifying principles of and using termination process of, intervention to enhance consumer functioning.	1	2	3	1	2	3
17. *Differential intervention approaches*						
—Identifying and using activity group skills.	1	2	3	1	2	3
—Identifying and using behavior therapy techniques.	1	2	3	1	2	3
—Identifying and using principles of family treatment.	1	2	3	1	2	3
—Identifying and employing crisis-intervention techniques.	1	2	3	1	2	3
—Identifying and using cognitive therapy techniques.	1	2	3	1	2	3
—Identifying and using group techniques.	1	2	3	1	2	3
—Identifying milieu treatment and working in that type of setting.	1	2	3	1	2	3

	Knowledge			Skill		
	Don't Know	*Need to Know More*	*Know Enough*	*Can't Do It*	*Need More Practice*	*Can Do It*
—Identifying techniques and working with self-help groups.	1	2	3	1	2	3
—Identifying principles and using natural systems.	1	2	3	1	2	3

E. Working Across Boundaries to Deliver Services

18. *Managing information*

—Identifying and using interview process and techniques.	1	2	3	1	2	3
—Identifying and using observational and descriptive techniques.	1	2	3	1	2	3
—Identifying and using recording techniques (recordkeeping, agency records, etc.).	1	2	3	1	2	3
—Identifying and using reporting techniques (preparing and presenting reports).	1	2	3	1	2	3
—Identifying and using information management techniques.	1	2	3	1	2	3

19. *"Supervising "up"*

—Identifying components of the supervisory process.	1	2	3	1	2	3
—Identifying ways of using supervision effectively.	1	2	3	1	2	3

20. *Managing transitions*

—Understanding stages of organizational change.	1	2	3	1	2	3
—Being skilled in the dynamics and emotions accompanying rapid change.	1	2	3	1	2	3
—Knowing different types of boundaries created and encountered in human services and being skilled at crossing them.	1	2	3	1	2	3

21. *Integrating*

—Identifying assigned responsibilities.	1	2	3	1	2	3

	Knowledge			Skill		
	Don't Know	*Need to Know More*	*Know Enough*	*Can't Do It*	*Need More Practice*	*Can Do It*
—Clarifying connection between assigned and felt responsibilities.	1	2	3	1	2	3
—Defining quality requirements for performing tasks from multiple perspectives.	1	2	3	1	2	3
—Conducting self-assessment using a variety of instruments.	1	2	3	1	2	3

E X E R C I S E

6

ASSESSING FEELING AND ACTIONS AT WORK[7]

Human service organizations can be stressful. While stress is a normal part of work life, it can sometimes become too much to handle. One way of ensuring a healthy work life is to pay attention to how you feel about your work and how you are behaving at work. Human service organizations, like all work organizations, are a maze of explicit and implicit structures that make up their "culture." Understanding how to operate within this maze can spell the difference between career growth and failure in the workplace. Monitoring your behavior and your feelings in the workplace are critical to keeping stress within healthy limits. The exercise below is one resource for doing this. It should be administered on a regular basis and used to develop an action plan—especially for those items that are causing excessive strain. Check your responses to each item.

Step 1: Complete the inventory.

Step 2: Count how many "checks" you made for each column. For example, how many times did you check "very much like me"?

Step 3: Ask your supervisor and one co-worker to complete the inventory in terms of how they see you.

Step 4: Compare your responses with how others see you and talk about it. What do your responses suggest to you about how well you handle stress?

Step 5: Develop a brief action plan to address at least one issue that might help you to enhance your career growth.

---

[7]This exercise is from Dennis T. Jaffe and Cynthia D. Scott, *Take This Job and Love It* (New York: Simon & Schuster, 1988), pp. 212–214. The exercise has been slightly changed from the way it appears in the text.

	Very Much Like Me	Somewhat Like Me	Not Sure	Somewhat Unlike Me	Not at All Like Me

How Effectively Do You Use the Support and Help of the People Around You?

1. I ask for help from others.
2. I know who to ask when I need something.
3. I have a close person I regularly confide in.
4. I learn a lot from the people I work with.
5. I seek out other people to find out what is happening at work.
6. I know informal ways to get things done at work.

Do You Experience a Sense of Empowerment in Your Work?

1. I am able to accomplish what I want to at work.
2. I let go of things when I get overloaded.
3. I listen to both sides of an issue.
4. I know how to say "no" to people.
5. There is usually a way to solve a problem.
6. I know what my priorities are at all times.

Do You Draw on Your Inner Resources to Make Your Work Effective and Satisfying?

1. I always think about what can be done in a situation.
2. I feel that I am competent and effective in my work.
3. I encourage myself to try new things.
4. I am able to say what I feel to others.
5. I don't let negative feelings build up until I explode.
6. I listen to my hunches.

Are You an Effective Master of the Changes Taking Place Around You?

1. I enjoy doing new things.

	Very Much Like Me	Somewhat Like Me	Not Sure	Somewhat Unlike Me	Not at All Like Me
2. When I find myself upset about a change, I can change my feelings.	_____	_____	_____	_____	_____
3. I'm not likely to blame other people for my problems.	_____	_____	_____	_____	_____
4. I feel the future is likely to be better than the past.	_____	_____	_____	_____	_____
5. When I experience a lot of change, I take time off to get my bearings.	_____	_____	_____	_____	_____
6. When something doesn't work, I look for another strategy.	_____	_____	_____	_____	_____
7. There's always a better way to do things, and I try to find it.	_____	_____	_____	_____	_____

Do You Have a Clear Sense of Your Personal Mission, Meaning, Purpose, and Goals at Work?

1. I know what I stand for.	_____	_____	_____	_____	_____
2. I am willing to take a stand for my basic values.	_____	_____	_____	_____	_____
3. My workplace shares the same basic values I have.	_____	_____	_____	_____	_____
4. I have a vision of where I want to be going.	_____	_____	_____	_____	_____
5. My work feels meaningful and important.	_____	_____	_____	_____	_____
6. I like what my agency stands for.	_____	_____	_____	_____	_____
7. I feel that my life is organized around some basic goals.	_____	_____	_____	_____	_____

How Much Does Your Agency Encourage You to Use Your Fullest Capacities, Stay Healthy, and Grow?

1. My agency has a clear and consistent set of values.	_____	_____	_____	_____	_____
2. I am included in decisions that affect me at work.	_____	_____	_____	_____	_____
3. I feel that my supervisors have my best interests at heart.	_____	_____	_____	_____	_____
4. I am expected to help my agency improve and do a better job.	_____	_____	_____	_____	_____
5. I am learning new things in my job.	_____	_____	_____	_____	_____
6. My workplace is concerned about my health and encourages me to pursue healthy behavior.	_____	_____	_____	_____	_____

	Very Much Like Me	Somewhat Like Me	Not Sure	Somewhat Unlike Me	Not at All Like Me
7. People's feelings and needs are respected in my agency.	____	____	____	____	____
8. My agency regularly changes in response to new information that suggests changes are appropriate.	____	____	____	____	____
Total	____	____	____	____	____

EXERCISE

7

ASSESSING THE QUALITY OF WORK GROUP PERFORMANCE[8]

The questions below can be used by a group of workers to assess the quality of their performance. Typically this assessment would be completed by everyone in the work group, then the answers would be summarized and discussed by group members (e.g., during a staff meeting or a staff development program). Part of the discussion would include identifying items the group would like to address and specific actions each member would take to improve the quality of the group's performance. Circle your responses.

Step 1: Talk with your supervisor and co-workers to see if they might be interested in assessing the quality of the group's performance. This might be the subject of a future staff or team meeting, for example.

Step 2: Decide who will ask everyone in the group to complete the questionnaire as well as why. For example, you or your supervisor might announce it at a staff meeting, or circulate a memo, or do it more informally in one-to-one discussions.

Step 3: Ask everyone to either return the questionnaires to one person (who will tally the responses), or share how they answered each question during a group discussion (where the agenda would be to discuss group performance item by item).

Step 4: As a group, select the top one to three items that you would like to improve. Then, for each item, develop a list of action steps the group will take and who will be responsible for each.

---

[8]Adapted from Beverly Whiddon, "The Effect of Congruence on the Relationships Between Participation/Job Discretion and Staff Performance." Unpublished Ph.D. dissertation (Tallahassee: Florida State University, 1982), cited in Patricia Yancey Martin and Gerald G. O'Connor, *The Social Environment: Open Systems Applications* (New York: Longman, 1989), p. 225.

Step 5: Readminister the survey in about six months to a year to set a new quality improvement agenda and to see how well the first one was achieved.

	Strongly Disagree	Disagree	No Opinion	Agree	Strongly Agree
In general, the direct staff in my work group:					
1. are energetic in their jobs.	1	2	3	4	5
2. try to find the best alternatives in offering services to consumers.	1	2	3	4	5
3. use the supervisory relationship to its fullest advantage.	1	2	3	4	5
4. do required assignments, such as federally required paperwork, on time and accurately.	1	2	3	4	5
5. seem familiar with state and federal laws that affect their consumers.	1	2	3	4	5
6. take pride in their individual work.	1	2	3	4	5
7. work cooperatively with other staff.	1	2	3	4	5
8. take the initiative and are "self-starters" in their work.	1	2	3	4	5
9. seem reluctant to just "go by the book" in offering services to their consumers.	1	2	3	4	5
10. demonstrate knowledge of and make use of departmental regulations.	1	2	3	4	5
11. demonstrate knowledge of and make use of professional skills necessary in working with their consumers.	1	2	3	4	5
12. take pride in the work of their group.	1	2	3	4	5
13. seldom wait to be told what to do.	1	2	3	4	5
14. demonstrate flexibility in dealing with consumers.	1	2	3	4	5
15. seem interested in giving an extra effort to do their jobs well.	1	2	3	4	5
16. often make use of other community resources when these might be appropriate for consumers.	1	2	3	4	5
17. seem to do as much as possible to fulfill the requirements of their jobs.	1	2	3	4	5

	Strongly Disagree	Disagree	No Opinion	Agree	Strongly Agree
18. act as advocates for consumers within the parameters of the regulations and laws.	1	2	3	4	5

EXERCISE 8

CONSIDERING ADDITIONAL READINGS ABOUT THE SKILL OF INTEGRATING

Integrating for competent practice is indeed an ongoing process. It is also an effort that requires a high degree of skill. Chapter 12 was a preliminary introduction to a complex but important topic. The readings below will provide further information. Review this list as well as the footnotes in Lessons 1 and 2. Place a check mark beside those that interest you and make a commitment to review them by some future date. Also consider identifying other ways to learn more about the skill of integrating.

Accountability/Competence/Effectiveness

Biggerstaff, Marilyn A. "Licensing, Regulation, and Certification." In *Encyclopedia of Social Work,* 19th ed., 1616–1624. Washington, D.C.: National Association of Social Work, 1995.

Bloom, Martin, Joel Fischer, and John Orme. *Evaluating Practice: Guidelines for the Accountable Professional,* 2d ed. Englewood Cliffs, N.J.: Prentice-Hall, 1995.

Briar, Scott. "The Age of Accountability." *Social Work* (Jan. 1973): 2.

Fischer, Joel. *The Effectiveness of Social Casework.* Springfield, Ill.: Charles C. Thomas, 1976.

Gaither, Gerald R. *Assessing Performance in an Age of Accountability.* San Francisco, Calif.: Jossey-Bass, 1995.

Hodkinson, Phil, and Mary Issitt. *The Challenge of Competence (for the Caring Professions): Professionalism Through Vocational Education and Training.* New York: Cassell, 1995.

Murchison, Irene, Thomas S. Nichols, and Rachel Hansen. *Legal Accountability in the Nursing Process.* St. Louis, MO.: Mosby, 1978.

Rock, Barry D. "Goal and Outcome in Social Work Practice." *Social Work* 32 (Sept./Oct. 1987): 393–398.

Strom, Kimberly, and Ronald Green. "Continuing Education." In *Encyclopedia of Social Work,* 19th ed., 622–623. Washington, D.C.: National Association of Social Work, 1995.

Personal Growth

Bridges, William. *Job Shift: How to Prosper in a Workplace Without Jobs.* Reading, Mass.: Addison-Wesley, 1994.

Eldridge, William D. *The Challenge of Maturity: A Comprehensive Guide to Understand and Achieve Psychological and Social Self-Actualization as We Grow Older.* Lanham, Md.: University Press of America, 1995.

Gardner, J. W. *Self Renewal,* 4th ed. New York: W. W. Norton, 1981.

Grossman, Stephen R., Bruce E. Rodgers, and Beverly R. Moore. *Innovation, Inc.: Unlocking Creativity in the Workplace.* Plano, Tx.: Wordware, 1988.

Heath, Douglas H. *Fulfilling Lives: Paths to Maturity and Success.* San Francisco, Calif.: Jossey-Bass, 1991.

Jaffe, Dennis T., Cynthia D. Scott, and Glenn R. Tobe. *Rekindling Commitment: How to Revitalize Yourself, Your Work, and Your Organization*. San Francisco, Calif.: Jossey-Bass, 1994.

Quality

Brown, Stephen W., Evert Gummesson, Bo Edvardsson, and Bengtove Gustavsson. "Empowering Consumers with Public Human Services." *In Service Quality: Multidisciplinary and Multinational Perspectives*. Lexington, Mass.: Lexington Books, 1991.

Carr, David K., and Ian D. Littman. *Excellence in Government: Total Quality Management in the 1990s*, 2d ed. Arlington, Va.: Federal TQM Services, Coopers and Lybrand, 1993.

Dickens, Paul. *Quality and Excellence in Human Services*. New York: Wiley, 1994.

Evardsson, Bo, Bertil Thomasson, and John Ovretvelt. *Quality of Service: Making It Really Work*. New York: McGraw-Hill, 1994.

Gunther, John, and Frank Hawkins, eds. *Total Quality Management in Human Service Organizations*. NY: Springer Pub., 1996.

Juran, J. M., and Frank M. Gryna. *Juran's Quality Control Handbook*. New York: McGraw-Hill, 1988.

Martin, Lawrence L. *TQM in Human Service Organizations*. Newbury Park, Calif.: Sage, 1993.

Woody, Robert Henley. *Quality Care in Mental Health: Assuring the Best Clinical Services*. San Francisco, Calif.: Jossey-Bass, 1991.

Integration

Berger, Robert L., James T. McBreen, and Marilyn Rifkin. "The Integrating Framework." In *Human Behavior: A Perspective for the Helping Professions*. New York: Longman, 1996.

Goldstein, Howard. *Social Work Practice: A Unitary Approach*. Columbia: University of South Carolina Press, 1973.

Gordon, Suzanne, Patricia Benner, and Nel Noddings, eds. *Caregiving: Readings in Knowledge, Practice, Ethics, and Politics*. Philadelphia, Pa.: University of Pennsylvania Press. 1996.

McMahon, Maria O'Neil. *The General Method of Social Work Practice: A Problem-Solving Approach*. Englewood Cliffs, N.J.: Prentice-Hall, 1990.

Mehr, Joseph. "Integrating Contemporary Strategies, Personal Relationship Skills, and the Supervisory Process." In *Human Services: Concepts and Intervention Strategies,* 5th ed. Boston, Mass.: Allyn & Bacon, 1992.

Parsons, R. J., S. H. Hernandez, and J. D. Jorgensen. "Integrated Practice: A Framework for Problem Solving." *Social Work* 33 (Sept./Oct. 1988): 417–421.

Teare, Robert J., and Bradford W. Sheafor. *Practice-Sensitive Social Work Education: An Empirical Analysis of Social Work Practice and Practitioners*. Alexandria, Va.: Council on Social Work Education, 1995.

Reflective Practice

Bisman, Cynthia. "Practitioner Observation: The Self-Monitoring of Practice." In *Social Work Practice: Cases and Principles*. Pacific Grove, Calif.: Brooks/Cole, 1994.

Dean, Ruth G. "Ways of Knowing in Clinical Practice." *Clinical Social Work Journal* 17 (Summer 1989): 116–127.

Goldstein, Howard. "The Knowledge Base of Social Work Practice: Theory, Wisdom, Analogue, or Art?" *Families in Society* 71 (Jan. 1990): 32–43.

Harrison, W. David. "Reflective Practice in Social Care." *Social Service Review* (Sept. 1987): 393–404.

Klein, Waldo C., and Martin Bloom. "Practice Wisdom." *Social Work* 6 (Nov. 1995): 799–807.

Mezirow, Jack, and associates. *Fostering Critical Reflection in Adulthood: A Guide to Transformative and Emancipatory Learning*. San Francisco, Calif.: Jossey-Bass, 1991.

Palmer, Anthony, Sarah Burns, and Chris Bulman, eds. *Reflective Practice in Nursing: The Growth of the Professional Practitioner*. Boston, Mass.: Blackwell, 1994.

Rein, Martin, and Sheldon White. "Knowledge for Practice." In *Handbook of the Social Services,* edited by Neil Gilbert and Harry Specht, 620–634. Englewood Cliffs, N.J.: Prentice-Hall, 1981.

Schon, Donald A. *The Reflective Practitioner: How Professionals Think in Action*. New York: Basic Books, 1983.

Smith, Robert M. *Learning to Learn Across the Life Span*. San Francisco, Calif.: Jossey-Bass, 1990.

Thomas, Alan M. *Beyond Education: A New Perspective on Society's Management of Learning*. San Francisco, Calif.: Jossey-Bass, 1991.

Yolloly, Margaret, and Mary Henkel, eds. *Learning and Teaching in Social Work: Towards Reflective Practice*. Bristol, Penn.: Jessica Kingsley, 1995.

Ethical Dilemmas

Corey, Gerald and Marianne Schneider Corey. *I Never Knew I Had a Choice*. Pacific Grove, Calif.: Brooks/Cole, 1993.

Gorovitz, Samuel. *Drawing the Line: Life, Death, and Ethical Choices in an American Hospital*. Philadelphia, Pa.: Temple University Press, 1991.

Hugman, Richard, ed. *Ethical Issues in Social Work*. Great Britain: Routledge, 1995.

Kane, Rosalie A., and Arthur L. Caplan, eds. *Everyday Ethics: Resolving Dilemmas in Nursing Home Life*. New York: Springer Publishing, 1990.

Monagle, John F., and David C. Thomasma. *Health Care Ethics: Critical Issues*. Gaithersburg, Md.: Aspen Publications, 1994.

Ogloff, James R. P. "Navigating the Quagmire: Legal and Ethical Guidelines." In David G. Martin and Allan D. Moore, *First Steps in the Art of Intervention: A Guidebook for Trainees in the Helping Professions*. Pacific Grove, Calif.: Brooks/Cole, 1994.

Reamer, Frederic G. "Ethics and Values." In *Encyclopedia of Social Work,* 19th ed., 893–902. Washington, D.C.: National Association of Social Work, 1995.

Rhodes, Margaret L. "Social Work Challenges: The Boundaries of Ethics." *Families in Society: The Journal of Contemporary Human Services* 73 (Jan. 1992): 40–47.

Royse, David, Surjit Singh Dhooper, and Elizabeth Lewis Rompf. "Ethical Dilemmas." In *Field Instruction: A Guide for Social Work Students,* 2d ed. New York: Longman, 1996.

ANSWERS TO SELECTED QUESTIONS AND EXERCISES

Answers to Chapter 1, Lesson 1

A N S W E R
1

The correct answers to Frame 7 are indicated by a check mark:

	Generic Content	Setting-Specific Content
1. Being able to identify the diagnostic labels used to classify consumers receiving mental health services.	____	✔
2. Being aware of the values underlying human service work in a variety of settings.	✔	____
3. Understanding the formulas used to determine whether a consumer is eligible for a particular form of financial aid.	____	✔
4. Being skilled in the role of collaborating with (helping) consumers to empower them to acquire needed services and behaviors.	✔	____
5. Being familiar with the causes, processes, and treatments for drug addiction in particular populations.	____	✔

Return to Frame 8, Chapter 1, Lesson 1, p. 15.

A N S W E R
2

The four key elements in the learning model that uses experiences as the sources for understanding and generating knowledge are indicated by a check mark:

✔ 1. Finding patterns in your experience.

____ 2. Writing down learning goals.

✔ 3. Thinking about your experience.

____ 4. Using a variety of resources to meet your learning needs.

✔ 5. Having concrete experience.

✔ 6. Experimenting with new behaviors based on your experiences.

_____ 7. Charting your progress toward learning goals.

_____ 8. Taking extensive notes to document what you have learned.

Turn to Frame 9, Chapter 1, Lesson 1, p. 16.

ANSWER

3

The learning habits in column B are matched to their characteristics in column A (see the boldface letters).

Column A *Characteristics of Learning*	Column B *Learning Habit*
C 1. Questioning the rationale for a particular answer choice and suggesting an alternative.	A. Observing sensitively
E 2. Being able to learn from a variety of situations—such as self, instructors, supervisors, consumers, and television.	B. Listening to understand
A 3. "I learn a lot by keeping my eyes open."	C. Thinking critically
B 4. Being more interested in what another person is saying than in how you are going to respond.	D. Increasing self-awareness
F 5. Taking someone to lunch whose beliefs you do not share.	E. Cultivating variety
D 6. Keeping a journal of the feelings you have as you complete the program of learning in this text.	F. Openness to change

Return to Frame 12, Chapter 1, Lesson 1, p. 18.

Answers to Chapter 1, Lesson 3

1. The systems approach or systems thinking stresses:

	True	*False*
A. wholeness.	✔	
B. relationships.	✔	
C. arguments about what is and is not a system.		✔
D. environments.	✔	
E. using drawings and tables to display the system.	✔	
F. searching for the one complete model.		✔
G. understanding the purpose or goal of a system.	✔	
H. that all systems are equally complex.		✔

4. Why should a human service worker consider the four levels of system complexity—the framework system, the control system, the biological system, and the human or social systems? *To appreciate that human systems are likely the most complex of those we know and to use this sensitivity to cultivate an attitude of humility that recognizes we'll never be able to fully understand any human situation; but we can use the systems approach to come closer to understanding and being better able to help.*

Your answer might be similar to this—or you might have other ideas. Return to Frame 5, Chapter 1, Lesson 3, p. 46.

1. The Jones family has been served by at least two of the five program subsystems described in Frame 5 of this lesson. Recall that these five program subsystems were health, mental health, education, social welfare, and criminal justice. The first human service worker to help the Jones family was from the education subsystem. The agency to which the family was referred is probably part of the ___*mental health*___ subsystem.

2. The agency to which the Jones family was referred was intervening in two primary areas of functioning. They are ___*emotional*___ functioning and ___*family*___ functioning. *You might also have identified education.*

3. Two approaches to service delivery are the comprehensive service center and separate independent agencies. Which approach to service delivery is illustrated in the Jones's case? ___*separate independent agencies*___

4. Two ways of viewing consumer populations are by broad categories, such as age or nature of the problem, and by level of helping. If you were to describe consumer populations in the Jones's case by age, which of the following would apply?

_____ Infants

✔ Children

_____ Adolescents

✔ Parents

_____ Elderly

5. If you were to describe the levels of consumer populations or levels of helping in the Jones's case, which of the following would apply? That is, at which level(s) were services provided in this case?

✔ Individual

✔ Family

_____ Organization

_____ Community

_____ Society

Return to Frame 7, Chapter 1, Lesson 3, p. 53.

Answers to Chapter 2, Lesson 1

ANSWER
6

If you correctly matched every statement with the obstacle, your answers will look like this:

1. P   **2.** R   **3.** C   **4.** E   **5.** E   **6.** R   **7.** C

How did you do? If you missed more than one or two, you might review Frame 4 on page 70 before going on. Otherwise, go on to Frame 6, Chapter 2, Lesson 1, p. 71.

ANSWER
7

Analysis of Mrs. Collins's Needs

Areas of Need	Levels of Functioning					Obstacles to Functioning
	(1)	(2)	(3)	(4)	(5)	
Physical functioning				X		Mrs. Collins has a personal deficiency, a large tumor, that requires immediate medical treatment.
Emotional functioning				X		Her emotional state is near panic, and she is refusing to face her situation realistically. This is also a personal deficiency.
Education and employment			X			Since she is receiving public assistance, it is highly probable that she is either unemployed or is able to earn only low wages. This is probably an environmental deficiency.
Financial functioning		X				Although she manages her income well, it is a very limited amount that she is apparently unable to increase through employment. Rigid laws fix public assistance grants at unrealistically low levels.
Transportation*	X					
Family*	X					
Housing*	X					
Safety and security*	X					
Spiritual and aesthetic*	X					
Leisure and recreation*	X					

*Since this is a crisis situation, the focus is on the major problem. No information was received that any of the remaining areas were causing problems.

Turn to Frame 8, Chapter 2, Lesson 1, p. 74.

Answers to Chapter 2, Lesson 2

ANSWER

You should have selected C: a combination of individual and family responsibility supplemented by some public aid and private charitable organizations.

Return to Frame 6, Chapter 2, Lesson 2, p. 84.

ANSWER

9

You should have answered as follows:

Question 1 = B. The social changes during the industrial age helped the growth of a comprehensive human service system.

Question 2 = A. Social changes during the industrial age created new concerns about problems of unemployment, poverty, working conditions, and civil rights.

Go on to Frame 8, Chapter 2, Lesson 2, p. 87.

ANSWER

10

You should have selected C: social changes during the information age have brought a new ideological approach to human services focused on efforts to reform delivery systems, reduce federal expenditures, eliminate or cut back programs, and increase competition for scarce resources.

Return to Frame 10, Chapter 2, Lesson 2, p. 88.

Answers to Chapter 3, Lesson 1

ANSWER 11

Look back over your answers and see if you can detect a trend. For example, do you see yourself as a helping person? Do others see you that way? Do people, rather than things, catch your attention? Are you comfortable with yourself? Do you share yourself with others to develop closer relationships?

Return to Frame 6, Chapter 3, Lesson 1, p. 144.

ANSWER 12

Your answers should be as follows:

1. dignity and respect
2. self-determination
3. confidentiality
4. competence
5. privacy

If you missed any of these, return to Frame 8. If you correctly identified all five human values, congratulations! Now turn to Frame 10, Chapter 3, Lesson 1, p. 148.

Answers to Chapter 3, Lesson 3

A N S W E R

13

You should have underlined the following responses:

1. dominance
2. social well-being
3. creativity and challenge

Return to Frame 5, Chapter 3, Lesson 3, p. 176.

A N S W E R

14

The correct answers are:

A. people
B. data
C. things

Return to Frame 7, Chapter 3, Lesson 3, p. 177.

A N S W E R

15

The correct answers are:

A. 4
B. 1
C. 3
D. 2

Return to Frame 9, Chapter 3, Lesson 3, p. 178.

A N S W E R

16

A. brokering
B. consumer advocating
C. mobilizing

Return to Frame 11, Chapter 3, Lesson 3, p. 180.

Your answers should look like this:

(Relating to consumers)   _3_   A. Worker introduces self to consumer and talks about feelings and needs in order to establish an open and trusting relationship for the future.

(Collaborating)   _2_   B. Worker evaluates efforts to achieve helping goals in order to determine the future course of the helping process.

(Intervening)   _1_   C. Worker leads regular group sessions of residents using reality therapy as the treatment modality in order to modify individual behavior.

Return to Frame 13, Chapter 3, Lesson 3, p. 181.

You should have underlined the following responses:

1. managing information
2. supervising "up"
3. integrating

Return to Frame 15, Chapter 3, Lesson 3, p. 182.

Answers to Chapter 4, Lesson 1

ANSWER

Your answers should look like this:

	Informal Resource System	Formal Resource System	Societal Resource System
1. City of Big Bend Welfare Department	___	___	✔
2. Big Bend Red Cross	___	___	✔
3. A Girl Scout troop interested in volunteer work with the developmentally disabled	___	✔	___
4. Federal Social Security office	___	___	✔
5. A private agency that tests the developmentally disabled	___	___	✔
6. A Salvation Army center	___	___	✔
7. A privately owned day care center	___	___	✔
8. Relatives of developmentally disabled clients	✔	___	___
9. Special classes for the developmentally disabled offered by the public schools of Big Bend	___	___	✔
10. Neighbors of parents of developmentally disabled children	✔	___	___

If you did not classify all these resources correctly, you need to review Frames 1 and 2 before you go on. If you classified them all correctly, return to Frame 4, Chapter 4, Lesson 1, p. 199.

ANSWER

20

In order to get to know her community and the resources that are available, Alice could (1) try consulting any directories that the city of Flatlands or its chamber of commerce may have published; or (2) start developing her own resource file by talking to other workers in her agency and different residents of Flatlands; or (3) try visiting some of the other agencies in the community and get to know some of the workers in these agencies.

You have completed Lesson 1, Chapter 4. Continue with Lesson 2 and keep up the good work.

Answers to Chapter 4, Lesson 2

ANSWER
21

You could have answered by checking number 8. Kim was able to help Mr. Lane to recognize a need he could address by using all the skills identified. Do you agree? Why or why not?

Return to Frame 4, Chapter 4, Lesson 2, p. 204.

ANSWER
22

Some of the ways in which Seth might facilitate Jason's approach to employment are: (1) talking with Jason about his feelings toward getting a job and seeking help from the welfare department; (2) involving Jason in planning how he might find and use a resource that can help him and possibly rehearsing with Jason ways of approaching a resource for help; and (3) describing the types of resources that are available to assist him in locating a job.

Return to Frame 6, Chapter 4, Lesson 2, p. 206.

ANSWER
23

In proper order, the best ways to help George are as follows:

___3___ Get an appointment for George with some of the resources that can help him and make sure George has this information.

___4___ Spend time helping George to keep his appointments, possibly escorting him for his first visits.

___1___ Talk with George directly about his situation, explaining the resources you might refer him to for assistance.

___2___ Contact the resources you and George have agreed might offer him assistance with his needs.

If you had any trouble with this task, return to Frame 4 for a review. If you answered correctly, go on to Frame 7, Chapter 4, Lesson 2, p. 206.

ANSWER
24

Your follow-up with Eric has shown you that he needs your assistance in getting medical attention. Some of the ways you might help Eric get this service are (1) telephoning or going to see the nurse in charge and trying to enlist her support in getting an appointment as soon as possible; (2) discussing the situation with Eric to see if he behaved in a way that resulted in his request being refused; (3) finding out whether you had adequately prepared Eric for this referral—that is, whether he knew what to do and how to get the appointment; and (4) going to your supervisor and asking for assistance in the matter. In addition to these actions, you can probably think of a number of other ways to help Eric.

You have now completed Lesson 2, Chapter 4. Go on to Lesson 3, p. 209.

Answers to Chapter 4, Lesson 3

ANSWER

You should have circled the following:

A. Not helpful
B. Helpful
C. Not helpful
D. Not helpful
E. Helpful

If you missed *any* of these, you need to return to Frame 3 for a review.
If you answered all of these examples correctly, go on to Frame 5, Chapter 4, Lesson 3, p. 211.

ANSWER
26

You should have selected C. Art is talking informally with Mrs. Lane and is using this opportunity to find out if she knows of any residents in the community who might be helped by a new program that is being developed.
Return to Frame 7, Chapter 4, Lesson 3, p. 213.

ANSWER
27

Correct. Marty has used the technique of observation to discover an individual who needs assistance. The best thing for Marty to do would be to reach out by introducing himself to this woman and finding out if there is anything he can do to help her.
Go on to Frame 8, Chapter 4, Lesson 3, p. 213.

ANSWER
28

We don't think this is the best approach for this situation. Even though Marty is not assigned specific work in the waiting room, he has observed an individual who may need assistance. The best thing for Marty to do would be reach out and offer to help this individual.
You may want to review Frame 5 on page 211 before you go on to Frame 8, Chapter 4, Lesson 3, p. 213.

Answers to Chapter 5, Lesson 1

ANSWER

29

You should have checked A, B, C, and D. If you answered correctly, you have a good understanding of why consumers sometimes need worker advocates.

If you had any trouble with Frame 2, return to Frame 1 for a quick review. Then go to Frame 3, Chapter 5, Lesson 1, p. 221.

ANSWER

30

Sorry, but if you were to take this action, your attempt to help Marcy would probably fail. Before you decide to begin advocating on behalf of any consumer, you should (1) try other means of solving the problem, (2) discuss the situation with the consumer and get the person's consent, and (3) make certain the complaint or grievance is legitimate. Return to Frame 4, Chapter 5, Lesson 1, p. 221 and see if you can choose the correct action to take in this situation.

ANSWER

31

Excellent! This action shows that you are carefully considering Marcy's situation and are first making an attempt to solve her problem by discussing the situation again with the head nurse. You are also involving Marcy in your actions, and both of you are making certain that her complaint is legitimate. You've demonstrated a good understanding of the three factors that are important to consider before any advocating begins. Go on to Frame 5, Chapter 5, Lesson 1, p. 222.

ANSWER

32

This response demonstrates that little effort is being made to understand Marcy's situation and indicates a patronizing attitude toward Marcy by attempting to exclude her involvement. You should return to Frame 1 on page 219 and start Lesson 1, Chapter 5 on page 219 again.

ANSWER

33

These are some of the reasons Mike's attempt at advocating on Eric's behalf failed:

1. Mike did not take the time to find out from Eric what specific actions he felt were cruel and unjust, who specifically was treating him unjustly, and what he wanted changed.
2. Mike was also unsuccessful because he did not make any effort to find out exactly who he should contact. Running to the first doctor he saw in the hall made it likely that his efforts would fail.

3. Mike also failed to check whether Eric's complaint was legitimate before he made his hasty and irresponsible decision to begin advocating.

Did you think of any other reasons why Mike's efforts failed? We hope so, since this situation is a good example of the need to consider a consumer's situation carefully before you begin advocating. It is also a good example of what can happen when you fail to practice the three basic principles of any advocating technique.

Go on to Frame 8, Chapter 5, Lesson 1, p. 223.

ANSWER

34

Yes, Roy has done a good job of clearly stating the problem situation to Mr. Mann. Return to Frame 9 and see if you can underline exactly where Roy made his clear statement of the problem to Mr. Mann, then go on to Frame 10, Chapter 5, Lesson 1, p. 225.

ANSWER

35

You should have underlined the following sentence: "We would like you to allow Doris to stay in her apartment, and we assure you the rent will be paid."

If you had any trouble identifying this statement, you may want to review Frame 8 on page 223. Go on to Frame 12, Chapter 5, Lesson 1, p. 225.

ANSWER

36

Are you sure you read the last paragraph in Frame 10? Roy did remember to make use of the fourth part of persuading by restating what he and Mr. Mann had agreed to before they hung up. If you are still uncertain, you may want to review Frames 8, 9, and 10 on pages 223–225. Otherwise, go on to Frame 13, Chapter 5, Lesson 1, p. 226.

ANSWER

37

Right. Roy did remember to use the fourth part of persuading before they hung up by restating what he and Mr. Mann had agreed to regarding Doris. Return to Frame 13, Chapter 5, Lesson 1, on p. 226.

ANSWER

38

Situation 1. You should have checked C, blunt assault, since this worker is not taking any time to find any common ground, nor is he simply trying to be frank and honest and lay his cards on the table. He is bluntly saying to this supervisor that he is opposed to the decision that denied a consumer treatment and that he is going to fight the decision in any way he can.

Situation 2. You should have checked A, common ground, since this worker is starting his persuading efforts by trying to find where he and the receptionist can agree before he starts to reveal the facts concerning the consumer who needs the information.

Situation 3. You should have checked B, cards on the table, since this worker is being straightforward and frank concerning Mr. Blink's situation and what action needs to be taken.

How well did you do? You should have answered all three of these situations correctly. If you did, go on to Frame 15 on page 228.

If any of your answers to the situations in Frame 14 were incorrect, you should review Frame 13 on page 226 before going on to Frame 15, Chapter 5, Lesson 1, p. 228.

ANSWER
39

No, persuasion involves making an effort to understand the other side's position, but this is usually *not* the case when pressuring is employed. Return to Frame 16 on page 228 for a review of pressuring before you try Frame 17, Chapter 5, Lesson 1, p. 229 again.

ANSWER
40

Correct. Pressuring differs from persuasion in that it involves the use of *forceful action*. In persuasion, the emphasis is on understanding the other side's position and appealing to reason. Go on to Frame 18, Chapter 5, Lesson 1, p. 230.

ANSWER
41

No, both *persuasion* and *pressuring* involve making appeals to reason in order to change decisions and actions. Return to Frame 16 on page 228 for a review of pressuring before you try Frame 17, Chapter 5, Lesson 1, p. 229 again.

ANSWER
42

No! Pressuring is a powerful advocating technique and must be used with a great deal of planning and caution. Should you think there is a need for pressuring, you should discuss the situation with your supervisor and fellow workers. Return to Frame 16, Chapter 5, Lesson 1, p. 228 for a careful review.

ANSWER
43

You are partially correct—but there is one other thing to remember when pressuring is being used. Return to Frame 18, Chapter 5, Lesson 1, p. 230 and select a more complete answer.

ANSWER

44

You are partially correct—but there is one other thing to remember when pressuring is being used. Return to Frame 18, Chapter 5, Lesson 1, p. 230 and select a more complete answer.

ANSWER

45

No. Pressuring is not undertaken just because a consumer is dissatisfied with agency decisions affecting him. There are other activities and other advocating techniques that should be tried *before* you decide to turn to the pressuring technique.

Review Frame 16, then answer Frame 18, Chapter 5, Lesson 1, p. 230 correctly.

ANSWER

46

Right. Pressuring is an advocating technique that should be used with a great deal of caution *and* with strong support and a great deal of assistance from your supervisor. Return to Frame 19, Chapter 5, Lesson 1, p. 230.

ANSWER

47

You are way off the mark with this answer. Remember that pressuring is a powerful technique, and since it relies on the use of force, it must be used with a great deal of caution. Review Frame 16 on page 228 about the technique of pressuring before you answer Frame 18, Chapter 5, Lesson 1, p. 230 correctly.

ANSWER

48

You should have checked 2, 4, and 6 as items that are *not* included in a written summary for a hearing. Review Frame 16 on page 228 if you answered incorrectly; otherwise, turn to Frame 20, Chapter 5, Lesson 1, p. 231.

Answers to Chapter 5, Lesson 2

ANSWER
49

You should have checked C. Legal rights are those recognized by law or policy and are theoretically enforceable. Human or natural rights belong to people because they are human beings and are not always enforceable because not all are recognized by law or policy. Proceed to Frame 3, Chapter 5, Lesson 2, page 235.

ANSWER
50

The correct answer is False. The concept of natural law is one that has been the subject of debate throughout history. There are many different interpretations of natural law, and some believe it does not exist at all. If you answered True, turn to Frame 1, Chapter 5, Lesson 2, page 233 for a review. If you answered correctly, proceed to Frame 3, Chapter 5, Lesson 2, page 235.

ANSWER
51

Correct. The right to the least restrictive alternative means that a developmentally disabled person should not be institutionalized if other services and programs in the community can meet his or her needs. Return to Frame 7, Chapter 5, Lesson 2, page 240.

ANSWER
52

No. The question asks about the meaning of the right to the least restrictive alternative for developmentally disabled persons. You chose an answer that describes aspects of consumer rights under circumstances of involuntary commitment. You may want to review Frame 5 before you consider the correct answer to Frame 6, Chapter 5, Lesson 2, page 239.

ANSWER
53

Yes, in most states developmentally disabled residents in institutions are entitled to fair wages if they perform work for the upkeep of the institution and if someone else would ordinarily be paid to do the work. Continue to the next question in Frame 8, Chapter 5, Lesson 2, page 240.

ANSWER
54

The correct answer is A. The right to treatment for the developmentally disabled means that people who are involuntarily institutionalized for a mental illness generally have the right to a professionally acceptable treatment plan. Recall that people with mental disabilities who do not live in an institution, and are therefore not in state custody, generally have no rights to community-based services under the Constitution. Turn to Frame 9, Chapter 5, Lesson 2, page 240.

ANSWER

You should have checked B, C, and E. If you missed any of these, review Frame 10 before proceeding to Frame 12. If you answered correctly, go directly to Frame 12, Chapter 5, Lesson 2, page 243.

ANSWER

56

Yes, in this situation, if you decided that Joe should not be allowed to attend sick call, and your only reason was that you were busy and did not want to be bothered, then you were denying Joe his right to receive adequate medical treatment. Even if you are working in a state thar does not give inmates in correctional settings clear rights to adequate medical treatment, you, as a human service worker, should try to see to it that inmates get the medical treatment they need. Continue to Frame 13, Chapter 5, Lesson 2, page 243.

ANSWER

57

The correct answer is D. Notice of rights means that an inmate will receive adequate advance notice of what conduct will result in discipline or punishment and written notice of any charges against him. Return to Frame 14, Chapter 5, Lesson 2, page 243.

ANSWER

58

The correct answer is False. At this writing, many homeless children experience difficulty accessing public education. This difficulty is due in part to inability to furnish required documentation concerning immunization records and proof of residence. Return to Frame 16 to answer statement B—Chapter 5, Lesson 2, page 245.

ANSWER

59

The correct answer is False. The right to adequate shelter is not guaranteed except by very few state constitutions. Return to Frame 16 to answer statement C—Chapter 5, Lesson 2, page 245.

ANSWER

60

The correct answer is True. Some states have indeed expanded how they define a resident of a state in order to ensure the homeless can exercise their right to vote. Return to Frame 16 to answer statement D—Chapter 5, Lesson 2, page 245.

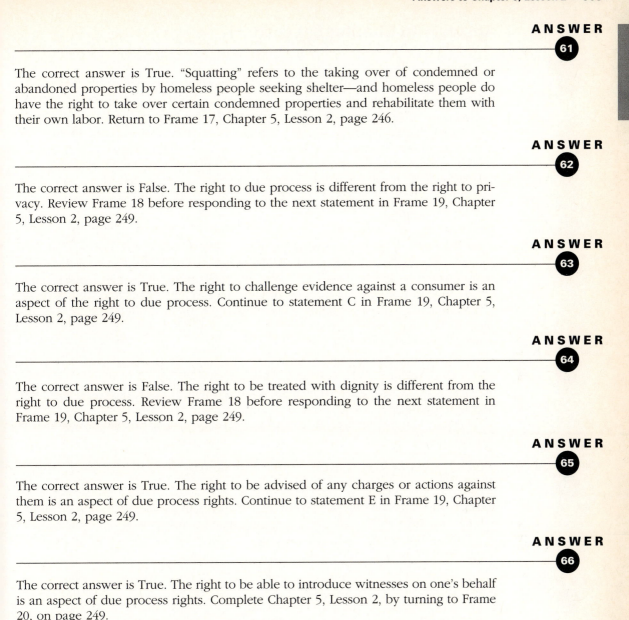

A N S W E R

61

The correct answer is True. "Squatting" refers to the taking over of condemned or abandoned properties by homeless people seeking shelter—and homeless people do have the right to take over certain condemned properties and rehabilitate them with their own labor. Return to Frame 17, Chapter 5, Lesson 2, page 246.

A N S W E R

62

The correct answer is False. The right to due process is different from the right to privacy. Review Frame 18 before responding to the next statement in Frame 19, Chapter 5, Lesson 2, page 249.

A N S W E R

63

The correct answer is True. The right to challenge evidence against a consumer is an aspect of the right to due process. Continue to statement C in Frame 19, Chapter 5, Lesson 2, page 249.

A N S W E R

64

The correct answer is False. The right to be treated with dignity is different from the right to due process. Review Frame 18 before responding to the next statement in Frame 19, Chapter 5, Lesson 2, page 249.

A N S W E R

65

The correct answer is True. The right to be advised of any charges or actions against them is an aspect of due process rights. Continue to statement E in Frame 19, Chapter 5, Lesson 2, page 249.

A N S W E R

66

The correct answer is True. The right to be able to introduce witnesses on one's behalf is an aspect of due process rights. Complete Chapter 5, Lesson 2, by turning to Frame 20, on page 249.

Answers to Chapter 6, Lesson 1

ANSWER

You should have underlined the words *unmet* and *met,* since Mrs. R.'s need for low-cost day care is not being met, although the community need for day care is being met. There may be many reasons for the fact that Mrs. R.'s need is not being met. When human service workers or others in a community find several such cases, it is time to mobilize resources to deal with this as an unmet community need.

Go on to Frame 3, Chapter 6, Lesson 1, p. 258.

ANSWER

68

Hank has remembered questions 1, 2, and 3. He has neglected, however, to find out how nonresidents—merchants, professionals—and so on—see the problems; consequently, he has no basis for comparing their perceptions with those of community residents. If you had trouble with this question, review Frame 1 on page 256 before going on to Frame 4. Otherwise, proceed to Frame 4, Chapter 6, Lesson 1, p. 258.

ANSWER

69

Identifying unmet needs in a community is the activity that must take place *before* mobilization can begin.

Review Frame 8 on page 261 before answering Frame 9, Chapter 6, Lesson 1, p. 262 correctly.

ANSWER

70

When a human service worker is meeting people with problems in the community and helping them obtain assistance, he is engaging in *brokering,* not mobilizing.

Review Frame 8 on page 261 before selecting the correct response to Frame 9, Chapter 6, Lesson 1, p. 262.

ANSWER

71

Correct. Mobilizing refers to the process of developing new services or linking existing services to fulfill an unmet community need.

Go on to Frame 10, Chapter 6, Lesson 1, p. 262.

ANSWER

72

You should have checked 2, 4, and 5, since many groups do not (a few do) make their needs known, and community resources are often resistant to changes in the policies and types of services offered. This makes it difficult to identify unmet needs, and also to mobilize resources to meet those needs that are identified.

Return to Frame 11, Chapter 6, Lesson 1, p. 262.

A N S W E R

73

You should have checked statements 1, 4, 5, and 7. Statements 2 and 3 are objectives of brokering, while statement 6 is an objective of advocating. Mobilizing objectives include making known resources accessible, getting resources to change their services or coordinate with other resources, gathering support, and assisting in establishing new services—all to help meet unmet community needs.

Return to Frame 12, Chapter 6, Lesson 1, p. 263.

A N S W E R

74

The most important step in the mobilizing process is carefully determining community needs. It makes little sense to mobilize a wide range of community resources if a related program or service already exists or if the girls in your halfway house are the only ones in need. If only your girls need the service, you could develop a small program in the halfway house itself, with as much community involvement as necessary.

The answers to how you would proceed are as follows:

1. How would you determine the need? Meetings with high school guidance counselors, employment service counselors, and chamber of commerce representatives might provide you with preliminary information on the extent of the need for specialized job training in the community.

2. How would you bring existing resources together? Once you have been able to at least estimate the number of girls who could benefit and the number of employers who would support the program, with some documentation, an interagency task force could be established by the local social planning agency or by your own agency.

3. How would you gather community support and acceptance? After several meetings of the task force, representatives are better able to identify resources and usually more prepared to share their own resources. Significant community leaders could then be approached for financial and/or moral support. A campaign to educate the public through news releases, public speaking, brochures, and so on, could also be an approach to gathering community support.

As you can see, the process of mobilizing involves the use of organizing and planning skills as well as skills needed for working with groups.

Go on to Frame 13, Chapter 6, Lesson 1, p. 263.

A N S W E R

75

No, a city commission is a group of individuals already formed to handle the business of a city. It would not be formed on a temporary basis.

Review Frame 13 on page 263 before answering Frame 14, Chapter 6, Lesson 1, p. 264 correctly.

ANSWER

Right! Committees can be formed on permanent and temporary bases to work toward the solution of a problem. Other community groups are formed, for the most part, to handle long-term problems.

Go on to Frame 15, Chapter 6, Lesson 1, p. 265.

ANSWER

No. A club is usually formed around a common interest in some activity, not for solving a specific community problem.

Review Frame 13 on page 263 before answering Frame 14, Chapter 6, Lesson 1, p. 264 correctly.

ANSWER

78

If you answered "an existing consumer group," you are right! It was not necessary for Wanda to form a committee or a council. Nor was it necessary for her to go to an official organization of any kind, since a consumer group interested in dealing with such a problem already existed within her community (the hospital).

If you answered anything else, review Frame 13 on page 263 before going on to Frame 16, Chapter 6, Lesson 1, p. 265.

ANSWER

79

The correct answer is E. To help get a service or program started that will meet a need, you should develop a plan of action, gather support, and recruit residents to form a group that will be responsible for either establishing a new community service or bringing together existing resources to meet the need.

Go on to Frame 17, Chapter 6, Lesson 1, p. 265.

Answers to Chapter 6, Lesson 2

ANSWER 80

You should have put an *I* next to items 2, 3, and 6, and an *F* next to items 1, 4, and 5. Generally in informal meetings, while all take part, one person assumes the role of leader. If this does not occur, little will be accomplished.

Return to Frame 3, Chapter 6, Lesson 2, p. 269.

ANSWER 81

You should have circled *formal* in the first case and *informal* in the second.

Go on to Frame 4, Chapter 6, Lesson 2, on p. 269.

ANSWER 82

No, sending letters is not necessarily the best way to get people to attend meetings, particularly a first meeting. It should be used only as a last resort, although it is a good way to remind people of the meeting once they have been contacted in other ways.

Review Frame 1 on page 266 before answering Frame 4, Chapter 6, Lesson 2, p. 269 correctly.

ANSWER 83

Excellent! By taking the time to visit each individual on a personal basis and explaining the purpose of the meeting and the importance of his or her attending, you are conveying to that person that he or she is important to and needed by the group.

Go on to Frame 5, Chapter 6, Lesson 2, p. 269.

ANSWER 84

This may be a useful second alternative, but it is not the best method. Calling may also be a useful way of reminding people of the meeting.

Review Frame 1 on page 266 before answering Frame 4, Chapter 6, Lesson 2, p. 269 correctly.

ANSWER 85

The best course of action would be to go by and visit Mr. Cranston again. His absence at the first meeting may have been avoidable. However, *do not* question him about why he did not attend. It is sufficient to say that he was missed and you hope he can make the upcoming meeting. To "write him off" because he missed the first meeting would be a mistake; Mr. Cranston may well have the potential to make valuable contributions to the group.

If you answered incorrectly, review Frame 1 on page 266 before going on to Frame 6, Chapter 6, Lesson 2, p. 269.

ANSWER
86

Two of the key activities in preparing for a meeting are:

1. Preparation of an agenda for everyone
2. Preparation of a meeting report to be sent to all those who attended and those who did not attend

Go on to Frame 7, Chapter 6, Lesson 2, p. 270.

ANSWER
87

You should have checked all the items. If you had any trouble, review Frame 1 on page 266 before going on to Frame 8, Chapter 6, Lesson 2, p. 270.

ANSWER
88

The correct answer is D. An agenda may be useful in helping members know what is going to happen at a meeting as well as for giving direction to the meeting.

Return to Frame 10, Chapter 6, Lesson 2, p. 271.

ANSWER
89

In addition to her success in keeping this committee moving forward, Mrs. Pope is probably also helping the committee to do the following:

1. See problems through to a solution and then move on to another one.
2. Take time at the end of each meeting to plan for the next one.
3. Plan meetings so that there will be time for all members to participate if they so desire.

Did you state at least two of the above? If so, go on to Frame 11. If not, review Frame 8 on page 270 briefly before going on to Frame 11, Chapter 6, Lesson 2, p. 271.

ANSWER
90

No, the enabler helps the group function independently. Return to Frame 11 on page 271 for a review before answering Frame 12, Chapter 6, Lesson 2, p. 272 correctly.

No, the organizer establishes groups by recruiting residents to work on solving problems. Review Frame 11 on page 271 to examine the five major roles before answering Frame 12, Chapter 6, Lesson 2, p. 272 correctly.

Correct. The gatekeeper's role is to keep the channels of communication open among members of groups by encouraging and facilitating participation of all members.
　　Return to Frame 13, Chapter 6, Lesson 2, p. 273.

No. There was a correct answer among the three choices given. Review Frame 11 on page 271, then select the correct role described in Frame 12, Chapter 6, Lesson 2, p. 272.

Correct. The enabler helps the group function better and become independent.
　　Go on to Frame 14, Chapter 6, Lesson 2, p. 273.

This is close, but not correct. The organizer helps establish groups to work on solving community problems. Once the group is formed and has selected a leader, the organizer shifts to become more of an enabler.
　　Review Frame 11 on page 271, then select the correct answer to Frame 13, Chapter 6, Lesson 2, p. 273.

No. The gatekeeper facilitates communication. Review Frame 11 on page 271 before answering Frame 13, Chapter 6, Lesson 2, p. 273 again.

No, the role of follower is a passive role. The follower rarely provides information or advice. Review Frame 11 on page 271 before choosing the correct answer to Frame 13, Chapter 6, Lesson 2, p. 273.

ANSWER

98

It would be difficult to fulfill this task until the problem has been clarified. Review Frame 14 on page 273, then answer Frame 15, Chapter 6, Lesson 2, p. 274 correctly.

ANSWER

99

Right! The first stage in problem solving is to help the group clarify the problem. This can be accomplished by obtaining information, complaints, and so forth, from those experiencing the problem.

Go on to Frame 16, Chapter 6, Lesson 2, p. 274.

ANSWER

100

Group members would have a difficult time deciding on the result they wish to achieve before they know what the problem is.

Review Frame 14 on page 273 before answering Frame 15, Chapter 6, Lesson 2, p. 274 correctly.

ANSWER

101

Yes, once the problem is clear and before ways are identified for solving the problem, it is necessary to decide on the desired results.

Go on to Frame 17, Chapter 6, Lesson 2, p. 275.

ANSWER

102

The task of identifying those methods to be used in solving the problem should not be taken up until another task is completed.

Review Frame 14 on page 273, then answer Frame 16, Chapter 6, Lesson 2, p. 274 correctly.

ANSWER

103

This would be premature. Before planning and organizing for action, methods for solving the problem should be identified and discussed.

Review Frame 14 on page 273 regarding the stages in problem solving, then answer Frame 16, Chapter 6, Lesson 2, p. 274 correctly.

In order to find out whether the group is accomplishing its goals, they must continuously evaluate the progress made to date. Lastly, follow-up action is needed to check on the solution to the problem. This will lead to information about how effectively the problem-solving process has worked and will identify additional unmet needs in the community, thereby setting in motion another problem-solving process.

Continue now with the Chapter 6 summary on p. 276.

Answers to Chapter 7, Lesson 1

ANSWER

1. Good eye contact.
2. Sitting in a position facing the consumer.
3. A relaxed (but not slouched) sitting position with a slight forward lean.
4. Open position (uncrossed arms and legs).

Return to Frame 4, Chapter 7, Lesson 1, p. 286.

ANSWER

You should have listed *what, how, when,* and *why. Why* questions are the least desirable because they tend to demand too much from consumers or put them in a defensive position.

If you missed any leads, review Frame 4 on page 286; otherwise, go to Frame 6, Chapter 7, Lesson 1, p. 287.

ANSWER

2. Male college student
  A. (Paraphrase): You said it is difficult to talk with your parents and they never seem to listen to you.
  B. (Reflection): You feel frustrated because your parents just offer money rather than listening to what you are trying to communicate.

3. 40-year-old man
  A. You have full responsibility for the house and children, a responsibility that you have never handled before, and although you do not miss your wife, you miss female company since your wife has been in the hospital. You find that it is difficult to work full time and take care of the household.
  B. You feel overwhelmed by your new double role as breadwinner and housekeeper. *(You often cannot be certain from a printed statement which feeling the person is experiencing. In this example and the preceding one, feelings other than "frustrated" and "overwhelmed" may also be correct answers. In this exercise you have to guess, whereas if you were actually interviewing the person, you would know the feelings he was experiencing from his nonverbal affect coupled with his words.)*

4. Male college student
  A. You have been dating someone you like for several months and did not realize she was also seeing someone else.
  B. You are angry and probably hurt and disappointed to learn that someone you like very much is going out with someone else while dating you.

5. 10-year-old girl in foster care
  A. You miss your parents and miss living at home. You don't like having to do chores and homework and haven't made friends in your new school.

B. You feel lonely for your parents and frustrated that you cannot go home.

6. 30-year-old woman
   A. You don't see any change in the problems in your life since you began seeing me two months ago.
   B. You feel that coming here is a waste of time, and you are angry with me because your husband is still drinking and your children are still in foster care.

7. 21-year-old woman
   A. You went to a weight-control group and were successful in losing weight, but since the first four weeks of attending the group, you have not stayed on your diet and have gained back the weight you lost.
   B. You feel discouraged and disgusted with yourself because you have gained back the weight you lost while attending a weight-control group.

8. 15-year-old in juvenile corrections facility
   A. You are doing everything you are supposed to do; your mother needs you at home, and you want to know what you can do to get out of here.
   B. You feel frustrated that you cannot leave here and help your mother at home.

9. 50-year-old alcoholic man in treatment center
   A. You know that you are an alcoholic, but now that you have dried out, you think you can handle the problem without attending AA meetings and can be a social drinker without any problems.
   B. You feel you have successfully completed this program, and you feel competent to handle your drinking on your own.

If you had difficulty, review Frame 7 on page 288 and write new responses to the statements. Try practicing paraphrasing and reflecting in your conversations with friends, with classmates, and with consumers if you are currently working in a human service setting. If you were able to paraphrase and reflect feelings accurately, go on to Frame 8, Chapter 7, Lesson 1, p. 290.

A N S W E R

108

---

1. A. Summarization (from past).

   B. Open request for information.

2. A. (3) is an open-ended question.

   B. Paraphrase or repeating key words.

   C. (4), (8), (10), (18).

3. Words used by consumer that need further definition: depression, shyness in public (how was this enacted?), insecurity, uncomfortable with the way my life was going.
   Since this was a termination interview, the worker's goals were to cease frequent contacts, evaluate progress, and assess whether the consumer wanted additional services at this point. The worker already knew what the preceding words actually meant to Ray.

4. A. (5) verbal follow
   B. (6) interpretation, support

C. (7) information giving
D. (9) reflection of feeling
E. (12) interpretation
F. (14) praise/support

5. The confrontation stimulated the consumer to explore further and deepen his self-understanding as expressed in Ray's response to (18), (19), (20), and (21).

Return to Frame 11, Chapter 7, Lesson 1, p. 295.

Answers to Chapter 7, Lesson 2

A 15-year-old female in a group home

1. A. This response misses important parts of the message and ignores all the consumer's feelings. Return to Frame 3 on page 302 and select another response.

B. This response is premature advice. The worker decided to ignore the consumer's feelings and overlooked an opportunity and need to express empathy. Had empathy been expressed, the worker would have had an opportunity to learn more about the situation. This response will only end communication. It is unlikely that the advice will be heeded; the advice only tells the consumer that talking with the worker will get her nowhere. Return to Frame 3 on page 302 and select another response.

C. This response expresses for the consumer the feelings that go with the situation and tells the consumer you are with her and are ready to continue trying to understand the situation. This is laying the base for developing a helping relationship and a helping plan. This is the appropriate choice.

D. This response refers to feelings but is not an accurate reflection of the consumer's feelings. It also closes discussion, as it draws a conclusion too quickly. Return to Frame 3 on page 302 and select another response.

A 19-year-old female college student

2. A. Making the assumption that the consumer became dependent is a premature interpretation and does not address the consumer's feelings. Return to Frame 3 on page 302 and select another response.

B. If you selected this response, you are on the way to learning to identify accurate empathy.

C. This addresses feelings, but incorrectly. The worker is reading his or her own script into what the consumer tried to communicate. Even if this were the case, it is the worker's job to address the *consumer's* feelings, not those of the consumer's significant other. Workers sometimes err in focusing attention on the person the consumer is concerned about rather than on the consumer; it is not helpful to attempt to understand the feelings of someone you have not met. Return to Frame 3 on page 302 and select another response.

D. The worker is looking for an interpretation of the consumer's behavior that is irrelevant and inaccurate and does not address the consumer's expressed feelings. Return to Frame 3 on page 302 and select another response.

If you missed the empathic responses, reread the section on empathy. If you identified the empathic responses, go on to Frame 4, Chapter 7, Lesson 2, p. 303.

ANSWER

1. The common error the worker made was to give premature and irrelevant advice. In both instances the ideas came from the worker's head; perhaps these were things the worker would have done for her- or himself, but they were not necessarily helpful ideas for the consumer. In fact, the worker did not bother to find out what the consumer wanted or what the sources of difficulty were.

2. This worker used closed-ended questions more frequently than any other skill. Closed questions and premature advice are common errors of beginning interviewers.

3. Of course there are various ways to restate the questions so they are open requests for information. A few examples of how this might be done include:

(5) "Do you go out at all?" could be stated as "What kinds of things do you and your husband do together?" or "What do you enjoy doing?" or "Give me some examples of things you and your husband have done together." It is unclear in the context of the interview why this question was asked; it implies an assumption on the part of the worker, namely, that because the consumer said her marriage was boring, she and her husband must not go out.

(8) "Tell me what is boring about your life," or "Can you tell me what 'boring' means to you?" *plus* "What would make your life more interesting?"

4 No. The worker does not follow closely what the consumer is actually trying to communicate. The worker seems to make assumptions and at times follow his or her own agenda.

5. Empathy. The worker does not reflect feelings and there is little expression of empathy with this consumer.

Return to Frame 5, Chapter 7, Lesson 2, p. 304.

ANSWER

1. Genuineness is a complex concept with multiple dimensions. It is not possible to point to *one* verbal or nonverbal behavior and say that it is genuineness; however, we think the characteristic exists, is important in the counseling relationship, and can be recognized as absent or present. Check to see if your answers included several of the following:

A. Using words the consumer can understand.

B. Not using jargon that is not part of your everyday style of communicating.

C. Congruence between your verbal and nonverbal behaviors and between your real feelings and what you express verbally.

D. Spontaneity.

E. Absence of defensiveness.

F. Avoidance of strong emphasis on a formal helping role and professional jargon.

G. Consistency between your values and your behavior.

H. Ability to be open and to share yourself honestly when this is helpful.

2. Several ways to express respect:

A. Demonstrate and *communicate high expectations* for the consumer; expect more of the consumer than the consumer expects of him- or herself.

B. Perceive the uniqueness of the consumer; express *unconditional regard* for the individual (we may not approve of some actions of people, yet we accept their unique, essential self).

C. Show your *willingness to work with the consumer,* your availability to the consumer, and your willingness to work on the consumer's issues and concerns.

D. Express your *commitment to self-determination* through implementation of the empowerment principles and through allowing and emphasizing consumer selection of goals and means for achieving goals.

Review Frame 5 on page 304 for other ways of expressing respect, then turn to Frame 7, Chapter 7, Lesson 2, p. 306.

ANSWER
112

No. The reason that Sue has failed to establish a helping relationship with Rose is her fear that their relationship would be damaged if she had to tell her that the assistance grant was being cut off. Sue is focusing too much attention on keeping things "pleasant and friendly" no matter what the circumstances, and this is not a characteristic of a helping relationship.

Return to Frame 11, Chapter 7, Lesson 2, p. 309.

ANSWER
113

1. A. (–) This response includes no empathy; it minimizes and generalizes the problem and ignores the consumer's feelings.

   B. (–) Again, the response ignores consumer feelings. This is a change in focus from the consumer's concern; it probably reflects an idea or a solution of the worker's, namely, that the consumer does not understand how hospitals work and that once the consumer understands this, the problem will be resolved. The worker ignores the consumer's concerns; also, a closed, irrelevant question.

   C. (–) This is advice; it is a good suggestion and might be more helpful if the worker had first reflected the consumer's feelings and then made the suggestion.

   D. (–) This is really ignoring the consumer's feelings and concerns. It is inappropriate advice giving that minimizes as well as ignores the consumer's feelings.

2. A. (–) A minimal prompt that does not express empathy.

   B. (–) This may be an attempt to express empathy; however, it is not accurate.

   C. (–) This is another attempt to express empathy, but it's off the mark. The consumer did not specify employers and did not express this much anger.

   D. (+) This seems to hit the mark and to include consumer feelings without distorting the message or adding the worker's ideas.

3. A. (+) This shows active listening, paraphrasing to validate the problem situation the consumer describes, and empathy to surface expressed but not yet labeled feelings of excitement and worry.

B. (−) Not accurate; it's more an interpretation than an expression of empathy.

C. (−) This is advice giving and a minimization of the problem.

D. (−) The worker ignores the consumer's feelings and responds with her or his own feelings; a judgmental remark and an appropriate self-disclosure.

4. A. (−) The worker ignores the consumer's expression and interprets the consumer's feeling.

B. (−) Again, ignores the consumer's feelings; minimizes; remark is manipulative and shows a lack of respect and a lack of genuineness.

C. (−) Response is inappropriate and probably not a truthful self-disclosure; also, it shows an absence of respect and genuineness.

D. (−) This response changes the topic focus and ignores the problem—the worker may have decided that this consumer sees all workers as not liking him, thus interpreting the consumer's statement without taking the time to find out what is going on. The worker also asks an inappropriate closed question.

5. A. (−) The response ignores consumer's feelings and experience and interprets consumer's reactions prematurely and probably inaccurately.

B. (−) Again, the response ignores consumer's concern, minimizes it, and attempts to change the focus.

C. (−) Again, the worker ignores the consumer and prematurely interprets the consumer's reaction; this might also be called a judgmental remark.

D. (+) This is close, though it could be improved had the worker said that the consumer feels that she or he is not receiving help from the psychiatrist.

Go to Frame 12, Chapter 7, Lesson 2, p. 312.

Answers to Chapter 7, Lesson 3

ANSWER
114

Check to see if the four items you listed are included below:

1. Ability to stand back
2. Ability to learn from others
3. Ability to respect differences in beliefs and views
4. Ability to see the ways of others as preferable
5. Ability to respect differences in the ways people do things
6. Ability to respect the choices of others
7. Ability to respect the values of others
8. Ability to value different lifestyles and coping styles

Turn to Chapter 7, Lesson 2, Frame 6, p. 321.

ANSWER
115

There are a number of ways to complete this ecomap; there is no single, correct way to draw the connections. Nevertheless, think about any differences between the way you completed the map and the ecomap shown on page 626..

You have completed Lesson 3, which is also the end of Chapter 7 on relating to consumers. Go on to the chapter summary on page 326.

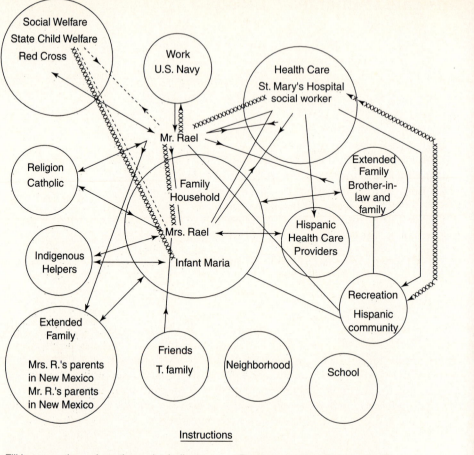

Instructions

Fill in connections where they exist. Indicate nature of connections with a descriptive word or by drawing different kinds of lines. In practice, ask consumers how they experience the relationship.

Draw arrows along lines to signify the flow of energy, resources. Identify significant people. Fill in empty circles or add others as needed.

——————— Strong relationship
- - - - - - - Tenuous relationship
xxxxxxxx Stressful relationship
No line means that there
is no relationship.

Answers to Chapter 8, Lesson 1

Step 1: Anticipatory empathy is something the worker practices before meeting the consumer; however, some of the worker's statements reflect that she had taken time to think about how the consumer was likely to feel. Thus, you should have written (12) in the space for Step 1, for this is where the worker shows anticipatory empathy. Examples of anticipatory empathy are "I know this is not a trip you wanted to make" and "You are probably feeling that we are all against you."

Step 2: There is no evidence of Step 2 in the dialogue. Preparing a comfortable physical setting is done before the worker meets with the consumer.

Step 3: There are several instances of Step 3. The following numbered sentences are steps in an appropriate initial greeting: (1), (2), (3), (5), (7), and (8).

Step 4: The orientation process is exemplified in (12), (13), and (15). Given that this was a nonvoluntary, angry consumer, the worker needed to take time initially to explain the agency's goal and her goals and intentions. The worker simply began by trying to increase the consumer's comfort and by trying to help the consumer develop positive feelings and expectation.

Step 5: No examples of opening statements.

Continue reading Frame 3, Chapter 8, Lesson 1, p. 337.

You should have underlined and circled the words listed below.

Inference (words that should be underlined):

disoriented
wandering aimlessly
abusive
angry
messy
poorly dressed
had not bathed for days
disturbed
disconnected
rambled

Behavioral descriptions (words that should be circled):

stopping individuals, asking them for money to buy food
brought him into the mental health center
wearing a jacket that was two sizes too big for him; it had tears in the sleeves and was covered with dirt and spots
did not know the day of the week or the year
looked away from the worker when he talked
did not answer questions
described situations that did not relate to the worker's questions

You may infer that someone is "wandering aimlessly." A behavioral description would be: "Robert walked around the same six blocks for an hour." "Abusive" and "angry" also are inferences, unless examples of Robert's behavior that led to this conclusion are given. In describing appearance you would express what you actually see, rather than infer that Robert is "messy" and "poorly dressed." Further, it is helpful to describe what Robert does rather than simply state that the consumer is "disturbed." "Disturbed" may mean different things to different people. Without knowing what the consumer is doing, we do not have the information we need either to make an assessment or to pinpoint targets for change. This segment of a case record would be strengthened had the worker included an example of a situation described by the consumer that did not relate to a question asked him by the worker.

Go to Frame 6, Chapter 8, Lesson 1, p. 339.

ANSWER
118

Possible responses:

1. *Consumer strengths:* The family has been together consistently for a long time; flexibility and some adaptive skills as shown in Mrs. Coe's going to work and the family's move from a farm; concerned about grandmother and children and about providing a home for them; recognize problems and ask for help.

2. *Situational strengths:* Own their own home; children like the town; some resources for mother and son.

3. *Family and community factors:* Close family, commitment to helping family; tradition of contact with extended family; need more information on community contacts and neighborhood relationships; adults may miss the relationships enjoyed in country—need more information on this. Family interactions: husband's role is threatened due to unemployment; recent changes, such as wife working; adolescent son beginning to conflict with parental expectations; mother sees youngest child as never doing anything right.

4. *Physiological and medical factors:* Need more information on youngest son, probably a psychological evaluation; grandmother's mental and physical health deteriorating.

5. *Cultural, ethnic, and religious factors:* May need to ask about these issues to get a picture of their culture as a farm family; do not have information about religion.

6. *Past history:* Parents met in high school and married two years after Mrs. Coe completed high school (they have been married 18 years); no problems with eldest two children as they were growing up; current problems with eldest and with youngest child. Grandmother and father had difficulties adjusting to the new community; father was "breadwinner" when they lived on the farm and continues to work, but employment opportunities sporadic.

7. *Potential for change:* Need more information; no indication they are not motivated to change; change in attitudes about youngest child may be difficult, as mother has had negative expectations for a fairly long time. Coping styles need to be explored—how did they handle past problems? Mother is able to request help. Have they had other experiences with human service workers?

8. *Behavioral excesses:* Mother may be too negative in interacting with youngest child (this needs to be further explored and observed, preferably through home visit or specific data from mother regarding her interactions); conflicts with eldest child.

9. *Behavioral deficits:* Grandmother losing ability to care for herself and help around the house; parents' skills in communicating with eldest son and youngest son may be lacking (need more information); Mr. Coe may need job-seeking skills or additional work skills to secure more reliable employment; adaptation to new environment and lifestyle; husband's ability to adjust to wife's new role as income provider; husband may need more skills around the house and in interacting with children.

Some of your responses or choices may vary from those given above. You may pick up a component not included above, or you might have decided that a particular factor belonged under a different component than the one it was placed under here. This does not mean that your choice was incorrect, since there is no one correct way to complete this exercise. It would be an interesting and valuable learning experience to discuss your responses and perceptions with your classmates. Go to Frame 9, Chapter 8, Lesson 1, p. 344.

Answers to Chapter 8, Lesson 2

ANSWER

119

1. The importance of the concern to the consumer.
2. The seriousness of the concern and the potential severity of the consequences if there is no change.
3. Your estimate of how difficult it will be to change the goal or targeted concern.
4. Expressing concern in positive terms.

Turn to Frame 3, Chapter 8, Lesson 2, p. 351.

ANSWER

120

You should have checked 1, 4, and 5.

There is no evidence that behaviors are easier to change than are thoughts or feelings, nor that consumers are more likely to change a difficult problem simply because they are ordered to do so. If you checked 2 or 3, reread Frame 1 on page 348 and then go to Frame 4, Chapter 8, Lesson 2, p. 352.

ANSWER

121

Pinpoint Practice Form

Self-Behaviors	*Evaluation*	*Consumer Behaviors*	*Evaluation*
number of pages read	✔	self-esteem	vague unless you use as standardized scale
eliminating number of minutes over conference time period	✔	anxiety in groups	vague
yelling at home	yells (no -*ing*)	percentage of verbal participation	✔
calories consumed	✔	truancy	days or classes missed
nail biting	nail bites		
promptness	too general	obsessive talking	vague
focus on the topic during conferences	✔	leaving child unattended	number of times leaves child
hanging up clothes	eliminating	positive comments to child	✔
patience	too vague; specify behaviors	going to bed on time	in bed on time
verbal participation in class	number of words or number of times person talks	improve self-functioning	vague
turning in records on time	records turned in on time	clean house	specify tasks
		staying home	"dead man"

Self-Behaviors	*Evaluation*		*Consumer Behaviors*	*Evaluation*
omitting inferences in written records	✔		alcohol consumed	measure amounts
interruptions in interviews	✔		compliments to spouse	✔
			activities with children	✔

Return to Frame 6, Chapter 8, Lesson 2, p. 355.

ANSWER
122

Date	*Time in Minutes*	*Number of Negatives*	*Rate*
10/21	300	12	.040
10/22	120	27	.235
10/23	405	14	.034
10/24	405	13	.034
10/25	405	11	.027
10/26	405	9	.022
10/31	405	15	.037
11/1	405	25	.061

Return to Frame 8, Chapter 8, Lesson 2, p. 358.

ANSWER
123

1. Improve parenting skills.
   Behaviorally specific goals:
   A. Say "Thank-you" to child for helping with housework.
   B. Spend 30 minutes a day with child, just talking about the day's activities or playing a game selected by the child.
   C. Specify a reward for putting clothes away and give it to the child consistently at the end of each day.
2. Establish a stable environment.
   Behaviorally specific goals:
   A. Serve dinner each evening at 6 P.M.
   B. Arrange for child care in own home when you are going out for the evening.
   C. Let children know a day ahead of time when you will be out.
3. Stop abusive behavior.
   Behaviorally specific goals:
   A. Do not hit child.
   B. Do not use curse words when addressing child.
   C. Do not lock child in bathroom.
4. Improve attitudes toward children.
   A. Think about and write down two good things each child did each day at the end of the day.
   B. Spend one day out without the children each week.

C. Give the children chores to do at home and rewards for completing them.

Return to Frame 8, Chapter 8, Lesson 2, p. 360.

ANSWER

The two possible themes reflected in suggestions 1–5 are (A) involving the consumer in developing contracts and (B) documenting the service plan. Did you see any other themes? If you missed these two points, review the first five suggestions before going to Frame 12; otherwise, continue with Frame 12, Chapter 8, Lesson 2, p. 364.

ANSWER

In writing contracts, specify the following:

A. What is the consumer to do? What is the worker to do?
B. When should goals be achieved—target dates?
C. What consequences will occur if goals are not accomplished?

Review suggestions 6–10, then proceed to Frame 13, Chapter 8, Lesson 2, p. 365.

ANSWER

126

There are a number of ways to respond to the problem. One goal would be to increase communication between Mr. and Mrs. Coe and Mrs. Johnson. Mrs. Johnson apparently was trying to stay out of the family's way, while the family hoped for more help from her and worried because she was spending so much time alone in her room. Thus, you might list arranging additional joint informal interviews with the Coes and Mrs. Johnson as the worker's responsibility.

The worker needs to find or develop services not readily available to provide help to Mrs. Johnson at home and transportation so that she can attend activities at the senior center and church and get to the doctor. The advocacy role is needed here. The worker may want to contact community leaders and organizations in the local community and on the state level, such as the state department on aging. The worker may also want to encourage the Coes to contact local leaders regarding gaps in services. Other consumers have likely experienced these gaps. Documenting them and encouraging other workers to do the same may be first steps in getting needed services.

Through mutual discussion and some individual work with Mrs. Johnson, additional ways that she could help around the house could be worked out.

Resources for medical expenses and for nursing home care need to be explored further, should nursing home care be the family's ultimate choice.

Return to Frame 16, Chapter 8, Lesson 2, p. 368.

Answers to Chapter 8, Lesson 3

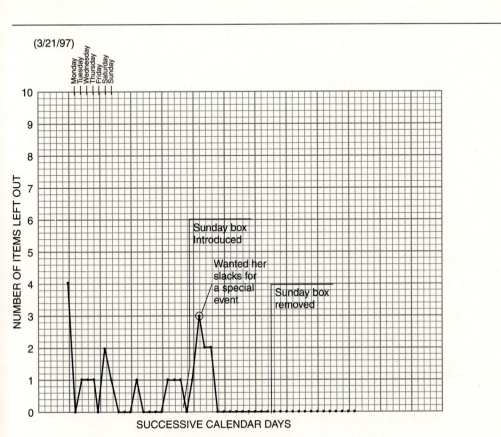

Return to Frame 4, Chapter 8, Lesson 3, p. 379.

Date	Rate
11/19	0
11/21	.05
11/23	Thanksgiving Holiday
11/26	0
11/28	0
11/30	0
12/3	.02
12/5	0
12/7	0
12/10	.02
12/12	.04
12/14	.06

ANSWER

128

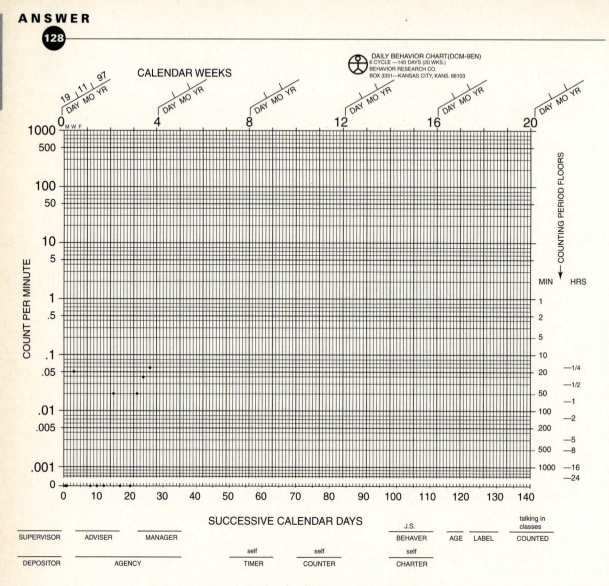

Return to Frame 7, Chapter 8, Lesson 3, p. 382.

Answers to Chapter 8, Lesson 4

ANSWER

The correct answer is True. The child welfare worker is part of a consumer team rather than a team of service providers. The child welfare case manager also links consumers to services. If you missed this question, review the definitions of the case management models in Frame 2 on page 389 before continuing to Frame 4, Chapter 8, Lesson 4, p. 390.

ANSWER

The major activity that occurs in a case conference is information sharing. Case conference activities also include (1) problem solving; (2) sharing ideas about the consumer's problems; (3) exchanging ideas about how to provide help to the consumer or ideas for new service plans; (4) evaluating the effects of current service plans; (5) providing support to workers who have difficult problems to solve; (6) sharing information across agencies; (7) peer supervision; and (8) coordination of services. If you mentioned any two of the preceding activities, continue to Frame 7 on page 394. If you were not able to list at least two central activities that occur in case conferences, reread Frame 5 on page 392 before going to Frame 7, Chapter 8, Lesson 4, p. 394.

ANSWER
131

Correct. The worker's observations of the consumer are included in the summary. There are many problems presented, but the major problem is not clear, and there are no reasons stated for sharing the information with the group. Turn to Frame 9, Chapter 8, Lesson 4, p. 395.

ANSWER
132

There is no clear statement of the consumer's problem, although there are allusions to many problems that Ms. Harold is having.

Return to Frame 8 on page 394, reread the summary, then answer the question correctly before proceeding to Frame 4, Chapter 8, Lesson 4, p. 395.

ANSWER
133

There is no reference whatsoever in the summary to the worker's reasons for sharing this information with the other workers; nor are any specific questions stated that the worker wishes to discuss.

Return to Frame 8 on page 394 for a review before answering the question correctly. Then turn to Frame 9, Chapter 8, Lesson 4, p. 395.

ANSWER

134

Paragraph 2 explains Ms. Harold's service needs; it is not a summary of the results of any treatment used.

Return to Frame 9 on page 395 and answer the question again.

ANSWER

135

Paragraph 3 gives an explanation of Ms. Harold's immediate problems; it is not a summary of the results of treatment used.

Return to Frame 9 on page 395 and answer the question again.

ANSWER

136

There is no information in paragraph 4 regarding the results of any treatments used.

Return to Frame 9 on page 395 and select the correct answer to the question before continuing on to Frame 10, Chapter 8, Lesson 4, p. 396.

ANSWER

137

Correct. The results of the services provided to help Ms. Harold solve her most immediate problem are presented in paragraph 5.

Turn now to Frame 10, Chapter 8, Lesson 4, p. 396.

ANSWER

138

This is incorrect. The writer has explained the results of a service provided to help Ms. Harold solve a pressing problem.

Return to Frame 9 on page 395 and select another answer.

ANSWER

139

Right. A tentative service plan is outlined in paragraph 4. Go to Frame 11, Chapter 8, Lesson 4, p. 396.

ANSWER

140

Return to Frame 8, Chapter 8, Lesson 4, p. 394 and review it carefully. There is a tentative service plan outlined in this case summary, so see if you can find it now.

ANSWER

141

Some of the possible questions that the worker could use to gain help from other workers are as follows:

1. What suggestions do you have for providing Ms. Harold with continuous services to help meet her needs?
2. Is the suggested plan a possible solution?
3. How can I provide more than just crisis services?

Did you mention one or another of these? Turn now to Frame 12, Chapter 8, Lesson 4, p. 396.

ANSWER
142

Your summary should include the following components:

1. Identifying information
2. A clear statement of Ms. Harold's major problem
3. The service plan
4. A summary of the results of services provided
5. Reasons for sharing this information and specific questions you need answered about the problem areas

Return now to Frame 13, Chapter 8, Lesson 4, p. 397.

ANSWER
143

Right—but consider the entire field of answers before settling on this one. Read the list of choices in Frame 15 on page 399 again, then make an additional selection.

ANSWER
144

An important facet, to be sure. But the consultant will need more than just this. Make another selection in Frame 15 on page 399 and check your answer.

ANSWER
145

Although this might be helpful, it is usually not necessary in order for the consultant to determine if he or she has the resources to help solve the problem.
Review Frame 14 on page 397, then select the correct answer.

ANSWER
146

Correct. Continue with Frame 16, Chapter 8, Lesson 4, p. 399.

ANSWER
147

One of the choices precludes another. Read them carefully before checking off another answer to Frame 15, Chapter 8, Lesson 4, p. 399.

A N S W E R

You should have numbered A, B, C, and D as 3, 1, 4, and 2. If you misplaced some, review Frame 14 on page 397 and then work out the logic behind the answer.

Answers to Chapter 8, Lesson 6

The correct answers are as follows:

1. The consumer has *experience* in living.
2. The consumer has a *readiness* to learn different things because she is facing different challenges and tasks.
3. The consumer is sensitive to *failure* and may have to overcome doubts and fears about learning.
4. The consumer has an interest in the *immediate usefulness* of new knowledge.

   Did you miss any? If so, go back and read Frame 1 on page 409. If you got them all right, move on to Frame 3, Chapter 8, Lesson 6, p. 411.

Sorry, but this is exactly what you should *not* do. Return to Frame 3 on page 411 for a review before you answer Frame 4 correctly.

No, this is not the best answer in this situation. Remember that teaching will be most effective when it is presented in terms of the adult's past experience and when it focuses on immediate problems. Return to Frame 4 on page 412 and answer correctly.

Correct. Proceed to Frame 5, Chapter 8, Lesson 6, p. 413.

You should have checked answers A, C, and D as some probable reasons why Wayne has not been a very successful teacher. You can probably think of a number of other reasons. This situation simply demonstrates the importance of following the basic steps of educating when you are trying to teach a consumer new skills.

   Go on to Frame 6, Chapter 8, Lesson 6, p. 413.

ANSWER

154

That's half the answer. You have overlooked one other important reason why evaluation is important in educating. Return to Frame 7 on page 414 and select the complete answer.

ANSWER

155

Incorrect. You do not evaluate your teaching activities to see how popular or well liked you are. Review Frame 6 on page 413 before you try Frame 7 again.

ANSWER

156

You've got half of it. A careful rereading of Frame 6 on page 413 will show you there is one other important reason for evaluating your teaching activities. Return to Frame 7, Chapter 8, Lesson 6, p. 414 and select the complete answer.

ANSWER

157

This is not a primary purpose of evaluation. In evaluation, your primary concern is to find out how well the consumer is progressing. Consumers have the right to follow and adapt your instructions in ways that are most helpful to them personally.

Return to Frame 6 on page 413 for a review.

ANSWER

158

Right! Evaluation will assist you in determining the progress you and the consumer have made; it will also aid you in identifying any additional areas in which the consumer may need educating.

Go on to Frame 8, Chapter 8, Lesson 6, p. 415.

ANSWER

159

You have included one incorrect answer with this choice. Return to Frame 7 on page 414 and choose the correct answer.

ANSWER

160

You should have checked A and C as actions that are *not* helpful in educating. If you had any trouble with this question, review Frame 8 on page 415; if you answered the question correctly, you have reached the end of Chapter 8, Lesson 6.

Answers to Chapter 8, Lesson 7

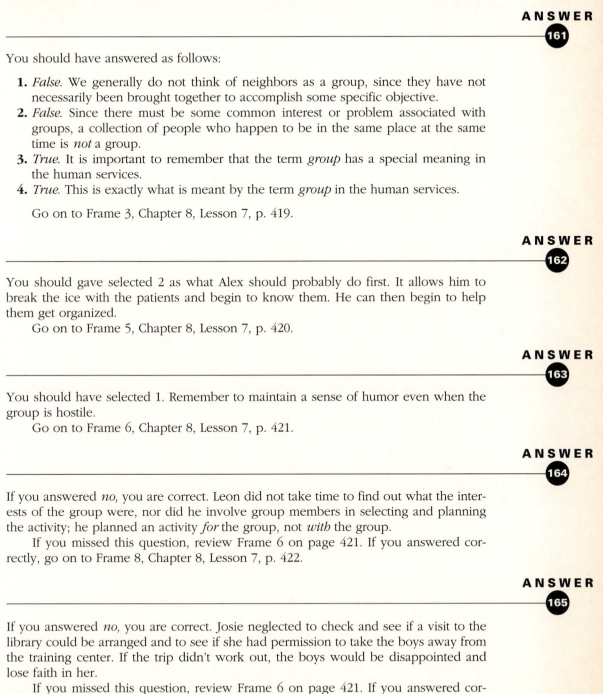

ANSWER
161

You should have answered as follows:

1. *False.* We generally do not think of neighbors as a group, since they have not necessarily been brought together to accomplish some specific objective.
2. *False.* Since there must be some common interest or problem associated with groups, a collection of people who happen to be in the same place at the same time is *not* a group.
3. *True.* It is important to remember that the term *group* has a special meaning in the human services.
4. *True.* This is exactly what is meant by the term *group* in the human services.

Go on to Frame 3, Chapter 8, Lesson 7, p. 419.

ANSWER
162

You should gave selected 2 as what Alex should probably do first. It allows him to break the ice with the patients and begin to know them. He can then begin to help them get organized.

Go on to Frame 5, Chapter 8, Lesson 7, p. 420.

ANSWER
163

You should have selected 1. Remember to maintain a sense of humor even when the group is hostile.

Go on to Frame 6, Chapter 8, Lesson 7, p. 421.

ANSWER
164

If you answered *no,* you are correct. Leon did not take time to find out what the interests of the group were, nor did he involve group members in selecting and planning the activity; he planned an activity *for* the group, not *with* the group.

If you missed this question, review Frame 6 on page 421. If you answered correctly, go on to Frame 8, Chapter 8, Lesson 7, p. 422.

ANSWER
165

If you answered *no,* you are correct. Josie neglected to check and see if a visit to the library could be arranged and to see if she had permission to take the boys away from the training center. If the trip didn't work out, the boys would be disappointed and lose faith in her.

If you missed this question, review Frame 6 on page 421. If you answered correctly, proceed to Frame 9, Chapter 8, Lesson 7, p. 422.

A N S W E R

You should have checked all the principles listed. If you had any trouble with this question, review Frame 9 on page 422. If you answered correctly, continue to Frame 11, Chapter 8, Lesson 7, p. 423.

Answers to Chapter 10, Lesson 1

1. Additional reasons to keep consumer records include identifying the consumer and the need; facilitating supervision and consultation; providing data for administrative tasks; and providing data for human service education and research.
2. Some reasons you might suggest for not keeping records are the additional work for human service workers and administrative support staff, the additional cost, and space problems. However, when you compare these with the reasons for keeping records, how strong a case could reasonably be made not to keep records?

Return to Frame 3, Chapter 10, Lesson 1, p. 483.

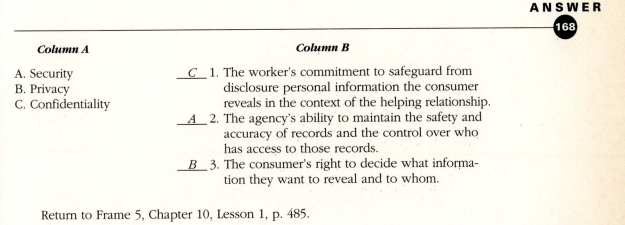

Column A	Column B
A. Security	_C_ 1. The worker's commitment to safeguard from disclosure personal information the consumer reveals in the context of the helping relationship.
B. Privacy	_A_ 2. The agency's ability to maintain the safety and accuracy of records and the control over who has access to those records.
C. Confidentiality	_B_ 3. The consumer's right to decide what information they want to reveal and to whom.

Return to Frame 5, Chapter 10, Lesson 1, p. 485.

_B_ 1. Using secondary sources

A. The observer reads a story to the observed person, noting what the observed person is doing.

_D_ 2. Interviewing

B. The observer consults records and reports about the observed person to obtain background information.

_C_ 3. Spectator observation

C. The observer tries to place himself outside the observed person's immediate focus of attention.

_A_ 4. Participant observation

D. The observer conducts and directs a purposeful conversation with the observed person.

If you missed any answers, review Frame 5 on page 485. Otherwise, proceed to Frame 7, Chapter 10, Lesson 1, p. 487.

ANSWER

We think the best answer is 5. Margaret considered all these factors in deciding that the reasons for Allen's behavior should be explored before any conclusions were drawn.

Return to Frame 9, Chapter 10, Lesson 1, p. 488.

Answers to Chapter 10, Lesson 2

A N S W E R

171

The correct answer is E—all four would be considered a report within the definition cited in Frame 1; a report is the communication of information to someone who wants or needs it, in the most convenient and usable form.

Return to Frame 3, Chapter 10, Lesson 2, p. 496.

A N S W E R

172

You should have checked numbers 2, 3, 5, 6, and 7. Number 4 is probably not an agency report since it does not include a reference to a consumer or agency activities.

Return to Frame 4, Chapter 10, Lesson 2, p. 496.

A N S W E R
173

Numbers 3, 4, 5, and 7 are the correct responses. When preparing a report, you should be organized and use short, helpful notes pertaining to the main topics; then you should present the report without rambling, stick to the purpose, speak up, stand or sit erect, and concentrate on issues and information, not personalities.

Return now to Frame 7, Chapter 10, Lesson 2, p. 498.

A N S W E R
174

Numbers 2, 3, 5, and 7 are situations in which memos would probably be used, although 2 and 3 could also be oral communications in a small agency, unless you wanted it in writing for future reference. Memos are most frequently used in agencies to communicate with administrators or when you want something in writing in order to keep a record of the communication. Can you think of situations in which our answers would not be the preferred choices?

Return to Frame 9, Chapter 10, Lesson 2, p. 499.

A N S W E R
175

A and C are true statements. It can be assumed that Mrs. Wright's memo was unclear, since Mrs. Bright had trouble understanding what was expected of her. The memo by Mrs. Bright is also ineffective for reasons that you will be asked to identify shortly. There is insufficient time to complete the tasks expected of Mrs. Bright, and her request for a meeting on such short notice may be unreasonable, especially since the request was made of a busy administrator.

Return to Frame 9, question 2, p. 499.

ANSWER

Yes, this and brevity were the two positive aspects of Mrs. Bright's memo. However, she did not allow Mrs. Wright sufficient time to schedule a meeting and failed to identify the tasks that she could not understand. In addition, the purpose of the memo could have been made clearer.

Return now to Frame 9, question 3, p. 499.

ANSWER

Two days is probably not sufficient time for Mrs. Wright to receive the memo, schedule a meeting time, and send a reply. In addition, there is little time to prepare for the meeting. A week is usually considered minimum time for expecting feedback, unless a phone call is requested. However, these conditions are also a matter of preference and should be clarified among workers.

Return now to Frame 9, question 2, page 499, and answer the question correctly.

ANSWER

No, Mrs. Wright could not prepare for a meeting with Mrs. Bright, since the tasks to be discussed were not identified in the memo. Other pieces of information, such as when Mrs. Wright was free for a meeting, the specific memo that Mrs. Bright was referring to, and possible other topics of discussion at the meeting, were also missing from the memo.

Return to Frame 9 on page 499 and answer question 2 correctly.

ANSWER

In order to clarify the reason or purpose of any memo so that the receiver knows immediately what the sender is talking about, it is advisable to insert, just below the line telling who the memo is from, the word *Re,* which means "regarding." Or else one should simply write "Subject"; and then state the purpose, for example, "Re your memo of Sept. 1, 1997, pertaining to the tasks expected of me."

Return now to Frame 10, Chapter 10, Lesson 2, p. 500.

ANSWER

180

11–15–97

Memo
To: Mrs. Wright, Director
From: (Service worker's name)
Re: Your memo dated September 1, 1997, regarding tasks to be accomplished by November 20

    I have been unable to complete two of the tasks that you requested since I am unable to understand what you expected. These tasks include numbers 4 and 6 in your September 1 memo as follows:

4. (Explain task 4 here.)
6. (Explain task 6 here.)
Since the deadline for completion is November 20, perhaps you could clarify these tasks by phone as soon as possible or postpone the completion date.
I have enclosed reports on the completed tasks for your review and approval.
SW/pm
Enclosures

Although the form and terms used in your memo may be different from those above, you should have included the following items:

1. A brief statement that includes the necessary information.
2. An allowance for time to respond or comply with requests. In this case, a deadline was imminent so alternative possibilities were presented to allow sufficient time for Mrs. Wright to respond.
3. Clear, easily understood words.
4. Immediate statement of purpose using "Re," with further clarification in contents of memo.

Did your memo contain these elements? Good—go on to Frame 11, Chapter 10, Lesson 2, p. 500.

ANSWER
181

The correct answer is B—when gathering ideas and facts for your summary, you must keep the purpose of your report in mind and select only those ideas, facts, and activities that are relevant to the purpose.
Return now to Frame 13, Chapter 10, Lesson 2, p. 501.

ANSWER
182

We suggest A as the correct choice. Your second step would probably be to organize the information you have obtained from agency records concerning this consumer. Have you considered what method you would use to organize this information? Think about your answer and then turn to Frame 14, Chapter 10, Lesson 2, p. 501.

ANSWER
183

There is little if anything that could be said about this report to commend it. Mr. Davis would be justified in thinking that Mr. Armstead is an ineffective report writer.
Return now to Frame 15, page 502, and answer question 2.

ANSWER
184

Mr. Armstead has failed to organize his facts (answer B) in a way that would make them clear and understandable. What method would you suggest to help Mr. Armstead organize his facts? You might also have checked C—obtain the facts. This could be one of his omissions, since he was stating personal opinions and left out other facts that may be important for Mr. Davis to know in order to work more effectively with Rebecca and her family. However, he has gathered some relevant facts, and, therefore, this is not the major failure of the report.

Return to Frame 15, page 502, and answer question 3.

ANSWER
185

Answer C is probably one of the major problems with this report. The writer not only neglected to state the purpose at the beginning of the report so that the receiver would immediately know what it was about, but it would seem that he also failed to have any specific purpose in mind when writing it, except to finish quickly and be done with it.

Return now to Frame 16, Chapter 10, Lesson 2, p. 502.

ANSWER
186

Did you include the following in your report?

1. A statement of the purpose at the beginning of the report
2. Each of the major facts in chronological order by the year of occurrence
3. Detailed facts and statements based on the major facts
4. A summary of what you believe to be the needs of Rebecca and her family that regional rehabilitation can help fulfill
5. Clear sentences and specific concrete words
6. A concisely written page, with no excessive statements after the purpose of the message was fulfilled

If you are able to answer yes to five of the above, you have successfully completed this lesson. Go on to the chapter summary. However, if you failed to include more than one of the above, rewrite the report and make sure to include those points before you proceed to the chapter summary.

Credits

Page 4: From *The Fifth Discipline Fieldbook* by Peter Senge, Charlotte Roberts et al. Copyright © 1994 by Peter M. Senge, Art Kleiner, Charlotte Roberts, Richard B. Rosa, and Bryan J. Smith. Used by permission of Doubleday, a division of Bantam Doubleday Dell Publishing Group, Inc.

Page 7: Unless otherwise noted, the ideas in this frame draw on the synopsis of Robert M. Smith, *Learning How to Learn: Applied Theory for Adults,* © 1982, pp. 87–93. Reproduced by permission of Globe Fearon.

Page 19: From *The Social Work Interview* by Alfred Kaduskin. Copyright © 1992 by Columbia University Press. Reprinted with permission of the publisher.

Page 27: From Joseph Mehr, *Human Services: Concepts and Interventions,* 4/e. Copyright © 1988 by Allyn and Bacon.

Page 38: Naomi Brill, *Working with People: The Helping Process,* 5th ed. (New York: Longman, 1995), p. 19.

Page 41: Discussion from Richard Daft, *Organizational Theory and Design,* 3rd ed. (St. Paul, Minn.: West Publishing, 1989), pp. 14–15, as adapted from Kenneth Boulding, "General Systems Theory: The Skeleton of Science," *Management Science* 2 (1965): 197–207.

Page 56 (Figure 1.10): Source: Naomi Brill, *Working with People: The Helping Process,* 4th ed. (New York: Longman, 1990), p. 110.

Page 89: Reprinted by permission, United Way of America.

Page 90: This discussion is taken from Philip Popple and Leslie Leighninger, *Social Work, Social Welfare, and American Society* (Boston: Allyn & Bacon, 1990), pp. 2–24.

Page 91: Reprinted with the permission of Simon & Schuster from *Why Americans Hate Politics* by E. J. Dionne, Jr. Copyright © 1991 by E. J. Dionne, Jr. Afterword and introduction copyright © 1992 by E. J. Dionne, Jr.

Page 100 (Figure 2.1): Adapted from Jane Work in Joseph F. Coates, *Issues Management: How You Can Plan, Organize, and Manage for the Future,* p. 22; and Alice Chambers Wygrant and O. W. Markely, *Information and the Future: A Handbook of Sources and Strategies* (Westport, Conn.: Greenwood Press, 1988), p. 121.

Page 107: From *Wasting America's Future* by Children's Defense Fund, © 1994 by Children's Defense Fund. Used by permission of Beacon Press, Boston.

Page 109: From Michael Suroka and George Bryjak, *Social Problems: World at Risk.* Copyright © 1995 by Allyn and Bacon.

Page 137: Robert Scheurell, *Introduction to Human Service Networks,* p. 53. Copyright 1987 by University Press of America.

Page 141: Naomi Brill, *Working with People: The Helping Process,* 5th ed. (New York: Longman, 1995), p. 22–24.

Page 143: From Eveline Schuylman, *Intervention in Human Services: A Guide to Skills and Knowledge,* 4/e. Copyright © 1991. All rights reserved. Reprinted by permission of Allyn & Bacon.

Page 144: Steps from *Life Skills: Taking Charge of Your Personal and Professional Growth,* by Richard J. Leider, pp. 141–156. Copyright © 1994. Reprinted with permission of Prentice-Hall.

Page 145: *Life Skills: Taking Charge of Your Personal and Professional Growth,* by Richard J. Leider, p. 157. Copyright ® 1994. Reprinted with permission of Prentice-Hall.

Index